WAR, MASSACRE, AND RECOVERY IN CENTRAL ITALY, 1943–1948

VICTORIA C. BELCO

War, Massacre, and Recovery
in Central Italy, 1943–1948

UNIVERSITY OF TORONTO PRESS
Toronto Buffalo London

© University of Toronto Press Incorporated 2010
Toronto Buffalo London
www.utppublishing.com
Printed in Canada

ISBN 978-0-8020-9314-1

Printed on acid-free paper

Toronto Italian Studies

Library and Archives Canada Cataloguing in Publication

Belco, Victoria, 1952–
War, massacre, and recovery in Central
Italy, 1943–1948 / Victoria Belco.

(Toronto Italian studies)
Includes bibliographical references and index.
ISBN 978-0-8020-9314-1 (bound)

1. World War, 1939–1945 – Atrocities – Italy, Central. 2. Civilians in war
– Italy, Central – History – 20th century. 3. Reconstruction (1939–1951) – Italy
– Citizen participation. 4. Italy – History – German occupation, 1943–1945.
5. Italy – History – 1945–1976. I. Title. II. Series: Toronto Italian studies

DG572.B44 2009   945.091   C2009-906776-2

 Canada Council   Conseil des Arts
for the Arts   du Canada

 ONTARIO ARTS COUNCIL
CONSEIL DES ARTS DE L'ONTARIO

University of Toronto Press acknowledges the financial assistance to its publishing program of the Canada Council for the Arts and the Ontario Arts Council.

University of Toronto Press acknowledges the financial support for its publishing activities of the Government of Canada through the Book Publishing Industry Development Program (BPIDP).

For Lara Lammioni Lucarelli and Giuseppe Polverini

Contents

Acknowledgments

I first visited the Val di Chiana and the province of Arezzo in 1981, when I was a newly minted attorney, and with my husband rented a restored farmhouse on a vineyard just below Civitella. The owner, Lara Lammioni, and her husband, (the late) Giuseppe Lucarelli, were very much a presence in their tenants' holiday, and as we four often sat up late that summer, playing cards, drinking their Chianti, and watching old movies on their black and white television, Lara also told the story of what happened in Civitella during the summer of 1944. My husband and I returned almost annually for two or three week stays, with one child and then two, and over the years came to know the area and its recent past quite well. As I knew to look for the commemorative plaques and other markers, I saw, albeit in a limited way, what the massacres had done to Aretine villages that summer. Yet, aside from those markers (and a few pieces of shrapnel still in the Lucarelli's fields), there appeared little outward trace of war and massacre in the beautiful landscape of southeastern Tuscany and, aside from Lara's stories, life for Lara and the Aretines as we saw it seemed, on the surface, no different from that of others. How could there not have been a more permanent personal and physical toll, I wondered, and more fundamentally, how did people like Lara, who had lived through those events, get 'from then to now'? This book is my attempt to answer the second part of that question, at least for the very short period directly after, when getting on from 'then' – from the summer of 1944 – seems unimaginable.

This book has been more than ten years in the making, starting as a very long dissertation, becoming an even longer initial book manuscript, and now finally halved in length. Acknowledgments will be brief, however.

Thank you first to my dissertation advisor at the University of California, Berkeley, Susanna Barrows, to my other readers, Anthony Adamthwaite and Thomas Barnes (who, several years earlier, told this then criminal defence lawyer that becoming a historian really was a reasonable decision), to my outside reader, the late Allan Pred, who read and considered my work much more carefully than I expected and who made me realize that what I was seeing in Arezzo between 1943 and 1948 was transition rather than transformation, and to the French dissertation group that kindly took me in.

This book has benefited from several long research stays in Italy (long stays my daughter Teresa also had the benefit of) both before it was a dissertation and after, as it developed into a book, as well as shorter research trips to London, New York, and Washington, DC. This local study could not have been written without adequate time to spend searching the shelves of Aretine communal archives – and the permission to do so. In Italy, Giovanni Contini, at the Soprintendenza Archivistica per la Toscana, not only helped with archival access, but also introduced me to Emilio Polverini and Romano Moretti. In turn, their kindness, help, and introductions to the communal administrations of Cavriglia and Bucine, and to the towns and residents of Castelnuovo dei Sabbioni and San Pancrazio, respectively, were invaluable, as was their generosity in sharing their own years of research. Leonardo Paggi quickly got me access to Civitella's communal archive. It is impossible to acknowledge individually the many archivists, librarians, communal employees, association directors and secretaries, and others who made my years of research possible, so I thank them as a very large group. In particular, however, I thank those in the communes of Cavriglia, Civitella, and Bucine, who literally gave me the keys to their historical archives. The research process was enriched by so many experiences I imagine as unique to local study (particularly one in central Italy): the sindaco of Bucine reminding me to lock the front door to the communal offices as I was usually last to leave the building for the day; the citizens of the commune of Civitella who asked my advice on matters – assuming I was a communal employee because I spent so much time at the commune's photocopy machine; the noise of the children whose classrooms sat over Cavriglia's historical archive in the basement of the elementary school; Valeria Polverini welcoming me as an almost daily lunch guest; and the innumerable glasses of homemade vin santo drunk at kitchen tables of those who told me about their wartime and postwar lives.

Thank you to Ron Schoeffel and the University of Toronto Press for being patient.

And finally, thank you to my husband Bill Goodman, who carried more than his share of the domestic and economic load during much of this long process.

WAR, MASSACRE, AND RECOVERY IN CENTRAL ITALY, 1943–1948

Introduction: From War to Peace

This is a story of everyday life during war and in its aftermath. The setting is the small place that is the Tuscan province of Arezzo between 1943 and 1948, within the larger place that is wartime and postwar Italy, within the still larger place that is society at war. It begins with the country at war and with civilians who soon found themselves in the war's ruinous path. It ends with individuals, families, communities, and society recovering from the traumas of war, and with the process of rebuilding society well along on the course it would take for the next decades. In between are the fall of Fascism, the collapse of the nation, and the failure of the state and its institutions. In between also is a period when life's familiar patterns have been violently and utterly disrupted, and there is no state able to help solve postwar problems. In between is a society that fractured and came together on multiple old and new lines. Most broadly told, this is an account of what everyday life was like during a time of war and massacre and during a postwar marked by suffering, hardship, and deep division.

The line separating peace from war is not a neat one. As we surely know by now, the end of military battles does not always signify the end of violence and conflict. After victory (or peace) has been declared, life in the aftermath often continues to look remarkably like it did during war, or appears profoundly altered by war. Modern war and modern peace have grown to resemble one another, or more accurately, it has become harder to tell peace from war. This tendency really began with the Second World War, when the distinction between the home front and the battlefront ended, as war left the battlefields, taking over cities, towns, and farmers' fields to become an all-out war against civilians – and in some cases war between civilians – instead of a more recognizable war between soldiers.

A number of recent studies appropriately treat World War II and its aftermath as constituting an integrated period, or consider aftermath and consequences as closely related phases of the war itself. Focusing on themes that reach beyond traditional military history and international relations or the political history of war – themes of experience, trauma, gender, retribution, justice, narratives, commemoration, and especially memory, all broadly defined – historians are exploring the continuing relationship between war and society throughout the postwar and after.[1] Some have explicitly presented the time from war through peace as a period of societal as well as political transition, and that is the theoretical approach I take here – that the transition from war to peace, or to post-war, if not to veritable peace – constitutes a separate and logical histori-cal period.[2]

In this history of transition, my concern is with the variety of problems faced in everyday life and also with the nature and outcome of the transi-tion. Does such transition necessarily make for, or end in, societal transfor-mation – or, as more usually asked, does war really cause social change? Society never stands still, of course. It is always in transition, yet ordinary transition does not inevitably mean change or transformation. Transition is worthy of study in this particular modern war–total war context (as with post-1989 and other monumental transitions), because dramatic transi-tion generally presents a time when government and institutions are in flux or non-existent, when society is most vulnerable and more clearly dis-plays both its structure and structural flaws. Starting anew seems most pos-sible then, when life is more difficult but also in retrospect more interesting. What will change and what will not; why will some things change and some not? Does war act as a catalyst because its rupturing events make change possible? Or, as Tolstoy wrote of an earlier though nearly modern cam-paign of war, does war simply speed up the current of life without chang-ing its direction?

For Italy, the years between 1943 and 1948 form a natural, coherent transitional time to examine: 1943 marks the arrival of the war in Italy, the termination of the Fascist regime, the breakdown of the state and the nation, while 1948 marks the real postwar start of national and state re-organization. That benchmark year, 1948, brackets the far end when the Republican constitution was promulgated and the first democratically elected national government in more than twenty years brought Italy's postwar peace and reconstruction to a national level. It was also the year the political left became the opposition to the government in power, the year of the political schism in the briefly unified labour union confederation (CGIL), and the year of the attempt on Palmiro Togliatti's life. It was also the year the European Recovery Program (the Marshall Plan) began to function, the year NATO was formed, and the year the cold war began in earnest.

The years between 1943 and 1948 span the most intense period of war for Italy and the most intense period of the country's reconstruction. During those years, life changed unexpectedly, dramatically, and often tragically from day to day, until the very notion of 'everyday life' had no ordinary, expected, and understandable meaning. Society disintegrated more slowly, while the Italian state collapsed quickly. From the end of 1943 to 1948, Italy had essentially no centralized state wielding acknowledged national authority, and Italian society began to reconstruct itself without either benefit or hindrance of a state. The Italian disjunction between society and state thus appeared very clear. Moreover, local identities, local institutions, and local mistrust of the state were at their strongest during this time when Fascism had fallen, the monarchy had failed, and national (state and Fascist Party) institutions either no longer existed or did not function adequately. The gap between the 'local' and the 'national' was also most profound, as Italians expressed their lack of faith in Rome's ability to solve their postwar problems.

These were the years that gave rise to neorealism, that 'gritty social realism' characterizing postwar Italian film and literature and featuring Italian postwar suffering. Neorealism also characterized the daily lives of real people; postwar life and art shared a new kind of reality born out of destruction and hardship – part *Rome: Open City*, part *Paisan*, part *Shoeshine*, part *Bicycle Thieves*, and a very large part the less 'gritty,' more sentimental, and dead-on socially accurate Don Camillo and Peppone.[3] Life and society moved at greater speed. More vital issues weighed in the balance, as Italians on the local, as at all levels, approached life after twenty years of Fascism and five years of war. For Italians, it was a time when both need and politics – those twin offspring of war – were omnipresent in daily life and society, when need and politics brought people together and drove them apart. It was a moment of simultaneous desperation and possibility, of renewed public discourse and participation in civil life, and most of all, of deep disagreement about the nature of postwar, post-Fascist Italy. It was a time when people desperately wanted to 'return to normal life' but also saw the possibility of change, and when the unanswerable question always present was whether continuity or change would be the result of postwar struggles.

What happened to society during that transitional time? I acknowledge both continuity and change in postwar Italy; I am not firmly in the camp of continuity or the camp of change. In fact, when I go looking for social change in postwar Italy, I often find continuity, and then discover change when I expect continuity. My question, however, is given the dramatic, destructive, and massive nature of wartime and postwar effects on daily life, and on the nation and state, why did society not look radically different by 1948 and thereafter? Why did it not change more dramatically and fundamentally? To assert conclusions in this introduction, I believe the war and postwar events fractured society along so many lines, thereby preventing sufficient consensus that would have allowed for greater, deeper, or more widespread social change. I do not mean consensus in the sense of consensus for Fascism – the 'years of consensus' or the 'culture of consent' – though the sort of forced or cajoled consensus created and maintained during Fascism can direct social change from above. I mean consensus on what post-Fascist, postwar life should be.

In the postwar, real social change did not and could not take place from below (or within) because society divided so intensely and bitterly on so many different points. This was not entirely a bad thing, because fracture and division in some ways meant the opposite of Fascism, dictatorship, and attempted totalitarianism. The very freedom to fracture – to put it awkwardly – meant a new freedom of society, politics, and daily life; it granted a kind of agency and a voice to those who had not had it before; it meant more complex relationships between people and government, between women and men, between classes, between employees and employers, between owners of property and those without it, between former Fascists and former partisans, and between still more oppositional groups. Perhaps such increased social tension in itself constitutes recognizable social change, being a kind of recovery from Fascism and from war.

Given so much social tension and societal division, however, the pertinent question that follows is why society did not fracture more violently: why was there no postwar civil war in Italy – especially after the assassination attempt on Togliatti in July 1948? The short, blunt answer to the end of that question is, of course, because of Italian official willingness to shoot people on the street, and a slightly more attenuated answer has to do with American interference and money. A longer, more complete response, however, relates to the question Alexis de Tocqueville asked about a different society in a very different setting and context: what keeps society together and what breaks it apart?

In the postwar Italian context, what held society sufficiently together in that time of destruction, crisis, and transition when no strong force held it together from above? The question is a valid one for any society – particularly for any society in transition on account of war, political turmoil, or other sorts of crises that test society.[4] The observer can imagine a balance sheet or tally of sorts; on one side we can line up old and new commonalties, points of juncture, past events shared – especially a recent, momentous or traumatizing shared past – and a present of shared suffering; and on the other side list the fracture points that divide the society. Compare the number and quality of things that unite to the number and quality of things that divide. Overly simple and not always accurate, admittedly, and the cause and severity of the transition under examination naturally must be taken into account, as must the society's pre-transition cohesiveness and stability, but such an approach to any society in transition – including those which do not share Italy's particular 'national characteristics' – offers a way of conceptualizing why some societies have relatively smooth transitions after national trauma and others devolve into still more chaos, war, and civil war.

What most divided Italian society in the postwar? It was the war and its two most direct effects: need and politics. It was also prewar inequities and civil life as known before the war. What most united Italian society in the postwar? It was the shared suffering of war and the shared suffering of the postwar, as well as need and politics, and the vision of civil life as known before the war. I am certainly not the first to point out that Italian society has a tendency to fracture – especially along political and class lines, or that the goal of social unity has proved elusive, that Italians are a 'localist' or regional people, and that Italian society does not easily change. Cultural and national truisms are most clearly manifested when, as here, society is most disrupted.

War and Civil Life

On March 10, 1944, the police chief of Arezzo reported to the Fascist Republican head of that province that Allied bombings had 'disintegrated' civil life in that city, meaning as each day passed and more bombs fell, daily life went more and more to pieces.[5] In all of Italy, society's disintegration began with the collapse of Fascism and then abandonment by the state the previous year. The more immediate physical effects of war (as lived between opposing armies) nearly completed society's demise in Arezzo by the end of the summer of 1944. Intensive Allied bombing in the spring of 1944 damaged and destroyed buildings and made roads, bridges, and rail tracks impassable. Allied bombs drove citizens from their homes creating a refugee and evacuee problem of crisis pro-portions. That summer, many villages in the province experienced German atrocities against the civilian population of a nature and on a scale beyond comprehension, as hundreds of civilians were massacred and entire villages were burned. The arrival of the front battle lines then followed as World War II passed through central Italy during June, July, and August. Houses, farms, and businesses were destroyed, and people's most intimate, familiar possessions stolen. Schools and hospitals were closed or damaged beyond use; churches were burned. Families were separated. People wandered in the woods and abandoned villages; or they rushed aimlessly, not knowing where to go or what they would find. Survivors sheltered in caves, basements of burned houses, or under the roots of trees. People were buffeted again and again. Worse than the fall of a dictator or abandonment by one's monarch, society – with all its trappings, its meanings, and its supports – was destroyed by war.

Everything – every component of society from family life to commu-nity to government – needed to be reconstructed after the war. Communes rebuilt schools, hospitals, churches, and cemeteries, as well as rebuilding administrative government, associations, their traditional intensely so-cial life, and their very sense of community. Individuals, communities, and the nation simultaneously rethought (or chose not to think about) what it now meant to be Italian: what life would be after Fascism and af-ter a war that had uneasily combined defeat, Resistance, civil war, and liberation. For the villages that are the subject of this study, German mas-sacres of the civilian population were perhaps the most damaging blows the war delivered against local society. They added even more layers of complexity to the recovery and to what had to be carried out for the re-construction of society.

This history of transition tells how villages, communes, and ordinary citizens suffered and survived the war – how they lived from disintegra-tion to reconstruction, as the desire to return to normal life competed with attempts at change. Rather than a survey of physical and economic reconstruction, this is a look at local society's most immediate postwar problems and the solutions attempted. It considers how Italians alter-nately quick-stepped and dragged their feet on the post-Fascist path of change directly after the war. It searches out how society – individuals, families, and communities – recovered, returned, or 'came back' to life after five years of war and twenty years of Fascism. It focuses on the con-current relationship and dichotomy between the local and the national, between society and state at a time when the very concepts and existence of the nation and 'the state' were in flux – and in a place where until recently Mussolini had insisted: 'All for the State; nothing outside the State; nothing against the State.' It analyzes how local life, local level society, and local administrative institutions rebounded astonishingly quickly, if not smoothly and without conflict.

Although society is fragile enough that modern total war can cause its disintegration, society is also resilient – able to reconstruct, able to change, able to resist change. Examining the towns and villages of central Italy during the years 1943 to 1948 best illustrates this premise, because it is in central Italy that the centuries-old concepts of *la vita civile* and *civiltà* have been most clearly embodied, and where war broke down the way of life they comprise. The terms '*la vita civile*' and '*civiltà*' do not translate or travel well into English. Literally they are 'civil life' and 'civilization' (or 'civilizedness'), respectively, but mean both more and less than the English terms. Civil life is sometimes used interchangeably with civil society, which Paul Ginsborg and others locate between the private and the state; and it is nearly that. Civil life means more than 'public life,' however, and more than participation in civic and economic life.[6]

I employ here Sydel Silverman's illumination of the terms. Her ethnographical study of a small Umbrian hill town (population 350, 'nearly at the geographical center of Italy') was structured around the concepts of *civiltà* and *la vita civile*.[7] Civil life implies a town-centred way of life, as Italy is a town-centred country, a nation of cities small and large, though civil life also includes the rural areas surrounding a town or village.[8] On a different scale, this way of life entails membership in a politically organized society, participation in civic life, public life, work, and social organizations and events. On a smaller scale, it includes interpersonal relationships (including inter-class relationships), daily practices, daily interactions, and sociability. One is a member of a local community first, then a member of larger society. I would emphasize that, in Italy, one is a member of a family even before being a member of a community. These concentric memberships have always fit naturally and neatly together in the town and village society of central Italy. '[T]he town represents ... a way of life, which is celebrated in the idea of "*civiltà*."'[9] *Civiltà*, in turn, denotes an urban quality that also exists in central Italy's small towns and villages: 'it refers to ideas about a civilized way of life.' That civilized way of life, I believe, imparted a sense of order, and represents a reasonably well-defined way of life in which individuals, families, and communities know unspoken rules of interaction, have a clear sense of their value in the social scheme, and know how to behave in given circumstances.

When central Italian society disintegrated, and citizens and their communities were torn from their moorings, they still maintained the notion and ideal of civil life as social precedent, as 'normal life' to which they would return. Civil life and *civiltà* were the compass that had directed them for generations through all the vagaries of Italian national life. They were in large part what held society together in the aftermath. Civil life and *civiltà* do not mean that everyone in the community or the village agrees, gets along, or is the same; they certainly do not mean that individuals think of the community before they think of themselves or their families. They do, however, represent a general acknowledgment that society and everyday life have a certain pattern and certain boundaries – even if one does not concede them. And they mean that Rome and the state are far away, not in terms of kilometres, but in terms of trust and confidence.

The war in Italy was a local war, and postwar reconstruction was a local process, yet until recently it has not been studied as such.[10] The province of Arezzo supplies the ideal villages and communes for a local case study of 'how ordinary citizens survived the war' and a social history of war and transition. The province and its citizens lived through Fascism, Republican Fascism, and civil war. They suffered World War II in every brutal aspect. Wartime and postwar Arezzo provide local illustration for nearly every issue and problem, every strain on society that Italy faced during and after the war – and many that challenge any society beset by war. In addition, the place and period offer an opportunity to see how (and where) postwar politics and Italy's political parties made themselves part of everyday life in the vacuum created by the fall of Fascism and in the climate of need created by the war.

Although emblematic, the province, the communes, the villages, and the people chosen for this study cannot be microcosms of the entire country's experience of war and reconstruction.[11] Arezzo provides neither the nation in miniature nor the republic in the village. Instead of three almost neighbouring villages in central Italy, I might have chosen one town or village in each the south, centre, and north. That would have highlighted obvious, different wartime experiences and seemingly permanent regional differences, but still would not adequately represent all of wartime and postwar Italy. Paul Ginsborg has memorably stated that, 'in purely historical terms it would be better to talk not of three Italys but of three hundred.'[12] No single place, no three places – south, centre, north – can represent all of Italy at any time, most especially during wartime.

The south, centre, and north experienced war and occupation on a different timetable and at a different intensity. So too, when closely examined, every town, village, and city within each province and region experienced a somewhat different war and a different postwar – which is what I mean by a local war and a local postwar. Even among the villages of this study, the experience of prewar life, war, massacre, and reconstruction differed in details. The many large and small differences explain why a local level study is necessary to help understand the wartime and postwar periods and to remind us of war's human and societal costs.[13] Individual villages and a single province ground issues of continuity and change, and pinpoint where specific foundations for the future were laid. The reconstruction of society began quickly – and it began at the local level. Reconstruction commenced there, in part because the state and the nation were in even greater disorder, but more so because local, community, and communal-level society has always been Italy's greatest strength.

Italy in Context

This is an Italian story. Although illuminating, Italy's (and central Italy's) war and reconstruction is not a microcosm of Europe. For nearly the last two years of war, Italy lived simultaneously under three Italian governments and two foreign occupations, as Claudio Pavone has written.[14] Italy was 'cut in two' while Allied soldiers occupied and directed military affairs and civil affairs in the south (and then the centre), and while German soldiers occupied and directed affairs in the centre and north.[15] Italy was the first of the German-occupied countries to be liberated (piece by piece), and reoccupied by the Allies (piece by piece). It became the laboratory of Allied occupation: how soldiers would become governors, how inexperienced military men would direct 'civil affairs' once they had liberated the rest of Europe – an experiment on civilians now timely again.[16]

Italy did share many experiences of war, occupation, atrocity, and destruction with other countries of Western and Eastern Europe. Italy, as did other countries, had thousands of refugees and displaced persons to care for after the war. Countries other than Italy also had to rebuild after the massive destruction and losses caused by modern total war. Other countries also had to reconstruct government and the institutions of state and society. Italy experienced a level of war, massacre, and destruction similar to the occupied countries of Eastern Europe, close to that of Poland, Ukraine, and eventually Hungary. Liberated by the Soviet Union, the war-shattered countries of Eastern Europe took a very different postwar path from Italy's. Italy perhaps more closely resembled France. Both countries were occupied; both were 'cut in two' as it were; both were battlefields; both suffered massacres of the civilian population. Both had partisans, an armed resistance to occupation, and a civil war. Both had multiple, shifting wartime and postwar governments. Both had difficult, unsatisfactory epurations (or purges), official and popular. Both countries developed a comforting postwar resistance myth that grew over the following decades.[17]

Insofar as their prewar periods were more similar, the more fitting postwar comparison may be that between Italy and Germany. As studies comparing Italian Fascism with German Nazism have noted, the two regimes differed in some important respects, but shared a number of similarities.[18] They also shared similarities in their respective postwars. Both were physically destroyed in part. Both faced the abrupt end to lengthy, repressive regimes, which had attempted (with differing degrees of success) to nationalize individuals and society, and to absorb society within the state. Both were suddenly left without internal national direction. Both (together with Japan) had once been the enemy responsible (even if not equally responsible) for the world's worst war to date, but Italy much more so than Germany has avoided coming publically to terms with its Fascist past and its own wartime activities. Indeed, Italy has employed Nazi Germany as a point of reference against its own *brava gente* persona: to show how its own Fascist regime and its own wartime activities were not so bad in comparison. And, although Allied soldier-governors experimented first on Italy, Germany became the real laboratory for postwar reconstruction in ways far beyond those attempted in Italy. Italy was never institutionally reduced to 'ground zero,' never bisected by the victors, and never reconstructed in the opposing images of its opposing postwar occupiers.

Allied troops departed from Italy fairly soon after the liberation of the north and the end of the war. Although not leaving the country entirely to its own devices, the Allies did not continue to direct day-to-day affairs. Within limits – while still operating under much western economic and political pressure – Italy took its own postwar path towards reconstructing society. It was a uniquely Italian path, whose borders were defined by such varied elements as twenty years of Fascism; decades of political instability and social and economic disparity before the advent of Fascism; widespread postwar destruction and need; strongly competing visions on what postwar Italian government and society should be; together with an intense desire for order, normality, and the return to civil life in a country where the very notions of normality and order had multiple, often opposing reference points.

Another element made Italy's war and postwar unique – and served to unify Italians (at least temporarily) in the aftermath. Eighteen months of brutal war between Allies and Germans on civilian territory succeeded in transforming Italy from enemy-Fascist-perpetrator and active (if not entirely enthusiastic or successful) participant in World War II on the side of Hitler to a victim of war, of Fascism, and of Mussolini. The domestic termination of Fascism (although technically by the king from 'above') and hosting nearly two years of destructive war on their civilian landscape gave Italians the moral explanatory tools to distance themselves from the Fascist *ventennio* and from their participation in the first half of the war, in a way that Germans could not distance themselves from Hitler, Nazism, and the war. While Ernesto Galli della Loggia has argued the end of Fascism caused a national 'identity crisis,' and others argue that the ongoing 'Liberation dispute' later shattered any notions of unity and shared postwar collective identity, I believe the brutal war allowed Italians to form a new, not so temporary identity based on the shared experience of wartime victimhood and postwar suffering.[19] It was an identity both individual and collective – and one that both unified and divided.

Italians blamed Mussolini for the war, and blamed Mussolini, the Germans, and the Allies for their suffering. The country cast off Fascism and put on a new identity as quickly as some Italian soldiers discarded their uniforms and donned civilian clothes (or partisan weapons) after the September 8, 1943, armistice. The contents of state archives and especially communal archives allow an examination of interactions between the local, the provincial, and the state, and they make clear that postwar identity took shape as much locally (from below) as it did from above. Victimhood and suffering – individual and collective, local and national – is an always recurring subject in postwar life, with the massacred villages and massacre victims representing their epitome.

Nevertheless, not all remnants of the Fascist *ventennio* (or of pre-Fascist Italy) were abandoned. The second major – and recurring – subject is the common desire to return to normal life frequently competing with the desire for postwar change. Many people and the country itself in the immediate postwar chaos and poverty did not have the luxury or the desire to attempt dramatic change, to fix all old mistakes, and create a new, fairer society. Some Fascist era (and some pre-Fascist era) institutions and organizations still worked in whole or in part. Some were needed to keep postwar society functioning, while others were retained or rebuilt without good reason. Postwar reconstruction of society in Italy resembled the reconstruction of houses, bridges, and towns. Italians kept and reused what was usable, sometimes merely plastering over what should have been demolished. Then, using a combination of old and new materials, they rebuilt what could not be repaired.

'The simple truth is that Italians resist change,' Joseph LaPalombara famously put it, while Nicola Gallerano referred to 'the saga' or 'adventure of continuity' between Liberal, Fascist, and Republican Italy – and continuity is a term much in use when speaking of Italy.[20] Certainly, taking a wider and longer view, Italy missed (or sabotaged) the postwar opportunity to begin from 'social ground zero': to build a better, workable, more stable government, to bring the south into parity with the north, to build a more just society. But the postwar view from three massacred communes in Arezzo was one of smaller, more immediate concerns: where to sleep; what to feed the children; how to get water and medicine for the village; how to determine who were the most needy and how to help them; how to reopen the lignite mines; how to clear the farms of landmines; how to repair homes, roads, and bridges; how to create jobs for the hundreds and thousands of unemployed; how to conduct local elections; how to make local voices heard in Rome (and in the commune); how to bury and then honour the dead.

A great number of things did change, of course. Individuals changed as a result of their wartime experiences. Their goals changed; their opportunities changed. The war changed families and the contours of traditional family life. Children who saw their fathers or mothers killed grew up in city orphanages instead of in their villages. Young people who had expected to be farmers or sharecroppers like their parents and grandparents went off to work in industry or live in cities. Village life changed. Villages were rebuilt with electricity, an adequate water supply, better roads, and public housing. Ordinary people now ran the communes. The war and the end of Fascism also permitted new relationships between individuals and government, between the local and the state, while the pervasive climate of need created by the war allowed political parties and new political organizations to adapt and perfect old practices of *raccomandazione*, of patronage and clientelism: promising benefits, doling out assistance, and lending influence. In turn, however, needy individuals and communities made new kinds of demands on political parties and on the state.

This local study does not represent all of Italy or all of Europe after World War II, but it does have relevance for larger considerations of war, society, and transition wherever war causes widespread suffering, physical and institutional destruction; wherever war disintegrates daily life; and where the desire to return to normal life competes with attempts at change in the aftermath. By examining locally the details of destruction and the many areas of society that required reconstruction, and the difficulties in so reconstructing it, we can better understand why war generally changes society less than we might expect it to or less than we hope it will.

Situating the Villages

This province of valleys and hills is classic Tuscan postcard country. Rolling hills are terraced for cultivation and dotted with stone farmhouses. Lines of cypresses separate small farms planted with sunflowers and maize, or with olive trees and wine grapes. Fields of red poppies cover the valleys in the late spring and early summer, while fall brings wild mushrooms and chestnuts to the woods. Small, picturesque hilltop villages, remnants of the province's medieval past, enjoy breathtaking views over the wide valleys. Village streets are narrow and steep, not designed for cars (or army tanks); roads wind through the hills and valleys between farms and villages. Scores of bridges span the rivers and valleys. In this beautiful and tranquil place, plaques on communal walls, monuments in piazzas, and cemetery markers (these less likely to be seen by visitors renting vacation homes or touring the province's medieval and Renaissance sites) give the only hint of the terrible things that happened here during the summer of 1944.

Arezzo is the easternmost province in the region of Tuscany. Located southeast of the province of Florence and northeast of the province of Siena, it borders the regions of Umbria and the Marches to the east. The Chianti mountains bracket the west; the more difficult and inhospitable terrain of the Tuscan Appennines sits to the east. The province's four valleys and its forest make up its most characteristic features: the Val di Chiana south of the capital city, the Val d'Ambra to the southwest, and the Valdarno to the northwest. The Valtiberina lies east of Arezzo city, and the magnificent forested area of the Casentino is northeast. Three small towns – villages really – in three different communes are the most minute focus of this study.[21] These villages and their communes are all west of the city of Arezzo and south of the Arno River: Civitella in Val di Chiana in the commune of the same name, San Pancrazio in the commune of Bucine, and Castelnuovo dei Sabbioni in the commune of Cavriglia, though other Aretine communes and villages, especially Pieve

Santo Stefano, Laterina, Oliveto, Cornia, Meleto, San Giovanni Valdarno, and the capital city of Arezzo also have a role. Civitella, San Pancrazio, and Castelnuovo represent the three most common types of central Italian villages of the pre–World War II period,[22] and these three villages also represent the most horrific civilian experiences of World War II.

The village of Civitella in Val di Chiana sits on a hill at an altitude of 523 metres, with spectacular views over the northern end of the Chiana valley, while the remains of its castle and medieval walls present a distinctive silhouette when seen from below. As a minor character throughout the centuries of battles between Florence and Siena, Civitella and its castle often sheltered the bishops of Arezzo from both sides. First destroyed in 1252, the castle and village walls were reconstructed in 1273. During the battle of Campaldino in 1289, the castle passed under the domination of Florence, but the *podestà* of Arezzo managed to expel the Florentines from Civitella in 1303. Less than ten years later, the village was the chosen site of a peace treaty contemplating the end of hostilities between the Guelphs and the Ghibellines and their various factions. In 1347, Civitella passed definitively under Florentine control, and remained there until the death of the last of the Medici in 1737. In 1808, all Aretine territory became part of the *Dipartimento dell'Arno* and the Napoleonic Empire, and a *Maire* administered the commune until 1814.

The early years of the nineteenth century brought modernization to Civitella in the improvement of existing buildings and new construction. Streets were improved and new ones built; better connections were made between the village, the towns of the plain below, and the city of Arezzo. The area of the town proper continued to be delineated by its medieval walls and two gates, Porta Senese and Porta Aretina, and to be unified by its three piazzas: the lower of which looks directly over the Val di Chiana, while a loggia connects the two other piazzas slightly higher on the hill. The village's medieval well was rebuilt in 1849 (and remained the source of water for the village until World War II), and the church of Santa Maria Assunta in 1875, both located in what was then called Piazza Lazzeri – later renamed Piazza Vittorio Emanuele III and still later Piazza dei Martiri, or Piazza of the Martyrs. After World War I, the village monument to its fallen soldiers would be built in the adjoining piazza. The first rail line in the area in 1880 connected the cities of Arezzo and Sinalunga to the south, although the commune of Civitella did not have a train station until one was built at Badia al Pino in 1915. The government transferred the communal seat to that more accessible village two years later, though the commune has always retained the name Civitella in Val di Chiana.

The village of Civitella began losing population by the early 1900s to what had been the smaller centres of the plain below – Badia al Pino, Pieve al Toppo, Tegoleto, and Viciomaggio – but, with 865 residents, it still remained the most populated village of the commune until the beginning of World War II.[23] Until World War II, the village was also the most socially 'significant' in the commune, and those residents inside the walls considered themselves apart from the peasants living outside. The parish priest of Civitella was an archpriest to several parishes situated outside the village. The village had a small hospital and an old age home, built with the legacy of the former district doctor. Nuns, two nurses, a midwife, and two district doctors provided health care for the village and adjacent hamlets. More prosperous villagers together with the widow of the village's largest landowner had contributed to build a nursery school, also run by nuns. Three elementary school teachers taught a complete elementary school course, attended by children of neighbouring districts.

The village was also economically important to the commune. Civitella had two olive oil presses, a grocery store, a cooperative grocery, a jeweller, a clothing store for men, and a clothing store for women. It counted six blacksmiths, a mechanic, six shoemakers, three carpenters, a farrier, six bricklayers, and two bakers among its village artisans. The local butcher ran a small inn and restaurant. Several professionals and clerical workers for the commune also lived inside the village walls, as did those who owned larger plots of land outside the village. Small farmers and *mezzadri*, those Tuscan sharecroppers who worked portions of larger estates often owned by urban landlords and managed by a *fattore* (or estate manager), lived on the land and came to Civitella for goods and services.[24]

The village of San Pancrazio in the neighbouring commune of Bucine is only a few kilometres from the village of Civitella. Although smaller, 'poorer,' and less economically diverse, its hilltop location, panorama, and the quiet beauty of its surrounding woods rival Civitella's. At an altitude of 509 metres, it overlooks both the Valdarno and the Val di Chiana. Passing first the cemetery located a few hundred metres below, one enters the village at the top of a steep, winding road. Coming into the village, one also enters the main piazza; to its left is the seventeenth century building that was once the *podestà*'s seat, but which became the *fattoria* Pierangeli (or central farm building for the large Pierangeli farm) in the twentieth century. San Pancrazio had its own medieval castle, little of which remained, however, even by the seventeenth century. The castle and village fell under Florentine domination in 1340, a bit earlier than had Civitella.

More recently, in the years before World War II, San Pancrazio had a village priest and village church, of course, but only a very few craftsmen, and a single food shop. The village lacked a hospital, doctor, nuns, and nurses. Its nearest doctor was at Badia Agnano; the nearest large hospital at Montevarchi. Its prewar population numbered 650 inhabitants, fewer than half of whom lived inside the village and immediate environs.[25] The rest divided among four isolated nuclei and thirty even more distant farmhouses. Unlike Civitella, which had a more 'mixed' population, San Pancrazio was a purely agricultural village. The citizens of San Pancrazio were for the most part *contadini in proprio*, that is, owners of tiny parcels of land, subdivided ever smaller through the generations.[26] In addition to working their own small plots, many men also worked as foresters or woodcutters. The more fortunate also worked part-time as day labourers or farm hands for the *fattoria* Pierangeli or the *fattoria* at nearby Montaltuzzo, returning to work their own land in the evenings. About fifty *mezzadri* families occupied plots and houses in the area toward Civitella.

The village of Castelnuovo dei Sabbioni in the Valdarno, geographically in the centre of the commune of Cavriglia, shares a terrain of valley, hills, and mountain ridges similar to that of Civitella and San Pancrazio. This is a more barren landscape, however, with few farms or vines. The soil is not fertile, trees are scarce, and herbaceous vegetation sparsely covers the hills. Castelnuovo's importance is as much geological as it is historical, and as such is more recent than Civitella's or San Pancrazio's. Sitting in a lignite basin (known as the basin of Castelnuovo dei Sabbioni), the village derived its name from the sands (actually a fine-grained clay) and its economy from the lignite under its surface. Lignite is a yellowish-brown carbonized wood, which is the remains of prehistoric tree trunks and branches, with its original grain still visible. It burns like coal, though because of its looser texture it produces less heat and energy than coal. As mining of lignite deposits began in 1866 (part of Italy's late industrialization), lignite fuel helped develop the nearby metal and glass works of San Giovanni Valdarno. The construction of a large lignite-burning thermoelectric plant at the beginning of the twentieth century meant that Castelnuovo also furnished electricity to a large part of Tuscany.[27]

Miners and their families made up most of the population of Castelnuovo and surrounding villages. Before the First World War, the village population numbered about 1500, and the mine employed about 4000 workers. The population was more transient than those of Civitella and San Pancrazio, in that mine and factory workers moved more frequently to and from Castelnuovo and nearby Santa Barbara, Meleto, and

San Giovanni Valdarno. Most residents did not own or work on farms; land and property were not passed from parent to child. Because of the nature of their work, their labour and political organizations, and because of their comparative transience in a province and region where families lived for generations, the miners of Castelnuovo and environs and the industrial workers of San Giovanni Valdarno were considered more 'restive,' more politically radical – more troublesome – and threatening to the public order than the agricultural population of the rest of the Aretine.

Socialist Party and Catholic *Popolari* politics, and labour union activity (including anarcho-syndicalism) made Castelnuovo dei Sabbioni and its neighbouring villages the perfect setting in which new Fascist *squadristi* could operate in the years after World War I and where they found significant financial support. Indeed, the mining and the iron-works industries of the Valdarno contributed to the early growth of Fascism in a couple of ways. Owners and managers contributed financially to the new Fascist movement, whose violent methods they supported perhaps more than they accepted its rather vague and contradictory early ideology. In turn, the thugs or 'gangs of bullies' who had been employed to break up labour protests and to influence the miners and industrial workers in local election campaigns now made eager and ideal recruits for the Fascist squads.[28] Outside the mines and factories, the socialist and Catholic agrarian associations supporting the *mezzadri* and agricultural labourers in the Aretine countryside also provided a target for the *squadristi* in their work of terrorizing peasants, destroying workers' cooperatives, and social, political, and mutual aid organizations, while collecting contributions from large landowners.[29]

Politically, the province of Arezzo has been part of Italy's 'red belt' (though less red than some other parts), and the years after World War I started encouragingly for those who made it so. In the October 1919 elections, the first after the war, Socialist Party candidates triumphed in twenty out of forty communes; the Popolari (Catholic Popular, or Peoples Party) in eleven; the Liberals in none.[30] After the administrative elections of 1920, seventeen of Arezzo's communes had a Socialist Party majority; thirteen communes had a Popolari majority. However, the 'years of blood' (as one Aretine priest later referred to them) immediately followed these politically promising 'red years.' That is, the 'black biennium' followed the 'red biennium.' Civil unrest – 'almost civil war' – marked the time between 1919 and 1922 in the Aretine and in other parts of central and northern Italy where Fascism began to take hold.[31] In the

Aretine communes of Cavriglia and San Giovanni Valdarno, where many of the workers were socialists or anarchists, the response to encroaching Fascism and Fascist assaults on their organizations, their property, and their members was one of resistance, even armed resistance. In the spring of 1921, anti-Fascist resistance in the village of Castelnuovo exploded in violence greater than any yet seen in the province.

March 23, 1921, is a day famous in Castelnuovo's local history.[32] A number of elements in addition to local anti-Fascist sentiments were at work around that time, all causing tension among the miners. Errico Malatesta, an important anarchist leader, had been arrested and detained in Milan a few months earlier. Italian anarchists – including those in Castelnuovo and environs – protested his continued detention. In addition, Fascists had murdered the activist and anti-Fascist, Spartaco Lavagnini, in Florence a few weeks earlier. Closer to home, Attilio Sassi, an anarcho-syndicalist and anarchist secretary of the local Camera del Lavoro, was agitating the miners over Malatesta's detention and Lavagnini's murder. Maybe most important, 430 miners recently had been laid off in an economic move and their families were to be evicted from mine housing.

On the morning of March 23, three truckloads of heavily armed young blackshirts left Florence heading for Perugia, perhaps to assist comrades there in one of early Fascism's well-known 'punitive expeditions' or perhaps to celebrate the second anniversary of the founding of the Fascist movement (which had taken place in Milan's Piazza San Sepolcro). In any event, the road they took to Perugia passes through the Valdarno. Rumours of the pending arrival of a Florentine Fascist squad reached the mineworkers at Castelnuovo. Suddenly, at about two thirty in the afternoon, nearly 3000 miners left the mine gallery. Management activated the emergency alert siren, ordering the men to return to the mines. Instead, some of the miners, joined by a number of women, stormed the mine offices. Others overturned the flats for transporting lignite, using them to barricade the road to Castelnuovo, the bridge below the village, and the front of the consumers' cooperative. Armed with sticks, hunting rifles, dynamite, and other weapons, about 1000 headed towards San Giovanni to intercept the Fascists.

Coincidentally, Attilio Sassi happened to be at the mine that day to discuss with management the massive lay-offs of a few days earlier. Another, less political visitor, Agostino Longhi, a mining engineer from Grosseto, also happened to be visiting for a tour of the mine. About thirty miners forced entry into the directing engineer's office, demanding trucks and weapons. The director refused, and as events progressed, shots were fired, bombs were thrown, fires were set. Longhi was killed, and four others, including the mine director, were wounded. Eventually, seventy-four persons, among them seven women, were charged with complicity in Longhi's homicide and the attempted homicide of the director. Other charges stemmed from the damage caused to the buildings of the mine and the electric company; thefts of mine property; riots and disturbances of public order; threats; manufacture, possession, and explosion of dynamite and bombs; concealing arms; and setting fires. Some of those charged fled the area before being arrested, but the rest stood trial over a period of two years. The anarchist Sassi naturally was believed to have been the instigator. Engineer Longhi, an accidental martyr, entered Fascist hagiography.

Fascist 'action squad' violence also met anti-Fascist response in the Aretine countryside of the *mezzadri*. There, a more rural version of the Castelnuovo anti-Fascist uprising happened in the Val di Chiana a month later. On April 12, about thirty Arezzo city *squadristi*, together with blackshirts from the Valdarno and more from Florence, drove to the village of Foiano della Chiana to challenge the socialists.[33] They found the village deserted, however, as residents stayed indoors or took to the woods. Meeting no resistance, including none from the *carabinieri*, the Fascists marched through the streets singing as they destroyed the Camera del Lavoro office, the farmers' mutual aid assistance league, and the cooperative store.

The following Sunday, April 17, about twenty blackshirts returned to Foiano. Ten remained in the village, while the others headed towards Marciano about six kilometres away. All met up again that afternoon to return to Arezzo. When they passed through the hamlet of Renzino, two kilometres from Foiano, they were ambushed by a group of peasants. Armed with farm tools – axes and pitchforks – and with a few rifles and pistols, the farmers killed three of the Fascists and wounded others, including the captain of the Seventieth Infantry Division stationed in Arezzo (who had participated in the expedition wearing civilian clothes). Fascists from as far away as Siena, Perugia, Florence, and Città di Castello joined in the inevitable reprisals. They rampaged through the village and surrounding countryside, burning farmhouses and killing four citizens. For days afterwards, Fascists 'visited' the homes of socialists and other 'subversives' to threaten and assault them. The three dead men – these more of their own accord than poor engineer Longhi – entered Fascist hagiography as the 'martyrs of Renzino,' and provided the names for units of *fasci di combattimento* then forming.[34]

Thus, Fascism arrived in the Aretine much as it did in the other provinces of Tuscany, and in central and northern Italy, though perhaps with more force behind it – given Arezzo's proximity to Florence and the numerous active and enthusiastic Florentine *squadristi*.[35] Arezzo had its own share of blackshirts – even in Castelnuovo. By the end of 1921, the capital city's *fascio* counted 600 members and 220 women auxiliaries. As of May 1921, the province as a whole had 13 *fasci* with 1114 adherents, 19 sections and 1403 members by August that year, and 58 sections and 7000 members by May 1922. The first number of *Giovinezza* (November 27, 1921), boasted that the province of Arezzo 'in proportion to the number of its inhabitants, is among the foremost ranks of Fascist Italy.'[36]

The two-year period during which the miners of Castelnuovo stood trial began as a time of tension, antagonism, and violence, both on the part of the *squadristi* and their opposition. It was also a time of rapid and dramatic political transition in the Valdarno, in the Aretine, and in the rest of Italy. The trial began in Arezzo in a climate already hostile towards the miners on the part of the press, the court, the prefect, and some of the public. By the time the trial ended, with eleven acquitted and fifty-five convicted, Fascism had a firm political grip on the Aretine.[37] How completely Fascism captured individual hearts and minds, and how deeply it penetrated Aretine society as a whole is less answerable – and not critical to this study.[38] Twenty years of living the Fascist experience was a factor, but only one of the factors that shaped the postwar transition of society.

Fascism aside – and in the midst of Fascism – the villages of Castelnuovo, Civitella, and San Pancrazio, like the villages around them, were very much the villages of *Three Bells of Civilization*: places where civil life and *civiltà* structured society. There, the patterns and meanings of daily life were known and had been known for generations. They were taken for granted even as political change and violence began to spin out of control in 1920 and 1921 – and again in 1943.

PART ONE

War and Massacre

1 Italy at War

The sense of depression is accentuated by the events of war – which are not favourable to the Axis – and by the destruction caused by the frequent enemy bombings.

Questore, June 25, 1943.

To July 25, 1943

War can strengthen states or break them, but what it does to the people in those states is more complicated.[1] At its start, war's effects on the population may be as unpredictable as the final outcome for the state. As war continues, however, the more likely it is that it will lead to hardship, will disrupt and change the course of ordinary lives, and then end in individual and shared tragedy. A state's collapse will add to its citizens' (and to the nation's) immediate wartime difficulties, while lives remain altered and war-caused suffering continues after one state has ceased to exist and another has formed to take its place. Whether the war Italy entered on the side of Nazi Germany on June 10, 1940, would strengthen or break the Italian state and the Fascist Party was not a foregone conclusion, even given Italy's early misadventure in Greece. What ultimate, devastating effects that war would have on Italian lives – soldier and civilian – were inconceivable as the war began for Italy.

How deep or shallow was the ordinary citizen's support of or opposition to yet more war – and this on the side of Hitler – is difficult to gauge in the early months, as opposed to postwar hindsight, though some initial excitement and vocal support were apparent.[2] The experience of nearly twenty years of Fascist repression naturally constrained what reactions the population could express openly, and what most felt or remembered afterward was coloured by the second more brutal and local phase of the war that included bombing, invasion, occupation, and resistance. More local men were called or recalled to arms, and more depressing news arrived from the fronts, as was told around the village well or in the piazza in the evenings; but the horrors of Italian suffering and deaths in Russia, widespread destruction by Allied bombing at home, and war on Italian soil were still in the unimagined future. In many ways, life seemed to go on much as usual in Aretine villages for the first year or so of war.[3]

Fascism itself continued as part of daily life, certainly, and if Italian Fascism was a somewhat successful experiment in totalitarianism and was, at least in part, about nationalizing individuals, then Italy's entry into the war offered additional opportunities to further those aims and to strengthen both state and party at society's expense.[4] In the province of Arezzo, as elsewhere, the Fascist Party itself continued old activities as it took up many new ones, spurred first by Mussolini's increasingly totalitarian domestic policy and then by war.[5] When a party survey carried out from late 1937 to early 1938 showed that many *fasci*, including those in Arezzo, did not own the land or buildings that served as their headquarters, but instead utilized property owned by the commune or property belonging to private owners, the party sought to regularize its real estate situation.[6] It set out acquiring title to property – whether obtaining it by gift, intimidation, or very nominal purchase price – where *fasci* offices already sat or as sites for new *Case del fascio* and *Case littorie*, and it busied itself improving and expanding existing *Case* well into 1943.[7] In the province of Arezzo, in June 1942, the commune of Ortignano finally 'gave' to that commune's *fascio di combattimento* the plot of land, part of the commune's own *patrimonio*, on which the local party's *Casa* had sat for nearly two decades. That same month, the *fascio* of Palazzo del Pero in the commune of Arezzo purchased from a private individual, for an undisclosed sum, the site on which it intended to build a new *Casa del fascio* with a budget of 12,000 lire.

As late as the spring of 1943 – when surely the party and its *Federazioni dei fasci* had more pressing concerns – a dozen letters and other documents passed between the party in Rome, in Arezzo, and in the locality of the structure itself, exhaustively discussing the importance and correct method of using oil-based paint when repainting the *Casa del fascio* in Cortona – so as to minimize dust.[8] On July 21, 1943, nearly two weeks after the Allies had landed in Sicily, the *fascio* of San Giovanni Valdarno set aside the significant sum of 23,000 lire to reinforce the stairs and to relocate the projection booth of that *Casa*'s movie theatre.[9] The day after Mussolini's removal from office, Bruno Rao Torres, federal secretary of the federation of *fasci* for Arezzo, and apparently unaware of the most recent national events, reported to Rome on the number of members enrolled in the province's various *fasci*, the condition of their *Case*, and what repairs were urgently needed.[10]

So much material (and some frivolous) party activity during a seemingly inauspicious period can reflect a reinvigorated enthusiasm for Fascism and support for the war, or only the party's attempt to generate or claim both. Or the local *fasci* focus on very local Fascist Party property and accomplishments served to help divert attention from the increasingly difficult national and international situation, while simultaneously binding communes and villages more closely to the party and party programs. More telling than Aretine participation in that burst of party labours in the late 1930s and the early war years, Arezzo's prefect was able to report to Rome that no anti-Fascist activity had occurred in the province for the period from April to June 1942, and that subversive behaviour was insignificant from July through September that year.[11] How the prefect defined 'subversive' and 'insignificant' is not known, but apparently nothing characterized as sufficiently anti-Fascist or anti-war disturbed the public order (keeping in mind that the prefect's career depended on reports of inconsequential subversive activity).

How closely connected were the war and Fascism in the minds of ordinary citizens at the war's beginning and as it progressed? Did no anti-Fascist activity mean consensus for the war? Were Mussolini and Fascism already being blamed for getting Italy into this larger conflict, or would Mussolini become the scapegoat only after Italy was invaded, the war had been lost, and the Fascist Party had been dissolved? Support for or opposition to the war, as opposed to mere obedience to the commander-in-chief or head of state while the war had little direct adverse impact at home, is of some importance (if difficult to discern and measure accurately across the country) because of what the war would do and later would mean to Italy.

More meaningful, therefore, than the reported absence of anti-Fascist or anti-Mussolini manifestations were the many affirmative, supportive actions in the form of large and small monetary contributions that poured into the party from corporate donors (like the 50,000 lire sent by the Cassa di Risparmio di Parma) and from ordinary citizens (like the little boy who sent 10 lire he had been saving), to be passed on to families of the *combattenti* and the widowed families of those killed 'fighting communism' in

Russia.[12] The party had put itself in charge of assistance to families of current combatants and to families of the early war dead, using such private contributions in part, and handing out aid directly from and through local party arms (the *fasci*, the Opera Nazionale Dopolavoro, or party associations) or through the Communal Assistance Agency (Ente Comunale di Assistenza or ECA), which was funded through state and worker contributions and party-administered.[13] The party's national head of administrative services also asked for an additional state contribution of sixty million lire in February 1942 to cover the 'unforeseen expenses' of 'war year XX' – funds that would not be directed towards the war's conduct, but would support new party undertakings related to the war.[14]

Some of the state's increased contribution towards assistance also came from new taxes, but like the private contributions, it went out to whom, where, and as the party decided best.[15] Small grants were given to military families on the home front, while the troops received such morale boosters as cigarettes, 5000 leather cigarette holders stamped 'Gift of the PNF' (or National Fascist Party), a million litres of wine whose labels read 'Gift of the PNF,' thousands of packs of playing cards and table games, 10,000 pens stamped either 'Gift of the Duce' or 'Gift of the PNF,' and 40,000 pocket-sized photocards of the Duce himself, and another 30,000 of the king and the crown prince.[16] The party purposefully and very directly connected itself to the war (as did Mussolini of course). The war gave the party and the state more to do and more to control, and provided more opportunities for the party to make itself a larger part of everyday life. The war thus began as a source of invigoration for the party, strength for the state, and offered opportunities to expand what Emilio Gentile termed the Fascist totalitarian laboratory. The party, it seemed, most definitely wanted the war, or at least wanted to make good use of it. Party and state were utterly unprepared for the war they got, however, and with its pens and playing cards, the party helped remind soldiers on a daily basis just who had gotten them to Greece, North Africa, and the Russian front.

Paul Ginsborg has located the first domestic opposition to the war in the urban north in the spring of 1943. There, '[s]ections of the industrial working class were the first to express open discontent' against the war and the regime, when about 100,000 workers engaged in 'some form of strike action' in March 1943.[17] The thousands of Turin factory workers who stopped work throughout that month, demanding wage increases to counteract the increasing cost of living and to help recompense for Allied bomb damage, surely sent the strongest anti-war, anti-regime message to state and party to date, but they were not the first to demonstrate their displeasure with war-related current affairs. Food, not wages or the regime, became the first major source of discontent in wartime Arezzo, giving rise to small but concerted protests a year before the Turin workers took action.

Rationing made for an austere, restricted, and more nationalized life; it increasingly became the people's locus of resentment and cause of division against the war, the regime, the state, and against each other. Although Arezzo was an agricultural province where many citizens grew and raised much of their own food or had family in the countryside to supply them with basic foodstuffs, increasingly severe rationing and increased amassing requirements turned what began as an inconvenience into personal and family hardship – and into real dissent. Ration cards were not introduced in Italy until October 1941, but coffee and sugar had been immediately rationed as the war began, soon followed in autumn 1940 by limits on soap, fats and oil, flour, pasta, rice, and meat. Maize and then potato flour were ordered added to bread to cut the percentage of wheat flour used. Bread itself came to be rationed in October 1941 in the amount of 250 grams per person per day – lowered to an even less adequate 150 grams per day in March 1942.[18] By the spring of 1942, still stricter rationing implied the war was not likely to end soon, and that spring the protests began in earnest.

A few voices in a small place may speak as loudly as many voices in a larger place. In the small place that was Arezzo, coping with complaints and angry protests over rationing and food shortages kept Arezzo's prefect and the communal podestàs well occupied.[19] And as common when daily food and its procurement are at issue, women were the most vocal protesters.[20] On April 4, 1942, fifty women from the village of Ponticino in the commune of Laterina descended on the commune office demanding an increase in the recently lowered bread ration and finally obtaining a temporary increase to 200 grams per day.[21] That same month, a group of women and children from the farming hamlet of Strada in Casentino crowded into the local municipio in Castel San Niccolo calling for restoration of the supplemental bread ration for agricultural workers. They also complained about the unfair distribution of potatoes and beans, so escalating the situation that the local carabinieri unit intervened to plead for calm and to get the women to leave. The report of their protest reached all the way to the desk of the Interior Ministry in Rome.[22]

Protests occurred regularly: the citizens assailed their administrations each month with a common theme – too little bread and a meat ration that never seemed to arrive. Individual communes then complained (through their *podestà*) to the provincial prefect that they were being treated unfairly compared to other communes in the province, insisting that all others were receiving more meat, vegetables, and bread and in a more timely fashion. 'Discontent reigns,' reported every commune.[23]

'The province of Arezzo is principally agricultural,' Arezzo's *Questore* wrote in his June 25, 1943, report (his final report before Mussolini's fall), and therefore the 'rural population enjoys relative well-being, even during the current state of war.'[24] Censored mail during the spring and summer of 1943, in contrast, was filled with complaints about the high cost of living and shortages of good quality food. That and the frequency of demonstrations over bread, meat, vegetables, and unfairness belied the *Questore's* assessment of the population's relative well-being. According to one historian, Arezzo was among the provinces with the most food problems, and, according to contemporary informant reports, its citizens complained more about food and worried more about food than they did about other aspects or effects of the war.[25]

As the rationing system grew more inclusive, the black market became an integral part of the Italian economy, and Arezzo's as well. By November 5, 1942, the officially sanctioned market at Castel San Niccolo lacked every type of groceries, and most basic dry goods items. Both food and dry goods easily could be found, however, at exorbitant prices on the black market – which existed on a large scale.[26] Between April 25 and June 24, 1943, rationing infractions for Arezzo had increased dramatically from previous months: 110 merchants had been reported for hoarding goods, changing prices, and for other violations; 250 private individuals had been reported for various rationing infractions on the purchasing side.[27] Not enormous numbers compared to provinces with larger cities, but enough to alarm provincial authorities. The *Questore's* same June 25, 1943, report (which elsewhere had stressed Arezzo's well-being during wartime) reassured Rome that local police were carrying out surveillance of rationing with greater commitment than ever before, and catching ever more failures to follow national prices – a result that Rome could interpret in multiple ways.

The Aretines were more preoccupied with food shortages than with other aspects of the war between 1940 and 1943, because those other aspects – such as Allied bombing – had not yet hit central Italy. As the war progressed into the spring and the dry, hot summer of 1943 central Italy began to feel bombing's indirect impact. In early 1943, months before the Allies' July 10 landing in Sicily, daylight bombings by Allied 'Liberators' began over southern cities like Cagliari, Naples, and Trapani, and in the north over Milan and Genoa, creating thousands of internal evacuees and refugees who fled their bombed cities for the perceived safety of rural central Italy. The result for Arezzo was an unforeseen, unplanned-for influx of evacuees and refugees from other parts of Italy that strained the province's means, strained citizens' ability to cope, and quickly grew beyond the Fascist state's ability to regulate.[28]

Official and unofficial assistance to evacuees and refugees commenced with great enthusiasm and solidarity in 1943. As trainloads of refugees passed through central cities like Florence, members of the *Fasci Femminili* set up hospitality stations, offering coffee, soup, and pasta to the refugees.[29] Italians in parts of the country like the Aretine and the rest of Tuscany, which were not yet physically affected by the war (that is, not yet bombed), generously offered money, clothing, even temporary shelter. Aretine families volunteered to take in children from bombed cities. The party assigned the Fascist youth organization Gioventù Italiana del Littorio (GIL) the job of settling refugee children whose parents had remained at home, although many placements were made on a casual, private basis through acquaintances or through parish churches.[30] In March 1943, however, following orders from Rome, Arezzo's prefect ordered communal *podestàs* to terminate all private and informal initiatives for gathering or giving assistance. From then on, the Fascist Party alone was to organize and oversee aid to refugees and evacuees, though *podestàs* were told that, naturally, they and the communes' other citizens still were expected to assist the party with all means at their disposal.[31] Thus, social solidarity – more desirable and more necessary as the war escalated – also purposefully came under party control.

By July 1943, the Aretine, whose own prewar population was 319,754, had become home to 22,208 evacuees from other provinces.[32] As both the number of refugees and the price of food increased and as available food and housing thus became more limited, citizens in relatively untouched areas, like Arezzo, grew less welcoming to outsiders. They rather reasonably began to view the refugees as competitors for scarce resources and another unhappy consequence of a progressively more disruptive war. Philip Morgan has pointed to rationing and bombing – and the Fascist regime's inability to protect the people from bombing and to secure them enough food – as the main factors leading to Italians' dissatisfaction with Mussolini, Fascism, and the war that was clearly not going well for Italy.[33] As state and party tried to 'catch up' to the worsening situation, their inability to manage either war or the home front daily became more apparent to the increasingly frustrated and uncooperative population.

Now, the state mandated that every Aretine commune take in refugees and evacuees – up to its 'full capacity.' Government inspectors from outside the province threatened to come and check each commune's capacity, lest it purposely be understated.[34] Homes, farm buildings, schools, libraries, museums, private and public buildings all were considered potential housing for refugees, though a bit late in the game. Communes, on behalf of the state, officially requisitioned many privately owned buildings, while homeless refugees simply occupied some empty properties.[35] Sorting out questions of private property, entitlements to residency, and contentious evictions would continue for years after the war.

In May 1943, the commune of Civitella's prefectural commissioner wrote to a homeowner in the fraction of Tuori (in the commune of Civitella), who was then living in Brescia, that the continuing flood of evacuees required every house not occupied by its owner or by tenants be put at the commune's disposal for housing the 'unfortunate refugees.' The commissioner wished to give the owner the opportunity voluntarily to offer his empty house to a displaced family. If, however, the owner chose not to, and if his family did not return to occupy it within ten days from receipt of the letter, the commune had no choice but to requisition it. The commissioner concluded that the commune and Italy were '[c]ounting on your well known spirit of understanding towards our compatriots who, because of enemy barbarity, have been forced to abandon their own homes and property.'[36] The 'enemy barbarity' referred to, of course, was the Allied bombing of Italy.

The national spirit of understanding had practical limits in the village of Tuori as elsewhere. On July 17, 1943 – a week after the Allies landed in Sicily and just a week before the Fascist Grand Council voted to remove Mussolini from office – Arezzo's prefect (as directed by the minister of the interior, Mussolini) exhorted all citizens to take in refugees and to 'remain firm to the principle *that the evacuees who, under the terror of ruthless enemy bombing, have had to abandon their own towns and homes, often with loved ones wounded, should not have to wander from one province to the next to find a modest shelter.*'[37] When compelling citizens to open their property to evacuees, communal *podestàs* were directed to work with local *fasci* and, using 'efficacious and persuasive propaganda,' take every opportunity to rekindle fading sentiments of solidarity and generosity towards those who had suffered – and to rekindle sentiments of hatred for the enemy. By the time of that mid-July 1943 injunction, in Arezzo and elsewhere, sentiments of hatred were more commonly directed towards Mussolini – who had gotten them all into the worsening situation.

At the same time, other, somewhat less ruthless wartime enemies of the Italian nation and of Fascism already were present in the Aretine and sharing its resources with the townspeople, farmers, miners, and refugees. British nationals (and later, United States citizens), Greeks, Slovenes, Yugoslav nationals, and foreign Jews who found themselves in Italy when war was declared in June 1940, all were subject to internment or confinement, as were Italian anti-Fascists. Civilian internment camps – or concentration camps – existed in Italy as of 1940, with four of them in the province of Arezzo.[38] One camp, located in the village of Oliveto in the commune of Civitella, interned about seventy British citizens present in Italy when the war began, and Libyan Jews who had been living in Italy or who had been sent there after the first battle of El Alamein.[39] Another, larger camp, housing mostly Slavs, was located at Renicci near Anghiari, with the other two at Cortona and Bibbiena.[40] The camps' rudimentary accommodations generally lacked the barest necessities. The large camp at Renicci, for example, on which construction began in the summer of 1941, was only about half-completed when the first inmates arrived in October 1942; they spent the winter in makeshift tents, with only the ill and the children sleeping indoors on concrete floors in the uncompleted barracks.[41]

One hundred ninety foreign and Italian 'free internees' (that is, who were relatively free, in what was termed, *in stato libero*) lived in the city of Arezzo and some other communes in the province by the summer of 1943.[42] These included Italians and foreigners sent from other provinces to be 'isolated' in a different province, and those locals or foreign enemy residents not considered dangerous enough – or in some cases not physically strong enough – to be interned in a concentration camp. In addition were the 'unwelcome guests' (as opposed to enemies) whom the prefect described as for the most part 'undisciplined, conniving, and openly inimical to Italy,' over whom it was necessary to maintain strict vigilance, and who might be better off in concentration camps.[43] Although not specified, those 'undisciplined connivers' likely did not include the British nationals (including a number of elderly women) who had resided in Tuscany (usually Florence) for years before the war. Whereas some British expatriates (and later, Americans) who had long lived in Italy were interned (as at Oliveto); others were not.[44]

Some 'unwelcome guests' or official enemies of the state were not only interned, confined, or free, but suffered a bit of all three. June Adams, the daughter of an American mother and a British father, had grown up in Florence, where her father owned a real estate agency. She and her

father were arrested in May 1941 for 'having expressed hostile sentiments towards Italy and towards Fascism' and for 'having expressed satisfaction over the retreat of Italian troops' from Greece. The accusations
were false, but Miss Adams and her father were British and therefore
technically Italy's enemies. After spending a short time in jail in Pistoia,
they were sent to the province of Arezzo, where they were interned, not
in one of the camps, but in a run-down villa in the countryside. Her room-
mates there were other national enemies of Italy: two young Yugoslav
women and a Greek woman. Because her father was ill with ulcers and
because the villa had no heat, Miss Adams and her father were transferred to a hospital, where the father stayed until just before the liberation and where her mother joined them following Italy's declaration of
war against the United States. Miss Adams spent her days visiting nearby
farms to buy food. When her hospital room was needed for someone
else, Miss Adams lived with a local family, whom she paid for room and
board.

In July 1943, the Interior Ministry expressed concern that unspecified
'free' enemy subjects (these presumably British or American) might be
'carrying on in luxury hotels and pensions,' flaunting an 'extravagant
life-style' and 'provoking the indignation of the population,' rather than
observing the standard of living 'appropriate for those [enemies] in exi-
gent circumstances.' Arezzo's *Questore* and prefect promised that the enemy subjects living 'freely' in the province of Arezzo did not carry on
ostentatiously or provoke public indignation. According to the prefect,
all of the province's free internees comported themselves 'with discipline' and did not draw attention to themselves.[45] Moreover, the province had no luxury hotels in which they might carry on.[46]

Most semi-free enemies, like June Adams, could not have afforded to
flaunt themselves in luxury hotels, had any been available in Arezzo. Less
well-off subjects were even less able to contribute to the costs of their own
confinement or internment, something the government acknowledged.
The Fascist government confined or interned its enemies, but also recognized the need to assist them financially – though not by very much. The
Interior Ministry directed that the Communal Assistance Agency (ECA)
provide subsidies and assistance to both Italians and foreigners interned
or confined within Italy for national, political, or religious (racial) reasons.[47] That is, the ministry ordered living allowance subsidies paid to 'interned indigent Jews, conationals and foreigners' assigned to places of
confinement or internment. Individuals and families were granted 50 lire
a month to pay for lodging and food if confined rather than interned in a

camp. Interned heads of household ('the husband') were given 8 lire per day; the wife 4 lire, and 3 lire for each minor child authorized to live with the interned person.[48] In July 1943 – just before his fall – Mussolini raised all such relief amounts by one lira.[49] This was barely enough to keep a family from starvation and, moreover, it was not an entitlement in the legal sense, of course: no recourse was available if the few lire granted were not actually given, which most often they were not.[50]

The same combination of official harshness and token generosity extended to the administration of the camps. Camp guards were not always or completely unsympathetic towards the nation's enemy internees, and in Arezzo at least, camp regulations were not always strictly enforced. On May 6, 1943, in a small example of Italian consideration (and disregard for petty state regulations), the *Questore* of Arezzo easily dismissed a possible rationing and consumption tax violation on the part of the food purveyor to the Oliveto camp and some of its inmates. The local butcher had furnished 74 kilograms of veal to some of the camp's prisoners, who had paid for the veal themselves and paid to have it butchered – for their celebration of 'Jewish Easter' (*la Pasqua ebraica*). Surely, the *Questore* concluded, neither the rationing violation nor the tax violation was worth bothering about in such a case.[51]

Internees at Oliveto, as at other camps, were officially permitted to write letters only to those persons for whom they had received authorization (presumably from the *Questore*, the prefect, or the camp director), and they could write only one letter of twenty-four lines and one postcard each week. June Adams recalled, however, being allowed to write to whomever she wished as often as she wished wherever she happened to be held. In addition, the director of the Oliveto camp was sanctioned (along with the directors of the other three camps) in April 1943 for repeatedly allowing mail to leave the camp stamped 'passed by censor,' but without indicating on the envelope which office had censored it or whether it really had been read.[52]

A few acts of kindness in the realm of Passover veal or unread personal letters can be interpreted as basic acts of humanity typical of Italians (*brava gente*), as stubbornly individualistic reluctance to comply with the regime's policies towards national enemies who realistically posed no danger to the nation, or as local disgust with Fascism and the war. Individuals acting on the local level, however, were also what made possible the system of domestic concentration camps in which not all commandants were kind, in which many died, and from which some were sent on to forced labour in Germany or to death camps.[53]

Italian concentration camps were not designed to be part of the Nazi final solution, and Italians in those towns and villages where camps were located did not witness thousands of Jews and others enter camp gates but never leave. As Jonathan Dunnage has written, however, the 'existence of concentration camps in Italy before the German occupation,' and I would emphasize the number – the existence of some 120 to 130 camps in Italy well before the German occupation – should make one look at the pre–German occupation, pre–Republic of Salò period of wartime Italy and at Italians in a somewhat more German light.[54] These were not all Fascist true believers; these were ordinary Italians who governed, guarded, lived next to, and sold supplies to the camps and their inmates.

Italy's concentration or internment camps (before September 8, 1943) have been categorized as two types: those being *per scopi repressive* ('for purposes of repression') and those termed *a scopo protettivo* ('for purposes of protection'), with Italy's potentially dangerous national enemies 'locked up' or neutralized in the first type, and non-Italian Jews 'protected' in the second type. This 'bad camp'–'good camp' distinction in turn both reinforces and make more problematic the 'good Italian' or *brava gente* stereotype, especially as to those camps within Italy.[55] In Arezzo, was Renicci a 'bad camp' where Slavs suffered in dismal conditions? Was Oliveto, in contrast, a 'good camp' where British civilians whiled away the war and foreign Jews celebrated Passover? Such a distinction says something about existing racism, as it does about Italian recognition of who was more likely to be a real threat to the nation during wartime.

Italy was not the only World War II participant to intern national and racial (or ethnic and religious) enemies found on its soil when war broke out, of course (or, as in the case of the United States and Canada, its own nationals considered enemies). Nonetheless, while European Jews seeking safety had reason to turn to Italian authorities instead of German, Vichy French, or Croatian authorities in Axis occupied territory, what was the purpose of 'good camps' within Italy if not to separate 'others,' including Jews, from Italians? And, if the Italian state indeed intended 'good camps' in Italy to protect foreign Jews (rather than as a way to facilitate expelling them later), from whom did they need protecting before September 8, 1943, and unforeseen German occupation?

In the past decade or so, research attention has focused on Italy's actions during the first half of the war. Thus, until fairly recently, pre–September 8, 1943, perceived Italian military ineptitude or lack of enthusiasm, from which usually was deduced a widespread military and civilian reluctance to fight Mussolini's war against the Allies, had been used to distinguish the Italian from the German wartime case. The conviction that Italians, by nature, remained 'inherently good people' (*brava gente*) during that cruel war both fostered and was fostered by the distinction between Italy and Nazi Germany: Italians did nothing so bad (as compared to Germany) and any bad acts were the fault of Mussolini and a few committed 'bad' Fascists. As Italy's own war crimes and atrocities in the Italian colonies, in Greece, and in Yugoslavia now undergo critical examination, the picture of Italians at war has begun to change.[56] Italy's military activities outside Italy are not the only part of its wartime past to be reconsidered. Italy's treatment of enemies within its borders also makes up part of the blind spot of national memory. What Italian officials and civilians did locally to other civilians should not be forgotten as scholars scrutinize what Italian soldiers did during the period of war with Germany against the Allies.

One additional and important group – Allied soldier prisoners of war – had been more openly inimical to the nation of Italy, and POWs now also found themselves under Italian control, forcibly sitting out part of the war in the Aretine in the summer of 1943. Many of them had been captured at Tobruk and environs in North Africa in June 1942, and eventually were brought to POW camp 'Number 82' at Laterina, about fifteen kilometres from Civitella and San Pancrazio. Unprepared for waging protracted war and for protecting its own citizens during that war, Italy also was unprepared to accommodate the prisoners of war it took.

James Percival of the Durham Light Infantry was captured by German troops near Fuka, North Africa on June 29, 1942, and handed over to the Italians at Tobruk. He arrived at Laterina camp about August 6, 1942, and was one of its earliest inmates.[57] According to Percival, for the first few months, the prisoners lived in leaky tents made of ground sheets. The prisoners themselves helped build stone huts with cement floors, which finally were ready for occupation in January 1943. The Italian authorities had very little clothing to issue, so the men had to make do with their North African 'desert kit' through the bone chilling, wet Tuscan winter. They slept on thin straw mattresses. Water for plumbing and for washing clothes was infrequent, and showers were not available until April or May 1943. Food was inadequate as well; prisoners had 200 grams of bread and 20 grams of cheese per day, with meat only once or twice a week, but Red Cross parcels arrived fairly regularly.[58]

A daily bread ration of 200 grams was more than most Italian citizens were then allowed, and a number of prisoners received more when they went to work at local farms, as some fifty POWs from Laterina camp worked for Iris Origo and her husband at their estate in the Val d'Orcia in the neighbouring province of Siena for several months before the armistice. On May 7, 1943, Origo wrote of those prisoners, who did not seem too badly off in comparison with their Italian civilian 'neighbours':

> Their rations as a working-party are better than those they had in camp – four hundred grs. of bread a day, as opposed to two hundred, meat twice a week, etc. And they supplement their rations with magnificent Red Cross parcels (a five-kg. parcel a week for each prisoner) containing in each parcel a tin of butter, one of marmalade or treacle, cocoa, potted meat, dried beans or peas, bacon, fifty cigarettes and a cake of excellent soap – bounty at which we all gape.[59]

At the same time the *Questore* was writing of Arezzo's 'relative well-being during wartime,' the province's real circumstances (like Italy's wartime circumstances) seemed much worse to those living them than the official would admit. By the summer of 1943, respective situations were growing increasingly difficult for all of the various residents – POWs, enemy internees and confinees, refugees, and citizens – whose daily lives had become linked together, very locally, in the province of Arezzo. The *Questore* stressed that all was well, on the surface at least. According to that June 25, 1943, report, May 1 (Labour Day) and June 10 and 11 (the anniversary of Socialist Deputy Giacomo Matteotti's murder at the hands of Fascists in 1924) had passed without incident. A few 'subversive inscriptions' appeared on walls and some handwritten leaflets were left on the street at night, but these, he assured, were the work of 'individuals' rather than an organized anti-Fascist protest.

Although reluctant to undercut this positive note, the *Questore* did acknowledge that the people were anxious. The civilian population worried about what the coming months would bring; he said they feared more rationing, more refugees, more enemy bombing, more losses for the Axis. Lack of rain had hurt the crops. The cost of living was rising, though war had made unemployment in most industries basically non-existent. The largest and most assertive group of workers in the province – the 4000 miners of Castelnuovo dei Sabbioni – continued to concern the authorities. Enemy bombing and military takeover of railway transportation made conveying lignite to market more difficult, necessitating lay-offs and a shorter working day, and in turn causing protests by the miners and their families.

Notwithstanding the growing adversities of daily life, according to the *Questore* (for whom preserving calm, discipline, and public order constituted the point of his job), Arezzo's citizens maintained 'both calm and discipline' in the face of that challenging war and demonstrated an ability to meet whatever future events might unfold with still more calm.[60] How accurate was this reassuring picture of shared stoicism, discipline, and pervasive calm, drawn up for the prefect and for the state? Already, the more accurate shared experiences were those of disruption: one's food and one's property were no longer one's own and there was not enough of either to go around. People who had for years been one's neighbours were now the enemy in one's midst. Within a month, future events would take a sudden sharper turn, and further disrupt the 'calm and discipline' characterized in the *Questore*'s still optimistic June 1943 report.

The End of Fascism: July 25 to September 8, 1943

On July 25, 1943, Father Ferrante Bagiardi, the priest of Castelnuovo dei Sabbioni, briefly, matter-of-factly, and without further comment, recorded in his parish diary: 'At 11:00 p.m., the radio announced that His Excellency Mussolini has been dismissed as head of the government and that his highness the King has named instead His Excellency Pietro Badoglio.'[61] The Allies had landed in Sicily two weeks earlier on July 10, 1943, and the Italian army had put up some, but not enough resistance. Many Italians, including the members of Mussolini's Fascist Grand Council, recognized the Allied landing as the signal that the war (at least insofar as Italy was concerned) had been lost. One day after the Fascist Grand Council's July 24 'no confidence vote,' King Vittorio Emanuele deposed Mussolini as head of the government and Italians celebrated the 'end' of Fascism.

Before the fall of Mussolini, subversive and anti-Fascist incidents in the city and province of Arezzo normally had been minor and immediately subdued (at least according to the *Questore* and prefect), generally limited to a few anonymous leaflets and maybe a bit of graffiti. On the evening of July 26, however, widespread anti-Fascism openly erupted. Workers invaded and smashed *fasci* headquarters at Cavriglia and elsewhere. Armed troops prevented further destruction, until the prefect ordered the seats of the *fasci* for the entire province closed and locked. On the afternoon of the twenty-eighth, workers at the Fabbricone factory in Arezzo stopped work and demanded that 'all Fascist employees' be fired.[62] Father Bagiardi recorded that in Castelnuovo, the first feelings of astonishment at Mussolini's downfall rapidly gave way both to 'demon-strations of joy for the new government' and to 'reactions against some Fascist elements' – reactions which, he noted, resulted in serious cuts and bruises for those local Fascist 'elements' at the hands of the joyful demonstrators.[63]

Arezzo's prefect summed up the province's immediate 'post-Mussolini' situation for Rome:

– The course of military operations in Sicily is the cause of active concern: the people at all levels remain painfully shaken by it.
– The collapse of the Fascist regime has given place to evident, nearly unanimous manifestations of satisfaction.
– With the exception of sporadic and isolated incidents taking place in outlying locations in the province, order and discipline are everywhere maintained.
– The clergy and the organs of Catholic Action have clearly increased their activity.[64]

Arezzo's citizens may have been delighted at the fall of Mussolini, but they did not necessarily want Italy to lose the war. Thus, they were pain-fully shaken by the Allied landing (no doubt by the fact that the war had arrived in Italy and by the unmistakable inference that the war was going even worse for Italy than they had been told). Some unspecified 'inci-dents' (like assaults on Fascists in Castelnuovo) marred what the *Questore* and prefect kept insisting was the usual order and discipline during that most unusual time. And most intriguing of all to anyone studying the Italian postwar was the clearly increased activity by the clergy and by Catholic Action – quickly seizing the opportunity and already preparing to fill the political and governmental vacuum.

Fascism was 'over,' but what was left and what was coming next? Most Italians equated the fall of Mussolini and the end of Fascism with the end of the war. On July 29, hundreds of men who had heard the ru-mour of an armistice did not show up for their shift at the Castelnuovo mines, while on August 18, workers at the Fabbricone plant stopped work, as did fifty workers at the Boschi paperworks. All were celebrat-ing the rumoured conclusion of peace.[65] The rumours were false, how-ever, and war on the side of Germany continued under Marshal Badoglio's direction.

Meanwhile, over the days following Mussolini's fall, as the war went on and the Germans prepared for Italy's surrender and the arrival of the

Allies on the mainland, the political and political-institutional components of Fascism were terminated or dissolved – from above. On July 27, the king's royal decree abolished the Fascist Party, the Fascist Grand Council (which three days earlier had paved the way for Mussolini's dismissal), and the Special Tribunal instituted to try crimes against Fascism. July 30 saw the demise of the Chamber of Fasces and Corporations.[66] The Fascist Party youth organization, Gioventù Italiana del Littorio (GIL), which had enrolled young people between ages six and twenty-one, also was dissolved.[67] State and Fascist-state institutions – the offices of provincial prefect, prefectural commissioner, *Questore*, and communal *podestàs* – remained in place, however, though Iris Origo recorded that some prefects were placed under temporary house arrest.[68]

Italians and their remaining government also retained Fascist social and welfare organizations – ostensibly 'defascistized,' but otherwise unchanged. After July 25, the consensus-building leisure organization, the Opera Nazionale Dopolavoro (OND or *dopolavoro*) remained '*in vita*'; any sections that had closed were told to reopen.[69] Directed 'to reinvigorate themselves,' all *dopolavori* were obliged to institute at least one of the following activities: sports, excursions, theatre, culture (through a library or classes), music (bands, orchestras, or choruses), or rural initiatives (such as victory gardens or raising chickens).

Podestàs were notified on September 4, 1943, that the organization Gioventù Italiana was being instituted in place of the recently disbanded Fascist youth organization Gioventù Italiana del Littorio. What had formerly been 'GIL' was now just 'GI' – without the 'L' for *Littorio*. 'New' GI centres (which were actually the same old GIL community centres) would absorb all funds of the defunct GIL and were entrusted with all their predecessor's functions, especially assistance activities like children's summer camps and settling of refugee children.[70] The significance of the term *littorio* – and its elimination – was the symbolic 'defascistization' of an organization whose very purpose had been to inculcate the 'Fascist spirit' into the next generation through indoctrination and various physical, social, and service activities. Thus, peculiarly, the Fascist mass organizations GIL and OND quickly and easily ceased being agents of Fascism and consensus generators for Fascism. As many Italians would do within a very few days, they simply stopped being Fascist, yet they remained much the same.

Fascist 'spaces' and Fascist buildings could not be dissolved, of course, yet Fascist property or space also needed somehow to be 'defascistized.' Revitalized *dopolavori* were to separate themselves from former Fascist

Party officers and separate physically from *fasci* premises. Those *dopolavori* that had shared buildings or office space with the local *fasci* were to inventory precisely which items of property (such as furniture and supplies) belonged to the *dopolavoro* and which to the *fascio*. Current presidents and secretaries were to continue directing their *dopolavori*, but if any such officers also had doubled as political secretary of their local *fascio*, new officers were named in their stead. Persons enjoying the 'esteem of the citizenry' and possessing the necessary training and culture were eligible to take the positions, but *not* if they had ever served as leaders of their local *fascio*. On August 25, Civitella, Badia al Pino, Tegoleto, Tuori, and Viciomaggio in the commune of Civitella nominated new officers for their *dopolavori* because their former presidents had also been the political secretaries for the local *fasci*. *Dopolavori* presidents in Ciggiano and Oliveto had not simultaneously or previously held the office of *fascio* political secretary, and thus could remain at their posts – given that they no longer were exponents of the Fascist Party.[71] That is, those who had been political secretaries for the *fasci* were so compromised by their Fascist Party connections and activities that they could not retain their leadership of the *dopolavoro*, but simple members of the party were acceptable. *Dopolavori*, like GI, could be defascistized and now function as non-Fascist institutions, but *fasci* obviously could not.

Why were GIL (or GI) and the *dopolavoro* retained in their only slightly modified forms? By what criteria did the state or the newly defascistized government decide that an organization or institution was 'too Fascist' to be retained, cleansed, or renamed? How did they detach what was Fascist from what was not – like physically distinguishing *fascio* furniture from *dopolavoro* furniture? In the case of the GIL, only a partial name change was needed, dropping the designation of those who 'carried' the *fasces*.

Fascist social assistance and welfare-type agencies like ECA especially and like ONMI (Opera Nazionale per la Maternità ed Infanzia, the mother and child health and help organization) were more understandably preserved, being necessary to a society facing the ongoing exigencies of war and with nothing to substitute for them. And in most Aretine communes, as in Florence, the same officers remained in charge of the same day-to-day affairs. For those Fascist Party organizations which were maintained, their activities must have been otherwise acceptable, desirable, or valuable, and not entirely – or solely – defined as political.

The communes and their administrations also acted quickly to detach themselves from the former regime and the *fasci* they had supported freely or grudgingly throughout the *ventennio*. On September 6, 1943, the commune of Civitella requested the return of real property 'donated' to the *fascio* of Ciggiano in 1938, when the party was regularizing its real estate situation. On that parcel in question, the commune had paid for and built a three-room structure to house the offices of the now suppressed *fascio*. The building, no longer needed for that dissolved *fascio*, was ideal for a new school, which the commune greatly needed. The commune also noted the many other things it had contributed over the years. For example, 350 lire of communal money had been paid to acquire seven banners for the commune's seven *fasci*. Moreover, the commune had shared part of its own administration building with the village *fascio* of Civitella free of charge for more than twenty years.[72] The commune, it argued on its own behalf, was entitled to the return of its property now that Fascism was over.

The Death of the State

On September 8, 1943, two days after Civitella reclaimed its previously Fascist real property, Marshal Badoglio announced on radio the Italian armistice. Badoglio instructed Italian troops to cease fighting the Allies and not to attack the Germans, but 'to react to eventual attack from whatever quarter' – a quarter that could only have meant the Germans.[73] With that, Badoglio and the king fled for the safety of the south for the rest of the war, leaving no other guidance, plans, or leadership for the thousands of Italian troops or for the rest of the population – a fact long and bitterly remembered by both ex-soldiers and civilians.[74] Italy still had a monarchy and a head of state, but in name only; the structure they represented was no longer in place. The state truly had collapsed, and entire institutions with it. No longer was there a central, national government, no longer a supreme commander, a minister of war, or a general staff. Thousands of Italian soldiers then 'discharged' themselves. Helped by the local population, they changed from their uniforms into civilian clothes, and headed for home (and soon for partisan bands).

Despite the sudden absence of a central government (or head of government) in the capital, Arezzo's prefect continued to inform 'Rome' about public order and political developments in the province. He briefly telegrammed the Ministry of the Interior on September 15, 1943, about the events of the last few days, though one wonders who was there to read the news: On the twelfth, 'troops and officials abandoning arms and uniforms almost all dispersed.' On the following day, 'a unit of German troops arrived here, assuming military command of the city and direction of rail traffic, leaving the undersigned entrusted with the charge of public order.'[75] German troops occupied the Aretine almost immediately after the armistice, and also immediately began requisitioning goods and property.[76]

Father Bagiardi of Castelnuovo recorded that the Germans occupied Florence, Arezzo, and the other cities of Tuscany.[77] 'The Italian army is in complete dissolution,' the priest wrote. 'Rumours are racing. A moment of panic at the word that the Germans were at San Giovanni [Valdarno]. Actually it was troops passing through.' September 12 was calm. 'All the soldiers of the presidio have left to rejoin their families. Only the officers remain.'[78]

As Italian soldiers discharged themselves, thousands of Allied prisoners of war and civilian internees fled POW and concentration camps along with their guards. On September 13, when the guards at Laterina camp abandoned their posts, their prisoners also absconded.[79] James Percival described the events of September 8 and after:

> On the 8th September 1943 we got news of the armistice and were told to take it easy. We were notified to remain until Allied representatives came … On Sunday the Italians ran away and our … officers said we could please ourselves and I remained in the camp while others left. On the Monday the Germans arrived and said they did not want to bother us or be bothered by us getting out of the camp. At 4 p.m. however they came down in two sections and took over. They started to move No. 2 compound on the Thursday and No. 1 on the Friday, presumably for Germany. When we got to the station I went under the train with two others and escaped. I spent seven and a half months before getting through the Allied lines on 16th April.[80]

The following day, the civilian internees at Renicci camp near Anghiari also escaped when their Italian guards went home. Some of these escapees and more of the Allied POWs from Laterina, like Percival, hid in the woods around San Pancrazio, Civitella, and Castelnuovo, where, for many months in some cases, they received shelter, food, and civilian clothes from courageous and compassionate, and often pragmatic, local farm families.[81]

German Field Marshal Albert Kesselring had proclaimed all Italian territory occupied by German forces under German martial law on September 12, 1943.[82] A September 15 poster informed the citizens of Arezzo that German troops had arrived to 'collaborate' with Italian authorities in maintaining public order – 'collaborate' being an old word given new meaning in France in 1940. Another poster that same day announced the call for militia volunteers 'to assist police in keeping public order.'[83]

On the same day Kesselring declared martial law, Otto Skorzeny, the commander of a German Special Forces unit, rescued Mussolini from his internment on Gran Sasso in Abruzzo. From there, as is well known, Mussolini was brought to Germany. At Hitler's direction, he was set up in the puppet regime of the Italian Social Republic (the RSI), also known as the Fascist Republic, or the Republic of Salò on account of its location in the town of Salò in northern Italy. Father Bagiardi of Castelnuovo recorded for September 13, 1943: 'Radio Berlin broadcast the news that parachutists have freed Mussolini … and he is now in Germany where he is reconstituting the Fascist Party.' Two days later Father Bagiardi recorded another startling (but untrue) parachute manoeuvre – this one at the Vatican, where German troops had landed to protect the Pope from communists.

Mussolini's return to power, of sorts, and the formation of his new republican government were announced over radio on September 15. Father Bagiardi recorded that Mussolini addressed the Italian people from Germany on September 19, when he relieved officials and military officers from their oath of loyalty to the king. He also ordered all provincial, regional, and national military, political, administrative, and educational authorities who had been removed from duty after July 25 to retake their posts. On September 23, the new Fascist Republic named its new ministers.[84] On September 27, the new government of the 'Republican State of Italy' met for the first time.

By the end of September, Italy was no longer a single entity in the national governmental sense. From this point, as Claudio Pavone has distinctively described it, Italy lived the rest of the war simultaneously under three governments and two occupations. The kingdom of the south (of the king and Badoglio), the Fascist Republic, and the Committee of National Liberation (CLN, formed September 9, 1943, and made up of representatives of six anti-Fascist political parties) constituted the three 'governments.' The two occupiers were, of course, the Germans stretched from Naples to the north, and the Allies in the south, very slowly advancing north.[85]

This brief period between Mussolini's late July deposition and arrest (the 'end' of Fascism), the September 8 armistice, and the institution of the Fascist Social Republic a week later was one of utter political and practical confusion everywhere in Italy, but especially so in the Aretine and other areas suddenly comprising the new Fascist Republic. Who was now in authority? Telegrams, memoranda, reports, instructions, and orders passed from the new Republican Fascist government in the north to the provinces and the communes, as offices and institutions changed direction and directors again and again in the short space of a few weeks. Fascist Republican Bruno Rao Torres, who just a short time earlier had been cataloguing the condition of Arezzo's *fasci* while Mussolini was removed from power, sent word to the *podestàs* of the province that the state office of provincial 'Royal' Prefect had been abolished in the Fascist Republic as of October 25, and replaced by that of *Capo* ('head') of the province – of which he was the first.[86] Furthermore, communes were to eliminate or cross out the word 'royal' from all documents and letterheads, and to remove the royal coat of arms from all stationery. Portraits of the king were to be removed from all public offices and schools, to be replaced by portraits of Mussolini – whose portraits presumably were still readily at hand, having themselves been taken down from public walls barely three months earlier.[87]

The Fascist Republic took over – or took back – much of the government and its institutions. Fascist political organizations that had been dissolved only a few weeks earlier were reconstituted. *Fasci*, annulled at the end of July, now were reborn as 'Republican *fasci*.' Eliseo Bonechi became the new political secretary for the Republican *fascio* in the village of Civitella. According to postwar recollection, he took the post not because of ideological or patriotic loyalties to the old regime, but as a favour to the commune because no one else wanted it.[88] On November 4, 1943, the real property and chattels of that village's former *fascio* now were given to the new Republican *fascio*, in the person of its new representative political secretary Eliseo Bonechi. San Giovanni Valdarno's former *fascio di combattimento* now had its furniture 'legally' attached (lest the commune or some other competing group assert a right to it), pursuant to article 9 of Mussolini's January 23, 1944, Legislative Decree number 38, whereby ownership of all assets (furnishings and real property) of the terminated Fascist Party (PNF) automatically passed to the Fascist Republican Party (PFR).[89]

Youth organizations and their activities also were turned over to Fascist Republican control – or returned to Fascist control, depending on how one looked at the situation. On December 9, 1943, the new Republican president of the Arezzo provincial committee for the reborn Opera Nazionale Balilla (ONB), a former precursor of the former Fascist youth organization Gioventù Italiana del Littorio (GIL), informed the *podestàs* and prefectural commissioners of the province that all GIL former premises – which had very recently and briefly become GI premises – now were again at ONB's complete disposal and under ONB control.[90] This dizzying metamorphosis of government from Fascist to non-Fascist to Republican Fascist, and the competing transfers of rights and possession of property left people more disoriented with every change and every day.

The Communal Assistance Agency (ECA) was re-Fascistized in a way worth detailing. Before Italy entered the war, Fascist Party administered ECA had concentrated its relief measures on the unemployed, the permanently poor, the elderly, the ill and disabled, and needy families with a husband or father serving in 'the Ethiopian campaign.'[91] When Italy entered the war in June 1940, and as the war progressed, the numbers and categories of people needing relief expanded well beyond ECA's originally conceived mission, coming to include repatriates, refugees, evacuees, families of those recalled to arms, POW families, internees and confinees, and many others.[92] With the advent of the Fascist Republic, ECA underwent a division that created a new parallel body called the Fascist Communal Assistance Agency (Ente Comunale Fascista di Assistenza, or ECFA) – the added adjective making very clear who was to control it. The original ECA, instituted in 1937, most certainly had been a Fascist Party and government production, and Fascist Party members and Fascist women auxiliaries ran its day-to-day workings and made its assistance decisions. Now, in the Fascist Social Republic of late 1943 and 1944, ECA and ECFA existed side-by-side. In larger cities and communes like nearby Florence, ECFA had its own separate premises, its own Republican Fascist director, and its own (still mostly female volunteer) staff, operating in addition to regular ECA, which retained its own prewar, pre-republic president. In smaller communes, as in the province of Arezzo, no real physical split between the two bodies took place, in that they did not open or maintain separate offices or even separate staffs.

ECA and ECFA had separate duties on paper, however. Significantly, Fascist Republican ECFA charged itself with all assistance and relief relating to war victims and to the war in general. ECA directors or secretaries were told to turn over that ever-growing war-related portion of their relief and assistance work to the new political secretary of the new Fascist Republican Party for each commune. ECA officers may have been overjoyed to hand off that increasingly difficult job, but the question is why the Fascist Republican Party did not just take or retake the entire institution of ECA. And why take what was now the much larger, harder, and more expensive part of ECA's duties, leaving the relatively smaller part to old ECA? The new Fascist Republican Party, like the old Fascist Party

before it, saw the importance of connecting itself to the war, and wanted
to make sure that it was the one to control assistance and 'help' fellow
citizens in need during wartime. Any non-war-related needy were irrelevant in the social and political scheme by the end of 1943.

The Disintegration of Society

The September 8 armistice did not stop the war; neither did it slow down
Allied bombing or the flood of refugees into central Italy. Not only did
Allied bombs continue to crater large portions of northern Italy, but
bombs now began to fall on the Aretine.[93] Each commune once again
took stock of potential shelters, now to serve locals displaced by bombing
of their own province and their own houses. On September 17, 1943, the
commune of Civitella informed the prefect of the number of school
classrooms available to house local refugees if necessary: Badia al Pino
had five classrooms that together could house thirty people; Tegoleto
had four that could house twenty persons; Oliveto had two classrooms
that could house ten; Ciggiano had four that could house twenty;
Civitella had three that could house twenty; and Viciomaggio had two
that could house ten. No classrooms would be available for students, of
course, but 110 evacuees could be sheltered.[94] When Allied bombing
really got underway in central Italy in the spring of 1944, accommodations for only 110 refugees and evacuees would be woefully inadequate,
even for a single commune.

Thousands of Allied bombs fell over the Aretine between the fall of
1943 and the summer of 1944. Fifteen year old Almo Fanciullini kept a
detailed, illustrated war diary from September 9, 1943, to September 4,
1944, clipping news stories and making careful count of the number of
days and nights that Allied bombers flew over Arezzo and its communes,
where their bombs landed, and how many citizens were reported killed
and injured. The city of Arezzo, with its large railway marshalling yard
(located between Rome and Florence), was first bombed on November
12, 1943, between 7:10 and 7:25 p.m. One person was killed and thirty
were wounded. The second bombing, on December 11 at 11:22 a.m.,
killed sixty and wounded almost one hundred. The third, on December
20 at 8:45 p.m., killed ten civilians and wounded sixty.[95]

Very few parts of the province escaped bomb damage. By January 27,
1944, and the eighth major bombardment in two and one-half months,
the office of the prefecture was badly damaged, but employees were able
to transfer the most important documents to buildings yet untouched.

The republican *Capo* of the province moved his office to a villa outside of town and his family to San Giustino Valdarno.[96] Allied bombs destroyed more of the castle at Civitella than had the Guelphs and Ghibellines combined, and bombs hit the farms in the valley below. Bucine was bombed nearly as often as the city and rail yards of Arezzo. In the fall of 1943, air-raid sirens were heard at night and bomber squadrons passed over Bucine so frequently that the secretary of the commune, Aroldo Lucarini – like many others – decided to build a hut of tree branches in the chestnut wood a few hundred metres from his own house.[97] The hut had a straw roof, and was large enough to accommodate not only the Lucarinis, but also some neighbouring families. In the evenings, they sat in the hut – the Lucarini family, the family of the farmer, the family of the blacksmith – chatting and dozing in the dark, waiting for the siren to announce the 'all clear.'

The first daytime aerial bombardment hit Bucine on December 29, 1943, at about two in the afternoon – just after the Lucarini's one year old granddaughter had gone to sleep for her afternoon nap. The Allied objective was Bucine's large railway viaduct, only two or three hundred metres from the Lucarini's house. They scooped up the baby and rushed into the street, where they saw dozens of bombers flying overhead, fast and at low altitude. Then, a storm of bombs fell from the sky.[98] The Lucarinis threw themselves on the ground in the middle of the street, feeling the ground shake beneath them.

Realizing that the viaduct had been the intended target, the family decided that day to leave their house for some place far away from the station and that 'ill-fated' (*malaugurato*) viaduct.[99] Other residents of Bucine and neighbouring villages made the same decision. All swarmed into the countryside, filling the road with a procession of carts pulled by hand or by draft animals and weighed down with mattresses and other household objects. The next village was already filled with refugees, so the Lucarinis moved on. Reaching the village of Capannole the following day, they saw the *podestà* of Bucine, who with his family had abandoned the communal seat some time ago. He told them the widow Bettarelli had a room to let in the village. Such a situation was opportune, Signor Lucarini felt, because he and the *podestà* would be able to remain in contact over communal business, and also be able to keep track of rationing in the countryside.

Remarkably, Bucine's communal offices continued to function during this period. Signor Lucarini and his daughter Antelma, who worked in the commune's rationing office, bicycled from Capannole into Bucine every day, returning to Capannole in the evening. Bucine was bombed at day for the second time on January 3, 1944, just as Signor Lucarini and his daughter were on their way back to Capannole. They crouched in a ditch on the side of the road until the planes passed and the assault ended.[100] From then on almost every day, towards noon, they saw groups of Allied airplanes flying over Capannole, headed for the Bucine viaduct. The viaduct itself was never fully disabled, but with every attack the Lucarini's house near it suffered more damage.[101]

Father Narcisco Polvani, priest for the village of San Pancrazio in the commune of Cavriglia since 1901, began his daily entry for Monday, January 3, 1944, in his diary, as usual, with that day's weather: it was a beautiful sunny morning. A walk on that lovely day early in the new year lifted his spirits, despite the air-raid alarm sounding, despite his preoccupation over the distress of the people and the 'bombs dropped by the enemy' that had turned even that small district 'upside-down.'[102] This was not 'a war between two sides,' he said, but more accurately was 'murder.' Italians – 'divided, without an army, without an air force' – did not know how, could not defend themselves. 'How will it end?' On Sunday, January 23, he wrote that, at lunchtime 'as usual,' squadrons of airplanes – 'today most numerous so far' – passed overhead, but that day there was no sound of bombs. 'Where are these infernal machines going? It is rumoured that the enemy has landed at Ostia. Can it be true? Sad days for Italy! The population is terrorized … When the siren gives the alarm, people flee the villages and it is a truly pitiful sight. If the invasion continues, what will happen when even our district becomes a theatre of war?'[103] Almost daily at lunchtime, Allied planes headed for Arezzo city and its railyards or for Bucine's railway viaduct; the bombs that fell shook the glass in Father Polvani's windows and the nerves of his parishioners (as well as his own).[104] The 'drone' of the sirens, the 'incessant noise' of planes overhead, and then the sound of bombs in the distance (and soon the not so distance) were constant presences in Father Polvani's diary, as were the consequent fear and 'torment' of the people that 'wrung his heart.'[105] 'The population is very tired and lives in continual distress,' he said.[106]

Mixed in among Father Polvani's mundane entries on the weather, who came for dinner, how much he spent on food and cigarettes, who got sick and who slaughtered a pig, and the effects of total war on church going, is a compelling description of war every day growing closer and more intense, and of daily life growing more frightening, more disjointed and confused. It was written by a man who preferred the Germans (and entertained German occupation officers at lunch), who in 1944 still considered the British and Americans 'the enemy,' who felt that Italian partisans (or 'rebels') were dangerous and disgraceful criminals, and who privately disparaged a fellow priest of nearby Castelnuovo, Father Bagiardi, for 'inappropriate political behaviour' (that was, Bagiardi's warm relationship with the young anti-Fascists and communists of the area). Father Polvani's assessment of this new kind of war – aerial bombing of civilian targets and its effects on the civilian population – was, however, more astutely considered. Again and again, he commented that this was 'not war' but 'murder': 'Is this war? It is barbarity and the slaughter of innocents.' There 'has to be war,' he acknowledged, but it belongs 'on the battlefields,' not in the villages.[107]

Italians – even those without Father Polvani's national and political preferences – also might still have considered the Allies 'the enemy' in 1944 – or that the Allies and Germany now were equally Italy's enemies, both bent on destroying the country. Who but an enemy would drop so many bombs on the heads and houses of civilians? The Allied bombing of the province of Arezzo was part of a larger air campaign in central Italy called 'Operation Strangle.' Later characterized, inaccurately, as one of the war's 'outstanding' air campaigns, Operation Strangle's original purpose 'was to interdict the flow of supplies to the German armies in Italy through the systematic destruction of the enemy's rail and road network.'[108] The Allied design here was not to break the morale of the Italian civilian population; that already had been done. The basic idea was that halting supplies and disrupting communications would cause the Germans to retreat, thereby saving the Allies the necessity – and infantry deaths – of a ground offensive.[109]

The supply lines, the rail and road networks to be systematically destroyed belonged to central Italy, strictly speaking, and not to 'the enemy' – something the Allies did not appear to consider. The marshalling yards at Arezzo and at Pontassieve (near Florence), and the Bucine viaduct were operation targets 'A-1,' 'A-2,' and 'A-3' priority, respectively, and so received the Allied bombers' primary attention (figures 1–4).[110] The army-air force described its targets and its successes:

AREZZO – On the main Rome-Florence railroad line, a junction point for five important highways, and the northern terminus for a secondary rail route to the south, Arezzo was of tremendous value to the enemy supply network in central Italy. Between January 1 and July 15, bridges, highways and rail lines, as well as the Arezzo yards and locomotive repair shops, were

bombed 69 times, with nearly 18,000 tons of explosives blasting the targets
... Notable among Strangle's targets ... was the Bucine viaduct, which was
smashed by TAF when a train was crossing it. Wrecked cars still lie amid the
debris of the wrecked span. Other bridges in the area were also caught in
the bombsights as trains approached, with similar results.[111]

During the three-month period from the beginning of Operation
Strangle to the end of 'Operation Diadem,' the Allies mounted an average of 1352 effective sorties per day over a thin strip across central Italy,
with a daily average of 843 tons of bombs dropped.[112] Those daily tons
of bombs meant to destroy 'the enemy's' rail and road network fell on
the farms, homes, churches, schools, hospitals, and museums of co-
belligerent civilians, and those trains that Allied bombardiers liked to hit
just as they passed over viaducts and bridges also carried Italian civilians.
For the Allied Bomber Groups, Arezzo's civilian landscape was 'a target
of opportunity,' and the as yet unarticulated concept of 'collateral damage' was no deterrent.[113]

Despite thousands of tons of bombs dropped over the province and glow-
ing reports of success in hitting targets, the operation failed in the sense that
it 'did not achieve supply denial, which had been the objective,' making a
lengthy and destructive ground assault necessary.[114] The unit history for
Headquarters Seventeenth Bombardment Group (Medium) for April 14,
1944 questioned why Operation Strangle was not more effective:

> We're proud of the Group and proud of Joe, but we're letting him down
> these days. Today's results at Arezzo were another bad example. We've been
> enquiring around for reasons: The going home fever is reaching a new
> high, the briefings are too long, the targets are monotonously unvaried –
> the remark every day is heard, 'My God, that place again.'[115]

Concerns about bombing civilians did not enter directly into the
analysis.

Allied boredom aside, daily life became chaotic for the citizens of Arezzo
city and the provincial villages. Father Polvani and the Lucarini family, like
the rest of the Aretines who did not feel the same excitement as fifteen
year old Almo Fanciullini at the sight of so many bombers overhead, the
Aretines – and like the Seventeenth Bombardment Group receiving their
orders – must have exclaimed in dismay as more bombs fell daily: 'My
God, that place again.' Although it did not drive the Germans out of
central Italy, Operation Strangle successfully killed and injured Italian civilians, greatly disrupted civilian life, and severely damaged the civilian

landscape.[116] At the end of April 1944, only about one hundred people remained in the city of Arezzo, the chief of police reported.[117] For those who fled their cities and villages and kept moving from place to place as bombs destroyed more and more of central Italy, no place was safe.

The Aretine was physically under German occupation and was part of Mussolini's new Fascist Republic. And so, despite the armistice with the Allies, both the Fascist Republic and the German occupying troops expected Italians in the province to continue fighting for Germany. While Aretine communal officials puzzled over whether those September 8 'self-discharged' soldiers who now returned to their families were entitled to ration cards and rations, the Germans ordered all Italian soldiers – 'September 8 deserters,' they called them – to report immediately to the nearest German command – by no later than September 20 at 4:00 p.m.[118] In the coming months, both the Germans and the Fascist Republican government repeatedly demanded that ex-soldiers return and regularize their positions; they also commanded additional classes of men to report for the draft.[119] These continued call-ups provided great incentive for both *de facto* ex-soldiers and younger, newly draft-age men to be declared exempt from military service by going to work for the Germans repairing bomb damaged rail lines and building the Gothic Line defences – or to join the partisans.[120] Thus, one final critical group joined the unstable mix of participants in that local war in Arezzo.

While coping with Allied bombers trying to disrupt their supply lines, the German occupiers in the Aretine also faced the growing worry of local partisan bands. In the spring of 1944, Arezzo's *Questore* informed the Fascist Republican *Capo* that 'draft dodgers and runaway foreigners' from the POW and concentration camps were roaming the hills. Together they had formed armed bands that were committing 'occasional crimes.'[121] The *Questore*'s brief comment fairly described the early days of the partisan movement, though genuine desire to expel the German occupiers and to overthrow Republican Fascism also counted as important factors. Father Polvani's running judgment of the partisans and their relations with local society was, not surprisingly, somewhat harsher and did not credit them with bravery or with motives of patriotism or the desire to liberate Italy. 'Here they are speaking of bands of rebels taking refuge in our mountains,' he mentioned for the first time on March 16, 1944, 'and the people are frightened because they are heavily armed.'[122] A week later, he wrote of young men in the area who, not wanting to take up arms for the military, had 'deserted their families' and were living in the open countryside, suffering risks little different from the dangers of war.[123]

He first distinguished these locals from the well-armed 'ruffians' taking advantage of the abnormal state of affairs to intimidate residents of the countryside and extort sums of money, but the two groups soon merged. At 9:00 pm on March 30, 1944 (a day on which the weather had been uncertain and looked like rain), a 'band of rebels armed to the teeth' and 'with revolvers in hand' came to Father Polvani's door demanding 10,000 lire. They found and took only 9,500 – a theft which he promptly reported to the police and to the bishop.[124] 'There is no commander, no one in authority, things are heading towards anarchy ... They have escaped the war, they have left their families, they are living in the woods, finding themselves again in danger, living like bandits. God save Italy from such debasement!'[125] Bombing by day and 'rebel threats' at night made the local people afraid to walk in their own woods and afraid to be in their own homes. Father Polvani linked the daily Allied bombings and the activities of the rebels (the latter of which, according to the priest, consisted of stealing money from honest citizens and assaulting those who had sworn the oath to the Fascist Social Republic), together making for chaos and terror in daily life, and sure to bring about the ruin of Italy. 'Where will it end,' he implored after three armed 'rebels' appeared in the middle of the day (which had started as a 'splendid morning'), insisting that his parish chaplain give them more money. The chaplain, Father Cuccoli, gave them 500 lire, a loaf of bread, and a wheel of cheese, but in this small gesture, Father Polvani saw anarchy overtaking them: 'I never would have believed that our poor Italy would be reduced to this ... *God, let the good be spared and the bad be punished.*'[126]

Telling the good from the bad was not so easy, then or immediately after the war, except for those like Father Polvani who were very sure of the dividing line. Who were the good and who were the bad among the rebels and partisans robbing their neighbours and attacking Nazi-Fascists in order to liberate their country; the co-belligerent Allied pilots in their 'Liberators' daily dropping tons of bombs on civilians who already had surrendered; the Fascist Republicans and German soldiers trying to round up draft dodgers and strike back against partisans who engaged in guerrilla war against them; the locals who went to work building German defences; those who hid the Jews and escaped Allied POWs, and those who were afraid to hide them (like Father Polvani, who decided not to take in a family of Jews attempting to pass themselves as Sicilian evacuees, despite their 'pitiable predicament'); and those who just tried to make it through those very difficult days.[127] Life had become very confusing as well as dangerous: the partisans and the adherents to the Republic of Salò confused everything still more, and helped raise levels of tension and violence to civil war.

Italy's partisan movement – the armed Resistance – began during the national disorientation and disorder following the September 8 armistice.[128] The partisan bands, whom Italians (including Father Polvani) first called 'rebels,' then patriots and partisans, indeed were made up in large part of ex-soldiers still subject to the draft and younger men subject to later Fascist Republican call-ups. Partisan numbers, activity, and optimism grew rapidly during the spring and summer of 1944, followed by brutal German counter actions in late summer and fall.[129]

In Arezzo, already by mid-April 1944, about 3000 'rebels' camped in the upper Tiberina valley and 500 in Pratomagno, outnumbering the approximately 2500 Fascist Republicans in the province.[130] The autonomous band – 'Third Company Chiatti' – some of whose members took 9500 lire from Father Polvani and who harassed the Germans and Fascist Republicans in the commune of Cavriglia and the Valdarno, was about seventy strong and commanded by twenty-seven year old Nello Vannini from Le Màtole and Castelnuovo dei Sabbioni.[131] In April and May of 1944 in the area around Civitella and San Pancrazio (in the commune of Bucine) another partisan formation 'Banda Renzino' began to operate.[132] The band and its leader, twenty-four year old Edoardo Succhielli, son of a local family and formerly a lieutenant in the Parachute Corps, took their name from the hamlet near Foiano della Chiana, where in April 1921, armed peasants had killed three Fascist *squadristi*. The band was made up of 115 men, 36 of whom Succhielli said were escaped Allied POWs from Laterina, and headquartered around the farmhouses to the south and west of San Pancrazio.[133] A secondary road through the hills passed both San Pancrazio and Cornia and joined route 69 to Florence. The partisans attacked German motorcyclists and trucks heading towards Florence along this road, 'thus attracting attention to both these localities,' wrote a British soldier explaining later events.[134]

The German occupiers first encountered partisans in significant numbers after the fall of Rome on June 4, 1944. From that date, the partisans 'became more aggressive.' They became much more aggressive than Field Marshal Kesselring had reckoned with, and he later called that date 'the birthday of the all-out guerrilla war.'[135] On June 17, 1944, Kesselring wrote that the partisan situation 'particularly in central Italy has recently deteriorated to such an extent that it constitutes a serious danger to the fighting troops and their supply lines as well as to the war industry potential.' Therefore, he formulated 'New Regulations for Partisan Operations,' whereby the fight against the partisans was to be carried out with the utmost severity. Kesselring would protect any commander who exceeded 'our usual restraint, in the choice and severity of the means he adopts in the fight against partisans.'[136]

On June 20, 1944, as the battles for the Trasimene Line (near Lake Trasimeno, around Perugia to the southeast of Arezzo) got under way, Kesselring announced 'severe measures are to be taken against the partisans ... Every act of violence committed by partisans must be punished immediately.'[137] Because the partisans could rarely be caught in their acts of guerrilla war, civilians were to be punished instead for partisan violence. German troops posted notices that a proportion of a village's male population was to be arrested whenever evidence showed considerable numbers of partisan groups in an area. Civilian men were to be shot in the event of any act of partisan violence. If troops were fired at from any village, the village was to be burnt down. Perpetrators or ringleaders would be hanged in public. Anyone giving shelter to 'bandits,' or who assisted them with clothing, food, or arms was to be shot. Anyone knowing of a group or even a single rebel without reporting it to the nearest headquarters was to be shot. The fight against the partisans was thus to be a war of 'the utmost severity' against the civilian population.

Despite such threats against civilians, partisans continued their activities in the Aretine and some civilians continued to support them or join them. The squads carried out 'small actions' of interference and sabotage against the Germans and the Fascists, and 'in doing this, they did not always take into account the possible repercussions on the civilian population,' someone directly affected by those repercussions wrote years afterward.[138] The eventual repercussions – or reprisals – would be terrible.

In the spring of 1944, the *Questore* reported to the *Capo* of Arezzo that the public spirit was very depressed, both because of the situation in which the country found itself after September 8, and also because of the numerous bombings that had 'disintegrated' the 'civil life of the town.'[139] By June 1944, Arezzo's civilian population was caught between opposing foreign armies, and life for many had become a basic matter of searching for shelter and a moment of safety. In a very unnatural and dangerous kind of unity, the farmers, miners, priests, and other citizens shared their small part of central Italy with thousands of refugees and evacuees, with German troops, with Fascist Republicans, with Allied POWs in hiding, and with a growing number of partisans undeterred by German threats against the civilian population. Civil life would break down still further that summer. As the front lines of war came closer, violence and greater chaos would wreck what fragile equilibrium existed.

2 Variations on a Massacre

For them, every man was a victim, every house a bonfire.

Enrico Centeni-Romani, unpublished memoir

After Italy's September 8, 1943, armistice, the POW camp at Laterina again housed Allied prisoners of war, now under German control. Many of the prisoners this time around had been captured during the fighting at Anzio or escaping from other camps and they waited at Laterina for transit to Germany. Life in the camp was as bad as or worse than it had been under the Italians: the camp was overcrowded, without adequate latrines or washing facilities. The prisoners suffered from lice, lack of food, and all the ailments that resulted from such poor conditions.[1] During the summer of 1944, the camp saw a new exodus of prisoners, this one somewhat more planned than that set in motion on September 8. What survivors and British investigators came to call the 'Laterina death march' began about five in the afternoon on June 17, 1944.[2] With heavy Allied bombing overhead and Allied ground troops approaching the province, the ill, underfed, and poorly shod British and American prisoners of Laterina camp were forced to march the fifteen kilometres from Laterina to Montevarchi, presumably there to board a train for Germany.

Rumours circulated that Free French forces had landed on the Tuscan island of Elba, and the prisoners hoped the camp would soon be liberated. And so, when ordered to report, many sought to hide and wait for the French. German guards with dogs, guns, and grenades ably rounded up the approximately 1000 prisoners, however.[3] Organized into columns, the prisoners set out. Prisoner J. Mellon later told investigators: 'The prisoners were restive and Hoffmann [a German guard] shouted at the top of his voice that he would shoot the prisoners if they did not stand still. Some of the footwear of the prisoners was in a bad condition and some were marching barefoot. A number of prisoners, including myself, were suffering from dysentery.'[4]

Those who tried to escape, who fell out of line from exhaustion, or who were too ill to keep up were shot and their bodies left on the road. Anthony Olender survived his brief, unsuccessful escape attempt, but saw what had happened to others.

> Jim Woods and myself ran in amongst a bunch of the Germans who were apparently reinforcements, who were at the rear of the column ... We marched with these Germans about 10 or 15 minutes until we finally worked our way up into the last group of PW. After we got in amongst the last column, I stumbled over three dead bodies of Allied soldiers, in the centre of the road. I also saw another body lying by the side of the road.[5]

Stopping for the night in an open sports field near the station at Montevarchi, the prisoners did not board a train, but were marched back to Laterina the next morning. As the POWs returned to camp, they saw dead fellow soldiers left lying in the road, some shot, others killed by hand-grenades; but now the bodies had been run over and crushed by German trucks and half-tracks. J. Mellon remembered the horrible sight. 'On the return march we passed through the same village where I had seen the bodies lying. There I saw a number of bodies of prisoners which had obviously been run over by tracked vehicles and were lying in a mangled condition.'[6] Anthony Olender helped carry the bodies of two dead Allied soldiers to the side of the road. 'Some of the bodies had no heads. Trucks and half-tracks had run over them'[7] The next day, the surviving prisoners again marched from Laterina, this time only as far as a railway siding about seven kilometres away. Loaded into cattle-cars and trucks, they were taken to a prison camp in Moosburg, Germany, where eventually they were liberated by American troops.[8]

In the nearby village of Civitella on the day after the Laterina death march, events that would lead to a larger domestic wartime massacre began to unfold.[9] A retreating German division passed through that area in mid-June 1944, apparently on its way to regroup in Florence.[10] Seven or so of these German soldiers spent several days at a farmhouse below Civitella. On June 18, a rainy Sunday afternoon, four of them walked up to the village, joining the local men in drinking and card playing at the *dopolavoro*. The Germans shot off flares, either to amuse the village children or to signal their location to other members of their unit. They returned to the farmhouse for lunch, then went back to the *dopolavoro* when it reopened that evening.[11]

On that day, young partisan leader Edoardo Succhielli and his Banda Renzino were installed in the hills just outside Cornia, a very few kilometres from Civitella (figure 6). In his later statement to British investigating forces, Succhielli said he had received complaints from villagers about the behaviour of the four Germans in the village. Though initially reluctant to take any action against the Germans (as he later said), lest it be followed by German reprisal against the villagers, at about ten in the evening, he and several members of the band entered the club where, he later explained, he intended only to disarm the Germans. 'However, for some reason or other, he and the other partisans opened fire, killing two Germans and wounding a third.'[12] One young woman, whose parents had sent her to fetch her brother from the *dopolavoro*, saw the partisans enter just as she left the building – their red neckerchiefs attracted her attention – and she heard machinegun fire immediately after.[13] When someone extinguished the lights in the club, the partisans took advantage of the darkness and the confusion to gather what weapons they could find and then quickly fled.[14] The uninjured German soldier then carried his wounded comrade back to the farmhouse below. The division left the area later that night by car, while the bodies of the two dead Germans lay unattended in the *dopolavoro*.

Helga Cau went to Civitella the next morning, June 19, having heard about the shooting. She was Swedish and married to an Italian, a professor originally from Sardinia. They had evacuated from Florence with their three children to their farmhouse in Gebbia where, because she spoke German, she often interpreted for German troops in the area. Signora Cau and two sisters from the local hospital washed the bodies of the two dead German soldiers and prepared them for burial.[15] That night and the following morning, many of the villagers, but especially the men, aware of a German reprisal against civilians in the Aretine commune of Stia, in the Casentino, two months earlier, left Civitella and hid in the countryside.[16] Meanwhile, the Banda Renzino moved from Cornia to the hilly area of Montaltuzzo, about six kilometres west and midway between Cornia and the village of San Pancrazio in Bucine.[17]

On June 20, about twelve German soldiers appeared in Civitella and watched the priest officiate at the burial of the two dead Germans. Several women of the village and communal employee Luigi Lammioni also attended.[18] Although he insisted no one from the village had done the shooting, the soldiers told Signor Lammioni that he had until noon the next day to provide them the names of the partisans responsible.[19] That same evening German soldiers arrested six men (of the very few who had remained in the village) and fifty women. All were taken to a clearing outside of town, but soon released.[20]

More German soldiers began arriving in the area around Civitella on June 20 and 21. They pitched tents in the woods and billeted in local farmhouses.[21] And between June 20 and 23, Banda Renzino shot and wounded two Germans travelling by car on the provincial road near San Pancrazio. Villagers of San Pancrazio brought the injured Germans to the nearest hospital in the larger town of Montevarchi. During this same period in the same area, the band also attacked a small, retreating German unit and took fourteen prisoners, four of whom, Succhielli said, joined his partisans. They held the remaining ten German soldiers as prisoners at a farmhouse on Montaltuzzo. In his postwar statement, Succhielli maintained that he sent a message via Signora Cau to the German headquarters at Monte San Savino, warning that if the Germans took reprisals on the local villagers he would immediately shoot the ten hostages.

On June 23, an estimated two hundred German soldiers attacked the farmhouse and the partisan installation at Montaltuzzo. Greatly outnumbering the partisans, the Germans freed the prisoners and killed one partisan and a farmer.[22] While partisans battled German soldiers a few kilometres away, most of the residents of Civitella returned to their homes, reassured by either their priest or the *podestà* and by a German communiqué 'that the people of Civitella were not responsible for the murder, which is attributed to rebels.'[23] On June 27, German soldiers again entered Civitella, searching house to house and confiscating radios.[24]

June 29 is the feast day of Saints Peter and Paul. At about six-thirty in the morning, while many residents were at the village church for early mass, heavily armed German troops quickly invaded Civitella. Several wore camouflage and armbands inscribed 'Hermann Göring Division'; some, witnesses later said, appeared to be Italians dressed in German uniform.[25] Soldiers ordered the men, women, and children from the farms below Civitella to walk to the Palazzina bridge about a kilometre south of the village, where they held the civilians at gunpoint. Another group of soldiers passed directly to the centre of the village of Civitella, rounded up the men and older boys, and forced them into piazza Vittorio Emanuele. Still others burst into houses, immediately shooting men in front of their wives and children. Ten year old Dino Tiezzi, just waking up that morning, saw German soldiers shoot his father and older brother Bruno.[26] Gastone Paggi, who had brought his family to live with relatives in Civitella to escape the dangers of wartime Florence, was still wearing his nightshirt when he was shot in front of his wife and four children. German soldiers shot the six elderly residents (including one eighty-two year old woman) of the old age home. An elderly, invalid priest who had been evacuated from the city of Arezzo was shot as he lay in bed.[27]

Inside the church, with mass still going on, the parishioners heard gunfire and believed it might be the sound of the Germans retreating. As their priest, Father Alcide Lazzeri, was cautioning the congregation to let the Germans take whatever they wanted if they came into the village, a hand grenade blew open the church doors, and German soldiers ordered everyone outside. They separated the men from the women, shoving the men into the crowd already present in the piazza.[28] Two men and a boy who presented identification documents showing them to be refugees from Florence were spared and allowed to leave.[29]

Women and children were commanded to leave the village immediately, and many took the road to the nearby orphanage at Poggiali. Their chaotic flight was made more terrifying by the strong suspicion – and soon the knowledge – of what would happen to their men. 'The road was crowded with women and children, all fleeing from Civitella. As I left the village a woman [Elda Paggi] came up to me. She was only wearing a nightdress which was covered with blood, and had four children with her. She was screaming "They have killed my husband." Of course, she was referring to the Germans.'[30] The women and children sheltered at Poggiali for that night and for the nights thereafter.[31] 'Nearly all the women and children from Civitella were there and everyone was weeping and wondering what had happened to their menfolk.'[32]

In the piazza with the other men, Father Lazzeri realized what was about to happen and asked permission to say the benediction.[33] When the priest finished blessing the villagers, the Germans took the men's wallets and watches, and then separated them into groups of five. Thus, the men of Civitella were massacred – shot in groups of five, one group at a time, while the others watched.[34] The priest was one of the first group of five, and may himself have been the first man the Germans shot. They also killed the Fascist Republican *podestà* and Eliseo Bonechi, political secretary of the Republican *fascio* who had taken the job no one else wanted.[35]

Daniele Tiezzi, a young seminarian who had been serving at mass and was still wearing his cassock, was one of the second group of five.

The five of us formed up in a rough line by the German soldiers and another German soldier with a pistol came immediately afterwards and
pushed each of us into a more straight line. We were standing alongside the
bodies with our backs to two machineguns. The last mentioned German
soldier then stood clear of us and raised his pistol as though to signal to the
machine gunners. I saw the machine gunner on my left smile and nod to
the machine gunner on my right and heard a click as of a machine action
being cocked behind me, and acting on the spur of the moment, I turned
to my left and ran.

I passed the German with the pistol and he, possibly taken by surprise,
made no attempt to stop me. I ran as fast as I could along the back road of
the village, zig-zagging as I went.[36]

Although struck by bullets, he managed to jump over the village wall,
climb two more terrace walls, and make his way into the woods. Daniele
Tiezzi, whose father and brother had been shot in their bedroom, thus
escaped the massacre.[37]

Gino Bartolucci watched the shooting of Father Lazzeri and the
others; he also saw Daniele Tiezzi escape. In his group of five victims,
Bartolucci was second from the left. Those three to his right were shot
one by one.

It was then my turn. The German stood behind me and I saw, out of the
corner of my eye, him raise his revolver to the back of my head. I put my
hands to the sides of my face and as he fired, I, anticipating the shot, turned
my head to the left. I felt the muzzle of the revolver against my hand and
heard the report. I immediately felt a burning pain in both my hands, my
face, mouth and throat and realizing that I was still alive dropped voluntarily to the ground and lay there feigning death … I lay there without moving
until the Germans went away. As I lay there I heard many shots fired, all
single distinct shots and heard many bodies fall beside me. When the
Germans had gone I opened my eyes and saw around me the bodies of
many men all shot through the head.[38]

He survived, although the German bullet passed through his hands and
face. He later crawled over the village wall and made his way into the
woods.

Through these two eyewitness survivors, Daniele Tiezzi and Gino
Bartolucci, the details of the massacre at Civitella were told.[39] Aldo
Tavarnesi survived the massacre by hiding in the attic of his house. As that

burned, he fled to another.[40] Silvio Pasqui survived by hiding in the back of the church. Four women and two girls also died in the massacre at Civitella. An elderly woman from the old age home had been shot. Penelope Sandrini burned to death as she hid under a bed with her husband. Ines Bischi was shot on her way to the village. Maria Lammioni (wife of communal secretary Luigi Lammioni who had spoken with the Germans during the funeral of the two dead soldiers) and her two daughters aged five and two and a half years burned to death while hiding in their attic. Luigi Lammioni managed to save another daughter – the twin sister of the older girl killed – and himself by jumping from the roof of his house before it collapsed in flames.[41] Before departing, the soldiers set fire to the houses and threw many of the bodies into the burning buildings. The entire village was burned, including the church. The massacre and the destruction of the village were completed in less than two hours.[42]

The Germans left Civitella and went to the farms below, passing along the road through the tiny farming hamlets near Cornia: Caggiolo, Palazzina, Burrone, Solaia, and Gebbia. Here they killed all they met, including women and children.[43] No eyewitness escaped to tell how the massacres were carried out at these locations, but many bodies found there afterwards had been sprayed with machinegun fire.[44] The bodies of the women were found naked and burned. One daughter later found her mother's nude, blackened body, inexplicably lying beneath the burned carcass of a pig.[45]

At seven-thirty in the morning on June 29, Father Natale Romanelli, the priest of Cornia, was on his way to say mass at the church in Verniana, when he heard rifle and machinegun fire and saw smoke in the valley. Another man warned Father Romanelli that German soldiers were burning houses in the vicinity, and that he had heard sounds of shooting and screams from the direction of Burrone. The priest returned to Cornia and urged the villagers to leave. Most did so, except the priest's own elderly mother and his paralyzed sister. He himself hid in the woods on high ground about half a kilometre away, from where he could see Civitella burning. The priest returned to Cornia about six in the evening to find the houses on fire and the naked body of Rosa Pontenani, 'aged 52 years, lying dead in the road.' He also found his sister's body, shot and lying next to her overturned wheelchair. The next day, in a nearby house, he found the body of his mother and two other women. The furniture in the house had been set on fire and the bodies too had been partly consumed.[46]

Twenty year old Dino Amazzoni and his father, both sharecroppers in Burrone, began work as usual about six in the morning on June 29.

Returning home for breakfast at about nine in the morning, they heard rifle and machinegun fire, which they thought came from the Germans retreating. 'As we had heard that the Germans took young men with them when they left an area, my father told me to go and hide in the woods. I left at once and hid in a wood about five hundred metres away.' Amazzoni could see houses burning and hear gunfire that seemed to last about a half an hour. Returning home about two that afternoon, the young man saw eight dead bodies lying outside his house, every one of which he recognized. They included his father, his eighty-five year old grandmother, two fourteen year old neighbour boys, and two girls aged eleven and five. With the help of a neighbour, Dante Pasquini, he carried their bodies into his house. He then found the burned bodies of his landlord and the landlord's wife in the smouldering ruins of a straw hut nearby. 'I carried these bodies to my home and put them beside the other eight.'[47]

German troops also arrived at the village of San Pancrazio early the morning of June 29, at about six or six-thirty. They came in two Red Cross vans, in trucks, on motorcycles, and on foot.[48] As at Civitella, they rounded up the men into the piazza, but unlike Civitella, they did not shoot them quickly. The village men stood in the piazza all morning and into the early afternoon, under guard of about thirty German soldiers. At about one-thirty, another one hundred or so German soldiers arrived in the village, coming from the direction of Civitella. Now the women and children of San Pancrazio were ordered to leave the village – and told to walk for no less than two kilometres.[49]

As the men continued to wait, the Germans asked the whereabouts of the village's young men and local partisans, to which the men replied that the village had no partisans and their young men were hiding in the woods to avoid being drafted into the Fascist Republican army.[50] Finally, sometime after two, perhaps as late as three-thirty in the afternoon, the men were marched to the cellar of the *fattoria* Pierangeli, near the entrance to the village. They were searched and, as at Civitella, their watches and wallets were taken.[51] Father Giuseppe Torelli, San Pancrazio's village priest, pleaded with the Germans to kill only him and to spare the villagers. Unsuccessful and weeping, he told the men that the Germans were going to kill them all. At the priest's request, the Germans allowed the men to kneel in prayer and be blessed.[52] Then, five men at a time were made to enter the inner room of the cellar and were shot as they stepped inside. As at Civitella, the priest was among the first to be killed. One soldier then announced: 'If you know where the partisans are, speak now and save your life.'[53]

After about forty men had been shot, Ugo Casciotti (a caretaker at the *fattoria*) and four others, thinking that this might give them an opportunity to escape, told a German soldier that they knew where the partisans were. A guard pushed them aside.

> I awaited my opportunity and after about five minutes struck the German soldier who was guarding us and made a dash for freedom. Shots were fired at me, one of which wounded me in the left arm. As I jumped over a wall, a hand grenade exploded near me so I fell to the ground feigning to be dead. I lay there for several minutes then I crawled to some bushes and remained hidden until about 1700 hours. After this I … made my way into the woods where I remained until the arrival of the Allied troops about the 16 Jul 44. Upon my return to San Pancrazio, I found the majority of the houses had been destroyed, including the farm [*fattoria*] of Signor Pierangeli.[54]

Alfredo Serboli, a linekeeper with the electric company in the Valdarno, was herded with the others into the piazza and the *fattoria*, but spared when he presented identification documents showing him to be an essential employee. He, along with an evacuee from Siena, and the four locals who had volunteered information about the partisans were taken by truck to Monte San Savino, then to Florence, where all managed to escape.[55]

The *fattoria*, the bodies in it, and the entire town were then burned.[56] Dense smoke remained in the sky for days afterwards. From Duddova, where Aroldo Lucarini (communal secretary of Bucine) and his family had recently found shelter, they saw 'the sad spectacle' of San Pancrazio in flames.[57] At least three Italians were said to be among the Germans participating in the massacre at San Pancrazio. Witnesses commented on at least one soldier who spoke perfect Italian with a Tuscan accent. Survivors swore they recognized Fascist Republicans Dino Lugugnani from Ciggiano, wearing a black mask; Ezio Lammioni from Bucine, and Celso Pratesi also from Ciggiano.[58]

A smaller massacre played out more slowly near Civitella and San Pancrazio, beginning in April of 1944 when German officers belonging to a 'flak regiment' unit requisitioned the Carletti family villa located about two kilometres north of Monte San Savino, and lived there with the Carletti family (figure 6, for the location of the Carletti villa).[59] That particular German unit left the vicinity on May 1. On the evening of June 28, a different group of German soldiers came to the villa, bringing with them an Italian prisoner. Signor Carletti observed that all the soldiers had the name Hermann Göring on the bottoms of their sleeves. 'On one of the trucks they carried an Italian male civilian. One of the Marescialli [sic] demanded that I provide a room wherein this Italian, whom I was told was a rebel, could be confined.' At about ten in the evening, Signor Carletti told later: 'the Italian members of the household were told to go to bed and ordered not to leave the house.'[60]

Signor and Signora Carletti heard the sounds of motorcars approaching and leaving the villa all night. No one was allowed to leave the villa the next day.

> In the villa at this time were seventy or eighty German soldiers. We were forbidden to talk and anybody who approached the villa during the day was arrested and made prisoner in this room with us … About 2300 hours [on June 29], I was ordered to a downstairs room … I was then questioned … about a Signora Cau and afterwards taken back to the other room. The interpreter accompanied me and on our way I asked him for the reason of my detention. He told me that reports had been received concerning me, from Monte San Savino, to the effect that my family and I had been indulging in Anti-Fascist activities.[61]

Signor Carletti was held with the others until the next evening, again questioned about assisting partisans and escaped POWs, and warned he would be shot if he did not divulge the names of local partisans and the whereabouts of prisoners of war. 'About ten minutes after I was locked up I looked out of the window and saw my son Carletti, Luigi being escorted along the front of the villa by two German soldiers. I never saw my son again.'[62]

His son Luigi had been a partisan, and the family had assisted Allied POWs who had fled Laterina camp. One of the last people to see Luigi Carletti was the maid of a local family in the hills west of Monte San Savino on her way to fetch water from the village fountain about six on the morning of July 2. She saw two German soldiers escorting Luigi Carletti – whom she was able to recognize only because of her long acquaintance with him. He was badly bruised and unable to walk or stand on his own.[63] Luigi Carletti's beaten body was found on July 10, near the well on a neighbouring estate.[64]

Twenty-six year old Gina Polverini was a seamstress in Florence, but had returned to her parents' home in Gebbia in March of 1944 to escape the bombing of Florence. She saw fifteen heavily armed German soldiers arrive at the Cau house about ten on the morning of June 29. The soldiers also seized Polverini and kept her under guard at the Cau garden, then taking her, Signor and Signora Cau, and another young neighbour woman to San Pancrazio in an armoured car. There, at San Pancrazio, she too saw all the houses in the village on fire. From there they transferred to a larger vehicle at Montaltuzzo, and then went on to the Carletti villa at Monte San Savino.

At the Carletti villa, the German captain who had taken her from Gebbia closely questioned Signorina Polverini regarding the partisans. 'During this interview, an Italian of the peasant class was brought in. He was very badly bruised about the face, his clothes were torn and he looked as though he had been very severely beaten. He was asked if he knew me and I was asked if I knew him. We both denied knowing each other. Actually, I had never seen him before. After this I was taken back to my room.'[65] Detained alone in a room in the villa, Signorina Polverini was questioned several more times. Brought to Monte San Savino the next day, she saw the peasant of the day before: his body was hanging from a lamppost with a sign proclaiming: 'This is the way the partisans of Cornia are dying.'[66] That night, Gina Polverini was raped by one of the German soldiers. The following day, she was taken with some others to Florence for compulsory labour in Germany but managed to escape and went into hiding until the Allies liberated Florence.

On June 29, 1944, at least 211 civilians were killed: nine at Gebbia, forty at Cornia, somewhere between fifty-eight and seventy-two in and around San Pancrazio, and one hundred and four at Civitella.[67] The armed Resistance in the Val di Chiana ended that day. Still shaken from the 'battle of Montaltuzzo' and realizing there was nothing they could now do for the civilian population, Succhielli and the Banda Renzino decided not to take 'counter-actions' against the Germans.[68]

When a few of the women of Civitella returned to their homes later on the day of June 29 to look for their husbands, fathers, and brothers, the village appeared to be a different place. 'The place was deserted and I did not see a living soul,' one said; 'all the houses had been blown up and buildings were blazing everywhere.'[69]

As I got into the street the sight of death and destruction that I saw was amazing. There were bodies of men lying all over the place and all were covered with blood, some were even burning as they lay ... As I walked around the village it was like a place of the dead ... The gutters in the street were streaming with blood and articles of clothing were lying all over the place. Every house appeared to be burning.[70]

Most of the women waited to come back to Civitella the next morning. They found no men alive, and they worked together to find and take care of the dead. 'We women then got together and helped one another to remove the bodies or the remains of our loved ones. We carried them to what was left of our respective homes. There we washed what remained of their bodies. Then we wrapped them up in what white sheets we could find and carried them to the church ... Somehow we managed to clear up the church and then we laid out the bodies for benediction.'[71]

The women made coffins for some of the dead by collecting doors, floorboards, and odd bits of wood from all over the village. 'It was I, his wife, who made him his coffin and when his coffin was made as best as possible, we took a cart on which we placed my husband and two other men and took them to the cemetery where I dug his grave myself.'[72] 'We gathered up our dead ourselves, made the coffins ourselves, loaded them ourselves onto the cart used for collecting the town's garbage and, three by three, we brought them to the cemetery.'[73] 'We took [the coffin] to the church and managed to get my husband's body into it. The coffin was then put on a handcart, which already contained three bodies, and pushed to the cemetery by the women. Here he was laid at rest by me. There was no priest present and consequently no benediction.'[74] On Saturday, July 1, the women of Civitella by themselves buried their dead, but without the final sacrament (figure 7). 'There was no priest present at the cemetery, so we buried them as best we could.'[75]

The normal ritual of death and burial had been turned upside down in a terrible way. The image of the women alone, in the desolate and still smouldering village with blood still in the streets, coping with the bodies and the burials of their husbands, fathers, and brothers was evoked again and again in Civitella's postwar statements and in postwar memories. Though together, the women were utterly alone and on their own.

So many were in the same position – suddenly having to cope with so many dead directly in front of them. In Burrone, after Dino Amazzoni finished the work of moving the bodies of his family, his landlords, and his neighbours, he went back to hide in the woods, where he remained until the following morning.

About 0700 hours, Friday 30 June 44, I went to Cornia to get a Priest to attend to the burial of my father. The Germans however had also been to Cornia the previous day and everyone there was in the same position as myself. I returned to my home and got two oxen and a cart. Then I took the bodies three at a time to the Municipal Cemetery at Cornia. The priest Don Romanelli Natale officiated at the burial of everyone.[76]

After helping Dino Amazzoni move his family's bodies on June 29, Dante Pasquini of Burrone had gone to help another neighbour, Settimia Lazzeroni. At her house he heard someone crying for help, and found Palmira Caratelli alive but seriously wounded in the stomach and chest. He and Signora Lazzeroni carried her out and dressed her wounds as best they could. In the same room, still filled with smoke, he saw the dead bodies of five women and four men. The next day, he and some others removed the bodies from the house. 'The rest of that day I assisted in the making of coffins for these bodies. They were buried that day in a field outside the farmhouse as everyone was afraid to go to the cemetery in case the Germans were there. On Sunday 2 July 44, we dug the bodies up and took them to the Municipal Cemetery at Cornia where they were buried. The priest Don Romanelli Natale officiated at the ceremony.'[77] Father Romanelli officiated at the burial of thirty-four residents of Cornia killed on June 29, including his own mother and sister.[78]

Cavriglia

On June 29, the same day as the massacres at Civitella, Cornia, and San Pancrazio, Ivario Viligiardi of Castelnuovo dei Sabbioni, a twenty-four year old mineworker, saw a carload of German soldiers approach on the road where he was walking. It was, he decided, an opportune moment to dispose of the hand grenade he was carrying in his jacket pocket – not in an attempt to kill the Germans, but afraid to be caught carrying it. Although not a partisan himself, he knew Nello Vannini and his partisan band, the Third Company Chiatti. Viligiardi was caught, arrested, and brought to the town of Terranuova Bracciolini on June 30, where the Germans interrogated him about his connection to local partisans. Viligiardi later maintained to British investigators that he had denied all knowledge of the partisans. A bit later, however, he admitted that when his German interrogators threatened to carry out reprisals against Viligiardi's family, he told them that 'Vannini, Nello was the leader of the Cavriglia Partisans.'[79]

Viligiardi was questioned yet again – this time through an Italian interpreter – regarding the whereabouts of the local partisans.[80] Now, Viligiardi wrote out the names and addresses of three persons who he said were partisans. The interpreter later could not remember the names Viligiardi wrote, but did recall that two of them lived at Castelnuovo dei Sabbioni and one at Meleto. The interrogating German soldier informed Viligiardi that the place where (according to Viligiardi) the partisans were operating was not to be found on the map. Viligiardi 'then volunteered to accompany the Germans to the locality in question.'[81]

German units and groups of German soldiers were congregating in the area of Cavriglia at that time; their purposes and the connection between them are not definitely known from contemporary or later sources and have since been inferred in more than one way.[82] A few days earlier, on about June 25, a motorized German unit of some seventy men, described as an 'Anti-Partisan' unit and commanded by a Lieutenant Wolf, had come to Terranuova Bracciolini, near San Giovanni Valdarno. They established their headquarters in the house of Doctor Luigi Corsi on the Via Vittorio Veneto.[83] The following day, a section of the German Feldgendarmerie settled at San Cipriano. On June 29, an officer later identified as Ober-Lieutenant Gerhard Danisch, a Panzer Corps commander, other officers, and about thirty soldiers (some of whom were believed to be Italians in German uniform) also arrived at San Cipriano. That same day, another German officer, described as a major of the 76 Panzer Corps, his staff of five junior officers, and thirty additional soldiers commandeered an estate about four kilometres from San Cipriano for their headquarters.[84]

Still another German unit, later identified as the '11 Panzer Gren Hermann Göring Regiment,' located its headquarters in Cavriglia at this same time. And again, on July 1, another Hermann Göring unit 'about 100 men strong and with twelve vehicles,' streamed into the village of Montegonzi, about six kilometres from Castelnuovo dei Sabbioni. On the day of their arrival in the village, the major of this last unit sent for the village priest Father Ermanno Grifoni and asked if there were any partisans in the area. If so, he announced, 'I want you to know that any attacks made upon my soldiers by partisans will force me to carry out reprisals, as I did at Civitella della Chiana.'[85] Allied investigators later concluded: 'This appears to have been the commencement of a premeditated, pre-arranged and atrocious large scale reprisal raid against the male civilians of the aforementioned villages, because of the activities of the 3rd Company of Chiatti Partisan band.'[86]

On the morning of July 4, German soldiers blocked the entrances to Castelnuovo dei Sabbioni and stood guard. Between about six-thirty and seven-thirty in the morning, they began combing the village, passing from house to house searching for the men. Ivo Cristofani, a seventeen year old seminarian on an early summer vacation in anticipation of the passage of the front, was seized on his way home from serving mass.[87] The men were forced to piazza IV Novembre, at the bottom of the village below the church, and there the Germans carried out the massacre.[88]

By nine, about forty men were assembled in the piazza, some of whom had not been captured, but who had come voluntarily, in the apparent belief that it was safer to obey German orders.[89] After ordering the women and children to leave the village, the Germans allowed some, including Sister Maddalena Delfino, to retrieve a few things from their homes. When Sister Maddalena passed Castelnuovo's parish priest, Father Ferrante Bagiardi, standing together with the village men in the piazza, he told her to go into the church and chapel, and retrieve all the consecrated hosts. When she passed Father Bagiardi again, she gave one container to him, and took the other to share with the women sheltering in nearby Camonti.[90]

As the priests of Civitella and San Pancrazio had done (or were remembered to have done), Father Bagiardi offered his own life in place of the villagers. As in the other villages, the priest's offer was refused. The Germans did, however, permit him to give communion.[91] Several men attempted to escape before and immediately after Father Bagiardi distributed the Eucharist. Two were shot in the attempt, but two men managed to throw themselves over the west side of the village wall and hide in a ravine at its base, while three others ran into a house facing the west side of the piazza.[92]

At about nine-thirty, the men were positioned in front of the wall of the piazza, a machinegun on a stone slab facing them. Arduina Beni, watching from a hiding place near the wall, saw the men give up their watches and their identification documents to a soldier before they were mowed down by machinegun volleys. Agostino Foggi witnessed it all, watching from the window of his house overlooking the piazza.[93] Ernesta Borchi saw her husband killed, and Pia Bonci, watching from her garden overlooking the piazza saw her father and brother shot.[94] After the killings, the soldiers took wood and furniture from the houses, scattering it among the bodies. They poured gasoline over all and set everything on fire. Seventy-four men were murdered at Castelnuovo dei Sabbioni that morning. Their bodies were so thoroughly burned that surviving family members could not identify them.[95]

Ninety-three men were massacred that same morning at nearby Meleto. In similar fashion, German soldiers blocked off the village centre, gathered up the men in the main piazza next to the village's World War I monument, and ordered the women and children to leave. At least one of the soldiers was an Italian dressed in steel helmet and German uniform. His description matched that of Ivario Viligiardi – Allied investigators later decided – though at that moment Viligiardi was in Florence.[96] The victims again included the village priest. Father Giovanni Fondelli and the village men were divided into four groups, with each group taken and held in a different (apparently preselected) farmyard. Two men escaped, and two were spared.[97] All of the men who remained were machine-gunned, and their bodies set on fire. The houses in that village also were burned. Returning to Meleto that afternoon, the women saw 'heaps' of smoking corpses. Most were able to recognize the remains of their fathers and their husbands only by their clothing.[98]

At Massa dei Sabbioni, about fifteen very young (described by survivors as teenaged) German soldiers arrived at about noon. They calmly ate their lunch, then began searching and burning the houses. The village priest Father Ermete Morini, twenty-six year old Dante Pagliazzi, and seventeen year old Giuseppe Virboni were the first men captured, and were locked in a house farthest from the centre of the village.[99] The Germans took the priest into a barn, stabbed and shot him; then they did the same to Dante Pagliazzi, but Virboni was able to flee. While he ran, two Allied planes, whose pilots apparently noticed the Germans or the general activity, swooped down and dropped some small bombs, then passed again and strafed the road. Virboni got away, and ten more men held in the piazza also were able to take flight in the confusion. On the following day, the villagers found the burned remains of Father Morini and Dante Pagliazzi. They brought them to a corner of the cemetery, where they lay unburied.

On the following day, Father Giovacchino Meacci, the priest of neighbouring San Cipriano, learned of the massacre at Meleto. There, as with the other massacres, no men (or not enough men) were left alive to help carry the dead to the cemetery or to help with digging graves. The women of Meleto found a handcart, in which they wheeled their men's remains, a few at a time, to the cemetery. Those able to identify their relatives buried them in individual graves. Those bodies or remains they could not recognize were buried in ten larger common graves, after which Father Meacci attempted to record the names of the dead and presumed dead in the parish registry.[100]

The final massacre in the commune of Cavriglia took place at Le Màtole on July 11.[101] In the early afternoon, a truck carrying six or seven

German soldiers came upon a group of twelve men digging an air-raid ditch a short distance from the village. One of the soldiers, witnesses told later, 'was a certain Italian named Viligiardi, Ivario from Castelnuovo dei Sabbioni, dressed in German uniform.'[102] As the Germans rounded them together, one man was able to escape. The rest were marched forward, but after proceeding about one hundred metres, the men scattered suddenly and spontaneously: one escaped in the rush, one bled to death after being shot, and the remaining nine were recaptured. Their execution took place about five-thirty that evening and was viewed by many of the women in the village.[103] It was also witnessed by eleven year old Emilio Polverini who could see all of what happened from the half-open window of his grandmother's house. He and his younger brother were staying with their grandmother at Le Màtole, after their father had been killed in the July 4 massacre at Castelnuovo.[104]

War and Massacre

As Father Polvani had said some months earlier about the Allied bombing of civilian targets, 'this is not war, this is murder.' The actions of the Germans (and Republican Fascists) in the province of Arezzo in the summer of 1944 also were murder – the murder of Allied POWs, the murder of Italian civilians, of women and children. The distinction between soldier and civilian truly had disappeared. These were rural villages where city dwellers had come to find safety from the war. These were village piazzas where children played and residents chatted in the evenings, and which had been the centres of civil life and *civiltà* for generations. Now they were the sites of massacre and places where women went to recover the remains of their husbands, brothers, or sons, and where children identified what little was left of their fathers' bodies. War had transformed village piazzas into places of the most perverse sort of local unity, where all were massacred irrespective of politics, occupation, or class – shot together and buried together, as the women were united in their loss and in working together to bury their dead.

The central Italian massacres during the summer of 1944 prove at a minimum that the 'barbarization of war' was not limited to the eastern front or to the occupied countries of Eastern Europe.[105] Two additional questions must be considered, however. Why did the German soldiers do it (and it was not only SS troops, as Michele Battini and Paolo Pezzino have shown), and who was morally – if not directly – responsible? Assuming (for the moment) that the Germans carried out the massacres and related atrocities as retaliation or reprisal for partisan guerrilla activities, what had happened in the province of Arezzo to trigger such reprisals? At Civitella, local partisans had shot and killed two German soldiers and wounded another in the *dopolavoro* inside the village walls; moreover, comments made in the following days by German troops in the area imply retaliation for specific or generic partisan action. In addition, the peculiar fact that the Germans spared the few men who showed they were 'outsiders' – evacuees from Florence or essential workers – adds some weight to a conclusion that these villages and villagers were specifically targeted. Partisans had been 'active' in the woods around San Pancrazio, though those villagers also explained their massacre 'above all, because of the help given by the peaceful population to Allied prisoners escaped from prison camps who took shelter there.'[106] At Castelnuovo and the other massacred villages in the commune of Cavriglia, no partisan killings had taken place in the villages, but many citizens of Castelnuovo later attributed the massacres to their long, local tradition of anti-Fascism.

The best-known massacre – or reprisal against civilians – in Italy was that carried out near the Ardeatine Caves in March 1944, where in retaliation for the killing of thirty-three German policemen on via Rasella, 335 men and boys were executed on the outskirts of Rome.[107] Thus, German Field Marshal Kesselring's threat that ten Italian civilians would be killed for every German soldier killed by partisans was 'carried out.' The Ardeatine Cave massacre was an explicit and direct reprisal, the German order for which is clear: ten innocent Italian civilians (plus two extra) killed for each German dead on the via Rasella. At Civitella, San Pancrazio, and Castelnuovo, the 'ratio of reprisal' was more horribly disproportionate, however, and other than at Civitella the massacres did not appear to relate directly to specific partisan actions. Why did the Germans kill so many civilians in such brutal fashion (including women and children at Cornia) and destroy their villages so thoroughly – going well beyond Kesselring's published warnings of 'severe measures'?[108]

The tragedy of the Caus of Gebbia goes deeper. Because Signora Cau spoke German, because she had acted as interpreter for occupation forces in the area, because she had helped to prepare the bodies of the two soldiers shot in Civitella's *dopolavoro*, and no doubt because she was a foreigner and an outsider, locals believed she was a spy for the Germans. When no one (including the Caus' children) saw the Caus or knew what happened to them after the massacres, many concluded the couple had voluntarily accompanied the Germans to Germany. Allied investigators reported months later: 'Despite most exhaustive enquiries, which have been carried out from Monte San Savino to Florence, no trace of this couple can be found. The other prisoners were taken to Florence ... but it is not known whether the Caus ever left the villa.'[109] The Caus never left the villa, or at least not the village – their bodies were not found until 1951, in the furnace of a destroyed house. Most confounding then, why did the Germans kill Helga Cau, the foreign woman who translated for them, who prepared the bodies of their dead comrades for burial, and whom the locals distrusted?

Looking back from the present, instances of inexplicable violence (like murdering the Caus, or shooting and burning the women and children of Cornia), grossly disproportionate massacres of civilians, and massacres seemingly unrelated to any specific partisan action all argue against the massacres being precise quid pro quo for partisan violence, and argue for them being plain instances of wartime conduct, understandable at that particular point of that particular war – being what Leonardo Paggi has called 'ordinary massacres,' what Michele Battini and Paolo Pezzino have argued was the 'Eastern model of occupation' transferred to Italy, what Claudio Pavone explained as the final phase of the Nazi war in Italy when the 'entire civilian population became potential hostages in the hands of the occupiers,' or what I would cite as near perfect examples of the process whereby modern war had become total war against civilians.[110] If carried to its logical extreme, such interpretation leads to a conclusion that massacres and destruction (as carried out by German troops in Italy, sometimes with Republican Fascist help) would have happened with or without partisan acts of resistance, or even without partisan presence, because that was the stage the war had then reached.

By the summer of 1944, Allied troops in Italy advanced and German forces were in retreat towards an expected showdown at the Gothic Line, though neither advance nor retreat was orderly. A reasoned explanation of the massacres takes into account military need to 'cleanse' around Gothic Line defences and to subdue or neutralize the local population for protection of German troops in retreat, yet that explanation seems almost too rational when compared to the extreme conduct of the massacres. The massacres in Arezzo province went far beyond clearing the Gothic Line and intimidating the local population. As the Allies advanced and the Germans retreated, signs of an inevitable German defeat in the larger war (beyond Italy) were unmistakable: Soviet troops entered Germany in August 1944. Moreover, German forces in Italy were retreating through a country that had once been their political and ideological ally but was now 'hosting' the opposing side. Surely, revenge had its place in the massacres, as Battini and others also recognize. Thus, in all, provocation for indiscriminate German violence, massacre, and destruction would appear sufficient even without military need, even without Italian partisan goading, and even though Italians shared few or none of the characteristics of civilian victims similarly brutalized on the eastern front (not being 'Jews, Slavs, and Bolsheviks').

Should such bloody circumstantial evidence absolve the partisans of responsibility, however? During the summer of 1944, Italians, including the villagers of central Italy and the partisans themselves, knew that partisan violence against the Germans led to German reprisals against civilians. The citizens feared and expected reprisals, as confirmed by their flight to the woods after the shooting at Civitella's *dopolavoro*. Giovanni Contini and Ida Balò Valli both have presented the 'divided memory' of the Civitella massacre: how and why the widows of Civitella held – and those still alive continue to hold – the partisans at fault for the June 29 massacre. For many, partisan guilt is as great as German guilt for that village massacre, because they needlessly put civilian lives at risk.[111] Avoiding a historically meaningless 'cost-benefit' analysis, which asks whether the partisans' (or the Resistance's) accomplishments outweighed the negative 'costs' of civilian massacres – or, more succinctly: did the partisans actually shorten the war, help effect Italy's liberation, or restore an honourable, non-Fascist identity to Italy in a way that makes up for the massacres – questions remain whether and to what degree Italy (and history) can or should connect partisan actions to civilian deaths.

Should the partisans (especially the partisans in central Italy) have done nothing until the Allies arrived? Yet had they done nothing, they never would have proven themselves to the Allies and helped make possible northern partisan successes. Should they have turned themselves in, in place of the civilian victims, as some argued about the shootings on the via Rasella? That might have been an option if the massacres really were reprisals for partisan actions and if it really was the partisans the Germans wished to punish. Most importantly, in the last months of the war and first few years after, 'reprisal' (or *rappresaglia*) came to be the common term for any German military killing of Italian civilians in Italy, though reprisal for what was rarely specified. That means, I think, that as many Italians (officially and individually) perceived it, German soldiers killed Italian civilians simply *because* they were Italian, not because of what they (or partisans) had done.

More basically, were the partisans 'bad' or 'good,' to borrow Father Polvani's impossibly clear-cut terminology, in the context of that particular war? They were not the only Italians who took action against the German occupiers and Fascist Republicans, directly or indirectly. The lignite miners of Castelnuovo disrupted production that would have aided German troops and occupation forces, and factory workers sometimes did the same through strikes or sabotage. Food protests by Aretine women and food concealment by Aretine farmers also can be interpreted, in part, as anti-Nazi-Fascist, as can Italian acts of kindness to the nation's wartime enemies and POWs interned in their villages. Partisan actions are the actions associated with reprisals, however, and with the Resistance and the memory of the Resistance.

Debate over the partisans, their methods, and the postwar assessment became best defined after Claudio Pavone published *Una guerra civile. Saggio storico sulla moralità nella Resistenza*.[112] It is difficult to imagine what questions remain unasked or unexplored after Pavone's seminal analysis of individual and group responsibility, of reprisal as an 'imperfect war,' of the heavily charged word choice between civilian 'victims' and 'martyrs,' and of implications surrounding the choice whether to take action or do nothing. The answers become increasingly complex, however, as more research is carried out into the individual massacres and who conducted them, into the postwar political use of the massacres, and into how they have been remembered.[113] Although as former partisans, widows, and massacre survivors grow older and die, arguments about partisan guilt or heroism grow less intensely personal and painful, while greater scrutiny has shifted to the nature, meaning, and memory of the Resistance.

The scholarly and political claim often made (and analyzed) is that the predominant memory and predominant postwar Italian identity have been that of wartime resistance (or Resistance, with a capital 'R'). Paolo Pezzino locates the Resistance as the dominant narrative, memory, and identity in Italy from the 1960s, unchallenged until Pavone's reorienting 1991 study, while others cite 1947–8 as the moment when 'general anti-fascism of the Italian people' was selected as postwar common ground instead of a 'culture of crisis and critique of the fascist past.' Adopting the narrative of Resistance and adopting the Resistance as the 'founding myth' of the new republican Italy (whether adopted in 1947 or in the 1960s) relieved Italians of having to contend with a counter-narrative of apparent consensus for Fascism and all that entailed (including imperialism, war, and losing the war). Thus, selectively remembering (and identifying with) the Resistance – and agreeing to remember (and to identify with) the

Resistance, accepting the 'caesura of 25 April' as the 'starting date of the new Italy' – made it easier for Italians selectively to forget about the 'old Italy' of Fascism and war on the side of Nazi Germany.

The Resistance memory/identity and related *brava gente* identity are considered problematic (by those who assert Italy has not attempted to or does not know how to come to terms with its past), because focus on the Resistance has euphemized as anti-Fascist resisters the majority of Italians (who were not active resisters), while ignoring those who opposed the partisans rather than opposing Fascism or the Germans. Similarly, focus on Italian national natural 'goodness' during wartime has, until recently, excluded recognition of the unpleasant, troubling, and sometime murderous acts Italians engaged in during Fascism and during the war. This is what Claudio Pavone and others mean when they ask whether Italians truly know how to – and whether they choose to – 'come to terms with' the Fascist past.[114] Local archives, however, show no postwar moment when a Resistance identity was adopted and shared thereby to relieve Italians of any national self-examination; rather, Italians (in Arezzo, at least) easily acknowledged they had been Fascists until July 25 or September 8, 1943, but that Fascism meant little. Their wartime and postwar suffering was far more serious than their Fascism had been. After the war, Italians could most readily see themselves as victims of war, not among the perpetrators of wrongs carried out by or within Italy.

One less morally and factually charged question can be answered more definitively. Yes, there was a civil war in Italy between 1943 and 1945, at least in the parts of Italy where Republican Fascists and partisans operated, and where resistance (the Resistance) against the 'Nazi-Fascists' and against German occupation was carried out. Even Father Polvani referred to the 'half civil war' going on in his small zone during the summer of 1944, while the English advanced and the Germans retreated through the province of Arezzo.[115] In Arezzo, as in the rest of central and northern Italy, there were Republican Fascists and there were partisans, but the two sides were relatively small compared to the population overall, and they very rarely, if ever, engaged in actual fighting only against one another, without greater numbers of German troops involved. Without German occupation, there would have been no civil war in Italy then.

Clearly, a few Italians did participate in or were present with the Germans at the massacres in the province of Arezzo, something that would have continuing significance for postwar community feeling only

on the local level. And Italians in places other than Arezzo also participated in crimes, massacres, and atrocities against Italian civilians – their
fellow citizens. The Allies who investigated the central Italian massacres
did not push for war crimes trials in Italy stemming from those massacres. They believed the Italian government had neither the 'machinery'
nor the energy to try such cases, and that defendants might not receive
a fair trial. Moreover, the Allies (especially the British) did not care to
have emphasized how the partisan warfare they came to foster led to reprisals against civilians.[116]

What has come to be called *l'armadio della vergogna* or the Italian 'cabinet of shame,' filled with investigative records into German war crimes
against Italians, is now well known, as is the Allied decision not to prosecute German war crimes against Italians.[117] Both are generally put down
to an early cold war attempt to reconcile quickly with West Germany and
the Allies. That assessment, however, neglects to consider what no prosecution meant for Italy on the local level. It denied postwar justice to the
families of those murdered and to the communities in which the crimes
took place and, just as shamefully, protected guilty Italians together with
guilty Germans. Names and whereabouts of both Italians and German
suspects were known in many cases, but they were shelved for the sake of
postwar reconciliation within Italy as well. Selective prosecution of only
German perpetrators could not have occurred, because that would also
have revealed Italian participation.

3 Completing the Disintegration

War is war, and the consequences of it are distressing for everyone.
Don Narcisco Polvani, 'Diario anno 1944,' August 20

The period from July 4th to the 20th (which was the arrival of the first Allied vanguard) was the time of terror for us.
From the sindaco of Cavriglia's list of verified military offensives

Burying the Dead – Castelnuovo dei Sabbioni

Rumours of the July 4 massacres in Castelnuovo, Meleto, and Massa reached Bishop Giovanni Giorgis of Fiesole (in whose diocese the villages were located) through an 'irregular communication' from the Castelnuovo mine corporation the next day.[1] The news of tragedy was vague and impossible to investigate from that distance because all telephone and telegraph communication had been broken off. The bishop decided therefore to visit the commune of Cavriglia and see for himself what had happened. He asked one of his curates, Father Gino Ciabattini who was a native of Cavriglia and familiar with the region, to accompany him.[2]

Father Ciabattini said mass quickly and very early on July 8, and then departed with the bishop by six in the morning. The men were able to take a trolleybus (one of the very few still functioning in the city) as far as Florence, from where they reached Grassina by tram. After Grassina they walked: in the scorching Tuscan July sun, they walked forty kilometres along a road that had been cratered by Allied bombs and even then was being mined by German soldiers. They met German patrols along the way, and every so often saw Allied planes pass overhead – followed by German antiaircraft shooting wildly. Arriving in the village of

Gaville some twelve hours later, at about six in the evening, they stopped
for a brief rest and a visit with the local priest. Bishop Giorgis asked for
news of what had happened in Meleto and Castelnuovo, but no one
knew. They then went to the local German command set up outside of
town. With his few words of German, Father Ciabattini explained their
mission and obtained a pass from a young official that provided: 'The
Bishop of Fiesole and the priest Gino Ciabattini are authorized to visit
the villages of Meleto and Castelnuovo.'

Finally, they reached Meleto in the summer darkness. The village
seemed empty. Many houses were destroyed, but some frightened women
emerged from doorways to tell the priests their 'heartbreaking' story of
the massacre, and how they had buried their men in the local cemetery.
That night, the bishop and Father Ciabattini slept on mattresses on the
floor of the village school. Unable to sleep despite his exhausting day,
Father Ciabattini lay awake listening to the sounds of shelling, mines
exploding, and German trucks passing.

The next morning, Sunday July 9, the priest rang the bells, calling to
church those who remained in the village: '[T]hey were,' he said, 'the
mothers, the wives, the sisters, the daughters of the slaughtered.' Father
Ciabattini heard confessions, while the bishop said mass, prayed for the
dead, and gave a brief sermon attempting to comfort the survivors.
Trucks carrying German soldiers appeared in the village during the
mass, and one soldier wielding a pistol entered the church – terrifying
the already traumatized women.

At about nine-thirty in the morning, Father Ciabattini and the bishop left Meleto for Castelnuovo dei Sabbioni. Monsignor Pavanello and
Father Fani, having heard from residents of Gaville that the bishop was
on his way to Cavriglia, had walked from the town of Figline to meet
him. The four men proceeded together. 'Under the burning sun, we
crossed the country abandoned by the miners without encountering a
living soul,' Father Ciabattini told later. When they got closer, they
could see the Germans had blown up the enormous thermoelectric
plant and the lignite mine buildings, some of which were still burning.
Coming into the village of Castelnuovo, they found it deserted, except
for German soldiers preparing holes for landmines. Monsignor
Pavanello, fluent in German, explained the reason for their passage
through the countryside and received permission to proceed. In the
upper part of the village, they saw most of the houses either burned or
blackened with smoke.

Then, as they reached the piazza just below the church, suddenly they
met a 'horrifying spectacle.' A row of cadavers lay still smouldering –

blackened and unrecognizable. Unlike Meleto or Civitella, the bodies of the slaughtered men of Castelnuovo had not been removed from the piazza; the corpses now had been exposed to the July heat for five days, and gave forth a stench truly unbearable.[3] Some of the women came forward to tell the priests the events of their village massacre. Pressing a handkerchief to his face, the bishop unsuccessfully tried to find the bodies of Father Bagiardi and seminarian Ivo Cristofani among the piles. The bishop had intended Father Ciabattini to say mass in the church in Castelnuovo, but the church was locked and no one could locate the key. After blessing the corpses, they next headed for the parish of San Pancrazio (in the commune of Cavriglia).[4]

The priests arrived in San Pancrazio about noon, where Father Polvani greeted them. They appeared that 'hot and sunny' July Sunday, recorded Father Polvani, 'unexpected and in a sea of sweat.'[5] Father Ciabattini said mass for all the Castelnuovo victims, and the bishop instructed San Pancrazio's chaplain Father Aldo Cuccoli to oversee the swift removal and burial of the victims of Castelnuovo, lest the decaying bodies cause an epidemic.

On the next morning, the bishop and Father Ciabattini began the long walk back to Fiesole, stopping to rest at the village of Massa dei Sabbioni. There, they learned, the Germans had killed the priest Father Morini. Father Ciabattini and the bishop searched the hut in which Father Morini and Dante Pagliazzi had been killed and their bodies incinerated, but found only rubble and no additional remains of the victims. After blessing the ashes and bones, they continued home. Finally nearing Florence on Tuesday, July 11, they hoped to take the tram there from Grassina, but that line no longer functioned. Still on foot as far as Piazza San Marco in Florence, they found a trolleybus, and so did not have to walk the final kilometres to Fiesole.[6]

On July 10, the day Father Ciabattini and the bishop left Massa dei Sabbioni, Father Polvani and Don Cuccoli oversaw the burial in the local cemetery of three men killed in the woods outside San Pancrazio 'in reprisal' by the Germans.[7] Later that day, villagers brought still another body to the cemetery. This victim was unknown locally, and was most likely a foreign member of a local partisan band; they buried him as well.[8] Father Polvani and Father Cuccoli walked from San Pancrazio to Castelnuovo that same evening to bury the dead there. The constant shelling overhead and nearby bursts of machinegun fire frightened both the widows and the priests too much to continue, however, so they decided to wait until the following day. The priests returned to San Pancrazio that night.[9]

The next morning, Father Cuccoli again departed before dawn, now having obtained written permission from the German command to bury the dead.[10] The bodies were so numerous and so purulent that it was impossible for the priest and the women of the village to bury them alone. Some men had closed themselves inside the nearby mines, hiding from the Germans, but at Father Cuccoli's urging, 'in an act of true courage,' about thirty men emerged to help 'in this work of Christian mercy.'[11] Although the bodies were so badly burned and decomposed that they were unrecognizable, Father Cuccoli counted and examined the corpses one by one. Bullet holes were visible in the backs of the skulls. He was able to count seventy-three bodies and skulls, and tried to make a more precise and personal list by collecting names from the families who reported men missing.[12] With only a single horse and cart to transport so many dead, Father Cuccoli, the men from the mine, and the women of Castelnuovo passed six times up and down the steep street that led from the piazza to the cemetery, where the men dug a large communal grave.[13] The bodies were buried together, and Father Cuccoli said a funeral mass in a make-shift chapel. He then disinfected the piazza with materials obtained from the mining office and burned the cart that had carried the dead.[14]

After Father Cuccoli returned to San Pancrazio that night, three women had arrived from Le Màtole about ten in the evening to tell of the massacre in that village earlier the same day.[15] On the next day, with no other help and lacking even a horse or cart to carry them, the women of the village arranged the corpses one at a time on the rungs of a ladder and carried them one at a time to the cemetery at Castelnuovo. The women dug a mass grave next to that prepared just the day before.[16] Again, Father Cuccoli blessed the dead.[17]

The Front Passes – Civitella

After burying their dead, with their houses burned, their possessions stolen, and the front lines of war rapidly approaching, the women and children of Civitella had to look outside the village for food and shelter. Many continued to spend their nights at the Poggiali orphanage.[18] Others went to stay in nearby villages with family, friends, or with strangers who would take them in.[19] Still others lived in the woods, surviving on what food they could find. In the first days after the massacre, some young children, like Dino Tiezzi already traumatized by witnessing the massacre of his father and brother, became separated from their mothers and found them only days later.[20]

Dino Tiezzi's older brother Daniele, the young seminarian who was shot as he escaped the massacre, returned to Civitella and again encountered the Germans.

> Our house was destroyed and I was put to bed in my uncle's house ... A few days later, hearing that the Germans were preparing to defend Civitella against the British, I ... again took to the woods. Ten days later ... I was picked up by members of the Herman Goering Regiment and made to dig trenches near Arezzo. I returned to Civitella after the English had liberated the town.[21]

The other escapee from the massacre, Gino Bartolucci, also met up with the Germans again. 'About ten days after I got there [to the house of a friend] I was picked up by the Germans and made to work for them for a day carrying logs despite my wounds. I returned to Civitella some days after its liberation by the British.'[22]

Lara Lammioni's father, grandfather, two uncles, an aunt, and two little cousins had died in the massacre and the subsequent fire at Civitella. Now, she, her mother and sister, along with another aunt, four young cousins, her uncle Luigi, and his young daughter, all headed for Malfiano, Lara's family farm two or three kilometres down the hill from Civitella, joined by several other villagers with nowhere else to go.[23] Upon arriving at Malfiano, however, they found it occupied by German soldiers who had taken over all the stocks of food. As they could hear, the front was little more than a kilometre away at that point, leaving the exhausted, hungry, grieving villagers with no option but to stay.

The Allied offensive of July 4 had begun, and Allied shells regularly hit the farm. Their band of refugees – numbering about thirty-five – spent most of the time sheltering from bombs and artillery under the old stone archway of one of the Lammioni farm buildings. They cooked and ate the hens and geese that had been struck by shrapnel. The group avoided contact with the German soldiers, just as the Germans avoided them. The soldiers had only a single machinegun, which they placed in the first floor window of the farm building and moved from window to window, apparently to give nearby Allied troops the impression of a larger force. Its firing was a constant and nerve wracking presence.

One night the Germans set fire to their ammunition dump nearby, and the next night, finally, abandoned their position at Malfiano. Waiting in the dark, the refugees from Civitella expected the Allies to arrive at any moment. Instead, a small group of retreating German soldiers appeared. Immediately shooting and killing one of the few remaining men, they ordered the rest of the villagers into the hayloft. Two soldiers also pushed into the hayloft to ask in broken Italian: 'Where is the young lady?' They were referring to the only young lady of the group, Lara Lammioni, then twenty years old. Perhaps already almost two weeks after the massacre (the days had blurred), she was still wearing the stylish bright red dress she had put on early the morning of the June 29 holiday. In the barn, she covered it with a jacket the countrywomen wore when tending the vines. She rolled up her hair in a black scarf, rubbed dirt on her face and legs, and crouched near an old farm worker. The soldiers continued to demand the young lady ('[if] no young lady, [then] everybody dead'), shining their torches on each person's face in turn. Suddenly, an officer called to the soldiers; they left, bolting the barn door from the outside.

While the villagers remained locked in the barn, another Allied artillery offensive began. The noise was deafening: shells struck all around, and one hit the hayloft setting fire to the straw. The attack finally ended at daybreak. Inside the barn, Lara and the others were able to lift the barn door off its hinges. Just outside lay three dead German soldiers. The villagers agreed it was time to go find the English forces, but as no one was composed enough to decide upon a route, they all simply rushed ahead. As they hurried across the fields, they heard (and felt) machine-gun fire from the farm on the next hill only a few hundred metres away. Lara hid under the wall of a terraced field until the shooting stopped.

Finally, a lone soldier – the long-awaited Allied forces – appeared. He continued walking, barely glancing at the white cloth Lara waved at him. Lara suddenly realized that she was alone; the others apparently had taken another path after the shooting stopped. Continuing ahead, Lara first saw big lines of wire lying on the ground, then some large pots (for tea, she later learned), then at last more Allied soldiers. Unable to eat the food they offered her, whether because of nerves or after too many days without real food, she slept in an empty stable until an interpreter came to ask her about the German troops in the area and calmly listened to her story of the massacre at Civitella.[24]

The soldier in turn told her that a group from Civitella had taken refuge at the Dorna *fattoria* a few kilometres away. Lara found her remaining family there, and they stayed together for some days. Nearby, an Allied gun emplacement always pointed in the direction of the hilltop village of Civitella, which the Germans were still defending. After a day or two – Lara again lost track of days, but by now the front had passed – a truck from one of the local Committees of National Liberation (CLN) transported her small band of survivors to Foiano della Chiana. Although only a few kilometres from Civitella and San Pancrazio, it had remained relatively untouched by the passage of the front.[25]

The story of the massacre at Civitella began to circulate in Foiano, and the villagers offered them clothing, shoes, food, and much sympathy. Half a century later, Lara remembered being overwhelmed by 'a great variety of breads, all types of cheeses, prosciutto and salami, and fruit in abundance.' Still unable to eat, sick with fever, and an untreated jaundice-like ailment, Lara Lammioni lay in bed in her host's house, listening in the evenings to the sounds of young people dancing in the piazza to jazz records supplied by the Allied liberators.

The Lucarinis – Bucine

Until July 2, 1944, Aroldo Lucarini, secretary for the commune of Bucine, and his family remained at Duddova, where they had fled to avoid Allied bombing and the approaching front, until they saw German troops in the area.[26] Together with two other families, they decided to move further from main roads. The families pooled their remaining stock of flour, a few other provisions they could carry on foot, and a goat. They slept one night in a pigsty on the top of a hill, directly under German artillery fire. The next day they moved down into the valley. In the middle of a chestnut wood, they built a sort of round hut, with a layer of heather on the ground for a floor.

As the opposing armies drew closer, the Lucarinis, like the Lammionis at Malfiano and so many others, lived the antithesis of *civiltà*. '[L]ike primitive people,' they hid during the day, sleeping together at night.[27] In the hut, they all lay side by side with their feet towards the centre. Under them ran a stream, where they saw German soldiers washing up in the mornings. After a few days, they ran out of food except for about a kilogram of flour, so they decided to return to Duddova, where they found that village completely deserted. They were, however, able to catch two rabbits that had escaped their pen and were hopping through the abandoned streets. Finding nothing else, they took their remaining flour to a nearby farmhouse to try to make bread. As Signora Lucarini and one of the other women walked towards the farmhouse, Allied fighter planes patrolling the area fired on them. While the others watched, the women jumped into a haystack in the middle of the field.

Terrified, disoriented, and not knowing what else to do, they all walked back again to Duddova, where again they found nothing to eat. Now they began to look in nearby fields, hoping to find potatoes that farmers might have overlooked. Every day they found a few, and put them together in a pot. When the Lucarini's little group came upon a dead cow, the unintended target of Allied shelling, they hacked it into 'bloody pieces' with their inadequate knife. Cooking the meat with their scavenged potatoes, they felt 'these were feast days.'[28]

The German retreat and the Allied advance seemed to go on forever. The Allies would occupy a position only when absolutely certain that not a single German remained there. Signor Lucarini knew that the Allies were in the area, but since German artillery positions still were hidden in the surrounding hills, 'the Allies did not advance a step.'[29] The talk among the Lucarini group and other refugees and evacuees they met up with – confirmed by advice the Germans gave them – was to head north in the direction of Florence.

The Allies were still relatively distant from Florence, whereas the current zone was expected soon to be a line of German resistance rather than retreat. Their friends chose to remain, but the Lucarini family decided to walk towards Florence. Stopping for water after a couple of hours, Signora Lucarini declared she would go no further – 'trading uncertain evil for certain evil.'[30] They walked back to the hut and their friends. Hearing an unusual noise during the night of July 16, they peeked between the branches that made up the walls of their hut: German soldiers walked silently 'in Indian file' down the path from the hill where they had maintained their artillery command.[31] Finally, the Germans were withdrawing. And finally, the ground was clear for the Allies – who might not have advanced even then, had a group of partisans not gone to assure them that German troops had departed.

The Allies

As is the traditional nature of the discipline, standard military histories focus on commanders, decisive battles, and the capture of major cities or strategically important points. For the Italian campaign, this means that military historians proceed from Sicily to Salerno to Cassino to Anzio and Rome directly to the Gothic Line and on to the Po Valley and the Alps. It means that Field Marshal Kesselring and General Alexander are far more significant than the Aretine citizens and refugees who tried unsuccessfully to find some place of safety in the midst of war.[32]

Located between Rome and the Gothic Line, Civitella, San Pancrazio, and Castelnuovo were not the sites of major battles. They were, however, in the path of the British Eighth Army, specifically the Fourth Infantry

Division of the Thirteenth Corps. More narrowly, the communes and villages that are the subject here were located between the German delaying battles at Lake Trasimeno and the Arno River.[33] The passage of the front through this area – when described in British or American reports and histories – is mentioned only as difficult country necessarily fought through to reach the Arno, Florence, and on to breach the Gothic Line.[34]

The Allied Fourth Infantry Division began its advance 'to the abruptly rising ground about Civitella della Chiana and San Pancrazio' on July 4, 1944 – the same day German soldiers massacred the villagers of Castelnuovo, Meleto, and Massa dei Sabbioni.[35] After liberating Civitella and San Pancrazio almost two weeks later on July 16, 'the 4th Division, blocked on Highway 69, was compelled to shift its axis to a demolished country-road through Castelnuovo … From Castelnuovo the 2nd/4th Hampshires turned a minor German defensive line and secured Meleto. But every ridge and hamlet had to be fought for.'[36]

Something of the fight for 'every ridge and hamlet' and the ferociousness of the front can be gleaned from the Eighth Army contemporary telegrams and reports.[37] Field reports, like military histories, are not written from the perspective of the civilians who find themselves facing war. Like the earlier reports of Operation Strangle in the spring of 1944, when tons of bombs were every day described as dropped on the 'enemy's supply lines' instead of on civilians and their homes, the passage of the front through central Italy reads as if it took place on an empty – albeit topographically difficult – landscape, rather than one crowded with civilians trying to survive.

On the night of June 29–30, '22 Baltimores and 7 Bostons flew armed recces in the Iatoia, Bologna, Florence, Arezzo, Rimini areas and attacked scattered motor transport causing fires and explosions.'[38] June 29 was also the day of the massacres at Civitella, Cornia, and San Pancrazio. That night, while Allied bombers attacked German trucks, causing fires and explosions, Aroldo Lucarini watching from Duddova saw 'the sad spectacle' of San Pancrazio in flames. Dense smoke remained in the sky for many days afterwards.[39] Allied pilots may have seen the fire and smoke from German massacres along with that of their own bombs.

On June 30, '269 fighter bombers destroyed 2 bridges and damaged 3 bridges … and cut tracks in 8 places in the Bologna, Lucca, Faenza and Arezzo area. Destroyed 1 motor transport and damaged 11. Destroyed 1 locomotive and damaged 4. Destroyed 6 railroad cars and damaged 6.' The women and children of Civitella and San Pancrazio heard, and still remember, the sound of Allied planes and bombs overhead, and saw

Allied smoke mingled with German smoke, as they hid in the woods and at the Poggiali orphanage.

The Allies captured Siena on July 3 – one day before their push towards Civitella and San Pancrazio, and one day before the German massacres at Castelnuovo, Meleto, and Massa. '[L]eading troops now in contact with firmly held enemy rearguard position.' The Fourth British Division crossed the 'Canale della Chiana' and made contact with the enemy. On July 5, Allied troops were less than five miles from the city of Arezzo. On July 6, 'Civitella still strongly held [by the Germans] and no adv[ance] made in this sector.' On the night of July 7–8, '12 Baltimores, 26 Marauders, 52 Spitbombers, 137 Spitfires, 66 Kittyhawks and 46 Mustangs attacked roads and railways, bridges, gunsights and ammunition dumps in the Fano[sic]-Arezzo-Bibbiena-Cattonica and Florence areas.' On July 10, a British patrol finally made it as far as Cornia. The Fourth Division still repulsed counter-attacks from Civitella on that date. On July 11, artillery was 'very active on both sides.' On July 16, Civitella was captured, and '[t]he advance continues.' On July 19, the Germans still held Laterina, but Montevarchi was clear.

Cavriglia

Thursday, July 13, 1944, was a hot, sunny day in the village of San Pancrazio in the commune of Cavriglia; it was also, Father Polvani recorded, 'a morning of war – airplanes – shooting – cannons thundering.'[40] July 14 was 'a morning of peace' (from air attack), but for Italy on the ground it was 'true anarchy,' according to Father Polvani. Life was unrecognizable. The country lacked a government; the people did not know where to turn. About eight in the evening, some of the soldiers connected to the German command began to depart the area 'with gestures of gratitude and with admirable discipline,' according to Father Polvani[41] On the 15th, the cannons sounded again, and Father Polvani had a steady stream of villagers to the parish house asking for flour and other supplies: 'this abnormal condition somewhere between life and death is making everyone a little nervous.'[42] On Sunday July 16, the feast day of the Virgin of Carmine, the village's traditional procession with the statue of the Virgin did not take place – something few remembered ever happening before. Father Polvani could recall its absence only once before – when a flood had hit the area – in his forty-two years as parish priest. Residents in the centre arrived for the procession, but those who lived farther away stayed off the road, over which German vehicles were continually passing.[43]

Civitella, San Pancrazio (in Bucine), and the city of Arezzo had been liberated that morning, and Allied troops now approached the villages to the north and west of Arezzo. By that night, the front line had arrived in the village of San Pancrazio in Cavriglia, and the other villages of that commune. The German command had encircled the village with guns and fired them continually. What would happen when 'the enemy' responded, Father Polvani asked? He recorded that '[w]e are truly in the first line of fire.' The parish house was 'full of people and soldiers.'[44] Then, at midnight on July 17, the Germans dismantled their gun batteries and withdrew. Father Polvani again commented on the Germans' 'admirable discipline,' though he also noted that the local population was 'weeping' because the retreating soldiers – whose clothing was very worn – were letting themselves into people's homes and taking whatever linens and clothing they could find.[45] The German infantry then arrived in place of the retreating command. They did not take over the church or the parish house, which were already occupied by many of the villagers and residents from the countryside.[46]

San Pancrazio was still in German hands as of July 20; but on that day the Germans found themselves in direct contact with the 'enemy forces.' Guns fired continuously, and Father Polvani's cantina served as refuge for much of the population. At six that evening, he recorded, 'grazie a Dio' the parish was at last free – though it seems that Father Polvani was not referring to the Germans leaving the village, but rather to the villagers finally leaving his parish house. Instead of peace and quiet descending, however, a hailstorm of Allied grenades immediately drove the citizens back inside the priest's cantina.[47]

The following day, the villagers discovered that the retreating Germans had blown up all the bridges, including the bridge connecting the only access road to and from the village. Gunfire was still constant, but now sounded farther away. As a bit of calm returned, about half of the 150 people who had been sheltering in the parish house, cantina, and church returned to their homes to discover that the retreating Germans had taken what little remained of their food, as well as their clothes and everyday linens, and even their wedding trousseaus. Artillery fire suddenly began again nearby, and the citizens rushed from their ransacked homes back yet again to the safety of the parish church and cantina.[48]

Father Polvani closed his diary for the month of July 1944: 'And so ends the saddest month I have ever experienced in my 42 year tenure at San Pancrazio.'[49] The priest had sheltered more than 150 local citizens – 'always coming and going, asking and demanding' – every night for more than two weeks in the church, in the parish house, and the canti-na.[50] He had housed another forty evacuees for much longer. He had seen his best rooms taken over by the German command, which had treated the house as its own and taken away his supplies when it retreat-ed.[51] Who could have foreseen so much '*disfatta*' – meaning something like the 'overthrow of the normal order of things' – in such a remote place not even connected to a main thoroughfare? The parish had seen sad days before this, even 'days of blood' (*giorni di sangue*) in 1921, (re-ferring to the lignite miners' anti-Fascist protest in Castelnuovo and to Fascist *squadristi* retaliation). But never had anything happened like the barbarity of July 4, when three priests and over 200 'innocent victims' had perished in the commune.

Burying the Dead – San Pancrazio (Bucine)

Only a very few women of San Pancrazio in the commune of Bucine (next to Civitella) returned from the woods to the village immediately after the June 29 massacre. There, they saw their houses still smoking, the stone walls almost all collapsed, and a suffocating odour pervaded the air. After finding no trace of their men, the women retreated to the woods, where they remained during the passage of the front, going home only after the Allies arrived in San Pancrazio on July 16.[52]

Earlier, in the spring of 1944, when Operation Strangle had intensi-fied Allied bombing and it then appeared likely that the front might pass through the area, village men who had small farm plots outside of town dug holes five or six square metres in size under the roots of large oak and chestnut trees.[53] Each could hold three to four people. Using chest-nut branches, they also had built a couple of huts large enough for about twenty people. In addition, an area of rocky gullies northeast of the vil-lage also offered some protection. When the Germans drove them from the village on June 29, the women and children headed for these shel-ters. On the morning of June 30, the women, children, and the remain-ing men of San Pancrazio re-formed their village community amongst these shelters in the woods. The women, older children, and the few men left alive, in a gesture of pragmatic unity, immediately helped put together cover for those without.

At that time, most tried to believe or continued to hope that the men had been taken away for labour service in northern Italy or Germany. On Sunday, July 2, when the villagers heard their church bell ringing, they thought it a signal that the men had returned. As they began to run towards San Pancrazio, they saw the campanile explode in the air. The Germans had mined it and the other houses not previously destroyed, leaving villagers with no alternative but the woods.[54] At first, German soldiers stayed away from the villagers' shelters, but after a few days, they came into the woods to take food and take away the few remaining men to dig trenches and perform other labour. They also took the civilians' watches and searched the children, thinking their mothers might have hidden jewellery or money on them. After a few days more, the soldiers searched inside the huts, under the trees, and in the bushes – especially at night – looking for the women. The Germans took older women to carry out domestic tasks like cooking, washing, and sewing for the soldiers. Among the young women (as with Lara Lammioni) and their families, there was a well-founded fear of rape.[55]

On account of war and massacre, the events of daily life were reduced to a round of procuring food, hiding from the Germans, and trying to stay alive between opposing armies. During their time in the woods, the women of the village took over as managers of that new life, while the young women, girls, and the young men hid from the German soldiers. Boys between about twelve and fifteen years old had been young enough to have been considered children and ordered away from the village with their mothers before the massacre. Now, with new importance, they stood watch. They looked out for German soldiers and called warnings so the young men could hide deeper in the woods, so their mothers could hide the food, and so their sisters would not be raped. The boys also caught rabbits, or an occasional sheep – and once a cow – found roaming in the woods. Like the Lucarinis, without proper tools or skills to butcher them, the villagers simply cut the animals into crude pieces and took them to roast far away from the German soldiers.

The entire Tenth (German) Army withdrew on the night between July 15 and 16, and retreated northwards towards the Arno. On Sunday morning, July 16, the Allies entered San Pancrazio (Bucine), and the people returned to their village. The streets were so filled with the rubble of destroyed buildings that an Allied tank first had to pass through to make a pathway.[56] Written in German on the wall of the first house, the returnees saw the words: 'In this village they are all bandits' – that is, the Germans meant, partisans.[57]

Only after the village was liberated, did the women learn conclusively what had happened to their men. Ugo Casciotti, who had volunteered information about the partisans and then jumped over the village wall to escape from the piazza on June 29, knew the men had been massacred.

During the two and one-half weeks he spent in the woods with the women and children, he never told them of the other men's fate. The few others who knew about the massacre also let the women continue to believe that the Germans had taken their men for forced labour duty. Otherwise, they felt, the women could not go on.[58]

On July 25, nearly a month after the massacre, the citizens of San Pancrazio began to bury their dead. Ugo Casciotti later told British investigators:

> along with other men, I started to clear away the debris from the [*fattoria*] of Pierangeli. The building was an empty shell and all the debris had fallen through into the cellar. As we cleared the cellar we discovered the badly burned remains of a number of human bodies. They were in such an advanced state of decomposition that I cannot give an approximate number found ... This excavation took about twelve days to complete and a communal grave was prepared in the village cemetery of San Pancrazio, where the remains of the victims were buried.[59]

The women and children watched from outside while the cellar was cleared. Two Allied soldiers assisted with gas masks and lime and DDT for disinfectant.[60]

The bodies of the victims at San Pancrazio had been so badly burned and were by now so decomposed that their families could recognize them only by small, familiar objects.[61] Angiolina Rustici identified the body of her father by his waistcoat and by the cigarette lighter in his pocket.[62] Giulia Valenti recognized a pair of boots 'identical to those worn by my husband on the 29 June 1944.'[63] Emilia Arrigucci recognized a pair of socks that she had knit for her husband and that he had been wearing on June 29th, when the Germans took him away.[64] Eride Tiezzi recognized her father's leather belt.[65] Eugenia Panzieri found a small medallion that she had given to her husband a few days before June 29, but she could find nothing belonging to her missing father-in-law.[66] Maria Spini, the wife (now widow) of the manager of the *fattoria* Pierangeli did not go to the cellar to witness the exhumation, but some children later brought her two rings that she recognized as her husband's.[67] Santa Corsi, who had evacuated from Badia Agnano to San Pancrazio with her husband Dr. Alberto Corsi on June 22 – only a week before the massacre – recognized a silver cigarette case, a wedding ring, and a French coin belonging to her husband.[68] Ten year old Romano Moretti recognized the ring his father had always worn.[69]

Assessing the Aftermath

The immediate consequences of war and massacre differed from person to person and place to place in Arezzo, yet at some level it was a common, shared experience: all had suffered, all were victims in some way. For all, war and massacre would be their lives' defining moments. The things that divided them before the war (and that would divide them after) were temporarily ignored or obliterated. The villagers of San Pancrazio, Civitella, and Castelnuovo had been massacred indiscriminately: priests, labourers, craftsmen, sharecroppers, landowners, miners, doctors, Republican Fascist *podestà* and Republican *fascio* secretary, Italian army veterans, communists and Catholics. The widows and children fled to the woods, living together in a tragic, shared camaraderie. Bucine's communal secretary Aroldo Lucarini was a Fascist and then likely a Republican Fascist; his house was bombed, he and his family lived the life 'of primitive people' – hiding in the woods, dislocated and displaced, the same as those citizens who were 'mere Fascists,' non-Fascists, or anti-Fascists. Defining labels meant very little with Allied bombs overhead, German troops intent on slaughter, and the battlefront passing.[70]

If the massacred civilians, the newly made widows and orphans, and the thousands of displaced citizens are the victims, then the priests might be the heroes of this chapter of Arezzo's war and aftermath; though only the bishop and the massacred priests would retain that stature into the postwar. Father Lazzeri, Father Torelli, Father Bagiardi, and Father Morini were killed with their parishioners and, as were the priests in other massacred villages, were said to have offered their own lives if the Germans would spare the others. The bishop of Fiesole and Father Ciabattini made the dangerous and punishing trip on foot to bless the dead and comfort the survivors. Bishop Giorgis's journey – his long walk under hazardous conditions and in the July heat from Fiesole to Meleto and Castelnuovo – was and still is recalled at every memorial service and in every written and oral memory of the massacres and their immediate aftermath. At that time when daily life so violently had 'come undone,' the bishop's visit provided comfort as well as a desperately needed sense of normalcy and order in the midst of so much disintegration.

Father Cuccoli counted the bodies and skulls, and helped the women bury the dead of Castelnuovo and Le Màtole. Father Polvani had criticized Father Bagiardi's good relations with local anti-Fascists and young communists; he believed the partisans would be the ruin of Italy; he continued to refer to the Allies as 'the enemy' after they had become co-belligerents and until their arrival in the commune; and he dined with German officers – commenting favourably on their courtesy (*molto gentile*) and their 'admirable discipline' even after the massacres and as they departed the village with his poor parishioners' food, clothing, and linens in tow. Father Polvani, however, also had sheltered, fed, and prayed for dozens of his parishioners and neighbours during the lengthy and frightening passage of the front. Though he was extremely relieved when they finally returned to their own homes and left him in peace, his people had been a comfort to him, he felt, and he to them. The one good thing the war had done, he recorded, was to bring his flock closer together and closer to the church.

As the Allies rolled their tanks into the city of Arezzo on July 16, they found it 'much damaged by our own bombing and almost empty of civilians.'[71] On the heels of the liberating forces, the new Allied provincial commissioner also arrived at Arezzo on that date. He reported to Eighth Army Headquarters: '[p]ractically all the population of the town of Arezzo and a large percentage of other towns had fled to the country, many with just the clothes they stood up in. Some of the small towns and villages have been flattened, others such as Arezzo have lost about 30% of the houses.'[72]

Along with the provincial commissioner came his civil affairs officers (CAOs), who were to serve as the link between Allied occupation forces and Italian communal administrations, and whose first task was to obtain initial basic information on the current conditions of the communes to which they had been assigned. Even as about half of the Aretine (north of the city of Arezzo) remained in the front lines or still under German occupation, the Allies sought to determine the state of affairs – and the state of disorder – for the communes they now occupied. CAOs prepared reports within forty-eight hours of their arrival in the commune (the appropriately named '48 hour reports'), consisting of information supplied by communal officials (if any remained in the communes), from communal offices (if still standing), or from apparently reliable citizens. In their first forty-eight hours, CAOs had no time to tour or inspect anything beyond the communal seat. Communal officials and residents of the communal seat oftentimes themselves did not know the full extent of damage and destruction throughout their commune, especially in more remote or mountainous parts or those cut off from main thoroughfares by bomb damage to bridges and roads.[73]

The CAO assigned to the commune of Civitella gathered his '48 hour' information from unspecified sources in the communal seat at Badia al

Pino. He reported that the commune's current population was estimated at 9400; this was 1000 more than 'normal' or prewar numbers.[74] No banks were functioning; the communal treasury was empty of funds. The commune had no light or power, no motor transport. Only three doctors and five *carabinieri* officers were present in the commune; there were no other police. No hospitals operated; there were no medical supplies. Health and sanitation were nevertheless inexplicably 'good.' The water supply was 'normal,' in that water was available from those wells which were undamaged, but it would be 'necessary to draw the water by hand until [the] electric system is repaired.' The commune urgently needed flour, sugar, and oil, as well as salt, soap, and disinfectants. Approximately 15 per cent of buildings were destroyed, the CAO understood, and 25 per cent were damaged but reparable. 'Morale and attitude of people towards Allies and AMG' was 'good.'[75]

After their first forty-eight hours, CAOs went on to inspect the other parts of their communes accessible by army jeep, especially those villages said by combat troops to be the sites of particularly severe destruction. Thereupon, they usually discovered overall communal situations much worse than the first trip to the communal seat had shown. Although Civitella's CAO did not get to the village of Civitella during his first days in the commune, other Allied personnel did. Civitella was soon visited by the Eighth Army Red Cross supervisor, the AMG provincial legal officer, an AMG senior supply officer, and the AMG provincial agricultural officer, all of whom observed and reported on the village's bleak aftermath.[76]

The Red Cross supervisor who visited on July 27, noted that the women and children who had been driven away before the massacre were returning to the village 'daily.' About 30 per cent of the houses had been destroyed, with another estimated 50 per cent damaged but reparable. The many corpses had been 'dealt with' and the massacre sites disinfected. The villagers had no clothes, except what they wore; they had no blankets and no bedding. The village had no wells. Until recently, the residents of that hilltop village had collected water in cisterns filled by electric pumps. Now, without electric power, there was no water supply. The nearest water source was a kilometre away in the woods. There was 'no milk for babies, no sugar for invalids, no salt.' The last flour delivery (from the communal rationing office at Badia al Pino) had been a kilogram of flour per head for six days, 'now exhausted.'[77] The village did have an 'excellent little village hospital of 20 beds, with modern surgery and pharmacy, under the care of two nuns plus nurses.' The hospital was reasonably intact, but the pharmacy and its contents destroyed. The church was half ruined; three priests had been massacred, and no one had replaced them. 'The need for a priest is obvious,' considered the Red Cross representative. 'The people are crushed, but courageous and uncomplaining, they neither beg nor demand; their children are well dressed and cared for. They were all very friendly, courteous and dignified. I gathered that they preferred to stay in *their* village and see it through; much clearance has already been done. They need practical help and encouragement.'[78]

The Allied Military Government generated a plethora of assorted reports. Every CAO and every officer of every AMG/ACC subcommission reported to some other officer or commission weekly, biweekly, or monthly regarding his own portion of responsibility within the commune, and required statistics and reports from prefects and sindaci to complete their own reports. These many reports describe Arrezzo's and the communes' destruction, and the people's suffering in the post-front aftermath at the close of 1944; they also less eloquently quantified it.

All of Italy suffered materially from the war, Tuscany especially. 'Tuscany was one of the regions of Italy most damaged by the war ... This was a direct effect of the "*sosta*" of war [the war's 'pausing'] on its territory. The ... damage was enormous.'[79] As much as a tenth of the war's damage in Italy took place in Tuscany.[80] As for human losses, 13.2 per cent of the civilian victims of war in Italy were Tuscan.[81] Not all numbers so quickly gathered in those chaotic days were entirely accurate, of course, but usually they understated the damage.

In the commune of Civitella, eighty-seven private houses (totalling 696 rooms) were reported completely destroyed; 1100 houses had been damaged. The village of Civitella constituted the largest part of the commune's damage. In that small village alone, fifty-one houses had been destroyed; thirty-seven seriously damaged; fifty lightly damaged. The commune counted 1500 persons homeless, but all had found some accommodation with family, friends, in public or religious buildings, or other place less 'suited to habitation.'[82] That so many of those made homeless in Civitella and elsewhere found shelter somewhere shows both solidarity and desperation. Neighbours, friends, relatives, and strangers took in the homeless, but just as many lived in barns, huts, the basements of burned out buildings, or wherever they could find. Twenty-four bridges on communal roads had been destroyed, three on provincial roads, and eleven on national roads. Many of the roads themselves had been mined. Whole fields of landmines existed in the locale of Pian del Leprone, in the vicinity of the village of Albergo, along the bed of the

Leprone River, along the province's main north-south road, and along the Arezzo-Sinalunga railway line.[83]

The Germans had massacred 163 persons in the villages of Civitella, Cornia, and Gebbia. The Germans had deported three, and thirty-six other citizens had died from other war-caused events, such as bombing, artillery, and mines.[84] In that predominantly agricultural commune and province with large numbers of sharecropper and smallholder families, whose animals were their livelihood, the Germans had stolen (or killed) 129 head of cattle, 159 pigs, fifty-seven horses, 386 sheep, and three goats.

In the commune of Cavriglia, German troops had killed 192 persons 'in reprisal.' Another twenty-one had died from aerial bombs, mines, and artillery. 'Entire families were suddenly thrown into mourning and desperation, their dearest possessions stolen, without means of sustenance, without men to help the family, and often with children of tender years,' the first post-Fascist sindaco later described.[85] Fires had 'semi-destroyed' the village of Castelnuovo after the Germans had carried out the massacre there. Meleto was in worse condition, having been first torched by the Germans and then when nearby Castellare served as the site of front line combat for several days. Massa dei Sabbioni had been partially destroyed by mines. Massacres had not taken place at the other villages in the commune, but all had been heavily damaged by Allied bombing and then by mines and fires set by the Germans to destroy Italian property and slow the Allied advance.[86]

The electric plant at Castelnuovo had been completely destroyed, and the above ground installations of the area's lignite mines all had been seriously damaged or completely destroyed (figure 8). All of the mines were cut off from their head offices located in northern cities still occupied by German troops. Twenty of the commune's twenty-two bridges had been destroyed, and most roads were mined.[87] During July and August 1944 alone, landmines or unexploded shells seriously injured ten individuals.[88]

As of December 1944, 250 people were homeless, but had found temporary shelter somewhere. The commune of Cavriglia housed no foreign refugees or Italians returned from other countries, but did house 237 evacuees from other provinces, and 295 'temporary' residents from other provinces.[89] Beyond that, any definitive census on the housing situation was impossible. More than 1500 men, women, and children needed the most basic clothing and household supplies. Banks and the communal treasury were closed. Cavriglia's 'departing administration' left a deficit of 378,570 lire, an enormous sum for that time. Communal offices were disorganized, without a communal secretary and with only a few employees – the others having fled. Communal stores of grain were empty. The mills were all closed because there was no electricity and almost no water to power them, and so the harvest had not begun. The commune had no gasoline or oil. From that more industrial commune, departing German troops stole or killed 147 cows, 245 pigs, 151 sheep, and eight horses. From Father Polvani, German soldiers took five cows, seven pigs, a mare, and a farm cart.[90]

Stating a position and employing language soon to become common among cities, communes, and provinces throughout Italy, the post-liberation sindaco of Bucine (when requesting 200,000 lire from the Allied occupiers) asserted that his commune stood out from all the others, in that Bucine had suffered the most – and the worst – among the communes of the province. 'If all the Communes have suffered damages to their persons and their homes by the barbarous destruction of the Germans, unfortunately this Commune has to count a number of victims and present an accounting of private damages greater than the other Communes.'[91]

Although Bucine had been an economically poorer commune to begin with, its figures of destruction and death were comparable to those of Civitella and Cavriglia. In the commune of Bucine, the Germans had deported twelve persons and massacred 109. Thirty-eight had died from other causes of war. One hundred thirty-one houses had been completely destroyed; 123 had been damaged, but were reparable. Twenty bridges had been destroyed. Two hundred sixty families (comprising 944 persons) were homeless, and many of these were also 'without their family head and only breadwinner.'[92] The retreating Germans had stolen or killed 110 head of cattle, 200 pigs, 270 sheep, and ten horses as they left the commune.

It did not suffer civilian massacres on the scale of Civitella, Castelnuovo, San Pancrazio, or some other Aretine villages, but it was the commune of Pieve Santo Stefano and the village of the same name that became the symbol of destruction in the aftermath of postwar central Italy.[93] The war had ended for Arezzo city, for Civitella, San Pancrazio, Castelnuovo, and much of the rest of the province by the end of July. Florence was liberated on August 5. But, in an example of the strange mosaic that was World War II in Italy with its 'vague and shifting frontiers,'[94] after the front already had passed through most of the province and the Allied occupation government had already settled in, the worst of the war had yet to reach the remotest part of the province.

Pieve Santo Stefano is a small commune situated at the northeast limit of Tuscany, bordering Romagna to the north, with which it joins the Tuscan-Emilian-Marchean crest of the Appennine mountain range. On that crest, the Germans had built a portion of the defensive fortifications that made up the Gothic Line. The territory of the commune was never truly in the theatre of operations, in that German and Allied troops had not engaged in combat there as they had around Civitella and San Pancrazio, but the village and the area did not escape the violence and destruction of the war. As early as October 1943, the German army had settled in the area to construct the Gothic Line defences, hiring or forcing Italian civilians to work on and around the fortifications. Throughout the spring and summer, Allied bombing and shelling of roads, bridges, and motor transport had taken place there, as with the rest of the province. By June 1944, with their northward retreat beginning, it had become commonplace for German soldiers in the area to enter homes and farms of Pieve Santo Stefano and steal food and personal effects from the villagers and farmers. That same month, German soldiers killed four civilians 'for no good reason.' As the front mowed through other Aretine communes during July, German troops began to round up and plunder Pieve Santo Stefano's cattle, horses, and other livestock and barnyard animals, placing them in collection centres in preparation for bringing them north.

Then, on August 5, within the space of a few hours, German troops 'cleansed' the area in the most thorough fashion: they forced the entire population of the village of Pieve Santo Stefano, and much of the population of the entire commune, to the north. They drove the citizens away on foot, allowing them to take only what they could carry. Many families were separated. Some who refused to leave their homes were killed. People made their way to the regions of Emilia-Romagna, Lombardy, and Veneto, staying wherever and with whomever would take them in.

After thus removing the inhabitants, German forces systematically mined and burned the entire village – the seat of the commune, including houses, churches, and public buildings.[95] They bombed all the bridges over the Tiber; they mined all roads and fields. By August 31, the destruction was complete. The first British patrols arrived on September 2, though retreating German troops continued shelling the commune for several more days. One of the earliest Allied reports provided bluntly: 'Referring to the town of S. Stefano, there seems to be an enormous problem; the only remaining building is a church in the center of the town, apart from this one may safely describe the town as a heap of rubble.'[96]

The citizens of Pieve Santo Stefano slowly began to return in the autumn of 1944 – to their heap of rubble. Some of the returning population sheltered in the surrounding countryside in the few houses not destroyed. About 1000 persons lived among the ruins 'in conditions of inconceivable hardship.'[97] Not until the war ended the following spring did the final 2000 citizens come home. In the village of Pieve Santo Stefano (the communal seat), 276, or 99 per cent of residences had been destroyed; 30 per cent had been destroyed in the rest of the commune. More than 2550 were homeless.[98] Of the animals throughout the commune, 95 per cent of the cattle, 95 per cent of the horses, 98 per cent of the pigs, and 40 per cent of the sheep had been plundered or killed. No draft animals remained to be counted. Twelve hundred hectares of land were mined, while 103 kilometres of roads were not passable either because they had been mined or destroyed by bombs in various parts.[99] Twenty-three bridges on communal roads had been destroyed, eighteen on provincial roads, and fourteen on national roads.[100] Twenty-two citizens were known to have been killed by the Germans; fifteen were presumed killed. Twenty had died from other causes of war.

Throughout the province of Arezzo as a whole, though the accuracy of all figures is unverifiable, nearly 4000 private houses on farms and in villages and towns had been destroyed; more than 11,000 damaged.[101] Seven factories had been destroyed; one damaged. Four hundred fifty-six bridges on communal roads had been destroyed, 137 on provincial roads, and 102 on national roads. In that province of countless hills, valleys, and rivers, the destruction of so many bridges paralyzed communications and what few means of transportation remained.[102]

The Germans killed 1093 persons in the province and deported 5578.[103] The now familiar 'other causes of war' – Allied bombing, artillery fire, landmines – killed 1158 more civilians.[104] On September 1, 1944, with seventeen communes still to be liberated and numbers counted, the twenty-two already liberated communes had 11,508 refugees from other provinces (or countries) living in schools, movie theatres, makeshift camps, and in the open. The Germans took with them 15,581 head of cattle, 17,543 pigs, 20,291 sheep, and 3908 horses. In that agricultural province, sufficient quantities of cereals existed, but almost everything else was completely lacking: oils, animal fats, sugar, salt, pasta, rice, fresh meat, cheese, butter, jam, coffee. No means of transport to bring supplies from other provinces was available, and in any event could not have passed over ruined roads and bridges.[105]

As for Arezzo's provincial administration, ever since the provincial offices had been transferred from the centre of the city because of Allied bombing, 'the Prefecture found itself in a series of difficulties,' so the *Questore* reported with characteristic understatement.[106] The last Fascist Republican *Capo* of the province, Melchiore Melchiori (Bruno Rao Torres's successor), along with a contingent of other Republican Fascists, had absconded to the still German-occupied north on June 14, taking with him the entire provincial treasury of 19,000,000 lire, as well as all the typewriters and the stencil machines from provincial offices.[107]

German troops (authorized by Melchiori just before his flight) occupied the villa to which the provincial offices had been moved, and would let no provincial employees or officials inside to take records or documents away for safekeeping. And, before they left in July, the Germans set fire to what they could not carry with them. While most office furniture was stolen, the greater part of the province's accounts, as well as the general archive containing tax files and records of the communal treasuries were destroyed. 'So, in short, these are the events of the office of the Prefecture, whose situation is doubtlessly serious and difficult,' one of the few remaining officials succinctly summed up.[108]

When the Allies arrived to liberate Aretine villages from which German troops and Fascist Republicans already had departed, and to post their occupation proclamations, they had to pick their way through piles of rubble and remains of ruined villages. They found the shaken civilian survivors, the victims of bombing campaigns, massacres, and the passage of the front. Yes, this was war – the assorted residents of postwar Arezzo surely could tell Father Polvani. In its aftermath, the war left widows and orphans, the wounded, the homeless, refugees and evacuees, former partisans, former Fascists and Fascist Republicans yet to return, returning deportees and prisoners of war, veterans, Allied troops, and the Allied occupation government all sharing the ruined Aretine in the summer and fall of 1944.

PART TWO

Life in the Aftermath

4 Life with the Allies

What did you personally observe in the attitude of the Italian people and Government that gave you a great deal of encouragement that they were trying to pull themselves up by their bootstraps and not just lying back on their Allies? There have been a great deal of reports saying that the Italian people are apathetic, that they are letting us do their thinking and working for them, their planning for them and they are lying down. Is that true?

September 1945 press conference question to S.M. Keeny

Although the front had not passed completely and German shelling continued, one of the first actions of the newly arrived provincial legal officer for the Allied Control Commission (ACC) of Arezzo was to visit the village of Civitella, on July 20, 1944 – only four days after the area had been liberated. Major Walter D. Stump had received orders from Eighth Army Headquarters to look into reported German atrocities in the province. Stump found Civitella to have been 'almost completely destroyed by the Germans on June 29, 1944, the few remaining residents being chiefly women and children.' He informed headquarters how the men had been shot in the piazza, and that '[l]arge areas on the pavement adjacent to this wall are still covered by dried up pools of blood, mute but powerful testimonials to this exhibition of brutality ... The village is now a place of utter desolation.'[1]

In the province of Arezzo, which had seen so many local massacres, Stump proceeded from one village to the next. Each report grew more graphic and more immediate, as if Stump had been there to witness the horrible events. On September 1, he recounted the massacre at Meleto:

The men who were apprehended ranged in age from 14 to 69 years, one being the village priest and some being ill at the time. These men were ... then taken to different buildings of the village where all ... excepting several who succeeded in making their escape, were lined up, and usually in groups of five ... and shot down with machine guns. The dead and wounded were then thrown in heaps in the houses adjacent ... then more or less covered with furniture taken from nearby houses on which some petrol was thrown and then set on fire. The bodies of the dead and the wounded were entirely consumed by fire except some small pieces of bone ... After setting the fires, these soldiers sat about in the general areas of the fires and joked, laughed and smoked as the fires consumed their victims. Afterwards the soldiers went about the village setting fire to many of the homes and engaged in general looting of the village.[2]

He concluded the massacre at Meleto was inexplicable and unwarranted: unlike Civitella where partisans had shot two German soldiers inside the village walls, no partisan activity had occurred in or anywhere near Meleto. The following day, he described for headquarters the massacre at Castelnuovo dei Sabbioni:

The women and children were warned to leave their homes at once and a number of them were herded together in the village cemetery. These scenes were carried out ruthlessly and with dispatch by the German soldiers as members of the bewildered and terror-stricken families of the village took final farewells of each other. The German soldiers maintained a cynical and utterly indifferent attitude toward these people, spurning with disdain and impatience, their entreaties and appeals.[3]

Major Stump's superiors did not appreciate his lengthy, emotional evocations (and interpretations) of such tragic events or his sympathy for Italian victims so recently the enemy. An ACC Rear Eighth Army officer scolded Stump for preparing reports that were 'too long and too detailed.' He reminded Stump that ACC was not there to investigate alleged war atrocities against civilians; Stump's job had been only to assure 'the briefest possible details reported to this HQ for the attention of the investigating auth[orit]y.'[4] Major Stump subsequently stuck to legal matters at hand as he settled into his job as Arezzo's provincial legal officer.[5] Despite the fact that he was in charge of prosecuting Italians for violating ACC proclamations and committing other crimes against the Allies, and perhaps recalling his arrival in the province, Stump nearly always expressed both sympathy for Italian suffering and optimism regarding Italy's national reconstruction.

In contrast, however, Arezzo's first provincial commissioner (the highest Allied military authority for a province) took a very different attitude towards the citizens of Arezzo, their wartime and postwar adversity, and their future. When he left the province in mid-October 1944 as Arezzo passed from Allied army area control to regional command, Lieutenant Colonel J.O. Thurburn, ended his final monthly report on the province and the people he had governed since the previous July, as if the war and its destruction had provided Italians with a welcome opportunity for shiftlessness: 'I might add, that most of these people have no desire to work if they can obtain relief or subsidies of any kind.'[6]

Thurburn's successor as provincial commissioner, Lieutenant Colonel G.W. Quin Smith, shared that sorry assessment of Italians. Quin Smith's acerbic views on Italians in general, the Italian character, and the citizens of the Aretine permeated his communications up to Eighth Army Headquarters and down to his civil affairs officers (CAOs).[7] When rolls of Allied military telephone wire went missing, Quin Smith noted that 'petty theft' 'unfortunately was always a characteristic of the Italian countryside.' The continued characteristic of petty thievery did not bode well, he added, 'for the moral revival [*risorgimento*] necessary to line [align] Italy with the modern nations.'[8] A much needed 'moral revival' or 'moral renaissance' made for a frequent theme in Quin Smith's missives.[9] Not only would a moral revival bring Italy in line with modern nations (meaning the victorious Allies – limited to Britain and the United States – which themselves presumably had no need of a moral realignment as they were winning the war), but would also assure Italy's postwar pursuit of a democratic future.

Quin Smith saw the Allied Control Commission's role (and his own) as unappreciated leaders of that moral revival, striving to guide a people who obstructed him at every turn and who had no real commitment to their country's moral rebirth. His comment also shows how he and most of the other non-Italians now in charge of governing postwar Italy considered the country a defeated enemy nation, still 'the other side' in the war. Father Polvani's continued characterization of the Allies as 'the enemy' contained much truth (but for reasons different from the priest's personal and political sympathies).

The post-battlefront Aretine was occupied, governed, and assisted by Allies who ranged in attitude from Major Stump at one end to lieutenant colonels Thurburn and Quin Smith at the other. Some, like Stump, were truly moved by the plight of civilians caught in the war and who now coped with devastation and a difficult reconstruction. Others found the Italians routinely grasping, lazy, inefficient, dishonest, and uncooperative in response to heartfelt Allied attempts to make them 'good, democratic citizens.' In all of Italy, from General Alexander on down, Allied soldiers and governors were undecided whether to treat Italians as victims, friends, or conquered enemies, and so treated them as all three (but mostly the third).[10]

The Allies came to Italy in three distinct but closely interconnected bodies. They came as armed forces or liberating and advance troops. They came as administering and governing forces: the Allied Military Government and the Allied Control Commission. And, they came as relief workers and aid givers. The first group was most numerous and disruptive. The second group intruded most into civil, daily life. The third group (governmental and NGO) was naturally the most welcome (and will be considered in the following chapter). The Allied presence affected Aretine citizens every day – because troops were living in their buildings and eating their food, because dozens of Allied directives regulated their daily affairs, and because Allied assistance meant a hot meal, a pair of shoes and an overcoat, and means to repair a destroyed village.

Allied Military Government (AMG)/Allied Control Commission (ACC)/ Allied Commission (AC)

Once the first joys of liberation had passed, the Allied occupation and administration of Italy was not an especially happy situation for either the Allies or the Italians. One problem was that as they settled into an area, the Allies usually discovered the physical situation to be far worse than they had expected or estimated from intelligence received – and far worse than they were prepared to handle. Another problem was that untrained, inexperienced soldiers, most of whom knew little about Italy, about Italians, or about the rudiments of administration, suddenly were thrust into the complex business of directing a foreign country's ruined civil and economic affairs in the middle of a war.[11] Furthermore, what territory the Allies had to occupy and govern kept shifting. For eighteen months – from the day of the armistice until the end of the war on May 5, 1945 – Italy was a country cut into pieces that kept changing in size and shape, and whose pieces were fought over by multiple, competing governments.

The Allied Military Government began as two separate organizations: the Allied Military Government (AMG) and the Allied Control Commission (ACC).[12] The AMG administered territory very recently liberated, while the ACC supervised the administration of territory that ostensibly had been 'restored' to the Italian government because fighting had passed and the area was considered stable.[13] The AMG-ACC distinction ended on January 24, 1944, when ACC was reorganized and AMG was integrated with it, with AMG thereby losing its separate identity and role (though ACC often continued to be referred to as AMG/ACC or as AMG alone).[14]

By the time the Allies arrived in Arezzo in the summer of 1944, the reorganized ACC functioned in three phases. In areas 'where operations were progressing' (called 'Army Areas' – that is, where combat was still taking place or troops were advancing), a team of ACC officers was attached to the headquarters of each army. This army 'team' 'set up the initial phases of Military Government in a liberated territory as the Armies move[d] forward.' They posted Allied proclamations and orders and remained in charge until an area was 'secure' enough for army troops to leave. The area then was turned over to Allied 'Regional Command' for the second phase: combat troops had moved on, but ACC continued in absolute control of civil affairs. These 'secure areas' behind the armies were divided according to regions under the command of regional commissioners, and further subdivided according to provinces governed by provincial commissioners like Quin Smith. In the third and final phase, when the Allies 'returned' an area to Italian government control, ACC officers remained as advisors to the Italian government, and the number of Allied officers present was then drastically cut. Moreover, once an area returned to Italian control, Allied advice was no longer binding on the Italian administration, and the returned area's citizens were no longer subject to Allied proclamations.[15]

ACC's original purpose was to 'arrange for the procurement, shipment and distribution of imports necessary to avoid disease and unrest.'[16] The Allies acted not so much out of humanitarian concern, but so that the Allied war effort and safe passage of troops up the peninsula were not endangered by an ill and restive native population. Feeding the population and preserving public order were the two most immediate and closely connected tasks. ACC efforts, however, went well beyond basic measures to 'avoid disease and unrest.'

Precisely what its name declared, the Allied Control Commission was a military-run administrative organization devised to control Italy and life in Italy. At the end of October 1944 – as a gesture to the Italian government – the term 'Control' was dropped, and the ACC technically became known as the Allied Commission, or AC. The actual degree of Allied control exerted over Italians and over the Italian administration changed not at all, however, and most who were part of it continued to refer to the Allied Control Commission or ACC, or still AMG/ACC or AMG. David Ellwood has stated that the 'structures of control set up in Italy were those designed for total occupation in enemy territory.'[17] ACC reached into every corner of civil life, and Allied governors tried – with some success – to control everyday life as well.[18] Like Quin Smith, some also wanted to have a deeper moral impact on the people whose activities they controlled. The Allies imposed a state of sorts – one quickly fashioned on military occupation, control, and order – upon a temporarily stateless society. The state they imposed did not succeed in producing a moral revival; but by its pervasive and oppressive regulatory nature, ACC government did succeed in preventing unrest at the same time it postponed the internal reconstruction of society. It also contributed to a widespread sense of continued victimhood at Allied hands.

The citizens and refugees in the province of Arezzo spent the year after the passage of the front under phase one and phase two of Allied governance. Allied officers arrived in Arezzo having already had some ten months experience in administering Italian civil affairs, but the reorganized ACC operated no more smoothly in the summer of 1944 than had AMG/ACC after the Allied landing at Salerno in 1943.[19]

ACC provincial headquarters for Arezzo province set itself up for the first phase temporarily at Città della Pieve on July 1, 1944, moving to the city of Arezzo when the Allies liberated it on July 16.[20] Three months later, the province passed from the first phase, that of army area control, to the second phase, that of regional command on October 14, 1944, as Thurburn departed and Quin Smith arrived. Arezzo then spent the rest of the war under Allied regional command. (Tuscany made up ACC Region VIII; see figure 9.) On May 10, 1945, a few days after the war ended, Arezzo passed to (the third phase) Italian government control, just as the more northerly provinces of Florence, Lucca, and Pistoia passed from army area to regional command control.[21]

Arezzo's thirty-nine communes were initially divided into three districts, and later into six communal districts, with each district under the supervision of a civil affairs officer (CAO), who oversaw the activities of newly installed communal sindaci (who took the place of Fascist era *podestàs*), kept abreast of what went on in the communes, and provided weekly reports on their district to the provincial commissioner.[22]

The Allied occupation of the Aretine first got under way with the distribution of poster-size copies of AMGOT (Allied Military Government for Occupied Territory) general orders and proclamations to the communes.[23] Proclamations addressed all sorts of behaviour and criminalized a wide range of everyday activity, including making it an offence against the Allied Forces punishable by fine or imprisonment to remove or damage any proclamation or order posted under AMG/ACC's authority.[24] Through their proclamations and their physical presence, the Allied occupiers directed every imaginable, ordinary pursuit – from mailing a letter, to reading a newspaper, to selling potatoes.[25] Proclamations restricted the possession of wireless sets and carrier pigeons. They absolutely banned taking 'photographs of any sort, whether indoors or out-of-doors, and whether by still or cine or other type of camera.' They prohibited all meetings and assemblies; only gatherings 'for religious purposes' (baptisms, weddings and funerals) and courts of law could be held without first obtaining a permit. Neither the Italian flag, nor the colours of Italy, 'or of any other country at war with Great Britain or the United States,' could be publicly displayed – phrasing which implied, of course, that Italy was still at war with Britain and the United States. The singing and playing of the Italian national anthem and any other patriotic or political song or music of Italy 'or any such country' also were forbidden.[26]

Allied governors constrained Aretine life in the most fundamental local ways: food, movement, socializing, and honouring the dead. They disallowed a planned ceremony to commemorate the one year anniversary of the German massacre of civilians at Vallucciole – for reasons of public order, they said.[27] They threatened to seize carts and draft animals, and to incarcerate the owners found on the few Aretine roads which remained passable, but which Allied directive closed to Italian traffic. They arrested Italian soldiers who, having joined the Allied Army, now attempted to drink in Arezzo's bars and cafes reserved for Allied soldiers.[28] They prevented a farmer from milling his grain without first obtaining the proper documents and without filing the proper reports, and they prosecuted farmers for turning over their produce to Allied troops that demanded it. Although peace had reached the province of Arezzo, the Allies kept the bread ration there at the wartime level of 200 grams. In the commune of Cavriglia on August 22, 1944, they 'absolutely' vetoed – until further notice

– the sale of wine and alcohol in public shops, *dopolavori*, and other recreational and social circles.[29]

The Allies set curfew and travel limitations, infractions of which made up the bulk of Allied, then Italian prosecutions, and filled Arezzo's jails. For the month of September 1944, for example, ACC kept busy prosecuting 273 cases, the majority of which were curfew and pass offences, and a smaller number of wrongful possession of Allied property.[30] A curfew violation (being out after seven in the evening.) brought a sentence of between seven and ten days in jail and a 400 lire fine, while a travel violation (travelling more than ten kilometres from home without a permit) sent the malefactor to jail for anywhere from one month to three months.[31] Throughout the occupation, the vast majority of 'Allied interest cases' involved travel and curfew offences.[32] Cases of wrongful possession of Allied property increased as the months went on, but pass and curfew crimes always constituted the vast majority. Ordinary Italians really did go to court and go to jail for the ordinary crimes of staying out late and venturing away from home.

Newspapers and all other publications were closely scrutinized. Unlike the Allied censoring officer in Carlo Levi's postwar novel *The Watch*, who barely glanced at the newspaper he was assigned to monitor, Quin Smith took his responsibilities seriously. Quin Smith even precluded the bishop of Arezzo from circulating his monthly 'Bolletino.'[33] Other – defiantly political – papers were published and circulated illegally, and Quin Smith long sought the editor and publisher of *La Falce* ('the sickle' – as in the hammer and sickle), believed printed in Florence, and which offered frequent articles critical of ACC governance (methods which included keeping some former Fascists in provincial administrative positions).

Quin Smith directed his CAOs that no publications were 'allowed without authority and this includes any form of publishing information. There is only one paper and that is the "Informatore Aretino." It is non-party and censored.'[34] The *Informatore Aretino* itself was briefly suspended from publication in December 1944, after its editor published a lengthy letter from Arezzo's sindaco objecting to a particular instance of Quin Smith's invective against the Italian 'character.' Quin Smith explained:

A few small posters have been put up [by Quin Smith] in prominent places, such as over the CCRR's [*carabinieri*] head and the prefecture, declaiming against the Italian disease called 'Inganno' [deceit or shiftiness]. The Sindaco of Arezzo saw fit to answer with a tirade in the local paper. Result: paper suspended for a short period and editor warned his permit was for news and not mud-stirring.[35]

Apparently Quin Smith did not feel that publicly branding Italians and Italian officials as 'crooks' might have constituted 'mud-stirring' on his part. The action made plain to all his estimation of Italians.

Quin Smith's greatest venom, however, was reserved for anything that even remotely smacked of politics or political activity. Being caught outdoors in the evening would get you seven days in jail, but being caught outdoors talking politics was far more serious. 'In order to avoid disturbance and to keep men's minds on their work, no PUBLIC political manifestations have so far been permitted,' he emphasized.[36] All political gatherings were absolutely prohibited – and Quin Smith defined 'political' very, very broadly. CAOs were warned to be on the alert for political meetings held under the guise of a baptism or other religious service.[37] CAOs were to visit village *dopolavori* and other recreational circles frequently to make sure that political talk did not take place along with card playing. Wearing political emblems or political 'colours' ('particularly communist' red) was forbidden.[38] Quin Smith threatened to punish a group of Italian soldiers who had been overheard singing 'political songs.'[39] Citizens were not allowed to celebrate May 1, or 'Labour Day whatever that may mean.'[40]

Liberalism and even Christian Democracy threatened the new *risorgimento* almost as much as did socialism or communism, it seemed. Four prominent and conservative Italians were convicted, fined, and sent to jail for holding a political meeting in the town of Cortona without permission.[41] 'Generally we try and let it be known that we are interested in only one party – called "AMG,"' he reminded.[42] 'Politics generally is to be discouraged till Italian Government takes over: it is bound to damage the "Risorgimento" that we are trying to stage. Latter is one of WORK; we can leave TALK to Rome.'[43] For Quin Smith and the Allies, the hard work of reconstructing Italian society was something completely separate from politics. To most Italians, the two were impossible to separate.

The rationale for any single one of the many regulations and prohibitions is easy to understand. Outlawing all firearms and ammunition; censoring newspapers; prohibiting photography; monitoring carrier pigeons, dances, and the selling of potatoes; keeping civilians indoors between nine in the evening and five in the morning; not letting them travel more than ten kilometres; and criminalizing politics – each had some logical relationship to protecting troop safety and army property and to maintaining public order so that Allied troops could pass to forward areas. The types of regulations were not so unusual for an occupied country during wartime. It was the sheer number of regulations, the micro-level to which they reached, and the criminalization of normal traditional activities that made life with the co-belligerent Allied occupiers so oppressive.[44]

The 'tone' of the regulations and of the occupation itself made it very clear on a daily basis who had won and who had lost the war. Moreover, Quin Smith, who trusted Aretine integrity (and morals) not at all, devised still more ways to regulate civil life and to humiliate and humble Italians, beyond even those ACC officially formulated. Regarding much needed assistance in the form of clothing received from abroad, he directed, 'Red Cross Clothing. Has arrived and will be distributed. To avoid its being sold on the black market, CAOs should direct C[ommunal] committees to keep a list of stuff issued and MAKE all recipients wear it to a parade monthly. This is easy to arrange. No parade, no kit. This clothing will be the source of a deal of bickering and letters.'[45] No evidence in communal archives or in surviving local memory suggests that forced monthly Red Cross clothing parades ever actually took place. And, indeed, Red Cross and UNRRA donations and distributions of clothing and other basic necessities were a rich source of local bickering, angry letters, and occasional theft. But treating Arezzo's widows and orphans and other needy war victims as petty thieves and black marketeers was hardly the way to father a moral rebirth in the province.

ACC was to achieve its primary objectives of preventing disease and unrest not only by regulating the smallest details of daily life while providing Italians with quantities of food and medicine, but also by creating and maintaining 'efficient local government.'[46] Occupation and control were to be carried out on the provincial level, because ACC considered the province the most local, yet feasible level of control. Even before their invasion of the mainland, Allied planners had determined that the 'person and institution of the provincial Prefect' would be the key figure and existing institution to connect Allied government to Italian administration. The relationship envisioned was not an equal one, however. 'In this system, the Senior Allied Provincial Administrator ... sits, not in the chair of the Prefect, but in a chair at his side and tells him what the Military Government wants done. The Prefect then issues his own orders, to his own subordinates, in his own name, at the direction of the Provincial Administrators.'[47] This seemingly 'indirect' system of control had the benefit – from the Allied viewpoint – of not making ACC appear to be a colonial government, but rather one that would 'encourage Italian self-determination' and democracy. The Allies also believed that local 'subordinate personnel' would be more likely to obey their own prefect than they would a foreign officer.[48]

The ventriloquist's 'dummy' system of government, with two chairs behind every provincial desk (one for the Italian prefect and one for the Allied provincial commissioner giving him the orders he was then to issue) did little to obtain efficient local government or allow for much self-determination, however. Provincial commissioners like Quin Smith made it patent they were the true governors of the province and that the Allied–Italian relationship was significantly more unbalanced than Allied officers tactfully whispering suggestions into Italian official ears.

Despite the prefect's traditional institutional role as the link between the communes and province (locally) and the government (nationally), Quin Smith sharply scolded Arezzo's prefect for writing directly to the Italian minister of the interior in Rome. The prefect was 'prohibited in every respect from writing directly to the Minister of the Interior on any subject.' All such communications first had to be given to Quin Smith, who would decide whether to pass them on to the appropriate AMG/ ACC subcommission – which might then inform the Italian ministry of the prefect's concerns.[49] These 'hoops' through which Italian administrators had to jump did nothing to promote an easy transition to the Italian self-determination, responsibility, and 'self-democracy' that Quin Smith and the Allies kept stressing.[50] They also did little to foster local respect for post-Fascist administrative authority.

Administrative job security in the province and the communes depended not on efficiency and self-determination, but on whether Italian actions pleased the Allied occupiers. The prefect and communal sindaci were appointed – and often summarily dismissed – by ACC.[51] Sure ways to displease Quin Smith personally and the Allies generally were for prefect or sindaco to make an independent decision, to listen to anyone other than ACC, or to 'be political.' Provincial Commissioner Thurburn named two prefects in rapid succession directly after Arezzo was liberated. The first lasted only a few days before being replaced. He then was reappointed on July 25 to replace his replacement, who did 'not fulfill his task in a satisfactory manner.'[52] Thurburn dismissed him again on August 19 because he was so disliked by the townspeople and by his own subordinates that he could accomplish nothing.

Out of five possible replacements, Thurburn strongly recommended Colonel Guido Guidotti Mori to the ACC regional commissioner:

He is extremely well spoken of by the Bishop, the Senior Judicial Officer present here, the leader of the Partisans, etc. and I am very favorably impressed with him. He is a retired Army Officer and a landowner, who was Podestà of Arezzo from 1926 to 1929. He was Director of Alimentation [rationing] here later, but was imprisoned this year by the Republican Government on a false charge. He was inscribed as a member of the PNF, but was always anti-fascist. He is a strict Catholic. I should say he was democratically minded but anti-communist.[53]

On the morning of August 23, 1944, the Committee of National Liberation (CLN) for the province of Arezzo handed Thurburn a written protest against Guidotti Mori's appointment – opposed both because of Mori's Fascist past and because the provincial commissioner had not consulted CLN before making such a high level appointment.[54] Thurburn refused to be budged, however.

Duly appointed, Guidotti Mori lasted only a few months as prefect. He had done nothing wrong from the Allies' point of view, but by the time Lieutenant Colonel Quin Smith replaced Thurburn as Arezzo's provincial commissioner in early October 1944, much of the population joined the CLN in calling for Guidotti Mori's removal. In November 1943, with Republican Fascists in charge of the Aretine, Guidotti Mori had served as director of the province's rationing office (SEPRAL). The Fascist Republican *Capo* had him arrested for 'defeatism,' after Guidotti Mori had distributed biscuits for the communes to hold in reserve in case the Allies arrived and it became impossible to bake bread. This vaguely anti-Fascist act, however, did not make up for the facts that Guidotti Mori had been a very early member of the Fascist Party and had been the first Fascist *podestà* of the commune of Arezzo.[55]

Quin Smith supported Guidotti Mori at first, but soon reported to the regional commissioner that he had 'considered this matter further since our last correspondence and have now concluded that the Prefect Dr Guido Mori is too old and not strong enough to pursue a clear cut administration free from political bias and should like him replaced as soon as possible.'[56] Guidotti Mori made the situation easier for the Allies when he submitted his resignation on November 3, 1944, asserting he had accepted the appointment only temporarily and as a favour to Thurburn. Now that the provincial situation had improved, Guidotti Mori wanted to return to his children and to his country property.[57] The people had been allowed to speak in this instance, or at least Guidotti Mori heard them.

Quin Smith's concern was 'to effect Mori's removal in a way that will not brand him as a fascist nor indicate that he has been put out of office by the CLN,' although the CLN had played a significant role in Guidotti Mori's departure.[58] Like many other local citizens, the CLN objected that the man who had been the first Fascist *podestà* of Arezzo would now serve as the first post-Fascist provincial prefect. And, as the first and most important post-Fascist political figures or political body within the province and the communes, CLN members strongly objected to the Allies making such an important appointment without their input.

As elsewhere, the CLN was the most irritating political Italian thorn in Thurburn's and then in Quin Smith's side during their tenures in Arezzo. The partisans, whose disarmament would pose difficulties in some of the more northern areas of the country, were less problematic here. Except for occasional instances of partisans holding onto their guns, robbing citizens, or taking the epuration (or purge of Fascists and collaborators) into their own hands, Arezzo's partisans caused ACC much less worry than did the CLN.[59]

The first national CLN – made up of representatives of the major non-Fascist political parties – had formed in Rome in September 1943, after the armistice and flight of Badoglio and the king, while provincial and communal-level committees throughout Italy soon followed this central committee.[60] Serving as local government in many places during the brief period after the departure of the Germans and before the arrival of Allied governors, provincial and communal-level CLNs were understandably reluctant to give up their authority to the Allies and take on the minor – non-political – tasks the Allies considered appropriate.

In his first report as PC, Lieutenant Colonel Thurburn informed headquarters: 'In some communes the Committee of Liberation with the Patriots continued to issue orders etc. after our occupation, but I think they all now realize that the normal Italian Administration under AMG is the only authority.'[61] The perceived realization was short lived, as soon thereafter Thurburn directed his officers,

> to see the Committee of Liberation in each Commune and ensure that they realize that now the one and only authority is [in?] the Commune under the CAO or Provincial Officer is the Sindaco and that their duty is to give help to the Sindaco when he wants it and not to interfere with his duties. In numerous ways they can be of assistance like any other good citizens.
>   a. Seeing that wheat is taken into the Granai.
>   b. Watching for black market operators.
>   c. Watching bakers and millers etc.[62]

CLNs wanted to do more than oversee the collection of grain or spy on black market violators.[63] They wanted a real position and a voice in post-war administrative life.

CLNs attempted to act as advisors to the sindaci, to the prefect, and even to the ACC. Arezzo's provincial CLN informed ACC of the 'absolute necessity' of raising the bread ration from 200 to 300 grams – effective immediately.[64] The communal CLN of Montevarchi urged the prefect to authorize distribution of goods left behind when Republican Fascists fled north to the needy families of the commune – with the CLN overseeing that distribution.[65] In its publicly circulated protocol of September 15, 1944, Arezzo's CLN stated that while it did not necessarily oppose the Allied appointment of both the sindaco and the *giunta* for the commune of Bucine, the committee wanted both the sindaco and *giunta* to know that they must always consult with the CLN on 'problems of administrative character' and follow CLN's lead.[66]

Quin Smith felt even more strongly than did Thurburn about the appropriate place of CLNs, an organization that offended Quin Smith's views on Allied authority, and more importantly on politics. His first memo to CAOs provided:

> CLN. This has NO official position. It can be allowed to act on the lines of the British and US legion i.e. for social purposes only. They will have NO part in administration and will not be consulted as a body. Their members can be treated in all respects like any other respectable citizens (where such is the case). Their chief danger is trying to keep on the power that the interrenum [sic] period gave them. (Many did nothing till we actually arrived) CAOs should take the greatest care to see that S[indaci] are not being 'run' by them or any other 'party.'[67]

In November 1944, less than a month after his arrival in the province, Quin Smith directed the Arezzo provincial and communal committees to 'dissolve themselves.' 'If I find that they are still carrying on as a unit I shall know how to deal with them.'[68] He formally ordered CLN 'to suspend all activity' and to close its office by November 29. In December, however, he found, 'that in spite of the C.L.N. having been told to quietly dissolve themselves and seek more up-to-date channels for their loyalties they were still keeping on their offices and staff.'[69] New prefect Elmo Bracali had to vow to Quin Smith that he had never consulted the provincial or communal CLN on questions of political or administrative character, and moreover had directed the CLN not to meddle in administrative affairs of the communes and province. He did receive and listen to their views, Bracali acknowledged, as he did with 'any other private citizen who asks to confer with me for reasons of public interest.'[70]

In one of his last reports to headquarters, however, Quin Smith conceded his battle against the CLN, which had neither dissolved nor depoliticized its activities.

> The C.L.N. continues active and restive against the restrictions that have been placed upon it in regard to publications. Though they have been constantly told that as citizens their advice and influence will always be welcomed, their committees are never tired of trying to impress their *party* strength on the people. Our recent 'avviso' to the Prefect on the subject was copied to your office. In some ways C.L.N. form a counter to the communists and so tend to keep a balance BUT their influence is seldom economic and usually political.[71]

In November of 1945, six months after the province had returned to Italian government control, and just before all of Italy did so, Arezzo's CLN invited the prefect to its first provincial congress. The meeting took place on December 1, at which the prefect publicly and politely thanked the committee 'for the effective collaboration that the Provincial Committees and the Communal Committees have given me in my difficult job of governing the Province.'[72] Quin Smith and the ACC were not mentioned.

Allied Troops

The thousands of Allied combat soldiers who passed through the Aretine after the summer of 1944 had a different, but also significant impact on daily life after the passage of the front. ACC prevented the citizens of Arezzo from staying out after nine in the evening, from flying flags, and from selling potatoes. Allied troops by the thousands took over Italians' property and ate their food. The Aretines had the Allied army living in their homes and farms, in their factories and schools. Allied soldiers ate and drank in their restaurants and bars, bought up their crops, took their resources otherwise needed for reconstruction, and lastingly destroyed their historic landscapes.[73]

In that province, which had already experienced so much disruption and every day saw the arrival of more refugees, the ongoing troop presence was as destabilizing as the much smaller number of ACC officers who controlled most aspects of daily life. When the war stalled south of

Bologna over the fall and winter of 1944, troops stopped in the Aretine. These were not occupying forces, but larger numbers of troops eventually heading north where the war continued, and somewhat later included those awaiting demobilization and the promulgation of a peace treaty with Italy after the war ended. Thus, they were under army command, rather than that of ACC. ACC officers tasked with preventing 'disease and disorder' in that war ravaged province also had to cope with thousands of fellow Allied soldiers – over whose movements and actions they had no control.

At the end of October 1944, Army HQ Fifty-five Area moved into the 'much damaged city' of Arezzo with nearly 300 units, including the 'independent' Poles.

> Many of these [units] are in or round the city. In addition, there are certain Polish units which form the base for the operations of the Polish Corps further North. The latter are often difficult to treat with and are inclined to be independent; certain clashes with local police and military have occurred. Generally, the presence of so many troops all clamouring for covered accommodation, plus the large number of their vehicles, places a burden on administration, comparable to that caused directly by war conditions.[74]

In mid-October, the mining village of Santa Barbara in Cavriglia awaited an influx of 6000 members of the Reserve Brigade Group of the Sixth South African Armoured Division. The group's commander had been ordered to find a location nearer the front line. He felt 'acquisition' of such a rural 'settlement' would be less disruptive than occupying a town, 'as his Tanks … etc. could be dispersed in the surrounding fields and outbuildings of an adjacent lignite mine.'[75] Eight hundred stunned and intimidated residents of Santa Barbara were turned out of their homes on November 4, 1944, to make room for the South African troops. Extra *carabinieri* were called in to deal with protests or refusals to leave, but the 'evacuation was carried out without incident.'[76] With the arrival of the South Africans, more than 10,000 Allied soldiers inhabited the three adjacent communes of Montevarchi, Cavriglia, and San Giovanni – communes whose own populations totalled only 35,225 (not counting refugees).

As the war in Italy moved northward, the Allied army forcibly evacuated civilians living in 'forward areas,' sending them south of the battle lines. This meant that as the front lines passed Florence, evacuees from places north of Florence were pushed south into the Aretine – which already housed many refugees from southern Italy and now was rapidly filling with Allied soldiers. By autumn 1944, several hundred civilians from the north and from Livorno and Pisa areas had to be placed in locations throughout Arezzo. Quin Smith complained to headquarters, '[w]e are now faced with the threat of several hundred refugees from the Bologna area. If we appear statistically unhelpful when they come, it is to be noted that much room which might be available for refugees in the communal families has been taken up by the army.'[77]

There simply was not enough room for everyone, and it was the civilians (like those at Santa Barbara) who got evicted. Private villas were taken over for officers' residences, for hospitals, and for housing Allied nurses.[78] Troops and an Allied transit POW camp occupied the former POW camp at Laterina, which otherwise might have sheltered refugees or locals whose homes had been destroyed. Polish forces used the former internment camp at Anghiari as a rest camp.[79] Temporary evacuee camps had to be set up for refugees.[80]

Not all Italians were as quiescent as the displaced residents of Santa Barbara. ACC, which had to find shelter for both soldiers and refugees, sometimes hoped that the 'political reaction of the civil population as evinced by censor's reports will bring home inadvisability of pressing co-belligerents too far.' By 1945, the censor's reports showed a population heartily sick of the disruption and very ready for both soldiers and refugees to go home.[81] 'An interesting example of the "temper" of the population is provided in regard to the reconstruction of some of the bridges over the Arno,' said Quin Smith. 'Although villages to the north of the river are cut off from the industrial area to the south, they seem to prefer this to having bridges which would enable the army to come in and requisition property and billets!'[82] The local people would rather remain without bridges, if that meant Allied troops had no means to come and fill up their town.

While Quin Smith hectored Arezzo's provincial inspector of schools to reopen the schools, to get children off the streets, and to begin indoctrinating them for the moral *risorgimento*, villages complained that Allied troops were living in their classrooms and so they could not reopen the schools.[83] The Army Fifty-five Area town major grudgingly agreed to derequisition the school in the village of Marciano della Chiana at the end of December 1944, but Polish Corps troops living in the elementary school in the commune of Subbiano and in schools in other communes farther north were more difficult to dislodge.[84]

In October 1944, the unit '7, Madras Engineer Battalion I.E.' occupied seventy-one of the one hundred rooms at the seminary in Cortona, leaving only the remaining twenty-nine rooms for the friars and seminarians. Most of the students had fled about a year earlier when the Germans commandeered the place. Now, students and teachers were returning every day from other convents where they had taken refuge – but which now were, in turn, taken over by Polish and other troops. The rector wanted to reopen the seminary, but was told that it was the only building in Cortona then fit for Allied troop accommodations.[85]

Other property was taken over as well. Clementina Gilli owned five hectares of farmland in the province, worked by *mezzadri* (sharecroppers). Soldiers of the 694 Tank Troops had been camping on two of the hectares, and now the Allies requisitioned the rest for occupation in late October 1944. Both Signora Gilli and the inspector for the Italian Ministry of Agriculture asked that the three hectares not yet occupied be spared, so that her sharecroppers could plant winter wheat. The request was denied – 'given the continued influx of troops into the province of Arezzo.'[86] Less wheat planted meant less wheat grown and amassed, and of course, less wheat available to raise the bread ration, and less work and income for the province's sharecroppers and small farmers. Father Polvani wrote of the 'liberators' who cut the electricity and lowered the bread ration.[87] Still grateful for the Allied liberation, the population was nevertheless very tired of a bread ration of only 200 grams, tired of their property not being their own, and tired there seemed to be no prospect of life getting back to normal any time soon.

An Army Area unit took over the tobacco warehouses at Bibbiena that same month of October 1944. Winter frosts were imminent and about one hundred tons of leaf tobacco on surrounding farms went unharvested, because no other storage facility existed.[88] The ACC provincial supply officer warned that amassing of the tobacco crop could not take place without storage space, and would result in more private and black market tobacco sales.[89] When vacated the following spring, the warehouses were immediately requisitioned again, this time by South African troops. By the end of February 1945, the army had taken nearly all the warehouse space in the province and turned it into military barracks.[90]

Many requisitions, like Signora Gilli's wheat fields and Bibbiena's tobacco warehouse, interrupted or deferred the province's reconstruction. Repair of the Florence railway branch lines into the Casentino, the Valtiberina, and Val di Chiana was delayed, because 'army have just transferred its local workshops, against our [ACC] protests, to the I[talian] S[tate] R[ailway] at Chiusi.' Because the army continued to reside in the Arezzo gas works throughout the winter of 1944–5, coal had to be transferred to the Casentino cement works – effectively keeping both the gas works and the cement works out of commission.[91] Troops bivouacked in the farm consortium buildings throughout the province, preventing the storage of crops and other foodstuffs. Allied soldiers occupied the sulphur factory at Castiglion Fiorentino, so that no sulphur could be produced, though the factory was ready to commence work. They also slept in the brickworks, thus preventing the manufacture of bricks sorely needed for rebuilding.[92]

Buildings 'essential to the [Italian] public administration' were expressly exempted from Allied requisition and occupation unless needed for Allied 'operational purposes.' Because 'operational purposes' could cover a great deal, that exemption did little to prevent requisition and occupation.[93] Allied troops took over the prefecture, the post office, and most administrative and other public buildings throughout the province 'for operational purposes,' which purposes entailed housing for their own offices, recreation facilities, and troops.[94] 'Having exhausted possibilities of eviction of private persons, shops, etc.,' the army 'are continually asking us to move parts of the administration,' Quin Smith complained.[95]

Historic buildings and monuments also were protected against Allied requisition, but that protection was worth very little to Allied armies looking for a place to sleep and for wood to build temporary bridges. The ACC monuments and fine arts officer objected to Quin Smith directing the Italian Office of Civil Engineers to use the Casa Vasari in Arezzo – 'the dwelling house of the great Florentine architect, painter and writer on art' – as work space, on account of its protected monument status.[96] There was nowhere else for the civil engineers, however, having been pushed out of their own offices by the Allied army.[97]

Perhaps most permanently damaging was the Allied assault on the historic forest surrounding the eleventh century Benedictine monastery and hermitage of Camaldoli. The forest, which was made up of mostly enormous and ancient silver fir trees was, like the hermitage and monastery, an Italian national monument – and one which the Allied Second Forestry Group had been clear-cutting since the beginning of November 1944.[98] By mid-March 1945, the army had cut over 10,000 trees (an average of forty-one tons of wood daily since November 1). Their commander, Major Hodge, who was himself a forest officer in civilian life, was reported to have stated, 'frankly that the destruction of this great forest by means of "clear-felling," *i.e.* cutting out entire tracts without regard to appearance or to the future of the land, was a terrible thing, justifiable only by military necessity.' He pointed out the 'urgent requirements for wood for bridges in forthcoming operations.'[99] When he learned of it, even Quin Smith urged his superiors to 'preserve what is left of the great, historic forest of Camaldoli.' 'It is felt that the damage to the forest if subject to military needs only with no regard to its aesthetic value may leave an irreparable mark on the story of our occupation of central Italy.'[100] Cutting did not stop, but was moved to another part of the forest, farther from the hermitage at the top of the mountain.[101]

The army's 'growing need for petrol' usually meant that local industry and Italian civil transport often had none.[102] The army also had a monopoly on electric power, doling out a bit to civilian use only 'after the "needs" of the army have been satisfied.'[103] Allied 'wood-cutting parties' cut trees from public and private woods, or simply took away wood that had already been cut.[104] The army requisitioned supplies from Aretine factories – coal, steel, bricks, roof tiles, charcoal, and wood – either stealing it outright without any payment or guarantee whatsoever, or by presenting a purchase order, but too rarely showing the cash that owners desperately needed to pay workers.[105]

When the South African Armoured Division arrived at the mining village of Santa Barbara, they discovered that the lignite mines were not only a good place to park their tanks, but also offered a ready, seemingly endless, and free source of fuel. In mid-October 1944, the ACC 'Industry Division' reported an available lignite stock of 220,000 tons, including 20,000 tons of briquettes (lignite processed in a form ready to burn; the lignite equivalent of coal briquettes). By the end of October, various army units were taking away 'small quantities' of the stuff, and the Army Railway Services also 'were interested' in the briquettes.[106] By December 1944, the lignite mines were losing 'by their estimate 50 tons of fuel per day which is being taken away by military lorries.'[107] Most of it was being taken away by Allied troops who did not bother tendering a purchase invoice – or even a promise to pay.

By February 1945, only about 40,000–50,000 tons remained of the more than 200,000 ton supply that the mine had started with just five months earlier. Military 'sales' were rarely for cash, but for 'chit,' and what little income the mines received from civilian and some army sales was far less than it was costing to operate, to pay the miners, and slowly to repair the war damage to the mine installations. Moreover, ACC estimated that the American Fifth Army had simply stolen at least two-thirds of the total amount of lignite originally available for sale. The lost sums at issue were 'something in the region of 90,000,000 lire.' The mine owners had had to borrow 7,000,000 lire in the previous two months just to stay in operation. Quin Smith worried – 'not on behalf of the [Italian] owners' – 'but [naturally] from the point of view of public security and Army security ... Miners throughout the world are never easy people and are always liable to cause trouble and I gather the Valdarno miners are no exception.'[108]

Lignite was probably the most valuable commodity stolen outright in enormous amounts, but the Allied army also violated ACC food controls and its own instructions on army food procurement. Troops quartered in Arezzo bought up huge quantities of vegetables, potatoes, chickens, and eggs, all of which were controlled. Authorized to buy 200 eggs per week, Army Fifty-five Area was buying many more, and paying 13 to 15 lire per egg, while the controlled price was 7.50.[109] In addition, they used AMG/ACC currency, more valuable and desirable than the lira, to buy 'ALL the more attractive items of food' not controlled, and that otherwise should have come on the civilian market. Troops also used government rations, cigarettes, and chocolate as trading material to procure local produce.[110]

Soldiers from outside (especially from Florence Command) also came to the agricultural province of Arezzo to 'forage' (as they called it) – illegally buying chickens, rabbits, vegetables, and eggs – violating the ban on inter-provincial sales.[111] Army 'food pirates' (another contemporary term) came from other provinces and other regions as far away as Naples, driving up prices and taking food needed by the population and the troops within the province.[112] Arezzo was suffering a serious potato shortage in the spring of 1945, when a U.S. Army truck was 'endeavouring to get back to Florence on a road recently opened to farm traffic by the construction of a light wooden bridge' able to support a maximum of two tons. The truck was found lying on its side and the bridge badly damaged: with its illegal overload of potatoes, the truck weighed about six tons.[113]

The *carabinieri* had 'black market blocks' on all roads to stop and search for unauthorized food traffic, but were not allowed to stop and search Allied military personnel driving military trucks and holding military passes. The CAO of Bibbiena district himself stopped a three ton Allied truck from Florence. The driver was carrying thirty-two live lambs and one hundred kilograms of potatoes he had bought in the province of Perugia, and three turkeys he had just purchased passing through the Aretine village of Poppi on his return. They were, he explained, for his unit's Easter dinner. A farmer in Sansepolcro was convicted in ACC court and ordered to pay a substantial fine of 12,000 lire for violating an ACC order controlling the harvesting and private sale of potatoes. He had illegally sold 437 kilograms of potatoes to Eighth Army troops. 'I dug my potatoes on the 3 Oct. 44 and when the military came along and said they wanted potatoes I gave them [for 6 lire per kilo] because I thought it was obliging for us to sell to the English military.'[114] The fine he paid was several times what the British soldiers paid him for the potatoes. The Eighth Army was aware of ACC's regulations on the sale of potatoes, of course, and the likelihood that the farmer might go to jail for his 'obligingness' to the English military.

In addition to taking their resources, Allied soldiers also committed occasional crimes against the persons of the civilian population. A 'few cases' of rape by Allied soldiers were reported, including the rape of a woman by an Indian soldier, but the soldiers were rarely identified and undoubtedly more rapes went unreported.[115] Indian soldiers murdered a civilian at Monte San Savino, motive unknown. Elsewhere, a British soldier forced his way into a civilian house, pulled his gun, struggled with the owner and was shot, leaving the owner charged with homicide. When a group of Italian soldiers were ordered to leave the Bar Roma in the city of Arezzo, being told it was reserved for Allied and Polish troops, they exchanged punches and kicks with the Allied military police called to eject them and with Allied soldiers who joined in the fray.[116]

Local civilian complaints about Allied army behaviour often had to do with Polish troops. Censored letters mentioned Polish troops taking over people's houses, being 'overbearing and drunk.'[117] A trattoria owner in Sansepolcro reported that two Polish officers had remained drinking past curfew, asked for women, and eventually assaulted the owner's daughter.[118] Handwritten posters appeared in the village of Montevarchi speaking against the Polish troops, and elsewhere, street fights between civilians and Poles broke out.[119] The Polish soldiers, in their turn, objected that townspeople excluded them from civilian dances to which British soldiers were invited.[120]

Some encounters between Italian civilians and Allied soldiers really were more pleasant. Father Polvani met a British captain and his driver attending Sunday mass and was surprised to find them 'truly educated.'[121] A few women married the men their families had sheltered as escaped prisoners of war or whom they met later during the occupation.[122] Italian women engaged to marry British soldiers had to undergo a medical examination and present a medical certificate, after which an ACC provincial officer then interviewed them, pronouncing upon their cleanliness and moral character, and deciding whether there was any objection to the marriage from a social, moral, or security point of view.

Consent was usually given – albeit reluctantly – if nothing was found to prevent the marriage 'apart from the general undesirability of Englishmen marrying Italians,' as the Army assessed such matches.

Far more often, Italians and Allied soldiers mingled less permanently at authorized (and no doubt some unauthorized) dances. Allied occupation officers gave rather exclusive dances, while the lower ranks danced – sometimes not without incident – with the locals.[123] One party in Cortona in October 1945 turned into an unplanned 'boxing match,' *La Nazione del Popolo* reported, when drunken New Zealand soldiers grabbed a bottle of gin without paying for it. The evening, organized coincidentally by the Cortona Sporting Society, ended with broken glasses, shattered bottles, and two smashed chairs.[124] One Aretine CAO requested that curfew for civilians be extended from 2200 hours until midnight, 'as we sign up to 2500 curfew passes a week, chiefly for troops' dances,' and more than one intercepted letter complained that the young Allied soldiers, like young Italians, thought about nothing but dancing in the aftermath of war.[125]

On December 30, 1945, when the last of the Allies (except for the Poles, who had nowhere much else to go) had departed the province, prefect Bracali made a final report to the minister of the interior regarding the 'Behaviour and feeling of the population in its dealings with the Allies.'[126] His citizens' conduct had always been correct and respectful, inspired by a sense of dignity and appreciation. Their conduct belied their true feelings, which were, he said, contrary to their conduct. The Allies' prolonged stay in Arezzo had brought great hardship to the population. Troops and officers had occupied public buildings and private homes, driving many local families to join the ranks of the evacuees. The Allied presence had delayed the recovery of public services, rebuilding, and normal life. On yet another level, Bracali explained, everyone (even the ordinary people) openly regretted the Allied treatment of Italians: the unfair terms of the peace settlement, and their refusal to acknowledge the Italian contribution to the Allied victory and the great Italian sacrifices of property and lives.

Some Italians claimed things were better under the Allies and some charged things were worse, while others repeated the 'usual refrain,' saying, 'the musicians have changed but the music is the same.'[127] They meant that life under the Allied occupiers looked pretty much like life under the German occupiers. While it was going on, the impact of the Allied occupation and the presence of Allied troops was that of continued disruption in daily life and delay in the reconstruction of civil life

– as well as the prevention of disease and unrest. Their more lasting impact on Italy at the national level was, as others have recognized, to slow down or even prevent the reorganization of the state while some chance (or hope) existed for a real coalition government that would have reflected and served Italian society.

Such a depressing achievement occurred on the local level as well. While in the provinces and the communes, in the towns and the villages, as in Rome, the Allies prevented self-determination and self-government, 'pausing' political (and social) reconstruction while the left and right became more polarized and less likely ever to compromise or work with one another. The Allies were not the cause of that polarization, and it would be unjust to blame them and their months of occupation for Italy's entire local and national political predicament. Italy surely would have fractured along party lines anyway, but might have had greater opportunity for a workable, unified coalition government (not just an interim government) had one begun sooner and without Allied interference.

The months of Allied occupation had another result, as prefect Bracali recognized and articulated. The Allied occupiers had treated Italians 'unfairly.' They had treated Italians unfairly, not only by the terms of the peace settlement and their refusal to recognize Italian wartime sacrifices and contributions; they also treated Italians unfairly by the nature and tenor of the occupation. Not every Aretine citizen came into daily contact with CAOs or military judges, or was on the direct receiving end of one of Quin Smith's jabs at the Italian character, but enough Italians were made aware of and did experience the very unequal relationship they were in with their liberator-occupiers. Italians did not necessarily feel they had been 'defeated' in the war, or that they were members of a defeated nation, which was one reason so many were so indignant about the terms of the peace settlement. Through the occupation and all that went with it, however, the Allies persisted in reminding Italians in a variety of direct and indirect ways, that Italy indeed had lost the war. 'The English care little about our situation,' Father Polvani wrote, 'and just go on ahead to victory, which for them is already assured.'[128] 'The English prove to be polite,' he noted a couple of weeks later, 'but they treat us like conquerors, "looking down on us."'[129]

The victorious Allies who fought the Germans in Italy, then occupied Italy, assisted the country financially and then presented it with a humiliating peace settlement, saw Italy as a country that had started the war and affirmatively done its share to carry out the war. To postwar Italians, the perception was different. In his 1945 Christmas address to Italian prisoners of war waiting to return home, Alcide De Gasperi – as leader of Italy – spoke of the 'disastrous war provoked by the Fascist dictatorship.' Similarly, in his first postwar pastoral letter, the bishop of Arezzo gave thanks for the end to the 'terrible war that no one in Italy had wanted, and that had been caused solely by one man.' The references were to the first phase of the war (Italy's 'parallel' war to Germany's war) that transformed into the second phase of the war: the brutal, destructive foreign war fought on Italian soil. The identity of the 'one man' was obvious: responsibility for the disastrous, terrible war was quickly transferred to the dead person of Mussolini.

One of American army soldier, war commentator, and popular cartoonist Bill Mauldin's wartime drawings of the Italian campaign shows a frustrated and furious Italian peasant housewife, standing in front of the remains of her bombed and burned house, left with only a broken chair and a dented cooking pot. Hands on her hips, she glares at an American infantryman who responds intuitively: 'Don't look at me, lady. I didn't do it.'[130] He had done it, of course: the Allies had bombed and helped to flatten Italy (as had the Germans); but the Italians had 'done it' too. Allied occupation presence told Italians they had gotten what they deserved in the war (or at least what the Allies thought they deserved). To Italians, this was unfair. They pointed to their ruined country and their great personal sacrifices and physical suffering; they pointed to war and massacre on their soil – none of which (as prefect Bracali pointed out), the Allies appreciated fully. After the war, with Fascism 'over,' Italians would see themselves as victims of war, not among the perpetrators of the war and of the many wrongs that had been carried out by and within Italy. Italy and Italians had been martyred.

Liberation Day

The Allies did not 'botch' the occupation of Italy, as a more current Allied occupation has been characterized. Cultural differences between Italians and their occupiers were not so great that they could not be overcome, and although the Allies initially had come to Italy as 'the enemy,' the liberation they effected was collectively desired – or nearly so. The arrival of the Allies in an area was welcomed because it really did mean that war there was over. Moreover, the Allies achieved their relatively modest occupation goals in Italy: they succeeded in preventing disease and unrest. More gratuitous ambitions of 'bringing democracy' or leading a moral renewal were what rankled. Italians preferred to fight it out among themselves what postwar society and the postwar government would be.

Just ten days before the province reverted to Italian control, Quin Smith concluded that the attempted moral *risorgimento* had failed – but through no fault of the Allies:

> In total, the immense task of starting the risorgimento at the proper place is clouded by other political difficulties. A recent suggestion that the one building standing in a village – the church – should be temporarily used on week-days as a school, was considered revolutionary and all combined to suggest alternatives. This points a most important moral in present-day Italy.
>
> It is the considered opinion of this office that no amount of talk or politics will put the people on the track of modernity unless certain basic characteristics are eradicated from the mass of the people … The need is for:
>
> a. Public-spirit and citizenship.
> b. Public dignity and scorn of pettiness.
> c. Broadmindedness and charitableness.
>
> No one looks beyond his own nose; no one is willing to 'give way' on his own without waiting for someone else to give the lead. No one has confidence that unselfishness will bear any national, material, fruit.[131]

The village with only one building left standing was Pieve Santo Stefano, and Quin Smith's extrapolation of such extensive civic and moral failings from that devastated village's choice not to have its church – which was all that remained of the former community – used as a school building, was very much in keeping with his views on Italians' unwillingness to recognize their own faults and greater unwillingness to address them. With that parting shot at the Italian national character, and a rather incisive, early deduction about Italian individualism and 'amoral familism,' the Allies departed the province.[132]

Italy celebrates the date April 25 as Liberation Day, a national holiday that often makes for the bridge to a long weekend in the beautiful days of early spring. The choice of date does not coincide with the more usually acknowledged 'end' of the war in Europe; it is a date unique to Italy (or rather to northern Italy), and why it was chosen has become a sore point. April 25 (24 through 26) was the date popular insurrection and partisan fighting drove German occupation troops from northern cities – before Allied forces arrived. Thus, the anniversary of the day is most definitely not one for honouring the Allies for having liberated Italy, or even for thanking them for their help in preventing starvation, disease, and unrest. What April 25 and Liberation do mean is complicated by the fact that Italy was physically, politically, and socially divided on the original April 25th (in 1945) and appears to be more politically divided sixty-plus years on, at least insofar as the significance of April 25 is concerned. It has become a day to argue about liberation or Liberation as much as to celebrate it. In recent years, the polemic over April 25 has become particularly bitter, centring on the question of just whose holiday it is, who it includes, and just what it celebrates, with some of those on the political right calling for its end.

In April 2003, the situation came to something of a head and authorities feared possible violence at the celebration in Rome. In the days before April 25 that year, President Carlo Azeglio Ciampi (as the voice of reason) stayed away from the problematic question of who did the liberating and the fact that the date left out a good part of the country. He cast the Liberation as the founding moment of democracy in Italy and of the democratic constitution and therefore reason enough to celebrate; he pleaded that it be 'a holiday of unity,' 'not a day of clashes.'[133] The president of the senate urged, 'let it be celebrated because it meant the end of three wars.'[134] Berlusconi pointedly did not attend the national ceremony in Rome and instead spent the holiday at one of his houses on Sardegna. Others continued to go at it over which Italians really were part of the liberation (or Liberation) and who could take credit for the Resistance, whether there had been a 'real' Resistance, over the role of Fascist Republicans, over the partisans and the reprisals they triggered, over the deaths of the thousands of soldiers trapped on the island of Cefalonia when Italy unexpectedly surrendered, and over the treatment and fate of Italy's Jews.

Italy today is less unified regarding its WWII 'wars' than it was directly after them when Italians together faced the task of rebuilding and when blame for it all could be laid on Mussolini, the Germans, and the Allies.[135] The days leading up to the important sixtieth anniversary of the holiday in 2005 were marked by Berlusconi's government crisis; escalating debates over the proposition to give military combat veteran status with attendant rights and benefits (as '*militari belligeranti*') to 'Repubblichini' soldiers, the 'orphans of Salò,' those who fought for the Fascist Republic; and by Alleanza Nazionale (AN) adherents insisting on using the holiday also to honour the dead of the Fascist Social Republic. Before his governing coalition fractured, Berlusconi had announced his intention to appear in Milan next to President Ciampi, and along with the general secretaries of the three labour union confederations CGIL, CISL and

UIL. The AN and the Northern League announced that they would continue to 'desert' the holiday.[136] Reconciliation about war and liberation, even temporarily, seemed unlikely to be achieved in time.

The sixtieth anniversary celebration went well most everywhere it was observed, although Milan's sindaco disapproved of the large number of red flags in that city, saying they were reminiscent of the Soviet dictatorship; the Northern League and the AN did officially stay away while also continuing to insist that Fascist Republican militia members be recognized as war veterans; and a number of public speakers (including those who had been part of the Resistance sixty years earlier) called for an end to current revisionism regarding Fascism, the Resistance, and the civil war. In Rome, before the ceremony there, Berlusconi, having been recalled to office by the president, cordially shook hands with his future opponent Romano Prodi. President Ciampi spoke in both Rome and Milan, calling the day one of 'unity and harmony.' He listed the many domestic sacrifices and losses that had contributed to the Liberation, but also included Allied soldiers who came from 'every continent' to liberate 'Europeans from vicious Nazi-Fascist tyranny.'[137] He stressed especially the importance of the Republican constitution for all Italians, and movingly declared that the spirit of the Resistance remains alive in the text of that document which formed the foundation of the country's liberty and (inclusively) guaranteed the liberty of all.

In language unintentionally reminiscent of one Allied occupier of sixty years earlier, the president said that the constitution had made possible the 'moral and material rebirth of our nation [Patria].'[138] The emphasis on the constitution as a document for all Italians and on the holiday as a day to celebrate that constitution was intended to warn against altering that constitution. Highlighting the constitution, however, along with the enumeration of Italy's many wartime sacrifices also allowed the day to be one of unity and inclusiveness. Those Italians who declined (and decline) a national, postwar identity derived from the Resistance could nevertheless appreciate Italians' shared wartime suffering and embrace the constitution that followed from such suffering.

5 True Victims and the Truly Needy

Distruzioni. Necessità. Bisogni.
> Sindaco of Pieve Santo Stefano to president of the council of ministers,
> February 17, 1947

All the families are left without their breadwinner, without a roof overhead,
without clothing, and without provisions.
> Sindaco of Bucine to the prefect, September 29, 1944

The war in Italy struck Aretine villages Pieve Santo Stefano, Civitella, San
Pancrazio, Castelnuovo, and Meleto, and people in those villages, particularly hard. As Arezzo's prefect often emphasized during the postwar years,
however – generally when asking the ministries of the interior and of postwar assistance for funds – no commune in the province had made it through
the war unharmed. Every commune in the province of Arezzo, every town
and village, every citizen had suffered. The province as a whole was left with
ruined landscapes, houses and public buildings bombed, churches burned,
fields mined, personal possessions and livestock stolen, thousands of persons displaced, thousands of refugees and Allied troops to deal with, little
food, inadequate water supply, no electricity or fuel, few means of transportation or communication, destroyed bridges, often no passable roads,
no public services, few hospitals, no functioning schools, and families with
one or more members – usually a male breadwinner – killed.

Allied Assistance

The Allies' most welcome role in Arezzo, and in all of Italy, was that of
aid-givers. After the front passed through Arezzo, provincial coffers were

empty and communes were deep in debt. The Fascist Republican *Capo* had fled northwards taking the entire funds of the provincial treasury. In the commune of Cavriglia, the previous administration (which also departed with the approach of the Allies) had nothing to take when it went north. Instead it left a deficit of 378,570 lire in the communal treasury.[1] Banks throughout the province, including the Bank of Italy, were closed. The Fascist era welfare agencies ECA and ONMI had had their funds and supplies stolen or destroyed by retreating German troops and fleeing Republican Fascists.

The Allies arrived with much needed money and supplies for immediate relief (figure 10). The newly arrived ACC provincial finance officer quickly wired headquarters, 'I am desperately in need of funds here as Arezzo Commune needs are dire and, being a Commune of 65,000 people considerable sums will be required. Can you let me have ten million? Bank of Italy not functioning yet … Please come to my rescue pronto.'[2] The ACC funded most of every commune's budget during the period of occupation, and in the first months after the passage of the front, most of every commune's budget went for food, clothing, medicine, and shelter for its devastated citizens and refugees. For the single month of March 1945, ACC contributed 1,000,000 lire to Arezzo ECA's budget, to be used by the communes for general assistance.[3]

Along with liberating forces and the ACC came British and American secular and religious voluntary societies devoted to relief work – and more sympathetic than Quin Smith to Italian victims of war. The Red Cross (first the American, then the British), the American Friends Service Committee, the (British) Friends Ambulance Unit, the American Jewish Joint Distribution Committee all arrived in Tuscany, lived among the ruins, and worked under the direction of ACC.[4] After ACC departed, volunteers from a variety of service organizations stayed to work with Italian and foreign refugees, in part, helping to choose which displaced, foreign Jews would be allowed to immigrate to Palestine, attempting to assist other refugees to integrate into Italian communities, and aiding Italians in rebuilding their destroyed or damaged homes.[5]

The National Agency for Distribution of Relief Supplies in Italy (Ente Nazionale per la Distribuzione dei Soccorsi in Italia, or ENDSI) was the first major assistance organization to carry out its own relief program managing its own funds, rather than acting at ACC's direction with ACC's funds. The creation of Myron C. Taylor, who was chairman of American Relief for Italy, Inc. and President Roosevelt's personal representative to Pope Pius XII and the Vatican, ENDSI was a pre–cold war, pre-emptive strike in Italy by the United States and the Catholic Church. Instituted in Rome on September 13, 1944, ostensibly under the 'control of the Presidency of the Council of Ministers' (honorary chairman Ivanoe Bonomi), the agency's purpose was 'to provide for the free distribution of relief supplies to the civilian population: A) sent by American Relief for Italy, Inc., in accordance with the intent of the donors; B) assigned by the Italian Government; C) provided by legacies and donations of other governments, agencies and private persons.'[6]

In addition to its national committee, ENDSI formed provincial and communal committees.[7] Provincial committees included the prefect or his delegate, the bishop or his delegate, and the president of the provincial committee of the Italian Red Cross or his delegate. The sindaco or his delegate, a parish priest or his delegate, and a local representative of the Italian Red Cross or a communal district doctor made up communal committees.

ENDSI's manifesto to the communes set forth the particular categories of needy war victims who were to receive its help: '1) above all refugees, and persons who on account of the war or for other reasons are homeless; 2) abandoned elderly persons and children; 3) families deprived of their head or seriously affected by the misfortunes of war; 4) particularly large or numerous families; 5) pregnant women and nursing mothers; 6) the disabled; 7) the unemployed.'[8] These categories certainly represented the most numerous and traditionally sympathetic victims of war and the poor in general. While not specifying – and not requiring – that recipients be either Catholic or anti-communist, the fact that the assistance provided them came from the Catholic Church or from the United States in conjunction with the Catholic Church was made very clear. ENDSI early and openly connected much needed relief and assistance with the Catholic Church, United States' generosity, and the desired political direction of postwar Italy.

The United Nations Relief and Rehabilitation Administration (UNRRA) was the final important Allied entry into Italy and assistance there. UNRRA was only slightly less political than ENDSI, but was non-religious. The UN agreement establishing UNRRA was signed on November 9, 1943, and UNRRA's first session was held in Atlantic City, New Jersey, between November 10 and December 1, 1943. According to UNRRA's basic mission, the United Nations would supply medicine, food, and other necessities 'to the peoples freed from Axis control.' The United States was to be the largest financial contributor among the nations, while each of the other forty-four member countries would contribute 1 per cent of gross income.

UNRRA was a mission initially difficult to sell to the United States. Lest they believe that they were merely giving charity, by helping former enemies, victims of war, or those from other countries less fortunate than themselves, the president assured Americans that it was 'a clear matter of enlightened self-interest and of military strategic necessity.' Early UNRRA pamphlets told the U.S. pre–cold war public in alliterative terms that this 'relief for the liberated' was a 'first fundamental for a free world.' It was 'not a charity,' but 'help for those who help themselves.' It was the 'promise for secure peace,' and the 'first step in the direction of post-war economic progress.'[9]

UNRRA's 'Out of the Chaos' pamphlet for the American public said that aid would go to 'those countries which were invaded, and whose resources were so completely depleted that they do not possess enough foreign exchange to pay for the supplies which they must import.' UNRRA funds were '*not* expected to help the German or Japanese peoples.'[10] Technically, Italy fully met the criteria of having been invaded and having its resources depleted. To much of the United States and the congress (as to ACC and Allied troops), however, Italy was more like Germany and Japan than it was like 'war victim' countries such as Greece, Yugoslavia, Poland, Czechoslovakia, and China. As an ex-enemy nation, Italy originally was not entitled to UNRRA aid at all, or only 'against full payment' by the Italian government. The war had put Italy's civilians in a heartrending situation, however. In September of 1944, the UNRRA council considered providing limited relief for Italy, primarily to the true innocents: women, children, and foreign refugees in Italy, but later extended aid more broadly.[11]

UNRRA and ACC overlapped only briefly in Arezzo. In Tuscany, in April 1945, the Italian Displaced Persons Section was the first UNRRA program. Later in 1945, a program commenced to provide welfare services for children and for nursing and expectant mothers, for medical and sanitary aid and supplies, and for assistance in the care and return of displaced persons to their homes.[12] In August 1945, the UNRRA council made Italy eligible for full-scale relief during 1946. A regional office for Tuscany and Emilia-Romagna (as a combined region) eventually opened in February 1946 in Florence, after Allied troops and the ACC had left Arezzo.

Throughout 1946, UNRRA's Emilia and Toscana region had branches devoted to public information,[13] 'special relief projects' (meaning Italian displaced persons), welfare, health, non-Italian displaced persons, statistics and reports, agriculture, food, industry, ports and shipping, and finance and administration. It made sure that Italian recipients were as aware as the American public that UNRRA would help only those who helped themselves. An UNRRA poster provided as the twelfth and final 'aspect' of UNRRA activity for Italy: 'UNRRA can only lay the foundations for the reconstruction of Italy, and provide temporary aid. THE REST FALLS TO THE ITALIAN PEOPLE – THAT IS TO EACH OF YOU.'[14]

UNRRA's help was indeed temporary (though critical). The regional office for Tuscany and Emilia closed in February 1947 when UNRRA field activities in the region ceased. In its short life, it touched individuals on a local level (which the Marshall Plan would not do), and provided desperately needed immediate relief through food and clothing, generally without emphasizing Italy's 'subject' status.[15]

The Allies also had a more prospective effect on welfare in the postwar Aretine and all of postwar Italy, resuscitating Fascist era welfare institutions and organizations. Both the Communal Assistance Agency (ECA) and the maternal and child health and welfare agency (ONMI) owed their continuing postwar existence to ACC and UNRRA, in that both ACC and UNRRA would employ ECA and ONMI as mainstays in their own assistance work. ACC policy, and later UNRRA policy, was to make 'maximum use ... of local agencies with the purpose of strengthening those that are needed for the long-term rehabilitation of Italy.'[16] The Allied military and UNRRA had not based their policy of reusing local agencies or institutions on study or analysis of the effectiveness of those existing bodies, but simply on the fact that they were in place and they could work.[17] 'It is apparent that there is no time for theorizing or permanent social planning until the needy Italian people are better clothed and fed,' they recognized.[18] And then, once the needy Italian people were better clothed and fed, the old organizations remained firmly in place as the Allies departed.

Indeed, nothing was inherently or fundamentally wrong with ECA or ONMI, except for once having been Fascist Party tools used to penetrate and shape society, something the Allies recognized.[19] ACC, nevertheless, regarded ECA as the most important province-wide welfare agency and determined it would play a 'large role' in the 'new Provincial Welfare picture.' On April 14, 1944, the Italian government (with Allied direction) decreed that ECA and its communal committees be reconstituted in every commune.[20] ECA was to be 'the *principle organ of assistance*' operating in every commune.[21]

On September 9, 1944, the interior minister also provided for reorganization of the provincial and communal branches of ONMI. In 'agreement with the Allied Control Commission,' reorganized ONMI would carry out its same Fascist era functions, but change slightly the names of its administrating bodies. [22] For the sake of continuity and efficiency, directors, presidents, secretaries, and members of the former committees of both ONMI and ECA could be kept on if otherwise 'suitable' and 'unobjectionable' – meaning they were not subject to the official purge of public employees or so loathed by the population, because of Fascist era or wartime activities, that they could not carry out their duties. Many communes, therefore, enjoyed continuity in the administration of relief services.

The Allies eventually left, taking their money with them. Whatever initial gratitude, then growing impatience, irritation, and resentment Aretine citizens felt about the Allies in residence, they regretted their absence deeply in one respect. 'With the passage of the Province of Arezzo to the Italian government,' the prefect recorded, 'the Allied Military Government has left the province and every enterprise has passed to the appropriate Italian ministries.'[23] The commune of Cavriglia was 'plunged into difficulty' when the Allies left. 'All AMG financing stopped, and from that moment the communes had to function with their own revenues – which were less than their expenses.'[24] Bucine's sindaco found the commune and himself in 'great difficulty' in June 1945, resulting from the lack of Allied aid 'that up until a few months earlier had arrived with a certain abundance.'[25] The financial situation of all the communes 'became critical.' Although happy to have their civil and moral lives back to themselves, Arezzo's administrators and the province's citizens missed the 'certain abundance' of Allied aid deposited directly into communal budgets and handed out as in kind relief.[26]

The Hierarchy of Need

Almost everyone in Arezzo – as in central Italy, if not in all of Italy – was a victim of the war. Not only were individuals and families 'victims,' so were villages, communes, and provinces.[27] Every victim was also in need, and the needs were of the most basic sort. The first post-liberation sindaco of Cavriglia listed the three immediate and fundamental problems facing his own and the other war torn communes. They were: provisioning (or 'feeding,' *alimentazione*), unemployment (*disoccupazione*), and aid (*assistenza*) to needy victims. 'Needy victims,' he elaborated, included the families of those slaughtered, the evacuees and those displaced, and 'many other categories of persons.'[28] 'Victims,' 'needs,' and what to do about both developed into major topics in the life and discourse of postwar Italy.

Every sort of aid was urgently required: food, clothing, shelter, medicine, money, jobs; but the need for assistance far exceeded what there was to give (even while the Allies were there to assist). And so, not everyone in need could be helped. Introducing a letter from Emilio Sereni (then minister of postwar assistance), an editor for the newspaper *Resistenza* summed up the situation facing Italy and Sereni's new ministry: 'Certainly the needs are infinite in this wretched postwar of ours, but it is not possible to provide for them all.'[29] A September 1945 clothing distribution exemplified the problem on a very local level, when the commune of Bucine received 200 pairs of shoes from UNRRA to allocate. The commune reported fourteen partisans, seventeen veterans, 146 prisoners of war already returned, 138 prisoners yet to return, twenty-nine other men, 177 widows of political victims, ninety-six orphaned children between the ages of seven and fourteen, nineteen younger than six – all of whom needed shoes and clothing – far more than what was available. The massacred village of San Pancrazio, which claimed most of the widows and orphaned children in that commune, received only ten pairs out of the 200 pairs of shoes.[30]

Because need was so widespread and assistance so limited, the whole problem of need and assistance required a selective (or rational) approach. The providers and the administrators of aid – whether Allied or Italian, public or private, local or national – had to decide who among the needy should be helped with limited resources – or, who out of a village's hundreds of needy would get the ten pairs of shoes available. The process began with organizing war victims into groups. Thus, when the sindaco of Cavriglia recounted the commune's three fundamental postwar problems, he spoke of providing assistance to the needy families of the slaughtered, to evacuees, the displaced, and 'to many other categories of persons.'[31] That is, victims of war were separated into 'categories of persons' according to how and what they had suffered.

Citizens were not just war victims or needy victims; they were more specifically war orphans, civilian war widows, unemployed veterans, injured partisans, the politically persecuted, and so on. Before the war, ECA already had divided poor relief (or 'welfare') recipients according to more traditional categories such as the unemployed, the elderly, and the disabled. Narrower, newer classes of Italians repatriated from abroad or from the colonies, families of men recalled to arms, refugees, internees and confinees were added and given assistance priority at the beginning of the war. As the war intensified, it supplied many more theretofore unforeseen categories of victims, and categorization became progressively more elaborate and specific throughout the war.[32]

After the war, the Ministry of Postwar Assistance continued the practice of categorizing victims according to what harm they had suffered. A former political internee, a Jewish returnee from a concentration camp, a forced labourer returned from Germany, a former partisan, a wounded soldier, a returnee to the ruined village of Pieve Santo Stefano, and the widows of men murdered in Civitella, San Pancrazio, or Castelnuovo all were victims of the war. While all were likely to need assistance, whether they actually received it was determined first according to their membership in a particular category (their victim status), and then granted depending on their degree of need (their place in the hierarchy of need).

Official categorization is consistent with state bureaucratization, and granting assistance in an *ad hoc*, particularist, and incremental manner is a hallmark of a 'non-universalist' welfare system such as Fascist and post-Fascist Italy's.[33] Categorization (both official and informal) was also a means of creating a measure of order within the overwhelming and disordered postwar task of assisting an infinite number of needy. Moreover, victims somewhat naturally had fallen into categories as the war successively generated new harms. In any event, organizing the war's needy victims into basic categories was a relatively simple first step towards rationalizing need and assistance during and after the war. Both ENDSI and UNRRA operated in terms of categorizing eligibles; so did communal ECAs and the new Ministry of Postwar Assistance (Ministero di Assistenza Post-Bellica, or APB).[34] Instituted in June 1945, just weeks after the end of the war, APB was to consolidate postwar assistance into a central ministry, with peripheral provincial offices and communal level committees.[35]

The ministry of APB addressed itself to those who had suffered 'most directly and most deeply' from the war. As in earlier postwars, when the distinction between soldier and civilian had been very clear, those initially deemed to have suffered most directly were those who had borne arms for the nation. This most recent war, fought on civilian territory, however, had caused equally direct and deep suffering for the civilian population. APB therefore categorized war victims potentially eligible for assistance as: 1) partisans; 2) veterans; 3) prisoners of war; and 4) civilian victims of war. The first three classes were self-explanatory, though their numerical order (with partisans preceding veterans and POWs) is worth noting.[36] Civilian victims, being a new and less self-explanatory category than the first three, then were divided into subcategories of refugees, evacuees, and others displaced or homeless; civilians repatriated from foreign countries; civilians returned from internment and from deportation; families of civilians killed or missing on account of the war; civilians wounded during the war; and co-nationals who were no longer receiving remittances from abroad because of the war.[37] Thus, not only were those with a strictly military connection to the war recognized as deserving victims eligible for assistance, so too were civilian victims like the residents of Arezzo, Civitella, San Pancrazio, Castelnuovo, Pieve Santo Stefano, and much of the rest of Italy.[38]

Falling within a particular category – whether articulated by APB, ECA, UNRRA, ENDSI, or another institution or organization – did not, however, assure one of assistance after the war or the passage of the front. In that time and place where needs were infinite and it was impossible to provide for them all, aid was not an entitlement for needy civilians, veterans, or partisans.[39] Being 'made whole' was not a right for any victim, even those who had suffered 'most directly and most deeply.'

Postwar needs pervaded local and national life to such an extent that a hierarchy of need quickly developed, by which only the very neediest could and would be helped. To receive assistance, a victim had to be not merely needy, but 'truly needy.' He or she had to be the neediest among the needy, the 'true victim' (within his or her category) among the many victims in Italy. The hierarchy of need governed not only individuals: victim villages, communes, provinces also were in need and in competition for limited assistance. Communal sindaci appealed to their prefect, and prefects petitioned the government ministries and foreign aid organizations, asserting that theirs was the most damaged and needy commune or province among all the others and therefore required more assistance than they currently were receiving.[40]

Although the hierarchy was mostly unofficial, it was explicitly articulated as a hierarchy. Arezzo's prefect directed the committees in charge of distributing UNRRA garments in the communes to select the 'neediest' (i più bisognosi) refugees and civilian returnees by dividing them into the following categories:

A) those not having immediate need of clothing;
B) those having need of clothing, but not urgent need;
C) those having extremely urgent need of clothing [bisogno urgentissimo].[41]

The prefect elsewhere emphasized that 'assistance to victims of war presumes first of all an actual and real state of need.'[42] He chastised sindaci of every commune in the province for certifying too many families as indigent because of the war (thereby making them officially eligible for certain forms of state assistance or for precedence in assistance). Given the general state of postwar need common to the great mass of citizens, only 'the really and truly indigent' should be certified for inclusion on the rolls of the poor.[43] Similarly, Arezzo's APB provincial committee announced it would grant aid only for need that was 'beyond normal' – not need 'of an ordinary nature' such as that deriving from unemployment (a condition from which so many were suffering that unemployment constituted a normal postwar state of affairs).[44]

The vocabulary of the hierarchy of need permeated postwar assistance from the ministries in Rome to the most local village level.[45] On October 1, 1945, APB announced a temporary subsidy for 'returnees to civil life,' a large category including veterans, partisans, former internees, deportees, and political prisoners, in order to ease their return. In addition to showing proof of partisan, veteran, POW, or civilian deportee status, however, claimants had to verify two additional conditions: that they were involuntarily unemployed because of lack of work, and that they were in a state of real need.[46] Similarly, families of the fallen (those killed in the war) came within ENDSI's second category of eligibility for assistance, but even they were to receive assistance only if 'real conditions of need' had been determined.[47]

The Treasury Ministry announced that anyone in the nation who hoped to receive government assistance had to be 'in a state of particular, or special need.'[48] When determining the order in which citizens should receive state compensation for war caused property damage or loss, the superintendent of finance would give priority to families 'most affected and needy.'[49] Communal sindaci were to submit names to the prefect, limiting their lists to ten families each week. In Civitella's first compilation, all ten families were 'seriously needy' and inscribed on the rolls of the poor. A somewhat later selection included 'the neediest persons and those most deserving of aid.'[50]

Wool blankets from Prato were to be distributed in Arezzo – but only to needy persons and those communes in the province 'most affected' as a result of the war.[51] A Christmas package of tinned meat and fish from the provincial committee of UNRRA was intended only for 'the neediest people' of Bucine and 'the categories least well-off.'[52] The sindaco of Cavriglia asked the local CLN to gather names of those among the population in 'real need,' who would then be eligible to receive clothing sent by the American Red Cross. In Castelnuovo dei Sabbioni alone, 151 families were in such 'real need.' In Meleto, 677 men, women, and children were in 'real need' of shoes, coats, underwear, and other most basic items of clothing.[53]

Italy's children constituted one infinitely large, directly suffering category of postwar needy victims. The children who suffered were not as in previous wars only those whose fathers had been killed or injured in battle. Now, they were children who had seen their parents massacred and their houses torched by the Germans. They were children themselves wounded or disabled during the bombing, the passage of the front, or from landmines. They were children whose families were refugees and evacuees. For all of these poor children, the hierarchy of need was very much in effect. Each commune and each village within the communes listed its orphans 'in order of need' to submit to the National Association for War Orphans, as only the very neediest might receive distributions of clothing and other items.[54]

The provincial branch of the Action Party supported a proposal to send war orphaned Italian children to the United States to be adopted by Italian-American families if orphaned of both parents, or to live temporarily with an Italian-American family if orphaned of one parent.[55] No one in the massacred villages of the province of Arezzo, which had significant numbers of children orphaned of a father (and some of a mother), chose to send a child to Boston, Chicago, or New York, but, following centuries-old practice, many did seek temporary care for their children in orphanages and *collegi* in Italy.[56] Because so many wanted to place one or more of their children in an orphanage temporarily, a surviving parent or other relative had to prove the child's neediness beyond that shared by all war orphans. One girl, almost twelve years old and orphaned of her father by the war, was not accepted into an orphanage – given the considerable number of needier, 'more deserving' orphans, who were 'of more tender years and also deprived of a mother,' concluded the National Association for War Orphans.[57] The same organization also declined to contribute towards sheltering a little boy who, along with his brothers and sisters, had been orphaned of his father. So many other 'extreme cases of absolute need' existed that funding was not available 'merely' for an orphan member of a large family.[58]

When the organization 'Bimbi di Napoli' asked the communes of Civitella and Bucine for the names of country families willing to take poor Neapolitan children into their homes for a period of time, the communes responded that because of German massacres and their position in the war's front line, they already had more of their own truly needy and orphaned children than they could assist. Conversely, when Bucine's sindaco asked the president of the National Committee for Political Victims for special assistance on behalf of the orphans of San Pancrazio, he was told that Rome's 800 terribly needy orphans had precedence over other orphans.[59]

Even within a single family, one child could be deemed 'needier' than the other family members, either because of age or physical condition. One child might be lucky enough to receive a hot meal provided by UNRRA or other aid organization, while his brothers and sisters were not deemed needy enough. The hierarchy broke down in those instances: 'No power on earth could convince a mother to give the luxury of one good meal a day to her neediest child while her other children ate the normal sub-standard diet at the same table,' commented an UNRRA field worker.[60]

Need – whether for a bowl of soup, a blanket, an unemployment subsidy, or shelter for a child – had to be 'truly exceptional' and 'urgent' to be recognized and met in that time and place where most everyone was in need.[61] Assistance was limited to those 'in conditions of real need,' to the 'truly needy,' 'the desperately needy,' and the absolute 'most needy.'[62] Such qualifying terms came to constitute a recognizable vocabulary of need, employed both by those who gave aid and those who hoped to receive it. 'Needy is a relative term,' wrote an UNRRA worker in Italy. He was referring to those living in refugee camps, who he said were not to 'be considered the most needy in the country' (out of the millions of 'needy war-displaced and homeless persons' in Italy). Refugees in camps were fortunate at least in having some form of accommodation. The ones in a true 'state of desperate need,' he said, were those Italians living in caves, shacks, cellars, and the ruins of their destroyed homes.[63]

Determining the Truly Needy

When Arezzo's prefect passed on 2000 lire for the communes to divide between the neediest (*più bisognose*) mothers or widows of those killed in the war, ECA divided that very small sum among four women. They included a mother whose son had been killed by the Germans in the massacre at San Polo, a mother whose three sons were killed by the Germans in the massacre at San Pancrazio, a widow whose husband was killed by the Germans in the massacre at Meliciano, and a woman whose two sons and son-in-law were massacred at Meliciano.[64] How were those four women chosen among all the other 'neediest' widows and mothers?

If only the neediest among the needy could be helped, then of course the truly needy and desperately needy somehow had to be discerned and distinguished from the merely needy. It was a decision mothers apparently could not make regarding which one among their children would eat a nourishing meal. It was also a decision beyond the ability of the sindaco of Pieve Santo Stefano, where everyone 'without exception' was in need. 'Conditions of wretchedness exist for everyone,' so he informed the prefect.[65] The sindaco of the commune of San Giovanni Valdarno told the prefect and the UNRRA provincial committee that he could not determine which families should receive one of the 1000 lengths of wool UNRRA had provided – and for which over 1500 families had applied. It was impossible to reject so many requests, 'all being truly the *neediest* cases' and all falling within UNRRA and ECA categories. Instead, he suggested, UNRRA should send the commune an additional 500 pieces of fabric.[66] Similarly, the sindaco of Bucine wrote to inform the UNRRA provincial committee that its assignment of food rations for forty-five children in San Pancrazio was not sufficient. At least sixty children there were 'in absolute need of assistance' every day, without fathers and without the barest necessities. It was impossible to make some do without.[67]

Choosing the truly needy among the infinite numbers of needy had to be done, nonetheless, especially when no additional lengths of wool or meal rations were forthcoming. That unhappy task fell most often upon those traditional, institutional figures who presumably best knew the truly needy, because of their close, local level contact with the population: parish priests and the local police.[68] In November 1944, Bucine's sindaco requested the priest of each parish within the commune to supply a list of the neediest families, according to which the sindaco then would distribute a modest, one-time financial subsidy. In that commune battered by Allied bombs, German massacres, and front line combat, one priest came up with only a single family 'in a state of real need.' Another priest found six; one named sixteen. One priest listed eleven, specifying whether each family was merely needy, in a state of real need, desperately needy, needy because their belongings had been destroyed, or homeless and needy.[69] Bucine's priests later had to select which needy children in their parishes would receive the very few pairs of shoes UNRRA provided.[70] When ECA for the commune of Florence decided that only the 'neediest' would be fed at communal soup kitchens, it assigned parish priests the job of choosing them.[71]

Communal level aid or assistance committees – for ECA, APB, UNRRA, ENDSI – always contained one or more parish priests, and sometimes a nun from the local nursery school.[72] The new archpriest of Civitella declined to serve as a member of the communal committee for UNRRA distribution. Given his limited time in the area, he said, he would not know how to 'rank' the needy, and so would not be a useful member of the committee.[73] Two priests (as 'Representatives of the Church') joined the nine member Cavriglia communal committee for the distribution of clothing given by the American Red Cross.[74]

In addition to priests, the local arm of the *carabinieri* or *Questura* also was called upon to separate the truly needy from the merely needy. Whereas parish priests had to select which smaller group of individuals or families from the larger village group would receive soup, shoes, or a subsidy, the police instead generally examined the 'need quotient' of potential individual recipients. Communal sindaci or the prefect would direct police officers to investigate and report on the family background and current economic condition of those individuals who petitioned for subsidies, clothing, housing, jobs, and other postwar assistance.

'Needy' was a subjective term as well as a relative term, when assistance was neither a right nor an entitlement. The criteria used by both police and priests (or by the various assistance committees) for selecting the truly needy never were definitely articulated. What 'true need' meant, or how it differed from ordinary need or mere need was never particularly clear.[75] Reports on who was neediest and why varied from investigator to investigator (whether priest or police officer), from village to village, and from needy person to needy person. Some were found not truly needy because they had a son who worked, or because they sharecropped a bit of property. Some recipients were designated 'truly needy' – or not – with no explanation or supporting factual basis. Notably, conclusions of real or insufficient neediness often included comments about a potential beneficiary's pre- and postwar politics, standing in the community, and moral worthiness; and interestingly, comments on political position and moral worthiness were more common in police reports than with a priest's list of the village's neediest persons.

The absence of objective national standards is not surprising. Who would have delineated and overseen them in the postwar interim state? How would they have made sense across Italy, between north and south, city and country? The absence of objective standards locally, however, made for some not so surprising practices. The emphasis on requiring real, true, exceptional need – without any real, objective standard as to what constituted that exceptional need – required those seeking assistance not only to be truly needy (however that might be interpreted), but also compelled them to argue convincingly to sindaci, priests, police officers, committees, or to whomever was distributing some form of assistance, why they and their family ranked at the top of the postwar hierarchy of need. It also resulted in complaints of unfair treatment, and assertions that others 'less needy' were receiving more than the truly needy, as in Castelnuovo when a group of widows crowded into the *carabinieri* office, demanding an explanation as to why they had received smaller ECA subsidies than other widows in the village who were no needier: 'A. had less than R.' 'C. had more than the others, although she was in a more advantageous condition, having a son employed.' 'Signora C. from Massa lost everything and was homeless, but had received no subsidy at all.'[76]

Communes were in the same position as the widows of Castelnuovo. The sindaco of Pratovecchio expressed both astonishment and anger that his commune had not been included in the prefect's register of 'victim communes' (*i comuni sinistrati*). As a result of that omission, Pratovecchio's citizens received less assistance from UNRRA and ONMI, while other communes 'less damaged' or less victimized than Pratovecchio now received more aid.[77]

The provincial representative of the American Red Cross sought to avoid the widespread and 'deplorable favoritism' in the distribution of donated clothing, reminding communal committees that distribution was to be based only on need and calling for the 'scrupulous examination of each individual's degree of need.'[78] UNRRA program directors stressed to field workers 'the careful selection of eligibles' and 'distribution on the bases of comparative need.' ENDSI told its communal committees to be inspired by criteria of absolute impartiality and objectivity, while always remaining independent from interested pressures.[79] The director general of the Italian delegation for UNRRA cautioned provincial prefects that UNRRA assistance was to be 'strictly apolitical' – a warning timed for the 1946 elections: individual recipients were to be chosen independently from their beliefs, and from political and religious orientation.[80]

In spite of the warnings they gave and precautions they took, Allied-funded assistance organizations continually expressed surprise and frustration at the 'deplorable favoritism' shown in granting assistance – at how subjective and political the assistance process was in Italy.[81] Favouritism in assistance decisions (that is, subjective decisions based on recipients' position, background, and whose influence they could bring to bear) was a long-standing tradition, and one perfected even more during twenty years of Fascism when local Fascist Party members had the power to make assistance decisions regarding their neighbours and fellow citizens.

Thus, in addition to arguing their own cases, hopeful individual recipients employed the traditional practice of *raccomandazione*: enlisting others more articulate or influential to speak for and recommend them. These included traditional spokespersons like doctors, lawyers, teachers, land-owners, and employers, but now, of course, no longer included Fascist Party influentials.[82] Instead, now the local secretary or representatives of the Communist or Christian Democrat Party were much sought after.[83] The provincial secretary of the Christian Democrats would write to a commune's Communist sindaco recommending a particular person for a job in the communal administration, an apartment in newly built public housing, or a larger subsidy from ECA. The Communist Party secretary would write to the parish priest or the director of a Catholic orphanage, asking for assistance for an applicant. Occasionally, petitioners were able to obtain letters from both Catholic and Communist supporters (or patrons, more accurately). Communes as well as individuals utilized connections whenever possible. The Aretine and the Aretines could call on prominent PCI member Giulio Cerreti at one end, and DC notable and Pieve Santo Stefano native, Amintore Fanfani at the other.[84]

In a country with longstanding traditions of clientelism and patronage, and with centuries of organized charity driven by more complex motives than simply helping the poor, petitions pleading one's own neediness and enlisting more influential individuals or groups to support one's claim reached a new level in Italy's 'wretched postwar.' Aretine archives are rich with hundreds of handwritten letters and typewritten petitions, attended by supporting documents asking the sindaco, the secretary of ECA, communal and provincial assistance committees, the prefect, sometimes even the ministers of postwar assistance and of the interior, for blankets, clothing, food packages, a temporary subsidy, a job with the commune, or an apartment in a recently constructed block.

Politicizing the Truly Needy

Postwar determinations of who was neediest and who should be helped were even more intricate during the years 1944–8 than they otherwise might have been, because they were made in the politically charged, pre-election atmosphere of post-Fascist Italy. Unlike the Allies and foreign aid workers, Italians (politically active or not) accepted that politics related directly to assistance – and vice-versa – and that the political parties would engage in the work of assistance. All of the major political parties were invited and all sent representatives to the National Convention of Assistance Organizations organized by Florence's ECA and held in Florence in October 1947: the Socialist Party and the Socialist Workers

Party, the Communist Party, the Christian Democrats, the Liberals, the right-wing L'Uomo Qualunque, the Action Party, and the Democratic Workers Party.[85]

Patronage, clientelism and *reccomandazioni* were nothing new, but assistance now became politicized in a couple of new ways: one intentionally, the other less so. Dozens of communal level committees were formed (sometimes spontaneously, but generally named by the sindaco and communal councils, with input by the prefect) to oversee distribution of aid from the Red Cross, ENDSI, ECA, ONMI, the provincial office of social assistance, UNRRA, and other governmental and non-governmental organizations. These committees included representatives of different (and often opposing) societal and occupational groups, such as farmers and landowners, labourers and professionals, property owners and the homeless, and different ends of the political spectrum to insure full societal representation and, consequently, some degree of fairness.[86] Well-meaning attempts at inclusiveness served inadvertently to politicize assistance, however. Inclusiveness guaranteed that Communists and Catholics – selected because they were Communists and Catholics and specifically acting as Communists and Catholics – and the right and the left had a great deal to say and influence to wield regarding who in the commune should and would be assisted.

The church and the Christian Democrat Party (DC) had significant influence over assistance because, as seen, parish priests always sat on communal committees, and because sindaci called on priests to provide names of the neediest persons in the villages. Because the local administrations of many Aretine communes had a Communist (or Socialist) sindaco, and a majority of Communist and Socialist members on their communal council or *giunta* – and who also sat on communal aid committees – the PCI (the Italian Communist Party) also was able to make its presence felt and voice heard in assistance determinations.

Italy's nascent political parties attempted to influence the distribution of aid given by others, but more intentionally they themselves quickly entered the business of assistance. Politics thus played a very direct role when the parties selectively gave out their own hot meals, food packages, and trips to the seashore for poor children. In Arezzo, the battle over assistance soon came down to the DC and the PCI – the Catholics and the Communists. The Christian Democrats were the party with the greatest resources, especially as time grew closer to the 1948 national election. A young school teacher in a small mountain village in the province of Arezzo recorded how promises of a new road, an aqueduct, and electric light for their war damaged village had convinced the poor villagers to vote DC in the 1946 Constituent election.[87] The PCI had been a bit quicker off the mark (than the DC) in the field of assistance, however, at least in the red province of Arezzo. The PCI also benefited greatly from the work of the very active Union of Italian Women (UDI), and from UDI's close connection to the Communist Party and to the assistance activities of UNRRA and ONMI.

UDI was ostensibly apolitical and open to women of any or no political views. When asking for Allied permission to form local chapters immediately after liberation of an area, UDI listed its proposed activities as 'striving for social and economic emancipation, and giving assistance to soldiers and their families, and to poor children.'[88] As volunteers for ONMI and for the National Association for War Orphans, UDI helped make decisions as to which poor children would be given a place at funded summer camps (or colonies) and which would be accepted for shelter in an orphanage or schooling in a *collegio*.[89] And within a short time, UDI would also sponsor its own nursery schools, meal programs, and summer camps for select, needy children, and received some communal funds for its assistance programs, as we will see.[90]

Angelo Ventrone has written persuasively of DC and PCI key roles in creating a new postwar democratic Italian citizenship.[91] By penetrating society at all levels, and by incorporating individuals (especially women and young people) into politics, the parties forged a closer relationship between citizens and their government than had before existed in Italy's history. What Ventrone argues is correct, though his closer relationship was more a local than a national one, at least in the early postwar years. Had it not been for such widespread need and so many needy victims, however, the parties – women members included – would not have been able to penetrate so quickly and deeply into daily life and society on the local level, using assistance to do so.

Among Other Victims

Arezzo's needy war victims shared their province and its scarce postwar resources with 'others' – those whom local political parties were not particularly eager to help, and whom communal administrations fervently wished would go away. And, if asked, Arezzo's citizens would have agreed with the UNRRA field worker who wrote that refugees living in camps should not 'be considered the most needy in the country.' Refugees and evacuees from other provinces and other countries arguably should have ranked quite high in the hierarchy of victimhood, but the local perception

– and later the national – was something very different. Refugees were the 'others' whom Aretines complained received more assistance than they who were living in the ruins of their own homes and villages.[92]

An enormous number of refugees and evacuees inhabited the Aretine during and after the war. When the Allies first invaded and Mussolini fell in July 1943, the province already had become the temporary home to 22,208 refugees from other provinces or repatriated from other countries.[93] Of course, Arezzo was not alone in receiving large numbers of Italian refugees. An August 1944 survey showed about 26,000 refugees in the neighbouring province of Siena.[94] At the end of 1945, the commune of Florence had over 6000 evacuee and refugee families to feed and shelter.[95]

By the time most of the province was liberated, every commune in Arezzo sheltered Italian evacuees and refugees – some in the hundreds – from other communes within the province (many from the city of Arezzo, who had fled to escape the bombing), from other provinces, or from other countries.[96] ACC estimated that Civitella had a refugee population of one hundred at the beginning of September 1944.[97] A month later, the commune reported 250 refugees and evacuees from all parts of the country, including Florence, Milan, Rome, Naples, and farther south.[98] For the communes of Bucine and Cavriglia in September 1944, ACC calculated 200 and 800 refugees, respectively, noting that the 'situation is still very fluid,' despite the fact that for 'military reasons, movement is prohibited.'[99] Throughout the post-front and postwar period, getting an accurate count of – and getting control over – the number of Italian and foreign refugees was impossible. Refugees came, stayed, and went, not at will exactly, but as conditions drove them.

As the war advanced northward from the province during the late summer and fall of 1944, ACC officials in Arezzo were directed to take in still more refugees. 'Operations are, as you know, producing large numbers of refugees and it may be necessary to allocate up to 10,000 to the Southern part of Region VIII during the coming 2–3 weeks ... It may be necessary to send anything up to 1000 or even more refugees to your Province.'[100] Despite frantic messages from PC Quin Smith that Arezzo was 'not in a position to absorb any outside refugees,' that it could not 'possibly be asked to accept further refugees,' and that '[i]t is out of the question to take any more,' hundreds more refugees continued to arrive throughout the fall.[101] Because refugees and Allied troops so outnumbered what rooms were available in the province, refugees also lived in schools 'under very unfavourable conditions,' in any other public buildings available, in theatres, and in four 'mass shelters' or camps located in the communes of Foiano, Lucignano, Monte San Savino, and Castiglion Fiorentino, in the Val di Chiana.[102]

More than 200 refugees 'from provinces already liberated' (that is, from southern Italy) already lived in the city and commune of Sansepolcro by the summer and fall of 1944. Despite the opportunity to return home once the province of Arezzo had been liberated, and the offer of transportation to do so, they refused to go – 'for reasons not entirely plausible' according to Sansepolcro's sindaco.[103] Thirty local families whose houses had been destroyed sheltered in the commune's schools, and now ACC notified the sindaco to find shelter for 300 evacuees from the Bologna area who would arrive at any time. Had the prefect any advice on how to dislodge the stubborn southern refugees from the commune, the sindaco asked? The prefect suggested the sindaco simply revoke the southerners' ration cards in order to 'encourage' them to leave the province and return home. The sindaco feared, however, to do so would cause them to riot.

They chose to remain, the sindaco believed, because of the easy assistance they were receiving. Against the sindaco's advice, an ACC official had ordered 480,000 lire specially distributed over a thirty-day period. Now that those funds were exhausted and local ECA could not provide more, what did the prefect and the ACC propose the commune do? The sindaco wrote in frustration to the prefect: 'How I would like to do something for all these people, but I ask Your Excellency with what means?'[104]

In the fall of 1944, 640 evacuees (mostly southern Italians) resided in the commune of Monte San Savino, 260 of them (apparently all southerners) in a single mass shelter.[105] A communal health official wrote to the sindaco and to the provincial medical authorities; the sindaco in turn wrote to the American Red Cross and to ACC about the shelter's deplorable health and sanitary conditions.[106] One case of typhoid already had been diagnosed, and there were many cases of tuberculosis. Scabies and lice were rampant. Residents were sleeping together on straw, which more than once had caught on fire. The commune could do nothing to improve the camp or to help the camp residents – but not because the commune chose to do nothing.

While Quin Smith deplored the morals of Italians in general and Aretines in particular, the Aretines in turn complained about the southerners. 'The moral and intellectual level of the evacuees renders useless every gesture on their behalf, and grouping them together [in shelters] simply multiplies their moral wretchedness,' decried Monte San Savino's sindaco.[107] When the local citizens – themselves in need – had charitably donated goods to the camp, the evacuees had immediately sold them on the black market in order to buy wine. That fact might seem humorous, he said, 'if it were not so tragic, and showed what a moral low point the evacuees had reached.'[108] The sindaco pleaded with ACC forcibly to transport the southerners back to their home provinces in military vehicles. The camp situation in Castiglion Fiorentino was no better. There, the refugees lived in tents until a convent and a movie theatre were requisitioned for their use. The convent served primarily as a hospital, but 150 of the refugees moved into the small theatre, all sharing two toilets.[109] When 'an influx of Bolognesi' arrived in the commune from the north in November 1944, the only solution – or so the citizens and authorities of Castiglion Fiorentino hoped – was to send the camp's current residents south or to camps in Siena province.

Attempts to return southern refugees to their homes or just to get them out of the province did not meet with much success, and even the Allies could not get them to budge. 'The number of persons living in Rome or South, who left [Arezzo] by available transport, was only a small percentage as they refused to avoid [avail?] themselves of this opportunity. This problem complicates all plans for clearing Comunes of south refugees as CAO's and Sindaci in Comunes affected tried a number of schemes to enforce departure but with little success.'[110] The Naples segment of Roberto Rossellini's 1946 film *Paisan* shows what conditions were waiting for many of the southern refugees when they returned home, and life in a mass shelter in Arezzo must not have seemed so bad in comparison. Aretine complaints about the continued presence of amoral or immoral southerners illustrate more, however, than Italian regionalism played out on a social level. They also reflect the postwar hierarchy of need, and where Aretines believed they should rank in relation to Italian 'outsiders.'

Whereas most of the earlier internal refugees had come from the south, the autumn 1944 influx of refugees began from the nearby provinces of Livorno, Pisa, and Bologna, as the war stalled there.[111] Pisans and Bolognesi were more acceptable, but like the southerners, the large numbers of Livornesi were seen as 'creating a real problem' for the Allies and more so for the communes that had to take them in.[112] The Allied regional welfare office, the provincial commissioner, local officials of the displaced persons and repatriation subcommission, and the sindaci all wanted the Livorno evacuees out of the Aretine as quickly as possible, or at least contained in additional 'holding camps,' rather than freely circulating.

In addition to the southern refugees crowded in Castiglion Fiorentino, ninety-three evacuees from Livorno now lived in a single building in the town in the autumn of 1944. How they had arrived or taken over the building, neither the commune nor ACC officials could say for certain. They had simply appeared and now they would neither leave nor agree to be 'contained.' What unpleasant things the evacuees from that port city did while in the province of Arezzo were not spelled out, but the Livornesi were as unwelcome as the southerners whose morals were debased and who sold charity on the black market to buy wine. Their standards of *civiltà* differed significantly from those of the Aretines. 'The conditions are very bad, due in part to the character and habits of the Livornesi,' wrote the American Red Cross welfare representative to Quin Smith regarding the refugee situation in Castiglion Fiorentino.[113]

Neither the Allies nor the Italians knew how to manage the spiralling refugee and evacuee situation in their midst. Italy was the Allies' first training ground for dealing with large numbers of refugees, just as the country had served as practice on being an occupation force, managing civil affairs, and quickly constructing a welfare system. Plenty of practice was available, but methods were never perfected. 'The whole problem of refugees seems to be one which is shunted from one unit to another without much consideration for either the organization receiving the bodies or for the poor refugees' welfare,' complained an American Red Cross representative to Quin Smith.[114] Quin Smith wrote to his own supervisors, '[i]t is again emphasized that the present patchwork policy of dealing with the refugees is not only inefficient but definitely bad for the prestige of AMG. The refugee baby is being passed so continually that it is doubtful if the cure is not worse than the disease.'[115]

The ACC did not want to establish additional mass camps or large shelters, fearing that they would become a provincial and an ACC responsibility, and so pushed instead for compulsory billeting among residents in the communes. The communes and the citizens of those communes on the other hand, not surprisingly, fought orders to crowd southern or northern strangers into their homes. Moreover, given that Operation Strangle and Arezzo's position in the war's front lines had made for large numbers of local refugees, homeless and displaced, few communes in the province were in good enough shape to provide housing for large numbers of refugees from outside the province.[116] Mass shelters made for a terrible and unhealthy situation for the refugees, but suddenly forcing communes to place dozens or hundreds of outsiders in the damaged homes of needy citizens – themselves so recently bombed and living in a war zone – seemed far more unfair to the locals.

No acceptable solution was found by Italians or the Allies, though both compulsory billeting and expanded mass holding camps were employed.[117] 'This W[elfare] O[fficer] has been present upon the arrival of refugees in a number of communes and in his opinion based on what little he has seen, the situations thus created are terrible and he feels that our worst enemies should not be subjected to the hardships and heartaches that many of the people undergo simply because of the absence of careful advance study and preparation.'[118] There were hardships and heartaches on both sides: it was not that the Aretines did not understand the refugees' predicament, but felt the Allies and the authorities were alleviating the refugees' suffering at the Aretines' expense.

Then, in the winter of 1944–5, while the province coped with northerners arriving, tried to get southerners to leave, and wondered how to handle the disruptive character and habits of the evacuees from Livorno, a large group of very needy, very internal war refugees returned from the north to their ruined homes in Pieve Santo Stefano. Unfamiliar with the events of that village's destruction, PC Quin Smith and provincial welfare officers were caught unawares when Eighth Army trucks dropped 1000 people in the ruined village, with no warning, no permits, and 'no previous application to the prov[incial] HQ.' Upon inquiry, however, the ACC regional commissioner found that 'the 1,000 refugees sent to Pieve Santo Stefano were not refugees in the true sense, but were, in fact, Italians returning to their home commune.'[119]

The forcibly evacuated villagers of Pieve Santo Stefano very much considered themselves 'refugees in the true sense,' however, as did their neighbours. The returning citizens of Pieve Santo Stefano were viewed far more sympathetically within the province by both Aretines and Allies than were displaced southerners or evacuees from Livorno. The sindaco and citizens of neighbouring Sansepolcro were a good deal more amenable to taking in evacuees from Pieve Santo Stefano than they were to keep providing for the southern evacuees in their commune, or for the 5000 Allied soldiers who also had moved into the commune of Sansepolcro about the same time. Arezzo's ACC welfare officer first tried to convince the returnees to live with willing families in Sansepolcro, 'but the people insisted that they wanted to remain in Pieve in spite of conditions.'[120]

The initiative and love of place shown by the citizens of Pieve Santo Stefano contrasted sharply with the actions of the southern and Livornese refugees, in the minds of the Aretines. Even the ACC was moved:

The condition of the village is appalling. W.O. [Welfare Officer] was unable to find more than three buildings in the entire place which had not been completely destroyed or severely damaged by demolition ... Several families are crowded in a large room of the badly damaged theater and also in the two completely whole buildings of a dwelling character. Others found shelter in one or two remaining room[s] of buildings that unquestionably should be completely leveled because of the hazzards [sic] of falling walls and masonry. The people are thoroughly aware of the hazzards and large numbers of men and women at work clearing the rubble and doing what they can to eliminate the most serious dangers though heavy snows which are common to the region will multiply the dangers many times. The W.O. was amazed at the comparative cleanliness of the rooms he visited and the absence of filth ... W.O. was informed that the local Sindaco is an architect by profession and very capable. He is quoted as saying that if they could secure tiles the people could solve their own shelter problem ... The main local church is relatively undamaged and possibly could be used as a shelter that is at least safe from falling walls but they do no[t] want to do so partly from lack of glass for the windows and apparently mainly because of sentimental reasons.[121]

Aretines, who preferred to be homeless in their own homes, could not understand why southerners and other refugees did not want to return to theirs. The citizens of Pieve Santo Stefano were true victims, even if not true refugees according to Allied definition.

As the war ended, more Italian refugees, both military and civilian, began to pour through the province heading from north to south.[122] Arezzo was an important way station, because of its central position between Florence and Rome. On May 5, 1945, 145 refugees arrived in the city of Arezzo. On May 6, 305 arrived; 530 arrived on May 7; and on May 8, another 390 arrived.[123] By the middle of May, the city saw as many as 600 new refugees a day. Fortunately for the province, many of these latest refugees stopped only briefly for a day or two, and then by foot or by train proceeded on.

The province (working together with the Allies and the ACC displaced persons subcommission) instituted two transit camps in the city of Arezzo after the war. The city's military barracks (with capacity for 500) was turned over for use as a 'reception centre' on May 6, 1945, and became an overnight shelter for civilian refugees going south. The other transit camp served Italian soldiers, partisans, and POWs. In addition to the transit camps, a more permanent 'very overcrowded' mass camp functioned in the capital city of Arezzo between 1945 and 1948, sheltering both foreign and Italian displaced persons, including Italians repatriated from North

Africa. When that closed, another refugee camp was instituted at Laterina, the former site of the large POW camp.[124]

Foreign refugees – including numbers of Jews from Polish and German concentration camps – also began to flood into Italy in the summer of 1945. Entry into Italy was relatively easy for almost anyone right after the war. As Italian POWs and Italian civilians (such as those who had gone to Germany as volunteer or forced labourers) returned to Italy across the Austro-Italian border, along with them came thousands of displaced foreigners. As of August 15, 1945, UNRRA supported 720 foreign refugees in the Emilia and Tuscany region, spending 2,450,000 lire each month. By February 1946, UNRRA maintained 1900 non-Italian DPs in the region living in and outside of camps in Emilia-Romagna and Tuscany.[125] In June 1946, UNRRA had a 'caseload' of 691 foreigners in Tuscany requiring 'out of camp' assistance, while Emilia-Romagna had 1070.[126] Although these were not enormous totals compared to Italian refugees, and the number of entering foreign DPs decreased further when Italian officials tightened border controls in the winter of 1945–6, neither Jews hoping to reach Palestine nor other displaced foreigners were particularly welcome in Italy.[127] As the communes of San Pancrazio and Civitella had too many of their own needy war orphans to take in additional needy children from Naples, and as the citizens of Castiglion Fiorentino and Sansepolcro wanted the southerners and Livornesi out of their communes, so Italy as a country not unreasonably considered it had far too many of its own needy citizens, including its own needy refugees, to allow temporary entry or a permanent home to foreigners. For Italian 'refugees proper,' the ministry of APB and UNRRA provided the figure of 78,752 for the 'whole region' of Tuscany and Emilia for the month of March 1946. For that month, the Italian populations in the twenty-nine refugee centres throughout Tuscany and Emilia-Romagna remained 'fairly static, a total of about 11,000 persons,' while the remaining 65,000 plus lived outside of refugee centres.[128]

In February 1947, UNRRA's Italy Mission tallied the numbers of Italians still 'homeless' ('war displaced and homeless Italians') – but counted only those receiving assistance from the Ministry of Postwar Assistance.

It must be remembered, however, that the number of those 'homeless' unemployed persons to whom this Ministry pays its small sussidio of 20 Lire per day, or of those persons living in the Ministry's camps, does not include very large numbers of other homeless persons who are in a very real state of need. They show, nevertheless, the existence of a specific group of approximately 800,000 homeless persons in a state of severe need, of which number over two-thirds come from certain particularly devastated areas.[129]

Thus, as late as 1947, Italy had 800,000 homeless and needy Italian refugees either still living in camps or whom it was supporting with UNRRA help. Italy, in addition, had uncountable numbers of other homeless citizens 'in a very real state of need,' but who were living somewhere and somehow getting along.

Although a large number of its own citizens continued to be homeless in the technical sense that their homes had been destroyed or were not habitable, Arezzo had fewer than 300 of its own refugees (citizens of Arezzo province) living in refugee camps. Arezzo's crowded camps housed Italians from other provinces and Italians and foreigners from other countries, and it was these foreign and domestic 'others' who were still living in Arezzo's camps and shelters two years and more after the war had ended.[130] Seemingly permanent refugee camps and their populations were especially problematic for postwar reconstruction and the return to normal civil life throughout Italy. Camp residents had nothing to occupy their time and no contribution to make to postwar society. They received food, clothing, and shelter from UNRRA, from the Italian government, and sometimes from the communes; and, an UNRRA official warned:

> It is clear that, unless more determined and effective action is taken to empty these camps in the very near future, Italy will be faced with a substantial group of people whose moral and physical deterioration, often already far advanced, will be close to unremediable [sic]. Not only are these camps 'running sores' but they are also an expensive burden on the national exchequer.[131]

APB Minister Emilio Sereni recognized that camps and refugee shelters had been necessary during the country's time of 'serious hardship' to provide war refugees with some level of economic and social stability, and that the devastation suffered by some provinces prevented many refugees from returning to their homes for at least a year after the end of the war.[132] By the summer of 1946, however, the continuing situation, had resulted in a 'peculiar social condition, with a related mentality,' the so-called 'professional refugeeism.' Refugee centres, Sereni said bluntly, had become seats for a permanent population who had developed a mental habit of making demands and claiming the right to support 'on the back of the state.' For them, postwar life would not get back to normal, and he feared they would leave Italy a 'sad heritage of idleness, vice, and parasitism.'[133]

Refugees and evacuees – both foreign and Italian, in and out of camps – were a postwar problem that did not go away quickly, in Arezzo or elsewhere. The refugee camp at Laterina closed only in 1963. At some point, however, it did not matter if refugees were from the next commune, from Naples, North Africa, Bulgaria, or Poland. What mattered was they ate the food, occupied housing or other space, and took the assistance that 'belonged' to the citizens of that commune and that province. Not only did the refugees engender feelings and comments that they were receiving more than the local population and that they were less truly needy than the local population, they also delayed the reconstruction of society. From the Aretine perspective, refugees contributed to societal disorder, to unemployment, to health problems, to food shortages and the black market. The citizens of the Aretine could not return to civil life, or recreate their own life of *civiltà* with so many refugees among them.

These feelings were localism and regionalism at work, to be sure; even nationalism was involved as Italy strove to deny entry and to expel needy, foreign refugees. And so, it might appear from the hierarchy and politicization of need that postwar need served only to separate people and drive them apart. Widespread need and inadequate assistance did cause Italians to be divided into more and more distinct and competing categories of victimhood. Widows were necessarily pitted against other widows, orphans against other orphans, partisans against veterans, the merely needy against the truly needy in determinations of who would receive the one hundred blankets, the forty-five hot lunches, the twenty undershirts, or the ten pairs of shoes. Communes also competed with other communes, and provinces with other provinces for limited government funds and international aid.

Need united people on a local level, nevertheless, because families, communities, villages, and communes could point to others – other villages, other communes, southerners, foreigners – who were taking what should have gone to themselves; and they could point to Rome and to the Allies who never provided enough. Need, like trauma and suffering, contributed to a common, local identity. No one outside the village, or the commune, or the province understood – or cared – just how bad conditions were and how the locals had suffered and continued to suffer. As the sindaco of Pieve Santo Stefano wrote to Alcide De Gasperi, president of the interim counsel of ministers, despite the village's total destruction and the commune's suffering, no one from the Ministry of Public Works had visited – 'not even for an hour' – to see the horrendous damage firsthand; yet ministry representatives had toured and assisted other, less damaged communes in the province.[134]

Shared victimhood was national as well as local. Poor Italy: 'Povera Italia!' as one intercepted letter said in 1945.[135] Italy saw itself like the widows and orphans, like the village of Pieve Santo Stefano, like the citizens of the Aretine who had lost everything and were living in their ruins of their destroyed homes: a true victim on a national scale. Their country had been destroyed and their lives turned to infinite hardship. Italy had been martyred, ordinary citizens and the government agreed, but others outside Italy did not acknowledge the enormity of what had happened. No one outside of Italy fully understood or appreciated Italy's contribution, the magnitude of Italy's suffering, and the extent of Italy's need.[136]

6 Restitution, Reparations, and Rewards

> Among the difficult tasks of reparative justice entrusted to this Ministry ... I have particularly at heart those which concern the assistance, shelter, and the reeducation of poor children and adolescents physically disabled by the war.
>
> Minister of Postwar Assistance

One victim was not content to petition for immediate relief in the form of a blanket, a pair of shoes, a meal for his children, or a small temporary financial subsidy. Pasquale Migliorini may or may not have been truly needy, but as a political victim of Fascism, he sought much more in the way of comprehensive restitution for his loss and reparation for his suffering. In 1921, Migliorini had been a clerk in the Anagraf and Civil State records office in the commune of Cavriglia. Forced from that post because he refused to enrol in the Fascist Party, he left Italy for Paris. He lived in France until the end of April 1942, when he was arrested there because of his known opposition to Fascism. Transported back to Italy and confined on one of the Aeolian Islands, he was eventually liberated on September 10, 1943, two days after Italy's armistice and the collapse of the state. In January 1945, Signor Migliorini found work as a temporary clerk at Cavriglia's communal rationing office. He wrote to the sindaco that he now felt the need to see his situation 'definitively settled' – as in the 'settling of accounts,' rather than as in 'settling back home' after more than twenty years.[1]

Basing his demand on unspecified (and non-existent) 'provisions of law' whereby those harmed by Fascism (for example, having been deprived of jobs or livelihood), now had the right (*diritto*) to be taken on again in those previous jobs with all retroactive claims, Migliorini asked to be reinstated in the position he had held twenty-four years earlier, with retroactive benefits to 1921, and a fair salary to satisfy his family's needs. Communal records do not reveal the unlikely occurrence of Migliorini's return to his old job with twenty-three years of back pay. His reference to a 'right' to have accounts settled after wrongs done because of Fascism is important, however. Although no decree or statute was promulgated requiring the state, the province, or the commune to 'make up' for Fascist era iniquities or deprivations – financial or otherwise – the state did undertake limited attempts to repair some of the wrongs perpetrated by the Fascist state and the harms caused by war.

Assistance, in the form of immediate relief, began as a fix (or 'filler') for need during and directly after the war, but the goal and forms of assistance soon advanced to a higher level. Some of the more progressive types were still partially, or initially, dictated by the hierarchy of need, others were not. For all, specific victim status or inclusion in a particular victim category remained critical. The more advanced forms of assistance all were monetary and went beyond filling need. All were rooted in the principle of restitution – reimbursement (or pay back) for specific losses; or in the principle of reparations – payment for unquantifiable loss or suffering; or in the principle of reward – imbursement for services provided, even if provided unwillingly. The government did not articulate a break down of payments into those three groups as such, but the three principles are apparent in practice. They all derived from the postwar Italian state's attempts at societal reconciliation, as well as from a desire to make Italians 'whole' again after the war, and from a commitment to acknowledging Italian suffering.

Italians believed that the Allies did not recognize or appreciate Italians' 'great sacrifices of property and lives,' or Italy's contribution to Allied victory.[2] In contrast, acknowledging its citizens' sacrifices and losses would be a cornerstone of the postwar Italian state. Nearly all victims (nearly all citizens) – wounded partisans, wounded veterans, war orphans, civilian war widows, children injured by landmines, internees and deportees, citizens whose homes had been destroyed by bombs, and others torn from their prewar civil life – came to be recipients of state subsidies, awards, indemnities, pensions, school scholarships, and other forms of assistance more meaningful than blankets, overcoats, and tinned meat. The process would eventually bring Italians closer to the state and make them expect more from the state. It would also unite Italians and divide them.

From the chaos of 1944 to the democratically elected national government of 1948, the interim postwar Italian state began to structure itself in terms of financial and moral commitments – restitution, even true reparations – to the large percentage of its citizens who had suffered for the nation during the war or at the hands of the Fascist state. No clear, planned trajectory began with immediate aid and poor relief (whether from the state, the Allies, or a foreign aid organization), then moved on to state-devised and financed subsidies for needy categories, and then to restorative or reparative awards from the state, and from there arrived at pensions and entitlements for certain groups irrespective of need. In the 'vast field of postwar assistance,' different forms co-existed between 1945 and 1948, and thereafter.[3] But a discernible transition did take place, and it was a loosely chronological one compressed within a very few postwar years.

Subsidies

The new state Ministry of Postwar Assistance (APB) – entrusted with the difficult task of reparative justice – was intended to consolidate much postwar assistance under itself. As seen in the previous chapter, APB formulated and provided a number of one-time ('extraordinary') and temporary subsidies to groups that fell within its charge. APB announced its first subsidy (*sussidio*) on October 1, 1945, to recent 'returnees to civil life': partisans, soldiers discharged after May 8, 1945 (excluding, of course, members of the Fascist Social Republican forces), military prisoners of war repatriated after May 8, 1945, and civilians whom the Germans had deported outside of Italy for forced labour after the September 8, 1943, armistice – who now were unemployed and in a state of real need.[4]

The purpose of the subsidy was to provide financial means for the returnee and family for the first ninety days of 're-entry to civil life.'[5] This temporary subsidy was not to continue longer than ninety days, as calculated from the date of re-entry or return, and could not be joined with other subsidies or emoluments provided by the state or local organizations.[6] Returnees were to receive the state's help, but only if they were needy, unemployed, and not receiving any other monetary benefits. That is, the state briefly subsidized its citizens whom the war had uprooted from civil life. It did so to ease a needy citizen's return to civil life, but did not attempt to make up for wrongs done or harms suffered in the uprooting.

The kinds and numbers of postwar state and parastatal subsidies (*sussidi*) are too numerous to list with any hope of including them all. Some subsidies were temporary in nature or given only once. Others, however, came to be given on a regular monthly basis, were the precursors of pensions, and were closely tied to the wartime practice of granting assistance according to categories of war-generated harm. Most subsidies were granted only to those who fell within a specific category and who truly needed the money; but because so many Italians fell within more than one victim category and because so many were needy, many people often were eligible for more than one type of subsidy. The same family could be war refugees as well as having a son or husband who served in the Italian military or as a partisan, for example. Another family could have had a civilian member killed by the Germans, and yet another member deported for forced labour service. Individuals and families may have suffered several harms (and thereby fell into more than one category of eligibility), but generally could not collect multiple subsidies. That is, at this point, subsidies were not given to compensate for every wrong suffered. Specific harms were not being addressed and redeemed in and of themselves, but rather the state recognized that the breakdown of civil life meant need.[7]

Almost a year before the war ended, on August 14, 1944, the interim state, in the form of the minister of the interior, Ivanoe Bonomi, had authorized a subsidy to 'political' ex-internees and ex-confinees, both Italian and foreign. This subsidy recognized those who had directly suffered at the hands of the previous state, and offered a bit more than the more general 'returnees' would receive from APB a year later. Those eligible included Italian anti-Fascists; British, U.S., Yugoslav, or other then enemy nationals living in Italy when the war broke out; and foreign Jews, all of whom had been subject to confinement or internment.[8] The subsidy did not automatically go to all former political prisoners, but only to political ex-confinees and ex-internees liberated as a result of events following July 25, 1943 (the deposition of Mussolini) *and* who still (in August 1944) found it impossible to return home.[9]

The decisive points were previous confinement or internment and now the inability to return home and take up work – that is, to return to civil life. For Italian citizens, the 'political ex-internee subsidy' also depended on their current degree of need. Nevertheless, some minor element of reparation was present for those foreigners whom the previous regime and state had treated as enemies, in that they could get the state subsidy without proof of need, if international events prevented them from returning home to their normal occupations. The subsidy carried no time limit for Italians or foreigners; it could continue until an ex-internee or ex-confinee's situation changed.

On October 23 of 1944, Bonomi, as interior minister, directed prefects of liberated areas to pay (through ECA) political ex-internees and ex-confinees in zones liberated after that date, the sum of 75 lire per day up to a maximum of fifteen days following liberation.[10] The following January, Bonomi specified that 'the subsidy' should not be paid to ex-internees who currently had remunerative employment that provided for their support.[11] A month later, however, he clarified who was to receive it. All (*tutti*) ex-internees and political confinees liberated in zones after October 23, 1944, were to be given what he now referred to as the *premio* (bonus or award) of 75 lire per day for fifteen days.[12]

> The payment of such subsidy – which is extraordinary and is the first financial help to those categories – ought to be executed with the greatest possible promptness; this does not of course preclude them from a regular subsidy, but is intended to be limited only to those persons who were [themselves] subject to internment or confinement and not to family members eventually authorized to go live with them.[13]

Moreover, he added, '[i]t is to be more precisely understood that the request for said extraordinary indemnity can be made two, three or more months from the date of liberation, and in a locality other than the one in which they were interned.'

The interim state thus formulated an inclusive grant, conceptually different from ECA general subsidies to needy, unemployed war victims (*sinistrati*) and different from the state's earlier subsidy for needy, unemployed former confinees and internees not yet returned home. Now, a political ex-internee and ex-confinee could be awarded the daily (though temporary) 75 lire – even if back at home, employed, not truly needy, and receiving other subsidies. In early June 1945, Bonomi distinguished the earlier (August 14, 1944) need-based subsidy, calling for tightening measures around its distribution: 'The granting of the daily subsidy to ex-confinees and political ex-internees, instituted in August 1944, has, as is well known, the object of meeting the needs of those who, formerly affected by police measures and then liberated on account of the events of July-September 1943, found it impossible to return to their own homes and are in need.'[14]

Other subsidies, including the August 1944 daily subsidy and that first granted by APB in October 1945, were monetary grants in the exact

sense of subsidizing: giving citizens (and some foreigners) something to
tide them over until they could get back home and back to work – until
they returned to civil life. Bonomi's October 1944 award for former political internees, in contrast, constituted a first example of reparations
from the state, given irrespective of a recipient's need or ability to return
home, to employment, and to civil life.

I Premi

With in kind assistance and subsidies, the state (and other organizations)
addressed need by dividing and arranging the needy into categories
based on different types of harm as a way of organizing or systematizing
the granting of assistance. When the state shifted focus to the harm or
wrong itself, need became either less relevant or irrelevant. The requirement of need distinguished state subsidies from state *premi*, in that the
former required it, but the latter did not. *Premi* implied, instead, some
sort of service or suffering to be recognized and rewarded. The state
came to decide that certain harms or wrongs caused by Fascism or by the
war especially must be officially recognized and compensated – monetar-
ily and morally – not necessarily because the citizens who so suffered
were in need, but more so because state and society wanted to acknowledge the enormity and severity of Italians' – and Italy's – suffering.

In August 1945, to mark the liberation and the end of the war (and the
partial departure of the Allies), the council of ministers granted a
'premio di Liberazione' to state and public employees in those provinces
returned to Italian administration.[15] As a separate *premio*, the clerks and
other communal workers in the commune of Cavriglia, like those in
many other communal administrations throughout Italy, received an additional small financial bonus for extraordinary service in keeping their
commune functioning during the difficult final six months of 1944.[16] In
addition, the high commission 'per i Reduci,' under the auspices of the
council of ministers, authorized a substantial 5000 lire *premio* to wounded partisans, men and women – 'due' them because of injuries suffered
in the struggle for liberation.[17]

The postwar was a fertile time for giving and receiving *premi* and rewards for service rendered and suffering undergone – and for more
complex reasons.[18] On January 14, 1946, APB's minister announced an
important *premio* in the amount of 20,000 lire for families of fallen partisans and for families 'of those slaughtered during German reprisals.'[19]
Civilians or partisans 'wounded or invalided at the hands of Nazi-Fascists'

would receive half of that, or 10,000 lire. Thus, the widowed families of Civitella, San Pancrazio, Castelnuovo, and other communes of Arezzo were to receive the significant sum of 20,000 lire because they lost a member in one of the German massacres carried out during the summer of 1944. APB did not require a showing of true need – or any need – for this special award. It went without saying, certainly, that most of the widowed families were in desperate need, but they did not have to demonstrate it or enlist someone to argue it for them. The state was recognizing their sacrifice and loss, not their need. Neither did the families have to assert or prove cause and effect (or quid pro quo) between partisan action and German reprisal. That is, they did not have to convince authorities that the massacres truly had been in reprisal.

The 20,000 or 10,000 lire *premio* was called the Premio di Solidarietà Nazionale or Award of National Solidarity, a title that carried a number of interesting postwar connotations. 'National solidarity' and 'national unity' were terms in wide use after the war. National unity often meant overlooking differences to accomplish shared postwar goals. The interim governments in Rome were the so-called 'governments of national unity' or 'national solidarity' from 1944, until De Gasperi set up his fourth cabinet in May 1947 with Christian Democrats, Liberals, and Republicans – excluding Communists and Socialists, and thereby ending national political unity. 'National solidarity' also was called upon whenever groups or associations of any political stripe collected donations or held fundraising events for various victims of war. Thus, the rubric of 'national solidarity' could encompass anything from a short-lived postwar experiment made up of political parties holding opposing views on what shape postwar society should take, to showing support for partisans injured while battling Nazi-Fascists, and for villages of grieving widows whose husbands had been murdered by Nazi-Fascists.

The state was recognizing those civilian and partisan victims certainly, but postwar national solidarity and unity were being propounded – not rewarded – by the state's 20,000 lire *premio*, to place it more correctly. Demonstrations of national solidarity on the part of those murdered civilians through their ultimate contribution to the Italian war of liberation had been unwitting, and the deaths were deeply regretted by their surviving families. The state, not the victim families, chose to conjoin civilian victims together with partisans as its demonstration of national solidarity.

In the months following APB's announcement of the *premio*, Arezzo's sindaci readied lists of men and women massacred, but the underlying procedure leading to qualification for the *premio* took a somewhat circular path. In order to be considered for the 20,000 lire solidarity *premio*, families, widows, and widowers first had to obtain recognition for their dead relatives as 'having fallen in the struggle for liberation,' which recognition was granted by the pre-existing National Committee for Political Victims or one of its subcommittees.[20]

The National Committee for Political Victims (Comitato Nazionale pro Vittime Politiche, also sometimes called the National Committee for Civilians Persecuted for Political Reasons) formed in Rome directly after the city's liberation in June of 1944, to assure monthly allowances for families of those murdered by German troops (including families of the Ardeatine Cave victims), families of deportees and 'racial victims,' other 'political victims' of Fascism, and families of partisans 'killed in the struggle for liberation.'[21] The National Committee for Political Victims thus undertook long-term, monthly assistance (something like a proto-pension) for a fairly large group of Italians – before APB and the state took over that duty. Its payments ceased and the committee for political victims phased itself out of business when APB distributed the National Solidarity *premio* and as state war pensions were fashioned for civilians. From its inception, however, it was one of the most active and effective of the impermanent postwar assistance associations, and it had begun to provide monthly grants for some victims of war and Fascism as early as the end of 1944, and for the massacred villages of Arezzo in early 1945.[22]

'Political victim' and 'struggle for liberation' – like 'national solidarity' and 'national unity' – could be inclusive (and flexible) terms after the war. Fallen partisans were identified as political victims because they had given their lives to the cause of anti-Fascism and Liberation (with a capital L). They had died in the struggle for liberation, killed because they were partisans, although their own personal politics could have ranged from communist to liberal to monarchist. The committee for political victims also recognized civilians killed in Nazi-Fascist massacres as 'having fallen in the struggle for liberation,' and so APB then in turn recognized those same persons as victims of Nazi-Fascist reprisals for purposes of the 20,000 lire Award of National Solidarity.[23] Thus, civilian massacre victims became political victims too.

Titles, terms, and three different categories of postwar status became conflated, though Italians could have obtained any one of them under very different circumstances. A 'political victim' originally meant someone who had been prosecuted or persecuted for anti-Fascist sentiments or activities sometime during the Fascist regime. Someone 'fallen in the struggle for liberation' usually meant a member of a partisan band killed fighting the German occupiers or Fascist Republicans (or the Nazi-Fascists) between September 8, 1943, and 1945, while those 'slaughtered during Nazi-Fascist reprisals' instead meant civilian victims like those massacred at Civitella, San Pancrazio, Castelnuovo, or the Ardeatine Caves.

Conflating them all after the war was not the result of inadvertent linguistic sloppiness, however, but was deliberate. That is, the state sought to join together political victims, wounded or fallen partisans, and massacred civilians in recognition that all had contributed to the struggle for liberation (or Liberation). Civilians massacred by Nazi-Fascists were considered 'victims of Nazi-Fascist reprisal,' of course (as all German or Nazi-Fascist massacres and atrocities came to be called reprisals, even without direct evidence of reprisal motives), but also were considered to have 'fallen in the struggle for national liberation,' and then consequently deemed 'political victims' (though whose politics they had been 'victim to' becomes somewhat troubling if one follows the reasoning to its end). Everything was political after the war, and victims were no exception.

Some wartime massacre victims inadvertently had been omitted from earlier lists, or else confusion existed whether someone really had been victim of a Nazi-Fascist reprisal – that is, a political victim whose death contributed to the struggle for liberation, or who had died by some other less significant means. In such cases, APB's provincial officer asked communal sindaci to confirm whether a particular individual was a civilian victim of a Nazi-Fascist reprisal (had been massacred by Nazi-Fascists) – and if possible to describe more specifically how he or she had died. The request was always an 'urgent' one, given that the victim's family could not receive its *premio* without advance recognition by the political victims committee. Arezzo's communal sindaci then affirmed to the provincial APB office that a particular person really was a 'political victim' – giving dates and details of his or her slaughter by Nazi-Fascists during a reprisal (or what the village, commune, and authorities termed a reprisal).[24] Those unfortunate victims of war who had died stepping on a landmine planted by retreating German troops, who had been killed by Allied bombs, or who had been struck on the road by a speeding German or Allied truck were not considered political victims fallen in the struggle for liberation, and their families were not eligible to the 20,000 lire *premio*, although they were just as dead from war-related events.

The much anticipated *premio* was slow in coming, however. Bucine's sindaco wrote to both the prefect and to the National Committee for Political Victims in Rome on May 13, 1946, to ask why the widowed families of San Pancrazio had not yet received the money promised by the minister of APB back in January. The committee had stopped providing its monthly subsidies that January in anticipation of the *premio*, and so the women now had no income at all. The sindaco wrote again ten days later, setting forth in the strongest language the suffering of the widows and orphans of that village. He also appealed to ECA to provide some support in the way of monthly subsidies – as it had done for the widows of Civitella – while the widows continued to await their *premio*.[25] By September 1946, however, the money still had not arrived. Despite repeated telegrams to the ministry in Rome, and notwithstanding the many reminders given by Arezzo's representatives in Rome, and even an insistent delegation of Arezzo's widows directly to the APB minister in Rome, neighbouring provinces had received their *premi* from the financially-strapped state, but Arezzo for some reason had not.[26]

Indemnities

Many more civilians suffered from the war in less tragic ways than having been incarcerated for years or having had family members massacred. Citizens who had suffered property loss or damage as a result of bombing campaigns were to be the beneficiaries of a bombing indemnity (*indennità di bombardamento*) that was explicitly restitutive – and less loftily phrased than the Award of National Solidarity. The Fascist Republic originally had established an indemnity in November 1943 to compensate for enemy (Allied) bomb destruction.[27] Italy's post-Fascist treasury minister continued and expanded indemnity coverage for losses caused by additional 'war offensives' for communes where such indemnities were needed after June 1944 – the month of so much destruction in Arezzo and central Italy.[28]

The state's intention to provide restitution was clearly present in that indemnity, but the money was no more forthcoming than was the National Solidarity *Premio* for Arezzo's widows. Although Aretine communes were no longer in the battle lines after the summer of 1944, the war continued for nine more months, the interim government continued in disarray, and very few citizens of the province received any monetary compensation for property damage suffered. At the end of the war, at the same time the APB ministry was founded in the summer of 1945, a separate office of undersecretary of state for war damages (il Sottosecretario di Stato per i Danni di Guerra) was instituted within the Treasury Ministry to handle such claims.

To obtain the indemnity for war-caused damage to real property, chattels, or other possessions, the head of a family submitted a form declaration to the Danni di Guerra provincial office. Arezzo's office 'left much to desire,' however.[29] Of the 56,882 claims for damage compensation and the additional 29,444 claims limited to the loss of household furnishings that had been submitted in the province from 1943 until a year after the war, only 1834 had been paid by June 30, 1946. The pace quickened a bit after that, but only an additional 2291 accounts had been paid between August 1, 1946 and January 31, 1947, leaving more than 82,000 still not reimbursed almost two years after the end of the war.[30]

Anyone who could procure from their communal sindaco a 'certificate of indigence on account of war damage' was to receive priority in payment. The willingness of sindaci to certify their fellow citizens' indigence in hopes of speeding up the indemnity process gave rise to the prefect's order that such certificates should be granted only to the 'really and truly indigent' – to those in greater need than the 'current general state of need common to the great mass of citizenry.'[31] Even armed with their certificates of indigence on account of war damage, however, the residents of Civitella, San Pancrazio, Castelnuovo, Pieve Santo Stefano, and other ruined villages continued seeking payment and precedence for payment to the end of 1948 and beyond.

From the perspective of sixty-plus years later, the issue is not whether all widows and war victims promptly received the subsidies, *premi*, and indemnities formulated for them and promised to them. The historical institutional point is the very process: the interim postwar state – itself unstable, in flux, inadequately financed, and divided – considered, constructed, and set out increasingly inclusive programs designed to provide restitution, reparations, and rewards for its citizens, rather than simple *ad hoc* relief and assistance. The contemporary point important to victims like the widows of the massacred villages of Arezzo, of course, was very much whether and when they were ever going to see the money the state promised them.

The activities of what I call the 'ministries of aftermath' – the APB, undersecretary for war damages, secretary for war pensions, and so on – exemplify how Italy's postwar government was and would be shaped by the war's effects on society for many years to come. In a variety of ways, the state purposefully acknowledged that its citizens had suffered and sacrificed, and thereby the state also contributed to a shared postwar sentiment and victim identity. Without payment behind that acknowledgment, however, the state did little to instil confidence in its citizens that their government really could solve their postwar problems.

Pensions

The state pension of war was the next, and arguably ultimate level of state restorative assistance or reparative justice. Pensions resembled subsidies, *premi*, and indemnities in that they were intended to help those whom the war had victimized, but pensions undertook payment longer-lasting and more personal than did a temporary subsidy to tide over ex-confinees as they returned to civil life, an indemnity for property damage, or a substantial one-time award from the state in hopes of generating national unity from a shared meaning of partisan contribution and civilian sacrifice. The postwar war pension looked to the future and took into account how the war had permanently changed lives; it also became a true right or entitlement.

War pensions (*pensioni di guerra*) had gone to veterans or their surviving families after the Libyan campaign, after World War I, and after the war in Ethiopia.[32] In this most recent postwar, they went to families of war dead and to those seriously wounded by war – whether the war wounded and dead were soldier or civilian. Injured or disabled partisans were given war pensions, and APB extended war pensions to 'injured civilians' at the end of 1945. Families of civilians killed by Nazi-Fascists in reprisals, who earlier had received a monthly subsidy from the National Committee for Political Victims and then the *premio* of National Solidarity, also were entitled to war pensions – as were families of those dead from war-related accidents or causes which lacked even a remote 'political' connection.[33] Thus, the men, women, and children maimed or the families of those killed by exploding German landmines or by Allied bombs were granted war pensions, even though they had not been eligible for the Award of National Solidarity.[34]

By the end of 1946, the widows and widowers of Civitella, San Pancrazio, and Castelnuovo were included in war pension provisions through the loss of their civilian husbands or wives, with benefits dating back to the day after the massacres at their respective villages.[35] As with other slow starting (or slow paying) forms of state aid, some widows who were eligible for pensions and who had applied for them, still had received nothing by 1948.[36] The amount of a pension logically was indexed to the seriousness of an injury, the loss of a family breadwinner, or the number of minor children in a family; it did not depend on or vary with need.[37] And, whereas subsidies were not cumulative when a victim fell within more than one category of assistance eligibility, a woman whose husband had been massacred by the Germans and who herself had been injured from a war-related cause was entitled to two war pensions from the state: one through her dead spouse and one on her own account. A widow who remarried lost the pension received on account of her husband's death, but their orphaned children did not.[38]

Death of a husband by Nazi-Fascist reprisal or one's own injury from an exploding landmine was fairly easy to substantiate, because the cause of death or injury could be specifically located in time and place. For something less physically apparent or less directly derived from a precise event, however, proving a 'war-caused injury or illness' could be a long, difficult, and sometimes traumatic matter for a male or female civilian. After the Germans killed her husband and destroyed her home in Castelnuovo dei Sabbioni on July 4, 1944, Signora Giorgina Polverini and her two young sons fled into the nearby woods, where she remained until after the liberation of the village. While living outdoors, Signora Polverini contracted bronchitis, which went untreated as no medicine or medical treatment was available when she returned home to the ruins of Castelnuovo. She became affected with pleurisy in 1945, and then contracted tuberculosis in September 1948, which sent her to a sanatorium in Arezzo in October of 1948 and again after a relapse in 1950.[39]

Although she received a war pension because her husband had been massacred by the Germans, Signora Polverini originally was refused a separate war pension for her own illness. The reason for the denial was state obstinacy, not because she already received one pension after her husband's death and so could not receive another. In Signora Polverini's case, the front lines had passed Castelnuovo by August 1944, whereas her pleurisy did not arise until 1945, and tuberculosis did not strike until 1948. In appealing the denial, she called a *carabiniere* officer to give an account of the massacre of her husband and the other village men, the destruction of the village, and the flight of the women and children to the woods until the passage of the front and the arrival of Allied troops. The antitubercular consortium of Arezzo also supplied a declaration asserting that the September 1948 and 1950 bouts of tuberculosis had been caused by the episode of pleurisy suffered in 1945.

Not until more than a decade after her last attack of tuberculosis in 1950, however, did the state (through the court of accounts) finally concede that her years of debilitating lung ailments were 'caused by the war.'[40] The 1961 court decision recalled the suffering undergone during the summer of 1944:

On July 4, 1944, German soldiers passing through the area seized Signor Giuseppe Polverini (husband of the claimant), shooting him a short time later together with other hostages in the main piazza of the village. That same day, her house was occupied by German troops and she was forced to flee into the nearby woods, from which she was able to return at the end of August 1944, after the Allies liberated the village. During her stay in the woods, Signora Polverini contracted bronchitis, that she could not treat adequately whether from lack of medicines, or the pain from the tragic death of her husband, or from having to assist her two sons, the one nine years old and the other eleven.[41]

Signora Polverini's own postwar illness, according to the court, was the product of the German reprisal.

Status and Solidarity

Signora Polverini, like hundreds of women in Castelnuovo, Civitella, San Pancrazio, and other massacred villages were widows. More precisely, their position was that of war widows; even more precisely, however, they were civilian war widows of victims killed during reprisal, victims who were thus political victims having fallen in the struggle for Liberation. The state's approach would extend to the victims' children as well. War orphans, like war widows, made up another traditionally recognized war-related status group, and like widows, the orphan group increased by many thousands as a result of the war. The way a child had been or-phaned also mattered for the receipt of assistance or other postwar ben-efits and consideration.[42] War-related causes of a parent's death, in general, were not enough. Communes carefully drew up lists of their war orphans for the National Association for War Orphans, just as they com-piled names of massacre victims for the National Committee for Political Victims and for a family's receipt of its solidarity *premio*.[43] The National Association for War Orphans requested communal *sindaci* to distinguish those who had a civilian parent massacred by the Germans in reprisal from the 'general orphans of war,' the latter being those children who had a soldier parent killed in battle or a civilian parent 'killed by bombs, mines, artillery, etc.'[44] One child's dead father was said to have been killed by an exploding mine, whereas his death certificate stated that he had been killed in a 'reprisal' (*rappresaglia*), and so the organization sought clarification from Bucine's *sindaco* before granting any assist-ance. The child's father had indeed been killed in a landmine explosion on July 16, 1944, at ten in the morning. The child was a war orphan, yes, but not the orphan of a political victim.

Many postwar benefits designed for orphans thus were intended only for the orphans of political victims. The restriction was, in part, an extension of the difficult postwar selection dilemma presented by limited resources and an infinite number of needy, but there was also more to it. Orphans of political victims, like the widows of political victims and like political victims themselves, had a different position from the rest of Italy's war victims in the postwar scheme. Certain orphanages, for example, were available only to orphans of political victims. In November 1944, ONMI renamed its Rome Asilo Materno, Monterotondo, as 'Figli d'Italia,' turning it into a shelter or orphanage for both sexes, but only the orphans of fallen partisans, of those killed in Nazi-Fascist reprisals, or of other political victims were eligible for admission.[45] The term 'political orphan,' unlike political victim, never became part of the postwar vocabulary, but such status dictated future support even for orphaned children.

Requests for admission into the Rome orphanage had to be presented to ONMI through the National Committee for Political Victims, the National Partisans Association of Italy (ANPI), or directly by the orphan's family, and supported by a number of documents including a declaration from a 'competent authority' on the family's economic condition.[46] Only one orphan per family could be admitted, though in exceptional cases ONMI might admit two. In 'extremely pitiful cases,' children who were not orphaned of a parent – but who had a surviving political victim parent – might also be admitted.

Several children from San Pancrazio went to ONMI's 'political victim' Monterotondo orphanage in Rome.[47] The National Committee for Political Victims had acted as intermediary for one widowed mother's request that her child be placed there, while in many cases, the sindaco wrote on behalf of the mothers and orphans.[48] One widow, whose husband had not been killed by the Germans during the June 29 massacre in that village but who had died on the Montenegrin front, was left with the care of her three children and her elderly in-laws. She asked that her two older sons (ages six and eight) be accepted at Monterotondo, pleading, '[g]iven our distance from populated centres and lack of financial means, I look with pain upon my sons growing up in bleakest misery and ignorance.' Even though their father had not been a political victim (or a reprisal victim), the children were nevertheless in their own way 'sorely affected by the war and deprived of a father's aid,' their mother beseeched, implying that her orphaned children suffered equally with those whose fathers had been massacred.[49]

Why were reprisal (or massacre) victims said to be political victims having fallen in the struggle for liberation? And why were their widows and orphaned children considered and treated differently from other war-made widows and orphans? The answers have to do with partisans, and with unity and reconciliation. Partisans were neither military veterans nor civilian victims; in many instances, they came to rank higher than either in the postwar world. Disarmed by the Allies, shut out of a direct role in national postwar politics, and occupying a sometimes ambiguous position in local society after the war, partisans were nevertheless outspoken, well represented, and frequently recognized by the state.

During the summer of 1945, as seen, the government awarded a 5000 lire 'wounded partisan bonus' or 'award' (the *premi partigiani feriti*) and, a year later, the *Premio* of National Solidarity to partisans wounded or families of those killed in the struggle for liberation.[50] Along with these acknowledgments of partisan contributions, the state took further steps to organize and formalize its position towards partisans and to determine partisans' place within the postwar state among those who had suffered and sacrificed for the nation. An August 21, 1945, decree mandated the institution of regional commissions to examine the qualifications of those claiming partisan status, and to consider proposed rewards or compensation for partisans' 'military valour.'[51] The commissions created an extremely detailed system, and one under which recognition was definitely worthwhile to obtain.

According to the system of qualifications, one could be recognized as a 'partisan combatant' (so long as he had served at least three months or provided noteworthy help to a partisan formation), a 'fallen partisan,' or a 'patriot,' and the effect of recognition as a '*partigiano combattente*' was significant and rewarding.[52] In the postwar scheme, *partigiani combattenti* were at least the postwar equals of military volunteers who had served in a more organized military capacity 'in the war of liberation engaged in a zone of operations in actions of war.'[53] That is, those recognized as *partigiani combattenti* were entitled to the same economic and other government benefits as soldiers who had enlisted in the Italian army after September 8, 1943, and served in a combat theatre. Thus, qualified partisans were entitled to a raft of benefits retroactive to the beginning of their partisan service. On a cash basis, they received the military stipend or military salary, the military family allowance, additional amounts for family or cost-of-living increases, a Christmas bonus for 1944, and a *premio di Liberazione.*[54] Scholarships or places in job training programs also were available to partisans as to military *reduci* (veterans, prisoners of war and military internees) but were not extended to civilian victims of war (or their orphans).[55] Partisans, along with military veterans, received statutory, mandatory priority in hiring for public sector jobs.[56]

The legislation more recently proposed (and opposed) in Italy to extend military combatant status to those Fascist Republicans who fought for Mussolini's Republic of Salò would also extend the same military combatant and partisan combatant benefits – even though they had, in essence and in fact, fought against those military and partisan combatants, as well as against Italian civilians. Definitely not intended as a tardy gesture of reconciliation or national unity, the proposed law is considered a contemporary and very politicized revision of Fascism, the war, Republican Fascism, and Liberation.

While raising difficult questions about the meaning of patriotism *versus* the value of recognizing when a cause is obviously lost, rewarding Republican Fascist combatants is also a slap in the face both to partisans (part of the point, of course) and to military veterans who fought with the Allies after September 8, 1943. Equating Salò soldiers and militiamen with the partisans and soldiers who fought for the liberation of Italy from Nazi-Fascism is meant, at least in part, to denigrate the partisan contribution, because it equates them not only for potential state benefits (many of whose recipients will not live much longer to collect them), but also gives them a belated but equal part in the history, representation, and memory of that period. It certainly complicates – and is intended to do so – any shared postwar national identity of anti-Fascism and Resistance.

Status (by which I mean being part of a recognized group) meant a great deal in the official postwar arrangement of restitution, rewards, and reparations. Even so, definitions were conveniently flexible then (as they seem to be again in the case of Salò soldiers), either because victims – political and otherwise – and the causes of victimhood were so plentiful, or because postwar national unity and solidarity were rapidly proving to be elusive goals once the struggle for Liberation was completed. One met the qualification of 'fallen partisan' having 'fallen in the struggle for liberation' if he: 1) died during partisan actions, from wounds suffered during partisan action, or from illness contracted in partisan service; 2) was assassinated by Nazi-Fascists as a political prisoner, a hostage, or because of a reprisal; 3) was a political prisoner who died from maltreatment suffered in prison or in a concentration camp.[57]

Thus, the men massacred or assassinated at Civitella, San Pancrazio, and Cavriglia (and presumably the women and children massacred at Cornia) also were partisans fallen in the struggle for liberation – despite the fact they had not joined the partisans (or had chosen not to join the partisans). Giuseppe Polverini, a mineworker, a husband, and father of two young sons, was shot and burned in the July 4, 1944, massacre at Castelnuovo. He had been 'killed in reprisal' (though reprisal for exactly what was not critical) and thus was a political victim fallen in the struggle for liberation under the state's definition, but he had never been a partisan. In 1946, however, Signor Polverini's widow and orphaned sons received an unsolicited state certificate recognizing him as a partisan.

Why did the postwar government term him a partisan, and what was its purpose in conflating – or uniting – him and other massacre victims with partisans as having fallen together in the struggle for liberation? How had their deaths together or separately furthered the struggle for liberation, and why were the Polverinis and the many other families who had the awful misfortune to live (and die) in villages where massacres took place political victims? Massacre victims, in the end, were no different from apolitical civilian victims who stepped on a landmine or were killed by Allied bombs, and so why not conflate civilian massacre victims with victims of bombing, landmines, or 'other causes of war'? Their families' losses and suffering was neither greater nor less. Were they not all victims together in the postwar – especially if the state's purpose was inclusiveness, unity, and national solidarity?

The postwar government's transparent and nobler intention was to acknowledge its citizens' sacrifices and suffering, to recognize that all had suffered, to help restore and make them whole, to help make up for the war and the past regime – not just to help fill their postwar needs. If that were the case, however, why were all sacrifices not equal? If suffering and sacrifice had contributed to the struggle for liberation, then all Italians (except some Republican Fascists, Mussolini, and the king) had suffered and sacrificed and thus all had participated in the struggle for liberation. All had experienced food rationing and shortages, the call and recall to arms of family members, terrifying and devastating bombing campaigns, the death of a soldier-family member or his absence as a POW, the deportation of civilians, the passage of the front, property damage or total loss: all had experienced at least some of the hardships of war. Why did the state decide that some suffering and sacrifices were worth more than others – or, more accurately, that some sacrifices were more meaningful to post-Fascist, postwar Italy?

Some sacrifices were of a different nature from others, of course. Those who had been arrested, imprisoned, or otherwise persecuted under the Fascist regime, because of anti-Fascist activities or beliefs, were political victims in the obvious sense that their anti-Fascist politics, or their clash with Fascist politics, had caused their suffering. Partisans, fallen or injured, or who had sacrificed months from their civil lives living under conditions of hardship to fight German occupation and the tail end of Fascism could also be considered political victims. Whether motivated by political beliefs, duty, love of country, avoidance of the Fascist Republican draft, a bit of excitement, or by the intention of contributing to postwar social and political change, partisans were necessarily in opposition to Nazi-Fascism.

To answer the question of what made the massacre victims political victims (or the equivalent of partisans) requires going back to the earlier question of whose politics they were victim. Their own politics did not make them victims. In their postwar statements to Allied investigators, the recent widows emphasized the 'political innocence' of their murdered men. Alduina Menchetti's husband had been seized by the Germans and murdered in Civitella the morning of June 29, 1944. She told British military investigators a few months later: 'My husband Menchetti Torquato, aged 28 years, had never been a partisan and had never taken any part in any of their actions. Neither was he interested in politics nor did he belong to any political party. He was a Fascist until the collapse of Mussolini, like everyone else. He had to belong to this party or starve but that was the only time in his life that he belonged to any political party.'[58] Gina Magini said the same. 'My husband and cousin had never been partisans and had never helped them. They were not interested in politics of any kind. Previously they had been Fascists as everyone had to be or starve but they never even took this seriously.'[59] The widows, the sisters, the mothers said the same: the murdered civilians were innocent of partisan activity. Most were innocent of politics – Fascist or anti-Fascist. They were innocent of wanting the war. They may have been Fascists before the fall of Mussolini (like everyone else), but that was all.

The massacre victims could not be singled out as victims of Nazi or German politics, because every Italian who felt the brunt of the war after September 8 was a victim of German military occupation and, thereby, Nazi politics in some sense. And if, as the postwar government and many Italians wanted to call it, Italy's entry into the war – and everything that followed from that enormous misstep – had been the fault of one man, and that one man had been the head of the Fascist regime, then everyone in Italy was also a political victim of Fascism. The explanation of their political victimhood, however, is the civil war within the larger war, as recognized by the postwar government. Civilian victims killed in reprisal for partisan activity were victims of that smaller, very political war of Italian against Italian, while in a parallel way those killed by landmines, bombs, or shrapnel were victims of the larger, international war that did not hold equal meaning for Italy.

In *Uomini e no* (*Men and Not Men*), the important first partisan and political novel to be published in postwar Italy, Elio Vittorini gave a particular meaning to massacred civilian victims.[60] In the novel, forty 'innocent civilians' are to be selected and shot in retaliation for the killing of four Germans. "'I am wondering what I would think if I were one of them,'" muses 'En 2,' the nameless-nicknamed urban partisan (or *gappista*) in Milan. "'We don't have the right to ask,'" says another. "'But,'" En 2 persists, "'if I were one of them? If I were one of the forty who will be shot tomorrow morning? What would I think of being shot along with thirty-nine others for four bastards cut down by the patriots?'"[61] And then comes one of the most problematic lines, not only in Vittorini's novel, but also as a central strand of the intended postwar appraisal of the partisan resistance and the necessity of its human consequences. Grey Moustache, another member of the urban partisan band jumps to his feet and asks indignantly, "'[a]re you saying it's not worth sacrificing ten of our people every time we get one of the enemy?'"[62]

With that, was Vittorini saying it was worth it? What about when the ratio of sacrifice was 200 to one, as at Civitella and at San Pancrazio? Grey Moustache goes on to emphasize that the partisans would have laid down their lives from the very inception of Fascism – believing 'it was worth the blood of a thousand of us' – had they been able to strike against the regime some twenty years earlier. For Grey Moustache, and for En 2 as well, resistance – meaning the partisan, anti-Fascist, anti-Nazi Resistance (with a capital 'R') – was more than just a way of driving the Germans out of Italy and definitively terminating the years of the Fascist regime. Resistance was also a struggle for the renewal – or redemption – of Italy. Such redemption would not and could not take place through partisan actions alone, but would come with the spilled blood and the deaths of civilians slaughtered in reprisal. It would come through civilian – human – sacrifice.

A bit later in the novel, Berta sees the corpses of some of those sacrificed (or massacred) on the streets of Milan in retaliation for the partisan killings: the two fifteen year old boys, the little girl, the two women, the old man with the white beard, 'the dead in the sunshine on one sidewalk, the dead in the shade on another sidewalk, then the dead on the Corso, the dead at the foot of the monument,' and so on.[63] Though the scene is a horrific one, and Berta and the other passers-by ask each other 'why,' the answer and the explanation are quite clear and straightforward. They – the dead – died for 'us' (and not only for the organized, anti-Fascist partisan 'us'). They died for 'the liberation of each of us' – even for those who did not take part in the fight. The dead themselves speak and tell Berta that they died for her – even for her – to make her free and to establish true human relationships between human beings.[64] The dead victims are not angry or bitter at having been sacrificed. They 'understand everything.' They seem resigned, even honoured, awfully enough, to have been slaughtered for Berta and all the others – including for those who have not participated in the fight. Moved by the sight of the bodies, Berta herself is both 'exalted and dismayed' that so many people, innocent people unknown to her, have been sacrificed for her.[65] She *is* grateful.

Vittorini crafted an optimistic and hopeful meaning for the massacre, with an obvious reference to the sacrifice of Christ and to rebirth. In the novel, innocent beings are necessarily sacrificed for the salvation and redemption of the larger society. Unlike real life, neither the dead nor the living blame the partisans for their choices or their methods in trying to kill the Germans (and Fascist Republicans) – choices that postwar Italians believed made massacres into reprisals. Massacres and civilian victims were an indispensable part of the redemption process that would end Fascism and German occupation, and make for the beginnings of a better, more humane postwar Italy and postwar world. In postwar literature, the outcome of the war is already known, of course, and the dead can rationalize. The reasons and meaning they tell the fictional living can be carefully phrased.

All of this was what made civilian massacre victims political victims – and why it did not truly matter if German massacres really were specific reprisals. This conclusion has not strayed so far, as it appears, from the beginning of the chapter and the postwar state's 'difficult tasks of reparative justice.' The state, like Vittorini, wanted to make the Resistance and Liberation inclusive, rather than exclusive and divisive. A shared and unchanging memory of the Resistance would prevent on a national scale the 'divided memory' Giovanni Contini located in Civitella.[66] There was a need to restore the nation and repair the social fabric after war and after Fascism, processes that would not succeed by focusing on the recent civil war and the many things that had divided Italy and Italians during the preceding decades. Concentrating instead on Italy's sacrifices and suffering would be more effective in doing so.

PART THREE

The Return to Civil Life

7 Restoring the Community

[Y]ou should present lists of the names of prisoners, who because of their previous jobs are needed for the revival of civil life in Italy.

Directive to prefects

We are convinced that the authorities and the law will do their duty so that no guilty person will remain unpunished.

La Nazione, Cronaca di Arezzo, no. 118, May 18, 1945.

Dancing … is like a mania that has possessed young people and adults after the end of the war. The moral danger is great.

Don Gino Ciabattini, parish diary for
Castelnuovo dei Sabbioni, August 12, 1945.

The Aretines (like the rest of Italians) lived through the war and its aftermath not only as individuals, but also as members of their communities, and as part of a larger nation victimized by war; that is, the experience of war was both unique and common. At the end of December 1945, Arezzo's prefect reported to the Ministry of the Interior that, among the citizens of the province, an 'individual and collective sense of loss' flowed from their 'shared suffering,' and from which the people found it 'hard to recover.'

[The population] suffers from the sorrows and the grave sacrifices endured first during the period of the war, then from Nazi-Fascist oppression, and finally from the passage of the front. This became embodied in the loss of so many lives through aerial bombardments, artillery battles, reprisals at the hands of Nazi-Fascists, mine explosions, etc.; in the destruction of lines of communication, railways, and roads; in the destruction and damage of many buildings, and even entire villages and towns; in the theft of furniture, linens, farm equipment, seeds, farm animals, etc.[1]

The prefect was not mistaken. In communities and in a society where little appeared to have changed for generations, life so rapidly had become unstable and unpredictable.

The personal and communal consciousness of loss that so pervaded the atmosphere of postwar life, and from which citizens found it difficult to recover, begot a natural aspiration to return to life as it had been before the suffering and destruction of war. That wish for restoration coexisted – sometimes harmoniously, sometimes in conflict – with desires to make a new beginning and change certain aspects of society, but many articulated a longing for order, reconstruction, and rebirth explicitly in terms of a 'return to civil life' and a 'return to normal life.' The return involved getting on with life, which for many meant getting on with life as it had been before war and destruction – but which no longer meant being Fascist. One obstacle to societal reconstruction then was what to do about former Fascists and about Fascism, and that was a postwar problem solved with surprising ease.

The connection between the return to civil life and the reconstruction of society was clear, however. Central Italians equated the return to normal civil life with the reconstruction of society and of Italy. Italy and society would be reborn only when civil life had been restored; but conversely, civil life could not revive until societal (and physical) reconstruction was underway. The return to civil life had symbolic, tangible, and some disputed meanings that influenced the conduct of daily life after the war. The ministries in Rome also spoke of a return to civil life, but their return involved creating national unity and instituting larger scale, nationwide programs to rebuild the country and to compensate victims of Fascism and war. The return to civil life for individuals and communities entailed a more finely detailed process.

Returnees

The war had uprooted so many from their families and their communities that a most literal aspect of the return to civil life meant the physical return of individuals to home, farms, villages, and cities. Three displaced Italians wrote in imperfect, though moving English, to the

ACC provincial commissioner of Arezzo in October 1944 for permission to return to Florence from Arezzo:

> The named below, with their families, were considered by fascist laws as belonging to the race of Jews and since 6 years they suffered persecutions and particularly since 8-9-43 when the Fascist Government requisitioned all their things and they were without any means to live.
>
> They were compelled (also in order to avoid the arrest) to escape from their city and to go in little localities. They lived only with those few means that they could find.
>
> After having been in numerous localities and after having suffered awfully, they are actually [currently] in Arezzo without means to live and they have not the necessariest clothing especially for Winter.
>
> In order to return to their normal life they ask you for going back to Florence where they hope to find a part of their personal clothing and where they certainly will begin again their normal activities.[2]

Those Italians articulated most poignantly the postwar longing to return home to 'normal life' and to 'begin again their normal activities.' It was a feeling widely shared.

'Returnees' brought to mind officially those absent from home because of military service.[3] Many more Italians and others were returnees in a broader sense, however.[4] June Adams and her parents, together with other British subjects or U.S. citizens interned in Italy during the war, also hoped to return to Florence, or the other Italian cities they had long considered home.[5] Young, resourceful, and without far to travel, Miss Adams made her own way from the Aretine countryside back to Florence where she quickly found work with the Allies. An elderly Italian couple, the Martellis, were not so fortunate. They too found themselves in the province of Arezzo after the passage of the front. Arezzo's bishop presented their 'truly pitiful' case to ACC Provincial Commissioner Thurburn: Signor Martelli was ill and needed to return home to Rome. They required Allied permission to travel, as well as some means of transport. They could not – as the bishop so aptly phrased it – 'take the way of the refugees': the Martellis were not able to walk from Arezzo to Rome.[6]

The trip from Arezzo to Florence or to Rome was not a particularly long or difficult one, comparatively speaking. In that war which had affected civilians as much as soldiers, and which had created human displacement on a scale never before seen, millions were taking the way of the refugees, making their way on foot across the European continent. Others had shorter distances to travel, but their dislocation and returns were often equally tragic. Arezzo's civilians had fled to the woods during the spring and summer of 1944 to escape bombing, artillery fire, and German massacres. Reflecting on the difficult situation in the commune of Cavriglia as it had been when he took office on July 25, 1944, the sindaco stated, '[i]t must be considered moreover that the population, which took refuge in the mines or in improvised shelters, returning to their villages, found their own homes in part or completely pillaged, and completely destroyed in those places [which had been] hit by the savage reprisals.'[7]

These civilian returnees recalled their homecomings most clearly – and the disappearance of what had been their normal lives. 'When we came back to our house, there was nothing there. Everything had been burnt; they had even killed our pigs,' remembered one child who returned home from the woods outside San Pancrazio, after the massacre and the passage of the front. 'We came home and there was nothing,' said another. 'Our animals were gone too, even my cat ... All we had left were two bed sheets that my mother had hidden in a sack in the woods.'[8]

A resident of Duddova, near San Pancrazio, described how she, her husband and child, and their neighbours returned from the woods to their homes on the morning of July 16, 1944, after the village was liberated. When they had fled to the woods the month before, she and her husband had managed to save a cart and a pair of oxen, which they kept with them as they sheltered from the passage of the front. In the days after liberation, her husband used the oxen and cart to assist others, 'since in those sad days all of us helped each other carry back to our homes whatever we had been compelled to bring in the woods.'[9] One fellow refugee asked for assistance in retrieving household effects he had brought into hiding. Her husband agreed, of course, but just as they began the trip home, only about a hundred metres from where they had started, a German landmine exploded. The blast destroyed the cart, killed one of the oxen and wounded the other (which died later that day). Allied soldiers transported the woman's seriously wounded husband to hospital, where he died the following day.

Her family's longed-for return home – after the commune was liberated and the war in their part of Arezzo finally ended – had turned into the most 'sorrowful occasion.' Instead of returning to normal life, now she was a widow with sole care of her nine year old son. Beyond that, husband and wife were sharecroppers, and as such she was now financially responsible for half the cost of the dead oxen and the ruined cart. Still worse, she could not manage to work their plot alone. She and her young son would go live with her brother-in-law and his wife, and in the years that followed, she would help them with the plot they share-cropped, no longer wife and mistress of her home.

In the villages that had seen their men massacred, so many widowed and orphaned families would never return to their 'normal lives' and 'normal activities.' The *fattoria* Pierangeli had been the largest employer in the village of San Pancrazio in the commune of Bucine. The *fattoria*'s foreman consequently had been one of that village's more prosperous and influential citizens. He also had been among the village men whom the Germans shot and burned in the *fattoria* cellar on June 29, 1944. His widow left San Pancrazio and found work as a maid for a family in Rome. His fatherless son went to the orphanage Monterotondo, set up for the orphans of political victims in Rome.[10] The boy's mother visited him there every Sunday, bringing with her a small bag of food he kept in the cupboard by his bed. The orphaned children of Bucine's district doctor (who also had been killed in the San Pancrazio massacre) went to live in Perugia at a state orphanage for the children of health workers.[11]

Life in an orphanage or *collegio*, separation from home and the re-maining parent (usually their mother), was the final, or ultimate trauma for some children who had lived through bombing, the violent murder of a parent, and the terrifying passage of the front. Dino Tiezzi had seen German soldiers burst into his bedroom on the morning of June 29, 1944, shooting and killing his father and oldest brother. Another broth-er had been shot escaping from the piazza in Civitella where the Germans had gathered and killed the village men. Dino himself fled to the woods with his mother, but became separated from her for several days in the fear and chaos after the massacre. He went to a *collegio* at the age of ten. Though not physically injured himself, he inexplicably lost the ability to speak for several months while there. Today the diagnosis most likely would be selective mutism brought on by trauma and unabated stress. More than fifty years later, he remembered being able to hear, but una-ble to make words come out of his mouth.[12]

The three children of Signora and Signor Cau of Gebbia, near Civitella, had last seen their parents on the morning of the June 29, 1944, massacre, when the Germans had taken them away in an armoured car. That summer, after the passage of the front and amidst persistent local rumours that the Caus had gone north with the Germans, the chil-dren and their elderly Swedish grandmother unsuccessfully tried to dis-cover their whereabouts. The Allied public safety officer was able to confirm only that the Caus had not been seen in their apartment in

Florence for the past several months. The children and their grand-mother eventually got to the Swedish embassy in Rome, after a stay in Arezzo's Displaced Persons Camp at Castiglion Fiorentino, and apparently then to Sweden. The Cau children would not learn until seven years later that the Germans had killed their parents and abandoned the bodies not far from where they had been first taken.

Other citizens of Arezzo waited and hoped for family members to return home. Almost everyone in Arezzo, it seemed, had a close relative absent on account of the war, whether a soldier or partisan, POW, political prisoner, or deportee. Those citizens deported for forced labour, or to concentration camps, or to clear the way for retreating troops, began to return home after the war ended in the spring of 1945. In the village and area around Pieve Santo Stefano, from which the Germans had deported almost the entire population of 3000, more than 1000 deportees had not yet returned by June 1945.[13] Two sisters managed to get home to Pieve Santo Stefano earlier, on December 7, 1944. Both schoolteachers, they applied for reinstatement to a school post as soon as they arrived, but were told that 'the date of application expired on October 5.' 'We have no homes, no clothing, and no means of living,' they wrote to the Allied CAO in Sansepolcro, asking for his intervention on their behalf.[14]

Every commune numbered their citizens deported, just as they counted the number of buildings destroyed and damaged, livestock stolen, and persons homeless, in their postwar assessments of war damage. The Germans had deported twelve citizens from Bucine, four from Civitella, communes where far more members had been murdered.[15] The commune of Stia, which had 126 of its citizens massacred, recorded that the Germans also had deported 171 persons, some of whom they had sent to concentration camps, others to work camps.[16]

The extent – and definition – of deportation was complicated by the civilians who voluntarily had gone to work in Germany while Italy and Germany were allied, and who found themselves working for the enemy after the September 8, 1943, armistice.[17] In addition, Italian soldiers whom the Germans had taken prisoner after September 8 had been offered the 'opportunity' to work for Germany, and those who chose not to avail themselves of that opportunity remained in prison camps. Refusal to assist the German war effort after the September 8, 1943, armistice meant a longer delay in coming home after May 5, 1945. Alcide De Gasperi, as minister of foreign affairs, expressed his hope to UNRRA mission head S.M. Keeny that the Allies might facilitate the return of Italian deportees and internees in Germany 'taking into consideration that their status of detention and the hardships suffered are due to the refusal they made in the interest of Italy and the United Nations to lend any form of collaboration to the common enemy.'[18]

From the summer of 1944, the ACC considered lists of Italian military prisoners held in Allied hands (rather than German prison camps). The lists, submitted by Italian provincial authorities, contained names of those deemed 'necessary for Italy's reconstruction' to be given precedence in repatriation. Those who might thus receive an earlier release were to include 'skilled workers of various organizations, of important agencies, banks, etc.' who 'because of their previous jobs were needed for the revival of civil life in Italy' and POWs essential to the maintenance of their families (that is, if the family had no other means of support).[19]

American Army enlistee Benedict Alper spent a year in Rome helping devise and implement the program to speed the return of 'necessary' Italian POWs to their homes. In his October 29, 1944, letter home to his wife, regarding his second day on the job, Alper wrote, '[t]he importance of this for present and postwar conditions is very great. It is all part of the business of getting people back where they came from, and I feel that no reconstruction can really begin, much less continue, until people are home. I have seen published figures that at least a million Italian prisoners are away from home.'[20] The citizens of Arezzo and the rest of Italy immediately would have recognized and agreed with Alper's connection between 'getting people back where they came from' and reconstruction. The reconstruction that could only 'really begin' once people came home (or went home) encompassed for the Aretines both physical and societal reconstruction.

In March 1945, shortly before the end of the war, Arezzo's PC Quin Smith assured the prefect that repatriation of Italians would be 'definitively an Italian question' and not one handed over to ACC. That same month, ACC's provincial finance officer for Arezzo sought the return of Felice Ricciarini 'who is a tax official urgently required for work in this Province.'[21] Arezzo's gas works, through PC Quin Smith, asked for the return of Francesco Bianchini – a *key worker* – from a POW camp in Algeria that same month.[22] Essentialness and indispensability were in the eye of the beholder, and were never really an Italian question so long as the Allies occupied the country. When one woman asked that her husband, a POW in South Africa, be sent home because the extended family was going to subdivide their small property in the commune of Laterina and she needed him to work the farm, ACC headquarters for the region of Tuscany simply returned her request. In the wife's eyes, her husband was essential to the maintenance of his family, but '[n]o useful purpose whatsoever would be served by submission to higher authority as no repatriation of Italian P's O.W., is being allowed unless such action is in direct furtherance of the Allied war effort.' It was the Allied war effort more than the reconstruction of Italy that mattered while the war continued.

Families wanted their POWs home not only so that reconstruction could begin, but also in the expectation that their return might ease desperate postwar financial situations. One woman whose husband was a POW in Germany wrote to him from their home in Poppi in March 1945 that her 'wretched' government subsidy of 20 lire a day for three people had not arrived for eight months. She had sold her uncle's shoes for nearly 3000 lire, but that had quickly been spent. 'To live today, you need a hundred lire a day, not the 20 they give me; a single egg costs 20 lire. Tell me, how am I supposed to live?'[23]

De Gasperi's 1945 Christmas radio address to Italian prisoners of war told them to 'have courage' – that their wait would not be much longer.[24] Along with that message of hope, however, he informed them of the sorry conditions to which they would return: 'you who, after so many years, cannot imagine the shape of our country – covered and devastated by a disastrous war provoked by the Fascist dictatorship.' The country had been 'sowed with ruin,' De Gasperi told the POWs. Italy's communications, transportation, and industries were paralyzed. The nation was 'pervaded by sicknesses that are the companions of war and of defeat, threatened above all by hunger that has already seized the throat, and will worsen if the Allies and especially America does not send wheat and coal.'

De Gasperi nevertheless wished to reassure both POWs and civilian internees that, despite such a precarious situation, any rumours they may have heard regarding the Italian government purposely delaying their return were false. 'Rather we have always insisted and we do insist that your return be quick and complete.' About 900,000 prisoners and internees already had returned to Italy by December 1945, and another 400,000 were 'being awaited with open arms,' he said.[25] Rumours that the government in Rome hoped to slow down the return of military and civilian prisoners, and that the authorities thus were not actively working for the prisoners' return, did circulate within Italy and among the prisoners. The government, it was widely said, feared the return of so many men when unemployment had reached catastrophic proportions and the Communist Party was busily signing up new members.[26]

Retribution

In that Christmas address to Italian prisoners of war, De Gasperi spoke of the 'disastrous war provoked by the Fascist dictatorship,' and elsewhere the bishop of Arezzo referred to the 'terrible war that no one in Italy had wanted, and that had been caused solely by one man.'[27] While guilt for Italy's participation in that disastrous war could be narrowly assigned, guilt for Fascist wrongs, especially more local ones, was a somewhat more difficult issue. Communities and the nation both recognized that the reconstruction of society and the return to civil life required the return of the prisoners, deportees, and internees whom the war had torn from their families, from their communities, and from Italy. For other citizens, either voluntarily absent or quietly at home in their own villages, postwar relations with their neighbours had a different tenor.

One citizen of San Giovanni Valdarno wrote to a friend expressing his assessment of the eventual renewal of society, '[m]any years and, above all, much good will on the part of Italians will be needed for revival. The years will pass, but for now it does not seem that good will, the spirit of sacrifice, harmony, the desire to give and to work are stronger than the desire for revenge and destruction among Italians.'[28] The immediate desire for revenge was strong in Arezzo and in other parts of Italy, just as in France and elsewhere where wartime events had split many communities and their citizens into opposing sides. Contrary to the pessimistic judgment of the writer from San Giovanni, however, revenge was a necessary part of the revival process, and the reconstruction of society also depended on what to do about, and with, former Fascists. Both official purges and some private acts of vengeance helped to reorder community relations after Fascism and the upheaval of war, and both were over quite quickly.

On March 24, 1947, the communal council for Cavriglia, in closed session, voted to relieve immediately from service one particular communal employee.[29] Giorgio Calvi had held the post of assistant secretary for Cavriglia's archive and for communal protocol. He had also previously been 'subjected' to official epuration (or purge) as well as criminally convicted by Arezzo's court of assizes, and sentenced to eight years and nine months in prison for complicity in a voluntary homicide. The homicide for which Calvi was convicted was not a recent one, however. It had taken place long before the war, even before the march on Rome and Mussolini's grasp of official power. The former communal employee had been one of the original thirty-one members of the town of Cavriglia's *fascio*. The commune's first three *fasci* had formed in the villages of

Cavriglia, Castelnuovo, and Meleto in the days immediately after the March 23, 1921, anti-Fascist uprising at the Castelnuovo mines, to which the enthusiastic new, local *squadristi* had responded, in part, by assaulting members of the farmers' and consumers' cooperative at Castelnuovo, and attacking their houses and cooperative store. One co-op member, the father of four children, was killed in a fire set by *squadristi.* Nine of the new Fascists were arrested for homicide, but soon released.[30] Now, twenty-six years later, Calvi was found guilty of participation in the crime.

Signor Calvi was not present for the council's vote or to receive a copy of their deliberation after the verdict – he 'was nowhere to be found.'[31] From wherever he had fled well before his criminal conviction, however, Calvi did manage to petition the council to reconsider his dismissal from service – a petition which the sindaco and most of the council members rejected for the following reasons: 'a) Because the crime, which so resonated in local public feeling, will inevitably matter [be of importance to the communal population], even if his appeal [from his criminal conviction] goes forward ... b) Because his absconding proves his guilt.'[32]

Community memory was long, and Calvi's Fascist crime had resonated with the public for more than twenty-five years, although no real action had been taken against him until that much later trial, conviction, and dismissal from his job.[33] Signor Calvi's Fascist guilt still mattered and was worth revisiting because, as one of that commune's earliest adherents to Fascism and its violence, he had helped create the Fascist regime on a local level and helped put an end to local citizens' post–World War I attempts to effect political and social change. More tangibly, while acting as a Fascist, he had been involved in, and arguably was responsible for, the death of another member of the community. The postwar was a time for reckoning and provided the opportunity to settle scores – including some very old ones.

Community memory may have been long in some instances, but the period of official and popular reckoning was a short one, compared to the length of the regime.[34] About a month after Marshal Badoglio's brief tenure ended and Prime Minister Bonomi's first coalition government commenced – and just after the war ended for the province of Arezzo – the most important decree for sanctions against Fascism, DLL 159, of July 27, 1944, was promulgated.[35] Then, not quite two years later, in June 1946, with the vote against the monarchy and the election for the Constituent Assembly completed, the official purge effectively ceased. The High Commission for Sanctions against Fascism had formally ended on March 31, 1946,[36] followed by Prime Minister De Gasperi's approval of justice minister and Communist Party leader Palmiro Togliatti's proposed amnesty on June 22, 1946.[37] By then, popular vengeance had also lost most of its intensity.

Although the time for official epuration and local revenge was relatively brief, both played important roles in the return to civil life. The processes took official and popular forms. Officially, DLL 159 had created the High Commission for Sanctions against Fascism and established four subcommissions to oversee different aspects of punishing Fascists. One subcommission oversaw property confiscated from the Fascist Party, and one dealt with sequestered Fascist profits. From a community viewpoint, the two more important subcommissions were those charged with prosecuting Fascists and with purging local Fascists from government and public employment. In a country where Fascism had been in place for more than twenty years and had touched nearly every aspect of society and public life, deciding which Fascists should be purged and punished was not an easy task.

With the passage of the front, the arrival of the Allies, and the formation of new communal councils in the summer of 1944, many Aretine communes summarily fired Fascists from public employment without evaluating specific cases until several months or even a year or more later.[38] Alternatively, some communal or state employees were not terminated immediately, but had their political pasts reviewed first. In the spring of 1945, just before the end of the war in the north, the provincial delegate of the high commission directed every commune, public entity, and parastatal organization to gather and consider information on Fascist Party membership and Fascist activities of each employee – whether previously fired or not.[39]

Questions were designed to elicit the length and closeness of an employee's relationship to Fascism.[40] Qualifications which years earlier might have been claimed (whether truthfully or not) to obtain a job, higher salary, or other benefits, now returned to the detriment of those who had claimed them. Presence in Milan's Piazza San Sepolcro on March 23, 1919, for Fascism's first meeting, holding the qualification of *squadrista*, early membership in the party, participation in the 1922 march on Rome – all were significant, but by themselves not enough to bring sanctions. More seriously, had an employee benefited financially from membership in the party, or held high office in the party? Most critical, however, was membership in the Fascist Republican Party, having sworn the oath of loyalty to the RSI after September 1943, or having aided the Germans.

Communal archives house completed sworn declarations from all communal and public employees – from communal secretaries, to assistant typists, to schoolteachers and district doctors, to the men and women who swept the streets – in regard to their Fascist pasts. Cavriglia's CLN, as requested by the sindaco, drew up lists of those in the commune to be included within categories of *Repubblicani, squadristi, antemarcia e marcia su Roma, sciarpa littorio,* and *gerarchi.* The town of Cavriglia counted at least fifty-eight of its citizens (not necessarily all public employees) within those categories, while the commune overall listed sixty-seven public employees, including several women, potentially compromised by such qualifications.[41] Some communal employees were dismissed, but retained rights to their pensions. Others were dismissed with the proviso that 'their compatibility to serve again in the public administration [was] acknowledged.'[42] Real penalties or permanent dismissal from employment were the rare exception, not the rule.

Purge commissions frequently decided as they did for one public employee of the commune of Civitella on February 28, 1946: 'Taking into account that [Signor A.], although enrolled [in the Fascist Party] before the march [on Rome], never displayed serious fascist factionalism, but in fact maintained a good moral and political attitude – it is decided that no sanctions be applied except the obligation to reimburse the Administration for every economic advantage obtained on the strength of his fascist title.'[43] Thus, one could have been an early adherent to the party, perhaps even have benefited financially from party membership or position, but nevertheless have exhibited good moral and political behaviour (or attitude) – so long as he or she had not engaged in 'serious Fascist factionalism.' The term was key, but what constituted 'serious Fascist factionalism' was not defined on a national, official level. It generally meant, interpreted locally, as having engaged in Fascist violence or otherwise having shown a commitment to Fascism that caused serious detriment to the community or to its citizens, as had Signor Calvi in 1921.

The criteria for sanctions were too vague to provide strict guidance for purge commissions, but their very vagueness allowed for flexibility and made them workable on a local level. Vague standards meant that those facing purge or other punishment could be considered as individuals, rather than in strict accordance with the Fascist Party labels they bore. Individual actions and extenuating circumstances were therefore viewed in light of community experience and local opinion, rather than by firm national norms which might have required, for example, that all who had marched on Rome (or once had claimed to) be fired from their jobs.

When the provincial delegation of the high commission considered the case of Carlo Luzzano, a communal employee for Civitella and a former Fascist, the sindaco and the local CLN each presented very different pictures of the man. The delegation relied, therefore, on the *carabinieri* investigation and lengthy report.[44] The investigating officer had discovered that Luzzano exhibited good moral and political conduct, and had no criminal record. He had joined the 'now-suppressed' Fascist Party on August 22, 1922, but had never joined the Republican Fascist Party. Neither had he ever engaged in 'harmful political activity' towards persons or property, either before or after September 8, 1943. Perhaps equally importantly, he was 'a person endowed with scant initiative or authority.' He had a wife and three unmarried daughters – and it was said publicly that 'even at home, everyone gave orders but him.' He came from a well-off family that had been 'reduced to poverty' through his own bad financial administration and that of his dead father. It was not Luzzano, but his older brother who had gone so far with his commitment to Fascism as to follow the German troops in their northward retreat. In contrast to hen-pecked Carlo, the brother remained 'an ardent Nazi-Fascist,' and had not yet returned to the area.

The *carabinieri*, one could see, believed that Luzzano deserved derision or sympathy more so than epuration, and Arezzo's provincial high commission concluded, 'on the basis of information received,' that he should receive only a sanction of censure.[45] Signor Luzzano probably never saw the report painting him as a fairly ridiculous character rather than a serious Fascist factionalist. He saw only the commission's censure – which he felt was too harsh. In his petition for reconsideration, he emphasized 'yet again' that he had been only an ordinary or 'simple fascist' (*sempre semplice fascista*). Why then had he received such punishment?[46]

Time and again, those subject to purging insisted that they had done nothing more – and been nothing more – than had their fellow citizens: they had always been just ordinary Fascists. So many neighbours and fellow citizens had been 'mere Fascists' or 'simple Fascists' including, like many others, those massacred by the Nazi-Fascists, but their Fascism counted for little. As Gina Magini said of her husband and cousin, both killed at Civitella on June 29, 1944: 'They were not interested in politics of any kind. Previously they had been Fascists as everyone had to be or starve, but they never even took this seriously.'[47] On July 25, 1943, when the king removed Mussolini from power, and again at the September 8 armistice, everyone who had once been a 'mere Fascist' (like everyone else) received an opportunity to renounce Mussolini and Fascism, and most did so.[48]

Alba Bonichi of Civitella spoke for many when she described her father's situation to Allied investigators after the June 1944 massacre. 'My father was not a Partisan and he had never assisted them in any way. He was not interested in politics or any political party. He had been a Fascist and was in the Italian Army until September '43, but after the collapse of Mussolini he had not bothered about anything Fascist.'[49] Alduina Menchetti's husband, also murdered by the Germans at Civitella, also had been 'a Fascist until the collapse of Mussolini, like everyone else.'[50] As expressed in retrospect, almost everyone had been Fascist, but almost no one – apparently – had ever taken Fascism seriously. In a nation where so many had been Fascist for so long – if only 'merely' so – they were reluctant to condemn their neighbours for having been the same.

The bright line test dividing 'bad' Fascists from a wide spectrum of 'simple Fascists,' 'mere Fascists,' and 'ordinary Fascists' was loyalty to the Fascist Social Republic. Those who, unlike everyone else, continued to 'bother about' Fascism and took it seriously enough to adhere to Mussolini's Fascist Republic after September 1943 now made distinct targets once the front had passed. In August of 1944, one distraught woman wrote to the prefect for news of her husband whom local authorities had arrested the previous month. Since then, she had heard nothing of him or from him. 'He was a fascist and a *squadrista*. I don't ask that he not be judged and eventually punished; I ask only that it be done fairly. Others in this place were fascists and *squadristi* like him; they did things he didn't do, and yet today they are peacefully with their families where no one has harassed them.'[51] The husband had been a Fascist and a *squadrista* – as had others. Unlike them, however, he had sworn loyalty to the Fascist Republic at the end of 1943. He also had 'collaborated assiduously' with the Germans, and acted as 'an informer for the Nazi-Fascist SS.' Thus, his situation differed distinctly from the many other former Fascists who had stopped 'bothering' about Fascism in 1943 and were now at home 'peacefully with their families.'[52]

Another family also had adhered to the Fascist Republic. On August 13 and 14, 1944, partisans forced their way into the family's home, sheared the daughter's hair, and arrested the father and two teenaged sons. The father and sons were incarcerated at a local military barracks previously occupied by German troops, where they were killed when a German time bomb went off on August 18. The sindaco then requisitioned the family's printing shop – not because of the family's Fascist Republican leanings, so the sindaco asserted, but because two women (mother and daughter) could not run the business alone. The daughter neither accepted nor believed the sindaco's explanation. Rather, 'it was all political,' she was certain. She countered that her family had joined the Republican Party from the 'pure spirit of Patriotism and not for Favouritism to the Germans nor hostility to the Allied Government.' She also argued – equally unsuccessfully – that a person's political past should be forgotten after death, and insisted that she and her mother were perfectly capable of running their small printing plant. Instead, she complained, the sindaco had employed three workers to take over the shop – including one of the very same 'Partisan Communists' who had arrested her father and brothers and who was now earning 50 lire a day 'while spending his work hours in idleness.'[53]

It was not 'all political' (or forgettable) after the war; it was personal as well. In general, prewar and wartime relations with one's fellow villagers most often served as an indicator of public willingness to overlook – or not – a less than sympathetic political history that included support for the RSI. Relations with the German occupiers also carried weight. As in France and elsewhere the Germans occupied, the charge of collaborationism was a heavy one right after the war. In Italy, Fascism had been the norm for twenty years, but in places like Arezzo, where the Germans had destroyed entire villages and massacred civilians, having been a collaborator was infinitely worse than having been 'a mere Fascist' until 1943.

Allegiance to the Republic of Salò sometimes merged into accusations of collaborating with the Germans. The claim – as advanced by the printer's daughter – that one might have adhered to the RSI out of innocent, misguided, or pure patriotism, rather than from a wish to see one's fellow citizens suffer, really was a hard one to make after the war. The director of the local Fascist Republican newspaper *Giovinezza Repubblicana* was charged with the crime of having collaborated with the 'German invader' after September 8, because he had published inflammatory claims such as 'the renegades [partisans] are worse than the enemy and should be treated without pity and without mercy.' He had used propaganda, the charge read, to 'incite the massacres of citizens and patriots.'[54] One woman faced the charge of collaboration because during the German occupation she had spread 'shameless' (*sfacciata*) Republican propaganda and 'made herself disliked by the population.'[55]

Accusations of collaboration often were laid against those who were private or privately employed citizens, because they were not subject to dismissal from their jobs or purge from public life. Denouncing them as collaborators was the only way – other than through private acts of retribution – that local citizens could confront private individuals who had

'made themselves disliked by the population,' but who had not committed any specific 'Fascist crimes.' One large – usually absentee – landowner in the commune of Castel San Niccolo, had sworn allegiance to
the Fascist Republic and spent the period of German occupation in his
home in Florence. Upon return to his property in the province of Arezzo,
he found his house there occupied by refugees. He promptly turned
them out – 'notwithstanding that one of these refugees was a woman in
an advanced state of pregnancy' – and promptly found himself charged
with collaborating with the enemy.[56]

As in these situations, a charge and a finding of collaboration had a
good deal to do with the accused having done something to bring about
the local population's dislike – and that something might have been only
tangentially related to affirmatively aiding the Germans. The prefect
later characterized the case of Antonio Civita in just such a way. 'The
dispute,' he reported, 'basically was connected to the personal position
of Engineer Antonio Civita.'[57] Civita was a mining engineer who had
been general director of the main mining company in the Castelnuovo
area. Arrested as a collaborator after the passage of the front, he was released from Allied custody in June 1945 and returned to service at the
mine despite warnings from the *carabinieri* and even from ACC Provincial
Commissioner Quin Smith that he was likely to get a 'bad reception'
from the local inhabitants.'[58] The 'main accusation against him,' according to the Allies, was that 'he continued to operate the mine in collaboration with the Germans while Civita claims he was only doing his duty.'
Like all local stories, however, it was more complicated than that.

After another charge of collaboration (this one brought by the miners), a brief suspension, and a court dismissal of the charge, Civita again
returned to work, whereupon on March 1, 1946, more than 2000 miners
went on strike to protest the court's action and Civita's return.[59] The
prefect convinced the miners to resume work the following day, in exchange for arranging a meeting to discuss their complaints. The timing
of the strike contributed to the prefect's interest in reaching a quick
resolution: it took place just as the 1946 administrative election campaign began. Everyone then got involved in the case, including representatives of the Communist Party, the Action Party and Liberal Party,
representatives from the mine employees' internal commission assisted
by representatives of Arezzo's Confederation of Labour (CGIL), and representatives of Castelnuovo's CLN, as well as representatives of the national and provincial federation of miners. The swiftly organized March 4

meeting, which all attended, was held at the Florence office of the Tuscan Liberation Committee (CTLF) (Florence's CLN).[60]

A 'long and contentious discussion' ensued, as the prefect described it in detail to the authorities in Rome, but it boiled down to this: As the main representative of the mine 'during the difficult period of German occupation and the passage of the front' and because Civita's job as general director had been to safeguard the mine corporation's property and keep the mine working, Civita necessarily had contact with the German occupiers. He 'therefore found himself in opposition to the mineworkers, who were almost all communists' and 'unshakable enemies of the Germans,' and who wanted to sabotage the mine. Because the German occupation 'had culminated in the cruel massacres of July 1944,' an 'incurable rancour' remained against those, like Civita, who had contact or relations with the enemy occupiers.

The story had an interesting subplot, however. The prefect admitted that Civita did appear – 'in a rather indirect way' – to be politically compromised, and compromised in a way that had little if anything to do with collaborating with the Germans. In early March of 1944, the Castelnuovo miners had gone on strike for a raise in pay and an increase in food rations. Civita had called in the Fascist Republican police, claiming the strike was a political one. So, had Civita's offence been to keep the mine going for the German occupiers, or had it been to call in the Fascist Police to break the miners' March 1944 strike?

In contrast, extenuating circumstances and community feeling could outweigh both one's documented status as a *Repubblichino* and appearance as a collaborator. Giuseppe Picchierri had remained in service as *carabinieri* marshal for the village of Ambra in the commune of Bucine for the entire period of the Fascist Republic; he had even sworn the Republican oath. 'It turned out,' however, that Picchierri was a good man as well as a 'good officer.' In June 1944, the marshal had tried, unsuccessfully, to use his position to prevent the killing of two young men who failed to report for the Fascist Republican draft.[61] Moreover, his 'limited collaboration' could principally be attributed to 'reasons of a financial character,' given that he had a 'rather burdensome' large family to support. The president of the commune's CLN also spoke up for him, explaining how in May 1944, the marshal had allowed a band of local partisans to 'disarm' him and his men. He had peacefully surrendered all the weapons in his barracks, and urged the San Giovanni Valdarno barracks to do the same.[62] He was neither prosecuted nor removed from his position after the war.

Although his reasons for swearing allegiance were mercenary, and so technically he had received financial gain, Marshal Picchierri also had tried to use his Republican connection to help the community during the difficult period of German occupation and civil war. Picchierri was by no means the only Italian who had joined the Fascist Party or even the Republican Fascist Party because he had wanted to get a job or keep a job – or to keep his family from starving, as the widows of Civitella phrased it. Whereas the motive of financial gain, in principle, provided grounds for sanction or censure, the extremely common refrain that 'I joined the Party because I had a family to support' was considered a different motive and was received with understanding, so long as no sufficiently aggravating facts existed.[63]

Individual actions, public feeling, and the September 8 watershed – as well as a pragmatic recognition that twenty years of Fascism often made it difficult to separate the guilty Fascists from the mere Fascists – complicated and contributed to the official postwar process made up of administrative purges, criminal proceedings, and drawn out determinations like Antonio Civita's. They also contributed to acts of popular justice and community-based retribution carried out without the niceties of *carabinieri* reports, courts, or other due process.

Upon arriving in the commune of Bucine, the ACC ordered the arrest of the Republican Fascist *podestà*, Marco Capobussi. In his place, ACC named local attorney Nello Signorini as sindaco, and a five person communal *giunta* that included the parish priest of the village of Duddova and at least one former partisan.[64] At their first meeting, the new administration proceeded to fire 'almost all the clerical staff and other workers,' naming new communal employees. The new employees, 'chosen for the most part from among the partisans, were all absolutely incapable of performing the services with which they were entrusted.'[65] They were also chosen without consulting or even informing the commune's long-time secretary Aroldo Lucarini, and it was he who described the new hires as 'incapable.'

Along with the rest of the community, Signor Lucarini and his family had suffered through Allied bombing and the passage of the front. In the spring of 1944, Allied Operation Strangle badly damaged the home he had saved for years to build. After the family left that house located dangerously close to the large target of the Bucine viaduct, he and his daughter dodged Allied bombs as they bicycled to work in the commune office from their rented room in a nearby village. When the fighting intensified, his family fled to the woods where, from their hiding place, he had seen the village of San Pancrazio in flames after the massacre. A few days later, with his family and some neighbours, he searched for ever-dwindling food and shelter and watched the Germans in retreat. During all of the chaos and dislocation, he had tried his best to maintain the functioning of communal offices and to keep communal records from harm. He also, however, most probably had sworn allegiance to the RSI in the fall of 1943.

Neither the Allies nor the partisans arrested Signor Lucarini after the province was liberated in July of 1944, and both the Allies and the new communal administration permitted him to continue in his job as communal secretary. His work, he later related with intense emotion, could not proceed with the 'necessary calm,' however, because of the 'bloody and brutal reprisals by the party in power against all those who had joined the Fascist Party or who simply had sympathized with them.'[66] Under the 'pretext of punishing political adversaries,' the 'more ruffianly and sinister individuals' gave 'vent to personal hatreds and grudges with impunity.'[67] The Allied authorities, according to Signor Lucarini, allowed them a 'free hand,' ignoring the 'daily acts of cruelty' they committed. These same individuals also attacked the local *carabinieri* barracks, forcing the marshal to reach a sort of compromise: 'Live and let live.' So, while the Allies and the *carabinieri* looked the other way, partisans and 'other ruffians demanded bribes, robbed, beat people to death, and went around armed and undisturbed in their acts of reprisal.'

Signor Lucarini provides a rare, very personal, and very subjective look into what it was like to be on the receiving end of community and popular justice. The terror he and his family experienced was to him not unlike a continuation of the civil war itself.

On a daily basis, gangs broke into the homes of those they disliked, dragged their enemies outside, leaving them bloody and exposed to the ill-treatment and insults of the crowd. The women were stripped and left exposed to jeers; many of them had their hair cropped ... We lived in an atmosphere of anxiety and terror, afraid of what tomorrow would bring ... Given our continual ... anxiety, and the fear that, sooner or later, some trouble would arrive for us, we spent hours and hours behind the shutters watching what went on outside. I could thus give account of the atrocities that were committed without anyone daring to raise a voice in protest or even of disapproval.

Lucarini's turn to face the community came on the afternoon of August 15, 1944. He and his wife and daughter were, as usual, behind their shutters watching and waiting, when a crowd gathered outside and called for him. Signor Lucarini immediately realized what was happening; but nevertheless asked what they wanted. Some ordered Lucarini outside, while others swore at him and threatened him. One spit in his face through the bars of the gate. The *carabinieri* marshal, who stayed a good ways off, ineffectually tried to calm the situation. Someone grabbed Lucarini by the arm and dragged him out. Within a moment, he was in the middle of the crowd, 'overwhelmed and manhandled' – so seriously that he later had to seek medical treatment. His wife and daughter 'did not hesitate' to follow him into the crowd. But, as 'their reward for showing their devotion and to save him from greater harm,' they were shorn of their hair – by their own neighbours – in the centre of the piazza, in the town where they had spent their entire lives. Writing with great feeling eight years after the events, Lucarini said that he could forgive, if not forget, the insults and the blows he had received. He would never be able to forgive, however, the 'many blows and bruises' his wife had suffered trying to protect him.

Aroldo Lucarini and his family experienced the first round of local justice, conducted during the summer and fall of 1944 just after the front passed. As the war ended the following year, citizens confronted Republican Fascists who had fled north and who now returned home. Throughout the spring, summer, and fall of 1945, shots were fired and bombs were thrown at houses of ex-Fascists and ex-Republicans. As Signor Lucarini said, individuals were threatened, robbed, and beaten. Many of these acts were attributed (and not only by Lucarini) to partisans, communists, and other 'anti-Fascist parties,' who were said to be taking the law into their own hands and purposely creating an atmosphere of terror – all apparently under the 'very noses of the Allies.'[68]

Targets of popular epuration included women – like Aroldo Lucarini's wife and daughter – who were related to Fascist Republicans or who themselves had supported the Social Republic, who had consorted or collaborated with the Germans (and sometimes those who consorted with Allied soldiers), or who earlier had engaged in questionable or otherwise unpopular activities.[69] And, as happened elsewhere to female collaborators during this period, as indeed throughout history, a most common manifestation of community reprisal was a shearing or forced hair cut.[70] *La Nazione* reported on the 'epidemic' of women – 'the shorn girls' (*le ragazze tosate*) – who ventured into beauty shops wearing hats or turbans and asking for privacy. 'I've had typhus' and a fever, they always said, 'so I had to have my hair cut off.' 'There's a lot of that particular ailment going around this year,' *La Nazione* sarcastically commented on the so-called typhoid 'epidemic.'[71] The newspaper treated the shearing light-heartedly, but cutting hair, like tossing bombs through windows or dragging men into the piazza for a beating served as public punishment and humiliation to its victims, and as a sort of forced atonement. It also functioned as catharsis in those small communities where everyone had to live together in the months and years after the war with the facts of what had happened during the war.

What was happening – or would happen – to the most egregious Fascists and collaborators was of great community interest. Alongside articles about the return of POWs and deportees, political party activity, upcoming distributions of rationed foods or donated assistance, and the many problems of reconstruction, the newspapers reported daily on which local Fascists had been arrested, either in the north or upon their return home.[72] Olivero Caporali had been political secretary for the *fascio* of Laterina until July 25, 1943, and then served as secretary of the Republican *fascio* until June 10, 1944, when he fled north with his family. Returning home in early June 1945, he was arrested. *La Nazione* described him as 'one of the most *violent* elements during the fascist period' – who had also organized dances for the Germans at Laterina.[73] 'The entire population greeted his arrest with satisfaction,' the newspaper stated. Bruno Rao Torres, the former (and first) Republican *Capo* of the province was arrested in Milan and jailed in Varese in June of 1945.[74] The arrest of Mario Baldassini, whom the newspaper described as 'a zealous fascist,' was 'greeted with joy' by the population of Castelnuovo dei Sabbioni.[75]

Citizens responded to the return and arrests of the worst Republican Fascists and their delivery into the justice system with satisfaction and joy, according to the press, but also with more deadly violence. Before the Fascist Republican Agenore Palmini could be arrested on his return to Meleto from the north, he was lynched by the crowd and died en route to the hospital.[76] Crowds also killed the Republican Francesco Borghi in May 1945. Pasquale Cherubini and Giustino Fattorini were murdered in Montevarchi the following September.[77] Eugenio Franchi and Ovidio Pierazzuoli were shot on the streets of Soci.[78] While the Allied commission still governed the province, someone aiming at former Fascist Francesco Rosai shot and killed his sixty-one year old father instead.[79]

Arezzo's *Questore* reported in July and again in December 1945 that the return of the *Repubblichini* and persons compromised by 'the past regime' had given rise to many 'episodes of popular violence,' and what was clear was that not only 'communist partisans' were taking part.[80] The prefect reported in December 1945 that no amount of persuasion or explanation could calm the citizens – especially the women – in those places where Nazi-Fascist reprisals against the population had occurred.[81]

A crowd in Castelnuovo dei Sabbioni, which included at least three women, killed Pasquale Badii in May 1945. Father Ciabattini, parish priest for that village since the previous November, recorded that they dragged Badii from his house while beating him with clubs. Other persons joined in, and 'the popular fury grew.' Badii tried to flee, but the crowd kept at him until he finally fell to the ground. The women then continued to strike him, all the while screaming curses: 'Go to hell; not even a priest will bless you!' In that village where so many men had been shot and their bodies burned in the piazza, the women then poured gasoline on Badii, setting him on fire while he was still alive and watching him burn to death. The priest also noted in his parish diary that, a few weeks later, before the first anniversary of the July 4, 1944, massacre of their own men, the women came to ask forgiveness for the murder of Pasquale Badii. Father Ciabattini, who himself had seen the immediate aftermath of the July 1944 massacre at Castelnuovo, including the remains of men's burnt bodies still lying in the piazza, termed the killing of Pasquale Badii 'horrifying.'[82]

On October 17, 1946 – several months after the official amnesty for Fascists – some 200 women, widows and mothers of the men killed by Nazi-Fascists in the area of San Giovanni Valdarno, carried out a 'hostile demonstration' at the seat of the local court of assizes against defendant Adolfo Noferi. While armed guards escorted him into the court, the crowd of women attacked him with their fists and with stones. The police had to rescue Noferi 'from the popular fury.'[83]

Those purged and convicted would soon have their punishments significantly reduced or remitted entirely. The Arezzo section of the Florence-based newspaper *La Nazione,* made the much-debated amnesty its headline for June 22, 1946: 'La Repubblica porta la Pacificazione & l'Amnistia è stata Promulgata.' 'Broad measures for common offences – For political offences: death sentences are transmuted to life imprisonment; life imprisonment to thirty years in prison; amnesty for all other penalties – Remission of sanctions up to 500,000 lire.'[84] On the following day, June 23, the newspaper reported that about fifty thousand persons would benefit from the amnesty.[85]

Even before the amnesty, some purged public employees had been rehired, either because they had been suspended only temporarily, or because the commune later reconsidered, deciding their Fascist pasts had not been so serious in retrospect. After the amnesty, other employees who had lost their jobs on account of the purge and who remained out of work appealed. A former Fascist and former communal clerk in Cavriglia, petitioned the provincial administrative *giunta* to return to his communal post and be given back pay for the time he had been suspended.[86] On June 2, 1947, Cavriglia's communal council considered that it needed instruction on the law governing 'such a delicate problem,' because the man's petition for his rehiring and repayment raised not a 'unique question,' but one that would affect 'all those who had been purged.'[87]

The council directed the *giunta* to hire legal counsel, but the *giunta* delayed, 'not only to save money, but also to give the sindaco a chance to find an alternative way.'[88] A year later, in July 1948, with no compromise reached, the *giunta* finally hired an attorney to represent the commune in that case. The commune might well have saved the money it spent on legal advice. Earlier in 1948, De Gasperi clarified which 'particular situations related to the past epurative activity of the public administrations' might be re-examined. Just as sentences and fines were remitted, epuration judgments that had removed former Fascists from their public jobs could be expunged. Perhaps most importantly, those employees (like the man in Cavriglia) who had been dismissed because of their Fascist pasts could – and in some cases should – be rehired and awarded back pay and other benefits for the period of their suspension.[89]

The commune of Bucine had suspended five communal employees from service and from their salary in the summer and fall of 1944, pursuant to DLL 159. All were rehired, and in 1948, the commune paid more than 152,000 lire to reimburse the five ex-Fascists for their suspension.[90] Not an enormous sum, especially given that the 1948 value of the lire was a fraction of what it had been in 1944 and 1945, it was nevertheless significant to poor communes like Bucine or Cavriglia, which still had massive unemployment in 1948 and communal budgets deep in the red.

Rehiring and reimbursing former Fascists who had been purged from public employment made for acrimonious relations within communities and with those who had never been Fascists or who had always been anti-Fascist. Recounting the events of his initial term, Priamo Bigiandi, the first elected postwar sindaco of the commune of Cavriglia, recalled and wrote bitterly (in 1951) of those 'purged' from public employment and of the amnesty that soon thereafter cancelled out their political pasts. Purges in the commune had not been an act of vengeance, he stated. 'But there is quite a difference between this and the law that grants preferential treatment to those whom all political factions of the CLNs recognized as guilty of the *ventennio* of tyranny and of all the misfortunes of the Nation [*Patria*].' Bigiandi himself had been one of the participants in the March 1921 anti-Fascist uprising at the Castelnuovo mines. Charged and convicted, he had served nearly six years in prison for his opposition to Fascism. As president of Castelnuovo's CLN after the war, he had been one of those who formed the local epuration commission in 1945.

Sindaco Bigiandi could understand a law that permitted re-employment for a certain number of those public employees compromised by Fascism and by relations with the Germans. What the sindaco could not understand – or, rather, understood 'only too well' in the context of the 1951 political climate of Christian Democrat domination and failed national unity – was the commune's obligation to pay such people their salary 'ever since the first day they abandoned ... the communal offices to flee north with the Nazis and the Black Brigades.' Instead of requiring those who profited from Fascism to repay even 'an infinitesimal amount,' the Christian Democrat state made the communes (not the state) reimburse the Fascists.[91]

Roy Palmer Domenico has described how, on a national level, different political parties and different societal sectors strongly disagreed on the purpose, extent, and procedures of the purge. The quick amnesty was intended, in part, to end those divisive disputes, to contribute to postwar unity, and allow Italy to put its Fascist past behind it as swiftly as possible. While some, like sindaco Bigiandi, objected to the reappearance of former Fascists in public life and employment (and with back pay), others were happy to close that chapter in Italy's history.

By the end of 1947, more than a year after the amnesty, local feelings generally had calmed. In November of that year, the principal of the elementary school for Foiano della Chiana – the village that had been the scene of the bloody 1921 anti-Fascist attack by peasants against *squadristi* and bloody *squadristi* reprisals – decided to relocate her office from one room to another.[92] She directed six students to carry teacher Ferruccio Billi's few pieces of furniture from his classroom to her office, and vice-versa. While transporting *maestro* Billi's desk, the boys opened the drawers – making the startling discovery of old picture cards (*cartoline fasciste*) depicting Fascist martyrs. The incident immediately came to the attention of Foiano's sindaco, Signor Gervasi. Gervasi was not only the sindaco and father of one of *maestro* Billi's young pupils, he was also the Communist Party deputy for the commune. A further search turned up a whole trove of Fascist cultural memorabilia, including forty-one booklets entitled 'Fascism and Europe Twenty Years Later,' twenty-one picture cards of one local Fascist martyr, the book *Youth and Fascist Legislation,* and three gramophone recordings of 'Giovinezza,' the Triumphal March, and other Fascist tunes.

Sindaco Gervasi demanded an adequate explanation from the principal, as well as from Signor Billi, regarding the material's provenance. The principal enjoyed a blameless past, untouched by Fascist connections. Billi, however, had been a *squadrista*, had marched on Rome, held the *sciarpa littorio*, and was an early member of the Fascist Party. He had also been purged – briefly suspended from his teaching job and 'discriminated against' – and then readmitted to service as an elementary school teacher after the amnesty.[93] A *carabinieri* investigation and much discussion within the community determined that this was not dangerous, neo-Fascist activity; rather, this was old, unimportant 'mere' Fascist activity. 'Despite his political past' and his strange choice to hold on to multiple copies of Fascist lore, Billi 'enjoyed esteem among the population of Foiano.' No one, the authorities and the community concluded, still cared about the school's old inventory from the Fascist regime. The Fascist past already was behind them; people could get on with their normal lives and the community could get on with reconstruction.

Fascism was easy to dismiss, but the question 'why' remains. The widespread ability to put it in the past so quickly can support an argument that Fascism sat only lightly on the surface of Italian society for a full twenty years, as R.J.B. Bosworth has argued based on much more extensive evidence.[94] More usually, the quick dismissal of twenty years of Fascism has been employed to make the argument that Italians chose not to examine and come to terms with their Fascist past, preferring instead a different memory and a different identity which concentrated instead on 1943–5. Part of the answer, however, aside from human nature, is that Fascism – like Fascist – has always been difficult to define. Fascism was never monolithic – not simply one thing for all Italians. Important to recall in this regard – after July 25 and September 8, 1943 – is the widespread satisfaction and joy recorded and how quickly communities and communes disposed of attributes of Fascism on the local level.

The determination to get on with life and stop 'bothering' about anything Fascist prevented further internal division of communities, villages, and the nation, halting the separation of those who had been Fascist factionalists from mere Fascists, from anti-Fascists, and from 'afascists' – all of which was healthy, in a sense, for immediate postwar life and society. Reconstruction, physical and social, was more important at that difficult moment than was allotting blame to oneself or to others, or for taking responsibility for what seemed already long in the past, as compared to the more immediate shared sufferings of war. Later, reflection was unnecessary: the population had always been victims, 'good Italians,' been anti-Fascist or non-Fascist, or at worst had been 'mere' or 'simply' Fascists – as everyone else had been.

A Mania for Dancing

The young teacher assigned to Civitella for the 1946–7 school year recorded that the village had not succeeded 'in shaking off its funereal atmosphere assumed three years ago.'[95] He also wrote of one of the villagers who, almost every evening, 'sang and accompanied himself on the guitar – that is Andrea, one of the four or five men who miraculously escaped the massacre.'[96] 'While he waited with the others to be shot,' the teacher recorded in his diary, Andrea suddenly ran and jumped over the wall. Shot in the legs, he fell, pretending to be dead until the Germans left – 'and so he saved himself.' 'He sings very well,' the young teacher poignantly noted, 'in a low voice, with melancholy.' Andrea's melancholy was to be expected. He had to balance the miracle of survival against the guilt of being one of the very few men to survive. Ruggero Franci, the teacher and village observer, heard Andrea's life-affirming story of survival along with the women's stories of the massacre – again and again throughout the year.[97]

Postwar community life was a strange combination of joy and melancholy – and balancing the two sometimes proved difficult. Arezzo's *Questore* reminded every sindaco in the province about the prohibition against 'noisy and rowdy games' being played near churches and school buildings. The minister of the interior had received complaints that in piazzas and especially near churches and school buildings, gangs of children were 'with impunity' practising '*il foot-ball*' and other 'noisy and dangerous games, completely incompatible with the dignity of citizenship.'[98] That government and religious authorities would begrudge an exuberant game of soccer to children who so recently had lived through bombing and massacre and had witnessed the battles of armies, sounds terribly harsh, but who could know what constituted appropriate public behaviour in that difficult time?

Perhaps more so than any other single postwar activity, dancing exemplified the complex problem of sheer joy and the beginnings of a more normal civil life conflicting with feelings of melancholy. Once the ACC departed and Aretines were free to host their own, dances were held in every imaginable venue to show solidarity, raise money, celebrate events, or just express sociability and postwar pleasure. The Workers Recreational Circle in Badia al Pino requested permission to hold a dance in May 1945 to benefit evacuees and other victims, 'to alleviate the sufferings caused by war.'[99] War-caused suffering was to be alleviated by using the entrance fee for assistance, but dancing itself also helped alleviate war-caused sadness. In September 1945, a dance held 'for the reconstruction of Arezzo' raised 32,000 lire, while another earned 10,000 – large sums by immediate postwar standards.[100] The Tegoleto section of the Association of Returnees from Prison held a dance on Sunday, February 24, 1946, from three to seven, followed by a more elaborate ball for the *reduci* themselves, beginning at eight-thirty. A 'fine orchestra' played and 'excellent bar service' was available. The Aretine committee of the Italian Red Cross held a benefit featuring tea, dancing, and bridge the following Tuesday evening 'to assist abandoned children.'[101]

Requests for permission – for a *licenza ballo* – arrived at the desks of the sindaci, the *carabinieri*, and the prefect from every organization in nearly every village, The requests as often were for blanket future permission as they were for a single evening. The Socialist Party of Mercatale Valdarno asked for a general licence for 'dance parties.' The ENAL circle of Poppi (which had its own dance floor) asked permission to hold dances on weekends throughout the summer of 1946.[102] Local ENAL circles (that is, Ente Nazionale Assistenza Lavoratori) held so many weekend dances that its Aretine provincial office directed all circles which intended to hold dances to present their dance requests before Thursday of each week directly to the provincial office, to give sufficient time to consider them.

Dancing was not without its complications, of course. Politics also made their way to the dance floor. The *carabinieri* for Badia al Pino intended to issue no more permits for dances there, on account of the 'great commotion' caused by opposing political parties at previous dances.[103] Arezzo's provincial director of education reminded sindaci again and again that the use of schools and schoolrooms for parties and dances – by and for whatever organization – was illegal.[104] Sestino's sindaco informed the director, in the spring of 1947, that he was helpless: members of the recreational circle connected to the local ENAL 'arbitrarily' had taken over the schoolrooms for dances in the village of Palazzi, making it impossible for the school to function.[105] In October 1946, the Red

Cross sought to evict the People's Cooperative from the two-storey building in Tegoleto (which the co-op rented from the Red Cross), because
the co-op had turned part of the place into a dance hall. The local population wished to reclaim the space, the prefect sternly told the sindaco,
for its rightful and 'higher assistential use.' The sindaco was not so certain about the local population's true wishes, especially since the co-op's
dances were always very well attended.[106]

Father Ciabattini recorded in his parish diary for the twelfth of August,
1945, how, in the village of Castelnuovo dei Sabbioni, they celebrated
the feast of San Donato, patron saint of the parish. 'The girls sang holy
mass, directed by the Sisters.' While parishioners worshipped inside of
church, things were noisier outside: 'Local leaders inaugurated a new
dance floor, built in the middle of the woods. Dancing attracts numerous
persons. It is like a mania that has possessed young people and adults
after the end of the war. The moral danger is great.'[107] Father Ciabattini
directed his reprehension not only towards those risking moral danger,
but also towards the 'local leaders,' most of whom were communists and
who purposely chose the local religious feast day for the inaugural dance
party, so he believed.

The mania for dancing also raised a troubling question of how much
joy was appropriate after war and so much suffering. Lara Lammioni remembered young villagers her own age, happily dancing in the streets to
jazz music in July 1944, while she lay ill and weeping after the massacre
of much of her family and the destruction of their farm.[108] In early
January 1945, one man wrote from his home in Foiano della Chiana,
commenting on the disorder of daily life: 'Life is so chaotic here that you
can't imagine, but the people and the English [soldiers] don't even feel
ashamed about dancing – there are so many dances now.'[109] They should
feel ashamed, the writer clearly believed, dancing while life was such a
mess. The refugees in one Arezzo camp – supported at Italian public
(and UNRRA) expense – were reported to be 'conducting a standard of
life without control.' They 'wiled away the evening going dancing.' Not
hesitating 'to abandon their own children,' they returned to the camp
'at all hours of the night.'[110]

In July 1945, at the minister of the interior's suggestion, Rome's direc-
tor of public security ordered all dance halls closed in that city. Dance
halls had 'blossomed in great numbers recently' in every part of Rome.
The measure was taken 'for reasons of order and public morality.'
Authorities had verified frequent 'incidents' during dances and parties.
The incidents that threatened public order may have been drunken

fights, prostitution, or confrontations between those with opposing political views. More subtly, however, in those days 'still so grave and difficult,' some argued that no one should make a spectacle of 'excessive carefreeness.'[111]

Should citizens have felt guilty dancing in the midst of so much suffering, their own included? How much carefreeness was excessive? In the communes of Arezzo, council members and citizens often argued that money would be better spent helping widows or engraving plaques in honour of those massacred by the Germans, but was instead going to build dance floors and fund dances. Dancing in the piazzas and the schoolrooms and the many new dance floors was a new aspect of civil life, one not widely seen before in small rural villages before the war, but one reflecting a feeling that life would be normal again, and so also helped to restore the community. Even Father Polvani, while noting the 'shamefulness' of so much music and dancing during those 'sad moments,' understood that 'youth will be youth' and full of life after all that had happened.[112]

8 Rebuilding the Commune

The commune is in the hands of extremists, and from it everyday arrive orders on top of orders. We don't know how to behave. If things stay the same, the small landowner is doomed. The commune is an administrative body, but here it legislates, taxes, and causes trouble and oppression.
Don Narcisco Polvani, 'Diario anno 1944,' September 21, 1944.

Arezzo's *Questore* and ACC Provincial Commissioner Quin Smith – whose daily work in somewhat different ways included maintaining public order, monitoring the province's political situation, and keeping their thumbs on the pulse of the citizenry's mood – both repeatedly commented on the population's mistrust of the state and the popular conviction that the 'authorities,' whether in Rome or the provincial capital, were not capable of solving Italy's postwar problems.[1] In July 1945, the *Questore* reported to the prefect: 'The public mood is quite depressed, mostly about three matters: the high cost of living, the problem of housing, [and] unemployment. The population is convinced that the authorities are not able to tackle such problems, and from this [conviction] arises indifference towards the various political parties.'[2] Likely meant to reassure the prefect that the influence of the increasingly active parties was limited, a conviction did exist that 'the authorities' – whether those in Rome or the prefect in Arezzo (as the state's representative) – could not solve the problems of the postwar, and that conviction was widely shared.

That result was nothing new. Ordinary Italians traditionally felt distant from the state and mistrusted most national institutions – sentiments which five years of destructive war and postwar chaos only exacerbated. Community practices and communal institutions were more important and meaningful than the state in the lives of central Italians (if not all Italians), and remained important even after Mussolini and Fascism attempted, with some success, to nationalize Italians. After the war, as Aretine villagers waited increasingly impatiently for the war indemnities, *premi*, and pensions that the state promised but was slow to deliver, and as citizens demonstrated for jobs and called for reconstruction to begin, the state proved its ineffectualness every day. It was the communes that filled the gaps between citizens and the state.

The dichotomy between the 'local' and the 'national' was clear during the first postwar years.[3] The state and the nation had collapsed with the fall of Fascism, Italy's surrender, Badoglio and the king's abandonment of the army and the people during the midst of war. Moreover, as Arezzo's prefect reported, the population suffered the losses of war individually and collectively. Not everyone in Aretine villages lost a family member in German massacres or had a house destroyed by bombs, but collectively as members of communities, they lost their priests and churches, their schools, hospitals, and public buildings. Together the villagers fled to the woods to await the passage of the front, and often returned to find their villages in ruins. The citizens of every village and commune suffered together the Allied occupation and the continuing disruptive presence of refugees. Their immediate postwar centre was their shared local experience and their shared local problems, as little tangible solace arrived from Rome.

This is not to say that unity and solidarity reigned on a local level after the war on account of shared suffering, or that citizens enjoyed a common vision for societal reconstruction and the return to normal life. Arguments and dissent were very much part of postwar community and communal life. Indeed, the many disagreements – and just plain bickering – furthered the revival of a vibrant civil life. The return to civil life and the reconstruction of society began at the local level, in the rubble of ruined villages, in village piazzas, in makeshift council chambers and during noisy public meetings, during disputes over who should be hired and fired, over complaints about continued rationing and scarce housing, and through difficult decisions about what rebuilding projects should have precedence.

The previous chapter expanded the meaning of the return home and to normal life, treated the official purge and popular justice as aspects of local life vital to the postwar community, and ended with citizens balancing postwar joy and melancholy, while this chapter focuses on the institution of the commune in which community and daily life were embedded.

The Structure of the Commune

Whereas communities within Italian villages, cities, and countryside are conceptual (that is, without precise physical boundaries), they exist within the very real, defined and bordered institution of the commune. Communes are local governmental, administrative, and demographic units; they also comprise multiple communities. The commune as institution, local administration, and civil authority, played a major part in the return to an everyday life that both resembled 'normal,' prewar life and helped make up for the losses and destruction of war.

Below the national level, three levels make up the country and government of Italy. The country is divided into regions; each region into provinces; each province into communes (sometimes referred to as municipalities). Communes then consist of the communal seat or main town (in which the communal offices, or *municipio*, are located) and a contiguous group of towns, villages, and communal 'fractions.' The city of Arezzo is, thus, the communal seat of the commune of Arezzo, as well as the capital of the province of Arezzo, which, in turn was made up of thirty-eight additional communes.

The communal level of administrative government has been important since unification, though communes were poorly financed during the Liberal era and one nationalizing goal of the Fascist regime was to limit their autonomy. Communes traditionally were responsible for public health and sanitation (including water supply and sewage), local policing, public works, maintenance of public property, and the supervision of hospitals, welfare services, and public charities. Communes decided, levied, and collected their own taxes on five sources: 'a local property tax; a local consumption tax; licenses on commerce, industry, trades, and the professions; a tax on domestic animals; and a family income tax.'[4] Basically, communal administrations decided who and what should be taxed within those five overall categories, they could also amend tax rates, and could exempt certain persons or items from tax. Taxing was a critical communal function, naturally, because it provided a direct source of revenue. Communes also maintained records of vital statistics: registration of births, deaths, marriages, changes of residence, records of property ownership. They provided the land and structures for elementary schools, social service and welfare organizations, public markets, public lighting, and as seen, during the Fascist era often for *fascio* headquarters, offices, and *dopolavori* as well.

With the Fascist takeover in 1926, local elected councils were dissolved and sindaci dismissed. A *podestà* or prefect's commissioner, appointed by the prefect, replaced the elected sindaco, and 'consultative bodies' replaced elected, local councils. Prefects, state-appointed career civil servants, remained as an institution representing the state, in charge of the provinces, and took greater control over local administrative government than they had before.[5] After the war, and after administrative elections for sindaci and councils were reinstated, the prefect retained that greater authority attained during Fascist days. He could veto communal council decisions on grounds of illegality or on financial grounds – grounds that were within his discretion to determine. He could also dissolve the council, and suspend a sindaco. In the postwar, and especially during the early months when local, provincial, and state government were in flux, disputes between sindaci, *giunte*, and communal councils on the one side, and prefects on the other, were frequent, and often became drawn out battles of will over large and petty issues.

Communal administrations were fluid directly after the war, in part because of Allied interference, then as the purge of Fascists from public life removed some long-time communal employees from their positions. Before administrative elections in 1946 and especially while the war continued in the north and the Allies occupied the country, battling CLNs over local and communal authority, communal officials often had little say over the workings of their commune.[6] Communal administrations stabilized (at least for the term of office) with the spring elections of 1946, when citizens cast votes for communal councils for the first time in two decades. Even then, however, the functions of the communes were not clearly defined as communal administrations faced countless postwar problems. What were a commune's 'precise duties' after so many years of Fascist rule and after the destruction of war?

Whereas Aretine communal records for the Fascist period share a wearisome annual sameness of budget preparation, employee compensation, and attestations to widespread popular support for the regime, post-Fascist communal annals are very different. They offer illustrations of difficult local circumstances, yet very active civil life after war and Fascism. In council members' (and their audiences') implacable differences of opinion and their impassioned discussions and votes on every conceivable question, communal records reflect postwar democracy and engagement on a local level.

Democracy then and there meant free elections and party organization, but it also meant direct popular participation in public affairs. Ordinary citizens – including younger men, former partisans, and those with strong political identification now benefited from a more widely shared (though certainly not universal) postwar, post-Fascist public belief that local government should involve the local population. Members of the working classes – labourers, smallholders, sharecroppers – entered public political life and ran for local elected office against more traditional elements. Father Polvani complained to his diary – and more publicly – that the commune of Cavriglia was 'in the hands of extremists' and that their 'schemes' were ruining the commune.[7] In Monte San Savino, a socialist who was a cloth salesman (pedlar) by trade, took over as sindaco in February 1945. The *giunta* replaced him two months later with a Communist Party member who was a sharecropper. Career communal secretary Aroldo Lucarini described the first as 'absolutely lacking every qualification to carry out his office.' The second, however, Lucarini said, was 'although deprived of education, an intelligent and active person.'[8]

The career prefect and some more experienced communal civil servants 'resented the political immaturity' of the postwar communal councils. Council deliberations, the prefect considered, were inspired more by the 'programmatic direction of the political parties' (especially after the 1946 administrative elections) than by getting things done. The new public interest and public participation also served to slow down communal business. Council meetings often had to be held in a commune's largest standing building rather than the usual council chamber, because so many citizens wanted to be present not only to hear deliberations and votes, but also to have their own say on matters. 'The public which often is present at the [council] sessions,' complained the prefect, 'actively intervenes in the discussions and directly influences the decisions ... as frequently happens the Council chambers are transformed into public meeting places, where everyone feels authorized to interrupt and where everyone puts forth his own opinion, sowing discord and delaying reconstruction and the resolution of the most impelling problems.'[9]

Communal decisions did not get made as quickly as they might because of the public's involvement. The prefect described this public concern and 'direct interference' in communal affairs as 'demagogy.' He heartily disapproved of it, appointed state official that he was. It was not demagogy, contrary to the prefect's characterization, because there was no one demagogue appealing to the people; it was instead the people all talking at once. Postwar problems needed to be addressed and solved, nevertheless, but how would that happen with the people all joining in and with the so-called 'political immaturity' of communal councils?

Dozens of communal-level and provincial-level commissions and committees were born almost immediately after the passage of the front to take on the many local difficulties. Their general purpose was to bring a range of citizens into the local reconstruction process and to assure that different groups or categories would be represented or have some say in the multiple aspects of postwar reconstruction. Committees thus served a 'proto-democratic' function, by providing the population a voice (or at least a representative voice) in the early problem solving, decision making postwar process.

The initial act of Bucine's communal council, during its '*straordinario*' first meeting on August 12, 1944, was the 'appointment of various commissions,' all of which related to the many problems the commune now faced.[10] Bucine's council named a commission for agriculture, a political commission, a provisioning commission, an assistance commission, an employment commission, and a building commission. Every commune in the province formed similar commissions and committees to address postwar daily life and reconstruction. There were communal committees on hiring,[11] and communal committees 'against' unemployment, layoffs, and firing.[12] Communal committees existed to verify that agricultural labourers or sharecroppers did not take non-agricultural jobs, and that the appropriate men replaced women in public jobs.[13] Agricultural committees attempted to locate farmers whose oxen had not been lost to the Germans or to Allied bombing, so that those few remaining draft animals might be shared for plowing and harvesting.[14] 'Vigilance committees' existed to monitor prices, making sure that their commune's prices were in line with those of other communes, and to assure that local merchants abided by official prices.[15] Committees formed to see that rationing went smoothly and fairly – or at least as well as could be expected – and to guarantee that their own communes got their fair share within the province. Every commune where 'actions of war had destroyed or damaged a significant number of buildings' was required to name a building repair committee.[16] Committees joined to improve conditions for 'those compelled to live in refugee camps,' while others gathered assistance for soldiers returned from prison camps and for civilians returned from deportation, concentration camps, or forced labour.[17]

The makeup of local and communal committees says something important about post-Fascist and postwar society. It was expected that certain officials and those holding positions of traditional importance in the local community would routinely serve on one or more relevant committees. Sindaci and council members doubled as members of various committees, making up part of the earliest agriculture, political, provisioning, assistance, employment, and building commissions. Former schoolteacher, former partisan, and then again schoolteacher, Elio Scala sat on the communal council, the political commission, the employment commission, and guardian committees for several orphaned children.[18] Priests, as noted in chapter five, always served as members of assistance committees. Bucine's council named 'all the parish priests of the commune' along with a lay representative from each village to the first postwar assistance commission. Committees and committee life brought more 'ordinary' people into the local process of reconstruction and into public life as well. Smallholders and sharecroppers, and in some places *braccianti* too, served on agricultural and other commissions along with sindaci, *carabinieri*, large landowners, priests or the bishop's representative. Renters, the homeless, the unemployed served together with property owners, landlords, and business owners on housing, employment, and building commissions.

Committee life was an essential component in reconstruction and the return to civil life. That is, committees were seen to be a necessary precursor to reconstruction, even if women were underrepresented – or unrepresented – on many committees in the newly democratic society. Day-to-day activities of the many postwar committees are not available for review. Local and provincial committees did not record their deliberations, decisions, or results, though some can be gleaned from other sources, usually council minutes or communications to sindaci and the prefect. Few committees lasted very long; only a very few persevered until 1948 or 1949, having fallen victim to discouragement or fracturing rather than disbanding because reconstruction had been successfully completed. Those who served on committees, not surprisingly, now remember little about their work and the debates of so many years ago, except that arguing was commonplace for most issues.[19]

Postwar committees did not accomplish all they were formed to do, but they never had the tools or means to do so much. They did not accommodate every homeless family; they did not make sure that every field was plowed; they did not find a job for every unemployed person; they could not guarantee that every poor widow received her fair share of UNRRA goods, but neither did they expect the state or any other entity to do it for them. The sheer number of committees, their composition, their duties, and the expressed expectations of what needed to be done and that they might accomplish it were what mattered. Committees (and their makeup) reflected local society and emphasized that local reconstruction had to be started by the people themselves.

Communal committees in general have been overlooked in the study of the formation of the Republic in postwar Italy, despite their undeniable contribution to postwar civil life. As argued earlier, attempts to guarantee representative fairness through assistance committees made up of opposing political parties, of priests, partisans, and more oppositional others had the result of politicizing assistance and assistance decisions. Similarly, housing committees made up of owners, landlords, tenants, and the homeless and employment committees consisting of employers, employees, the unemployed, the chamber of commerce, and the unions meant, and were intended to mean, that all were represented. Such inclusive participation also increased the level of contention in local postwar life, with the result that less was agreed upon than otherwise might have been if committee members had not stood on opposing sides of every issue. Nevertheless, recognizing that every citizen should have a say in the important problems of reconstruction was worth more than pure efficiency. Committee life – especially during the period before an elected government – was the essence of democracy and the opposite of Fascist dictatorship, even if not the solution to the problems of reconstruction.

Feeding the People

First among the three most 'fundamental problems' facing his commune directly after the passage of the front, recalled Cavriglia's first post-Fascist sindaco when the 1946 elections ended his appointment, was that of provisioning, or 'feeding the people.'[20] Not among a commune's traditional duties, overseeing rationing, amassing crops, enforcing local prices, and just making sure citizens had enough to eat came to rank among the most pressing post-front and postwar concerns for communes and their sindaci, as did fighting for each commune's fair share within the province.

Food, getting it and paying for it, preoccupied Arezzo's citizens as well. The postwar food situation was a continuation of invasive mandatory wartime sacrifices. Now, Fascism and the war had ended, but the large part of life revolving around food and food difficulties was not likely to return to normal anytime soon. Just as they had earlier during the war, a large percentage of Aretine letters intercepted during the Allied occupation repeated themes of high food prices, the black market, continued rationing of basic foods like bread and pasta, and how to circumvent both rationing and price controls.[21] One resident of San Giovanni Valdarno wrote to a friend in January 1945: 'It is not possible to manage to earn enough to eat without starving, without thinking of how to clothe oneself or do other things; we need a minimum of 600 or 700 lire a day.'[22]

Similarly, monthly reports from the *Questore* to the prefect and from the prefect to Rome always described the population's frustration over the food situation. 'Regarding rationed foodstuffs, the people complain about the shortages; while for those things available on the open market and for common essentials, they complain about the exorbitant prices,' reported the *Questore* for July 1945 – and every month thereafter.[23] Over a year later, he told the prefect of the population's anger over such small distributions of olive oil, bread, pasta, and other still-rationed necessities.[24] Another year later, he recorded the population's complaints about the increased price of bread.[25] 'The public mood is rather depressed as regards the provisioning and economic situation,' the *Questore* routinely revealed with typical understatement.[26]

Not only the *Questore*, but also the *carabinieri*, the provincial alimentation (rationing) section (SEPRAL), communal alimentation commissions, and – before they left the province – a plethora of Allied officers all said much the same every single month, varying only in lesser or greater detail.[27] The citizens of Arezzo were dispirited, even irate, about shortages, inadequate or late rations, high prices, about those who got rich on the black market, and over the continuing duty to consign produce, all of which now had been going on for years. And as with other postwar problems, they tended to blame the government in Rome (and their prefect) for the entire state of affairs.

Each commune naturally considered its own citizens' needs first, and with transportation and communications still problematic, remote communes often suffered worse than larger, more central communes. Although SEPRAL's job was to assure uniform distribution across the province, rationed goods frequently arrived late to distant communes and villages – or ran out before they were dispatched from a central location, just as they had during the war. Residents of Arezzo's mountainous zone (and even less mountainous zones like Civitella and San Pancrazio) regularly bemoaned to family and friends in other places, and to their communal administrations, that they were receiving much less than city and town dwellers: 'In this mountainous country, we don't find all that they get in the cities. Moreover, SEPRAL treats us unfairly, sending us less than what they send to the city ... [This month] we got no vegetables, no canned goods, no sugar, a tiny bit of salt; we are still waiting for the pasta.'[28]

Remoteness sometimes had its own rewards, however. The residents of the poor mountain village, Petrella di Sestino, ate polenta and potatoes every day. They ate very little bread (still rationed) and no fruit, and drank wine only on Sundays, according to the young schoolteacher who

taught there for the 1945–6 school year. Living far from provincial officials (and even communal officials) who had the power to limit what animals could be slaughtered and to control how much of their own meat,
poultry, and eggs farmers could keep and sell, Petrella's citizens ate a
great deal of pork, lamb, chicken, and eggs – items in great demand and
short supply elsewhere.[29]

Both individuals and communes violated (or simply ignored) provincial amassing or consignment requirements, distribution amounts, and
price controls where possible.[30] And Arezzo being part of Tuscany, where
olive oil is a year round daily staple, and where the annual pressing of the
olives and production of *olio nuovo* is a much celebrated event, many violations on both the supply and receiving ends had to do with olive oil.[31]
Sindaci and communal commissions routinely distributed more than
was allowed, while local producers failed to consign what was required.
The sindaco of Castiglion Fibocchi ran into trouble with the Allied occupiers for ordering a distribution of olive oil in his commune far larger
than anywhere else in the province of Arezzo, while Father Polvani, who
owned property in the commune of Cavriglia, himself was 'caught out'
evading the olive oil amassing decree.[32]

These were only two of the many engaged in what Provincial Commissioner Quin Smith termed 'the widespread disregard of the law' regarding olive oil in particular and amassing and distribution in general.[33] 'All
true patriots ought to consider such general evasion of the law of Italy a
dishonor.' Violations could not be carried out so freely, he emphasized, if
communal sindaci made more of a real effort to stop them. 'The position
of Sindaco is honorary, and therefore honorable,' he reminded them. 'I
would very much like to see a Sindaco who has the courage to enforce government orders, and actually to report those who do not have the loyalty to
carry them out.'[34] Sindaci, however, had more loyalty to their communes
than to the state.

Prices, as set by provincial committees for the coordination and enforcement of prices, were supposed to be consistent throughout the province,
but communal administrations could set prices within their own communes subject to the prefect's approval. Thus, prices were often determined on a very local level and based on micro-concerns; so in June 1945,
the commune of Cavriglia both fixed the price of bread and raised the
price of bread flour higher than elsewhere in the province because of the
distance Cavriglia's bakers had to travel to the nearest functioning mill.[35]
Foiana della Chiana set its poultry prices so high that farmers from the
nearby commune of Torrita di Siena, in the neighbouring province of

Siena, clandestinely travelled to Foiana to sell their chickens there, leaving Torrita's market without chickens for sale.[36]

In September 1946, that provincial committee, along with Arezzo's prefect, decried the habitual local violations of provincial price settings (especially for meat) and the persistent failure of local officials to carry out rulings against the violators. For their part, the provincial committee added, sindaci and communal-level commissions showed 'a truly deplorable acquiescence' to 'public defiance.'[37] Despite accusations of laxity and complicity in infractions, sindaci and local commissions generally did attempt to keep prices under control and the rationing situation in order, even as they sometimes looked the other way in the case of amassing violations and while contributing to distribution violations.[38]

Sindaci found themselves caught between the needs of their fellow citizens within the commune (as well as the determination of local producers to keep more) and regulations they were expected to enforce for the greater benefit of the province and the nation. 'They had to provide the goods indispensable for feeding the people; a difficult thing,' conceded communal secretary Aroldo Lucarini. Sindaci had not only their own citizens to worry about, but also the many refugees 'with their needs and complaints.' It all meant 'continuing worries' for sindaci and everyone else in the communal administration.[39]

The black market was ever-present and was something completely beyond communal administrative control. 'The black market is widespread in this Province also,' reported the prefect to Rome at the end of December 1945. '[I]t represents an unfortunate and unavoidable necessity, given the insufficient quantity of goods rationed for normal provisioning.'[40] It continued everywhere so long as rationing, amassing, and price controls were the law. The prefect did reassure the Interior Ministry that Arezzo's black market prices were generally lower, however, than those in many other provinces and cities. Black market prices remained constant for sugar and oil, he noted in August 1946, and even decreased a bit for flour and pasta as more foods became available and their prices rose on the legal market. Nevertheless, the 'black market still exists,' said Arezzo's *Questore* every month throughout 1946, 1947, and after.[41] The *borsa nera* (or *mercato nero*) existed not just for food, but for all items made scarce by the war. The teacher Ruggero Franci paid an entire month's salary of 3000 lire for a pair of black market leather shoes towards the end of 1945.[42] One commune found itself sanctioned by the prefect for spending more than double the regular market price when buying bicycle tires on the black market. The commune had been unable to locate any tires on the legal market, however, and could not wait for scarce tires to appear because communal guards and other public employees needed bicycles (and tires) to carry out their everyday duties.

In October 1946, when Arezzo's prefect publicized new penal sanctions for those who dealt on the black market and those who evaded consignment of their grain and olive oil, he noted such transgressions being verified 'with worrying frequency.' Those antisocial actions, he scolded, convinced the public (especially those who did not farm, but who lived 'with only the proceeds of their labour'), that 'every abuse was possible' and that 'the organs of the State are impotent to end the sinister and detrimental activities.'[43] State organs most assuredly were powerless to control much of those activities at the local level. The citizens did not need much convincing about the state's ineffectiveness.

The Normal Duties of a Commune in an Unusual Time

Even traditional communal administrative functions took on new dimensions on account of war. In addition simply to counting and keeping track of citizens, census and demographic records now were relevant for obtaining postwar pensions or state aid, and communes needed to determine how many of their citizens had been killed in the war – by bombs, by the Germans, or in combat.[44] An accurate communal count also meant that the correct number of ration cards might be issued, the correct amount of rations received, and that sufficient olive oil, grain, and other produce were amassed. Moreover, the number of potential electors – male and female – needed to be finalized before the first elections.[45]

Similarly, communal responsibilities included building and repairing communal roads and streets. While kilometres of roads needed to be cleared of mines and otherwise rebuilt after the war, communes also changed street names to mark the end of Fascism and memorialize the horrors of war. Streets earlier named for Fascist 'martyrs' or to commemorate dates like the march on Rome now returned to their pre-Fascist names.[46] Other village streets and piazzas were renamed to observe where and when German massacres had been carried out during the summer of 1944.[47] Streets and piazzas in nearly every central Italian commune honoured not only their own wartime dead, but also national figures martyred for their anti-Fascism: Giacomo Matteotti, the Roselli brothers, Don Minzoni, and Piero Gobetti.

Children's return to school and schools' resumption of their usual functions were a large part of the return to normal life, and something only partly within communal control.[48] The traditional communal duty of providing the land and buildings for schools, and of maintaining elementary schools was complicated when so many school buildings were damaged or destroyed, and soldiers and civilians camped in what classrooms were still standing. Only 130 out of 420 elementary school buildings in the province of Arezzo were 'functioning' as schools in December 1944, while the condition of 131 other schools was still unknown, and the remaining 159 either were so badly damaged they were unusable or were occupied by refugees or Allied troops.[49]

Well after the Allied departure, many Aretine schools still had not reopened, either because necessary repairs had not been made or because there was nowhere else for refugees. At the end of 1945, refugees and evacuees still occupied a number of schools in the commune of Civitella, creating 'serious hardship' which further compromised the schools' 'renewal' after the 'harmful destruction of war,' wrote Civitella's sindaco, when he asked a number of residents if the commune might use space in their homes for the important business of schooling.[50]

The hamlet of Cornia, in the commune of Civitella, which had seen men, women, and children massacred on June 29, 1944, did not have its schoolroom in working order by December 1946.[51] The schoolroom in the village of Tegoleto (in Civitella) still lacked glass in its windows in December 1946 – the second winter the children would spend in a very cold classroom. Students in Badia al Pino were also spending a second winter in a school with at least half the windows broken.[52] That winter, the teachers took turns holding classes in the single room that had glass in all of its windows. The schools inspector for the district wrote in outrage to Civitella's sindaco that students were having lessons only twice a week ('I repeat: two times a week!'), because all had to wait their turn for the single classroom.[53] Schools without glass in the windows and with wind and rain blowing in are a common theme in communal archives and a common memory among those who were children or teachers in postwar Arezzo.[54]

A significant part of communal attention after the war went to the repair of schools, to plans for new schools, and to compensation for those who made their property available for temporary classroom use. In San Leolino (in the commune of Bucine), the badly damaged schoolroom was unusable, preventing the children from attending school for the academic year 1946–7. No suitable space existed for a makeshift classroom, and no other school was close enough for the children to attend every day. Lest the children lose another year of schooling, their teacher had been giving daily lessons in his home. The commune voted to reimburse him 100 lire per month for each of the 'poor children' he had been teaching, and whose families could not afford to contribute.[55] For the 1947–8 school year, the priest of San Leolino opened the parish house for classes to be taught there, until Bucine's communal administration voted funds for construction of a new school building in San Leolino at the end of 1948.[56] The commune also voted to pay Signor Rossi 3000 lire for allowing forty-five students to use a large room in a building he owned in Pietraviva: 2000 as rent for the period from July of 1945 to June 1946, and another 1000 to cover the damage students did to his adjacent orchard. On February 2, 1947, Bucine's communal council deliberated to borrow 1,200,000 lire exclusively for the construction of a school in that village.[57]

Villages without their own schools before the war now insisted on their 'right' to have a school. When provincial education officials and the prefect pointed out that, before the war, village children had walked upwards of five kilometres or more to attend the nearest elementary school or travelled as far as the city of Arezzo to attend middle or upper school, communes stressed that the situation should change given the end of Fascism and the suffering children had undergone on account of the war. Education should be more accessible to all in the new democracy, communal councils emphasized.

On January 8, 1945, Bucine's communal *giunta* voted to build a nursery school in the village of Ambra, where none had been before the war. A nursery school in that 'important village' was 'held necessary,' so that the children of labourers could be looked after and educated. While their parents worked, the *giunta* noted, young children often were left alone or in the care of persons and places unsuited ('for moral and hygienic reasons,' respectively) for that duty.[58] The prefect returned the deliberation 'denied' for the reason that the commune lacked sufficient funds for the project. Bucine sought the prefect's reconsideration – more than once. The commune eventually opened its nursery school with much village fanfare, despite the commune's budget deficit and the prefect's repeated vetoes. The commune also voted to contribute 100 lire a month so that twenty poor children could attend the new nursery school, where 'beyond receiving pre-elementary teaching, they also [had] lessons for moral elevation and psychological improvement for good training in life.'[59]

These examples of close attention to missing windows, substitute classrooms, lessons for poor children, and schools in villages which had never had them before represent only a few of many communal stories centred around the importance of schools, education, and children. Albeit, a commune's traditional duties included construction and maintenance of elementary schools within its boundaries. Even so, communes' interests in the condition of their schools, in educational opportunities for their children – especially the children of labourers and the rural poor, and in the moral value of education all became more pronounced after the war. Post-Fascist, postwar concern with education and the welfare of children stemmed from a voiced conviction that ordinary people deserved better than they had in the past, after the sufferings and sacrifices of war.

The most local of communal duties – and the most personal – was to supervise charity and welfare services. While the postwar state was determining a national response and national programs for its citizens affected by the war, communes based decisions on individualized and very local concerns. Bucine was a particularly poor commune, in part because its tax base consisted primarily of poor owners of tiny agricultural properties. Its communal records for the years 1944 through 1948 provide compelling narratives of the problems people faced after the war and the degree to which a commune intimately knew and cared for its poorest citizens. Something of a rural antithesis to the cold, uncaring urban postwar climate portrayed in Vittorio De Sica's *Bicycle Thieves* and *Umberto D.*, the commune's deliberations offer stories of both personal hardship and community concern. In these communal actions, council or *giunta* acted in unanimity; they debated certainly, but they always agreed. While so much of communal administration and everyday life throughout central Italy fractured along party and other social lines, communes easily reached consensus on society's neediest members. Those searching for postwar solidarity will find it here.

One woman born and raised in the commune of Bucine now had arteriosclerosis, was unable to work, and was alone in the world. The 'miserable pension' she received for her years employed as a maid at the Spanish consulate in Rome did not suffice to pay for her food or shelter. The commune agreed to send her to the Istituto di Mendicità (basically the poor house), and to pay the daily rate of 60 lire. Because the institute could not provide one, the commune also paid for a new horsehair mattress. In return, the commune took two-thirds of the woman's pension, leaving her the rest for 'her intimate needs.'[60]

The elderly without relatives to care for them, or with relatives who were unable to or who refused to care for them, were particularly vulnerable. The commune voted to pay 320 lire in annual rent, so that one 'poor' man could stay in the home of a 'kind friend' who took care of him and who asked for very little recompense. Another eighty-four year old woman suffered from chronic arthritis and, the doctor suspected, a fractured femur that had kept her bedridden since January 1945. She too had no family, but a neighbour had been assisting her and caring for her. Because the neighbour could not afford the woman's expenses for food and medicine, the commune voted to give the neighbour 300 lire each month for a year.[61]

Hospital and medical costs (*spedalità*) for the poor were traditional expenses for which the communes took responsibility, and their records cover a great deal of shelf space in communal archives. The many, many outlays for eyeglasses, physical therapy, leg braces, or trips to specialists in Florence or Pisa, were not automatic, however. In Bucine, as elsewhere, the communal decision to make them followed recitations of facts and supporting information on individual situations. Bucine agreed to reimburse 2580 lire for the anti-rabies vaccine (given with the 'utmost urgency') for a child bitten by a rabid dog.[62] It also reimbursed 2000 lire for orthopaedic shoes, without which, one man badly wounded in the war, would be unable to walk. It voted to contribute 3000 towards the 6000 lire needed for a pair of orthopaedic shoes for the son of a 'simple labourer without means of fortune,' who faced many other expenses for his little boy afflicted with polio.[63]

One woman had been ill for more than a year with a spinal ailment. Now she needed an orthopaedic brace for her back, but she also owed money to the hospital. Her husband had recently been laid off from the Castelnuovo lignite mines. The couple had no savings and no family member to help them. Bucine's *giunta* voted unanimously to contribute towards her hospital debt and to pay for the back brace.[64] A former partisan suffering from tuberculosis needed treatment with the antibiotic streptomycin. The man was in a sanatorium at Terranuovo Bracciolini, and his family, which was in 'the most straitened financial circumstances' could pay nothing. The commune could afford to contribute a little, but not enough to pay for the 30 grams of the 'precious medicine' needed. Bucine's sindaco wrote to the provincial office of the Ministry of Postwar Assistance asking for help in that 'most pitiful case.'[65] The sindaco also appealed to the commune's citizens for contributions to assist 'one who had fought against the Nazi-Fascists.' The commune sent one forty-four year old widow to the psychiatric hospital in Florence. She had suffered a mental breakdown and continued depression after her husband was massacred by the Germans. She began 'to have insomnia and think of suicide,' according to the *giunta*'s deliberation.[66]

When Angiolo Ermini left the post of sindaco for the commune of Bucine on June 23, 1945, and Giuseppe Scaramelli took his place, the communal treasury had a deficit of 2,045,805 lire.[67] In December 1945, Bucine could not pay the 141,686 lire it owed a hospital in Siena (where several of its citizens had been treated) 'on account of the absolute lack of funds in the treasury.' Neither could the commune pay the 221,680 lire it owed the hospital of Terranuova Bracciolini. The prefect urged the commune to pay at least 50,000 lire on account, as the hospital's own financial situation was disastrous because so many others had not paid.[68]

To pay for these financial outlays on their citizens' behalf, and to pay for other communal expenses that included replacing typewriters carried off from communal offices by the Germans and Fascist Republicans, and astronomical sums for bicycle tires for their communal guards and messengers, communes had the power to set and collect their own impost or use taxes within a few traditional categories.[69] The very few private cars and carts not driven off by the Germans were taxed. Store signs were taxed at 30 lire for each letter or number, 50 lire for each figure or symbol. Tariffs also applied to advertisements or posters publicly displayed, with amounts varying according to the permanent nature of the advertisement, whether it was illuminated, whether it was distributed on the street or carried on the side of a vehicle.[70] Ownership of an espresso machine was taxed. In the commune of Civitella and elsewhere, machines that prepared a single cup were taxed at 1500 lire; machines with two spouts at 3000; another 1000 lire tax was calculated for every additional spout.[71] A piano tax amounted to 800 lire, whereas a billiard table was taxed substantially higher at 2000 lire if in a private residence, and at 3000 lire in a public place or recreational circle. Those who employed domestic servants were taxed 400 lire for the first, 1500 lire for the second, and an additional 2500 lire for each additional servant.[72] Poor agricultural communes like Bucine acquired very little in the way of tax revenue from owners of pianos and billiard tables, or those who employed three maids. For the year 1945, Bucine collected not a single lira in taxes on domestic help or on pianos. It did receive 750 lire on one coffee maker and 2000 lire for a billiard table, however – but nothing remotely close to what it spent on supporting its poor and elderly.[73]

Consumption taxes applied to meat, fish, chocolate, cheese, butter, and pastries – all luxuries in Arezzo's immediate postwar world.[74] Impost and consumption taxes may not have been great moneymakers, but fines for evading them generated some income for the commune. In August 1947, Bucine fined 101 of its residents for contravening the consumption tax on wine reserved for direct producers (meaning those who made wine but had not paid tax on what they kept for their own use). The fines netted the commune 100,000 lire – with individual fines ranging from 200 to 5000 lire per violator, depending on the family's size, economic condition, and the quantity of wine not reported.[75] The commune had to give 45 per cent of that to those who reported the violators, however, and another 5 per cent to the state, leaving only 50 per cent for the commune.

The commune of Cavriglia now looked beyond traditional taxation categories, seeking to increase its income by the novel method of taxing the lignite mines that had supported the local labour force for so long, but had never provided money directly to the commune itself. Debating a proposed 5 per cent production tax, in October 1945, the communal *giunta* noted: 'a) that the road network [which the commune built and maintained] extends more than 75 kilometres; b) that the population is essentially labourers; c) that the [mine] is a corporation and thus exempt from the [usual communal taxes and imposts]; d) the many and important lignite-bearing industries bring the commune no financial benefit.'[76] The commune emphasized the contradiction that the road system, which the commune built and maintained, served the mines almost uniquely for transporting lignite, while the lignite itself brought 'no tangible contribution to communal finances, *but only to the national economy.*'[77] The 5 per cent lignite tax became one of those local postwar subjects avidly discussed in the piazzas and that drew hundreds to communal council meetings, where members of the public demanded to have their say on the matter. The issue was of great local interest not only because of the commune's urgent financial needs, but also because of the new notion that the commune's administration – now including ordinary labourers – had the power to legislate taxation of 'the many and important lignite-bearing industries' that had directed the life and economy of the commune for decades.

Rebuilding Communal Identities

Decree, DLL 1, of March 1945 required each commune to formulate a plan for reconstruction, and soon thereafter the undersecretariat for press, spectacle, and tourism directed communes formulating their reconstruction plans to take into consideration not only homes and basic public works, but also 'touristic resources.' Those incipient or pre-existing resources should be developed, making tourist attractions 'one of the Nation's richest resources.' Communes therefore were to pay particular attention to hotels, historic and artistic centres, and thermal and other natural sites as they planned for rebuilding after the war. Postwar reconstruction not only offered 'the opportunity to rebuild a commune's most appealing features,' the state commented from Rome, but also provided an unforeseen chance to 'eliminate all those discordant elements' that jarred 'the environmental and scenic character of the individual zones.'[78]

Although the province of Arezzo has many artistic and architectural treasures and much natural beauty, to interpret the rubble of Civitella, San Pancrazio, and Castelnuovo, or the total destruction of Pieve Santo Stefano as a happy opportunity to weed out unattractive attributes, something along the lines of a giant closet cleaning, definitely classed as looking on the bright side of adversity. Whether Aretine communal administrations saw their tragedies in quite that light is doubtful – especially when state contributions towards reconstruction of any sort were so slow in coming. Responding to a questionnaire about his commune's 'touristic patrimony,' Civitella's sindaco noted that the commune had no hotels, no *pensioni*, no rooms for rent, no restaurants, no theatres or movie theatres, no swimming pools, no sports grounds, no tennis courts, no ski centres, no health resorts, and no telephone service. Bus service between the village of Civitella, the communal seat Badia al Pino, and the city of Arezzo did take place twice a week but was utilized by communal residents rather than tour groups.[79]

Surely, the call to put hotels, swimming pools, and tennis courts at the top of the communes' agenda for reconstruction sounded surreal in those places where a significant portion of the population was homeless, refugees were sleeping in the schools, roads were impassable, and every bridge (but two) over the Arno had been destroyed. State authorities thus proved once again how out of touch they were with local situations. Aretine communes all listed roads, bridges, schools, churches, hospitals, and local industries as the things most fundamental to their communal reconstruction plans.

Physical reconstruction, once it finally began in earnest, would signify the return to normal and civil life. Every commune, or zone, also had its particular features (some admittedly 'discordant' and 'jarring'): aspects considered most essential to the restoration of local life and local, communal identity. Two postwar examples followed very different trajectories – the Bucine railway viaduct and the Castelnuovo mines – and illustrate how communes handled what meant most to them (and made them what they were) as they strove to rebuild in the aftermath of war.

Today, as before the war in Italy began in 1943, the enormous Bucine railway viaduct dominates the landscape just below the small town of Bucine, communal seat of the commune of Bucine. It bridges a wide, deep valley to make up a section of the Florence–Arezzo railway. Because of its position on the critical north–south rail line, Allied bombers targeted the viaduct day after day as part of Operation Strangle in the spring of 1944, to interrupt German supply lines and troop movements. That massive bridge not only represented the war's destruction to those who lived near it, its destruction also had a serious, practical impact on transportation between north and south, and seriously affected the area's economy. Dispensing the 'Latest News from the Valdarno' in early 1945, a member of the Allied PWB, wrote about the commune of Bucine: '[Bucine] is situated in the Val d'Ambra, but economically is closely linked with the Val d'Arno. Owing to the destruction of the Florence-Arezzo railway it has become isolated and has lost much of its former importance.'[80] Lacking industry and a mixed economy, the commune had not had much importance before the war either – except for its position on the rail line.

Rebuilding the rail viaduct meant reopening a major rail line. That project thus was critical to the region and the nation, but, locally, it was an essential step in the return to civil life for the people of Bucine. To the local population, it did not happen fast enough. They believed the Allied occupiers first, and then the state, delayed unreasonably in financing the viaduct's reconstruction. The PWB report continued: 'On the whole the people are disappointed as they had hoped for more effective aid from the Allies. Above all they had hoped for the repair of the railway on which Bucine largely depends for its livelihood.' The neglect shown by both the Allies and the Italian state was, the administration and the citizens of Bucine considered, simply another manifestation of the distance between their commune and the authorities in Rome, and Rome's disregard of problems endured at the local level. The sindaco, the *giunta*, and crowds of unemployed labourers called again and again for a beginning to the bridge's reconstruction, and loudly protested when state contributions failed to materialize as promised.[81]

When it did commence, state monies financed the rebuilding and some outsiders were employed, but it was nevertheless a very local event with great significance for the revival of local life, as much of the rest of the commune and the province still awaited repairs and reconstruction. Local photographers and even those from Florence recorded the progress. The commune celebrated its completion: labourers and residents joined for a communal meal laid out on the viaduct itself (figures 11 and 12).[82] The reconstructed Florence–Arezzo rail line was inaugurated at a more formal ceremony on Sunday, March 31, 1946, in the presence of the minister of transportation. The first train to pass along the newly rebuilt line stopped briefly at Bucine, on the railroad bridge, to the joy of local citizens.[83] Because it was completed relatively early in the postwar reconstruction period, even as so many other public works and private structures remained untouched and unfunded, the restored Bucine viaduct embodied optimism about postwar reconstruction, about the future, and about the possibility that everyday life would soon return to normal.[84]

The postwar story of the Castelnuovo mines has a much less happy ending. A more active presence and a larger component of the local economy than the Bucine viaduct, the lignite mines were central to the community of Castelnuovo and its commune, Cavriglia, in multiple ways. 'The mine – cursed and loved – [was] experienced as the social and cultural identity by an entire community,' not merely as an 'element of the landscape.'[85] The mines were indeed part of the landscape, given that the lignite basin covers some five kilometres in the commune of Cavriglia and into the neighbouring commune. The mines' economic effect on nearby towns and villages was such that nearly every family in the extended area had a member who worked for the mines or who derived income less directly (as shop owner, for example) from the existence of the mining industry. The postwar 'crisis of the mines' – the rapid decline of the Castelnuovo mines' financial viability and the resulting dismissal of their workforce – would touch everyone.

Lignite mining in the commune of Cavriglia had begun on a significant scale in the last quarter of the nineteenth century – made possible, coincidentally, with the completion of the Bucine viaduct and the Florence–Arezzo rail line which facilitated transportation of the lignite to market. As both the number of employees and output grew, so did political awareness and labour activity. From the turn of the century, worker action at the Castelnuovo mines reads like a history of Italy's radical labour movement – and predictable management response to strikes with lockouts and layoffs. The year 1921 marked the beginning of the 'crisis of the first postwar.' When the spontaneous anti-Fascist uprising of March 23, 1921, turned violent, wounding the mine director and killing a visiting engineer, Fascist *squadristi* rampaged in response, and the corporation, in turn, shut down the mines and fired workers. Using the events of 1921 as 'a pretext,' management then reduced wages and working conditions worsened.

Conditions became so bad and worker morale fell so low that even the Fascist union representatives called for improvement.

Production increased in the late 1930s, spurred on by Mussolini's autarkical policies and Italy's lack of coal.[86] From an annual production rate of 303,896 tons in 1934, lignite production almost doubled to 604,193 tons each year between 1935 and 1939. Many families who had left the commune in the 1920s now returned; the corporation renovated existing facilities and constructed a new briquette-making plant and a new extraction plant. The first year of the war, 1940, saw an even greater production increase – to 950,024 tons. Allied bombs and the passage of the front effectively halted production in the spring and summer of 1944, and in July, German troops that massacred the civilians of Castelnuovo and Meleto also blew up the electric power station, the briquette-making plant, and all above-ground mine installations. The mines then remained closed until a mine engineer employed the motor of an abandoned German tank to help generate electricity. That cleverly improvised but marginal source of power could not make up for the many other immediate postwar difficulties, including no means to transport lignite to market and Allied forces that considered Castelnuovo's lignite stocks theirs for the taking.

In 1945 and 1946, production and sale of lignite 'recovered a rhythm.'[87] Allied troops departed the province before completely depleting existing lignite stocks, and mine facilities were repaired (though the electrical plant was not). By the end of 1945, everyone connected with the mines was hopeful. Father Ciabattini noted in his parish diary for Castelnuovo dei Sabbioni on the December 4 feast day of Santa Barbara, patron saint of miners, for the year 1945, that the 'managers and many workers [together] were present at high mass.'[88] Moreover, reconstruction of the Bucine viaduct and reopening of the Arezzo–Florence rail line in March 1946 meant that lignite again could be delivered to markets. When the miners struck that same month against the return of former mine director Antonio Civita, the prefect, the corporate owners, and the political parties all treated the workers' demands seriously, and during this same period the indebted commune of Cavriglia sought to tax the corporation based on lignite production

The regained postwar situation proved fragile, however. The initial return to normality for the mines and mineworkers coincided with the arrival of UNRRA and U.S. shipments of coal and other fuels provided at fixed prices lower than the Castelnuovo mines could offer.[89] Simply put, wide availability of cheaper and more efficient foreign supplied fuels immediately and sharply decreased the demand for Valdarno lignite, resulting 'in a rapid worsening of the financial situation of the lignite producers that within just a few weeks became untenable.' The influx of cheap foreign coal was thought to be only a 'temporary abundance,' but together with inflation-spurred rising production costs locally, it was enough to kill the mines.

The situation for the mineworkers unravelled with disorienting speed. As the political struggle between Christian Democrats and Communists heated up in Castelnuovo, Father Ciabattini recorded the 'usual festival of Santa Barbara' taking place on December 4, 1946. That year, management attended high mass, but only 'a small number of workers' did so.[90] On February 3, 1947, about 2500 mine workers with the aim of obtaining a 'pay raise' began a work slowdown – reducing normal production by 50 per cent.[91] The workers had little leverage when there was little demand for their product.

The secretary of the Miners Federation, along with the former anarchist, Attilio Sassi, and other representatives, travelled to Rome to meet with the minister of labour. After negotiations between management and the miners' shop committee stalled, then restarted at the prefect's urging, the workers occupied the mine on February 27. The strike committee declared that production would be maintained under worker control. It was, the committee said, neither an expropriation of mine property nor an experiment in cooperativism, but a sincere attempt to keep things going while the parties reached a solution. At that point (when the workers took over the mine), Labour Minister Giuseppe Romita's interest – and willingness to intercede in this local matter – grew keener.[92] Then at the close of the second shift on March 3, the workers at the Castelnuovo mine terminated their occupation, returning control to the corporation. On the morning of March 4, with the beginning of the first shift, the workers began regular production, while 'confidently awaiting' the 'prompt outcome of negotiations' through the minister of labour.[93] Cavriglia's sindaco, Priamo Bigiandi, spoke for the miners.

Months later, by November 1947, nothing had been resolved in favour of the miners, and the corporation's financial position became increasingly desperate. The company futilely asked that the politically fixed price of foreign coal be reset according to the market price of lignite (that is, that a tariff be applied to imported coal), and requested that the state give the mine a reduced rate on state railways for transporting the lignite. On Santa Barbara's feast day the following month, Father Ciabattini recorded that the holiday was celebrated 'as usual' with attendance at mass on the part of the mine managers and 'a fair number of workers.' He also noted that 'symptoms of another crisis in the local lignite mines were beginning.'[94]

The new year did bring further crisis to Castelnuovo's lignite mines. In February 1948, the corporation dismissed 400 workers. In March, the corporation dismissed an additional 200 labourers and forty clerical workers. Workers responded with a forty-eight-hour general strike in solidarity, and constituted a miners' management committee – with the intention of reoccupying the mines. Intervention by Arezzo's prefect, together with the prefect of Florence, helped bring about an agreement to reduce the number of dismissals and to fix a truce in the dismissals until the end of the month. The following month, insisting the dismissals were necessary, the corporation announced that it would dismiss another 930 workers in May. The layoffs gave rise to more 'agitations,' requiring the prefect to call in the police to maintain public order.[95]

Writing on May 1, Labour Day, that year, Father Ciabattini recorded that the 'festival of Labour' was celebrated in that red village with the 'same social-communist display as usual': a parade and red flags. The priest – himself a local man – saw the mine crisis not in economic terms of inflation and the artificially reduced price of foreign coal against the higher price of inferior Italian lignite, however, but in very local, political terms. Sandwiched between diary entries on the results of the April 1948 national political elections and the children's First Communion on the Feast of Pentecost, he laid the blame for the crisis squarely on the communist unions and their 'activists' who planned to 'seize' the mine. 'The mine has carried out layoffs. The red unions promote agitations and incite the workers to walkout. Only a few workers have the courage to resist intimidation by the activists. The aim of the walkouts is to place the corporation in bankruptcy and then to take over for themselves the exploitation of the mines.'[96]

The workers had not intended the corporation's bankruptcy, of course; the mine's financial health was critical to their continued employment. No matter how much or how quickly it was produced, however, given postwar inflation and the availability of cheap coal, lignite could not be sold for enough to cover production costs.[97] By May 1948, about 2500 mine workers and mine employees were out of work, with many owed more than two months back-wages.[98] On May 18, the corporation halted all activity, and on May 24, it fired thirty-nine female employees and ten security guards. On July 5, 1948, the *Tribunale* of Florence turned over mine operations and administration of the corporation to an outside council under oversight of a judicial commissioner. In September 1948, more than 1700 workers formed a cooperative they called 'La.Mi. Va.' (Lavoratori Miniere Valdarno), and themselves both worked and essentially ran the mines.[99] The feast day of Santa Barbara was 'celebrated in a very modest way on account of the mine situation' that year, Father Ciabattini recorded.[100]

In so short a time, from 1946 to 1948, the mine workers went from successfully protesting the return of engineer Civita, to fighting for their jobs, to struggling to keep the mine going at all.[101] The commune went from hoping to balance its postwar budget with a lignite tax to struggling to assist hundreds of unemployed miners and their families. The outside management terminated on February 28, 1949, but the workers occupied the mine – 'communist workers' Father Ciabattini pointed out – and continued to run it on their own. 'This fact ruined the critical economic situation even more,' the priest asserted.[102] Not really a political crisis, it was more than an economic and employment crisis; it was also a commune-wide social crisis.

With reconstruction finally underway in other villages and communes, the Castelnuovo mines – whose restoration had seemed so promising in 1946 – were dying, while mineworkers, their families, and the commune itself were determined not to let the mines go. Other lignite mines in the area continued in operation, declining more slowly than Castelnuovo's, but that mining region never returned to what it had been before – and immediately after – the war.[103] The postwar reconstruction of the Bucine viaduct meant the reconstruction of local life and return of the commune's place in the larger life of the nation, whereas the crisis of the Castelnuovo mines marked the end of a way of life. For Castelnuovo and surrounding villages, normal life – as it had been and as its citizens expected it to be – would not return.

After the first, post-Fascist, postwar democratic administrative elections in March of 1946 (and just before the crisis of the mines began), Cavriglia's newly-elected council and sindaco Priamo Bigiandi listened to outgoing sindaco Leonardo Lusanna's 'Report on Activities Carried Out,' prepared for the inaugural communal council meeting on April 2, 1946. The outgoing sindaco had been appointed by the CLNs of Cavriglia and Castelnuovo, and had begun his activities on behalf of the commune after the passage of the front, on July 25, 1944. He served as sindaco during the difficult immediate post-front and postwar period, in a commune where more than 200 civilians had been brutally murdered by the Germans, and whose mines and electrical plant had been nearly destroyed.

In written form, the report covering nearly two years condensed to only ten pages, but the public reading of its contents was a highly emotional event. 'After more than 20 years – today, 2 April 1946 – the Communal Council elected by the people has gathered. I am thankful therefore to address a goodwill greeting and to account for my activities.'[104] The outgoing sindaco described the postwar condition of the commune – the destruction, semi-destruction, and damage to every village and nearly every home; the damage to its industries; the empty food stores; ruined mills; no electricity; no means of transportation; ruined roads and bridges; unemployment; and a large communal budget deficit. He then set forth the first steps towards local reconstruction: how the commune had found means of assistance for the families of massacre victims, had put the unemployed to work repairing the roads and bridges, had devised a system of power generation from abandoned automobile engines to open the lignite mines and to power the mills so that flour could be ground. The state made up no part of that immediate postwar process – it was the commune and local activity that began the work of reconstructing Italy. The sindaco's report ended with the one aspect of the commune that could never be restored. He called to mind the commune's massacre victims and related them to the nation's rebirth: 'I close this report by inviting all those present and the population to turn their thoughts with reverence to the victims of barbarousness and of violence, because their sacrifice might serve as warning to the future and be a stimulus to harmony and to the work of reconstruction, essential to our martyred Italy, to raise it again from the catastrophe that has struck it.'[105]

The outgoing sindaco's report on Cavriglia's postwar – especially recalling Nazi-Fascist atrocities in Castelnuovo and Meleto – brought tears to the eyes of the twenty newly elected council members and the many members of the public who were present for that historic, democratic session of communal business. The council subsequently deliberated that sindaco Lusanna's report be published at the commune's expense, so that 'such disasters suffered by the commune of Cavriglia might be recorded for posterity and be a warning to the coming generations.'[106]

9 Private Property, Public Good, and the Housing Crisis

> This year the chestnut harvest should be plentiful, but too often they're wasted or ruined because they are not yet ready ... Our woods are filled with men and women searching for chestnuts. The farmers are in despair, but they don't defend themselves. Insulting words, threats: they have to suffer it all. They say that yesterday more than 30 *quintali* of chestnuts were pilfered.
>
> Don Narcisco Polvani, 'Diario anno 1944,' October

> The widespread destruction of homes and property in Italy by the war is without question one of the paramount problems weighing upon Italy's post-war recovery.
>
> Memorandum, Expanded UNRRA Lire Fund Housing Reconstruction Program, February 1947

Property suffered a thorough upheaval during the war, not only in Arezzo, but nearly everywhere in Italy where bombs had fallen, where refugees and evacuees sheltered, where the front passed and the Allies occupied. The damage, ruin, or occupation of so much property heightened the sense of proprietorship as the exigencies of war challenged traditional notions of property and the rights to its possession and use. Within just a few years, even with a continuing housing crisis, and as sharecroppers struggled to increase their share of ownership, ideas about property settled down almost where they had been before the war. Indeed, the Italian Republic, through its 1948 constitution, explicitly affirmed what custom and rules of law had long assured, and what war and postwar political action had not changed. Article 42 of Title III, provided in relevant part: 'Private property is recognized and guaranteed by law, which determines the methods of its acquisition and enjoyment and the limitations designed to assure its social functioning and render it accessible to all.'[1] This chapter considers the problem of property and property's place during transition and the return to civil life.

Private Property in Flux

When UNRRA Italian mission head, S.M. Keeny, held his October 9, 1945, press conference at UNRRA headquarters in Washington, DC, regarding a requested new – and increased – funding for Italy, given widespread destruction and poverty throughout the country, he was asked: 'While these poor people are suffering so, is it true that there are still great amounts of rich people [living] in luxury and idleness and wealth in Italy? No attempt has been made to compel them to share part of this Italian burden, either by us or by the Italian Government?'[2] Why were the American people being asked through congress to provide funds for Italy, Keeny's questioner skeptically posed, if 'the Italian government itself has not attempted very strongly to squeeze some of the money – to take care of the poor – from the rich of their own country?'

Keeny responded, 'I think the Socialist and Communist Parties would make such a charge rather strenuously. They would want further division of the land and further capital levies, and that is one of the issues on which the election will be fought – as to how far this should go.' Keeny's remonstration that a proposal for the Italian government to force money from the rich to give to the poor amounted to a redistribution of wealth and property – which, in those slightly pre–cold war years, screamed communism to American listeners (exactly what the United States hoped to prevent in Italy) – sufficed to divert the press conference onto topics safely removed from the suggestion that wealthy Italians be made to share with their fellow citizens.

Certain property would have to be shared, however (though not redistributed on a permanent basis), because there simply was not enough to go around, while citizens would battle one another acrimoniously over who was entitled – or more entitled – to distribution of property (especially in the context of public housing). In addition, some property had no owner after the war, some property had once had an owner, and other property definitely still had an owner – and that owner most definitely wanted to retain the property without interference from the state, the commune, or fellow citizens. A surprising number of novel questions and predicaments about property presented themselves after the fall of

Fascism and the chaos of war. As with so much else, answers were not easy – even who had authority to give the answers was disputed – while solutions generally were *ad hoc*, motivated by immediate necessity as well as political concerns, countered by tradition, and sure to be unfair to some of those involved. Property served to divide people not only along the old lines of class (the 'haves' from the 'have-nots'), but also on local administrative and more personal grounds.

Small but unprecedented questions of ownership followed the German retreat and passage of the front. German troops withdrawing during the summer of 1944 had left a cart near one sharecropper's plot in Duddova (in the commune of Bucine). The *carabinieri* had temporarily 'assigned' the cart to another man in the village of Pietraviva, who also had 'care' of a horse abandoned by the Germans in Montevarchi, and who was using horse and cart together in his health services work in the commune of Bucine. In the spring of 1945, the commune of Montevarchi wanted the horse returned there, but Bucine's sindaco argued that his commune had no other means of transport, and declined to give back the animal.[3] The horse belonged neither to the commune of Montevarchi nor to Bucine, of course. Then, the sharecropper sought to reclaim the cart – it was *his* cart – rightly considered 'his,' according to Bucine's sindaco. The sindaco urged its prompt return, because the sharecropper intended to institute legal proceedings.[4] The man must have intended to proceed in court under some universal 'finders keepers' theory; otherwise, his 'right' to property which the now absent Germans likely had stolen from someone else and then abandoned rested on rather shaky grounds.

Alberto Barni, a sharecropper near Sansepolcro asked the local Allied CAO ('Mr. Governor of A.M.G.') to intervene in his similar property dispute. The property at issue in his case was a German 'motor-lorry' that retreating Germans had wrecked and left lying near Barni's farmhouse. Barni had suffered sorely on account of the wrecked truck, when other German soldiers passing through a few weeks later thought Barni had sabotaged the truck and hidden its tires. As a result, the soldiers had 'illused' Barni and treated his family 'with the utmost cruelty, to such a degree as shooting my poor brother ... before his wife's eyes. The Germans damaged also my house and stole all my cattle.'[5] He wrote (or someone wrote for him in English) in defence of his position: 'When the Allied forces arrived here and civil life begun [sic] to resume, two different Transport Firms of this city tried to appropriate the remains of the lorry, without any regards to me, contesting between themselves the priority of their advances and their presumed rights to this sort of booty.'[6] Signor Barni sought 'full possession' of the wrecked truck, which certainly was a 'sort of booty' of war, although a very poor sort. He, more than any transport company, he argued, should get the vehicle, considering all the trouble it had brought him and the fact that it had been abandoned on his plot of land. Who had 'priority' of right under such unusual circumstances?

More so than abandoned German property, Fascist property – or what had been either Fascist Party property or the property of former Fascists – offered some of the most complicated local and national circumstances. When Fascist Republicans in Arezzo fled north at the approach of Allied troops in spring and early summer 1944, many took what valuables (their own and others) they could carry, but left real property (naturally) and bulky chattels and other personal property behind. Property left behind was not necessarily abandoned; unlike retreating German troops, village *Repubblichini* presumably would (and did) return at some point. Among their first acts, reconstituted communal councils or *giunte* named temporary conservators and administrators of property owned by former Fascists now voluntarily absent from the area. Those designated frequently were partisans or others with some postwar status, but not necessarily with expertise, property management experience, or disinterest in the eventual outcome of the property.[7]

Beleaguered prefect Guidotti Mori thus ordered every Aretine commune to form a three-person committee for overseeing preservation of Fascist-owned land, farms, and buildings within its territory. Committee members were to be 'honest persons,' with one of the three 'knowledgeable in agricultural matters.'[8] Absent Fascists also had their bank accounts frozen, with funds overseen by an additional three-person committee chosen by the sindaco and local bank directors. Cavriglia's new sindaco adopted the *giunta*'s nomination for that commune's three-person 'Commission for the Preservation of Real Property belonging to Preeminent Fascists or Persons compromised by the Past Regime' as his second official decision, and adopted the nomination for a 'Commission to Block Bank Funds of All Preeminent Fascists or Those Compromised by the Past Regime' as his third decision.[9] Perishables, such as foodstuffs, generally were turned over to communal rationing offices for distribution and furniture often was used in government offices, but less immediately usable property was conserved and cared for.[10] Only when a former Fascist Republican was dead (or assassinated), did the commune seek to acquire his property for communal use.[11]

The end of Fascist institutions, the end of the Fascist Party, and then that of the Fascist Republican Party made for another disputed, domestic 'sort of booty.' The Fascist Party, now 'defunct,' would not be returning for its property, and so, in every commune, the property of a village's 'ex-*fascio*,' the buildings and contents, and its treasury thus became available. How formerly Fascist Party property would be used in post-Fascist Italy was a subject of intense debate. Who should get it fuelled local and local–national disputes. Should *fascio* funds go to local rebuilding efforts or to assisting the victims of war, as was often proposed? How should Fascist space be transformed into post-Fascist space? Should it house new post-Fascist organizations or otherwise be used for the common good?[12] The post-Fascist state, quite naturally, considered former Fascist Party property to belong to the state. Communes, equally naturally disagreed, arguing much like farmers who found German trucks abandoned in their fields, that formerly Fascist property now belonged to the communes in which it was located.

The clearest cases from the communes' point of view involved the return of real property and structures that communes had built for or provided free of charge to their local *fasci* sometime during the *ventennio*. Less clear was what to do with real property and buildings that even earlier had belonged to local associations such as workers' or consumers' cooperatives or *Case del Popolo* before they were forcibly taken over by the Fascist Party very early in the regime, or property that had belonged to political parties outlawed after 1926. More complicated still was property the previous, now defunct Fascist Party had paid for itself or to which the Fascist state had contributed. In July 1941, for example, Mussolini had visited San Giovanni Valdarno, and 'personally' given a gift of 300,000 lire to build an outdoor theatre next to that village's *Casa del fascio*. Arezzo's provincial federation of *fasci* had deposited the money in a local bank, to be withdrawn by San Giovanni's *fascio* when the work was begun. The war had intervened, however, and the theatre had never been constructed or even begun. Now after the end of Fascism and the passage of the front, the money remained in the bank – plus interest accrued. The commune wanted to use some of the money for local assistance, and the rest towards expenses related to restoring war damaged public buildings, though who had the authority even to withdraw the funds was in dispute.[13]

Others argued that Fascist property, or at least some portion of it, should go to those who recently had fought Fascism. Father Fiorenzo Moretto, parish priest as well as an officer in the Monterchi communal section of the National Partisans Association of Italy (ANPI), complained

1 'Bucine viaduct near Arezzo, Italy made a beautiful target for the bombers of First Tactical Air Force. Months later, British troops took Arezzo, and saw what MAAF's "Operation Strangle" had done to cripple the Hun.' (On reverse of original.) U.S. National Archives, 342-FH-3A24806-61542ac.

2 'Notable among Strangle's targets near the city of Arezzo, Italy was the Bucine viaduct, which was smashed by TAF when a train was crossing it.' (On reverse of original.) U.S. National Archives, 342-FH-3A24799-52754ac.

3 'Bridges and marshalling yards at Arezzo, Italy were bombed 69 times by MAAF between January 1 and July 15, when the Allied Armies occupied the city.' (On reverse of original.) U.S. National Archives, 342-FH-3A24808-B61542ac.

4 'The shattered German gasoline truck caught by strafing fighter-bombers of First Tactical Air Force, and the Allied jeeps moving through the bomb damaged streets of Arezzo, Italy, tell much of the story of Operation Strangle, the air plan worked by MAAF to choke off all the Hun's supply routes through middle Italy.' (On reverse of original.) U.S. National Archives, 342-FH-3A24805-60439ac.

5 'Eighth Army: German Atrocities. This smouldering wreckage was once the picturesque mounting [mountain] village of Civitella, with a population of 400. In one day an estimated 140 of the villagers died.' (Original caption.) August 2, 1944. Photograph courtesy of the Imperial War Museum, London, NA 17296.

MAP OF CIVITELLA CORNIA AND SAN PANCRAZIO DISTRICTS

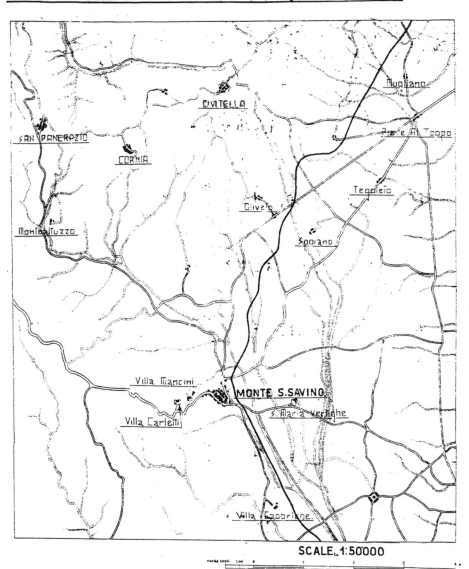

SCALE. 1:50000

REFERENCE.

CIVITELLA :- place where Partisans
    killed 2 German soldiers on
    18 June 1944 and where Ger-
    mans carried out reprisals
    killing 100 people on 29 June 1944.
CORNIA :- where 45 people were killed

MONTEALTUZZO :- place where
    Partisans had a battle
    with the Germans on 23
    June 1944
SAN PANCRAZIO :- where 67
    people were killed.

The following places are where the Germans, who took part in the atrocity on the 29 June 1944, were billeted :

MUGLIANO :- statement of PARETI
    Fabio. Page *401*
TEGOLETO :- statement of CANTUCCI
    Giorgio. Page *399*
SPOIANO :- statement of BONECHI
    E. Cesare. Page *382*
VILLA MANCINI :- statement of
    PAZIENZA Mario. Page *389*
VILLA FABBRICHE :- statement of
    BACCONI Augusto. Page *378*

PIEVE AL TOPPO :- statement of
    BONINI G. Batt. Page *386*
OLIVETO :- statement of GIANNINI
    Lorenzo. Page *385*
S. MARIA VERTIGHE :- statement of
    GIANNOTTI Corrado. Page *394*

VILLA CARLETTI :- statement of
    CARLETTI Licia. Page *360*

6 Map of Civitella, Cornia, and San Pancrazio Districts, prepared for Eighth Army investigative report on the massacres. Reproduced with permission of National Archives Image Library (NA/PRO WO) MFQ 1/1362.

7 'Eighth Army: German Atrocities. 103 bodies lie here. The survivors were unable to give so many a proper burial, so the bodies were laid side by side and earth heaped on for sanitation.' (Original caption.) August 2, 1944. Photograph courtesy of the Imperial War Museum, London, NA 17297.

8 Ruins of the electric plant outside Castelnuovo dei Sabbioni. Photograph taken by Leo Camici. Reproduced with permission of Alessandra Camici.

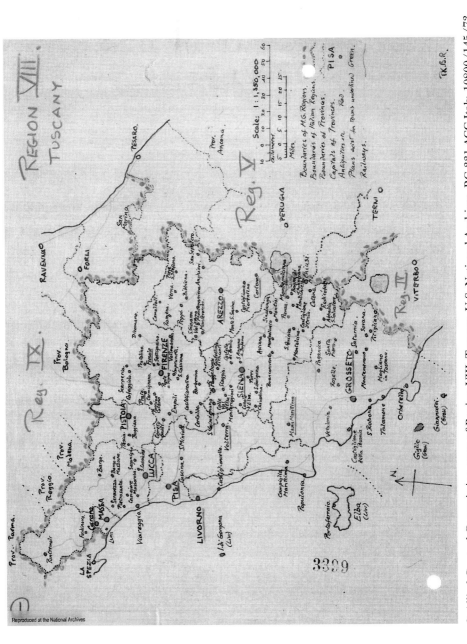

9 Allied Control Commission map of Region VIII, Tuscany. U.S. National Archives. RG 331 ACC Italy, 10800/145/73.

10 Allied food distribution, Castelnuovo dei Sabbioni. Photograph taken by Leo Camici. Reproduced with permission of Alessandra Camici.

11 The celebratory meal on the Bucine viaduct. 'The luncheon was a party, but it was also a worry because it meant the end of the work; from that moment many laborers would be sent home.' (Caption from the 1996 anniversary exhibit, my translation.) Photograph taken by Foto Vestri (1946). Reproduced with permission of the Commune of Montevarchi. Archivio Storico del comune di Montevarchi – Archivio fotografico Vestri, FC 1002.

12 The celebratory meal on the Bucine viaduct. 'The luncheon was set up on tables made of scaffolding.' (Caption from the 1996 anniversary exhibit, my translation.) Photograph taken by Foto Vestri. Reproduced with permission of the Commune of Montevarchi. Archivio Storico del comune di Montevarchi – Archivio fotografico Vestri, PR 70.

13 Castelnuovo dei Sabbioni celebrates the Republic. Photograph taken by Leo Camici. Reproduced with permission of Alessandra Camici.

14 Castelnuovo dei Sabbioni celebrates the Republic. Photograph taken by Leo Camici. Reproduced with permission of Alessandra Camici.

15 Piazza IV Novembre, the site of the July 4, 1944, massacre at Castelnuovo dei Sabbioni. The church is at top, above the piazza. Photograph taken August 1944 by Leo Camici. Reproduced with permission of Alessandra Camici.

16 The crowd at the Piazza IV Novembre massacre site for the first anniversary of the July 4, 1944, massacre at Castelnuovo dei Sabbioni. Photograph taken by Leo Camici. Reproduced with permission of Alessandra Camici.

17 Speechmaking at the Piazza IV Novembre massacre site during the first anniversary of the massacre. The speakers are standing on the balcony of the building to the left of the massacre site, as seen in figure 15 (where only the top floor balcony is visible). Photograph taken by Leo Camici. Reproduced with permission of Alessandra Camici.

18 On the second anniversary of the July 4, 1944, massacre at Castelnuovo dei Sabbioni, the bishop of Fiesole inaugurates the chapel built in memory of the victims on the massacre site in Piazza IV Novembre. Photograph taken by Leo Camici. Reproduced with permission of Alessandra Camici.

to Arezzo's prefect that, in Monterchi in February 1945, they seemed to be back in the 'middle of the fascist regime.'[14] Father Moretto was 'shocked' by communal authorities' 'negative attitude and conduct' towards ANPI and the partisans. That 'negative attitude' helps evidence local variants of feeling towards the armed Resistance as well as the ambiguous position held by partisans (and by partisan-priests on occasion) in central Italy: the sindaco declined to provide either rooms for ANPI's local offices or financial support for the association's charitable activities. ANPI had asked to utilize just one of the premises belonging to the ex-*fascio* of Monterchi. Instead, the priest complained, the sindaco permitted five former Fascist Republicans, who 'actually had served in the Republican army,' to manage the former *fascio*'s theatre. While those former Fascists kept the formerly Fascist theatre in operation, partisans from the commune were still risking their lives in the north fighting for the nation, Father Moretto argued, adding that others in the commune had died at the hands of the Germans – betrayed by Fascists. Thus, the theatre should more appropriately be in ANPI's possession and under ANPI's management, with proceeds used to 'assist the families of our comrades and our fallen.' ANPI and the priest took their own postwar moral justice position (ultimately unsuccessful) between the state's and the commune's competing claims for the property.

Property sometimes had passed through several hands from the *ventennio* to the postwar. With the passage of the front in August 1944, the reformed recreational workers' circle of Castelnuovo dei Sabbioni claimed 'full possession' of the building that had been the village *fascio*'s seat. That same building had been the *Casa del Popolo* for the socialist workers' recreational circle nearly twenty years earlier until the local Fascist Party had seized it from them in the early 1920s. When the reborn workers' circle finally physically retook the premises in 1945, nothing of the *fascio*'s (or the original circle's) furniture remained (except for a lengthy inventory list of it); the place had been stripped bare, but by whom was not clear.[15] The Castelnuovo *fascio* and its sister *fascio femminile* had closed suddenly at the end of July 1943, leaving behind furniture and other items, all of which had been inventoried on August 4, 1943, during the very brief period after the fall of Mussolini and the dissolution of the *fasci*, but before the formation of the Fascist Social Republic.

Slightly later in 1945, the furniture and other items still could not be located when the state superintendent of finance insisted it all be accounted for. Between August 1943 and August 1944, first Italian troops briefly occupied the building, then Fascist Republicans had taken it over;

German troops had requisitioned it briefly, until the 'well known reprisals of July 4, 1944,' and finally Allied troops had installed themselves. During that very busy year, any of the building's successive occupants might have carried away or destroyed the property, the commune told the state. While the commune pointed out the obvious, the workers' circle asserted that the building's missing contents by no means now belonged to the state or even to the commune.

The superintendent of finance also reminded the commune of Civitella of its obligation to maintain carefully all former *fascio* property as had been ordered inventoried in 1943 after the fall of Mussolini.[16] In March 1945, the Finance Ministry wished 'to ascertain immediately' the existence of all such goods and property, so as to include them in the registry of the state's patrimony. Civitella's sindaco tersely responded that it would be impossible to trace every single stick of furniture from the former *fasci* in the commune.[17] As for real property and buildings, a *fascio* building of three rooms had been built in the village of Ciggiano 'at the public's expense,' with the commune contributing the land. The commune had first sought return of the property in September 1943 when the Fascist Party was dissolved, but Republican Fascists had quickly turned the building into a Republican *Casa del fascio*. Now on the verge of taking the property once and for all, the commune insisted that that former *Casa del fascio*, which the commune had paid for, most definitely would not become part of the state's patrimony. 'The commune and the people reclaim their right of ownership,' the sindaco firmly asserted, and they intended finally to transform the building into the school the community had long needed.[18]

Post-Fascist battles over Fascist property further illustrate how communes often now portrayed themselves (and their citizens) as pawns or victims of Fascism during the regime, and how they saw themselves in opposition both to the Fascist and the post-Fascist state, perceiving that the state continued to act against their local interests. In 1947, when the state demanded that the commune of Bucine pay rent to the government for the commune's postwar use of the ex-*fascio* building in San Pancrazio, Bucine's sindaco stressed that the commune had used its own limited funds – with no help from the state – to repair that war damaged building. Before the commune even considered paying rent (for what the commune considered its own property), the sindaco insisted that the state acknowledge and offset what expenses the commune had undertaken to restore it.[19]

Public Taking and Private Use

The government – in the form of the state, the communes, and for a while, the occupying Allies – interfered in nearly every individual's property and its uses in one way or another, oftentimes in the name of the public good. After the passage of the front, farmers fortunate enough to have saved their oxen from the retreating Germans and from Allied artillery were obligated – without payment – to help transport material such as sand, rocks, bricks, tiles, lime, and cement that the communes needed to repair roads, houses, and buildings damaged by the war. In the autumn, they shared their oxen, pulling threshing machines from farm to farm. In the spring, Arezzo's prefect again ordered farmers to share their work animals, this time assisting in plowing and planting for those farmers whose own livestock had been stolen or slaughtered.[20] These mandated efforts contributed to unity and solidarity during that difficult period. Certainly, many farmers would have shared their animals and efforts even without a provincial directive, and most recognized that neither the communes nor the beneficiaries could reimburse the farmers for use of their oxen. Conversely, however, others resented the 'invasion' of their property and their neighbours' new (if temporary) entitlement to it.[21] Such forced sharing also contributed to a common sense of suffering and hardship – and the continuation of wartime sacrifices.

Citizens other than farmers had to share their property and possessions for the public – and the Allied – good. British troops requisitioned Signor Bagiardi's 'beautiful car,' one of the very few remaining, according to Father Polvani.[22] The English assured him it would be used locally, but Father Polvani believed that the automobile would not be seen again, and Bagiardi feared the same. The commune of Cavriglia requisitioned one man's Guzzi 250 motorcycle and another's unspecified motorcycle 'for the necessity of the commune' in August of 1944.[23] Bucine's sindaco asked a private citizen if the people of Rapale might use his well until the village fountain could be repaired.[24]

As communes began to rebuild, some private property became permanently public through a variety of means, not unlike the different ways real estate had come to the Fascist Party and local *fasci*. The village of Pietraviva, in Bucine, had only a single room for its elementary school, without even a toilet, and was 'in other ways inadequate and unsuitable' for the fifty students it held. Signor Raffaello Benini generously offered the commune – 'for free' – a piece of his land on which the commune could build a new school.[25] In 1947, the *giunta* of the commune of Cavriglia voted to pay 20,000 lire to the heirs of one man killed in the July 1944 massacres for a piece of property in the village of Meleto, on which the commune would build public housing.[26]

The commune of Civitella needed land on which to build the twelve residences (comprising forty-eight rooms) in Civitella and Cornia authorized by the Ministry of Public Works for 'those made homeless by the war,' as no adequate communally owned property was available in either place.[27] The commune also was very much in debt, and so asked the heirs of a man from that commune to donate their property 'as a gesture of solidarity towards the victims,' but the heirs declined, forcing the commune to acquire the property by eminent domain.[28] Similarly, the commune of Bucine condemned private land in San Pancrazio for a community sports park in 1946, when the owner would not donate it or sell it cheaply enough.[29]

The ongoing, post-front housing crisis also demanded that public property be used for public good in ways originally unintended. As seen, communes had Allied troops, refugees, and their own citizens living in schools, theatres, and any other available public buildings. The continuing need to shelter the thousands of homeless was obvious, but even with attempted solutions, disputes continued about the misuse and proper use of public property. By *giunta* vote, Bucine's incoming communal secretary and his family were permitted to live in rooms connected to the first floor of the schoolhouse.[30] The secretary and his family presumably behaved more decorously in their new home than did the woman living in a schoolroom in Ciggiano, near Civitella. During her recent visit to area schools, the local inspector for the Ministry of Public Instruction was appalled to discover the woman cutting hair in the village schoolroom.[31] How could the sindaco ignore such an 'abuse' of the property – and one which could also infect the children with head lice? The sindaco replied that the commune had permitted the 'poor woman, still homeless and sheltering in the schoolroom' to carry out her hairdresser trade only during school vacations, and assured the *ispettrice* that the room would be thoroughly cleaned before school reopened.

The superintendent of libraries for Tuscany complained to Arezzo's prefect – who, the superintendent assumed, shared his concern, given the prefect's 'well known interest in all cultural matters' – that the superintendent had found the books in a 'truly deplorable state' during his recent visit to Pieve Santo Stefano's communal library in the spring of 1947.[32] A family of refugees was living in one room of the library. Books were scattered on a bookshelf together with the family's food, and other books were stacked in a room where part of the ceiling was missing and rain fell in. These were not 'inferior or worthless' works, but 'very important books,' including beautiful editions of Italian classics from the first years of the last century. The superintendent realized the war had destroyed Pieve Santo Stefano, and that the problem of housing continued to worry everyone. Realistically, he was not asking that the family be evicted, or even that the library be repaired and reopened to the public. He asked only that the most valuable books be transferred elsewhere temporarily, perhaps to neighbouring Sansepolcro. Refugees who were then living in the Communal Hall could move into new public housing units when they were completed, thereby leaving room in the Communal Hall to store the library's most valuable books.

One family lived in Arezzo's bomb damaged archaeology museum for more than four years, until the end of 1949, preventing at least part of the museum from being renovated and reopened.[33] The use of schools, libraries, communal offices, and other structures as homes for the homeless not only raised issues variously relating to traditional communal duties and the delayed return to normal life, but also raised concerns over how far to 'stretch' the normal and regular uses of property. Recall the citizens of Pieve Santo Stefano who refused to use their sole intact building, their church, as a schoolroom during the week. Destruction and displacement meant continued disruption of daily life and contributed to the disoriented feeling that basic aspects of normal life fundamentally had changed. It also fuelled the longing to return to normal life as quickly as possible. And, in one grimly ironic private use of public, post-Fascist space, a widow whose husband was killed in the massacre of Civitella, and who was left homeless with her four children, asked permission to live in the village *dopolavoro*. It was the *dopolavoro* where the local partisan band shot two German soldiers and ignited the June 29, 1944, massacre.[34]

The Housing Crisis

That refugees and evacuee citizens still lived in schools, libraries, museums, huts, stables, and worse through 1949 and thereafter, shows how serious Italy's (especially central Italy's) housing crisis was.[35] The housing crisis (together with widespread need and unemployment) shaped postwar daily life – personal, administrative, and political – and was another large aspect of continued suffering. Local examples demonstrate the lengths to which desperate citizens went to obtain housing or keep what shelter they had, and local examples help explain the drastic steps communes took to solve the housing crisis. Local examples also demonstrate how the housing crisis helped political parties enlarge their 'social presence' and influence to become part of postwar daily life as they intervened in property disputes and decisions.

As in the early war years, when then enemy Allied bombs created the first phase of the refugee problem, those who had shelter had to share it. In central Italy in the later phase during autumn of 1944, after the passage of the front, Arezzo's prefect similarly ordered that no one within the province could keep more than one house for his or her own disposal.[36] Whoever possessed two or more residences immediately had to pick one, freeing the other or others to be assigned to homeless families. Individual rooms within occupied houses were requisitioned if an entire house was not available, with communal sindaci assigning two persons to every habitable room.[37]

Like farmers with their oxen, some citizens voluntarily shared with displaced family, neighbours, or strangers. Other property owners fought requisitioning, however, and their motives for doing so were interestingly varied. The countess who resided in Florence tried to block the order to give up two rooms in her villa in Arezzo, but she was not so selfish as she initially appeared: she earlier and willingly had turned over most of her villa for the temporary home of the provincial foundling hospital. Only those last two rooms she hoped to reserve for her own use. One absentee owner in Genova had allowed a group of nuns to use his villa in Chiusi della Verna as a rest and cure home for needy women workers, but the sindaco ordered the villa vacated to house refugees.[38]

Some owners did not regain possession of their own property even quite long after the war. At the end of 1948, once again in vain, Signor Luigi Pertucci requested the return of his villa in the city of Arezzo. German troops, who had been the first to requisition it, occupied the villa until the summer of 1944. Then, before Pertucci could return to Arezzo after the city's liberation, the house had been requisitioned by the commune's housing commissioner and assigned to homeless families.[39] Those families lived in the villa for four years beginning in August 1944, without ever paying rent (at least according to Signor Pertucci). He unsuccessfully attempted to dislodge the occupants by having the villa officially declared of 'artistic importance' and thus placed under the protection of the state.

Requisitioning residences often made for some strange and hostile bedfellows. In early August 1944, Arezzo's provincial CLN compelled or convinced Angelo Aiello to give over two rooms of his family's apartment – and shared use of the kitchen – to the four-member Ciofini family. Now, five years later, in August 1949, the two families were still flatmates. The Ciofinis had never made the slightest effort to find other housing, Aiello asserted to the prefect; instead the Ciofinis hoped the Aiellos would be the ones to decide to go, leaving them the entire apartment. What made the situation even more aggravating (and what must have made for years of lively kitchen conversation) was that Signor Ciofini was a member of the Communist Party (indeed the 'head of a cell'), 'always assiduously carrying out activity on behalf of the Party.' Signor Aiello, on the other hand, was a police sergeant, and 'therefore opposed to communism.'[40] After five years, he could no longer continue living with the Ciofini family – without putting his own personal safety in serious danger. How – or when – the stand-off ended is not known, but it is worth noting that Aiello and his family originally acceded to the sharing, something that reflects CLN authority at the end of the war, as well as the family's empathy with their displaced fellow citizens and the belief that the situation would be short term.[41]

In December 1944, a government decree had called for each commune to name a housing commission and commissioner to decide which property (or portions of it) would be requisitioned for lodging, and who would be assigned particular lodging.[42] Serving on the commission cannot have been an easy job. Both the commissioner and the vice-commissioner in the commune of Montevarchi quickly resigned – it simply was not possible, they said, to settle the 'infinite number of homeless families' in that commune.[43]

In Bucine, in a ten month period beginning June 1, 1946, the most recent commissioner there had composed six requisitions – all of which the prefect or the commune had annulled. He had, however, handled eleven other housing orders more successfully, without having to impose requisition orders. The statistics of those ten months spoke for themselves, said Bucine's sindaco; a housing commissioner ought to be making 'a real contribution' to placing the homeless and refugee families, but that was not happening. The sindaco had taken it upon himself to try (unsuccessfully) to place two poor families living in the village of Ambra. Moreover, an elderly couple had lived for two years in the hospital at Montevarchi, for which the communal treasury was paying an exorbitant sum every month. They could live more cheaply at home, with the commune paying for daily help to come in, but there was no home to put them in. Ambra's own district doctor had been searching – by himself – for months for a suitable place for himself and his family. The sindaco proposed a new commissioner to carry out the important duties of the job.

The sindaco of Pieve Santo Stefano, on the other hand, reported to the prefect that the housing commissioner of that commune – where about two-thirds of the communal population (which included the ruined village of Pieve Santo Stefano) was homeless – had made a 'good' contribution to solving the housing problem.[44] In most cases, settlement of the homeless within that commune had been 'accomplished in a conciliatory and friendly way.' Things may have remained so friendly there because, by the end of April 1947, the commissioner had signed only fifteen requisition orders, one of which had been annulled by a higher authority, and because so little property was left standing in that commune to be requisitioned.

Because most commissioners faced opposition both from owners whose property was requisitioned and from the homeless who felt they had not received a fair – or any – assignment in June 1946 communes formed an additional commission to examine and resolve complaints, with two members representing the homeowners and two members representing tenants.[45] Perhaps because communal housing commissioners had so little success in settling the homeless and solving the housing crisis, or because the housing situation had stabilized earlier in some other areas of the country, a June 1947 decree abolished the office of commissioner.[46] The position could be extended a year, until June 30, 1948, in communes with a population greater than 100,000 inhabitants or those having undergone particularly severe physical destruction of buildings due to the war.[47] The *giunta* for the commune of Sansepolcro voted unanimously to extend the office of housing commissioner for another year. That commune had a 'moderate' number of its own citizens homeless, but also had to cope with the many refugees from neighbouring communes of Pieve Santo Stefano and Badia Tedalda.[48] Montevarchi, Cavriglia, Bucine, Civitella, and most of Arezzo's communes also voted to continue their housing commissions for another year.[49]

The commune of Pratovecchio also voted for the extension, but the prefect declined to approve that commune's deliberation, pointing out that the one-year extension was 'reserved' for those communes having suffered 'particularly severe destruction' – a condition he considered inapplicable to Pratovecchio. The sindaco replied in disbelief regarding the prefect's assessment of his commune's condition. 'I was really astonished by your note in which you say that PRATOVECCHIO DOES NOT SEEM TO HAVE SUFFERED PARTICULARLY SERIOUS DESTRUCTION OF ITS BUILDINGS!'[50] He urged the prefect to visit the commune and see for himself the condition of the buildings and the destruction the Germans had caused – how they had blown up all the houses along the main streets to block the road against the Allied Army.

> Many families of this wretched place live in barns in a promiscuity lacking all human dignity, and the very few reconstructed buildings belong to private owners who themselves live in them. The Prefect's pronounced judgment is demoralizing, not only because it shows that the provincial authorities are completely unacquainted with conditions in the communes, but also because they feel they can issue such harmful judgments ... without first ascertaining the physical conditions of the communes damaged by the war.

Here was yet another, very clear example of the 'distance' between the state and the local. The prefect – who was only as far away as the city of Arezzo – had not even troubled to visit Pratovecchio, yet declared that the commune had not suffered. The state and its authorities, Pratovecchio's sindaco emphasized, showed just how little they cared about the conditions of the communes and the everyday suffering of ordinary people.

The state in the person of Interior Minister Parri had ordered a census of persons homeless in November 1945 in provincial capitals and other locales in which the 'housing problem' was grave. The census showed the commune of Arezzo with 8500 homeless out of a prewar population of 60,284, meaning about one in seven (not counting those originally from outside the commune) there was homeless.[51] 'Homeless' (*senza tetto*) did not necessarily mean that an individual or a family was living outdoors without any roof (*tetto*) at all, but generally meant that they were living in places 'not intended for' or not 'suitable for habitation.'[52] Bucine, with a prewar population of 9332, had 280 of its residents homeless at the end of November 1945, while Civitella had 344 out of a prewar population of 8126, and Cavriglia 550 out of 8969. A number of Arezzo's communes had fewer than one hundred of their citizens homeless, but most had between 200 and 600 homeless, and far more when refugees from outside the commune were included. Pieve Santo Stefano had the greatest number: 3850 still homeless, out of a prewar population of 5978 – almost two-thirds of its citizens.

A significant percentage of the many hundreds of written requests for aid received by communal ECAs in the province of Arezzo made prominent mention of the petitioners' housing situation and what had befallen their property. In the commune of Bucine, for example, the large victim population sought some assistance, because the Germans had carried off all of their belongings, and then destroyed their homes.[53] Many were entirely 'without a house' or any place to live: houses 'had first been set afire, then blown up – all reduced to a pile of rubble.' 'Blown to bits,' 'reduced to a heap of ashes' or a 'pile of rubble,' 'razed to the soil' – all were common and frequently repeated descriptions of what homes had suffered.

Phrases were repeated so often that, to one who reads them now in bulk, the letters and petitions appear formulaic. Certainly, the same schoolteachers or priests often helped dozens of inarticulate or illiterate citizens craft their pleas for assistance, which made for similarity. Such letters nonetheless show the magnitude of the crisis, and reemphasize how the population suffered the common experience of destruction and shared a collective sense of loss – very real property loss in this instance. Houses 'and everything inside them' had been lost. The Germans had carried off all personal possessions; the Germans had carried off 'everything they could find.' Many houses and some entire villages really had been reduced to 'a pile of rubble'; the citizens did not exaggerate. Women were widowed, had their houses destroyed, and were left alone and homeless with children and elderly in-laws to care for. One couple with an elderly mother, and three small children, one of whom was paralyzed from infantile paralysis, had lived in a horse stall for the last months. Another family of six shared a single room. Countless others were similarly 'without a home' and 'in pitiful conditions,' 'without even a bed to lie on.'[54]

Citizens similarly petitioned communal sindaci, the prefect, the housing commissioner, even the minister of the interior for help in finding any sort of lodging. The prefect generally passed the requests he received on to the sindaci of the communes from which the letters came, noting: 'This person has once again appealed to me for help in finding housing.' 'Have you considered [the petitioner's] present particular conditions of need,' the prefect would ask a sindaco, as he directed him to 'look into the matter further' for scores of petitioners who made repeated – sometimes monthly – requests for housing. 'The housing crisis has not been resolved in a little more than a month' since you last asked, testily responded the sindaco of Montevarchi (in September 1948) to the prefect's insistence, once again, that surely housing could be found somewhere, if sindaci would only 'look into it' more carefully.[55]

Repairing and Rebuilding

Aretine villages whose most recent public additions may have been a World War I monument, a well, a railway station, or a *Casa del fascio*, now needed to be rebuilt from their foundations, with housing usually the most critical element. Some truly desperate villages, like San Pancrazio and Levane, pleaded with the state to construct wooden barracks as an emergency measure to get the homeless through the winter of 1944–5.[56] Other places, especially Civitella, feared that construction of such temporary housing would adversely change the traditional character of towns and villages that already had suffered so many serious blows.[57]

The post-Fascist state formally had addressed the 'problem of war damaged property' in November 1944, in January 1945, and again in March and June of 1945.[58] Ideally, citizens whose homes were damaged, but reparable, would receive state monies to help pay for a portion of repair costs, while public housing would be built for those who were homeless and without homes to repair.[59] With the war over, the minister of public works established a central housing committee to coordinate the efforts of individuals, communes, provinces, and organizations in the repair and rebuilding of houses. Every commune where a 'notable number' of buildings had been damaged in the war was to form a communal reconstruction committee (or building repair committee) to draw up an overall plan of communal reconstruction. Each committee then was to make recommendations to the provincial office of the state civil engineer regarding the urgency of particular projects.[60]

In Bucine, as in the other communes, the sindaco served as committee president and the commune's secretary acted as committee secretary. One member – a homeowner – represented homeowners, while another member represented the homeless, and two other citizens served as technical consultants.[61] Committees were to do everything from designating damaged buildings capable of rapid repair; presenting plans for direct assistance on the part of the civil engineer in executing such repairs; encouraging homeowner initiative, especially in undertaking necessary repairs by themselves; to promoting and assisting the supply and transportation of necessary materials and tools; and generally encouraging the rapid execution of repair work.[62]

Generally, however, communal reconstruction committees were not so quick in 'providing the keen stimulus to reconstruction that was originally envisaged as their main function.' Committees could not make up for the postwar economy, the postwar materials shortage, and postwar transportation difficulties. Most homeowners did not have the funds to pay up front for building materials and for labour, even if the state would eventually repay them for part of their outlay. The government's June 1945 decree addressed that problem by allowing the civil engineer's office to purchase building materials on account for homeowners in 'devastated' communes who had suffered war damage to their property and who received approval from their communal reconstruction committee. Building materials, like everything else in the postwar world, were in great demand and short supply, however. Even when materials could be obtained locally, money from Rome to purchase them was very slow in making its way to provincial civil engineering offices.

The government's system of compensation was rather complex. For individual housing repairs that totalled 300,000 lire or less, the state (through a province's civil engineering office under the Ministry of Public Works) would contribute – or at least stated its intention to contribute – 50 per cent of that cost, plus an additional 10 per cent 'bonus' if the work was carried out within a given time. Communal reconstruction committees could approve and settle claims less than 100,000 lire without first obtaining approval from the civil engineering office. For repair work or rebuilding costing more than 300,000 lire, the state intended to pay one-third of the claim in sixty biannual instalments, from the date the work was completed. Mortgage loans (at 4 per cent interest) from credit banks or building societies also were made available to those whose repairs cost over 300,000 lire, though many homeowners were reluctant to seek them during that economically unstable time. The contributions constituted another large financial undertaking on the part of the state, but from the owners' end, as they stood surrounded by the ruins of what had been their homes, it seemed a token that they might be reimbursed, at most, only 50 per cent or a third of their expenses paid over a thirty-year period (and escalating inflation) – after they somehow managed to repair and rebuild on their own.[63]

At the end of 1945, Arezzo's civil engineering office had been assigned 20 million lire to advance or reimburse for works of reconstruction. Nevertheless, Civitella's sindaco complained the commune 'had never received much help' from the state. Homeowners in Civitella, who had repaired and reconstructed their own houses at their own expense, were waiting impatiently for the promised financing so that they might pay at least in part the expenses they sustained. By November 1945, the civil engineer had funded only four repairs.[64] A number of owners throughout the province who could not afford to make repairs and wait for government reimbursement were forced to sell at less than their property's prewar value and for money rapidly losing its value.[65] Despite such programs and legislation that acknowledged the enormity of destruction within Italy, slow payment (and sometimes no payment at all) compounded the popular conviction that the state was doing too little towards reconstruction, and was incapable of solving perhaps the most serious problem of the postwar.

Aside from difficulties in obtaining building materials, finding money to advance to labourers, and terminal slowness in state repayment, the very obvious flaw in the government's program was inflation. By 1947, the state's promise of a 50 per cent contribution towards expenditures of less than 300,000 lire, or of a third towards greater costs, did not go far in reconstructing a house that had been 'reduced to a pile of rubble.' Amounts were therefore increased. The state's eventual contribution remained 50 per cent of the repair costs (with a continued 'encouragement bonus'), but the ceiling was raised, on account of rapid inflation, to 500,000 lire for those whose houses had been damaged but were reparable for that amount.[66] Those whose houses were so badly damaged or completely destroyed that 500,000 lire would not cover the cost of repair remained eligible for state assistance in the amount of one-third the cost of rebuilding, now with an 'encouragement bonus' payable in a lump sum that varied from 40,000 to 80,000 lire according to the progress of the work and the size of the building.

Homeowners in those communes officially determined 'most damaged by the war,' enjoyed a slightly greater state contribution or compensation of 60 per cent of the cost of repairs.[67] That additional 10 per cent was important not only because it meant more money towards reconstruction, but also because it served to show, yet again, the distance and disinterest of the state. When the state inspector for Tuscany did not include the commune of Civitella among those 'most seriously damaged,' the shocked sindaco immediately objected to this example of how little 'the authorities' knew about local conditions. He reminded how the entire commune had been very 'hard hit' by both Allied offensives and the German retreat, and pointed to an earlier legislative decree recognizing the communal fractions of Civitella (Cornia, Tuori, and San Martino Montarfoni) as 'disaster areas.'[68]

The Ministry of Public Works oversaw this 'ordinary' repair, reconstruction, and repayment, while the Ministry of Postwar Assistance (APB) devoted part of its attention to a narrower group of ruined houses and showed that the state had in mind some purpose in addition to physical reconstruction. In 1945, APB expanded financial assistance for the reconstruction and repair of homes 'destroyed or damaged by Nazi-Fascists in acts of reprisal.' This was aid for those who 'during the partisan struggle – whether directly or indirectly – had their place of residence destroyed and thus have come to find themselves *in a state of serious need.*'[69] 'Such financial aid [towards rebuilding] should serve to return the residences to conditions of normal habitability,' the ministry explained. The aid had two aspects. It could come as 'provisional financing' up to 50 per cent (the same amount of state contribution pursuant to the more generally applicable June 9, 1945, statute) and as an 'extraordinary contribution' for the actual outlay towards reconstruction, excluding the cost of labour provided by the owner and family members – 'for which in no case was there entitlement to reimbursement.'[70] That is, the state (through APB) would advance some and vowed to repay the rest for houses damaged or destroyed during Nazi-Fascist reprisals, but would not do the same to return to 'normal habitability' those houses damaged or destroyed by other causes of war.[71] The state thus distinguished houses destroyed during German massacres from those destroyed or damaged by Allied bombs during Operation Strangle or by the passage of the front.

Arezzo's provincial office of APB, headed by the prefect, directed the reconstruction committees of each commune to set forth the number of houses destroyed or damaged in Nazi-Fascist reprisals; the sum required to repair or rebuild them; and 'an ordered classification' of those projects in which the committee believed APB should intervene first, either because the owners were especially 'deserving' or because the works were otherwise considered especially urgent. Committees were to consider a family's state of 'serious need,' and to give precedence to repairs that were important, but that would not exceed 300,000 lire. Reconstruction committees also were to choose first those projects for which owners themselves could do all or most of the repairs and rebuilding, for which labour the state would not reimburse.[72] Petitioners seeking APB financial assistance had to submit sworn declarations supported by the local *carabinieri* and setting forth the circumstances surrounding the destruction or damage and 'referring specifically to the actions of reprisal' which had taken place in the area (though not having to prove cause and effect or reprisal for what exactly, only that a massacre and accompanying property damage had taken place). The sindaco then confirmed 'the state of serious need of the petitioner' and the state of the petitioner's family.[73]

Once again the state pointedly equated massacre victims with the partisan struggle, and differentiated between reprisal (or massacre) victims and more ordinary or 'fortuitous' victims of war, this time down to the level of how their property had been destroyed. Once again, the state recognized the near universality of destruction and suffering, while distinguishing among victims within the same commune or even the same village. As with the 20,000 lire National Solidarity *Premio* granted to fallen partisans and to the families of those civilians slaughtered during German reprisals (or during more 'ordinary massacres' considered reprisals), the monies given to repair and rebuild reprisal damaged houses came from the state's 'Solidarity Fund' (*Fondo Solidarietà*). And again, the national gesture of solidarity to those considered to have contributed and sacrificed most for the cause of Liberation was there, but the money was slow in following.[74]

Housing for the Homeless

Ruined communes repeatedly told the authorities in Rome that their citizens could not rebuild on their own. Even with partial state assistance, the postwar economic condition of many property owners did not allow them to take on the financial burden of reconstruction and repair. Moreover, many citizens had never been homeowners, and therefore 'the population called for state intervention to construct a certain number of council houses.'[75]

A vast program (vast compared to anything Italy had seen before) of state-funded new construction made up a large part of the postwar plans of both the Ministry of Public Works and the Ministry of Postwar Assistance.[76] New 'houses for the homeless' (*case per i senza tetto*) would be financed entirely by the state, but turned over to the communes to administer – and for communes to make the local level decisions which of their homeless families would live in them.[77] Local civil engineers' offices recommended to the Ministry of Public Works how many would be built in a province and which communes should receive the houses. A percentage of the houses were to be reserved for 'returnees,' including veterans, partisans, POWs, returned deportees and internees, and returnees from forced labour.

A different public housing program, the *case popolari*, already existed. The Institutes of Public Housing (Istituti Case Popolari) were a depression-era Fascist creation, founded in 1935, which owned about 137,000 dwellings throughout Italy. They were state subsidized (so that rents were low), and located under the general jurisdiction of the Ministry of

Public Works, though provincial-level institutes had considerable autonomy (and so were more fully called Autonomous Institutes of Public Housing.[78] An administrative council made up of the local president of the institute, representatives of the civil engineering office and superintendent of finance, along with sindaci, selected the occupants of the houses, and administered and maintained the dwellings. After the war, most already built *case popolari* needed repairs, and new ones (an additional 135,000) were planned.

A third national-level program or agency paralleled those state programs: the United Nations Relief and Rehabilitation Administration – Comitato Amministrativo Soccorso ai Senzatetto. UNRRA-CASAS was founded in 1946 first to manage UNRRA-donated rebuilding aid and then, just as UNRRA itself began to close up shop and withdraw from Italy, to oversee the funds of the European Recovery Program (ERP, or the Marshall Plan) directed towards rebuilding. Intended to work closely with the state programs, but to remain independent from the state – and from political considerations and pressures – UNRRA-CASAS planned, helped finance, and helped to build housing for the homeless.[79]

The 'houses for the homeless' and the *case popolari* programs soon merged: newly planned state-funded housing came to be referred to as 'public housing for the homeless,' but not enough of it was being planned. Aretine communes called repeatedly on their provincial institute of public housing, the nearest UNRRA-CASAS representative, the prefect, Arezzo's civil engineer, and the Ministry of the Interior to repair *case popolari* already in their communes and to build new ones 'quickly.'[80] In November 1946, when the provincial civil engineer approved housing construction for the homeless of Massa in the commune of Cavriglia, Cavriglia's communal council met in a series of packed public sessions – not only to welcome the event, but to debate whether the houses should be built in Castelnuovo dei Sabbioni instead of neighbouring Massa dei Sabbioni.[81] The matter of building a small block of houses in one village rather than the next generated such public interest and heated public comment that the council chamber in the communal hall could not hold all those who wished to attend and speak. After much public 'input,' the council voted unanimously to propose that the housing be built in Castelnuovo instead of Massa. Because almost all the homeless of Massa were miners who worked in Castelnuovo mines, the council reasoned (though the residents of Massa did not), transferring the housing to Castelnuovo actually would be to their benefit. The imminent closure of the mines was as yet unimagined.

Local level debates and disputes over where housing should be built, how, and for whom often got in the way of the actual building, as did lack of funding. Discussions, arguments, and competing plans surrounding the construction of only one four-unit building in the ruined and very small village of Cornia, in the commune of Civitella, went on for several years before the structure was eventually built.[82] In August 1948, UNRRA-CASAS informed the commune of Bucine that limited funds prevented it from undertaking new construction of public housing, as urgently requested and needed, in the destroyed villages San Pancrazio and Badia Agnano. The sindaco begged the agency to reconsider: four years after the massacre and destruction in San Pancrazio, families were still living together in the 'most squalid misery,' many of them in barns 'crowded together like so many animals.'[83]

Arguments and disappointment stemmed from the very real fact that neither foreign aid nor state funds – or both together – would ever suffice to provide anywhere near the amount of housing needed, and thus a new aspect of the housing crisis began when some council houses finally were ready to be occupied in 1948. Like blankets, hot lunches, and other assistance given directly after the passage of the front, public housing in 1948 was in extremely limited supply, with not enough to go around. One man from the city of Arezzo, but now a local refugee in the commune of Civitella, requested a place in newly constructed public housing in Arezzo city. Civitella's sindaco wholly supported the request because, while displaced in the commune of Civitella, both the man and his son were unemployed and receiving public assistance from that commune. The sindaco of Arezzo commune informed Civitella's sindaco, however, that he had already received more than 1000 requests for the mere seventy available places in the city.[84]

Assigning housing – much like handing out shoes and overcoats – required (or allowed) those with authority and the decision making role to make assessments on the need, worthiness, and competing status categories of their fellow citizens, and it too generated hundreds of passionate requests and demands.[85] Not enough available housing also gave rise to just as many heated complaints, as well as frequent input from the political parties and anyone else with influence and *raccomandazioni* to share. By early 1948 and the important national election of that spring, the Catholic-Communist struggle was well underway in the province of Arezzo, as elsewhere. Intervening in the housing crisis on behalf of individuals and families served as another way by which political parties showed both their concern and their influence, and became part of daily life on a very local level.

One woman in the village of Sestino was a war widow whose husband had died on the Russian front. She herself had been deported to Germany for forced labour, which had resulted in her unwillingly vacating her lodging. Since her return to civil life, she lived with her parents and her two children, orphaned of their father, in a house with no running water. Her request for a 'modest apartment' was denied, even though Amintore Fanfani's private secretary (Fanfani was then minister of labour and social security) wrote to the prefect, asking him to intercede on the woman's behalf. The police officer who investigated the denial determined, however, that her current residence was sufficient and her economic condition was 'fairly good.' She enjoyed a teacher's salary, and also had a seven hectare parcel of land her children inherited upon their father's death. Moreover, the majority of houses in Sestino lacked running water; hers, therefore, was no worse than most.[86] Even a letter from Fanfani (or his secretary) was not necessarily enough.

Petitioners were widows with children orphaned of a father and elderly in-laws to support; entire extended families who were sharing a single room, or who shared with another family; they were living in a stable; they had no kitchen; they had left their homes to escape the bombing or the passage of the front, and found someone else living there upon their return or found nothing left at all. They were partisans, veterans of North Africa or the Russian front, state employees (and therefore, they argued, entitled to preference within state housing), and former prisoners in Germany. They were all '*senza tetto*,' all without alternatives, all desperate, and all likely to remain that way unless assigned a public apartment.[87]

Property owners petitioned for places in public housing on behalf of their tenants, either to free up space for their own use, or so that they could make apartments and houses available to others.[88] Employers petitioned for employees and party representatives petitioned doggedly for their constituents and supporters. Local politics and party interest were never absent from any aspect of postwar life including public housing, and when joined with existing personal and family disputes, they represent local postwar life at its most contentious and fractious. In Pieve Santo Stefano in the spring of 1948, when a *professoressa* requested an apartment in one of the new *case popolari* recently constructed in that war destroyed commune and the communal *giunta* voted to deny her request, she promptly took up the matter with the prefect. The sindaco explained that the commune then had only ten apartments at its disposal, while the commune also had at least sixty 'truly homeless' families. The available units each consisted of three bedrooms, a kitchen, and a living room, but the *professoressa*'s family consisted of only three persons: the woman and her parents. A unit would have been assigned them, the sindaco explained, if they chose another family with whom they were compatible – yet they refused to share.

Arezzo's provincial committee of the Christian Democrat Party pointed out that the family was currently living 'in a badly damaged place [with a rickety stairway], in continual danger for their personal safety.'[89] The communal *giunta* met again, and reconsidered the matter with the input of the secretaries of the main political parties and of the communal housing commission, deciding upon a solution, whereby the commune would pay for a new wooden stairway in the family's current residence. The *professoressa* refused the new stairway, however, and insisted again on an apartment in public housing, returning the dispute to the prefect's office.

The *carabinieri* investigated the matter painstakingly, reporting on all of the other families who had thus far been assigned the new public housing, and their comparative circumstances in relation to the *professoressa*'s. The others were all families with several children, and until given an apartment in public housing most had been living in schools, in the hospital, in government offices, or sharing a single room with no plumbing. Moreover, the communal housing commission had made the assignments with the agreement of all the major political parties. On the other hand, the reporting officer explained (demonstrating a real ability to present all sides of that very charged postwar problem), the *professoressa*, age forty-three, and her elderly parents currently lived in two rooms on the second floor of a badly damaged house, without a kitchen and with a temporary ladder-like stairway that posed a real threat of danger. Moreover, the *professoressa*, because of her social position, found herself uncomfortable (even disgraced) due to her living situation. The wooden stairway the commune offered would in no way have made up for the lack of space and the poor condition of the rooms.

Interestingly, the *professoressa* was first cousin to Pieve Santo Stefano's sindaco. The families were not on good terms, however, according to the *carabinieri*. Thus, one could not discount the possibility that the sindaco, as president of the communal housing commission, might have influenced the decision not to assign the family a house. The Christian Democrats' provincial vice-secretary stepped in to assert that 'we are persuaded by the state of things' that the prefect should institute 'a serious inquiry into the matter' and 'render justice' to the *professoressa* – justice which apparently included a new apartment. The poor woman found herself 'in desperate conditions' and intended 'to appeal directly to His Excellency Alcide De Gasperi.' That the local DC believed (or wanted the sindaco and prefect to believe) that De Gasperi himself would take an active interest in this local 'injustice' may have been yet another re-flection (or reminder) that Pieve Santo Stefano was the birthplace and hometown of Christian Democrat rising notable Amintore Fanfani (who would become the ultimate patron of sorts for the province – though not necessarily a successful one on the individual level). The *professoressa*'s appeal to De Gasperi, supported by her local party secretary, would have joined the many thousands that went from Italian villages and Italian vil-lagers of all political persuasions, all insisting that the state do something for them and do it quickly.

The sindaco, in his turn, reminded the prefect once again that the family indeed had been assigned a house – to share. The scarcity of lodg-ing and the numerous requests by those 'far more needy,' 'who lived in the most primitive conditions,' did not permit the sindaco to satisfy the woman's request 'to live in the way she desired.' The days of 'pulling rank' or claiming special treatment based on class or social status were over – a way of life ended by the war – the sindaco (her cousin) implied. The implication, and the reminder to the prefect that need meant more than position or influence after the war was belied countless times a day everywhere in Italy, of course.

Assignments to the next block of public housing were made, and once again the commune passed over the *professoressa*. Communal archives do not reveal who threw the final blow, or if the *professoressa* and her parents ever acceded to the new stairway, or found another place to live more befitting their social position. The fact that the sindaco, the *giunta*, the housing commission, the prefect, the *carabinieri*, and 'all of the major political parties' all got so deeply involved in individual cases time and again speaks to the sindaco's stubbornness and the *professoressa*'s refusal to take an official 'no' for an answer, but also to a time and place where everybody seemed very familiar with everyone else's business and cir-cumstances. On a larger scale, however, it also helps locate the shared and divisive place that property, housing, need, and local politics occu-pied in postwar daily life and postwar civil life. Here were cases where need and suffering made more for division than for unity.

Widespread destruction and loss of property caused displacement on a scale never before seen in Italy. That displacement and destruction constituted part of postwar need itself, and directly contributed to disor-der – down to the necessity of living in places 'not meant for habitation' or being forced to share your kitchen with incompatible strangers for the unforeseeable future. Disorder and the fear that life would remain filled with sacrifice and suffering made people want their normal lives back, but in some instances also expect that – after war and Fascism – they should be entitled to something more. They now demanded more of the state, but paradoxically, they continued (with some good reason) to believe the state neither fully recognized nor was capable of solving their postwar problems.

10 *Mezzadria* Struggle and Social Change: The 'Haves' and 'Have-Nots'

> Communism still leads the official race for prominence but it is still the undefined 'striving-for-something' after a disastrous political regime. No real signs are yet prevalent of nihilism – the dangerous side of the ideology: in fact the sense of proprietorship which characterises the Aretini will be a great obstacle to the more destructive side of communism.
>
> Provincial Commissioner Quin Smith, March 31, 1945.

> [N]umerically, the *mezzadri* constitute a leading force in the field of agriculture, as well as an economic force in some regions.
>
> National Union Convention, Florence, April 12–13, 1947.

In November 1944, the ACC provincial public safety officer (PPSO) for the Montevarchi district of Arezzo discovered what he described as 'subversive manifestos' circulating 'somewhat freely' in the Valdarno zone of the province.[1] Their author was the old, local anarchist, Attilio Sassi, and what Sassi sought to 'subvert' was the centuries-old contract between land proprietors and sharecroppers that governed the central and northern Italian *mezzadria* – or sharecropping – system of land cultivation. The 'subversion' called for was extremely modest, as will be seen; it certainly did not call for the 'nihilism' which Provincial Commissioner Quin Smith considered an inherent part of communist ideology, or even a seizure of land and estates. What Allied PC Quin Smith perceptively termed the Aretine 'sense of proprietorship,' even among those without property, would have prevented such a thing from happening. The particular Aretine 'sense' (on top of the general Italian sense of proprietorship) would also serve to limit postwar social change.

Property is an enormous and complex subject in general, in that property underlies much of the basic structure of society. But property is more than an institution or a legally defined category. Property can serve as a means to examine societal relationships – not only class relationships, but also interpersonal relationships, as well as relationships between individuals and authority, and those between people and the legally enforced customs of their society. It offers a way to structure the study of history through themes of continuity and change. Even after widespread physical and institutional destruction and in the midst of transition after war, during ongoing political turmoil, as in the case of postwar Italy, societies built on private property will see little rapid or deep transformation from below (or within) for social aspects relating to or arising from the institution of property, especially real property. Some temporary change may be necessitated or forced – or legislated – from above (as seen in the previous chapter) – but property and the customs that surround it are more likely to work against social change, and be instead a force for continuity. Law reflects this by reinforcing the importance of property and the stability of unequal relationships based on property.

Having property or not having it represents a great deal. In postwar Arezzo, not having it gave rise to a reassessment of and challenges to an old, traditional, structured way of life – the *mezzadria* (sharecropping) system. Or, rather, the postwar desire to change the centuries-old *mezzadria* system challenged patterns of property holding and division, as well as an embedded part of the prewar social system.

The *Mezzadria* System

The *mezzadria* system, typical of Tuscany, is referred to as the 'classic' form of Italian sharecropping (or *mezzadria classica*). The term *mezzadria* derived from the parties' contractual agreement (the *patto colonico*), whereby the sharecropper and the landlord each provided half (*mezzo*) – 'a perfect half' according to the Fascist era contract for the region of Tuscany – of the annual working capital and each was entitled to half the farm product.[2] Under this system, the landowner or landlord (the *padrone*) owned the plot of land (the *podere*) which the (male) sharecropper (the *mezzadro, mezzadri* in the plural, also sometimes called the '*capoccia*' for '*capo famiglia*') worked or farmed. The landlord also owned the farmhouse (*casa colonica*) in which the sharecropper, his wife (the *massaia*), and family lived, as well as the tools and working animals (usually oxen) the sharecropper used for farming. The *mezzadro* held only limited possessory contractual rights as temporary consignee of such property, all of which remained 'completely' the property of the landlord.[3] The sharecropping family owned no real property, and usually possessed little in the way of personal property. The sharecropping family, however, provided all of the labour needed to cultivate the land, to produce and harvest the crops. The landlord was to provide for necessary improvements to the land and for maintaining the farmhouse as habitable, as he saw fit. Habitability did not necessarily include glass in the windows or a source of water nearby. Until after the war (sometimes well after the war), it rarely included plumbing or running water.

The *mezzadria* system was firmly patriarchal and firmly fixed in both law and custom. As the *padrone* or his agent ruled the sharecroppers who lived on and worked his property, so the *mezzadro* or adult male head of the sharecropping household ruled the other members of his family as undisputed *capo famiglia*. In Arezzo, the family typically consisted of sharecropper, his wife, and children, but might also include adult sons or brothers together with their wives and children, depending on the size of the plot. The *massaia*, or wife of the *mezzadro*, in turn, ruled her daughters and daughters-in-law.[4]

Generalizing about any group, including all landlords or all sharecroppers and their families, is risky. Of course, an infinite variety of individual personalities and interpersonal relations played a role along with tradition and the contractual agreement. Not all fathers were domestic tyrants; not all sons and wives were mistreated; and not all daughters were isolated and overworked. Moreover, despite standardization and uniformity of *mezzadria* contract terms, not all landlords took advantage of their sharecroppers by refusing to complete annual accountings, by evicting them without notice, or by cheating them out of their full half. Not all refused to provide adequate farm equipment or decent, habitable housing.[5]

Generalizing about how the war affected relationships between landlord and *mezzadro* is a bit easier. As Catia Sonetti describes in her informative chapter on the transformation of Tuscan peasant families after the war and on account of the war, the relationship between *padrone* and sharecropper 'was either more despotic or more paternalistic' where a few landlords owned much of the property in an area and sharecroppers thus had few options to leave a despotic landlord for a slightly more congenial one nearby.[6] Mobility, in the geographical and employment sense of being able to leave an unsatisfactory situation and landlord and contracting for a better one, naturally was more feasible in places where there were more landlords and plots to choose from. That would have been true before the war as well, to the extent that Fascist era restrictive laws allowed transferring one's place of residence.

Relations between landlord and sharecropper, between sharecropper father and children, and between *mezzadro* and *massaia* underwent some war generated change, though such relationships certainly were not completely transformed. Men who had fought in the war, who had been POWS or partisans did not automatically settle into the same relations with landlords or fathers that they had had before the war. Women who had taken part in the Resistance, had hidden Allied POWs, or had managed farm plots when husbands were absent, or who themselves had provided forced labour in Germany would not always revert to the same prewar position they held with their fathers, husbands, and landlords.[7] Before or after the war, however, the relationship between landlord and sharecropper would never be an equal one so long as the *mezzadria* system itself existed. Inequality was inherent in the *mezzadria* contractual structure, its traditions, and the property-holding arrangement that divided the haves from the have-nots.[8]

The first written *mezzadria* contracts date from as early as the ninth century. The practice expanded throughout the thirteenth and fourteenth centuries, becoming the predominant form of agricultural organization in central Italy and much of northern Italy. Sharecropping began to decline in the nineteenth century, with the growth of urban centres, factories and wage labour, and landowners' increasing economic preference for salaried, seasonal labourers over sharecropping families, until the Fascist regime gave it a final revitalizing boost in the 1920s, employing the *mezzadria* system as a particular, backward-looking means of both land reform and social control.[9]

Fascism had a long and cordial relationship with large landowners, and an antagonistic one with sharecroppers, tenant farmers, and farm labourers. Sharecroppers in the regions of Tuscany and Emilia-Romagna had played a role in the unrests and uprisings of the red biennium of 1919–20. A significant number of sharecroppers together with farm labourers participated in strikes and demonstrations against particularly oppressive landlords and against unfair contract terms.[10] Some joined the Socialist Party or the new Catholic People's Party, the *Popolari* (PPI), electing Socialist and *Popolari* members to communal councils.

As a result of new organizational strength, strikes, and electoral victories, sharecroppers in a number of Aretine communes were able to obtain a slightly more economically beneficial contract (*patto colonico*) in the spring of 1919.[11] In addition, long-established unwritten contractual terms and conditions that served to reinforce the parties' socially and legally unequal relationship were modified or done away with in some areas. These terms – known as the *regalie* – included the sharecropper's obligation to provide the landowner with the gratuity of both eggs and poultry, and with part of every pig slaughtered – none of which was factored into the landlord-owner's 50 per cent share or the sharecropper's 50 per cent contribution. That is, the eggs, chickens, and pork came out of the *mezzadro*'s portion and went, without compensation in return, to the landlord. These were, in essence and custom, mandatory 'gifts' in tribute from the sharecropper to the landlord. A sharecropper also was expected to serve as a sort of an unpaid caretaker, maintaining the landlord's own grounds and gardens, while the *mezzadro*'s wife, the *massaia*, was to provide 'indoor' unpaid, personal services for the landlord, such as washing and ironing, housecleaning, and cooking.

Sharecropper victories in obtaining modest economic gains, in limiting landlord arbitrariness in refusing to complete annual accountings or in unfairly terminating contracts, and, in general, against *regalie* requirements were short-lived, thanks to Fascist 'squad' violence. So-called 'agrarian Fascism' constituted Fascism's first phase, as the nascent movement gained its earliest strength aiding large landowners in central Italy to maintain their positions of control and dominance. There, as is well known, *squadristi* smashed Socialist Party and newspaper offices, farmer and consumer cooperatives, social and labour union centres, and physically attacked socialists, some priests sympathetic to the peasants, and other activists devoted to organizing sharecroppers, agricultural day labourers, and small farmers.[12] The Fascist *squadristi* expedition to Foiano della Chiana in April 1921, the peasants' violent response in the nearby village of Renzino, and the Fascists' brutal retaliation provide the local Aretine example of the Fascist 'seizure of power.'

Once the regime was in power, Fascist agricultural policy superficially glorified traditional rural life and the roles of those who lived it. The reality, however, was the idea to eliminate the growing numbers of agricultural labourers in the countryside (the *braccianti*), 'as they represented a thorn in the side of the regime' – being potential political and social troublemakers – and to increase the numbers of *mezzadri* over day labourers, but Fascist agricultural policy certainly did not entail bettering the contractual bargaining strength or daily living conditions for *mezzadri*.[13]

In March 1926, the Fascist Union of Landowners and the Fascist Union of Farmers (or Peasants) reached a contract for the region of Tuscany, which included the province of Arezzo. The contract opened with the verbally bloated 'premise' that, 'the Tuscan *mezzadria* contract, based on the most intimate collaboration of classes and on the necessity of the existence of the most cordial relations between the parties representing "Capital" and "Labour," respectively, found that surest guarantee and its best application in the Fascist Syndical Regime.'[14] More specifically and less optimistically, the contract allowed the *padrone* to decide who and how many could live on the plot as part of the sharecropper's family, and reinforced the landlord's power to decide most everything else involved in working and living on the land. Although the contract was divided in terms of 'Rights and duties of the landlord' and 'Rights and duties of the farmer,' the rights for the most part lay with the landlord, while the duties fell to the sharecropper. The *mezzadro*'s rights and duties, as detailed, began with the duty to cultivate 'his' plot in 'strict adherence to instructions given by the landlord or his agent.'[15] Then, in December 1928, the national official Fascist *patto colonico*, which like the earlier regional contract marked a return to the oppressive, standard prewar contract, went into effect and remained in place throughout the *ventennio*.[16]

Directions of Change

Before the 1926 contract, in the years directly after World War I, while peasants, socialists, *Popolari*, and Fascist *squadristi* battled throughout the rural landscape, Attilio Sassi had been a political anarchist, an anarcho-syndicalist, and the anarchist secretary of the Camera del Lavoro in the commune of Cavriglia. As such, his professional concern lay more with the lignite miners of Castelnuovo dei Sabbioni and Santa Barbara in their struggles for a shorter working day and against arbitrary layoffs. He had been present at the Castelnuovo mine on March 23, 1921, to discuss with management the 430 layoffs of a few days earlier, when on that day, some 3000 miners rose up in a spontaneous and deadly anti-Fascist protest. Though he had not led or even triggered the riot, Sassi, along with others, was convicted.[17]

In November 1944, Sassi returned to the Valdarno, this time as a communist and as general secretary of an organization called the 'Mezzadri Farmers Union of the Valdarno Zone,' San Giovanni Valdarno section, and as an organizing force behind the cumbersomely titled 'Peasant Leagues [as] Bulwarks of Defence against Conditions of Life and Work for All Workers of the Land.'[18] In a November 1944 intelligence report on communist activity in Tuscany, the Allied psychological warfare branch

(PWB) proclaimed Attilio Sassi the major 'personality' in the Communist Party movement throughout, what PWB termed, the 'red' area comprising Montevarchi, San Giovanni, Castelnuovo, and Cavriglia: 'SASSI, Attelio [sic] born in Castel Guelfo 1876. Caused a riot in 1921 in which there were many casualties including one killed. Escaped to AMERICA and has only recently returned. Described as being a dangerous agitator.'[19]

ACC Provincial Commissioner Quin Smith ordered Sassi's manifestos turned over to Italian prosecuting authorities for 'appropriate action.' The Italian authorities advised, however, that no appropriate Italian proceeding existed to sanction Sassi for his activities, except that of *allontanamento* – whereby the police could order Sassi expelled from the commune. Montevarchi's sindaco proposed doing just that, because on top of circulating the manifestos, Sassi had held an unauthorized public meeting of 'workers and peasants' on December 24, 1944, during which he had encouraged sharecroppers to break their *mezzadria* contracts. In the course of the same meeting, Sassi also 'seriously offended the institution of the monarchy, the king himself, Marshal Badoglio, and the office of the *carabinieri*.'[20]

Montevarchi's public safety officer, Lieutenant Colonel D.E. Seymour Cousins, who had first alerted his Allied colleagues to the subversive manifestos, now convinced PC Quin Smith not to proceed against Sassi. Cousins had managed to wrest a written apology from Signor Sassi, which read (in its prepared English translation):

> While I hold firmly to the opinion that the present duties of tenants to their land-lords should be changed, I did not appreciate that in circularizing them as I have done, I violate an A.M.G. proclamation. I also recognize that the contents of the circular incited tenants to disregard the existing law. I therefore retract that circular during such time as A.M.G. or A.C. shall last and shall devote myself to bringing about a change in the law by democratic means only.[21]

Cousins suggested that Sassi's apology be published in Arezzo's sole Allied-authorized newspaper, *L'Informatore Aretino*, together with a statement 'to the effect that "in view of the following letter addressed to A.M.G. by Signor Sassi, his great age and his international esteem, it was on this occasion proposed to overlook his violation of A.M.G. proclamation."' Lieutenant Colonel Cousins did not explain further his change of heart, except to 'strongly recommend against any proceedings being taken … for various cogent reasons.'

Those cogent reasons may have had to do with fears of local public protests on the part of the miners or sharecroppers if the Allies tried and incarcerated the sixty-eight year old Sassi for handing out a few leaflets.[22] Alternatively, Cousins may actually have read Sassi's very moderate manifesto. Sassi and his comrades were not calling for a peasant takeover of the landlords' property, for redistribution, collectivization, or an end to the *mezzadria* system. Rather, they focused on the general unfairness of *mezzadria* written contract terms (as to rights and duties) and on the *mezzadri regalie* obligations to share their pigs and poultry with the landowner. Such was the limited extent of Sassi's subversive publication.

Another reason why Montevarchi's PPSO suggested no action against Sassi may have had to do with the fact that the Allies were not entirely clear on the details of the *mezzadria* system or the recent history of Italian sharecropping, though they recognized *mezzadri* discontent, of course.[23] Moreover, even Quin Smith, who typically opposed 'undemocratic' 'political activities' (that is, attempts to organize and demand change, rather than wait for social and economic issues to make their way to the national ballot), was not totally unsympathetic to the plight of poor sharecroppers who did all the work, while the owners, whom he pictured off in their Florentine palazzos, reaped the benefits. In his January 1945 report to headquarters, Quin Smith wrote:

A new form of agitation ... is that for the reform of the Mezzadria system in the Communes. Needless to say it takes a socialist form; i.e. the 'reform' is to be in favour of the contadini as opposed to the landlords ... In this Province it deals at present with details of division of products such as ownership of poultry and the feeding of swine. It is undoubtedly fostered by the large number of estate owners who live in Florence on the food forwarded ... from the estate, instead of living amongst their people.[24]

Despite Sassi's promise, a lengthier, more assertive manifesto appeared in January 1945. This one was unsigned, but its 'tone [was] reminiscent of the other notification bearing the signature of Signor Sassi,' according to ACC.[25] It commenced by addressing the *mezzadria* contract as drafted by the Fascist regime years earlier: 'The peasants demand that this *patto colonico* follow the same fate as the fascist regime and that another be drawn up in its place, which recognizes the right to a more humane life for the workers of the land.'[26] This manifesto urged organization of strong peasant leagues in every commune in the province, and it warned peasants not to wait for the end of the war in hopes that the still unformed postwar state would take the lead in instituting a new, fairer contractual system and a more humane working life.

A fairer contract, the manifesto stressed, would be imposed on the proprietors only 'through an organized and tenacious struggle.' The leagues were to press their demands to compel property owners (the *padroni*) to bear the cost of livestock lost through actions of war, and require that owners help restore the fields damaged by German mines, battles, and Allied military encampments. *Mezzadri* should refuse to consign eggs and poultry to the owners as established by the old *patto* and *regalie* traditions – 'not only because the custom [was] outdated, but also because the Nazi-fascists had stolen the poultry ... placing the peasants in the impossible position of having none to give.'[27]

The manifesto called for some more extreme measures as well, which went to the heart of the traditional *mezzadria* system. These included allowing the sharecropper two-thirds (rather than half) of the 'product' (crops produced) during the year. It would require owners to furnish more modern tools, such as plows, sowing machines, and hay cutters – 'for a more efficient and profitable working of the soil,' rather than leaving it to landlords' discretion how, or if, to improve the land and what tools to supply. Significantly, the manifesto's authors also insisted on abolishing the *mezzadro*'s and the *massaia*'s personal services for the owners, which 'recalled medieval conditions of feudalism incompatible with modern times and above all with the progressive democratic regime' that ought to prevail in Italy 'after more than 20 years of fascism.' That January 1945 document sought more specific and more extensive reforms than had the earlier version, but still did not seek to overthrow the system or to take over private property. Neither did its drafters expect the state and its provincial authorities to help advance the *mezzadri* cause or to take their part against the property owners. Any change, it stressed, would come through the *mezzadri* themselves, their organizational strength, and their struggle.

The story of Attilio Sassi and his manifestos stands for more than predictable Allied reaction to what they perceived as forbidden political agitation by a known 'leftist subversive.' It evidences how closely connected social questions were to property questions and to political concerns in that agricultural area. It also offers a realistic appraisal of how far poor sharecroppers would have to go to achieve the most basic social and economic justice. That even the old anarchist turned communist called for such modest change by such moderate means shows how deeply entrenched were traditional attitudes about property and the given roles of those in the *mezzadria* system. If attitudes, customs, and laws ever were going to change, surely it would be in that disordered and transitional time right after the war, when change seemed most possible – or at least those like Sassi, who sought to organize the *mezzadri*, so believed. The feeling that now with the end of Fascism, as after World War I, the potential for change existed and it gave the large population segment of propertyless *mezzadri* and farmhands the impetus to organize and the opportunity to voice their demands. The opportunity was taken up by some, though no means all.

PC Quin Smith reported to army headquarters at the end of April 1945 regarding 'several minor disturbances' in the area of the Casentino, 'in which Communists take a prominent part.' 'There is little doubt that one of the many contentious issues is that of reform of the system of mezzadria (farm tenure), which has a great appeal to the "have-nots" and the "have-littles" … The Prefect has been advised to publish the terms of the recent Government decree that mezzadria reform is to await consideration till one year after the end of hostilities.'[28]

The government decree referred to was the Gullo decree – or, rather, it was a part of the larger body of land-related legislation introduced by Communist Minister of Agriculture Fausto Gullo. While much of its attention was directed towards peasant organization and real land reform (or the beginnings of it) in the south, in the *mezzadria classica* farmlands of central Italy and Arezzo Gullo's decree extended all sharecropping contracts then in effect, according to the same conditions as previous years. That is, it postponed any action on or change to existing agrarian contracts for the period of one year. The decree meant a reaffirmation of the landlord's and sharecropper's fifty-fifty split of produce and all other existing terms.[29] While some considered the Gullo decree a clear victory for the owners, others viewed it as a promising indication that state-sponsored change would be in the works once the war ended.

In any event, the *mezzadri* and those who sought to organize them did not all wait patiently, despite the government decree or the hope of future state action as yet neither expressed nor promised. Organization that had begun on a small scale with the passage of the front in 1944 increased after the ACC departed from Arezzo province in May 1945 and Italians could once again hold public meetings and associate freely.[30]

Organization and agitation for a new contract and for basic change to the system was termed the '*mezzadria* struggle' (*la lotta mezzadrile*). Many of the difficult aspects of postwar life were phrased both officially and informally in terms of 'struggle' (or *lotta*). Indeed, much of postwar daily life was – and was expressed as – a struggle: the struggle for housing, the struggle against unemployment, the struggle against inflation and the high cost of living, the struggle to keep the mines open, and so on. 'Struggle' was a less martial vocabulary choice certainly than that of Mussolini's Fascist era campaigns: the 'battle' for grain, the 'battle' for land, the 'battle' for births. Rather, 'struggle' was postwar language that captured the ongoing quality of postwar daily life following the suffering of war. Struggle (or *lotta*) implied not a passive approach to postwar difficulties, however, but a very engaged response.

Agitation, Struggle, and Disputes

The number of those who stood to be directly affected by change in the *mezzadria* system in central Italy was significant. The population of the province of Arezzo in 1945 totalled about 319,754 persons (not counting outside refugees), of whom 158,066 were categorized as having 'interests' in agriculture. *Mezzadri* families numbered 15,655, comprised of 89,115 individual family members between twelve and sixty-five years of age – that is, of working age – and 30,525 individual family members younger than twelve or older than sixty-five. Families who owned anywhere between a small bit of land and a sizeable plot of land and who cultivated it themselves (*proprietari coltivatori diretti*, owner-cultivators or smallholders) numbered 13,420. Landowners who did not themselves farm the land they owned numbered 6000. Farm labourers on a regular salary numbered 1108. The province also counted 300 strictly seasonal and more specialized workers, and 350 higher-level agricultural workers such as estate managers and caretakers.[31]

That is, in 1945, 119,640 citizens of the province of Arezzo – more than a third of the total population – were part of *mezzadri* families, whereas 6000 persons owned the land that those thousands of others worked.[32] *Mezzadri* and their families were the largest status group in the province and made up a large portion of the population of Tuscany, as categorized by the work they did and the sort of life they lived. Yet, together with farm labourers they had perhaps the least in the way of property of their own.

Organizations representing *mezzadri* and farm labourers initially took a couple of forms, one less structured and one more so. Less structured were the original peasant leagues that Sassi called for. By January 1945, the first directing committee of the peasant leagues had been constituted in the commune of Arezzo, despite Allied warnings and Sassi's promise. Led by many *mezzadri* themselves, the initial Aretine committee undertook to extend these self-governed leagues to all communes throughout the province. More sophisticated in overall structure and governance, however, were the organizations (or suborganizations) that resided under the auspices of the provincial-level confederation of the Camera del Lavoro (CdL) and the national-level Italian General Confederation of Labour (Confederazione generale italiana del lavoro, or CGIL). Both the peasant leagues (working from 'below') and the more finely planned agricultural workers' sections of the CdL (working with CGIL from 'above') shared the general purpose of improving the political strength and contractual position of the *mezzadri*, as well as their living situation. The notion was, of course, that political strength was a necessary precursor to social and economic change.

The Camera del Lavoro is a difficult organization to translate and explain, as no equivalent body with an equivalent history exists in North America or Britain.[33] Very briefly, Camera del Lavoro (*Camere* in the plural) translates literally as chamber of labour. It began as a socialist innovation, mostly in central and northern Italy during the Liberal era of the 1890s and spread in the years before the First World War. The 'chamber' was a sort of 'one-stop' clearinghouse or umbrella organization for workers and their diverse associations, based on Socialist Party lines. Now, after Fascism, the Camera del Lavoro reformed quickly on the national, provincial, and local levels. No longer linked to the Socialist Party alone, it lay within (or as the base of) the multi-party framework of the nationally organized, united labour confederation, CGIL. CdL was very much an early presence in local reconstruction, as witnessed by Allied suspicions of its motives and activities, and Allied attempts to limit its activities to those that were 'strictly labour related.'[34]

In organizational structure, the Camera del Lavoro was a horizontal, territorial, and worker-centred association. That is, the CdL was organized or set up according to location, not according to kinds, categories, or sectors of employment. Each local CdL potentially covered all workers or employees who lived and worked in a particular commune or zone within that Camera's jurisdiction. Thus, the communal or local CdL ostensibly stood ready to represent workers in any field – whether factory workers, labourers, farmers, craftsmen, or teachers.[35] Importantly, it represented them in basically all areas having to do with work and working conditions – broadly defined – including acting in the immediate postwar years as an employment bureau or a hiring hall for labourers, arbitrating employment disputes, and serving as a leisure time, social, educational, self-help, mutual aid, and charitable centre.

The various, individual Camere within a province together made up the Camera Confederale del Lavoro (or Confederated Camere del Lavoro, CCdL) for a province. The CCdL was, in turn, a horizontal element (geographically based by province) within the national Italian General Confederation of Labour, CGIL.[36] CGIL formed on June 3, 1944 (at the time of the fall, or liberation, of Rome), signed into being – through the Pact of Rome – by representatives of the three main anti-Fascist parties: Communists, Christian Democrats, and Socialists.[37] CGIL, *via* the Camere del Lavoro situated beneath it, was intended to and did handle much more than what ordinarily would be considered labour or union issues, ably delving into realms of politics, political organization, social welfare, and social change.

Like the Committee of National Liberation (CLN), CGIL was affirmatively founded on principles of unity (or at least on the notion of anti-Fascist unity) and representation. While CLN had united Italians of differing political views and social backgrounds for the socio-military purposes of liberating the country from the Nazi-Fascists and beginning a post-Fascist, multi-party administration, CGIL sought to bring together Italians of different political beliefs, different classes, and widely differing occupations for the common goal of *unità sindacale*.[38] Thus established to carry out an infinitely longer-term and more difficult project than physical and political liberation of the nation, CGIL did not long survive intact. As the war in Italy was coming to an end, however, CGIL commenced both united and representative. CGIL and CdL were inclusive as to their members: they welcomed and spoke for workers of different ages and gender, of any political party, and of all occupations.

From its national inception, CGIL included a main premise of organizing 'workers of the land,' including everyone from agricultural labourers, to *mezzadri*, to direct cultivators. That premise mattered in Arezzo, where a significant majority of the population worked the land in some capacity. The plight of the *mezzadri* and strategies to better their situation appeared prominently in CGIL and CdL plans from the beginning.[39]

Early postwar associational activity among *mezzadri* and farm labourers in Arezzo should be considered together with and in relation to the neighbouring province of Florence and the somewhat more dynamic associations in Siena that set the lead for other provinces in the region. Siena's CdL representatives convened on September 10, 1944, not many weeks after the passage of the front, when along with measures unrelated to agricultural workers they also formed a province-wide Union of Agricultural Workers and a Provincial Federation of Agricultural Workers, action that the CdL of Florence and then Arezzo soon followed.

More structured from top to bottom, or more centrally organized than the relatively autonomous commune-based peasant leagues, the province-wide union joined all agricultural workers into a single category, and thus constituted the 'vertical' part of the postwar CGIL structure.[40]

The Sienese federation got to the heart of the current *mezzadria* situation quickly. Meeting on November 19, 1944, it voted to 'cancel' unilaterally the 1928 Fascist contract. That contract, the federation stated, 'no longer accorded with the legitimate aspirations of the *contadini*, in the new climate of regained liberty.' The Sienese union representatives also raised 'the grave problem of war damages' in relation to the peasants' 'great contribution of sacrifice and blood' in the war.[41] In essence, they argued that *mezzadri* and farm labourers who had been exploited and oppressed under Fascism, had also sacrificed and suffered more than their share on account of the war. Now was the time for change and a redistribution of agricultural 'rights' and 'duties,' though not necessarily for a redistribution of property. The *mezzadri* unions in the rest of Tuscany soon took up the argument.

The Union of Agricultural Workers soon metamorphosed slightly (at least by name) into the agricultural section of CGIL, known in short as Federterra. CGIL leaders had decided that all those who worked in agriculture, whether as sharecroppers, tenant farmers, small holders, other direct cultivators (excluding those who employed more than one permanent salaried labourer), or as paid labourers should be organized into a single union: the Federation of the Workers of the Land (Federazione Lavoratori della Terra) or Federterra, beginning 'competition' to an extent with the Christian Democrats' National Confederation of Direct Cultivators (Confederazione Nazionale Coltivatori Diretti), or Coldiretti.[42] Federterra existed on the local, provincial, and national levels, with each province divided into zones according to its communes, and each zone – or communal section – having its own secretary. The zones together then made up Federterra Provinciale.[43]

The sharecroppers of the province of Arezzo and the region of Tuscany saw a flurry of meetings in the early postwar months: meetings of Federterra locally, provincially, and regionally; of independent agricultural associations and peasant leagues more generally. Arezzo held its first province-wide Federterra conference on April 8, 1945, with the primary purpose of electing a directing committee.[44] Federterra had already enrolled some 2600 farm labourers, sharecroppers, and other farmers throughout the province, and 105 delegates attended the provincial conference.[45] The first Tuscan regional meeting took place in

Siena a month later, with representatives from Florence, Siena, Arezzo, Grosseto, Livorno, Pisa, and Lucca.[46] At this larger meeting, delegates focused on two main demands: a more equitable division of farm product (with a minimum of 60 per cent going to the sharecropper) and the formation of *mezzadro* councils. *Mezzadro* councils (also called *fattoria* councils or 'internal commissions') would run or have a say in the running of larger farms (*fattorie*) which were divided into several plots worked separately by several families. In smaller farms with a single or few plots, each *mezzadro* was to have the 'right of perfect equality' with the landlord to direct the workings of the farm.

Arezzo's provincial Federterra held the second meeting of its directing committee on July 14, at which it considered province-wide organizational progress over the last few months.[47] Secretary Martini noted that at the time of the first meeting in April, only fifteen communal leagues had formed throughout the province, twenty-five had organized by June, and now one month later, all but four of Arezzo's thirty-nine communes had a peasant league. Moreover, Federterra members now numbered more than 12,000, given that not only *mezzadri*, but *coltivatori diretti* and farm labourers were also joining Federterra.

Tempering that positive prospect, however, another provincial commissioner countered that although member numbers were indeed growing, they were still low relative to the large number of persons who worked the land in the province. The province had 'awakened too late' and had its 'hands tied' by Allied restrictions on travel, as well as by the 'absolute prohibition' on holding union meetings, 'not to mention' the destruction of roads and bridges, and the lack of means of transportation in that mountainous province, all of which made organization difficult. The association needed better, more persuasive speakers in the smaller villages, and an effective newspaper to counteract the landowners' influence.

The organizational situation in Arezzo was neither entirely bleak nor entirely promising. Then, as now, it appeared to have been both. Membership in Federterra was increasing, but still represented only a fraction of those who worked the land. Neither did those increasing numbers readily translate into progress for the sharecroppers, as illustrated by the unchanged aspects of the system and landlords' refusal to renegotiate contracts. Those doing the organizing, however, saw a direct connection between organizational numbers, unity, action, and results, whereby 'agitation' and then results (that is, change) naturally must follow from organizational strength. That July meeting in Arezzo thus also focused on the need to convince sharecroppers 'to agitate' unilaterally to alter the distribution of farm product for the current harvest season from fifty-fifty to sixty-forty in favour of the sharecropper, as had been resolved at the Tuscan regional meeting the previous month. A revolutionary redistribution of property (in the form of 10 per cent more for the sharecropper and 10 per cent less for the landlord) did not take place – not then at least, and not in the way initially envisioned; the sense of proprietorship and respect for property were stronger, as was, perhaps, fear of official and landlord response.

Arezzo's meeting ended with the decision that sharecroppers should take the additional 10 per cent, but 'set it aside' until the landlords agreed to serious negotiations with Federterra and the sides had definitely worked out a new contract that better corresponded to the needs of the *mezzadri* and the 'new democratic state.'[48] That is, in this early stage of the struggle, even those few *mezzadri* willing to retain the 'extra' 10 per cent of their landlords' property would not convert, use, or sell it until a new contract allowed them to do so, but rather would try and use it as leverage to force contract negotiations.

Yet organization and inscription in Federterra and farmer syndicates wielded some force of its own. As more sharecroppers and farm labourers joined Federterra, and as the political climate heated up more generally, the *mezzadria* 'struggle' (*lotta*) intensified and escalated into the *mezzadri* 'disputes' (*vertenze*). The phrasing really did change, as CGIL documents attest. Moreover, the word choice should be emphasized: 'struggle' implies a one-sided affair, while 'dispute' (like disputes between individual landlords and sharecroppers) signifies that two opposing sides are involved. The *mezzadria* struggle had begun to rouse landlords to the possibility that their percentage of farm product might be diminished and that their traditional position and relationship with their sharecroppers might be more fundamentally transformed.

The landowners, as the other side of the dispute, oftentimes through their own postwar representative organization, the Italian Confederation of Landowners, or Confida (Confederazione Italiana degli Agricoltori), now evidenced more concern about the changes demanded by sharecroppers and Federterra, with Confida insisting on landlords' contractual and traditional right to a full half the farm product.[49] And so, with landlords now staunchly in opposition, the disputes reached Rome. The country had only very recently seen the end of the war; Italy as a nation still faced widespread physical destruction and hunger. Soldiers, POWs, and forced labourers would soon be returning home adding to the difficulties of inadequate resources in food, jobs, and housing. In his telegraphed message to the provinces on July 17, 1945, president of the council of ministers and Interior Minister Ferruccio Parri expressed the seriousness of the agricultural situation, and the importance of stability and a good harvest that first year after the end of the war. He noted: 'In some regions of Italy disputes over the *mezzadri* contracts and agrarian contracts have given rise to agitation, conflicts and violence that disturb and damage the recovery, for which at this time agricultural production is more necessary than ever.'[50]

Maintaining both public order and amassing norms to ensure an adequate food supply was critical for national recovery; thus, Parri asked the CLNs and the unions to cooperate in working towards conciliation rather than spurring continuing conflict. Force would be used, he warned, if necessary, to ensure conciliation. Arezzo's prefect, in turn, emphasized to that province's sindaci, the provincial CLN, and to the CdL the 'greater public need' for sharecroppers and farmers to respect and comply with the 'normal and regular' work of harvesting the grain. That is, the immediate need for agricultural continuity and normality was greater – from the state's and the hungry, non-farming public's point of view – than was recognizing the opportunity for change in the *mezzadri* system. Everyone, the prefect reminded the province, was to show 'absolute respect for the existing laws,' and from the official point of view, normality and respect for existing laws meant adherence to the system as it was.[51]

'Agitation' – or action – on the part of the sharecroppers continued to be called for and threatened against the landlords, though what form it was to take on local, provincial, and regional levels (beyond holding back 10 per cent of crops) was not specific. In Arezzo, strikes were mentioned, but no widespread, concerted action took place. A few acts of violence did occur, especially in the Casentino, during the annual division of the grain between sharecropper and owner, but they were not directed against the land or crops. Membership drives, organizational meetings, and congresses continued, while membership numbers increased. As months went on, specific demands about *mezzadri* contract terms, wartime property damage and loss, and the proportional distribution of farm product were honed and frequently repeated between the local, provincial, regional, and national level associations.[52] Results did not follow, despite the clear sense that the situation and the 'disputes' were intensifying.[53]

National Federterra devoted its September 25, 1945, *Circolare* to 'inquiries and directives' relating to 'the major agitation and unrest of the *mezzadri* throughout Italy' as reported by various regional secretaries.[54] A fairer

division of crops was item A on the list, but other claims were equally important. The loss of livestock, tools, and crops from the passage of the front
and other events of war hampered sharecroppers' return to farming their
plots; and expecting them to pay half to replace what the war had destroyed
– and what they had never owned – seemed unfair as well as unrealistic.[55]
Settlement and reimbursement for such losses, either by landlords or by
the state, would have acknowledged and validated the sharecroppers' wartime suffering and losses in much the same way the state was recognizing
and reimbursing those citizens who owned real property, though the state
made no such parallel acknowledgment. An end to the *regalie* and required
personal services would have ended sharecropper families' traditional status as socially and legally subordinate to the landlords, while the withdrawal
of the Fascist era contracts would have marked a real end to Fascism and its
location of the *mezzadri* position in society.

The peasant leagues of the Val di Chiana ('all the Peasant Leagues of
the valley') met in Foiano della Chiana on December 17, 1945, and expressly adopted the demands common among the leagues of the province
and the region, under the auspices of Federterra and CGIL. Somewhat
more extensive than those set forth in Federterra's national circular, they
serve as a comprehensive example of the changes sought by the *mezzadri* at
the Aretine local level, and so are worth setting forth in detail. After 'am-
ple and exhaustive discussion,' the peasant leagues resolved: 1) to ask the
landowners to recognize the sharecroppers' right to divide the farm product and the profits by 60 per cent to the *mezzadro* and 40 per cent to the
landlord; 2) that the working livestock taken or killed by the Nazi-Fascists
or lost through causes of war be replaced in kind by the landlord at the
landlord's expense, while the landlord indemnified the sharecropper in
cash for other farm animals; 3) that the landlord give a bonus of 20 per
cent of the value of any livestock the *mezzadro* had saved from harm; 4) that
internal *fattoria* commissions be recognized on every farm in the valley
made up of more than five *poderi* (or plots), while those with fewer plots
recognize 'interfarm' or 'fractional commissions;' 5) that all the *mezzadri*
of the valley have the right to slaughter a pig for their families' own use
without any payment to or sharing with the landlord; 6) that every form of
obligation or *regalia* relating to poultry be 'completely and absolutely'
abolished; 7) that a province-wide contract regulate the old question of
tools (which tools and equipment should be supplied and paid for by the
landlord); and if the disputes were not resolved by the end of the year, the
mezzadri should not proceed with dividing the farm product or any earnings from livestock and poultry.[56]

Arezzo's prefect met with landowners first and then with the Val di Chiana peasant leagues later that month, after which Arezzo's provincial Federterra reported to the regional and national federations that a resolution to the *vertenze* seemed imminent. But by the end of December, with no agreement in sight, Arezzo's Federterra told the province's peasant leagues to hold off on dividing and accounting on the year's product and earnings until February 1, 1946, and the outcome of an arbitration decision awaited from Florence.[57] That decision, which was expected to serve as a model, was not easily reached, as owners there (like elsewhere) saw themselves asked to compromise while getting nothing in return. Local sections of provincial Federterra did report that instead of supplying landlords with rabbits, chickens, and other fowl and barnyard animals at Christmas and New Year, as custom and the Fascist contract required, sharecroppers gave them to local refugee shelters, orphanages, convents, and to UDI to distribute to the poor and the sick.[58]

By the end of 1945, some 13,000 persons had joined Federterra in the province of Arezzo. Of those, about 7000 were *mezzadri* heads of family and 3000 were other *mezzadri* family members (women and youths), 1400 were direct cultivators, and 1500 were agricultural wage and day labourers.[59] These membership numbers represented a considerable percentage of the *mezzadri* (some 10,000 out of 89,115) and farm labourers in the province, and a somewhat similar percentage of smallholders (1400 out of 13,420). At this point, though many made use of their local CdL, most Aretine workers of the land chose not to be represented by CGIL and Federterra, or by any organization (including Coldiretti), or had not yet made the decision at all. Was the absence of more vigorous associational activity in Arezzo a question of politics, apolitics, an expression of labour disunity, or sharecroppers' disbelief that the system could be changed? The alternative view that more than one in ten had so quickly joined Federterra (fewer than in Siena or Florence, though more than in the other Tuscan provinces) indicated that farmer and farm labour unity was very much alive in Arezzo.

The 1945 harvest season and the year itself passed in Arezzo, but the *mezzadria* disputes continued without sight of an agreement or solution. Parri did not succeed in resolving the *vertenze* before his short-lived government entered its own crisis. Prefect Bracali summed up at the end of the year: Federterra had contributed to the 'precariousness' of public order in the province by agitating for revisions in the *mezzadria* contract.[60] Such agitation was not justified in Arezzo, the prefect felt, where, as he said, much real property was 'considerably divided into small parcels,' meaning that land ownership (even if it was ownership of a very small agricultural plot) was wider spread in Arezzo than in many other parts of Tuscany and Italy. Economic conditions of both smallholders and *mezzadri* were relatively good, so the prefect asserted – indeed better than those of other, non-agricultural workers in the province, both manual and white collar, among whom unemployment levels were frighteningly high. Bracali concluded for his superiors in Rome that Arezzo's current turmoil had an 'exclusively political character' designed to attract the agricultural classes to the leftist parties (especially the communists) in view of the upcoming spring 1946 administrative and constituent elections. He did not see the *mezzadri* struggles or disputes as a property issue or as a call for social change.

From Disputes to 'Award' and 'Truce'

Whether they were motivated by party politics or were instead the *mezzadri*'s own call for transforming the old system of property tenure, division, and inequality, or some combination of both, *mezzadri* disputes with landlords continued in Arezzo and elsewhere. In March 1946, the national CGIL asked De Gasperi, who succeeded Parri as president of the council of ministers, to intervene personally – something he was very willing to do. A quick three months later, on June 26, De Gasperi rendered his judgment from Rome. In article 2, the most significant part of this 'judgment' (*giudizio*) 'on the *mezzadri* dispute,' De Gasperi recommended that landowners contribute a sum equal to the value of 24 per cent of the gross product (from the landlord's portion) from one year's agricultural income to make up for war damages suffered by the *mezzadri* and for production adversely affected directly or indirectly by the war.[61] The amount was to be paid in cash or credited to the *mezzadro* in two parts (14 per cent of 1945's income and 10 per cent from 1946's income); alternatively this could be paid by products 'in kind,' if the *mezzadro* so requested. The first payment was to make up for wartime losses suffered by the *mezzadro*, while the second payment was to be set aside for carrying out works of reconstruction or improving the individual plots of land.[62]

Essentially, that was it – and for many landlords and *mezzadri* both, that was very little. De Gasperi's judgment did address payment (or landlord contribution) to make up for war damage and to improve the land, although 24 per cent of one annual income would not go far in restoring heavily damaged areas like the province of Arezzo (unless that income was enormous). In unarticulated acknowledgment, it also rewarded *mezzadri* who had produced more for the nation (and the landlords) during the first two difficult postwar years, in that obviously, 24 per cent of a lot was more than 24 per cent of a little. The judgment treated sharecroppers' claims regarding loss and replacement of livestock in a less than satisfactory way, however. It called on landowners to replace working animals by October 1, 1946, holding landowners responsible for 70 per cent of the cost of some replacement livestock, with *mezzadri* still responsible for 30 per cent (though each party would have half, or 50 per cent ownership in the new stock). The judgment also directed landlords to reward *mezzadri* who had risked grave danger and successfully saved cattle or horses from being stolen or killed with a 1000 or 2000 lire *premio* for each horse or head of cattle preserved.[63]

The judgment gave *mezzadri* little else in the long run. For example, it 'forgave' the *mezzadri* their obligation to provide landlords with the gift of poultry for the two years covered in the award (1945 and 1946) – in consideration of *mezzadri* wartime losses – but did not mention permanently doing away with the traditional *regalie* obligations or the personal services that custom required of the *mezzadro* and *massaia*. Moreover, it specifically left the annual fifty-fifty division of farm product unchanged, and so disregarded what was the *mezzadri's* most fundamental demand and thereby maintained the very heart of the system: the division of what the sharecroppers produced and the owners got.[64]

This judgment, which came to be known as the '*lodo* De Gasperi' or '*il lodo*' (the term *lodo* was contained in articles 4, 5, and 7 of the judgment and meant 'award,' as in an arbitrator's award), satisfied no one.[65] While generally perceived then and now intentionally to maintain the traditional imbalance of power and to favour landowner interests over *mezzadri*, the judgment nevertheless did – or would – require landlords to do and pay more than many were willing to give. Moreover, from the proprietors' point of view, the *lodo* represented the state's interference with traditional rights and uses of private property, and with the very personal relationship between *padrone* and *mezzadro*. Proprietors acknowledged that war damage to their property had to be repaired and livestock replaced, so that their property and their sharecroppers once again could be productive, but they resented the government directing them how and when to do so, especially when the government itself was doing so little (so they perceived) for them.[66] For their part, the *mezzadri* saw the *lodo* as state disregard for their claims and condition, retaining the system in its essence.

The *lodo* De Gasperi, as first implemented, did not carry the force of law; thus, it neither legally compelled landlords nor entitled *mezzadri*.[67] It did, however, bring the interim state (and De Gasperi) squarely into the ongoing dispute and into this old and very particular realm of property, because the judgment also assumed that Federterra now would commit itself to end and renounce 'all agitation' on the part of the *mezzadri*, and to restore the 'state of legality' (or status quo) on the farms – including the elimination of *fattoria* councils.[68]

Arezzo's provincial labour office reported that the award had added only a 'little friction' to the ongoing *mezzadri*-landlord disputes, but had not caused any real disturbances. In general, *il lodo* simply was not applied or followed when first issued.[69] Federterra continued to 'threaten' taking 60 per cent of the farm product, but according to the provincial labour office after the fact, the *mezzadri* in most of Arezzo's communes were 'totally indifferent' not only towards attempting to avail themselves of the *lodo*, but also towards Federterra's continuing demands on their behalf.[70] Arezzo's prefect confessed to the Interior Ministry that his personal 'continued intervention' had not, in fact, brought the sides – Federterra together with the peasant leagues, and the landowners associations – any closer together or caused the landowners to adopt a more 'reasonable' position towards the *mezzadri*.

As the 1946 harvest season approached, the prefect expressed his intention to continue 'following developments carefully,' in order to protect both public order and the consignment of grain. The most important development during the summer of 1946 was Federterra's public warning to the landlords to adhere to the '*lodo* De Gasperi,' threatening that if they did not, the sharecroppers would keep the entire crop – not just an additional 10 per cent – and turn over the landowner's share for consignment to the cooperative stores.[71]

Such proposed action (however unlikely) naturally alarmed the prefect (yet again). Not dividing crops between land-worker and landowner represented 'a clear violation of the most basic principles of liberty and justice,' the prefect emphasized. This now went beyond merely altering a contractual agreement – and was something, the prefect pointed out, which could not be allowed. He promised the *mezzadri* all his support towards pressing landowners to accept the *lodo*. Nevertheless, in the event of a call for a general strike (something also proposed), he was prepared to maintain public order, he warned. Even a one-day *mezzadri* demonstration organized by Federterra and called for September 21 to demand landlord compliance with the '*lodo* De Gasperi' raised serious concerns in the prefect's mind about 'respect for property and individual rights.'[72] The property and individual rights that concerned him were the landlords' not the sharecroppers', of course.

In the end, property and property rights proved stronger than organization and agitation. Arezzo's provincial association of landowners eventually reached a 'provincial accord' with Federterra some months later, whereby both sides accepted the terms of De Gasperi's award, with one slight Aretine difference. Instead of the 24 per cent De Gasperi had advised, 20 per cent of the landlord's profits (divided between 1945 and 1946) would go to indemnifying the *mezzadro* for damages directly or indirectly caused by the war. The other 4 per cent would go towards paying labourers for community reconstruction works of an agricultural nature designed to help relieve unemployment. That 4 per cent to help unemployed, non-agricultural labourers came from what was to be the *mezzadri*'s 24 percent portion – the landlords did not contribute an additional 4 per cent.[73]

The 1946 harvest season in Arezzo closed with some 'deplorable episodes' not elaborated on by the prefect, but always 'ably repressed' by police, and without a general strike or the sharecroppers retaining more than their traditional share.[74] Arezzo's prefect pronounced the *mezzadri* disputes 'resolved' for that province in November 1946.[75] It was not much of a resolution, even according to the prefect. The *lodo* itself did become law in May 1947, which was seen as a victory for Federterra – and for the *mezzadri* – though many landlords remained intransigent.[76] After national-level negotiations, a *de facto* truce was declared (*la tregua mezzadrile*) in late June 1947, which finally modified the system to alter the division of produce between sharecropper and owner. The sharecropper now was to receive 53 per cent of the produce, and the landlord 47.[77]

After the fall of Fascism, the turmoil and destruction of war, after *mezzadri* struggles and disputes, the formation of peasant leagues and *mezzadri* committees, Communist Party and some Christian Democrat support, and the direct intervention of Federterra and CGIL, the *mezzadri* share increased by only 3 per cent. Moreover, a number of landlords in the province of Arezzo (and beyond) refused to abide by that modest new distribution ratio, and even resisted making their contribution to replacing livestock the Germans had killed or stolen.[78] Neither did the truce help equalize the relationship between *mezzadro* and landlord. Some owners acted as if the war and the *mezzadri* struggles offered no reason to alter the balance of power between landlord and *mezzadro*, and indeed not much had changed. Short of carrying out those threats of violence and unilateral redistribution, there was little the *mezzadri*, their organizations, or the communal administrations could do against recalcitrant landowners or their estate managers, though some sharecroppers occasionally took such matters into their own hands by refusing to follow orders of particularly tyrannical landlords and estate managers.[79] The law and the state remained firmly on the side of the owners.

Fundamental reordering of farm product sharing did not take place and neither did the formal abolition of the *regalie* and personal service obligations; landlords were not compelled to improve living conditions, and *mezzadri* families were not permitted to keep an entire slaughtered hog for themselves. But although sharecroppers were still fighting to realize a new contract well after 1948, *mezzadri* lives and positions did change.[80] In certain areas, albeit more often in the provinces of Florence and Siena than in Arezzo, peasant leagues were able to impose and maintain farm councils, as called for at the first Federterra regional conference.[81] In Tuscany, where the *fattoria* system of sharecropping predominated (as compared to Umbria or the Marches), this meant some greater say for the sharecropper (if not advancement of economic position) on the land he and his family worked.

More importantly, in the larger arena of community and communal life, sharecroppers took a post-Fascist, postwar role in local administration and government – as sharecroppers and as citizens. They formed *mezzadri* committees in the communes to present and deliberate issues important to them, and to assure that *mezzadri* representatives sat on other communal, aid, and reconstruction committees that would decide questions affecting them, such as proposed tax revisions on farm products, and the mandatory hiring of unemployed labourers to do agricultural work.[82] They ran for, were elected to, and served on communal councils throughout the province. Sharecroppers took roles in communal CLNs, in the Camere del Lavoro, in political party and election organizing, in every aspect of organized and casual postwar public life.

Mezzadri organization and growth also continued after the so-called truce in 1947 and after the 1948 split within CGIL, with Federterra membership numbers and activity increasing annually throughout the last years of the decade.[83] *Mezzadri* youth (male and female) and *mezzadri* wives joined and participated enthusiastically in Federterra meetings and events. Youth and female *mezzadri* members together outnumbered (by almost double) the number of heads of household and other adult male members in 1948.[84] By June 1951, total enrolment had increased to

29,499 members, who made up, in part, twenty-two youth commissions, fifteen women's commissions, and thirty-seven women's groups. Within the organization, as within individual families, *mezzadri* women and the young had voice and status they had not held before. As significant as this was, none of it was enough to change – or save – the system.

Iris Origo, whose diary of the war years in the Val d'Orcia was followed rather later by her autobiography, ended that more recent work with moving passages about social change on her and her husband's large, sharecropped farm in the neighbouring province of Siena, brought about by the *mezzadria* struggle and disputes. Being a landlord who cared deeply both about the sharecroppers and about the land, she saw much good in the *mezzadria* system, but recognized that it could survive only so long as both parties were convinced it was fair.[85] After the war, she believed, the sharecroppers became convinced it was not fair. Origo attributed the shift both to Communist Party persuasion and to hopes for a better life after the war. 'In the country ... it was particularly easy to foment social discontent, since it is not difficult to inculcate new hopes in times in which any change seems possible,' she wrote. Certainly, many sharecroppers – particularly those whose landlords had less social conscience than Origo and her husband – had found the system unfair long before the war. The disordering and dislocation of war that altered so much of normal life did give rise to new hopes of change and made change seem possible. The old anarchist Attilio Sassi and landowner Origo were in agreement on that point.

Transformation – more specifically, rapid and fundamental transformation – simply was not possible, because the system was so entrenched as a defined way of life, and so deeply based on long tradition, custom, and law relating to ownership of property. The *mezzadria* system was not transformed in Arezzo or elsewhere; instead, it slowly died away. Its death was not caused by lack of concerted popular action or by failed unity. The end came because one effect of war and its disruption was the offer of more life options, and one effect of postwar syndical organization and encouragement was the new sense of personal agency, especially among the young, that allowed individuals to choose among those alternatives. Sharecropping no longer appeared as the sole life choice to youth in *mezzadri* families, and as no longer the only choice, it became the least desirable one. The *mezzadria* system declined every year beginning in the early 1950s, as sons and daughters left the land, saying no to an isolated and backbreaking life as *mezzadro* or *massaia*.[86] Rural exodus occurred in the province of Arezzo, as it did in the rest of the agricultural areas of central and north eastern

Italy.[87] Unlike the more desperate peasants of the south, Arezzo's *mezzadri* youth did not head for Rome, Milan, or Turin, but tended to stay in the province itself, or in the region of Tuscany, moving only so far as urban centres like Montevarchi, the city of Arezzo, or Florence, to jobs in light industry in the Valdarno or elsewhere in the service sector.

In discussing the central Italian sharecroppers' struggle, Paul Ginsborg termed the '*lodo* De Gasperi' as the 'watershed' in that struggle: the struggle had 'ended in substantial, if not total failure,' but left a legacy of collective action and cooperation.[88] The struggles did indeed end in failure and their legacy of cooperation, as such, was not an extremely large one. Their historical legacy, however, provides more than Federterra membership numbers and a temporary contribution to syndical unity. The *mezzadria* struggles were central to postwar life in the agricultural province of Arezzo – and to notions and meanings of property, of ownership, of rights, and of individual identity, organization and unity, because of the shared sense of possibility that social change could occur quickly and from below. The struggles and the disputes had to do with private property on the one hand, and with those Italians who had nothing on the other.[89] They were not about *mezzadri* seizing property they had so long worked and produced, but concentrated on slightly changing the annual division of farm crops, on improving living conditions, and on equalizing the personal relationship between *mezzadro* and landlord. After the fall of Fascism and the sufferings and sacrifices of war, much about the *mezzadria* system – especially the traditional *regalie* of eggs and poultry and demeaning household duties the *massaia* and *mezzadro* 'owed' to the landlord – so clearly seemed a social anachronism.

No change could have been sufficient to save the *mezzadria* system in the long term. It was a way of life fewer and fewer people chose. Even had the sharecroppers quickly obtained the demanded 60 per cent share, an end to the *regalie*, and the right to keep all of their slaughtered hogs, their children still would have chosen to leave the land. Postwar social change to the *mezzadria* system finally manifested itself in that way – not with alterations in the division of produce, but with young people who saw the possibility for a better life only outside the *podere* their parents worked and others owned.

11 Unemployment

[T]he unemployment crisis in this commune appears to be growing ever more threatening.

> Giunta, Commune of Civitella in Val di Chiana, August 23, 1945.

Among the most serious postwar problems that today dominate the Government's attention, is that of assuring the most rapid employment of 'returnees' in public jobs and private productive activity.

> President of the council of ministers, October 23, 1945.

When the first post-front sindaco of Cavriglia listed the three most immediate and fundamental problems his commune faced, he named them as: feeding (or provisioning), unemployment, and aid to 'needy victims.'[1] No one in the commune, in Arezzo, or in Italy would have excluded unemployment from a list of the most serious postwar problems. Unemployment meant families without money to buy food, without money to replace possessions stolen by the Germans or destroyed during the passage of the front, and without money to repair or rebuild their homes. But unemployment comprised more than lack of a necessary income during an inflationary time. It meant jobless men, which in turn implied political agitation and potential public disorder. Deeper still, unemployment was a continuing assault on society and on daily life. Wartime suffering would not end and life could not return to normal so long as much of the population – especially men – remained without regular occupation. Unemployed citizens (meaning men) spent their days without structure; families felt the traditional family hierarchy shaken; communities saw their members outside their expected roles. The disorder brought about by postwar unemployment affected everybody (employed and unemployed) and frightened everybody. The perception of unemployment as a threat to family, to community, and to society (as Civitella's communal *giunta* expressed) was widespread. What to do about it was all consuming.

First, Fire All the Women

When Bucine's communal council constituted itself in August 1944, little more than two weeks after the commune's liberation, two of its very first acts were to fire Antelma Lucarini from her job in the rationing office, and to suspend Ricardo Betti as communal guard.[2] They were not dismissed for incompetence. Both communal employees had performed their work well for a number of years, including during the most difficult period of the war. Despite years of service, however, the post-Fascist council determined to suspend all male personnel who had held some office in the Fascist Party or who had some special 'merit' or rank in the party, and dismiss from public employment all female personnel – period. Betti had been a *squadrista* who had taken part in Mussolini's march on Rome twenty-two years earlier, whereas Antelma Lucarini was, of course, 'female personnel.' In addition to the fact that Betti's offence against the commune was to have been an active member of the Fascist Party from its inception, while Lucarini's was to be a woman holding a job that should go to a returning – and male – partisan or veteran, another difference between the two communal employees was that, after Togliatti's amnesty, Ricardo Betti got his old job back.[3] Antelma Lucarini did not.

Unemployment was widespread throughout postwar Italy among all classes and sectors. The war in Arezzo, which destroyed farms, livestock, the mines, and factories, left thousands unemployed, and their numbers increased every day as soldiers, partisans, POWs, and civilian forced labourers returned home after the war ended officially for the country as a whole. Demonstrations, sometimes involving hundreds of participants, occurred regularly in the communes and in the city of Arezzo, as the unemployed demanded jobs. Partisans and veterans, and their organizations and associations, were especially vocal and appeared particularly threatening. The memory of the years following World War I, when unemployed ex-servicemen had helped make up the core of violent Fascist 'squads,' was still present in many minds. Thus, it was not surprising that the prefect and others worried about the relationship between public order and unemployed men – especially soldiers and partisans. Neither was it surprising

then that women, especially those who had been hired for public employment during the war, would be fired to make way for men. With so much
damaged and destroyed, public administrative employment was one of the
few areas in which jobs still existed, and public employment was the only
sector that the province could control.

Some months after Lucarini's dismissal, Arezzo's provincial CLN made
the first move in what would become a postwar battle between local and
provincial administrations, and between women workers and those who
expected them to step aside for men. On November 3, 1944, Arezzo's
CLN sent a memo to 'all administrations' (with a copy to the prefect)
regarding the 'question of female personnel.' 'As a result of many complaints for a long time now,' the committee said it had decided to 'invite'
all administrations (communal and provincial administrations, and public agencies) to review the family position of all their female employees
and 'proceed to dismiss those who are not supporting their families.' In
substitution, the committee advised hiring men who were 'competent,
needy, and politically correct.'[4]

At this time, Arezzo's Allied occupiers were vainly attempting to limit
CLNs' local and provincial-level influence, and the Allied-appointed prefect was trying to please both the Allies and the CLN. Less than a week
after the committee's memo reached him, beset prefect Guidotti Mori
fired off his own informal directive to all sindaci and to every communal
administration, state office, and parastate office in the province:

> It has come to my attention that many female employees are still in service
> in this organization. Given that many men are unemployed, it is necessary
> to review – using very narrow criteria – the position of each female em-
> ployee and to discharge – naturally – all those who are not *heads of family*. I
> await your figures indicating the number of existing female personnel, the
> number let go, and the family situation of each (if any) kept on.[5]

In a detailed response, Cavriglia's sindaco informed the prefect that the
communal administration employed five women, all of whom the sindaco
would have to fire if he applied the prefect's directive 'to the letter,' because none was 'truly' head of her family. One woman served as both typist
and telephone operator; two assisted in the office of public records; and
two worked in the rationing office. They had worked for the commune for
some years – to the full satisfaction of the public and the administration.
All five performed their work with 'devotion, seriousness, and diligence';

each demonstrated 'competence, aptitude, and tact.' Because of such admirable personnel, the communal offices functioned with real speed and efficiency – something that would change with the substitution of new 'improvised' personnel unaccustomed to communal service. Men simply did not have 'sufficient cultural preparation' suddenly to be in a position of service, especially in service to a communal population made up almost exclusively of miners and sharecroppers.[6]

Moreover, the sindaco emphasized, taking on male employees in place of women would cost the commune an extra 50,000 lire a year. The commune paid the women 'very little really': only 433 lire per month each. For the same work, men would have to be paid 1200 lire each, and the commune would be responsible for benefits like unemployment and safety insurance (which it did not have to contribute for the women). All five belonged to families of 'the neediest labourers' and their small contribution helped alleviate the many economic difficulties in which the families currently found themselves. If the commune were forced to change personnel, it would be fairer to substitute from the many widows of men massacred throughout the commune by the Germans a few months earlier. They certainly now found themselves in the position of head of family, with no possibility of any other employment.

The range of argument and justification employed by the sindaco was impressive. In the space of two close pages, he pointed out that women would work for much less than men (in this case about one-third as much, and without benefits); they were more dedicated to their work; they were better suited (culturally and temperamentally) to interact with the public in a service capacity; they were better at serving poorer classes of people; and, finally, certain categories of women were actually needier – and more deserving – than the categories of unemployed men the prefect proposed.

Other communes and public organizations and their female employees argued equally fervently that individual and family need should permit a woman to keep her job, even if she were not technically head of her family. These communal battles with the prefect over firing women were another arena in which to show disdain for the state and its inadequate solutions to postwar problems, and they offer another look at the postwar on a local level. Arezzo's provincial branch of the National Agency for the Protection and Assistance of War Invalids had one woman as part of its three-person staff. The director asserted that even though the young woman's father received an invalid's pension from the First World War, her own salary as a clerk for that organization was the only other financial help the family had.[7] The commune of Arezzo expressly refused to dismiss across-the-board every female employee who was not 'head of her family,' as the prefect had directed. Arezzo's sindaco instead fired only one woman, and proceeded to battle the prefect for months afterwards over that single dismissal.[8] Agencies and communes explained that their few female employees not only were critical to the functioning of their offices, but also that the women all were in 'straitened' family circumstances: their fathers had been killed by the Germans, for example; they were evacuees; a brother or sister had died in the war; their fathers were labourers and the families had six, eight, or more members.[9]

On February 12, 1945 – coincidentally less than two weeks after Italian women were granted the right to vote – recently appointed prefect Elmo Bracali, Guidotti Mori's replacement, issued a more official statement on the subject of firing women. The wartime necessity of assuming 'numerous female personnel' no longer existed, while alleviating male unemployment now grew more necessary and urgent. Therefore, with ACC Provincial Commissioner Quin Smith's full approval, the prefect decreed:

(1) All female personnel hired as temporary employees by the administrations of local organizations or any organizations or institutes under the Prefect's control, must be gradually dismissed and substituted with suitable male personnel who possess the qualifications and education to accept public employment – with a preference for veterans and those who have been members of partisan formations.

(2) Women who can be considered head of family may be kept in service, as might those women who are members of families in which no other member is suited for employment, those who are part of large families, and those in a particular state of need.

(3) Female personnel should be kept in service for those specific duties to which they are well-adapted and not really substitutable [by men]: such as nurses, custodians and attendants for schools and institutes of instruction frequented by women, cloakroom attendants, kitchen and laundry workers, typists, stenographers, telephone operators, etc.[10]

Thus, under paragraph 3, women could keep jobs that were 'women's jobs,' jobs men did not want, and jobs that did not pay very much. Under paragraph 2, with recurrence of that common postwar phrase and condition, basically, they could keep any job, as nearly everyone in postwar Arezzo (and Italy) could argue a 'particular state of need.'

The newly arrived prefect may not have intended the result (or non-result), but, naturally, few firings ensued from the new decree. Women were either heads of family or the equivalent (many with husbands still in Allied or German prisons), they worked hours and for salaries men did not want, or they were very, very needy. The commune of Civitella had only two female employees: one who cleaned the communal offices, and one who cleaned the streets of Badia al Pino. Both were war widows and, thus, heads of their families.[11] Arezzo's National Association for War Orphans had one female clerk, herself an orphan as a result of the previous war, and so head of her family for the past many years.

Women ably pleaded their own cases too, of course, petitioning the prefect for exemptions from his decree. In the province of Arezzo, which had suffered so terribly from the war, many could claim more than one exception. One woman, a clerk in the communal offices of Cortona, had repatriated from France when the war began there, and then evacuated from the Italian port city of Livorno following the aerial bombardment there at the end of May 1943. Her father was 'ill' with pleurisy, and so was unemployed most of the time. Her family was in economic conditions of great hardship, given that hers was a large family and she was the only one earning money to support them all.[12]

Women simply refused to make way for men – for partisans and veterans – in public employment, thereby 'selfishly' impeding veterans and partisans in their return to normal, civil life, others argued. Women were not alone in stubbornly clinging to jobs. Not long after the prefect's February decree, the Sestino branch of the National Returned Servicemen's Association (Associazione Nazionale dei Combattenti) 'wished to bring to the prefect's attention' that communal administrations still employed women – as well as men who had never served their country either in war or in peace. What was worse, many of those 'still employed men' had been hired during the Fascist era, which carried the implication, of course, that the men had been hired for their public jobs because they were Fascist Party members.[13] The servicemen asked the prefect to join their 'sane, just, and humane' initiative of substituting meritorious individuals – that was, unemployed ex-servicemen – in place of all women and of men who had never served in the military.

On April 26, 1945, as partisan and popular anti-German uprisings were taking place in the north, leading members of Arezzo's division of the National Partisans Association of Italy (ANPI) sought a meeting with the prefect to discuss how the communal administration of Sansepolcro purposely prolonged the unemployment problem whereby 'elements

belonging to the old regime' together with the 'female element' prevented the hiring of former partisans in that commune. The prefect
quickly directed a worried memo to Sansepolcro's sindaco, regarding
the commune's 'needy partisans, deprived of employment,' while communal offices remained occupied by numerous women and by 'those
who have demonstrated attachment to the defunct political regime.' He
reminded the sindaco of his February decree (which had called only for
the dismissal of women). 'Naturally, when substituting female personnel
or male personnel compromised under the past regime, you should give
preference to veterans, disabled and invalided, volunteers and partisans,
who have the proper employment prerequisites.'[14]

The sindaco objected, demonstrating the less than clear position partisans held after the war (especially in parts of central Italy). Not a single
partisan had presented himself to the commune, the sindaco said, or
proffered documents attesting that his education, credentials, and aptitude made him suitable for public employment. In addition, the war had
only very recently ended (this dispute between commune, prefect, and
ANPI took place during the end of April and beginning of May 1945);
dedicated partisans should still be in the north with the Allied forces, the
sindaco noted. Furthermore, according to the sindaco, no one among
Sansepolcro's current communal employees had demonstrated any particular attachment to the defunct political regime; any such adherents
already had been suspended. Instead of generalized hints, the prefect
and 'his informants' 'should state *specific facts and name individuals*' – a
charge from which one can infer (as did the sindaco) that ANPI had
specific communal employees in mind.[15]

As for dismissing female personnel, the commune of Sansepolcro had
seen total destruction of its industries – including the Buitoni pasta factory
that had employed mostly women. Female unemployment was worse than
male – and only with the greatest difficulty could a woman find any job.[16]
Five women had been hired for the rationing office during the war and
carried out their services with care, intelligence, and particular dedica-
tion. One employee was a widow with three children – and thus exempt
from the prefect's decree. Even if not technically heads of their families,
the remaining four all provided the main support of their families.

In the summer of 1945, the prisoners of war began to come home.
Arezzo's provincial CLN alerted both the prefect and the *Questore* about
the need of finding work for arriving POWs, and what that meant in
terms of maintaining public order. CGIL also joined in, accusing the

prefect of having 'no concern' for the men returning from POW camps, from concentration camps, and from military and partisan service. Many returnees had told CGIL that 'even now in both public and private offices, there are too many women not possessing the requisite head of family status or recognized extreme need.'[17] That otherwise inclusive labour organization had little trouble dismissing its publicly stated commitment to women's right to employment. 'Although for us the question is absolutely disagreeable, because we struggle for women's right to work [*il diritto al lavoro delle donne*], nevertheless in the current situation it seems to us that girls [*ragazze*] who live at home – through a higher sense of social duty – ought to leave jobs for men and to wait until the situation gets better, and so allow everyone the moral satisfaction of knowing they are earning their own living.' Thus, there were 'women' who had the right to work (perhaps war widows who cleaned the streets), and there were 'girls' who lacked an elevated sense of social duty to give up their posts until labour and economic conditions improved.

The prefect reacted again, reminding provincial administrations, communal sindaci, presidents of public institutions, and assistance and charitable organizations of his February decree. 'It seemed' to prefect Bracali (undoubtedly because CLN, CGIL, veterans, and partisans all kept stressing the point) that not all organizations fully or equally applied the provisions of that decree.[18] As more POWs, along with returnees from internment camps, war wounded and invalids, and patriots and partisans who had taken part in the liberation of the *Patria* in the north were flooding back into the province. it was absolutely necessary that these men, who were 'truly deserving and who now found themselves deprived of all means of sustenance,' be given some occupation – to relieve them of 'uncertain futures and of their sense of depression and impatience to which forced inactivity was driving them.'

To guarantee compliance, on July 5, 1945, the following week, the prefect appointed a four man commission, which included provincial CGIL's general secretary, to examine each office's 'procedure' in dismissing its female personnel and substituting suitable, qualified male personnel falling within categories of veterans, war wounded, partisans, the politically persecuted, or member of a family of political victims. The commission would visit all offices in the coming days to carry out its investigation; the prefect warned: 'I think it opportune to advise you that ... aside from obvious social principles and exigencies of public order, it is necessary, especially in the current delicate moment, to eliminate every cause of uneasiness and justified impatience among those who deserve instead all our help and concern.'[19] That not very veiled language was intended to guarantee cooperation with his decree, and to stress social solidarity while raising the risk of outright violence – violence that was justified if those who had jobs to give (or give up) did not comply.[20]

Arezzo's UDI provincial committee and women members of CGIL expressed that postwar solidarity should include rather than exclude women. UDI returned to the alternative of eliminating instead all 'purgable elements' from public administrations *and* private businesses.[21] CGIL's female members also spoke in contravention of Arezzo CGIL's position on 'girls' who needed to display a higher sense of social duty. They entreated their communal CdL and provincial CCdL to intercede when five women workers were fired from communal offices in Cortona, quoting the general secretary of CGIL, who had spoken at a national meeting of the directive committee in Rome the previous month. They emphasized: '*The problem of unemployment has a particular aspect in the labour of women. We cannot resolve the problem of "returnees" by creating a problem of women; sacrifices, if there are to be some, ought to be made by all workers without discrimination by sex or age. Everyone has the right to work and to an equal wage. In any event, the fascists should be the first to be fired.*'[22]

Though hard fought, the dismissal of women workers proceeded, however slowly and 'in fits.' The commune of Cavriglia dismissed two of its female employees in the spring of 1946, and two others, expecting to be dismissed, resigned. One continued to work for the commune doing administrative work for ONMI. Two others were kept on through June 1947, so that the four male *reduci* hired to replace them could become accustomed gradually to the job.[23] Another was rehired, after the communal council later determined she really was head of her family. No 'amnesty' ever covered women sacked from their public sector jobs, as it did former Fascists. The latter were later ordered rehired because Rome (if not the communes) saw restoring them to their former positions as a component of postwar national reconciliation, whereas women, many believed, contributed to national reconstruction by being discharged to make way for returning veterans and partisans.

Not only in Italy – and not only after World War II – have women been encouraged, urged, or forced out of all sorts of jobs, with the idea that female unemployment would solve the problem of male unemployment.[24] In Italy, the 'problem of female employment' raised unresolved questions about the position of women postwar and unaddressed questions about who constituted head of a family after the war had altered the make-up of so many families. Did status as head of family still depend on age and gender, or was it based on earnings? Could a young wage-earning woman be head of family even if her father was alive? The phrase was manipulated to keep women in their jobs and to argue why they should go. More importantly, the 'problem of female employment' provided a focal point for those concerned with the horrific proportions of unemployed citizens after the war, and who despite war caused destruction, poverty, and suffering still believed 'girls' were taking up scarce jobs, working for pin money to buy magazines and movie tickets.

Firing women was not the solution, of course; that became obvious fairly early on. On a local village and communal level, the numbers of female public employees were extremely small, and communal officials personally knew each woman, her family situation, and her state of need in a way the state (in the person of the prefect) did not. Moreover, in postwar Arezzo, and postwar Italy as a whole, it was absurd for prefects, partisans, veterans, CLN, or CGIL to think that firing the few women communal or public employees would have any impact on unemployment.[25]

The 'Struggle against Unemployment'

As unemployment worsened,[26] the call to fire women and Fascists expanded to insistence on firing all single men, those with fewer than six in the family, any member of a family in which another member already had some employment, and all those who were not *reduci*.[27] Such drastic measures were never really implemented, but the fact that they were seriously proposed underscores the gravity of the unemployment situation and the desperation of the unemployed in postwar Arezzo.

The actual numbers of unemployed became an obsession for ACC, for the sindaci, the prefect, the provincial labour office, and the nation. Directly after the passage of the front, the Allies attempted to determine the number of unemployed in the province. Unemployment figures varied widely from commune to commune, and fluctuated from month to month, during the summer and fall of 1944 and after, as local citizens, Allied troops, and refugees came and went. The larger, more populous communes had the highest unemployment figures, naturally, as did the communes where industry and mining were concentrated. In August 1944, the province's first provincial commissioner, Lieutenant Colonel Thurburn, noted 'between 5000 and 6000 men unemployed in the communes of Montevarchi, Cavriglia, and San Giovanni, who worked in lignite mines or factories.'[28] In October 1944, 3960 men were unemployed in Arezzo commune and 3850 in Montevarchi. Cortona, with the second largest population in the province but with little industry, had 'only' 800 unemployed. The smaller commune of Sansepolcro, which saw its pasta factory, tobacco factory and processing plants, lumber mill, cement works, and ceramic works all damaged or occupied or destroyed by Allied troops, had nearly 1500 persons unemployed.[29]

Allied military and occupation presence slowed political and administrative recovery on the one hand, but on the other, the Allies provided needed employment opportunities for labourers to rebuild roads and bridges, and for service workers such as cooks and launderers. The Aretines felt that the Allied presence inhibited their return to civil life, while conversely, they feared what would happen when the Allies left and the jobs they provided came to an end. There is '[a]nxiety on part of the Allied employees as to what will happen to them when the front moves on and they lose their jobs. Unemployment in Castiglion Fiorentino is said to be virtually non-existent since all the workers there are employed in a British factory.'[30] Local unemployment numbers and anxiety increased sharply with the sudden departure of ACC in the early summer of 1945, when Arezzo's provincial labour office began keeping careful track of 'the state of unemployment.'[31] On August 9, 1945, Arezzo's prefect ordered the sindaco of each commune to provide – on the tenth, twentieth, and thirtieth of every month – the number of unemployed divided into separate categories for men and women, and insisting on the 'greatest exactitude' in the figures.

Communes were not to count sharecroppers or smallholders among the unemployed, or anyone who belonged to such a family or lived with those types of farming families. Neither were they to include persons physically unable to work, children under the age of sixteen, and 'in general, all those that have casual work, an irregular occupation, or who have the possibility of exercising an activity from which they could derive even modest means of subsistence.'[32] The definition of 'unemployed' was limited in part to exclude as many as possible from the calculation of unemployed and from claim to assistance benefits intended for the unemployed.

'Unemployed' thus did not include sharecroppers or small farmers (or anyone who lived with them), even if their fields could not be farmed because Allied troops had recently bivouacked there, because the fields had been bombed or mined, because farmhouses were uninhabitable, or because farmers no longer had the equipment, animals, or means to work the land. It did, however, include women, and in a few communes – as the sindaco of Sansepolcro stressed – the number of unemployed women rivalled that of men.

In August 1945, unemployment in that agricultural province where the majority were sharecroppers or small farmers amounted to 9120, including those in the city and commune of Arezzo: in the Valdarno mining and manufacturing zone, 1586 had been unemployed the previous month, now the number increased to 2092; the agricultural Val di Chiana counted 1403; the Valtiberina 1901; and the Casentino 1852.[33] A few months later, in October 1945, the situation had improved in some communes. Seasonal work in the upper zone of the Val di Chiana had brought the unemployment rate there much lower, as did a temporary government project of agricultural works and tree clearing. The number of unemployed men in the Casentino dropped dramatically that month because reconstruction on the secondary Arezzo–Stia rail line had begun. In the Valtiberina, however, unemployment numbers increased, especially in Sansepolcro, where 1145 men and 710 women were now unemployed in that commune alone, where light industries had not been able to make repairs on account of lack of materials.[34]

For the month of January 1946, the province as a whole counted 6750 unemployed men and 2643 unemployed women – according to the exclusive definition of the term. Eight hundred sixty more men and 240 more women joined the ranks of unemployed since the previous month, while 457 other men and seventy-seven women had found work since the previous month. Because the only agricultural workers who could be counted as 'unemployed' were salaried and day labourers, a mere forty-three men and ninety-nine women were unemployed in the agricultural sector for the month. In the building and road (repair and maintenance) sectors, 4369 men and forty-seven women were unemployed that same month.[35]

In the poor and war damaged commune of Bucine, officials counted no unemployed for August 30, 1945. They figured only thirty-one on February 20, 1946; thirty on April 10 that year; and forty on June 15 – because most of the commune's population was smallholders and sharecroppers.[36] Applying his own definition of unemployed, however, Bucine's sindaco counted 250 unemployed in July and 320 unemployed in October 1946.[37] Those numbers, he said, more accurately represented how many went out looking for work everyday.[38]

Throughout the province, the official number of unemployed persons hovered slightly below 10,000 throughout 1946, rose to over 10,000 for 1947 and the rest of the decade, occasionally climbing to more than 11,000.[39] In July 1950, the province still reckoned 9685 'officially' unemployed.[40] The 'real' numbers of the unemployed, as in the commune of

Bucine, were much higher when one considers that from a total provincial population of about 320,000, more than a third were members of *mezzadri* families, while smallholders and other direct cultivators constituted another several thousand.

The critical unemployment situation made for a volatile postwar climate as early as the autumn of 1944. Even with their authority and means of enforcing public order, the Allies worried what widespread unemployment – with no likelihood of early relief – might lead to. 'Particularly in the industrial area of the Val d'Arno, the dislocation of industry by the lack of transportation and power to run machines, has resulted in a situation which the CAO on the spot has characterised as "a volcano on the verge of eruption." It is hoped that this is exaggerated.'[41] That the unemployed embodied a volcano threatening to explode at any moment, may have been an exaggeration while ACC ran the province and it was still full of well-armed, Allied troops. As soon as those troops, Quin Smith, and the rest of the ACC officers departed, however, frequent mass demonstrations did erupt.

The *Questore* reassured the prefect in July 1945 not to worry about the possibility that growing unemployment would disturb public order, but that possibility almost immediately became a reality.[42] On July 16, in Pieve Santo Stefano, a 'large crowd of unemployed protested with shouts of "bread and work."'[43] They persuaded labourers who were engaged to stop their work, and they forced the closure of shops and public premises. On that same day, the Communist Party organized some 3000 people in Arezzo's Piazza Grande, who listened to impassioned speeches 'about the problem of unemployment and the purge of Fascists.'[44] All the political parties had much to say about unemployment, naturally, about what was not being done to solve it, and what each planned to do.[45]

Demonstrations regarding unemployment were common occurrences throughout the province from the summer of 1945 onwards, continuing and escalating especially throughout 1946. On January 12, 1946, unemployed *reduci* of San Giovanni Valdarno joined in the local *Casa del Popolo* to explain to the sindaco their 'conditions of distress and their deep desire to obtain any sort of work as soon as possible.'[46] On April 9, 1946, more than 200 unemployed *reduci* demonstrated in Subbiano. On May 9, 1946, thirty unemployed marched through the sole main street of the village of Rassina, carrying two banners that proclaimed 'We Want Bread and Work.' Separate 'agitation' took place in Castiglion Fiorentino, Cortona, Stia, San Giovanni, Sansepolcro, and the city of Arezzo during the month of June alone.[47] On July 5, 1946, 300 unemployed demonstrated in Cortona, demanding 'bread and work.' One hundred *reduci* protested their unemployment on July10, outside the prefect's office in Arezzo. The following day, 400 unemployed in Bibbiena called for jobs. During July 1946, fifty unemployed demonstrated in one commune, sixty in another, one hundred in another, and so on.[48]

By the summer of 1946, the *Questore*'s monthly reports to the prefect on 'public order' read like a daily chronicle of angry protests by the unemployed, despite the *Questore*'s admitted practice of including only the more 'significant' demonstrations.[49] In August, the unemployed of Bucine called for 'work at any cost,' and threatened to come *en masse* to Arezzo. They urged an immediate state contribution to begin public works in the commune. When the prefect agreed to meet with them, but then failed to arrive, he set off another angry demonstration. '*Lavoratori mal disposti*,' hurriedly telegrammed the commune's vice-sindaco.[50] On the last day of the month, more than 200 unemployed from Tegoleto, Ciggiano, and Civitella, organized by their Camera del Lavoro, travelled to the city of Arezzo 'for a protest at the prefect's office in order to obtain work.'[51] The following month saw 'significant' demonstrations in Anghiari, Sansepolcro, Badia al Pino, and elsewhere. A 'mass' of angry workers descended on the city of Arezzo 'requesting local authorities to relieve the suffering and the distress with which they had struggled so long on account of the lack of work.'[52]

About 200 unemployed workers in the commune of Subbiano went 'on strike,' demanding that the provincial authorities resolve the problem of jobs for labourers, by 'immediately beginning reconstruction of the Arezzo–Prato Vecchio–Stia railroad and other works previously promised.'[53] A few days later, the unemployed went on strike in the village of Pian di Scò, blocking the main road for the morning. In Civitella on the eighteenth of September, 350 unemployed declared a strike. They wanted the authorities 'to provide the work needed so they, in turn, could provide for the most urgent needs of their families.' Civitella's communal council deliberated the 'message' of the recent demonstration, agreeing that the sindaco, the prefect, the *Questore*, the Camera del Lavoro, and the head of the civil engineers all had a stake in both unemployment and reconstruction of the commune: 'it is advisable to begin some urgent and necessary works in the commune that could employ the most labourers.' The communal road which ran from Tegoleto to Badia al Pino remained in very bad condition since the passage of the front; repairing it would be at least a start in alleviating unemployment.[54] On October 2, 1946, 120 protested and 'threatened acts of violence' because reconstruction work – that would employ the unemployed – still had not begun there.

In Sestino, 200 demonstrated in the piazza, calling for the 'immediate start to reconstruction work to absorb unemployed labourers.'[55] A year later, in March 1947, about 150 unemployed workers in the commune of Sestino again protested in the piazza that promised reconstruction works that could 'absorb unemployed labourers' still had failed to materialize. The following month, 320 unemployed engaged in '*agitazione*' in Castiglion Fiorentino over a two day period.[56] More than one hundred labourers in Bucine were in '*agitazione*' over the lack of work, and they threatened 'to disturb public order' if reconstruction works to relieve unemployment were not promptly begun.[57]

These many examples represent only a few of the scores of protests serious enough to be reported during each of those postwar months and years.[58] The common theme of most 'public manifestations of protest' against unemployment in 1946 and 1947 centred around the failure of the state and the province to begin reconstruction of public works.[59] Unemployment and public order were closely connected from an official and administrative point of view naturally, in that communities hovered dangerously on the verge of disorder so long as large numbers of citizens remained unemployed and protesting. From the perspective of the unemployed (and many local authorities), the answer to unemployment was public works: 'projects to repair the damages of war and to relieve the unemployment of labourers.'[60] Unemployment could be solved, the unemployed argued reasonably, if the state and the communes began the many programs of public works – repair and reconstruction – so obviously needed throughout the province.[61] Reconstruction thus would doubly hasten the return to civil life, by returning the unemployed to work and returning the communes and the province to their prewar condition.

The provincial labour office's monthly report for April 1946 included a paragraph on the slightly improving situation in the field of agriculture and the worsening situation in industry – given that industries lacked materials and capital, and enjoyed little demand for their products (because the unemployed had nothing to spend). The director also reiterated a sentiment shared by most of the province and its unemployed: '*Given the current state of things, if we truly want to solve the problem of unemployment, we have to finance the reconstruction of public works, which are so numerous and important.*'[62]

The interim state recognized the obvious need to reconstruct public works and the closely related need to relieve unemployment. As early as August 10, 1945, the government authorized expending six billion lire over the rest of 1945 and 1946 to carry out urgent and extraordinary public works throughout Italy.[63] Projects were to be chosen not only because of their importance to public use, but also according to those which would occupy the greatest number of labourers. Communal reconstruction committees drew up lists of public works needed in their own communes, and sindaci met to consolidate a province-wide program. The earliest proposals in Arezzo – which included repairs to communal offices, to many schools, hospitals, public housing, aqueducts, sewer systems, public wells and fountains, well over one hundred bridges, city and village walls, cemeteries, roads, river embankments, and public lights – estimated the funds that would be needed for each project, and how many workers could be employed over the life of a project.

Anticipating its share of state funds, in August 1945, the commune of Cortona listed 147 urgent and necessary public works which it estimated would cost 136 million lire.[64] If even a portion of Cortona's proposed reconstruction projects were promptly funded and carried out, unemployed labourers would not have been an issue for several years to come in that commune. The smaller commune of Caprese Michelangelo requested more modestly that its most necessary bridges be repaired, so that some of the 'neediest unemployed workers' could be engaged, and its sindaco pointed out that those unemployed 'elements' most needy were also the most 'unruly.'[65] Putting them to work would help the commune, and would also alleviate the workers' need and keep them occupied. Again, ruined public works, unemployment, and public order were closely and clearly intertwined.

Actually obtaining the state funds to begin restoration of public works and to employ needy unemployed workers proved much more difficult for the communes than did planning the works projects and counting the number of unemployed needed to work on them. Exasperated communal sindaci wrote frequently to the prefect expressing frustration that the state was doing nothing about unemployment or about rebuilding their communes.[66] The commune of Bucine, the sindaco wrote in August 1946 (two years after the passage of the front), still needed to reconstruct fourteen bridges, as well as public buildings, and several schools. Four large provincial bridges situated within the commune's territory also awaited restoration, and more than a hundred kilometres of communal roads needed to be repaired.[67] If the government undertook even a few of those reconstruction jobs, it would substantially reduce unemployment and begin to restore the commune. In January 1947, Priamo

Bigiandi, sindaco of Cavriglia, wrote to the provincial office of civil engineers regarding eight urgent public works projects that the commune had submitted during the spring and summer of 1945. Despite the fact that nearly two years had passed, not a single one of the projects had been financed – let alone approved by higher authorities. The commune had attempted to begin the projects on its own, but could not afford to pay the labourers what was going to amount to several millions.[68]

The state eventually authorized money for reconstruction, but with rampant inflation, the enormous number of public buildings, roads, bridges, and other works in need of repair, and the thousands of unemployed needing jobs, the amounts granted were never enough and never seemed to arrive so that long-planned works could begin as scheduled. Having an 'in' with Rome did not always amount to much either, though political connections naturally were utilized and widely publicized at home. Undersecretariat of state for the Ministry of Transport, Christian Democrat Angelo Raffaele Jervolino notified Aretine native Fanfani at the DC offices in Rome on August 8, 1946, that 6,360,000 lire had been authorized for public works in the province of Arezzo ('because I know you also have at heart the situation of unemployed workers,' and presumably those in Fanfani's own province, in particular).[69] That amount, however, was far less than the single Aretine commune of Cortona had estimated its reconstruction costs in 1945.

Sums for reconstruction increased, but more was always needed, both because of inflation and because jobs did not materialize elsewhere. When the Ministry of Public Works authorized the 'final amount' (for the budget year 1947–8) of one billion lire for repair of war damage, Arezzo's prefect implored Rome to consider the extremely serious destruction suffered by the province, one hardest hit by the war and still facing industrial and mining crises that aggravated unemployment.[70] In 1948, the prefect resorted to using monies from the prefecture directly to finance smaller projects in the communes and to keep men working. The commune of Civitella received five million lire from the provincial treasury for one month to construct works of public utility (in that instance public toilets) and to relieve unemployment.[71] In March 1948, the prefect gave two million to the commune of Bucine to stem 'unemployment through urgent works.'[72]

Throughout 1948 and after, the notion of a 'plan of reconstruction works to relieve unemployment' still circulated as the solution to problems both of unemployment and reconstruction. That year, the Regional Association of Tuscan Communes, including the Association of Communes of the Province of Arezzo, held a region-wide conference in Florence at which Tuscany's sindaci, prefects, senators and deputies, and representatives of all the political parties met 'to examine the emergency situation in Tuscany following the notable increase in the number of unemployed and the slowness in which works of public reconstruction are financed by the bureaucratic organs.'[73] Both unemployment and the repair (or disrepair) of public works remained emergency situations that crossed party lines. At the end of 1948, the province of Arezzo counted 11,311 unemployed and well over three billion lire worth of public work projects yet to be carried out.[74]

Employment Strategies

The three-way connection between reconstructing public works, relieving unemployment, and maintaining public order excluded farmers, whether sharecroppers or smallholders. Only farm labourers (*braccianti*), meaning salaried or day labourers who did paid farm work for others, officially counted among the unemployed. Peasant owners and *mezzadri* were not to be considered 'unemployed' no matter their circumstances, but rather farms and farm property came to be seen as a potential, albeit temporary, solution to the unemployment of some non-farm labourers. In 1945, Arezzo, like some other predominantly agricultural provinces, took up the idea of putting unemployed, non-farm labourers to work in agriculture, apparently with the notion that there was always more work to be done on a farm.[75] The program began as a voluntary one and it was a matter of postwar solidarity (and expressed as such), in that farmers were expected to offer the unemployed work on their property. It was immediately unpopular.[76]

The 'assumption' program, as it was called, had several obvious flaws from its inception. Labourers were not the only ones unemployed: agricultural labourers (*braccianti*) also were unemployed, and surely it made more sense to urge farmers to 'absorb' them into any work that needed to be done. Even before the war, many small farms worked by their owners could barely support those owners, let alone several others. Additionally, on account of the war, passage of the front, and Allied occupation, many farms in the province were in very bad condition. Moreover, the majority of farmers in the province were sharecroppers who owned no land and many of whom were engaged in their own struggle with landlords at that time. Finally, unemployed labourers often did not make enthusiastic or efficient farm hands (no matter how desperate they were for employment to support their families), and relations between reluctant farmers, resentful at being told what to do with their property, and the inexperienced workers assigned to them often were not particularly cordial.

Asking farm owners to take on unemployed labourers was something like telling public agencies to fire their female employees or telling landlords to give their sharecroppers an additional 3 per cent: the state – in the person of the prefect – was stepping into the realm of local affairs and private property in an ineffectual attempt to solve postwar problems. The state was not welcome, and neither was the intervention of CGIL, which also supported the program. A few farmers and landowners initially took on unemployed workers, but most refused the prefect's and CGIL's first requests to 'absorb' them. One farmer with only three hectares in the commune of Castiglion Fiorentino generously took on fifteen workers. Some months earlier, even before the prefect's request, Father Polvani had agreed with the communal sindaco to take on ten men at the cost of 500 lire per day. [77] CGIL sent a not so subtle message to two less amenable farmers in the villages of Frassinetto and Policiano about the 'serious and related problems of unemployment and of maintaining social tranquility' in the province 'so tried by war.' While Arezzo's industries were being repaired, the prefect, the sindaci, and the industrialists all asked landowners to give some work to the unemployed, CGIL explained. In general, CGIL added, the result was satisfactory throughout the entire province, therefore the labour confederation found it 'exceedingly odd' that these two particular owners had 'refused to take on even one (and *we mean one*) labourer.'[78] The two uncooperative farmers were not alone, despite CGIL's singling them out. The result of the voluntary absorption program in the entire province was, in fact, 'not satisfactory.' Too few farmers followed the example of Father Polvani and the smallholder in Castiglion Fiorentino.

Then, on May 15, 1946, with public works stalled and the unemployment situation worsening, the prefect issued decree number 2213 regarding the 'obligatory assumption of labourers in agriculture.'[79] 'From that day on,' the matter would be regulated exclusively by the prefect's decree, under the control of communal sindaci assisted by local, communal hiring commissions, and under the added vigilance of the provincial labour office. The decree obligated both owners of large farms and direct cultivators who had a taxable annual income greater than 1000 lire, to take on unemployed labourers. Purposely omitted from the unemployed to be absorbed were those who themselves belonged to farm families of any sort.

That is, farmers ordered to absorb the unemployed were prohibited from taking on anyone who was a member of a farming family, including *mezzadri* and *mezzadri* family members. Landowners whose property was farmed by *mezzadri*, however, were obligated to take on unemployed labourers as well.

The prefect directed every commune to institute its hiring commission 'without delay,' and those commissions had the delicate task of setting the number of workers to be assumed by a farm, the duration of their assumption (a minimum of fifteen days was required), and the wage to be paid.[80] They also had to determine the effective state of unemployment – and need – of each unemployed labourer, with the neediest to be assigned first.

This was not a decree that promised to generate much in the way of local solidarity from the side of farmers and landowners, or to build unity among all involved. Not all absorptions of workers onto the land were adversarial and solidarity did exist, but it was by no means universal or widespread. Indeed, the decree's mandatory nature spawned immediate complaints and transgressions.[81] Farmers complained about the number of labourers they were forced to absorb, the amount of money they were told to pay, and the work projects that sindaci and communal commissions told them to provide – projects which under normal circumstances they either would have postponed, or never have carried out. Farmers' written protests to the prefect were vehement and filled with heavily underlined phrases emphasizing that all was being done '*against [their] will*.'[82]

The local landowners association objected on behalf of its members whose farms had suffered great damage during the war and now produced well below prewar output. *Mezzadri* complained that they lived in farmhouses without toilets, without ovens, even without glass in the windows, yet now had to share their plots with those who lived in much better conditions.[83] Sindaci reported that owners were not keeping labourers employed for the number of days they had been assigned, and wrote to local landowners who declined to comply with the prefect's decree, inviting them to their offices to reach some accord – or be referred to the authorities.[84]

From his vantage as communal secretary for Monte San Savino, Aroldo Lucarini observed that 'squads of unemployed' would go onto 'private property' on 'their own initiative' to dig ditches or channels for water, and then demand payment from the landowner. When the owners refused to pay for those 'superfluous' works, the workers followed up with threats – 'loudly proclaiming their right to work.'[85] Landowners in turn complained about continued official 'tampering with their indisputable right' (that is, the right of private property and the right to run their farms as they chose). In this 'atmosphere of competing interests' – and competing rights – 'the commune had the difficult duty of arbitrator and mediator.'

The sindaco of Monte San Savino called a meeting of all the larger landowners in the commune to try to find 'some middle ground.' He made the mistake of announcing such meeting to the general population, however, by ringing the civic bell. People hurried in from the communal seat and from the surrounding villages, blocking access roads and turning the meeting into much more than an arbitration session with local farmers. 'A handful of ruffians' took over communal offices, while a larger crowd 'hurled threats and insults' against the landowners and the vice-prefect (who had come from Arezzo) who had locked themselves (for both privacy and protection) in a meeting room.[86] The unruly crowd also occupied the telegraph office, making it impossible to inform Arezzo or to ask for police reinforcements.

'It goes without saying that the intimidated landowners found themselves forced to take on the labourers.' From a balcony in the commune building, the town crier called out the news to the crowd. After 'business' with the landowners was concluded, however, what had started as a protest against unemployment and landowners' recalcitrance now expanded. The 'mob' next demanded the dismissal of the sindaco and the firing of former Fascists 'whose names the crowd called out,' and to which the vice-prefect acceded.[87] Here came to life the official fear of men and women without work threatening social order, transforming protest over unemployment into a much louder (and broader) display of public discontent.

The prefect's make-work plan divided unemployed labourers against landowners. The postwar unemployment and agricultural situation also pitted labourers against sharecroppers, farm workers, and poor farmers who, some might have argued, all had more than a little in common with labourers in the way of class, poverty, and social treatment. At the same time small farmers and landowners were ordered to absorb non-farm labourers into agriculture, farmers themselves, members of farm families, *mezzadri*, and farm hands were being prevented from taking any sort of job outside of agriculture.

Farmers and farm workers who sought to leave the land first became an issue during the Allied occupation. The Allies, as would the Italian state, considered farmers and farmhands' departures from the land a danger to agricultural production and amassing of crops. In October 1944, Arezzo's ACC economics and supply division first reported on the consequences of farm labourers taking Allied-created non-farming jobs: 'With regard to the wage situation now, so many people are being employed by the Army at good rates, very great difficulties are being experienced by the farmers who are unable to pay the same rates. In consequence the whole agricultural program is being held up ... Without a law prohibiting the farm worker from leaving the land, and this savours of fascism and not liberation, little can be done.'[88]

The sindaco of Castel Focognano, near Bibbiena, also complained about the Allies employing farm labourers for non-farm work. The sindaco worried not so much about the detrimental effects upon local agriculture, but that the army's hiring of farm workers left the 'ordinary labourer' out of work and with 'no alternative means.' This labour quandary was one area of civil life which Arezzo's PC, Quin Smith, did not attempt to control. Quin Smith and the Allies were unwilling to overly regulate peasants' attempts to leave the land – perhaps because, as pointed out, that would have smacked of Fascism and not liberation. Italian authorities and citizens did not feel equally constrained.[89]

Sindaci, the *carabinieri*, and communal employment offices fielded complaints from unemployed labourers that farm workers and members of farm families were seeking and taking work outside of agriculture – unfairly, it was said, trying to have themselves counted as 'unemployed.'[90] Castiglion Fiorentino's CdL received permission from the prefect and communal authorities to conduct a new census among the 'officially unemployed,' because so many farmers and farm workers 'wrongfully' attempted to be included in that category.[91]

Arezzo's CGIL secretary wrote to the sindaco of Civitella denouncing 'farmers who work in industry.' Civitella's CdL had learned of a firm '*without scruples*' in Ciggiano that hired *mezzadri* and smallholders, instead of unemployed labourers.[92] The firm referred to had hired one *mezzadro*, one smallholder, and one smallholder from another commune, all of whom Civitella's sindaco requested be promptly dismissed. A provincial office in Arezzo made a similar mistake of hiring one member of a *mezzadro* family. The man was married, the father of two children, and shared a house and plot with his brother and the brother's family. Between the two families, they sharecropped seven hectares of land. Despite the *Questore*'s sad report that the families' combined economic conditions were 'miserable,' that the farm house they lived in had been partly destroyed during the war, and that the offending hire was in poor health, CGIL insisted that the man should be substituted by a 'more needy,' non-agricultural worker.[93]

It may have been true that those who owned small plots of agricultural land or even those who, as *mezzadri*, farmed someone else's land, had a bit more in hand in the postwar scheme of things than did an out of work labourer with no employment prospects. But the official notion that farmers and *mezzadri* and their families could not be termed 'unemployed,' and were not considered 'needy' enough as compared to out of work industrial workers and other labourers, no matter what their circumstances, makes the sharecroppers' own 'struggles' and paltry outcome even more poignant.

CGIL's attempt to organize sharecroppers and support them in their struggles against landlords, while at the same time actively working to exclude them both from unemployment statistics and from any non-agricultural employment makes increasing Federterra membership numbers impressive yet puzzling, as it became clearer that CGIL's real concern lay with industrial and urban workers, not central Italian farmers (something Coldiretti similarly noted). In a predominantly agricultural province, and a province where everyone – including farmers and sharecroppers – had so recently suffered the losses of war, massacres, and the destructive passage of the front, the way in which authorities, union and labour organizations, and workers themselves continued to deny the neediness of small farmers, sharecroppers, and farm workers served as another point of fracture in postwar society.

Categories and Hierarchies

Because those categorized as farmers or agricultural workers were prevented from taking jobs outside of farming, and because drought made the agricultural year 1945 'one of the saddest registered in the memory of man,' many farmers, farm workers, and farm family members sought officially to leave the ranks of 'farmer' and become industrial workers, either temporarily or permanently.[94] These formal requests for transfer of category (*passaggio di categoria*) and their consideration were procedurally complicated affairs. Job categories had been rigidly defined, in that norms regulating inclusion in a particular job category and limiting movement across employment sectors had been legislated years earlier as part of the Fascist regime's designs to manage labour and prevent physical migration from countryside to city. When Fascism fell, employment statutes nevertheless remained and communal employment offices – through which hiring was to be done – were reinstituted as a way to keep some control over unemployment and the unemployed after the

war. Those employment offices oversaw the hiring of unemployed labourers while they excluded sharecroppers and peasants (*i contadini*)
from the category of 'unemployed.'[95]

An Aretine farmer or sharecropper who disregarded the old laws or
the communal employment office could expect to be sanctioned both
officially and unofficially in that small and local place where unemployment concerned everyone and circumvention was sure to be found out.
As seen, a farmer or farm worker who did obtain a job outside his category likely would be soundly denounced by the local CdL, by unemployed workers, sometimes by his own sindaco – and dismissed. Change
of category – or sector – was not easily made in law or in fact, and obviously could not be done unilaterally by the farmer.

The commune's CdL had no objection when, in April 1945, Civitella's
sindaco issued *libretti di lavoro* for the son and nephew of a so-described
'peasant family,' so that the two young men could work for other farmers
or a large agricultural concern, given the family's own 'disastrous conditions.'[96] When the nephew formally applied to change category yet again
at the end of 1945, this time from agricultural worker (*lavoratore
dell'agricoltura*) to industrial worker (*lavoratore dell'industria*), however,
that application was denied. Civitella's sindaco had passed the request to
the prefect, who consulted with the provincial labour office. The prefect
denied the request because the provincial labour office had obtained
information that the man wanted to stop being a *colono* for the inadequate reason that he remained 'distressed by the war.'[97] A resident of
Ciggiano made the same request (to switch from agricultural to industrial worker) at about the same time. His application also was turned
down. In his case, the provincial labour office had made enquiries and
learned that he had 'always' been a *colono*, but now wanted to change
because he was on 'bad terms' with his wife and his father-in-law, on
whose farm plot he lived.[98]

If neither post-traumatic stress nor a failed marriage provided sufficient grounds to leave the farm, actual ownership of a bit of land or the
mezzadria contract to work it was even a stronger reason for denial. The
prefect denied the application for transfer of category made by one man
in 1946, who was a member of a family of four that owned and cultivated
a farm of 2.26 hectares. The prefect's preprinted rejection form cited the
minister of labour and social security's May 4, 1946, circular, number
3359 AGL, whereby denial was 'according to the norms intended to
check the phenomenon of unemployment in the field of industry that is
aggravated by, among other things, the flood of agricultural workers into

the field.'⁹⁹ Another man had his application denied, given that he belonged to a nine-member family which cultivated a farm of 12 hectares.¹⁰⁰ A *mezzadro* near Montevarchi, wrote to Amintore Fanfani (then minister of labour and social security) complaining that the provincial labour office had refused his request to leave the agricultural sector for industry, and asking Fanfani to overturn the decision. The labour office had determined that the *podere* he and his family worked was sufficient for their support, while the man insisted it was not.¹⁰¹

Job changes, that might be viewed as 'downward' or 'horizontal' moves so long as they remained within agriculture, were much more likely to be approved. In the fall of 1947, the provincial labour office questioned why Civitella had altered one man's title to 'worker' (*operaio*) from 'farmer' (*colono*) in the communal registry of his family's status. The sindaco acknowledged the commune had permitted the change when the man found work as an agricultural day labourer (*bracciante agricolo*). He and his remaining family had left their sharecropped plot more than two years earlier because they could no longer maintain it after the Germans had massacred his father and two uncles on June 29, 1944.¹⁰² The man was not moving into industry, the sindaco reassured, but simply working as a farm day labourer instead of living and working as a *mezzadro*. A year later, Civitella's communal commission decided favourably on the man's cousin's identical request to move into the category of agricultural *operaio* and work as a *bracciante agricolo*.¹⁰³ Young women could leave the farm somewhat more easily, if they sought to move into 'service' jobs as maids or seamstresses, and not into any jobs that might be done by men.

As CGIL, CdL, employment committees, veterans and partisans associations, and private individuals were vigilant in denouncing farmers who attempted to take jobs in industry, so they also reported citizens working in communes not their own and taking jobs that 'belonged' to residents.¹⁰⁴ The Fascist law against urbanization remained in effect, which meant that citizens, whether farmers or others, could not leave their own commune to look for work or to move to another.¹⁰⁵ Many did so anyway, of course, but it was more difficult to pass unnoticed in small, rural communes than it was in Rome or larger cities.¹⁰⁶ Those found out could be prevented from receiving social or employment services in the new commune, prevented from registering as a resident of the commune, or even be ordered to leave.¹⁰⁷ Unemployed outsiders were unwelcome even from neighbouring communes within the same province. Attempting to cross something so small as the boundary between two communes in order to find work demonstrated how local the postwar was.

Within the boundaries of the postwar unemployment crisis, out of work labourers and other non-agricultural workers were privileged, in a sense, over sharecroppers and smallholders. Not all were equal within the ranks of non-agricultural workers, however. Categories, hierarchies, politics, patronage, and one's wartime activities also played important parts in employment and unemployment in the postwar aftermath. When Arezzo's prefect announced a competitive examination for 250 posts in the police force, he also signalled that those who had participated in 'anti-German actions' in armed bands after September 8, 1943 (that is, who were recognized as partisans) were entitled to preference.[108] The competition for positions with the state railroad, under the Ministry of Transportation, was reserved for returnees (*reduci*) from prisoner of war camps, concentration camps, or from deportation; for ex-soldiers; for those wounded or disabled in the struggle for liberation; and for partisans who had seen fighting.[109]

In 1946, the president of the council of ministers required public administrations to dismiss workers who were not regular, permanent employees and hire an 'equal number of *reduci*.'[110] Twenty jobs were thereby created for *reduci* in the commune of Cavriglia, which had hundreds of its citizens unemployed. Subsequent state legislation and prefectural decrees required hiring only *reduci* for new openings in public administrations, whether the positions to be filled were those of white collar clerks, communal guards, or street sweepers.[111]

At its narrowest, the term *reduci* meant returning military veterans and partisans. More broadly, as seen, it had come to include former civilian prisoners, deportees for forced labour, the politically and racially or religiously persecuted, and others whose lives had been disrupted (in the sense of physically having left) and who were now returning to civil life after serving or suffering on account of the war. When the commune of Bucine fired four male employees in February 1946 because they were not heads of family, and fired one woman because she was no longer head of her family after her recent marriage, the commune had five positions to fill. Applicants, the commune required, had to be more than eighteen years of age but not yet thirty, and should be 'returnees' (*reduci* in the broader sense), or 'closely related' to someone killed in the war or killed in the struggle for liberation.[112]

Every public post (and many private ones) came to involve a competition between those who had fought in the war and those whom the war had made victims. A July 1947 competition for schoolteachers was open only to *reduci*, to war wounded and war invalids, to refugees who could not return to their homes, and to those who had suffered political and racial (religious) persecution. Teaching experience, education credentials, exam scores, and oral interviews all were taken into account, but being otherwise equal according to those criteria, applicants received critical, additional 'points' depending on what they had done or what they had suffered in the war. A teaching post, or even a substitute teaching post, thus depended on military service, on medals or decorations won, on partisan activity and the quality of partisan activity, on type of persecution undergone, length of time spent as a civilian deportee, or on status as war widow or war orphan.[113]

Competing for position of communal guard in the commune of Civitella, two men each argued his own preference for the post. Both were *reduci* in the narrower, military meaning of the term. More specifically, however, the returnee from a POW camp – who came in second – was also a 'war invalid.'[114] The other, first awarded the post, was both a military veteran as well as a war orphan (from World War I). After a long and complicated series of exchanges between the communal council, the prefect, the Opera Nazionale per gli Orfani di Guerra, and the Opera Nazionale per gli Invalidi di Guerra, the prefect referred to a 1921 (post–World War I) statute requiring communal administrations to hire at least one war invalid. He directed, therefore, that the post be taken from the war orphan and given instead to the war invalid. In that particular case, where both men had a military connection to the war in that both were veterans of the 1940–3 war, a war invalid 'outranked' a war orphan. Without the existing law to rely on, distinguishing between those two claimants in any rational fashion would have been even more irrational.

The absolute necessity of having to choose between multiple applicants and the resulting hierarchy of qualifications not directly connected to job qualifications or performance extended down to the job of street sweeper. The three final candidates to clean Badia al Pino's streets included a war widow with two young children, a man currently the gravedigger for the village, and another woman with no specified attributes or war related suffering. Not surprisingly, the communal council voted unanimously to give the post to the widow, 'insofar as she [was] a war widow and in a state of need.'[115] In Oliveto, the council chose three men as finalists for the same position (street cleaner): one, an ex-soldier had seen combat in North Africa; the second was a war invalid, and the third a returnee from prison. Eventually the war invalid was chosen – because he was 'better qualified.' Whether the preferred qualifications were war related or job related was not specified.[116]

More than their abilities, applicants necessarily elaborated their wartime and postwar suffering in the countless petitions and letters seeking employment.[117] Like entreaties for housing and for assistance, job requests also narrated harrowing experiences of war and massacre in Arezzo. One man applying for a clerk position in the communal offices of Civitella held the requisite diploma, but more compellingly though, on June 29, 1944, the Germans had massacred his father, who had been *cantoniere* in the commune for many years previously. He wrote to the commune: 'On the 29th day of July [sic], the German bandits killed my father with a revolver shot to the head, and in his turn threw him into a cantina and burned him (I found only some charred bones a few days later). They burned our house, stole our clothes and linens, and all the money my father had sweated and saved to support the family.'[118] He and his brother fled to the woods, where German soldiers found them together with several other men in hiding and put them all to work digging a large hole. At the end of the day, the Italians were shot, one by one, and pushed into the hole they had dug. When it was his turn, he ran, dodging the gunfire, but his brother and the other men all were killed. The applicant now was left without a home, and with a mother, a sister, and a little brother to care for, 'in hopeless conditions.'

The young man obtained a job with the commune soon after the passage of the front, thanks to the sindaco's influence and the compelling nature of his situation. As unemployment worsened and applicants were without work for months and even years, petitions became more anguished. One 'returnee' had 'done his duty as an Italian and a soldier' fighting first on the Libyan–Egyptian front, then in Russia. Now in December 1948, 'after three years of searching in vain for work in the country [he] had so faithfully served,' he would choose death – if not for the suffering that suicide would bring to his wife and three innocent children.[119] After what he had suffered and sacrificed for the nation, Italy was doing nothing to help him or make it up to him.

The Constitution of the Italian Republic, which took effect in January 1948, provided as the first of its twelve articles of fundamental principles that 'Italy is a democratic Republic founded on labour.' The nobility of labour – and the idea of a right to employment – made particularly appropriate foundations for a republic born in the midst of a national unemployment crisis. The immediate postwar story of work and labour in Italy is the story of unemployment and the attempts to end it. When the three secretaries of Arezzo's provincial-level CdL proclaimed in May of 1946, that the 'problem of unemployment' remained not only unsolved, but instead grew increasingly worrisome, they put it down to 'three essential factors': the stagnation of private initiative in works of reconstruction; the refusal of more than half of the province's large landowners to 'absorb' unemployed labourers for needed works; and the 'scarcity and insignificance' of public works undertaken.[120]

Citizens and communities had to take matters into their own hands, but infinite needs and the 'inability to provide for them all' also constrained self-determination, in that they limited just how much people could do to change their own circumstances. Nevertheless, the men and women of Arezzo sought and fought for work where and how they could. They protested and demonstrated; they pushed the sindaco, the prefect, the provincial labour office, private concerns, and communal hiring offices to create jobs, especially in the work of local reconstruction. They requested help or a recommendation, and they demanded it, from anyone or any organization that might conceivably speak for them or help tip employment decisions in their favour.[121] They utilized priests, politicians and political parties, postwar special interest associations, CGIL, and the CdL to help them find jobs and to influence hiring decisions. Self-determination was required to survive the many hardships of the postwar, and so citizens made public officials, politicians, and associations 'work' for them on their individual behalf. They, as a side effect, thereby helped further and entrench practices of patronage and *raccomandazione.*

If this reads like the postwar situations surrounding assistance and housing, it should. Unemployment made for unity insofar as unemployed individuals joined together to protest the lack of jobs, the slowness of reconstruction, and to demand work; they joined together in unions and labour confederations, and joined in sympathy to strike in protest against the killings of Sicilian workers, farmers, and union organizers.[122] Unemployment also made for solidarity in that donations were given and collections were taken to help the unemployed, and as those who had jobs agreed to work fewer hours, to share jobs, or to take 'turns' with those who did not, in order to make a little work for all.[123]

Unemployment was as much a divisive factor in postwar life. When a hundred unemployed persons competed for five jobs (just as when hundreds of needy competed for a dozen pairs of shoes or a few hot meals and when the homeless competed for a few places in new apartment blocks), some way had to be found to distinguish between the applicants and to decide who would get hired and who would not. Differences had to be found; and so, citizens were categorized and ranked according to wartime contribution and suffering. Although that process provided some rationalization for a situation that otherwise seemed impossible to sort out, categories and hierarchies also served to divide people because they accentuated differences – as indeed they are designed to do. Unemployment thus set women with jobs against men without them, and put unemployed labourers against property owners – and against share-croppers and small farmers who themselves were in no better position than the labourers. Unemployment thereby also divided citizens who were otherwise 'equals,' in that a few would obtain positions only through com-petitions that others would lose. It divided veterans and partisans, both of whom were *reduci* in very similar ways. Moreover, it divided veterans from one another and partisans from one another, as all used degrees of war related contributions and suffering to obtain an advantage. Society and its members focused not on similarities, but on differences, in attempting to solve the difficult problem of postwar unemployment.

PART FOUR

The Postwar Future

12 Pure Politics

He is a good type of man, without political views.
> CAO of Terranuova to AMG/ACC, August 16, 1944.

We held a course of preaching to bring the month of May to a festive and solemn close, and to beseech God for a good result in the upcoming elections.
> Don Gino Ciabattini, parish diary, May 26, 1946.

The prefect and the *Questore* usually commenced their monthly reports
to higher state officials with a section on the province's 'Political
Situation.' In a place that, by other evidence, teemed with political activity and with other activity that brought in party politics somehow (note
for example the party flags flying over the celebratory lunch at the
Bucine viaduct) (figures 11 and 12), the prefect and *Questore* noted that
'the people' and 'the population' took little interest in politics or in the
activities of the various political parties.[1] Early on, both men tied this indifference to the suffering and hardships Aretine citizens had endured
during the war, and to the many everyday struggles of reconstruction.[2]
With so much else weighing on them, the people had no thought to
spare for party politics. The Allied ban on all political activity may also
have contributed to the general public's reluctance to embrace party
politics until the ACC's departure in May 1945.[3] Public interest, along
with political party membership, began to increase after that, according
to the prefect. The population remained skeptical even then, however,
about the parties' ability to solve postwar problems any more effectively
than existing state authorities. In his December 1945 report, the prefect
commented that the educated members of society wished to 'wait and
see' what the parties actually would accomplish and deliver.[4]

Despite their officials' assessments, the population could not avoid politics: not everyone may have been interested, but party politics were everywhere in postwar Italy.[5] The political vacuum left by the fall of Fascism would quickly be filled, just as wartime destruction and postwar need created continuing opportunities for the parties and for politicization. Two stand among hundreds of other local Aretine examples highlighting the forces that contributed to the distinctive postwar political climate. The first, a formal note sent in October 1945 to Cavriglia's communal *giunta* from the Castelnuovo dei Sabbioni section of the Communist Party women's organization, UDI, the Union of Italian Women (Unione Donne Italiane), read:

> In the name of claiming women's rights that today place them on an equal plane with men, given the healthy and decisive contribution that women want and are able to make to the economic, political, and social reconstruction of the nation [*la Patria*], and considering the recent admission of female representatives to all the organizations, commissions, and committees of public administration, this committee asks for participation in this honourable *giunta* of at least one woman, appointed from the women of the entire commune.[6]

The prefect declined to modify the *giunta* to include the 'female element,' as he phrased it. His response, he said, did not 'in the slightest' constitute a refusal to acknowledge women's opportunity to join 'more intimately and more deeply in the civil, administrative, and political life of the Nation.' Rather, it reflected his belief that the appropriate way for women to obtain a place in the communal administration was through the upcoming administrative elections.

A brief August 1946 missive from Arezzo's *carabinieri* to the prefect regarding the month's 'political activity of the clergy' provides a second example. The clergy's political activity had been 'quite restrained,' the report said.[7] Nothing was really worth noting, he said, except the recent behaviour of Subbiano's parish priest, Father Benedetti. Benedetti was 'an old anti-Fascist,' who had been persecuted by the Nazi-Fascists for having 'blessed' weapons for the partisans. Now, however, the priest had taken up a position of 'open hostility' towards members of the Socialist and Communist parties. In addition, the priest of Castelfranco di Sopra also publicly manifested his 'open hostility' towards the 'parties of the left.' Exactly how the two priests demonstrated their hostility was not elaborated. The church did not begin excommunicating communists 'and those who subscribed to their doctrine of propaganda' until 1949,[8] and the reporting officer also mentioned that the local Catholic press had not published any 'addresses of a political nature' that particular month.

These exemplify two important political currents flowing through local life between 1944 and 1948. That is, women's place within the parties and in the new democracy was one such current, together with the importance of elections themselves. Like some, the prefect believed – or at least espoused – that elections would be the answer for women and for the rest of the population: elections would result in a new fairness and equality of representation. That result would not come to pass for women, who would not take an equal part in elected administrations, but who would extend their political presence in more traditional venues. The new position of women 'on an equal plane with men' and the promise that elections held for quick social change were fundamental subjects, but postwar political life in central Italy was also about Catholics *versus* Communists – and about the two groups' organizing and electioneering activities. Even those like anti-Fascist Father Benedetti and the communist ex-partisans, who so recently fought together on the same side against the Nazi-Fascists, now positioned themselves as irreconcilable opponents.

That irreconcilability, both a factor in and a result of postwar politics, coloured village life. After the war, Giovanni Guareschi's fictional Don Camillo did daily battle with his nemesis Peppone, the commune's communist sindaco, for moral and political authority over the local population in the 'red' Po Valley.[9] The priest's frequent conversations with Christ on the cross, as he sought to best Peppone, brought out a Jesus not the least reluctant to enter directly into that worldly postwar contest. As Don Camillo and Peppone clashed time and again, Jesus always gave good counsel on combining religion and politics. Giovanni Guareschi's charming and immensely popular stories of the priest's trials against Peppone and communism that spanned the late 1940s, throughout the 1950s, and into the 1960s, also reflect the development of the postwar Communist World–Catholic World construct as effectively as they describe the uniquely Italian postwar overlap of party politics, religion, and daily life.

Joseph LaPalombara called the Communist–Catholic conflict the 'basic postwar political struggle' in Italy.[10] That postwar social, political, and cultural war has provided material for case studies, party histories, interpretations of Christian Democrat tenacity (and fraud), and explanations of the Communist Party's first rise and fall.[11] Previous chapters have demonstrated how political parties became part of postwar life, most notably in the critical areas of assistance, housing, and employment. This chapter discusses everyday politics in their most overt sense: the activities of political parties during the early years of the struggle, as they led to the elections of 1946 and 1948. The Po Valley was home to Don Camillo and Peppone but they would have found an equally suitable setting in the hills and valleys of the province of Arezzo. The village of Castelnuovo dei Sabbioni and the commune of Cavriglia most quickly come to mind, with sindaco Priamo Bigiandi, frequent appearances by the old anarchist Attilio Sassi, and Don Aldo Cuccoli's and Don Ciabattini's indignant cries of 'that's not true!' in response to political speeches and communist taunts in the piazza.[12] In the communes of Arezzo, Garibaldi would never 'betray' Togliatti, but that did not lessen the struggle.[13]

Associational Politics

Party politics openly appeared in daily life once the Allies left the province, though not always without complaint. Memoranda dispatched from the provincial director of education to sindaci and party secretaries expressed outrage at the illegal uses to which schools were being put. Dances in the schoolrooms were bad enough, but holding political meetings there was even more inappropriate, the director scolded. The sindaco of Pergine Valdarno who had authorized Laterina's Communist Party 'cell' to use the local elementary school for its evening meetings lacked any jurisdiction to do so. School facilities were to be used only for the purpose of education and, moreover, 'in no case can the use of schoolrooms be authorized for political propaganda, given that – as is obvious – in a democratic regime, school has to be absolutely unconnected to politics.'[14] Laterina's Communist Party might well have countered that political meetings were education in themselves in post-Fascist, pre-election Italy, and therefore completely appropriate activity for the local schoolroom.

Arezzo's provincial labour office perceived equally serious problems in the physical proximity of government and politics – which, like schools and politics, should occupy very separate spaces, its director felt. The labour office, instituted during the Allied occupation, had been provided office space in the one-time offices of the formerly Fascist, now-suppressed Confederation of Industrialists. The Allied civil labour unit occupied the rest of the building, but when the Allies departed in spring 1945, the right-wing L'Uomo Qualunque Party rented the portion of the building left empty by the Allies. It was 'politically inappropriate,' the labour office insisted to the prefect, that it should be sharing an office building with L'Uomo Qualunque.[15] The office's director sent off another protest a couple of months later, as campaigning got underway for the March 1946 administrative elections. This time, the director pointed to the electoral campaign posters appearing on the outside walls of his office building. Such things had no place on those apolitical walls, he insisted.

Unlike the director of the labour office and the director of education for Arezzo, most everyone else (including the prefect) accepted party politics as an integral part of everyday life, and social-religious-political associations like ACLI (Associazioni Cristiane Lavoratori Italiani) quickly and easily melded politics with multiple aspects of daily life.[16] The women of UDI already had been active many months before they demanded inclusion in Cavriglia's communal administration in the autumn of 1945, granted early permission by the Allies to institute local circles throughout the province. David Kertzer describes UDI as 'formed in Rome in 1944 by a coalition of left-wing forces in anticipation of the postwar enfranchisement of women.'[17] Those left-wing forces were 'concerned' about socially and 'politically conservative' women, overly 'influenced by the church' and 'about to vote for the first time.'[18] An organization that began in order to 'educate' women to vote for the left grew into a much larger social presence on the postwar scene.[19] The organization expanded rapidly in the province of Arezzo and the rest of central and northern Italy, sincerely calling for members to 'this new organization that enters into national life inspired by the noble purposes of cooperating in the renewal and reconstruction ... for the future of the Nation so sorely tried.'[20]

The Aretine women's agenda, as expressed to ACC and Quin Smith, could not have been better or more neutrally phrased to please Allied male occupiers driving a moral *Risorgimento*, including their professed efforts directed towards economic and social emancipation of women and to the defence of democratic liberty. They extended invitations to 'all apolitical women' as well as to members of the political parties; they assisted soldiers and their families, and poor children. Arezzo's prefect elaborated independently on the women's organization, its benign nature, and its assistance activities. He assured the Allies that UDI had 'a national character and democratic tendencies, respecting the ideas and principles of all political parties' and 'aiming for women's participation in the economic and political life of the Nation.'[21] What otherwise suspicious Allied occupation officer could have disapproved of such a program? The fact that the *Presidentessa* and another member of the four-woman Aretine committee were enrolled in the Communist Party, while the other two had not yet 'precisely professed their political faith,' bothered neither the prefect nor the Allies.

The point is how UDI portrayed itself, seizing on traditional language and engaging in traditional women's activities that were both recognizable and acceptable. UDI members carried out work that Fascist women had done before them, and that Liberal era women had done before that. That is, they did traditional women's volunteer and assistance work – but in a masterful way that brought party politics into daily lives. UDI was closely connected to the male-dominated Italian Communist Party from its beginnings, and combined assistance, social, and political activities from the beginning.[22] But, a historian-observer might ask, did Communist Party (PCI) men press UDI women into 'women's work' to benefit the party, or, more appealingly, had the women already and independently recognized the significance of skilfully intertwining assistance and social work with party politics?

An examination of local records reveals how women carried out the organization's critical day-to-day work in the towns and villages – and how the population perceived that work. In the midst of longer discussions on the province's political situation in 1945, the *Questore* reported monthly to the prefect, and the prefect in turn to the Interior Ministry in Rome, that the Unione Donne Italiane 'continued its activity in the spiritual field.'[23] When UDI's Arezzo committee asked the communes for financial support in its 'first organizational phase,' Cavriglia's sindaco approved of the 'vast assistance program' assumed by the new association, which program – he quoted – consisted of providing moral help to the people 'without distinction as to party.' The sindaco deemed it 'right and proper' that the commune of Cavriglia, whose population had suffered so much on account of the war, might serve as an example 'through its interest and its aid' to encourage other private and public organizations. Cavriglia's sindaco therefore allocated 5000 lire from the commune's 'unforeseen expense fund' to the Cavriglia section of UDI, leaving barely 4000 lire remaining in the commune's entire fund.[24] Rather than give the money to the commune's poor through an existing charity, a communal assistance committee, or an official assistance agency such as ECA, the sindaco chose to pass it through the women of UDI.

UDI's assistance work was both vast and varied (and only touched on in chapter 5), in that the postwar aftermath offered much scope for assistance activities. UDI of Montevarchi held a charity fair in July 1945 for the families of the fallen, and was organizing a summer camp for children of needy families at Terranuova that same summer.[25] In September 1945,

Arezzo's UDI pressured the prefect, the provincial CLN, and the committee for ENDSI to do something more for the people of Pieve Santo Stefano ('without a doubt the most wretched village in our province').[26] UDI's provincial secretary had recently visited the village where all the houses had been destroyed and the poor families had no blankets, no clothing, and no shoes. On the January 6 feast of the Epiphany 1946, in the village of Canucia, UDI gave Befana gifts to 'all the children of working people who had suffered so much in these hard and sad times,' distributing candies, cookies, oranges, apples, figs, and nuts, as well as fifty much-needed pairs of shoes.[27]

Angelo Ventrone lists some general UDI nationwide undertakings, which included collecting funds for partisans and their families, setting up nursery schools for the children of labouring women, arranging for free medical services, offering cooking and educational courses, organizing singing and reading groups, and formulating a host of other assistance services and social activities.[28] And in spring 1947, it was UDI initiative (together with CGIL) that caused March 8, International Women's Day, to be celebrated throughout Italy. In Arezzo, all female communal and provincial employees received half the day off, and with pay, so that they could participate in the celebrations.[29]

UDI did much that was absolutely necessary and was socially worthwhile, while the group also seemed to have an eye on something else – and that something was party politics. The political direction assumed by UDI and especially by its individual members was 'fundamentally communist,' the prefect informed Rome once the Allies left the province, and UDI thereby had 'alienated the sympathies of women and young people of Catholic sentiments and faith, as well as women who shrink from organized political displays. These have swelled the ranks of [women's ACLI circles], who sympathize with the Christian Democrat Party.'[30]

In the middle of 1945, the various existing Catholic women's organizations, including the Movimento Femminile (MF), coordinated in a federated Centro Italiano Femminile (CIF) to carry out their own assistance programs and their own brand of political education and social reconstruction. Angelo Ventrone has described the sub-worlds and sub-struggle of Catholic and Communist women: 'UDI for its part, MF and CIF on the other, participated on opposite sides of the struggle for the conquest of civil society, but they also had, especially in this first phase of democratic rebirth, methods of operation and objectives that were very similar; first above all, the recognition of female capability in the public sphere.'[31]

Just as the *Fasci Femminili* before the war, now the Communist women of UDI and the Catholic women of CIF, took over volunteer duties, overseeing and offering assistance at the village and communal levels. Through their part in Catholic and Communist Party aid, welfare, and social work activities, Italian women had new opportunities for politically inspired accomplishments, though the limited venues for taking part in public life were not so new. Women's volunteer work in the field of charity and welfare (whether the welfare was politically sponsored or not) was nothing novel, but their active role as political party agents was. Ventrone and others have recognized and outlined UDI's and Catholic women's assistance work and its connection to their respective parties, but it deserves another look as an integral part of the very local, political postwar world. Local level assistance in the needy postwar was as important a weapon in the larger Communist–Catholic struggle as were labour unions, umbrella social associations (like ACLI, ENAL, and later ARCI), and election campaigns.

Fasci Femminili had faced no real competition in their domination of social welfare and assistance voluteerism during the regime. Now, however, the control of assistance – down to the minute level of foodstuffs to be served at nursery schools and summer camps – was hotly contested. Whoever gained control over food rations for their children's camp or lunch program in their own small village was that much closer to their party's successful and national 'conquest of civil society,' (to quote Ventrone). Political victory needed to be won at the very local level, women recognized, and it could be done thanks to widespread need and scarcity of resources created by the war.

Communist women were quickest to take up the cause of assistance – especially assistance to children – in the province of Arezzo. At the end of December 1945, the prefect noted that UDI's 'particularly active work' during the past summer had turned to sun therapy and health camps for poor children. Now the women were preparing 'still more active assistance pursuits' for the winter, with institution of nursery schools and hot meal programs. In March 1946, poor children from the city of Arezzo, all of whom were sons and daughters of the 'unemployed, of widows, or of prisoners of war' would be guests of Valdarno 'labouring families' for two months or more, to be cared for by 'the mothers of those working families.' Those long stays meant more work for the already hard working UDI mothers in the Valdarno, though the assistance was welcome (and was a welcome gesture of solidarity) to the parents of the needy children in Arezzo.[32]

The communist women of UDI soon met Catholic women in battle on the 'spiritual field' of assistance, where communist determination and organization confronted centuries of Catholic expertise in charity. Being the best organized and funded of the postwar parties, the two came to dominate the assistance field, in which the smaller parties could not compete.[33] In February 1946, the Papal Assistance Commission of Rome instructed its diocesan sections to prepare and inaugurate children's seaside and mountain summer camps – at the same time that UDI was doing the same. Sansepolcro's diocesan section of the Papal Assistance Commission contacted Arezzo's provincial UNRRA committee, asking for food provisions and linens for its planned children's camps. On May 7, 1946, a letter signed by the prefect and sent by Arezzo's provincial UNRRA committee granted the Papal Assistance Commission for the diocese of Sansepolcro 1120 daily portions of food.

Sansepolcro's own communal UNRRA committee also intended to start a separate sun therapy camp for children, and so also asked provincial UNRRA for provisions. That request was not made until May 27, however – that is, after Arezzo's UNRRA committee already assigned the meals to Sansepolcro diocese's papal assistance camps. A month later, on June 29, the provincial UNRRA committee suddenly blocked the meal rations previously granted to the papal assistance camps – now intending them for Sansepolcro's communal UNRRA camps, apparently at UDI's insistence.

On the next day, June 30, an urgently called meeting between Sansepolcro's communal UNRRA committee and delegates of Sansepolcro's Papal Assistance Commission took place. After much wrangling, both eventually agreed that, of the rations assigned for the camps managed 'within the jurisdiction of the diocese of Sansepolcro in the province of Arezzo, 150 now would be allowed to the communal UNRRA committee for its camp managed by the Unione Donne Italiane.'[34] Those rations would be handed over, however, only upon exhibition of a list naming the children to be admitted to the UDI/UNRRA camp. The issue had reached such proportions thanks in part to an article in the Aretine Communist Party newspaper *La Falce*, which faulted the prefect for not consulting directly with communal UNRRA committees before deciding how to allocate scarce provisions. One group of camps in Sansepolcro was run by Catholic women, and the other by UDI.

More significant than a hopelessly confusing argument over which group in Sansepolcro would get UNRRA-donated food for the children at its own particular camp, the incident says much about women in the postwar period and about the developing balance of power in local postwar politics. The dispute showed that UDI had a great deal of influence, and in some places had taken control over much of the actual UNRRA and other funded communal work. In retaliation, the local Papal Assistance Commission's agreement to turn over the 150 rations only when the list of children who would be attending the rival UDI/UNRRA camp had been published, acknowledged not that the UDI camp and its figures were fraudulent, but that the Catholic women and the papal commission expected the UDI camp to cater only to children of communist and socialist families.

That expectation was not without some factual basis then or later. In January 1947, UDI of Castiglion Fibocchi initiated a free hot meal service for children, which drew immediate protest from Arezzo's Christian Democrat provincial committee. Given that '*all* the children of labourers' already received a meal dispensed at the local nursery school, 'the communists and the women of U.D.I.,' now went from house to house to insist and propagandize so that the parents would take their children away from the nursery school lunch and 'give them to U.D.I.' Parents had not turned down the nursery school lunch in order to 'give' their children to UDI, however. No rational parent would turn down food for a hungry child in that postwar time. Nevertheless, the DC objected to UDI's additional meal and to the politics it represented. 'In substance then, what is the use of this second meal? Is it right that for electoral ends they ought to use up precious provisions?'[35] The lunches – the food itself – had become political, or at minimum a political tool.

The battle for the children whose parents held the power of the ballot continued. Two years later, the camp wars reached fever pitch in Castelnuovo dei Sabbioni, as interpreted by Father Ciabattini in his parish diary for August 1949.

> At this time, a spirited question over the running of camp 'Tregli' caught fire. The Prefectural Authority had entrusted the running of the camp to CIF, but the women of UDI did not want to accept that decision and so therefore some days before the date fixed for the opening of the camp by the CIF they gathered up a few children and occupied the premises. The lack of intervention by the local police, made it necessary to suffer even this injustice. The CIF camp was opened only after the Udine held the camp for about 20 days.[36]

Father Ciabattini attached to his diary a letter to the editor clipped from the August 30 edition of *La Nazione*. The letter was titled '*Udine terribili*,' and its author was no fan of the '*Udine*' (women of UDI). The author had 'sniffed out nothing less than UDI's famous seizure of the camp established in Castelnuovo dei Sabbioni in premises rented and paid for by CIF, and I smelled such an stink.' The entire rotten business was well known, the writer claimed, to the editor and to 'the good citizens of Castelnuovo.' The affair finally ended with a prefectural decree 'clarifying and settling thing so that the camp was to be returned to those who paid the rent' – that was to CIF.

That was not truly the end, however. On the night UDI was to vacate the camp on the prefect's order, the women lined up the children to sing 'a beautiful little song to the tune of "*Bandiera Rossa*"' (the Red Flag) as they marched through the village streets. According to the writer, the modified lyrics went: 'We are small but we will grow; we will kill [*ammazzeremo*] the Christian Democrats; priests, monks, and nuns will have to go to work.' The words were offensive enough, the writer asserted, but he also urged readers to consider 'those excellent women and girls of UDI, who often love to disguise themselves as ... angels of peace searching for ways to put the war behind us.' 'I don't know how these excellent persons can have the impudence to pretend an educational mission ... when after extolling so much love and peace, they look for ways to introduce into the virgin minds of children sentiments of hatred, of violence, the desire for blood, even before the children can understand what hate and love are.' The letter clearly shows where its author's sympathies lay, but the physical struggle over a camp for needy children also demonstrates the bitter polarization in that local postwar world so recently the site of very real massacres.

The Catholic and Communist 'worlds,' as Togliatti famously characterized the postwar division between Communists and Catholics, were separate and antithetical and, with women often on the frontlines, they frequently collided during those early years in the villages of Arezzo. Given Italy's history and the church's own history of patronage and control of charity, it should not surprise that the opposing Communist–Catholic worlds also fought their political battles through the *Udine*, CIF, children's camps, and competing good works during that time of infinite needs. Catholics and Communists carried their political struggle with them everywhere in the postwar years: to Sunday sermons, outings to Assisi, the Easter blessing of the houses, hot lunches, and children's songs around the campfire. The general population lived in the midst of political struggle – even if not all chose a side until they had to cast a vote. Political divisiveness and polarization were part of daily, civil life, though it was particularly intense in certain villages like Castelnuovo. A general disinterest in party politics, which the prefect and the *Questore* emphasized again and again, seems almost impossible to imagine for those politically intense years.[37]

Everything was political, but the early Catholic–Communist political struggle was very much about elections. Remaining disinterested must have been a challenge in the everyday life of election preparation and electoral politics. By the 1948 election, even the prefect (still insisting that the general public cared little about politics) acknowledged: 'The political agitation, ensuing from the antagonism between communism and Christian democracy, has been stirred up even more in this Province. It seems about to go beyond the bounds of a press campaign and fall into an open struggle.'[38]

Election Politics

From the fall of Mussolini and the Italian armistice, from the formation of CLN and CGIL, the parties – and the Allies – turned their thoughts to elections. While communes and communal budgets were in ruins, and Provincial Commissioner Quin Smith was prohibiting all political meetings and public manifestations of politics as part of occupation policy, Rear Admiral Ellery W. Stone (as chief commissioner for the Allied commission) was pushing the Rome interim government for early local administrative elections.[39] Any extended discussion of the constant Allied (American and British) interference in the timing, conduct, and outcome of the Italian elections is out of place in this local study.[40] Briefly, however, the initial Allied idea was to cobble together a government system for Italy that resembled a combination of Italy in 1915 and contemporary Britain and the United States. As party activity rapidly got under way, the United States especially – as is well known and sadly relevant again to current analogies – fretted about the possibility that Italian elections might result in anything other than American style democracy or something other than the democracy they envisioned for Italy.[41] 'The Government of the United States has continued to follow with closest interest preparations for elections in Italy,' the American Ambassador superfluously informed De Gasperi, president of the council of ministers, in January 1946.[42]

Well before the first administrative elections (but after the Allied occupation ended), political activity, heated discussion of the issues, and the figures of postwar public life filled Arezzo's days and public spaces.[43] On June 23, 1945, Professor Raffaello Ramat spoke in Arezzo on the theme 'the Europe of yesterday and the Europe of today.' The Communist Party committee held a meeting on the evening of June 24, 1945, in Arezzo's Piazza of the Anti-Fascist Martyrs, about the vote for women and the purge of Fascists. On July 8, 1945, Aldovrando Medici Tornaquinci of the Liberal Party 'laid out' his party's platform to around 500 listeners at Arezzo's Supercinema. On July 15, Professor (and prominent anti-Fascist) Piero Calamandrei of the Action Party held a conference in the Supercinema on the theme 'The Constituent,' attended by about 1000 people. That same day a few blocks away in Arezzo's Piazza Vasari, 'the Honourable Grieco,' representing the central Communist Party spoke to about 3000 listeners, also about 'the Constituent' as well as about socialization of industry and labour reform. A day later, on July 16, at a rally organized by the Communist Party and held in Arezzo's Piazza Grande, 3000 gathered to hear speeches on unemployment and the purge of Fascists.[44]

Smaller towns and villages were not left out. The *Questore* reported that 1000 people turned out in Poppi, Bibbiena, and Pieve Santo Stefano to hear about the Christian Democrat 'program.' Fanfani himself drew an even larger crowd when speaking in Sansepolcro (next to his hometown of Pieve Santo Stefano) on November 22, 1945. Talks and rallies did not always draw the hoped for crowds if the speaker was not a recognizable name, especially in the smaller towns – where more people showed up for the movies than for political speeches. Thirty people attended in Castelfranco to hear about 'Moral and Material Assistance to the Labourers of the Land.' In December 1945, only twenty in Caprese Michelangelo listened to two PCI and one DC representative members elaborate on 'the duties and the aim of Italian syndicalism for a close collaboration between all Italian workers for the reconstruction of the national patrimony destroyed during the recent war.'[45] Perhaps the pre-fect and the *Questore* inferred the general public's lack of interest in party politics from low local turnouts.

As the 1946 elections approached – the election for the Constituent Assembly in particular – every weekend brought new speakers to Arezzo, including some national figures. Pietro Nenni and Ignazio Silone were to speak at the Teatro Petrarcha in Arezzo on February 17, 1946, for the Socialist Federation. Nenni was indisposed on the actual day, but Sandro Pertini came instead.[46] The DC announced that it would inaugurate its electoral campaign for the Constituent Assembly (the election to be held on June 2) over the entire district on Sunday, May 12, 1946. To kick it off, Fanfani spoke at the Supercinema in Arezzo on the theme 'Christian Democracy and the New Italy.'[47] Speeches, whether in the provincial capital or the villages, generally treated grander themes of postwar life than party strengths or the villainy of the opposition, though the titles of the speeches tend to make a speaker's underlying views clear. 'On

Reconstruction and the Needy' might easily have been given by any of the parties, all of which promised to reconstruct the nation and help the needy, while 'Not all Proletariat, but all Proprietors' and 'Christian Democracy for a New Social Justice' were more obvious.

Communal council elections were the first postwar elections. Technically considered administrative rather than political elections, there was, however, nothing apolitical about them. Despite participation by all postwar political parties in the appointed interim communal administrations formed after the passage of the front, Communists and Christian Democrats, followed by the Socialists, claimed the majority of supporters in the province of Arezzo.[48] The *Questore* reported to the prefect before the first elections that while it was not yet possible to know the number of adherents to the different parties, 'beyond a doubt, the Communist Party and the Christian Democrat Party find the most favour with the population and have the greatest number of members.'

He estimated membership numbers roughly at about 16,000 for the Communists, 12,000 for the Christian Democrats, 5000 for the Socialists, a mere 1000 each for the Liberals and for the Action Party, and only about one hundred for the Democratic Labour Party.[49] The prefect (presaging scholars who would later reach the same conclusion) concluded that the Communist Party was the best organized from the start, having managed to preserve its structure clandestinely during the Fascist regime.[50] The Christian Democrats on the other hand, the prefect contrasted, had not yet achieved a complete organization, mostly because of a lack of leaders. The DC was able to count on the still somewhat 'circumspect' activities of the parish priests, and on the sympathies of the 'rural masses,' and so should be considered a real force – equal or even superior to the Communist Party with its greater numbers.

The prefect went on to summarize astutely the positions of the weaker parties, demonstrating that he really did monitor the province's political pulse. The Socialists had a significant number of faithful followers, but local members opposed the Communists' methods and were in favour of abandoning the 'unity of action' pact that joined the two parties. The Liberals, 'one might say' – and the prefect tended to agree – were a party of 'leaders without followers.' The Action Party likewise had appealing leaders, but few adherents; in the province of Arezzo, the masses saw little difference between the *Azionisti* and the Socialists. The Republican Party had a 'small though efficient nucleus,' but only in the Valdarno and the city of Arezzo.[51] Thus, the outcome of the first postwar election was predictable, but not definite.

1946

These were the first free elections in twenty years, while for women and younger men, these would be the first elections ever. For communes, running elections was an additional postwar challenge. Voting again after so long, or voting for the first time, presented more mundane local level issues and problems in addition to the personal decision whether to mark the Social-Communist or Christian Democrat list. Election preparation in the communes and villages was complicated not only because it had been so long since free elections, but also because the war had destroyed so much. In November 1945, as indebted communes prepared their budgets for the coming year, they had to consider estimated costs for registering voters, furnishing polling stations, and actually carrying out the elections. In Civitella, for example, existing 'electoral material' had been stored during the 'period of emergency' (the war in Italy) in the communal hall. That communal hall along with the electoral material stored there was destroyed during the 'brutal German reprisal' of June 29, 1944.[52] The widows had used any wood from old voting booths, salvageable after the reprisal, to make coffins to bury the corpses of the men killed in the massacre. The commune now could borrow tables from local schools (to hold the ballot boxes), but would have to pay a local carpenter to build new voting booths.[53]

Before the March 1946 administrative elections could be held, the communes also had to determine eligible voters by preparing the electoral lists. Compiling and reviewing the names of voters obviously meant specifying who would take part in the postwar democratic process, but also can be interpreted as still another aspect of the elaborate listing, sorting, and categorizing that went on after the war. On October 29, 1945, the prefect's 'urgent circular' to all sindaci set forth the 'need to follow with the greatest exactitude the status of compiling the electoral lists in the individual communes.'[54] First, commune-wide electoral commissions were named to prepare electoral list drafts. 'Tentative' electoral lists – separate ones for men and women – arranged according to electoral section or polling place then were approved by the sindaco. Bucine's sindaco approved the number of male voters at 3049, and female voters at 3079, for a total of 6128 divided among the commune's eight polling places. In Bucine, two of the eight polling places were 'mixed,' but the remaining six were either exclusively male or exclusively female (men and women did not vote together). This was not for moral reasons, but for organizational purposes and to lessen the possibility of improper influence during the actual voting.[55]

It was important that everyone eligible be included, and accusations of purposefully excluding certain voters from the electoral lists, usually women or members of religious orders, were often made. The DC provincial secretary complained that in Castelfranco di Sopra, Castel San Niccolo, and Loro Ciuffenna, names of men and women in religious orders and names of evacuees and refugees who were resident in the communes for at least the last two years had been omitted from the electoral lists. 'We would be grateful if you could see to this snag that can prevent some Italian citizens from the right to vote,' the DC secretary requested, while implying that something more obvious than just a 'snag' had kept those people off the electoral lists.[56]

Others definitely were to be excluded from the right to vote. In October 1945, Bucine's sindaco recommended five citizens be suspended from the commune's electoral list: one was the ex-political secretary for the Republican *fascio* of Montevarchi, another was the ex-political secretary for the Republican *fascio* of Bucine, and both were currently in prison camps. A third had enrolled in the German army and gone north with the Nazis. The fourth, a former major in the Italian army, had enrolled in the German army and become part of an SS battalion. The fifth was at that time on trial for crimes committed as a Fascist.[57] The likelihood that any of the five would return home that coming March and insist on voting in their communal election seems very small, but the gesture of publicly disallowing them from participating in the postwar, democratic civic life of the commune was what mattered.[58]

The *Questura* or *carabinieri* informed provincial electoral commissions which citizens had criminal records (and therefore forfeited their right to vote), but some criminal convictions made for difficult decisions.[59] Before the administrative election, the sindaco of Cavriglia requested the district electoral commission to 'reinstate' on the men's electoral list twelve men who had been convicted for crimes arising from the 1921 anti-Fascist uprising at the Castelnuovo mines.[60] The men had been deleted from the electoral list before the Fascist regime did away with elections and opposition parties a few years later. Their crimes were not ordinary ones, however, either when committed or in postwar, post-Fascist retrospect: they had been 'committed for reasons of a political character in the struggle against Fascism.'[61] The local Communist Party organized a two-hour miner's strike to urge authorities to annul the convictions and allow the men to vote, which led the electoral commission to agree to restore the men's names to their communes' electoral lists, dependent on the Court of Appeals granting their requests for 'rehabilitation.'[62] If the court did not issue the certificates of rehabilitation before the day of the election, the men would again be 'cancelled' from the electoral list, and prohibited (ironically) from voting in the first free election after twenty years of Fascism.

Less than two weeks before the March 1946 election, the court still had not issued the required declarations of rehabilitation, when the *carabinieri* warned that with all probability, demonstrations of 'protest of unforeseeable dimensions' would disturb public order throughout the commune of Cavriglia if the twelve men were precluded from voting. The commission thus revisited its decision regarding inclusion on the electoral list of those who 'during the Fascist period were convicted for anti-Fascist causes,' and one of whom – Priamo Bigiandi – now was running for Cavriglia's communal council. The *carabinieri* described Bigiandi as 'the most important representative of the local Communist Party, who aspires to the office of sindaco.' All persons currently inscribed on the electoral lists would be permitted to vote, the commission wisely resolved in time, including the twelve men whose convictions had not yet been expunged.[63]

The possibility of public disorder undoubtedly was a primary consideration, with historical justice somewhat secondary in the commission's decision to confirm the convicted men's right to vote. More profoundly, however, excluding from the first free elections in twenty years those who had reacted against the Fascist take-over of their communities at the very beginning would have meant continued, post-Fascist injustice. Priamo Bigiandi would become the first elected postwar sindaco for the commune of Cavriglia.[64]

The prefect also feared the possibility of violence during the course of the elections, apart from the registration problem in Cavriglia. Administrative elections did not all take place on the same day for the entire country, in part so that adequate numbers of law enforcement officers would be available. Some of Arezzo's communes, including Civitella, had their administrative elections on Sunday, March 17, while the rest, including Bucine and Cavriglia had theirs a week later on March 24. The prefect asked the Territorial Military Headquarters in Florence for a temporary force of 150 to ensure order during the March 17 elections in the Val di Chiana and Casentino communes.[65] For both electoral Sundays, all businesses selling alcohol were to remain closed, for obvious reasons, while restaurants and trattorias could remain open, with owners enjoined to serve wine only to those customers who also ate a meal.[66]

Civitella, Bucine, and Cavriglia (with the other mid-size communes in the province) would vote for twenty communal councillors: sixteen from the majority party and four from the minority.[67] This system gave rise to the fear that one party might cancel out another, leaving the third place party holding the minority. Thus, it also engendered a variety of party alliances, so that more than one party (usually the Communists and the Socialists) could share the majority. The alliance situation was fairly loose for that first election, with pragmatic considerations about the 'orientation of the masses' (as the prefect and others phrased it), and what combination of parties the masses might find most appealing mattering as much as shared political ideology.

Most communes had two candidate lists, usually with Communists and Socialists together on one list, and Christian Democrats together with various others on another. In Civitella and San Giovanni Valdarno, Action Party candidates also adhered to the Social-Communist bloc, while in the commune of Subbiano, the DC made a bloc with the Liberals, establishing the 'Peace and Labour' list. In Pieve Santo Stefano, both the Action Party and the Republicans joined the Social-Communist list.[68] The Action Party ran a separate, third list in Lucignano, where it won only thirty-seven votes. The parties in Pergine Valdarno also put forth three lists: Social-Communist, Independent, and Christian Democrat. In strongly communist Cavriglia, the Communist Party and the Socialist Party maintained separate lists, with the 'Independents' – who in that commune were primarily openly declared Christian Democrats – making up the third.[69]

Alliances made for some interesting amalgamated symbols. As in Bucine and elsewhere, the combined Social-Communist list took the sign of a hammer and sickle over a book.[70] Bucine's Christian Democrats (and their allies) ran their list under the DC sign of a cross within a shield and the word *Libertas*. In Civitella, list 1 (Christian Democrats) displayed the usual *Libertas* cross and shield, while shared list 2 (Communists, Socialists, and *Azionisti*) utilized a hammer and sickle and a flame. Most of the symbols, like the parties themselves, would regroup or separate into their own individual identities for the upcoming Constituent Assembly election. Before then, however, the first and very modest print campaign material offered by the parties in the poor communes of Arezzo depicted their combined signs and slogans as a clear and straightforward political message.[71] In Bucine, the Social-Communists' message simply excluded the opposition list altogether as it urged citizens to vote their list in its entirety – and at the same time reminded them exactly how to go about voting:

Friend worker!
Vote for YOUR list by making a cross (X) in the little box near the sign of the Parties of the People.

Before election day, the prefect ordered all sindaci to telegraph him three times during the voting, to keep him abreast of the results of the administrative elections and about public order.[72] Bucine's telegrams were brief and to the point, and must have reassured the prefect about public order, if not informing him about the election's outcome. The sindaco's morning telegram provided: 'Electoral section progress this Commune normal. Stop. Large crowd. Stop. Public order perfect. Stop.' That afternoon's was shorter still: 'Large crowd ballot box. Stop. Public order perfect. Stop.' The next day, the sindaco telegraphed: 'Total number voters five thousand two hundred sixty-three. Stop.'

Who had won, the prefect must have wondered. Why did the sindaco think the number of voters more important than the parties and names of those elected? Moreover, what was 'normal electoral section progress' after twenty years without elections? What constituted 'perfect public order' when 'political attitudes' really opened up on election day? Was it something short of pushing and shoving? Neither communal nor state prefectural archives contain reports of trouble or Communist–Catholic confrontation, though Father Ciabattini's diary mentions communist control of polling stations in his zone.

Local democracy in action during and after that first election exacerbated the Communist–Catholic divide, not surprisingly. Father Ciabattini described March 24, 1946:

> On this Sunday, the first administrative elections since the fall of fascism were held in our commune of Cavriglia. Three lists were presented: Communist Party, Socialist Party, and a list of 'Independents' which comprised elements moderate and favourable to the Christian Democrats. While the Communist and Socialist lists propagandized widely, the 'Independent' list did nothing. The elections took place with calm and order; however, the Communists who alone were in control of the polling stations, carried out much gerrymandering to their advantage ... The Communists, sure of victory, had a certain number of their members vote for the Socialist list, so that the Independents would not have the minority.[73]

The reader familiar with Don Ciabattini's diary, the postwar political atmosphere in the village of Castelnuovo, and with the Communist–Catholic struggle in general immediately senses that the priest could have – and would have liked to – more successfully taken DC campaigning into his own hands. In that case, you might imagine, the results would not have been so one sided. On the following day, March 25, he recorded only that 'the communists are demonstrating to celebrate their victory.'

When the first votes were cast, the earliest nationwide returns worried the Aretine left. *La Nazione del Popolo* reported on the 'electoral situation' in the 414 Italian communes throughout Italy that had cast their votes by midnight on March 14: 168 communes had voted Christian Democrat majorities, while 121 had voted Social-Communist.[74] The left need not have concerned itself, however, at least not in Arezzo. Communists and Social-Communists running together were victorious in the vast majority of Aretine communes. In Bucine, united Communists and Socialists dominated the communal administration, and so would share the majority between eight Socialist and eight Communist councillors, with four Christian Democrats making up the minority. In the commune of Civitella, the combined Socialists, Communists, and Actionists received about twice as many votes as the Christian Democrats. In Cavriglia, not surprisingly, the Communists swept the elections, receiving more than five times as many votes as either Christian Democrats or Socialists.[75]

Results in the massacred villages – including Civitella, San Pancrazio, and Castelnuovo – were consistent with commune-wide results heavily in favour of the Socialists and Communists, despite the solace the church and its priests had provided directly after the massacres. In Civitella's electoral section 4, for example, which included the village of Civitella, 158 votes were cast for list 1 (Christian Democrats), and 235 for list 2 (Communists, Socialists, and Actionists).[76] Results were more lopsided in Castelnuovo, naturally. There, only 190 out of 1687 voters voted for the (DC) Independents. One hundred ninety-seven (197) voted Socialist, and 1017 voted for the Communist Party.[77] Those massacred villages whose wartime suffering was greater than the rest of that war devastated province formed no special voting pattern of their own.

The percentages of those who cast their votes also were consistent with the rest of the province. Civitella's voter turnout was below the provincial average: out of 597 persons inscribed on the electoral list, 494 voted (which included two not on the list), but some other electoral sections (in other communes) where no wartime atrocities occurred had equal or lower turnouts. What would be interesting to know is how many of the non-voters in the village of Civitella were women – a figure which might provide some support for the provincial authorities' theory about political apathy and its cause. Unlike the other electoral sections in that commune, however, the number of voters in Civitella was not recorded by gender, and so Christian Democrat 'pockets' or rare sections with low voter turnout in the province cannot be directly tied to gender or to wartime experience.[78]

Women now made up half of the electorate. They also participated in communal election preparations by preparing and distributing electoral certificates, serving as *scrutatori*, and as secretaries or members of communal electoral commissions, but the prefect's suggestion that women would take their place in the communal administrations as a result of the elections was not realized. Many communes had no women among the more than thirty candidates running for communal council office. Ida Sappia, widow of a popular district doctor, ran on the Christian Democrat list in Bucine, and Laurina Bigazzi ran on the Communist list in Cavriglia; both were elected as council members, Sappia with the minority and Bigazzi, who came in fourth of all candidates, with the majority.[79] Emma Borsari, an elementary school teacher, Independent Social-Communist, and a widow, was elected to the council and to the *giunta* in Montevarchi.[80] Two women, both teachers, one a Communist, one a Socialist, were elected to the council in San Giovanni Valdarno. Only in the tiny commune of Castiglion Fibocchi (least populated of Arezzo's communes), was a woman named sindaco.[81]

Women in large numbers did not join 'more intimately and more deeply in the civil, administrative, and political life of the Nation,' but the men and few women elected to the communal administrations differed from those who administered the communes in pre-Fascist (or Fascist) days. Like postwar communal committees ideally made up of representatives from all classes, occupations, and political parties, the first elected postwar communal councils fairly accurately reflected the citizenry of the communes. In Bucine, the four Christian Democrat councillors had middle class occupations; they were landowner, bank clerk, *professoressa* (Sappia), and owner of a small trucking company. The majority Communist and Socialist members were smallholders, mechanics, carpenters, bricklayers, and elementary school teachers.[82] In Civitella, the Communist, Socialist, and Actionist members included labourers, shoemakers, and clerks.[83]

The Referendum and the Constituent Assembly

In January 1945, Prince Umberto of Savoy 'and his personal staff' visited the province of Arezzo, where Allied officers feted him with, among other things, roast turkey, gin, and cognac, according to the merchants' bills left behind.[84] A month later, on February 11, he 'suddenly' appeared in the village of Castelnuovo dei Sabbioni where he was welcomed by Father Ciabattini and 'a few people.' He visited the parish church and the rectory, Father Ciabattini recorded, then greeted the people. Some of the women whose husbands had been killed in the July 4, 1944, massacre 'set forth to the prince their sad facts.'[85] Photographs of the event show the prince in a finely tailored military overcoat and polished boots, carrying a walking stick, accompanied by Father Ciabattini and a small entourage of Allied and Italian soldiers.[86]

Why the prince visited that red village in that red province is something of a mystery, though presumably he intended to demonstrate solidarity and royal concern for his country and its people suffering so badly on account of the war. The war in Italy was still going on, however, and the royal family (most notably the prince in his elegant military overcoat) took no real part in it. The villagers of Castelnuovo, like much of the rest of Italy, could not disregard the king's flight to personal safety – away from responsibility for Fascism and the war – after the September 8, 1943, armistice. Already by February 1945, the royal family's future was precarious. A year later, *La Nazione* for May 8, 1946, commented that Vittorio Emanuele's expected, imminent abdication would not stop the 'electoral machine now in motion.'[87] The king did abdicate in favour of his son Umberto less than a month before the election, but neither his resignation nor Umberto's earlier visit to the province had the effect desired.

The Constituent Assembly portion of the June 2, 1946, election had a less predictable outcome than the referendum on the monarchy. The election for the Constituent Assembly was very much a political election, and it was a political election on a national level. The Allies, who had worried about Communist Party victories in the communal council elections, took an even more intense interest in the Constituent Assembly voting. The June 2 election would, in part, determine who would write Italy's constitution, and would also signal which party likely would eventually control the national government. For its part, the United States feared that the Constituent Assembly would not content itself with formulating a constitution, but might attempt to govern the country as if it were an elected government. The United States' ambassador passed along to De Gasperi the State Department's own interpretation of Italian law, to convince the interim Italian government of the Constituent Assembly's limited powers.[88] De Gasperi, who intended to keep firm hold on the national government, agreed.

Arezzo combined with the neighbouring provinces of Siena and Grosseto in a single college (the electoral college of Siena) to fill its allotted proportion of seats in the Constituent Assembly.[89] More than seventeen political parties (or movements, like the Movement for the Independence of Sicily) put up slates or candidates within the country as a whole, while a mere nine lists were presented in Arezzo (and the electoral college of Siena).[90] In list order, those nine included the Communist Party, the Christian Social Party, the Republican Party, the Socialist Party, the Action Party, the Democratic National Union, L'Uomo Qualunque, the National Bloc of Liberty, and the Christian Democrat Party.[91] Only two parties really mattered, however. Father Ciabattini recorded: 'They are holding the general election for the new Italian constitution and at the same time the referendum for the monarchy or the republic. For these elections also, there has been no propaganda on the part of the Christian Democrats. The Communists, however, have held meetings and more meetings developing their propaganda in an able and subtle way.'[92] This time, Father Ciabattini took campaign matters, at least some small matters, into his own hands. During the April 1946 pre-Easter, Holy Week blessing of the houses, less than three weeks after the strong Communist victory in the administrative elections, Father Ciabattini refused to bless the village *Casa del Popolo* (the PCI-sponsored cooperative social circle, which happened to be hosting two different variety shows during that holy period, the priest waspishly noted). Father Ciabattini's refusal gave rise to much comment in the village, especially among the Communists. At least twice when he blessed other houses of the village, residents had 'interrogated' the priest about his snubbing the more political 'house of the people.'[93]

The Christian Democrats did not bother to campaign in Castelnuovo dei Sabbioni – again – to Father Ciabattini's evident disappointment, leaving the Communists unchallenged. The same was not true in Petrella di Sestino, the small Aretine mountain village where Ruggero Franci taught during the 1945–6 academic year, where the Christian Democrats could expect a more receptive audience, and where the question of the referendum related closely to the Communist–Catholic struggle.

> In this village on a Sunday, very few are disposed to spend two hours walking to go to Mass, but politically they are all Christian Democrats, except for three or four who … are reds. The Christian Democrats, however, call it simply 'Democracy' and for them it is the only party worthy of existing. In arguments about this, their position, I have not thought it appropriate to raise some objections because the DC leaders have promised them a street, an aqueduct, and electric lights, but when I discovered that beyond just voting DC, they were also going to vote for the monarchy, I could not do less than tell them some recent historical facts to demonstrate that the blame for our recent misfortunes [that is, Fascism and the war] falls on that institution.

Many of them listened to my words, and at the end, I saw them go away thoughtful, but I don't believe I convinced them. For them at least, Republic means victory for the Reds and Monarchy means victory for the DC.[94]

On election day, June 2, 1946, Bucine's sindaco telegraphed the prefect at six-thirty that evening, with three and one-half hours of voting yet to go. This time, he let the prefect know the results straightaway. 'Constituent voting almost completed. Communist list prevailing. Christian Democrat and Socialist lists following [at a] notable distance. Public order perfect.'[95] The PCI had won in Bucine when the polls closed later that night, but the Socialists and the DC did not end too far behind. To the Communists' 1835 votes, the Socialists garnered 1252 and the Christian Democrats 1407 votes.[96] The Communist Party also won in the most populous commune of Arezzo, but not by a large margin: there the Communists received 9535 votes; the Christian Democrats 9190; and the Socialists 9045. The Socialist Party did surprisingly well, outstripping both the Communists and the DC in more than a third of Aretine communes. The commune of Civitella cast 1350 votes for the Socialist Party list, 1165 for the Communist Party list, and 1179 for the Christian Democrats.[97] The DC won a few of the smaller communes.

Thanks to communes like Cavriglia, however, where the Communist Party received the most votes in the province, four Communist Party representatives were sent to the Constituent Assembly.[98] The prefect summed up the socio-political results for the entire province for 'the very active month of June' to the Ministry of the Interior, acknowledging that the recent elections 'completely engaged the political attention of the citizens, the parties, and the various big shots.'[99]

The results of the Constituent Assembly signalled what future national political elections in the province of Arezzo – and the country – would bring. The Constituent Assembly election, Paul Ginsborg has said, 'at last gave an accurate indication of the relative strength of the three major parties,' an assessment with which Arezzo's prefect agreed.[100] Throughout the nation, the Christian Democrats took 35.2 per cent of the vote and attained 207 seats in the Constituent Assembly. The unitary Socialist Party received 20.7 per cent of the vote and 115 seats, while the Communist Party received 18.9 per cent and 104 seats in the Assembly.[101] The three main parties' relative strength would shift as the Christian Democrats and the Communists both grew stronger, and the Socialist Party divided.

'In the general results Christian Democracy has prevailed,' delighted Father Ciabattini, adding, '[i]n the referendum, voters in favour of the Republic have prevailed. The local communists are taking it badly because they were sure of a victory in the entire country. They are venting their anger with a parade to celebrate the republic.'[102] A republic was certainly not a bad consolation prize.[103] Casting out the monarchy helped make up for years of Fascism and war, and (like the popular execution of Mussolini) made it easier for Italians to disentangle Italy from its long connection to Fascism. The method of declaring the republic through national election rather than by the Constituent Assembly – or by revolution – also served as a symbolic first step in constructing a new, democratic state.[104] Teacher Ruggero Franci returned to Petrella di Sestino – that small Christian Democrat and Monarchist enclave – after the school vacation and the June 2 elections. In that remote place, the villagers still did not know the outcome of the referendum.

> As soon as they saw me, some of the villagers came up to me … I waved the newspaper in front of their eyes, saying 'squads' of republicans were travelling around to give just punishment to all those who voted for the Monarchy. Really, some of them believed the news was true, because at first they were all stock still, until one of them exclaimed with the air of one who believes he has just made a discovery: 'Oh! … and how will they know how we voted?' It ended in a laugh all around and with a nice glass of wine I offered to the health of the Republic, just born.[105]

The Prince of Piedmont had wasted his time on Castelnuovo and the province of Arezzo.[106]

The proclamation of the republic had 'no notable repercussions,' Arezzo's prefect reported, 'in a province already clearly oriented towards the Republican thesis.' The departure of the 'ex-sovereign,' when it happened, then 'definitely settled the matter.'[107] The few local, monarchical elements 'behaved absolutely correctly and were not harassed in any way.' Arezzo's prefect then telegrammed the sindaci of every commune to advise them that a 'celebration of the Republic' was to take place in all the communes on June 11 at seven in the evening.[108] On that day, the citizens of Arezzo city participated in 'a grand republican display' in Piazza San Francesco.[109] Castelnuovo's own parade to celebrate the republic brought out more than just communists 'venting their anger' over the DC victory in the Constituent Assembly. The village band led the way, followed by a crowd carrying banners proclaiming '*Viva la Repubblica*' and '*Viva l'Unione del Popolo Italiano.*' As slightly smaller numbers watched from the side, the citizens of Castelnuovo strode along the streets between houses flying the tricolour and still plastered with campaign posters from the election (figures 13 and 14).

Excitement over the new republic soon gave way to reality. Like distributing hot lunches or organizing summer camps, though on a much larger scale, drafting a constitution was a politically motivated and politically divisive act. The 'man on the street' thoroughly grasped the underlying situation, Arezzo's prefect believed:

> The first labours of the Constituent Assembly have given the exact feeling to the man on the street that in our country there is not yet formed that unity of political direction, which characterizes a mature and democratic people. In fact, opinion is rather widespread that the different deputies are bound more to a political group or ideological bloc, of the right or left, rather than to the specific function that they are called on to accomplish.[110]

The well-known conflict within the Constituent Assembly, as forces for fundamental change locked horns with forces for conservatism and continuity, resulted in a constitution that mostly reflected those second, more entrenched forces.[111]

Political party commitment in those days often seemed stronger than a commitment to the tasks at hand, Arezzo's 'man on the street' recognized and the prefect emphasized. According to the prefect, elected council members throughout the communes of the province also 'allowed themselves to be influenced more often by their political ideologies than by the necessity to work out, study, and resolve the serious problems of the commune according to the interests of the population.'[112] The 'politics of blocs' threatened 'to exhaust the better forces in a sterile political struggle,' he warned, instead of uniting them in 'constructive collaboration.'

1948

Delegates to the Constituent Assembly, members of communal councils, and the party organizers may have focused more on ideologies and 'bloc politics' than they cooperated on the day-to-day return to civil life because all were looking ahead to the 1948 political elections. The preceding elections were mere rehearsals for the all-important election to determine who would guide the new republic. Viewed in retrospect, given the patterns that emerged from the 1946 elections, the January 1947 split within the Socialist Party, De Gasperi's expulsion of leftist parties from his cabinet later that year, and constant American intervention, the actual national results in 1948 could not have been anything other than they were.[113]

Those indubitable results were again (in retrospect) even anticlimactic to the worry and frenzied local campaigning that preceded them. If Father Ciabattini fervently prayed for a 'good result' in June 1946, he prayed doubly hard in 1948 – and did not restrict himself to the power of prayer or withholding a blessing. Under the general diary heading 'March,' Father Ciabattini wrote, the 'electoral propaganda for the political elections set for April 18 has begun. The social-communists, who hide behind the symbol of the face of Garibaldi and take the name "Democratic Popular Front" attack the Church and the priests.'[114] The spring 1948 election campaign coincided with the Lenten course of preaching, opportunely allowing for some anti-communist propaganda – along with preparation for Easter – to counter Social-Communist attacks. The featured priest-orator visiting Castelnuovo jumped into the fray, dealing with 'topical subjects, speaking openly against communism and refuting [communist] slanders which are especially strong at this time. The communists who come to church are not reacting.'[115] Sizable crowds also attended mass to hear a visiting missionary 'who dares to speak badly of the communists even in this village of Castelnuovo which believes the feud with the reds is untouchable.'

Serious religio-political campaigning took place that spring of 1948. Between March 15 and March 20, Father Ciabattini carried out the traditional Holy Week blessing of the houses in his parish. This year, '[t]he reception in some houses was cold.' The villagers never turned him away, however, and with any who would listen, the priest seized the opportunity to carry on 'discussions about communism.'[116] Father Ciabattini did not characterize the priest-orator's or the visiting missionary's anti-communist preaching – or his own hectoring about communism woven into the Easter blessing – as electoral propaganda. Organized Catholic propaganda was utterly inadequate, he believed. 'The propaganda for the political elections is always more intense,' Father Ciabattini noted for the two weeks before the election. 'However, here in Castelnuovo and environs, only the communists make their voices heard. The propagandists for the Christian Democrats don't show themselves.'[117] 'They only manage to make propaganda by means of posters and leaflets that are posted and thrown by a group of young men from San Giovanni. The communists respond by gathering up the leaflets, setting them on fire, and throwing them back at the young men's truck.' Father Ciabattini did not acknowledge to his parish diary that the institution of the church and its servants were Christian Democracy's loudest voices in many villages, where 'in church we pray for a good outcome to the elections.'[118] 'At Holy Mass' on Sunday, April 11, a week before the election, Father Ciabattini 'read and commented on the instructions given by the Tuscan Episcopate regarding the duty of Catholics in regards to the elections.'[119]

Voting took place on April 18 and continued until two the following afternoon. Father Ciabattini, like everyone who took great interest in the election's outcome, was nervous. 'This is the day so awaited and so dreaded – the general political elections. The result of these elections is awaited with anxiety by everyone. The local communists are already convinced of their victory. They have prepared cakes to celebrate their triumph. It is rumoured that they have drawn up lists of people to eliminate, and at the top of the list are the priest and the nuns.'[120] Voting took place with order, 'perfect calm and regularity' in Castelnuovo and the rest of the province.[121] The percentage of voters was 'extremely high.'[122] Bucine's sindaco telegraphed during the course of the voting: 'All normal. Stop. Perfect order and calm. Stop.' By April 1948 and this third, and most anticipated postwar election, 'normal' now had some point of reference.

At six-thirty that evening, Bucine's sindaco telegraphed that the voting and counting was almost completed. Just as two years earlier, the current message went: 'Communist list prevailing. Stop. Christian Democrat and Socialist list [at a] noticeable distance. Stop. Public order perfect.'[123] The predictable communal results were available the next evening, but the population had to wait another day for the final, national results. In Bucine, 3073 citizens cast their votes for the Democratic Front and the face of Garibaldi, 1944 for the Christian Democrats, and only 337 for the Socialist Union. Civitella's results were somewhat closer (as they had been in the previous election): 2412 votes for the Democratic Front, 1668 for the Christian Democrats, and 283 for the Socialist Union. In the commune of Cavriglia, the Democratic Popular Front took 4880 votes. The Christian Democrats received a distant 1164 votes, the Socialist Union 141, and the other parties a total of one hundred. Among all Aretine communes, the Christian Democrats received 72,705 votes to the Democratic Popular Front's 101,507. 'The communists were surprised at the good success of the DC in this red zone,' Father Ciabattini was happy to record.

The DC enjoyed much greater success on the nation level, of course. 'At midnight the first results from Turin and Milan were announced. There is a clean prevalence for the DC,' the priest rejoiced. Father Ciabattini heard even better news a day later, on April 20, when the final results had been tabulated.

> The radio announced the results of the election: a clean and unexpected victory for the DC and defeat for the communist front. The communists remain bewildered: they are spreading rumours that the results on the radio are false. They are waiting for the arrival of *L'Unità*. To explain the mortification, the communist newspaper speaks of intrigues, of tricks, of intimidation on the part of the 'clericals' ... The communists have shut themselves up at home because they are waiting for a reaction against them.[124]

No local 'reaction' against communists took place; neither did the rumoured lists of priests and nuns to be 'eliminated' ever surface, yet each side plainly expected violent reaction from the other. Daily life and the Communist–Catholic struggle simply continued, but now at a somewhat gentler, post-election simmer.

Two final events represent more fully developed local currents of daily political life in the province of Arezzo. Both took place in 1948 and both relate, more or less, to the April 18 election. Nearly twenty-five years after the judgment originally was entered, on April 6, 1948, the penal section of the Court of Appeals in Florence, acting 'in the name of the Italian people,' finally granted Priamo Bigiandi's request to be 'rehabilitated' from his 1923 conviction for homicide and illegal possession of firearms resulting from the 1921 anti-Fascist uprising at the Castelnuovo mines. 'The defendant has given real and constant proof of good conduct from the day on which he had completed the sentence imposed until today,' the court concluded.[125] Less than two weeks later, on April 18, 1948, PCI candidate Bigiandi was elected to national office as a parliamentary deputy.[126] On July 14, three months after that victory and after the Christian Democrat national triumph, a gunman shot and wounded Communist Party leader Palmiro Togliatti outside the parliament building in Rome. For that frightening day that had so many ramifications, Father Ciabattini who usually had so much to say about the local and national political situation now had no comment. He recorded only the date, making no mention of its significance – as no mention was needed.[127]

Always on the losing end of the local political struggle, Castelnuovo's priest would be able to celebrate DC national victories for many years to come. Read as a sort of real life version of *The Little World of Don Camillo*, Father Ciabattini's diary offers local commentary on the Catholic–Communist struggle, almost as charming when read decades after those real facts. The real life struggle was much more serious, of course; occasionally it was deadly serious. The 1948 election marked the end to the possibility that the Italian Communist Party (with or without the Socialists) would govern the country, shape the postwar state, and help engineer its vision of a fairer society on a national level. In his social history of that single year, 1948, Marco Innocenti, wrote: 'April 18, a Sunday in spring: for the DC and for democracy it will be a national festival. And for the routed Communist Party it will be the true end of the postwar.'[128] The year 1948 meant the end of the postwar on account of the election and for a variety of other reasons, most especially the CGIL schism. Any chance of inter-party unity or cooperation and a shared mission had ended.

Not everyone in Arezzo or in Italy lived in a permanent, fevered political frenzy, worrying constantly about the opposition and its propaganda. Had they, a civil war would have been much more likely in July of 1948. The worries and hardships of daily life still took up much of the population's attention in 1948, as the prefect and *Questore* believed; yet those difficulties connected people to politics in a way. The political struggle must be studied in its postwar, local, social context, not only its political context. It was born in the proverbial 'world turned upside down' (as Father Polvani also referred to his own small district) – or more accurately, it began in a country turned into rubble. Such situation provided enormous scope for party politics – for conflict and opposing visions of how society should be reconstructed, and for struggle between the competing sides as to which would do the most to shape that reconstruction.

13 Honouring the Dead

Commune of Bucine
In the cellar of this fattoria on June 29, 1944 by the [hand of] Nazi-Fascists the martyrdom of seventy-two innocent victims took place. To pass on to history such a great infamy the communal administration of Bucine engraves their names.

Allied Control Commission (ACC) censors in Arezzo intercepted a letter dated January 4, 1945, sent from the Christian Democrat Party's provincial headquarters in Arezzo city, written by a party representative to the Carletti family in the town of Monte San Savino. The letter triggered the censor's interest because it mentioned 'political party activity' – something the Allied occupiers always remained alert to suppress. The activity described, or its objective more precisely, was of an unusual 'political' nature, however. It did not speak of party organization or future elections, mobilizing sharecroppers, miners' strikes, of *raccomandazioni* for party adherents for housing or jobs, or even of assistance activities. The Carletti family had unwittingly been connected to German massacres in Civitella, San Pancrazio, and Cornia when German soldiers took over their villa the night before the June 29 killings.[1] Signor Carletti had been repeatedly interrogated about local partisans, about Signora Cau of Cornia, and the whereabouts of escaped Allied prisoners of war. More tragically, he also saw his son Luigi 'being escorted along the front of the villa by two German soldiers.'[2] Luigi Carletti's beaten and bruised body was found near a neighbour's well on July 10.

The letter sent by the Christian Democrat Party to the Carletti family some six months after those events announced a 'competition among young people of any political leaning to honour the memory of Luigi Carletti, glorious victim of German barbarity,' and the aim of which was 'to promote youthful cultural and artistic activity.'[3] The portion of the letter copied by the censors makes no mention of the nature of the competition (was the prize a school scholarship, a monetary award, or just public recognition, for example) or of Luigi Carletti's own connection to or the family's interest in cultural and artistic activities. It does provide additional – somewhat superfluous – hints about local political party activity, however innocuous, during the Allied presence and despite Allied prohibitions. The fragment also gives a small preview of how (and how soon) the political parties would make their presence felt in the area of commemoration, as well as other aspects of postwar life.

Read more straightforwardly than another example of party participation in nearly every element of postwar life, the letter also evidences the strong and immediate desire to honour the war dead and thereby helps locate where and how the process of constructing postwar memory began. This chapter returns to those most direct victims of war, the war dead: soldiers, partisans, civilians, and especially the massacred civilians, to describe how fellow citizens buried their dead and honoured them – as they disputed the meaning and what would be the memory of the deaths in the first years after war and massacre.

Categorizing the Dead

Death was all around in central Italy during that final summer of the war, and making some sense of it was another immediate and pressing post-front challenge (though not one generally included in sindaci, police, or prefectural reports, as such). Compiling lists, fixing categories, and crafting hierarchies have been seen in a number of contexts before this: who most deserved assistance, housing, or jobs; who should be purged; who was a partisan; who was a *reduci* or who was a civilian victim of war. And, as already emphasized, such listing and categorizing were very deliberate steps towards order and structure in the overwhelmingly disordered postwar world.

Civilian dead were more complicated than military dead. Civilians first were categorized and then listed (within category) according to whether they 'had died' or 'been killed' during 'the struggle for national liberation and precisely during the period from September 8, 1943 to May 8 of the current year [1945].'[4] The timing was important in that a death (civilian or soldier) before September 8 did not count as a contribution to the struggle for national liberation. Civilians who had died within that later time period (during the second half, or second part, of Italy's war) then were divided and aggregated according to whether they died from wounds or poor treatment as political prisoners; as hostages; during reprisals or what were termed reprisals (as had most of the dead of Civitella, San Pancrazio, and Castelnuovo); from torture or mistreatment in German prisons, work camps, or concentration camps; or from bombs and artillery fire during the passage of the front.

The dead thus had their own kind of hierarchy. The commune of Civitella provided figures on its wartime human and material losses to Arezzo's provincial committee of the National Partisans Association of Italy (ANPI) in June 1947. ANPI had requested those figures from every commune in the province as support for its proposal that the national gold medal 'for partisan merits' (*medaglia d'oro per meriti Partigiani*) be added to Arezzo's official provincial crest.[5] The notion that the province would receive a military 'gold medal for partisan merits' based in large part on the large number of non-partisan (civilian) deaths and the extensive damage suffered there (arguably) in reprisal for partisan actions is – and was at the time – more than a little disconcerting to some. It conflated, as it was intended to do, partisan merits both with more traditional military merits and then, most especially, with civilian sacrifice. It meant, in essence, the more civilians massacred in reprisal by the Germans (and Fascists) in a province and the more damage done, the more successful partisans had been there and so the province was more deserving of the award. The partisans who made the proposal did not employ such cruel logic, but the path of reasoning leads directly there.

Civilian deaths, suffering, and destruction were situated together with partisan wartime accomplishments not only to bolster those partisan accomplishments; and to be sure, the province, its communes, civilian and partisan dead, and the survivors deserved national and local recognition on account of what they had suffered and lost. As seen, the state also conflated civilian massacre victims with partisans. The state undertook such acknowledgment with its *premi* shared between massacre victims and fallen partisans, and with certificates naming massacre victims as partisans, with grants to rebuild housing destroyed during Nazi reprisals, with shelter for orphans of political victims, and with similar forms of postwar recognition; from the material of civilian suffering the state also crafted a larger meaning of intended, voluntary self-sacrifice for national liberation, the rebirth of Italy, and the redemption of Italians from Fascism and participation in the first half of the war. From the state's point of view, that meaning could foster reconciliation and national unity – an important consideration during that postwar period rapidly becoming one of political disunity and social divisiveness.

National motives, like partisan motives, were not entirely selfish. Absent some proposed deeper significance, the violent deaths of so many civilians would be the empty, senseless net result of irrational wartime processes (like stepping on a landmine or being struck by shrapnel) without benefit of meaning to the post-Fascist, postwar nation and would be of little comfort to survivors. What the deaths had been 'for' therefore was the question. What (or who) had caused those deaths and who should be held responsible for them were related questions certainly, but ones that carried less emotional charge on the national (as opposed to the local) level and so generated less state interest. Nazi barbarity – or Nazi-Fascist barbarity – was the broadest agreed upon cause, whereas the difficult question whether partisan guerrilla actions or even the mere presence of partisan formations in a particular area more indirectly caused or triggered civilian massacres (which necessitated blaming the partisans) always was a more local matter, and one that soon would 'divide' local memory, as Giovanni Contini and Paolo Pezzino have shown.[6] That is why investigating and concluding whether Nazi-Fascist massacres really were reprisals was not particularly critical from the national point of view.

The existence of the *armadio della vergogna* demonstrates just how little interest the state had in finding and bringing to justice the German or Italian perpetrators factually responsible (and the pressure it felt not to pursue those perpetrators), while victim families and villages were unable to do anything about obtaining legal justice without the arm of the state. Direct evidence (that is, unambiguous proof) of 'why' remains lacking, although even existence of a direct order targeting certain villages and civilians still would leave unanswered questions about cause and responsibility. An explicit written statement or order found in German archives some day may show that the massacre at Civitella indeed was (or was not) carried out as retaliation for the *dopolavoro* shooting two weeks earlier. What sort of evidence, however, can ever satisfactorily explain why the women and children were ordered away from Civitella, San Pancrazio, and Castelnuovo before the men were killed, while men, women, and children were shot indiscriminately in Cornia and other places, or why the bodies of the men in Civitella were left where they fell, while those in Castelnuovo were covered with gasoline and burned?

To return to the question of what the massacres meant afterwards – or could mean afterwards – it must be stressed that the commune of Civitella rejected the proposal for a 'gold medal for military valour,' because its citizens – at least those in the village where the massacre happened – did not wish their place to be 'identified with' the partisan combatants. Civitella asked instead for the gold medal 'for civilian valour,' which it received in 1963.[7] The three underlying questions Aretines (and Italians) confronted when burying, remembering, and commemorating their military, partisan, and civilian dead are those any society faces when looking for and ascribing meaning after war or mass tragedy. Who or which among the dead deserves honouring? 'How much tribute is enough?' – as *New York Times* reporter N.R. Kleinfield asked in 2007 regarding the sixth anniversary of the September 11, 2001, attacks in the United States.[8] And finally, to whom do the dead – and their memory – belong?

In the commune of Civitella, 239 civilians 'had fallen' during the important period between September 8, 1943, and May 8, 1945: 188 died in reprisal killings, six from aerial bombs, thirty-five from landmine explosions, and ten by exploding hand grenades.[9] Such figures located where the commune ranked among those most harmed by the war (in a human sense as much as a physical sense) within the province and the nation. The numbers did not tell who had died, however. For ANPI's purposes in qualifying for the *medaglia d'oro*, numbers had more significance than individual names or, rather, names of who had died were not relevant for that purpose.[10]

Names and certain characteristics became more meaningful when, for example, communes prepared their lists of soldiers missing in the war. Fallen soldiers had first been divided into those known killed and those missing. The commune of Cavriglia counted twenty-two servicemen missing, presumed but not definitely known dead. That number alone sounds relatively insignificant compared to the number of civilians massacred or killed in that commune, and to the number of dead or missing soldiers reported by larger population centres. Yet when Cavriglia set forth its twenty-two lost soldiers and sailors in alphabetical order along with what information was known about their last whereabouts, each soldier's story unintentionally serves both as a small personal narrative and as a larger lament on Italy's lost war (the first period of Italy's war fought as part of the Axis, not the more heroic war of Liberation). 'Elio Balò, son of Clorindo [Balò] and of Giovanna Bigazzi, born in Cavriglia, April 8, 1921 ... Lost at war March 29, 1941, when the "R.C.T. Alfieri" on which he had embarked was lost at sea. His nearest relative is his father in Cavriglia.'

Enzo Billi, son of Giuseppe [Billi] and of Anna Rosi, born in Cavriglia, May 6, 1918 – unmarried. Soldier 57th Company Engineers ... The soldier wrote to his family for the last time December 10, 1942 from Russia. A soldier repatriated at the end of February 1943, Bianco Bindi of the commune of Bucine, the village of Capannole, has said that he left Enzo Billi in the beginning of February 1943 at Cercovo (Russia) with his feet frostbitten during the retreat.[11]

Amelio Caini, who wrote to his family for the last time on August 30, 1942, was reported missing in combat at 'Ruweins (18 km south of El Alamein, Egypt) on September 11.' Silvano Carapelli wrote to his family for the last time on January 9, 1943, from Russia. Nello Casprini was lost on January 23, 1942, when his ship the *Vittoria* was sunk in the Mediterranean.

That annotated list, like so many similar others in communal archives, makes for a moving record of Italian ships sunk and soldiers captured in North Africa and retreating from Russia on foot through deep winter snow without adequate clothing. For the 'nearest relative' – a father, widowed mother, wife, occasionally a brother – the information included as much as was known about a young man's death. Today, that poignant collection makes up part of a commune's historical archives, but the information itself is not important for most historical purposes. At that time, plainly put, Cavriglia's list of twenty-two soldiers and sailors contributed to an affidavit by which a family had its missing soldier legally declared dead.[12] Individual facts in those cases meant circumstantial evidence of a young man's certain death. That sort of list with its few grim details was not intended to honour the military dead or acknowledge their sacrifice for the nation (though it unintentionally did so), or even to explain how Italy had lost. Those details also explain why decisions – local or national – to honour soldiers were so difficult after the war, because honouring them meant retelling Italy's defeat.

Lists of civilians killed during the second part of the war in the massacres at Castelnuovo dei Sabbioni, Civitella, and San Pancrazio were similarly structured, but they told a different Italian war story. In June 1946, Arezzo's prefect announced 'an international exposition of war crimes' organized by the 'Allied nations' to be held in Rome with Italian participation, and whose purpose was 'to give adequate emphasis to the sacrifice suffered by our population because of Nazi barbarism.'[13] The prefect asked Aretine communes to send their 'available documentary material' – 'photographs, relics, lists of victims, and so on' – directly to the historical office of the president of the council of ministers in Rome.[14]

The aims of the Allied nations in presenting an exposition of Nazi war crimes – organized as the Nuremburg trials were ending and attempts already had begun to normalize the international position of West Germany – would be worth exploring further and do offer counter-evidence to Italian claims that the Allies did not fully appreciate Italian sacrifice and suffering. What form or size the exhibition eventually took, whether the many, lengthy lists sent by Arezzo's communes were displayed, or if any of the massacre survivors ever attended to view what must have been an unbelievably sad display of inventories, photos, and relics, are questions not answered in Arezzo's archives. Aretine communes did, however, send lists of their 'victims of Nazi barbarity' (occasionally with general reference to 'Nazi-Fascist barbarity').

Like others, Cavriglia's list was alphabetical; it included those 'killed, disabled, and wounded' in all the villages of the commune, setting forth very briefly the date, place, and cause of death. Cavriglia's citizens had been 'machine-gunned and burned' (*mitragliato e bruciato*) or 'shot' (*fucilato*). Very occasionally, a victim had been 'wounded by German artillery,' or killed in the lignite mines 'owing to explosives thrown by the Germans.' Most of the 197 civilians listed, however, had 'died July 4, 1944, at Castelnouvo dei Sabbioni Piazza IV Novembre,' or that day in and around Meleto, or on July 8 or 11 at Le Màtole, each having been 'machine-gunned and burned by German troops.'[15]

Lists of missing or dead soldiers told one part of Italy's war experience, while civilian victim lists reflected another. Those common and repeated words – 'machine-gunned and burned by German troops' – provided a sort of unintended chorus to nearly every civilian death, which emphasized the victims' common death and the commune's shared suffering and loss. Moreover, in a number of instances, two – or even more – brothers, cousins, or father and son are listed. Cavriglia's list, like those of other Aretine communes, thus also told of the massacres' terrible blow to village families and to communities. As only partial example, the two Bartolini brothers and the son of one all were killed. The two young Bonaccorsi brothers, the Pasquini brothers, the three Melani brothers, father and son Mugnai, father and son Neri, and eleven members of the extended Camici family were killed together.

As memorial plaques were engraved, or when it came time to erect monuments to the dead (civilian, partisan, and military), lists would be pared down to names in alphabetical order, as with First World War memorials in European village churches and town squares. After the war, the commune of Bucine prepared two simple stone plaques for its civilian victims.

Communal budget difficulties and postwar material shortages explain part of the reason for the simplicity of the two tablets. In the spring of 1945, in preparation for the first anniversary of the massacre at San Pancrazio, the communal *giunta* voted communal funds for a marble slab engraved with the epitaph quoted at the beginning of this chapter, followed by the seventy-two victim names.[16] The commune initially could not locate an appropriate piece of marble in time to have the plaque prepared for the first anniversary, and then could not afford to have it engraved.[17] The sindaco informed San Pancrazio's parish priest that the administration had 'searched in vain' even sending to Rapolano for travertine, but the anniversary ceremony would proceed nevertheless. With the communal administration participating 'in official capacity,' local citizens placed wreaths and flowers at the massacre site and then walked in procession to the cemetery, where Father Pecchi performed a 'solemn religious service.'[18]

Bucine's *giunta* had voted as early as February that same year for a more comprehensive tablet for all of the commune's civilian war dead, to 'record for posterity the infamies that the population of the Commune of Bucine suffered at the hands of Nazi-Fascist soldiers leaving communal territory in the period June 29 to July 16, 1944' and 'at the same time to honour the memory of those barbarously murdered by the Germans.'[19] When finally engraved more than a year later and affixed to the exterior wall of Bucine's communal hall in August 1946, the stone listed 115 names and the epigraph read:

> To remember the infamies carried out on the part of Nazi-Fascist soldiers in the act of departing the territory of this Commune ... the communal administration of Bucine lists for posterity the martyrs.[20]

Seventy-two of the names of the martyrs listed on that communal stone were the same as those later included on the tablet hung at the Pierangeli *fattoria* (the site of the massacre) in the village of San Pancrazio. The messages on the two plaques were not so different – both referred to the martyrdom of its civilian citizens at the hands of Nazi-Fascists – but two separate plaques were needed, nevertheless. The memory of San Pancrazio's seventy-two massacre victims – and their names – were part of the entire commune's wartime suffering at the hands of Nazi-Fascists during that final summer, but more specifically belonged to the village (and to the very spot in the village) where the massacre had taken place on June 29 and the surviving families lived.

The dead were 'segregated' for most purposes of commemoration: partisan from soldier from civilian – and civilian massacre victim from civilian victims of 'other' war generated causes of death. Each group represented a different war experience and each had different meaning for postwar society, especially in Arezzo where the relationship between partisans and massacre victims was sometimes problematic. Only in rare occasions and usually well after the war ended did names of dead soldiers (from the first part of the war) share space on the same memorials with names of fallen partisans and with civilian victims from the second part of the war.

Gathering and listing names of a locality's war dead were components of either immediate recordkeeping or permanent memorialization, whereas dealing with the bodies of soldier and civilian war dead was another, even more urgent part of post-front and postwar life. Twenty-five years on, those who buried the military dead of the Second World War had World War I precedent for treating their own and for strangers killed fighting far from home. In Italy, local administrations quickly buried foreign soldiers killed on Italian soil – enemy and ally alike – in their communal cemeteries. At the end of 1944, the sindaco of Monte San Savino spent scarce communal funds dedicating a special section of the commune's cemetery for the graves of thirty-three Allied (British) soldiers. Recently arrived communal secretary Aroldo Lucarini privately attributed the gesture to the sindaco's 'sincere admiration' of the 'English' as well as to his desire to 'cultivate the sympathy' of the Allied occupiers – and thereby maintain his tenure as sindaco.[21]

The sindaco cast his action in a more universal light, however: 'We are going to improve the little Cemetery in our town where the remains of 33 Allied soldiers lie. I think the respective families would be grateful to know that there is someone who is taking care of their dead relatives. This commune would like to write through your Red Cross to the families concerned, including, if possible, a small photograph of the place.'[22] German soldiers also were buried in the same communal cemeteries together with local victims of war, as Civitella had buried the two German soldiers shot in the *dopolavoro* of that village. Ten years after the war ended, the commune of Cavriglia exhumed its thirty German dead – having carefully maintained their names and other identification – so that they could be transported and reburied in a military cemetery in Germany.[23]

Dead civilians (or civilian bodies) were a much less familiar product of war than were dead soldiers, however, and were more difficult for survivors to cope with, especially when their numbers were so large, as in Civitella, San Pancrazio, and Castelnuovo, when most village survivors were female (widows), and when the circumstances of the victims' deaths had been so closely connected in time to the dangerous and disruptive passage of the front. In villages where massacres occurred, death (and dead bodies) made up part of the physical aftermath of war along with burned homes and bombed buildings. The experience of massacre differed for each village (as seen in chapters two and three), and thus what happened to the bodies of massacre victims differed for each village. Very soon, within a day after the massacre in Civitella, the women removed their men's bodies from the piazza and from the church and managed 'as best they could' to carry many of them home. There, they washed them, wrapped them in sheets, and carried them back to the half-destroyed church. Some women improvised coffins from what wood they could find. Because their priest was one of the victims, they themselves buried the men – with no blessing – in several mass graves (figure 7).

In Castelnuovo, the women left the bodies in the same piazza where they had been machine-gunned and burned, until the bishop and Father Ciabattini arrived from Fiesole some days later. Under the sight of the widows, Father Cuccoli, from the neighbouring parish, along with a number of men who had been hiding in the mine used a single horse and cart to carry the decomposing bodies a few at a time up the steep, narrow street from the piazza to the cemetery, where they were buried in a mass grave. In San Pancrazio, the Germans shot the men in the cellar of the *fattoria* near the entrance to the village, and then burned the *fattoria*. Not until nearly a month after the massacre in that village, after the front had passed and the village was liberated, did the widows, orphans, and other survivors return to excavate the cellar, identify and rebury what remained of bodies of the victims.

Finding the bodies of the dead, trying to identify them, and just getting them to the cemeteries and buried there were the most urgent tasks in the postwar aftermath for those villages where massacres had occurred. As life settled down a bit and physical reconstruction of homes, buildings, and public works slowly began between 1946 and 1948, citizens wanted to reorder local cemeteries and to regularize the graves and bodies of their dead in a more normal way. For the citizens of Civitella and Cornia, that meant removing their dead family members from communal graves and reburying them each in a separate, individual grave marked by an inscribed tombstone. The widow of Adolfo Caldelli requested communal permission for the 'transfer' of her husband's corpse 'from the common grave to a separate, distinct place.'[24] He had been 'killed in the reprisal at Civitella June 29, 1944' and buried in the cemetery there 'in the enclosure of the common graves.' Mario Falsetti asked that the bodies of his father and his two uncles, killed in the June 29 massacre, be exhumed from the common grave where they had been buried together with so many others. Now, four years after their deaths the young man recently had been able to acquire a separate plot for his relatives in the same cemetery. Giuseppa Cornelli (the widow Bozzi) asked that her husband Conforto and her three sons Pietro, Fernando, and Bernardo be moved and re-buried in separate graves in Civitella's cemetery.[25]

While they make for another recitation of the sad facts of the Aretine summer of 1944, the many requests for exhumation and reburial, and for permission to affix an inscribed stone in the communal cemetery, also show the importance – to families – that their dead be treated, recognized, and honoured as individuals and as civilians. Where it could be done, survivors wanted their dead buried separately and the graves marked separately. The physical separation of bodies and names within the common experience of massacre allowed families and villages some semblance of compliance, eventually, with recognized practice of burial as it normally took place for civilians in society.

Commemorative markers were placed in cemeteries and on individual graves where victims were buried. They also hung on the walls of the communal halls, both inside council meeting rooms and on exterior walls, thereby again, but less explicitly connecting those killed with sacrifice for liberation and the nation's rebirth. In addition, the exact sites where civilian victims had been killed would become meaningful places of commemoration as San Pancrazio's plaque at the *fattoria* Pierangeli illustrates. The citizens of San Pancrazio initially hoped to rebuild their parish church where the remains of the *fattoria* stood. The two buildings were located in different parts of that small village, and German soldiers had destroyed both parts on June 29. Signor Pierangeli, owner of the *fattoria*, told the sindaco and state officials that the families of the victims had a 'single, united desire': that the place of the massacre 'remain sacred to living and future memory' and that it 'become a place of pilgrimage and testimony to what barbarism had been suffered.'[26] Transferring the church to the site of the massacre would most definitely 'sacralize' the spot where the seventy-two men had died, and the request to do so exemplifies a local desire (in San Pancrazio at least) to shape commemoration and memory of massacre victims in a religiously sanctified manner. That conjunction of religious and secular space did not happen in that village, however. The church was rebuilt where it originally stood, and an impressive crypt later was built where the *fattoria* had been, with the underground room where the men had been shot reconstructed as a shrine.[27] Plaques, stones, statues, or larger commemorative structures, even chapels were placed to mark the specific, sometimes multiple locations where citizens or groups of citizens had been massacred within a village.

The commune of Bucine voted to place a stone 'on the same spot' in the piazza in the village of Ambra where two young men had been shot by Fascists, renaming the piazza: 'Piazza dei due Martiri.'[28] In the vicinity of Le Màtole, a small so-described 'monument-shrine' consisting of ten broken columns standing on a low square was erected where ten men had been killed. In Massa dei Sabbioni, a more elaborate religious-looking shrine with crucifix and altar was built on the spot of the shed in which Father Ermete Morini and Dante Pagliazzi had been shot and burned. And in Civitella, a marble cross and plaque on the village wall indicate where Father Alcide Lazzeri and most of the others had been shot:

> Here on June 29, 1944 in the tragic massacre of this place were killed the greater part of the innocent victims with their Archpriest. To the glorious dead, prayer and perpetual memory.

As some families, villagers, communal administrations, and parish priests sought to make the site of a wartime massacre a sacred place of 'pilgrimage and testimony' related to recent past suffering, so other citizens imbued locations where local killings had occurred with a somewhat different meaning. Arezzo's provincial section of ANPI, together with the local Communist Party, wanted to honour the memory of two young partisans murdered by Fascist Republicans on April 16, 1944, in the village of Ciggiano in the commune of Civitella. To commemorate their death, ANPI wished to mark with a plaque the very place where the men had been killed, a postwar gesture which, in and of itself, was not unusual. To mark the spot, however, required affixing the plaque to an exterior wall of the home of Signor Ezio Pratesi or otherwise placing it on his property in the immediate area of his house in Ciggiano.

The placement had more significance than would first appear. The idea was also to put the marker 'at the feet of those who committed the crime' – and, in this case, those feet belonged to the Pratesi brothers.[29] The Pratesis had been Fascists, then Fascist Republicans, allegedly involved in the killing of the two young partisans. Pratesi refused to have the stone on his property, not surprisingly. His attorney wrote to Civitella's sindaco, who had requested Pratesi's consent. The Pratesi brothers did not 'really oppose' the request, the attorney said, but had to consider the grave danger that placing a stone commemorating 'that unfortunate incident' in 'the immediate area of their residence could bring to their safety and that of their families.'[30] In fact, the attorney opined, it was not beyond a reasonable possibility that the place where the monument was to be positioned could 'become a meeting and gathering place for all political demonstrations happening in Ciggiano.' As 'that very sad episode' would be repeatedly evoked at demonstration after demonstration, the excitement of the crowd likely 'would explode in acts of hostility regarding those whom the crowd believes responsible for that massacre.' Pratesi's attorney reminded the sindaco, whom he personally knew to be 'a most reasonable man,' of his duty 'as first citizen of the commune' to safeguard everyone – 'without discrimination.'

Employing the same bizarre combination of polite euphemism and plain talk about homicide, ANPI replied that putting the stone, with Pratesi's consent, at the very place of 'that sad incident' actually would ease hard feelings between the local population and the Pratesi family, and would show locally that the Pratesi family really did value the partisan struggle and honour those who died for the liberation of the nation.[31] 'As regards any ceremonies in memory of the fallen partisans that might take place there, those will have no political aspect,' ANPI assured.

ANPI characterized the intentioned plaque not as a political statement or a comment on the two young partisans' and the assumed perpetrators' respective places in local history, but as part of a plan to put plaques or stones everywhere in the 'national territory' at the exact locations where partisans had fallen for Italy's liberation. There was a little more to it than that, as the Pratesis and their lawyer recognized. The proposed plaque and its placement were intended not only to honour the two young partisans at the very spot where they had died for the liberation of their country, but also to show the Pratesis that the public knew exactly what they had done and that it would not be forgotten. The permanent memorial would force the brothers to admit their guilt.

The Meaning and Memory of Massacre

The fight between the Pratesis and the partisans was about more than the awkward placement of a commemorative plaque. It also was about attributing meaning (as well as blame) to local events and local deaths in order to shape future memory, and even more so was about who would control that meaning and memory. That is, to whom did the dead, their meaning, and memory belong, and who had the authority to create shared, community memory?

Italy has had much to remember and much to forget in the years during and after the end of the Second World War. Only in somewhat recent years, however, has the remembering – or the call to remember the past more clearly and objectively – become as prevalent as the forgetting; it has been called the collective (and selective) amnesia which has characterized the Italian official, political, and individual approach to the Fascist era and the wartime past. The topics of postwar Italian memory and identity are generating a rapidly growing body of historiography (and scholarship in related disciplines) as well as fuelling a sometimes vitriolic public debate, particularly around the subject of April 25.[32] Memory, identity, and meaning are closely connected insofar as what people as a group choose to remember and forget collectively not only reflects who they are, but also who they want to be and how they wish to view their past and to view their place in that past. Furthermore, shared identity and collective memory are constructed from the same material, or the same events. Memory, like identity, is not necessarily about truth or based on the 'whole truth,' but about selecting, creating, assigning, or adopting an acceptable meaning to share.

The study of Italy's postwar memory (or disputed memory) is often approached as a problem with flaws to be corrected and 'gaps' to be filled.[33] That is, historians, political scientists, journalists, and others articulate what is the Italian memory of Fascism and war (and multiple issues included therein), what that memory leaves out (and why), and what Italy and Italians must concede in order to come to terms with the Fascist and wartime past. The most thoroughly considered studies demonstrate that memory (as is true also of interpretation, representation, and identity itself) has not been static over time, uniform across place, or free from bias and political considerations, as R.J.B. Bosworth and Patrizia Dogliani did in their 1999 edited volume.[34] Memories of civil war and Resistance, for example, have changed (or adapted) more than once between 1945 and today, according to the social and political climate and the passage of years. Moreover, memory then and now has always differed from centre to north, from city to countryside, from village to village, and even within a single village, based on differing experiences.

Study of problematic memory nevertheless tends to approach memory as seen from the objective present, rather than recreating how and where memory was initially fashioned, or tracing the path taken from actual events to the later memory of those events. Most recently, Robert Ventresca noted that, 'for the most part, historians of postwar Italian memory have limited themselves [himself included] to a rather confined conception of memory as created "from above."'[35] What is needed, he adds, and what is still in the very early stages, might be called an '"everyday history of memory" in postwar Italy.'

Alessandro Portelli and Francesca Cappelletto have taken a somewhat different approach to memory, interpreting oral histories and personal narratives of massacre and traumatic wartime experience. Both have carefully explored the local memory (and memories) of Civitella's massacre and focused on survivors' repetition of episodes within that memory. Cappelletto, an ethnographer, explains how the memory has been transmitted, and how Civitella's memory differs from other massacred villages in part because of the villages' different natures and different composition of inhabitants. Portelli has analyzed contradictions and lapses in survivors' memories to show all such 'divided memories' as multiple, 'fragmented and internally divided ... all one way or the other ideologically and culturally mediated,' instead of a 'spontaneous and pure communal memory versus an official and ideological one.'[36]

Memory, as is clear from the example of Civitella and through the work of Cappelletto, Portelli, Giovanni Contini, and Civitella survivor Ida Balò, is not crafted only from above, is not shaped only for political or ideological ends, and does not divide neatly into 'official' *versus* 'local' (and true). Memory creation is a process that also starts from below and starts immediately, most obviously in the case of local events or local experience of larger events. It is a complex process that, not only in Italy, tends to sift the acceptable from the intolerable, conserving (by emphasizing) the former, while suppressing the latter as an acceptable meaning is argued over or agreed upon. Not everyone's memory is the same, and the very notion of a group, public, or official memory is possible only by limiting the size of the 'group' to those who have agreed upon the same meaning. Alessandro Portelli asserts a 'multiplicity of fragmented and internally divided memories' as mediated by various factors; so too then, the meaning of important or traumatic events is multiple depending on how they were experienced and how (and by whom) they have been mediated.[37] Memory whether shaped from above or below is never one sided – and rarely only two sided. In postwar Arezzo, the process of creating local memory of the massacres began with 'deciding' on their meaning, a process as contentious and disputed at its ground level inception as is the current national end product of larger war and liberation memory sixty years after.

Father Aldo Cuccoli helped organize the ceremony marking one month after Castelnuovo dei Sabbioni's July 4, 1944, massacre. On

August 4, he came from San Pancrazio (in Castelnuovo), and together with Father Giuseppe Cicali and Father Giovacchino Meacci, priests from nearby parishes, said a series of masses for the massacre victims. Father Cuccoli recorded in Castelnuovo's parish diary that the church was 'draped in mourning,' and that the young people 'together with a good part of the population' took Holy Communion the evening before.[38] 'People of every class and from every neighbouring hamlet' attended the ceremony on the day itself: he 'saw the parish church packed with people,' and many 'received the sacrament.' On that first, one month anniversary, neither politics nor any other distraction intruded into the church and the religious ceremony. 'The sadness of the occasion prevented outside demonstrations of patriotism,' the priest wrote. The local CLN, 'however,' commemorated the fallen with a speech in Piazza IV November – the site of the massacre. Why Father Cuccoli would have considered demonstrations of patriotism unwelcome and something to be prevented is not apparent at that early date. Father Cuccoli may have defined patriotism (as Quin Smith might have) as the unwanted insertion of politics, broadly defined, into a service he hoped to keep strictly religious.

Castelnuovo's church was at the top of the village, while the piazza where the massacre took place was towards the bottom – directly below the church (figure 15). As sacred as the site of the massacre might be or become, especially after construction of the chapel in the piazza at the very wall where the men had been lined up and shot, the village space divided into two places for that first public memorial after the massacre. The CLN made its speeches in the piazza at the massacre site; the church carried out its services in the church. Both ended at the cemetery. 'At the end of the religious ceremony, the people carried wreaths of oak and flowers to the cemetery, where they stopped to weep at the tomb of the martyred.' There, Father Cuccoli gave the benediction.

The people of Castelnuovo, specifically those who attended mass and especially the widows of the massacre victims, wanted Father Cuccoli to be their priest, to replace the murdered Father Bagiardi.[39] Father Cuccoli had overseen the burial of the dead there on July 11. He had examined the burnt bodies, counted the skulls, and collected the names of men reported missing by their families. He had convinced the men hiding in the mine to help the women carry the bodies from the piazza at the bottom of the village where they lay, up to the cemetery and to dig a large communal grave. He had said mass for the dead, and then disinfected the piazza and burned the cart that had carried the remains of the bodies. Father Cuccoli had been an important part of the aftermath and had helped the women get through it. The director of Castelnuovo's mining company wrote to the bishop telling him of the people's wishes, but the bishop sent Father Cuccoli to nearby Massa dei Sabbioni and assigned Father Ciabattini to Castelnuovo dei Sabbioni.[40] Father Ciabattini also was a fitting choice. He was a local man (though not from Castelnuovo itself), and he had accompanied the bishop in the July heat on the long walk from Fiesole to Castelnuovo to investigate the massacres.

Father Ciabattini had arrived as parish priest of Castelnuovo in November 1944, and so already was established in the village by the time of the first year anniversary of the massacre at Castelnuovo on July 4, 1945 (figure 16). 'The crowd of people is enormous. The church is always, literally filled,' he recorded in the parish diary for that date.[41] Ten 'Holy Masses' were said. At the first mass, Father Polvani from San Pancrazio spoke 'a few words suitable to the occasion.' That evening they all walked to the cemetery 'as in a devout pilgrimage to the common tomb where the victims' remains had been collected.'

After 'the holy functions in church,' the more worldly service began (figure 17). A 'certain Diomiri' gave a speech in Piazza IV Novembre, 'and it was a speech stirring up hatred and revenge. All the labourers present applauded.' What hatred and revenge the unknown Diomiri incited were not directed towards the German soldiers responsible for the massacre or towards 'Nazi-Fascists' more generally.[42] He spoke, instead, of 'hatred for the church,' according to Father Ciabattini. His words were not noted, and Father Ciabattini (as was his wont) may have exaggerated the vitriol of Diomiri's speech. By next year's memorial service, however, the lines were clearly drawn for the battle that would take place where the men had been massacred two years earlier.

By July 4, 1946, the chapel commemorating the site of the massacre had been built. That previous winter, Father Ciabattini had taken up an initiative to erect a monument 'in memory of the fallen.' The entire population – 'even the political representatives' – welcomed the plan, the priest noted.[43] Eight Holy Masses were celebrated in the parish church and absolution given on that second anniversary. 'Afterwards, all made a sad procession to the new, holy monument.'[44] The bishop came from Fiesole to bless the chapel and speak a few words to all those present (figure 18). Those present included recently elected sindaco Priamo Bigiandi, the prefect, and 'other authorities.' Suitably, it was Father Cuccoli who said the first mass in the chapel, and then 'recalled the sacrifice made by the fallen, particularly extolling their Christian spirit and their heroic death alongside their priest.' Some of Father Cuccoli's extolling 'phrases' provoked 'comments' from those present, however. Father Ciabattini did not elaborate on 'the comments,' but one senses they were hostile.

'After the holy ceremony, the political orators began to speak.' The priests then retreated up the hill, where from the front of the church above, they listened to the political speeches given in Piazza IV Novembre below. First a communist, then a socialist, then the old anarchist Attilio Sassi spoke. Sassi's speech, according to Father Ciabattini, 'was nothing more than a continual incitement to hatred and was full of continuous insults against religion and all things holy.' So terrible were 'the slanders,' that Father Cuccoli could restrain himself no longer and called out a loud 'that's not true' from the church above. Father Cuccoli's shout then caused 'the communists' in the piazza to 'hurl abuse' at the priests, until the police finally stepped in to calm things down.

At Sunday mass, three days later, Father Ciabattini denounced the crowd's behaviour from the pulpit. No one in the church reacted, but outside, 'the communists tried to justify the event by publicly posting a placard and throwing the blame on the priests.'[45] Father Ciabattini and Father Cuccoli sent letters of protest to the local newspapers and to the prefect, and sent a lengthy open letter 'to the widows and the people' the following day, July 8. The ceremony had been a beautiful and moving one, the priests wrote, appropriately held in the place 'consecrated by the blood of the victims' and where their fellow priest had been sacrificed 'together with his people.'[46] Every other manifestation and 'profane word' had been 'out of place' and inappropriate to the sadness of the ceremony and the gravity of the moment, they added. Worst of all, the 'known revolutionary propagandist' Attilio Sassi, from the very first word of his speech, used 'false, anti-Christian expressions that revealed a heart of stone towards all those noble sentiments of compassion and religious faith of which the people had so approved just a little earlier.'

How had the people – at least some of them – turned so quickly from the religious ceremony to scorn the priests? Sassi's rhetoric most definitely was intended to insult and inflame, if the priests quoted at all accurately. Some of Sassi's more incendiary comments included: 'The widows can pray, but so many prayers are worth nothing,' and '[t]hose who tell them to pray are the same ones who yesterday blessed the weapons that performed the massacres.' What finally caused Father Cuccoli to explode with a shout of 'that's not true,' was Sassi's assertion that the chapel's 'inscription is a disgrace and a lie for the victims.' How the simple inscription over the chapel constituted a disgrace and a lie for the victims, and why that particular accusation bothered Father Cuccoli so much is puzzling, given that the inscription read only: 'the massacre victims of yesterday are the Immortals of today.'

By his comment so disapproving of the inscription, Sassi surely intended something more than a public expression of his own disbelief in an afterlife or in eternal life. Rather than view the victims as innocent martyrs now in heaven, perhaps he wished to cast them – as others also wished to do – as ones who had sacrificed their lives for an end to Fascism, for Resistance, for liberation of their country, for change, and for a better worldly life in the postwar. Or perhaps he meant simply to malign the church, provocatively challenging whether the victims and their memory 'belonged' to the church at all. Could they not have more than one meaning – if they had to have a meaning at all?

More disturbing should have been Sassi's accusation that the church (and, by extension, its priests) had supported the Nazi-Fascists, thereby indirectly 'blessing' the weapons used to massacre the very victims at the centre of the disputed commemorations. Many local priests like the murdered Father Bagiardi of Castelnuovo had supported the partisans and some actually had blessed the weapons of the partisans, though Father Polvani and others pretty clearly had preferred the Germans.[47] What bothered Fathers Ciabattini and Cuccoli the most, however (as they wrote to their parishioners and fellow citizens), was that the crowd did not turn against Sassi when he 'abused the blood of the martyrs' and 'insulted the faith and compassion of the people of Castelnuovo.' Rather, to the priests' 'surprise and consternation,' the crowd instead turned on them – the priests – with 'vulgar curses and rude words.' This was the same crowd (or part of it) which only a few hours earlier had shared in the religious ceremony, and listened to the bishop and Father Cuccoli. The two men appealed 'to the widows and to all the Christian people of Castelnuovo to express their disapproval of that behaviour which had offended and dishonoured' the village and the area. In the truth of that time and place, the hostile response was directed towards the church and its priests, and reflected the sympathies of much of the crowd. It had not been intended to derogate the massacre victims – only the church's approach to the massacre victims and decision as to the meaning of their deaths.

Would the civilian massacre victims get lost in the Catholic–Communist struggle, or would commemoration supply more fuel for it? What had once been a piazza in a village and then a place of massacre now had become the site of basic disagreement and contested meanings of postwar life. Serving that red zone caused Father Ciabattini and Father

Cuccoli grief over the years, not only during the annual July 4 commemoration ceremonies or during election campaigns. However, public vilification of the priests and the church as part of the political half of the yearly memorial services must have been especially demoralizing. The massacres were part of the two priests' own wartime experiences and identities. They had seen the immediate aftermath of the atrocities. They had touched the bodies. They had seen the widows' suffering and listened to their stories of tragedy.

The widows and families of the victims did publish a protest, asking that the events of July 4, 1946, not be repeated and that their dead 'not again be the opportunity for propaganda by any political party.'[48] The following year, Father Ciabattini recorded, fewer people attended church than in previous years, and the communists held an evening procession complete with red flags. That third anniversary of the massacre went without incident in the church or the piazza.[49] As time passed, the piazza as site of the massacre could serve both church and politics, if only one at a time.

In Castelnuovo, the dispute was not over responsibility for the massacres and the villagers' memory (or memories) never divided against the partisans, as in Civitella. But Castelnuovo was not the only place where fundamental disagreements developed around memorializing the massacres and honouring the victims, and deciding what form – and how much religious and political tribute – those procedures should take.[50] As fought out between the priests, the politicians, and sometimes the widows, the question in Castelnuovo and elsewhere was to whom the dead belonged. Who had the 'right' to decide (or mediate) the meaning of their deaths, to explain their martyrdom and determine for what they had been 'sacrificed'? That same question of who controls the meaning now gets asked and argued in the United States on the anniversaries of September 11, with some victims' families there, too, publicly beseeching that their dead not be used for political ends and that their memorial ceremonies not provide the stage for political and political-religious posturing.

In the massacred villages of postwar Arezzo, masses in memory of the victims and processions to the cemetery were standard. 'A solemn commemoration,' a 'solemn Office for the Dead,' a 'funeral mass,' a 'religious ceremony of remembrance' all described the memorial ceremonies in Civitella, Castelnuovo, San Pancrazio, Meleto, San Polo, and other villages in the province.[51] Families (and priests) did not insist that ceremonies in honour of their dead be purely religious, with nothing of the secular remotely involved, however. The victims had died in war, after all.

The state and its authorities rightly were expected to participate in ceremonies commemorating the deaths, to assure that tribute was 'enough.'

Communes as institutions generally had a presence at memorial ceremonies. The communal council of Civitella voted increasing sums every year to contribute to the religious services held to commemorate the June 29, 1944, massacre, as an 'official' gesture on the part of the communal administration.[52] Communal authority – in the person of the sindaco – and the nearest state authority – in the person of the prefect – were invited and were expected to attend every annual memorial service. When, for example, the director of the provincial office of social assistance sent regrets to Civitella, explaining that 'time constraints' prevented him from attending the first anniversary ceremony of 'the horrendous massacre of June 29, 1944,' both the sindaco and citizens were less disappointed at his absence than they were shocked that the director did not recognize the importance of the event, and did not consider attending to be a part of his work in the province.[53]

More appalling was the sindaco of Bucine's failure to attend the second anniversary commemoration ceremony for the massacre at San Leolino because he was 'not feeling well.' 'Only' ten men had been killed in that smaller massacre, but an official presence was called for, nevertheless. The massacre had been a vital part of the village's wartime suffering, which the commune (in the person of the sindaco) should have acknowledged. The vice-sindaco had not attended either, because unspecified 'urgent administrative business' had taken him to Arezzo. The communal secretary would have attended, but 'he could not make it until 11:30,' at which time the ceremony would already have been underway, and so his late presence would have been 'pointless.'

The vice-sindaco later sent a note to San Leolino's priest, apologizing that no 'representative of the commune' had been present: 'I beg you to have the courtesy to excuse the communal administration for the absence of a representative at the celebration of the ceremony, and to explain to the population how much pride the Commune of Bucine has for all of its best sons who held feeling for their country high in the face of German ferocity and had faith in Christ for the resurrection of our Italy.'[54] The vice-sindaco's belated message was a rather strange one. Communal administrative authorities had been invited to attend a solemn ceremony in honour and memory of San Leolino's ten civilians massacred by the Germans during the summer of 1944. The vice-sindaco appeared, at least from his note, to think that he, the sindaco, and the secretary had missed an event of a different character: one intended to honour those who gave up their lives fighting German occupation and Fascism to build a new nation. Faith was mentioned, but only in the context of Italy's resurrection. The note reads something like Vittorini's post-massacre scene in *Uomini e no.*

The men killed at San Leolino had not been soldiers or partisans. Presumably, the men had loved their country as much as did any Italian and wanted it free of the German occupiers, but these men had not acted out of patriotism. They had not acted: they had not confronted the Germans, throwing their love of country in Nazi faces. They had not gone to their deaths with a prayer on their lips for national resurrection, knowing they were giving their lives to Italy's rebirth – or intending to do so. They had simply been massacred. The question thus comes up again: what had their deaths been 'for.' An agreement on what they were being honoured for would have been consensus of the most important kind on what their deaths had been for, but neither kind of consensus was reached.

In considering commemorations and memorials for massacre victims, the reasons why other local victims of war were not similarly recognized should also be examined more closely. Local men lost or killed in Italy's war that ended on September 8, 1943, were memorialized somewhat later and in different ways from massacre victims, because their deaths had meant something different. The enemy had not killed them in the piazza before the eyes of their families. Moreover, although some asserted at the time that Italy 'had' to lose the war in order to show the world that Italians had not wanted the war, and although soldiers also thus could be perceived as victims of Fascism and Mussolini's war, military dead nevertheless represented that first part of the war, a part best not emphasized.

Local civilian citizens killed by landmines, by Allied bombing, in German camps, or by 'other causes of war' were more like massacre victims, but neither were they honoured equally. A few places would dedicate inclusive memorials to all Italian victims of the *lager* and even more inclusive ones to all Italian victims of Nazi-Fascism, but not local memorials to those townspeople killed by shrapnel during the passage of the front or by landmines left behind. Admittedly, a memorial to those whom Allied bombs had killed during the period of co-belligerency would not have been a particularly tactful postwar gesture. Such 'other' civilian victims were not responsible for their own deaths (just as massacre victims had not been), however, and many of them also had died in their own villages in front of their families and neighbours, yet they were not held to have contributed similarly to Italy's liberation and rebirth.

The vice-sindaco's expression of regret for his absence from San Leolino's commemoration ceremony exemplifies one side of a basic divide, as Civitella's unwillingness to have its suffering characterized by the gold medal for military valour exemplifies the other. Bucine's vice-sindaco represents the view that selected war dead (like conflating partisans and civilian massacre victims) could and should be utilized to wash away responsibility for twenty years of Fascism and participation in the first half of the war, then held up as generators of Italy's self-liberation (or Liberation) and the cause of national rebirth. Such a view gave meaning to the deaths of the massacre victims like the men of San Leolino and elsewhere, but it was a meaning created after the fact. It was a meaning that neither the Nazi-Fascists nor the victims had intended. The priests, of course, had another meaning in mind, which had more to do with worldly suffering and a different sort of rebirth.

Eventually, a sort of truce, or more accurately a postwar consensus would be reached over how to honour the victims at the annual ceremonies in the massacred villages, in which the religious would co-exist more peacefully with the secular (though not necessarily on the same day or in the same place).[55] Before then, however, Father Ciabattini and the political orators engaged in one more go round. Castelnuovo's July 4 anniversary ceremony fell on a Sunday in 1948, some months after the polarizing April national election and a few days before the assassination attempt on Togliatti. 'Being Sunday,' Father Polvani (visiting from the nearby parish of San Pancrazio in the commune of Cavriglia) said mass at nine in the morning at the chapel in Piazza IV Novembre. That evening, the citizens went to the cemetery for the blessing of the new tomb that had been built over the mass grave.

Also that evening, Father Ciabattini recorded, 'the local social-communists took advantage of the anniversary to hold a political demonstration.' In a procession and carrying red flags, they came to the chapel in the piazza. There, a certain Professor Francesco Tocchini, a communist council member from Florence spoke, and held 'a true political meeting.' In the course of his speech, he launched insults at everyone, but particularly at the priests. At a certain point, according to Father Ciabattini, he said 'these exact words,' calling priests 'those blockheads [barbagianni] who in church explain the Gospels and speak to you of charity and of love.' When, at another point, the professor began to speak of the Madonna of Assisi and 'maligned' as 'cretins' all those who made the pilgrimage to see her, the offended Father Ciabattini yelled loudly from in front of the church above: 'No, that's not true, it's false!'[56]

Cries and hoots came from the crowd in the priest's direction and someone came towards him in a threatening manner (so he said). The *carabinieri* intervened and restored order.[57]

That evening, together with a group of supporters, the priest wrote letters of protest to the minister of the interior, to the prefect, and to the
Questore. Angrier than he had been two years earlier when Attilio Sassi had
maligned the inscription over the chapel, Father Ciabattini also filed a
lengthy formal complaint.[58] He explained to the prosecutor for the
Tribunal of Arezzo just what had occurred in Castelnuovo on July 4, 1944,
and how the population now celebrated that sad anniversary with solemn
masses, processions to the cemetery, and blessing of the dead. At the very
spot where the men had died and where 'the faithful, in their compassion'
had erected a votive chapel, almost directly below the parish church, the
local social-communists had held a political meeting, at which the speaker
from Florence had railed against all constituted authority, against the
Catholic Church, and against the clergy. Father Ciabattini quoted the slurs
about the 'blockheads' and the 'cretins.' Also citing specific statutes, the
priest asserted (basically) to the court that the phrases used had offended
the official religion of the state, and so were grounds for prosecution.

The anniversary of the massacre the following year saw no incident,
perhaps because it did not follow such an important election. The religious celebration and the political demonstration both took place,
separately and at different times. Then, a couple of months later, on
September 29, 1949, the court handed down its decision on Father
Ciabattini's action against the professor. Despite the 'false testimony of
two witnesses called at the last moment' (according to Father Ciabattini),
Professor Tocchini was found guilty of the charges against him. Sentenced
to a month in custody, the sentence was suspended.[59]

Father Ciabattini was vindicated – at least a little. Extending the
Catholic–Communist struggle to the venue of memorials for civilian war
dead, or, vice-versa, placing commemoration and memorialization within its context meant that citizens (at least some citizens) made honouring
the dead another politicized aspect of postwar life. Moreover, especially
during that most volatile year 1948, the shared experience and the memory of village massacres served as another point of division. Father
Ciabattini and his opposition both wished to utilize the site of the massacre and the massacre. How to define the meaning of the place and of
the massacre, that is, how to insist the victims had not died in vain or how
to decide where they were spending eternity were different dilemmas
from that of how to make sure they were not forgotten.

The return to civil life – the return to normal everyday life – was most complicated here, in ways deeper than arguments and name-calling in the piazza that had seen so much death. The massacres of so many civilians had ruined individual, family, and community lives in ways that would continue to defy a shared understanding, even when citizens once again had enough to eat, when what to do about forgiving ex-Fascists and rewarding former partisans had been pretty much sorted out, when elections took place, and when life began to return to something approaching normality and stability. Why they had died and what their deaths meant would not have a single agreed upon answer, even when 'Nazi-Fascist reprisal' was part of that answer.

In 1947, the schoolteacher Ruggero Franci wrote that Civitella had not succeeded 'in shaking off its funereal atmosphere assumed three years ago.' Massacred villages finally would shake off their funereal atmospheres as years passed, as widows died and orphans grew up and raised families of their own. The victims will always be there, although the massacres will not much longer be part of living memory. The victims were always present in the postwar, but are present still only through annual ceremonies, and by way of plaques on communal walls and church walls, memorials and chapels at massacre sites, monuments over mass graves, and markers in cemeteries. Today those are the very few remaining traces in this landscape through which war and massacre passed.

Conclusion: After War and Massacre

On an otherwise 'beautiful morning for the grape harvest' in late September 1944, Father Polvani considered how the suffering of so many families all around him moved him to tears. In particular, the previous Monday he had met a group of women – widows seeking food and assistance – walking the eight kilometres from Castelnuovo dei Sabbioni to the communal seat of Cavriglia. 'How can they go on,' he asked himself.[1] The priest was not wondering how the widows could walk so far over ruined roads through the post-battlefront rubble, but how they could go on with life, how they would carry on after the murders of their husbands, the destruction of their homes, and the loss of all their possessions, now facing the sole care of their children.

The Second World War was a new kind of war whose battle lines crossed civilian landscapes instead of remaining on battlefields. War correspondent Martha Gellhorn said of World War II in Europe that it was a war in which civilians stayed home and had the war brought to them. Early modern warfare in Europe had also 'brought' war to civilians, as marauding armies descended upon towns and villages, besieging the civilian populations. The difference, however, was the modern brutality and more deadly effectiveness of the Second World War's methods against civilians. The history of war, even that of World War II, traditionally has, until fairly recently, been about battles, the movements of armies, and the decisions of generals, while the history of postwar was high politics, economic policies, the actions of governments and international relations. It has not been about the ordinary people who had war brought to them and who lived its aftermath every day. It has not been about the people who have to go on and how they go on with life.

In a 1964 preface to his *The Path to the Nest of Spiders*, Italo Calvino looked back on the birth of literary neorealism in the first days of the postwar, and recalled not only the 'vicissitudes' of postwar life, but also optimism at the end of the war and the stories ordinary people had to tell and that were worth telling.[2] Whereas neorealist films mostly depicted a 'black and white' postwar Italy of suffering, Calvino (nearly twenty years later) described Italians moving in 'a varicolored universe of stories' directly after the war. The word *disagio* appears again and again in the real-life stories and in the many official and unofficial documents of the time. In English *disagio* primarily translates as disorder, and in the postwar context it also had connotations of 'hardship,' 'privation,' 'want'; at that time it meant a particular kind of disorder. That setting of *disagio* is the setting in which the real-life experiences of both Arezzo and postwar Italy took place. The war's aftermath in Arezzo mirrors Italian neorealist film in its black and white bleakness, but also offers unbearably true, varicoloured personal stories. The ordinary citizens of the Aretine all lived 'irregular, dramatic, adventurous' lives (heroic and not) in the war and its aftermath: lives marked by war, massacre, unimaginable hardship, and difficult years of reconstruction.

These are otherwise unremarkable people who found themselves in the path of war and massacre and who had to go on through the aftermath. Father Polvani's young niece Lina was struck by shrapnel during the passage of the front and lost her arm. With no adequate tools, the doctor had to operate on her wound with work scissors.[3] Dino Tiezzi witnessed the murder of his father and brother, and then spent his childhood in a Rome orphanage. Lara Lammioni saw her family's farm ruined by Allied bombs. Her father, uncle, aunt, and cousins were cruelly murdered; their home in Civitella destroyed. She herself barely escaped rape by German soldiers. Young Romano Moretti lived in the woods with his mother and the other citizens of San Pancrazio after German soldiers murdered his father and the other men and then destroyed the village. Returning after the passage of the front, he was present as the burned and decomposed remains of his father were dug from the basement of the *fattoria* Pierangeli. From the half-open window of his grandmother's house, eleven year old Emilio Polverini watched the Germans massacre some of the men of Le Màtole. Only a week earlier, he had listened to the sound of machinegun fire and the screams of the men (including his father) coming from the piazza in Castelnuovo, and a day later had seen the burned bodies. After the war, on May 30, 1945, he saw villagers torture Pasquale Badii and burn him alive, and later he witnessed the battles over memory in Castelnuovo's piazza on the anniversaries of the July 4 massacre.

The war touched everyone, though it was particularly cruel to the women and children – the widows and orphans of the massacres – societal groups usually spared direct contact with war. That war did touch everyone, however. Whether someone was a soldier on the Russian front or a civilian protesting rationing; whether someone was interned in an Italian concentration camp or was selling food to the inmates of that camp; whether someone was a POW, a partisan, or a Republican Fascist; whether someone had been deported to Germany for forced labour, had fled her bombed home and was living as a refugee in a strange commune, or had repatriated from Italian Africa; whether someone spent the second half of the war sharing his villa with German officers or hiding under the roots of a tree; whether someone had sheltered escaping Allied POWs or had denounced a neighbour/enemy; whether someone had seen a husband or father massacred, or had blessed the weapons of the Fascists, everyone had taken some part in the war and everyone had to live together in the hardship of its aftermath.

Living together after the war often proved as difficult as living through the war, and so we return to the question of what kept postwar society together and what drove its members apart. Because war had touched everyone, albeit in different ways and different degrees, people shared a common experience. As the prefect had reported at the end of 1945, an 'individual and collective sense of loss' 'flowed from their shared suffering.' Everyone could point to some war caused suffering, whether it had been life shattering trauma or something more in the nature of serious inconvenience; the war had not been 'good' to anyone, particularly towards the end. 'All' Italians (or most, more honestly), in the most general way, could share the postwar feeling and opinion that Italy as a nation and its people had sacrificed and suffered grievously on account of that destructive war caused by 'one man' and wanted by 'no one' else.

More locally, Italians within a single area, commune, or town shared the experience of rationing and perceived experience of receiving less than other places, of bombing that was worse than in other places, of destruction worse than other places, of massacres not experienced by other places, of postwar hardship and need worse than other places, while they were given less assistance than others. Comparing themselves, their suffering, and their hardships with others, whether those others were from another country or another commune or another village, could unite people against the 'outside world' whether that outside world was truly outside or was really Rome, the neighbouring province, the neighbouring village, or was the refugee camp in their own midst. Citizens of Arezzo and central-northern Italy also had an ideal of civil life – of normal life – to which they very much wanted to return and which return, so it seemed, the Allied occupiers, the refugees, their neighbours, and the interim postwar state all were working to hinder.

In the first film version of the Don Camillo stories, at the end Don Camillo and Peppone, despite their stark, postwar political differences, are reconciled by the return (in flashback) to their shared anti-Nazi experience of having resisted against the German occupiers and having 'been against' the German occupiers. No mention of local Fascist Republicans or Nazi-Fascist sympathizers is made; there were only Italians against Germans. Of course, in real life, it was not so simple. Not all Italians had been 'against' the 'bad' Germans during either or both halves of the war. Nevertheless, enough Italians 'were against' the Germans during that second half of the war – in large part because of German occupation methods there and the continuation and intensification of a war that many hoped had ended in the fall of 1943 – so that the experience of German occupation and of war carried out by German troops in Italy also provided a strong unifying bond as well as the way to distinguish Italian wartime actions (as relatively harmless and not heartfelt) from German actions.

Perhaps less satisfactorily, though more elaborately done on the national level, the postwar interim state affirmatively strove to generate unity through reconciliation, by means of the amnesty for Fascists, by special assistance to widows of massacre victims, and by recognition for and benefits to those (or to their survivors) who had suffered or 'sacrificed themselves' for the Liberation and the rebirth of Italy. Forgiving the true Fascists as well as the 'mere Fascists' (as most had been) had to be done and done quickly, so that all could live together in the post-Fascist, postwar world. In doing so, however, the state neglected to recognize and reward adequately – or chose to ignore – those who had been anti-Fascist or who had resisted being even 'mere' Fascists, focusing instead on those who had been partisans or those who had been the victims of reprisals against partisans. This meant a conscious decision that Fascism (as opposed to German occupation) had not been so bad, but had been a normal state of affairs. The state's efforts to reconcile through recognition and rewards also slid over Italian actions during the war and did little to produce lasting postwar unity. Officially conflating such disparate groups as military veterans, partisan combatants, and civilian massacre victims, or

concocting an inclusive category of 'political victims' did not always successfully convince that thousands of civilian deaths had been necessary
and voluntarily offered for Italy's redemption.

The shared experience and sufferings of war could not overcome postwar differences, and those differences came more to the fore of everyday
life as the more immediate, unifying ordeal of war receded. The recent
memory of Fascism locally, civil war, and its local aftermath divided society,
sometimes violently, as the front passed and again when Republican Fascists
returned home. Even so, the feeling that Fascists (those who had been
more than 'mere Fascists') should be punished and excluded from public
life passed surprisingly quickly for most. Even before the amnesty, local
exceptions, and extenuating circumstances to the purge were the rule.

It was war caused need that was the most extensive divisive factor in
postwar life. Infinite numbers of needs and needy citizens reinforced the
fact that everyone had suffered, but when combined with too limited assistance, rationed food, too few jobs, and too much physical destruction,
need pitted people against one another both within and across categories. When a village has ten pairs of shoes to give and one hundred people who need them, or two jobs and two hundred unemployed, unity will
naturally give way, no matter how carefully need is rationalized. Except
most immediately after a tragedy briefly inspires unity and solidarity,
postwar Arezzo and postwar Italy prove how with desperate need, one's
own individual and family considerations will always trump unity (and
often solidarity as well).

Postwar politics also exacerbated differences and so also fractured
unity, as I am by no means the first to assert in the case of Italy. Political
polarization began quickly after the passage of the front, accelerated after the Allies' departure, and culminated in the climactic events of 1948:
the national elections (and the DC victory), the assassination attempt,
and the CGIL schism. Omnipresent politics and political considerations
were neither 'bad' nor 'good' in the sense of historical value judgments,
though they evidenced a lively appreciation of electoral democracy and
a newly sophisticated continuation of old practices of clientelism, patronage, and *raccomandazione*. Politics were simply omnipresent as a matter of fact: that fact made possible and nourished by the extent of postwar
need and too few resources to fill the need.

Postwar fracturing did not cause society to fall apart or to degenerate
into a second, larger round of civil war, because enough points in common existed to keep society together. Division, especially along new political lines and old class lines, did hinder postwar social change, however.

A four or five year period may be too short a time in which to expect to find real change, especially in an environment as fractious as Italy between 1943 and 1948. Yet it was during those years that Italians (some Italians) were most hopeful about remaking society. Change seemed most possible after the war had so fundamentally ruptured daily life, institutions, and government, whether change meant communism's 'moment to triumph' (according to Attilio Sassi), the opportunity to restructure the *mezzadria* system more fairly, or to create cross-sector, multi-party unity within a single labour union confederation. One important change did take place, though it was more evolution than change and again postwar need and party presence made it possible. The state from then on would be more responsive to the needs and increased demands of its citizens than it ever had before, even if it inspired no greater confidence and trust than it had before.

The premise that war causes social change (or makes it possible) must be countered by the reality that war's destruction will be met with a human desire to return to normality and rebuild as before, rather than to start entirely anew. Forces for continuity are as strong as forces for change. On September 5, 1944, a few weeks after the passage of the front yet before the entire province had been liberated, as Father Polvani worried how the women of Castelnuovo would carry on, and just a very few months after the *Questore* reported that Allied bombing had 'disintegrated' the civil life of Arezzo, an editorial in the first number of the first edition of the provincial newspaper *L'Informatore Aretino* noted that the 'life of the town is resuming its rhythm.' So short a time after so much devastation and in the midst of continuing suffering and *disagio*, and with years of both still to come, life was already getting back to normal.

In this study of transition from war to peace in the small place that is villages and communes in the province of Arezzo over the brief period of four years, the larger significance about the power of war and the strength of society should not be lost. War can destroy society, but not transform it. War has an immense power to affect people, to change the shape of daily lives and impose suffering, to destroy communities and institutions, to break states, and to influence actions and activities long after the battles have stopped and the aftermath has begun. Society is resilient, however. The ability of society and of individuals to rebuild and to go on with life surpasses war's power to destroy.

Abbreviations and Documentation

All translations from Italian are mine unless otherwise noted.

AC or ACC	Allied Commission or Allied Control Commission
ACLI	Associazioni Cristiane Lavoratori Italiani (Catholic Association of Italian Workers)
AMG	Allied Military Government
AMGOT	Allied Military Government of the Occupied Territories
ANPI	Associazione Nazionale Partigiani d'Italia (National Partisans Association of Italy)
APB	Ministero dell'Assistenza Post-bellica (Ministry of Postwar Assistance)
CAO	Allied Civil Affairs Officer
CdL	Camera del Lavoro (Chamber of Labour)
CGIL	Confederazione Generale Italiana del Lavoro (General Confederation of Italian Labour)
CIF	Centro Italiano Femminile (Catholic Centre of Italian Women)
CLN	Comitato di Liberazione Nazionale (National Committee or Committees of Liberation)
Coldiretti	Confederazione Nazionale dei Coltivatori Diretti (National Confederation of Direct Cultivators, Catholic inspired)
DC	Democrazia Cristiana (Christian Democrat Party)
ECA	Ente Comunale di Assistenza (Communal Assistance Agency)
ECFA	Ente Comunale di Assistenza Fascista (Fascist [Republican] Communal Assistance Agency)

ENAL	Ente Nazionale Assistenza Lavoratori
ENDSI	Ente nazionale per la Distribuzione dei Soccorsi in Italia (National Agency for Distribution of Relief Supplies in Italy
Federterra	Federazione Lavoratori della Terra (Federation of Agricultural Workers or Workers of the Land, within CGIL)
GIL	Gioventù Italiana Littorio (Fascist Party Youth Organization)
OND	Opera Nazionale Dopolavoro (National After-work Group)
ONMI	Opera Nazionale per la protezione della Maternità e dell'Infanzia (National Agency for Mothers and Children)
PCI	Partito Comunista Italiano (Italian Communist Party)
PC	Allied Provincial Commissioner
PNF	Partito Nazionale Fascista (National Fascist Party)
PPI	Partito Popolare Italiano (Italian Popular Party)
PPSO	Allied Provincial Public Safety Officer
PSI	Partito Socialista Italiano (Italian Socialist Party)
PWB	Allied Psychological Warfare Branch
RSI	Repubblica Sociale Italiana (Italian Social Republic, or the Republic of Salò)
SEPRAL	La Sezione Provinciale dell'Alimentazione (Provincial level rationing sections)
UDI	Unione Donne Italiane (Union of Italian Women)
UIL	Unione Italiana dei Lavoratori (Union of Italian Labour)
UNRRA	United Nations Relief and Rehabilitation Administration
UNRRA-CASAS	United Nations Relief and Rehabilitation Administration-Comitato Amministrativo Soccorso ai Senzatetto

Archives and Documentation

Documenting of Archives. The contents of communal archives I examined include everything from handwritten letters sent by local citizens to their sindaco, to bulletins and directives from the prefect and from officials in Rome to the communes. Basically, they include all the records and communications – demographic, personnel, financial, administrative, military, and other – of the commune. The communal archival material of Bucine, Cavriglia, and Civitella, like that of most small communes, is not indexed or catalogued. Records are generally organized according to a broad system of categories (category VIII for documents having to do with the military, for example), though interpretation of appropriate category was somewhat subjective, and careful ordering of documents was not a great priority during the war and postwar. I often found documents in surprising and unexpected categories. For the communal archives (other than the very well indexed communal archive of Florence) and their rich sources, my research method consisted of starting at one end of a shelf and working my way to the other end, and then moving on to the next shelf – examining every document in every file along the way for the war years and postwar until 1950 or so. In citing a particular document contained in the communal archives, I have simply recorded (and cited) everything that appeared on the cover of the folder or file that contained the document, except for deleting the word 'anno' before a year, deleting 'ogg.' or 'oggetto' before a file name, and condensing dates (as with 1943–5).

Italian State Archives

ACS	Archivio Centrale dello Stato (Rome)
ASA Pref. Gab.	Achivio di Stato (Arezzo) Prefettura Gabinetto
AS Florence	Archivio di Stato (Florence)
BNC Florence	Biblioteca Nazionale Centrale (Florence)

Italian Communal Archives

ASC Bucine	Archivio Storico, Commune of Bucine
ASC Cavriglia	Archivio Storico, Commune of Cavriglia
ASC Civitella	Archivio Storico, Commune of Civitella in Val di Chiana
ASC Florence	Archivio Storico, Commune of Florence
ASC Montevarchi	Archivio Storico, Commune of Montevarchi

Italian Association and Other Archives

	Archivio Diaristico Nazionale (Pieve Santo Stefano)
ACLI Arezzo	Associazioni Cristiane Lavoratori Italiani (Province of Arezzo)
ANVCG	Associazione Nazionale Vittime Civili di Guerra (Provincial Section of Florence)
ANFIM	Associazione Nazionale tra le Famiglie Italiane dei Martiri Caduti per la Libertà della Patria (Region of Tuscany)
CGIL Arezzo	Confederazione Generale Italiana del Lavoro (Province of Arezzo)

CGIL Toscana	Confederazione Generale Italiana del Lavoro, Centro Documentazione e Archivio Storico (Region of Tuscany, Florence)
CGIL Montevarchi	Confederazione Generale Italiana del Lavoro (Communes of Montevarchi and San Giovanni Valdarno)
ISRT	Istituto Storico della Resistenza in Toscana (Florence)

Foreign Archives

	Air Force Historical Research Agency
	Hoover Institution Archives
	Imperial War Museum
NARA RG 331	National Archives and Records Administration: Record Group 331
NA/PRO WO	The National Archives (formerly the Public Record Office): War Office
UN/UNRRA	United Nations Archives and Records Centre: United Nations Relief and Rehabilitation Administration

Oral Sources

I am not trained as an oral historian and, as a former trial attorney, I am aware of the weaknesses and many problems involved with 'out of court' statements (documents included). Taking into account problems (and flaws) of a particular 'declarant's' knowledge, perception, memory, bias, or self-interest relating to his or her statements, local history can, nevertheless, be enriched by interviews and conversations with those who were there. This local, social history is also about how people subjectively perceived and felt about daily life during war and its aftermath, and I was fortunate to be able to interview and speak with many who were children, widows, soldiers, ex-partisans, and those involved in local administration and assistance organizations during the period. Some contacts consisted of one-time interviews, while other conversations have gone on for a decade now (as with Emilio Polverini) or for more than two decades (as with Lara Lammioni Lucarelli). All such statements are offered as recollection or statements of memory, rather than for the truth of the matter asserted – that is, rather than as historical fact.

Notes

Introduction: From War to Peace

1 See, for example, Gregor Dallas, *1945: The War That Never Ended* (New Haven: Yale University Press, 2005); Susan Rubin Suleiman, *Crises of Memory and the Second World War* (Cambridge: Harvard University Press, 2006); Richard Ned Lebow, Wulf Kansteiner, and Claudio Fogu, eds., *The Politics of Memory in Post-war Europe* (Durham: Duke University Press, 2006); Richard Bessel and Dirk Schumann, eds., *Life After Death: Approaches to a Cultural History of Europe During the 1940s and 1950s.* (Publications of the German Historical Institute, Washington, DC. Cambridge: Cambridge University Press, 2003); István Deák, Jan T. Gross, and Tony Judt, eds., *The Politics of Retribution in Europe: World War II and Its Aftermath* (Princeton: Princeton University Press, 2000); Pieter Lagrou, *The Legacy of Nazi Occupation: Patriotic Memory and National Recovery in Western Europe, 1945–1965,* (Cambridge: Cambridge University Press, 2000); Jonathan Dunnage, ed., *After the War: Violence, Justice, Continuity and Renewal in Italian Society* (Market Harborough: Troubador, 1999); Helmut Peitsch, Charles Burdett, and Claire Gorrara, eds., *European Memories of the Second World War* (New York: Berghahn Books, 1999); Nancy Wood, *Vectors of Memory: Legacies of Trauma in Postwar Europe* (Oxford: Berg, 1999); Sarah Farmer, *Martyred Village: Commemorating the 1944 Massacre at Oradour-sur-Glane* (Berkeley: University of California Press, 1999).

2 On transition from war to peace generally, see Sheila Meintjes, Anu Pillay, and Meredith Turshen, eds., *The Aftermath: Women in Post-Conflict Transformation* (London: Zed Books, 2001); Claire Duchen and Irene Bandhauer-Schöffmann, eds., *When the War Was Over: Women, War and Peace in Europe, 1940–1956* (London: Leicester University Press, 2000); Megan Koreman, *The Expectation of Justice: France 1944–1946* (Durham: Duke University Press, 1999).

The first English-language study treating the war's 'lasting consequences' in Italy, and Italy's transition from war to peace and from Fascism to democracy is the collection of essays in S.J. Woolf, ed., *The Rebirth of Italy, 1943–50* (London: Longman, 1972). See especially Stuart Woolf's introduction and ch. 9, 'The Rebirth of Italy, 1943–50.' For more recent explicit treatment of one aspect of Italy's transition, see Ruth Ben-Ghiat, 'Unmaking of the Fascist Man: Masculinity, Film, and the Transition from Dictatorship,' *Journal of Modern Italian Studies* 10, no. 3 (2005): 336–65. See Anna Maria Torriglia, *Broken Time, Fragmented Space: A Cultural Map for Postwar Italy* (Toronto: University of Toronto Press, 2002) regarding the period as one of cultural transition.

Concentration on the transition from war to peace (or from the individual and collective trauma of war through recovery) parallels, to an extent, the increasing number of studies on transitional justice, violence, and memory, and on political, institutional, and economic transition (and democratization) after regime change, especially the post-1989 and post-1991 so-called 'post-Soviet transitology.' See, as only two (but excellent) examples, Jenny Edkins, *Trauma and the Memory of Politics* (Cambridge: Cambridge University Press, 2003); Ruti G. Teitel, *Transitional Justice* (Oxford: Oxford University Press, 2000)

3 Roberto Rossellini, director: *Rome: Open City* (*Roma: Città Aperta*) (1945), and *Paisan* (*Paisà*) (1946); Vittorio De Sica, director: *Shoeshine* (*Sciuscià*) (1946), and *Bicycle Thieves* (*Ladri di Bicicletta*) (1948). The first series of Giovanni Guareschi's Don Camillo stories was published in 1950 as *Mondo piccolo, Don Camillo*. The first Don Camillo movie, *Don Camillo*, an Italian and French production, was released in 1952.

4 Arthur Marwick described the 'test dimension' of war, whereby war imposes 'enormous stresses and strains to which a country's military, social, political and economic institutions must adapt if the country is to avoid defeat; indeed if the institutions are grossly inadequate they will collapse, as in Tsarist Russia.' In 1943, Italy failed that test. See Arthur Marwick, ed., *Total War and Social Change* (New York: St. Martin's Press, 1988), xv.

5 ASA Pref. Gab., busta 7 ('i numerosi bombardamenti subiti da questo capoluogo e che hanno disgregato la vita civile cittadina').

6 In the 1430s, in *Della Vita Civile*, Matteo Palmieri described 'the life of the model citizen, governing his own affairs in town and country and dutifully participating in the affairs of state.' J.K. Hyde, *Society and Politics in Medieval Italy: The Evolution of the Civil Life, 1000–1350* (New York: St. Martin's Press, 1973), 8.

7 Sydel Silverman, *Three Bells of Civilization: The Life of an Italian Hill Town* (New York: Columbia University Press, 1975), vii and ch. 1.

8 'The town ... also has its own reference points for identity and value; it is
   the focus of civic pride and *campanilismo*. The town piazza is a forum, a place
   for sifting information, for plotting intrigue, for personal presentation and
   public spectacle ... The piazza is a marketplace too, and all citizens, from
   landed aristocrat to humble shoemaker, are caught up in commerce. Their
   talk is about a piece of land for sale, about a deal someone has made, about
   an irregularity in the public accounts. And while the church looms large in
   the piazza, the values expressed are predominantly secular: respect for formal education and "culture," faith in written law and bureaucracy, and appreciation of quality and quantity in material things.' Ibid., 122.
9 Ibid., ix.
10 See the essays in Jonathan Dunnage, ed., *After the War: Violence, Justice, Continuity and Renewal in Italian Society*, one of the only English-language studies of
   various aspects of postwar society. Local study of the experience and actions of
   ordinary people living through the war is new in Italy as well. See Gabriela
   Gribaudi, *Guerra totale. Tra bombe alleate e violenze naziste. Napoli, il fronte meridionale, 1940–1944* (Turin: Bollati Boringhieri 2005); and Giulio Guderzo,
   *L'altra guerra. Neofascisti, tedeschi, partigiani, popolo in una provincia padana. Pavia
   1943–1945* (Bologna: Il Mulino 2002). See also Carla Forti, *Dopoguerra in provincia. Microstorie pisane e lucchesi (1944–1948)* (Milan: Franco Angeli, 2007).
11 The first postwar use of the phrase and concept 'Italy in transition' (that I
   have found) is G.R. Gayre, *Italy in Transition. Extracts from the Private Journal
   of G.R. Gayre* (London: Faber & Faber, 1946). An educational advisor to the
   Allied Military Government between September 1943 and March 1944,
   Colonel Gayre chronicled the daily problems faced by Italians and by Allied
   officials during the six months he spent in Sicily and southern Italy. A re-
   viewer faulted the title as 'misleading' because 'the problems of "the two
   Sicilies" cannot by any stretching be generalized to cover Italy as a whole.'
   Bernard Wall, *International Affairs* 23, no. 1 (1947): 112.
12 Paul Ginsborg, *A History of Contemporary Italy: Society and Politics 1943–1988*
   (London: Penguin, 1990), 2–3.
13 In his introduction to Jonathan Dunnage, ed., *After the War: Violence, Justice,
   Continuity and Renewal in Italian Society*, Mark Mazower stressed the importance
   of local and regional studies of postwar Europe: '[o]ne of the most fascinating
   results of the rich vein of local and regional historical analyses of the postwar
   period is how clearly it shows the dimensions of the crisis facing the machinery of state. Central power lies stripped of all its pretensions when viewed
   from the village. In the immediate aftermath of the war, it was the weakness
   not the strength of the state which most influenced the political process.'
   David Ellwood has suggested research into 'the behaviour of the mass of the

population as they survived all the torments of the civil war, the class war and the war of liberation' as a 'new, unifying theme' within wartime experience. D.W. Ellwood, 'Introduction: The Never-ending Liberation,' *Journal of Modern Italian Studies* 10, no.4 (2005): 385–95 (quote: 388–9).

14 Claudio Pavone, 'Tre governi e due occupazioni' in *L'Italia nella seconda guerra mondiale e nella Resistenza*, ed. Francesca Ferratini Tosi, Gaetano Grassi, Massimo Legnani (Milan: Franco Angeli, 1988), 423–52.

15 The reference is to Benedetto Croce, *Quando l'Italia era tagliata in due. Estratto di un diario (luglio 1943–giugno 1944)* (Bari and Rome: Laterza, 1948).

16 See David W. Ellwood, Introduction to *Italy 1943–1945: The Politics of Liberation* (Leicester: Leicester University Press, 1985).

17 Although they shared many wartime and postwar qualities, Italy does not have the equivalent of the Vichy syndrome. See Henry Rousso, *The Vichy Syndrome: History and Memory in France since 1944*, trans. Arthur Goldhammer (Cambridge: Harvard University Press, 1991); and Michele Battini, *The Missing Italian Nuremberg: Cultural Amnesia and Postwar Politics* (New York: Palgrave Macmillan, 2007), ch. 6.

18 See for example, Richard Bessel, ed., *Fascist Italy and Nazi Germany: Comparisons and Contrasts* (Cambridge: Cambridge University Press, 1996); Stanley G. Payne, *A History of Fascism 1914–1945*; Alexander J. De Grand, *Fascist Italy and Nazi Germany*; R.J.B. Bosworth, *Mussolini* (London: Arnold, 2002).

19 Ernesto Galli della Loggia, *La morte della patria: La crisi dell'idea di nazione tra Resistenza, antifascismo e Repubblica* (Bari and Rome: Laterza, 1996). Philip Morgan, *The Fall of Mussolini: Italy, the Italians, and the Second World War* (Oxford: Oxford University Press, 2007) and Michele Battini, *The Missing Italian Nuremberg*, make similar points about Italian suffering. See also D.W. Ellwood, 'Introduction' to 'The Never-ending Liberation,' *Journal of Modern Italian Studies*.

20 Joseph LaPalombara, *Democracy Italian Style* (New Haven: Yale University Press, 1987), 262; Nicola Gallerano, 'A Neglected Chapter in Italy's Transition from Fascism to the Republic: The Kingdom of the South (1943–1944),' *Journal of Modern Italian Studies* 1, no. 3 (1996): 391–9 (quote: 394). See also Claudio Pavone, 'The General Problem of the Continuity of the State and the Legacy of Fascism,' in *After the War: Violence, Justice, Continuity and Renewal in Italian Society*, ed. Jonathan Dunnage, 5–20; Guido Quazza, *Resistenza e storia d'Italia. Problemi e ipotesi di ricerca* (Milan: Feltrinelli, 1976).

21 I use the word 'commune' as the English translation of the Italian *comune*, the local administrative unit.

22 In all of Italy, in 1936, most people (48.2 per cent) worked in agriculture. Only 29.3 per cent worked in industry; even fewer, 22.5 per cent, worked in services.

23 Enrico Biagini, *Civitella. Un paese, un castello, un martirio* (Arezzo: Centros-tampa, 1981), Appendix IV.

24 Giovanni Contini, *La memoria divisa* (Milan: Rizzoli, 1997), 25, fns. 3 and 4 (citing the 1931 census). Also see Ida Balò Valli, ed., *Giugno 1944: Civitella racconta* (Cortona: Editrice Grafica L'Etruria, 1994), ch. 1; and Alessandro Portelli, 'The Massacre at Civitella Val di Chiana (Tuscany, June 29, 1944): Myth and Politics, Mourning and Common Sense,' ch. 10 in *Oral History and the Art of Dialogue* (Madison: University of Wisconsin Press, 1997). Thank you to Lara Lammioni Lucarelli and to Ida Balò Valli for describing to me Civi-tella as they remember it before June 29, 1944.

25 The commune of Bucine had a population of 9332 in 1939.

26 Giovanni Contini, *La memoria divisa*, 25–6. Thank you to Romano Moretti who introduced me to San Pancrazio and its residents, shared his research and ex-tensive collection of oral testimonies, and provided his own recollections.

27 Today it is difficult to get a feel for the village as it was before World War II. Castelnuovo dei Sabbioni is today two villages – one inhabited and one a 'ghost village.' The original village, owned by ENEL (the electric company), was closed and abandoned during the 1950s because years of mining togeth-er with the sandy nature of the subsurface had made the ground unstable. A new village was built nearby on more solid ground, at a higher altitude of 295 metres. Today a thermo-electrical plant operates at nearby village of Santa Barbara and dominates the landscape, making an eerie contrast with the empty village.

28 See Adrian Lyttelton, *The Seizure of Power: Fascism in Italy 1919–1929* (Lon-don: Weidenfeld and Nicolson, 1973), 71, 210–11; and F.M. Snowden, *The Fascist Revolution in Tuscany 1919–1922* (Cambridge: Cambridge University Press, 1989).

29 See Claudio G. Segrè, *Italo Balbo: A Fascist Life* (Berkeley: University of Cali-fornia Press, 1987), chs. 2 and 3, on Fascism's early 'agrarian phase.'

30 Ivano Tognarini, ed., *La guerra di liberazione in provincial di Arezzo 1943/1944: Immagini e documenti* (Arezzo: Provincia di Arezzo, 1987), 20. The Partito Popolare Italiano (PPI), led by Sicilian priest Don Sturzo, was a Catholic mass party, sometimes considered a precursor to the postwar Christian Democrat Party.

31 The term '*quasi-guerra civile*' in reference to the post-WWI era comes from Giorgio Sacchetti, *Camicie nere in Valdarno. Cronache inedite del 23 marzo 1921 (guerra sociale e guerra civile)* (Pisa: Biblioteca Franco Serantini, 1996). See Mimmo Franzinelli, *Squadristi: protagonisti e techniche della violenza fascista 1919–1922* (Milan: Mondadori, 2004); Adrian Lyttelton, *The Seizure of Power*; F.M. Snowden, *The Fascist Revolution in Tuscany*.

32 The facts that follow are taken primarily from Giorgio Sacchetti, *Camicie nere in Valdarno. Cronache inedite del 23 marzo 1921.* See also Giorgio Sacchetti, *Il minatore deputato Priamo Bigiandi 1900–1961* (Florence: Manent, 1998), ch. 1.

33 The April events at Foiano della Chiana and Renzino are set forth in Ferruccio Fabilli, *I mezzadri: lavoro, conflitti sociali, trasformazioni economiche, politiche e culturali a Cortona dal 1900 ad oggi* (Cortona: CGIL Valdichiana, 1992), 15–67; and Giuseppe Bronzi, *Il fascismo aretino da Renzino a Besozzo (1921–1945): Proposta di ricerca su studi e fonti d'archivio* (Cortona: Grafica l'Etruria, 1988), 9–13. The communes of Foiano and Anghiari were the two Aretine communes that voted for socialist majorities in 1914. See Ivano Tognarini, ed., *La guerra di liberazione in provincial di Arezzo 1943/1944*, 20.

34 Years later, a small partisan band adopted the name '*banda* Renzino.' See chs. 1 and 2.

35 A. Rossi (pseudonym of Angelo Tasca) provided a table based on data taken from official Fascist Party historian Giorgio Alberto Chiurco's, *Storia della Rivoluzione Fascista (1919–1922)* (5 vols.) (Florence: Vallecchi, 1929). Although admittedly extremely unreliable (the reports used extended only as far as May or June 1921 and they omitted large parts of Tuscany, Umbria, Latium, and several provinces), Tuscany and Venezia Giulia shared the distinction of having suffered by far the greatest amount of Fascist squad destruction of newspaper offices, cooperative societies, peasant leagues, mutual aid societies, *Camere del Lavoro*, union offices, etc. A. Rossi (pseudo.), *The Rise of Italian Fascism*, trans. Peter and Dorothy Wait (London: Methuen & Co. Ltd. 1938), 120–1. According to the table, in Tuscany in the first half of 1921, Fascists attacked a total of 137 buildings, offices, organizations, etc., including seventy Socialist and Communist Party clubs and offices, eleven cooperative societies, and twenty-four workers' clubs. See also 114–16: 'In "gentle Tuscany," however, fascist cruelty and violence reached their highest level.' See Roberto Cantagalli, *Storia del fascismo fiorentino 1919–1925* (Florence: Vallecchi, 1972). Adrian Lyttelton includes Arezzo in 'stage 2' of the Fascist seizure of power 'until July 1922,' rather than in 'stage 1' – the initial expansion during spring 1921. Adrian Lyttelton, *The Seizure of Power*, 70, and 436–7.

36 Giuseppe Bronzi, *Il fascismo aretino da Renzino a Besozzo*, 13–15.

37 One mineworker, Priamo Bigiandi, initially received a sentence of eleven years in prison. In 1946, he would be the first postwar elected sindaco (or mayor) of the commune of Cavriglia. Giorgio Sacchetti, *Camicie nere in Valdarno*, 49 et seq.

38 On the gap between Fascist rhetoric and ambitions and the reality of Italian life under Fascism, see R.J.B. Bosworth, *Mussolini's Italy: Life under the Fascist Dictatorship, 1915–1945* (New York: Penguin, 2006).

1. Italy at War

Epigraph: From the *Questore*'s June 25, 1943, report to Rome on Arezzo province's political and economic situation. ASA Pref. Gab., busta 7.

1 See Bruce D. Porter, *War and the Rise of the State* (New York: The Free Press, 1995), especially p. 15, regarding the proposition that war generally makes, strengthens, or consolidates states, but 'also sometimes breaks them.' See also Martin van Creveld, *The Rise and Decline of the State* (Cambridge: Cambridge University Press, 1999), ch. 4, characterizing war as the state's 'supreme test.'

2 See Aurelio Lepre, *Le illusioni, la paura, la rabbia. Il fronte interno italiano (1940–1943)* (Rome: Edizioni Scientifiche Italiane, 1989), describing early support for, or optimism about, the war. See also Miriam Mafai, *Pane nero*, chs. 1 and 2 describing 'happiness' and singing in the streets during the first days of the war. Enzo Collotti and Lutz Klinkhammer, *Il fascismo e l'Italia in guerra. Una conversazione fra storia e storiografica* (Rome: Ediesse, 1996), ch. 2, discuss the relationship between the war and consensus for Fascism. See F.W. Deakin, *The Brutal Friendship: Mussolini, Hitler and the Fall of Italian Fascism* (Part I, Revised) (Garden City, NY: Anchor Books, 1966) on Italy's military failures as the cause of Mussolini's (and Fascism's) fall.

3 Oral history of Lara Lammioni Lucarelli, and my interviews with her, and with Ida Balò, Dino Tiezzi, Amadeo Sereni, Emilio Polverini, and Romano Moretti, 1997–1999. (See my explanation under 'Oral Sources' in 'Abbreviations and Documentation.') In Civitella, a dominant local memory is the sense of the village's 'removal' from the war until June 1944.

4 See Emilio Gentile, *La via italiana al totalitarismo. Il partito e lo Stato nel regime fascista* (Rome: Carocci, 2d ed. 2001), *parte seconda*, on the extent and success of Fascism's (and the Fascist Party's) 'totalitarian laboratory.' As for the 'sacralization' of the state and of politics, or Fascism as civic religion (complete with symbol and ritual), see Emilio Gentile, *Il culto del littorio: La sacralizzazione della politica nell'Italia fascista* (Bari and Rome: Laterza, 2001 ed.).

5 When referring, as here, to the Fascist Party, I mean those Italians who were active members in party doings or active in running the party on the local level, as opposed to the many Italians who – as they would emphasize after the war – were 'mere Fascists': those who joined the party, but were not active participants.

6 ACS, fondo PNF Servizi Vari, Serie II, busta 847, fasc. Censimento proprietà immobiliari. The Aretine *fasci* of Anghiari, Bucine, and Civitella had enjoyed 'free use' of communal property 'for an indeterminate period,' without the technicality of a written contract or lease. Laterina's *fascio* shared a building

with the Italian Red Cross, without a regular contract, but for a nominal annual rent of 132 lire. Badia al Pino's *fascio* maintained its office in the premises of the *dopolavoro*, for which it paid rent of 100 lire per year.

7 ACS, fondo PNF Servizi Vari, Serie II, busta 845, fascs. 1, 2, 3, 7.4 and fasc. S. Giovanni Valdarno – Sede del gruppo rionale Elio Salvini; busta 846, fasc. Stia – Casa del fascio, fasc. Zenna – Casa del fascio; fasc. Castiglione Fiorentino – Immobile donato dalla Società Operaia di Mutuo Soccorso; and fasc. Censimento proprietà immobiliari.

8 ACS, fondo PNF Servizi Vari, Serie II, busta 845, fascs. 2 and 3.

9 ACS fondo PNF Servizi Vari, Serie II, busta 846, fasc. S. Giovanni Valdarno – Casa del fascio.

10 ACS fondo PNF Servizi Vari, Serie II, busta 846, fasc. Zenna – Casa del fascio.

11 For these reports, the prefect received a telegram of appreciation from Mussolini. ASA Pref. Gab., busta 6. The prefect was the highest state authority within each province, and the link between national government and local administration. He was a centrally appointed official, responsible for overseeing the communes, organizing the police, maintaining public order, punishing subversives, and informing Rome on events within his province. See Philip Morgan, 'The Prefects and Party-state Relations in Fascist Italy,' *Journal of Modern Italian Studies* 3, no. 3 (1998): 241–72; and Alberto Aquarone, *L'organizzazione dello stato totalitario* (Turin: Einaudi, 1995), 485–8, for the prefect's role during the Fascist period.

12 ACS, fondo PNF Servizi Vari, Serie II, Affari generali, busta 189, fasc. Fondi Duce, fasc. Contributi (1941–43); busta 193. Contributions also were sent from residents in the United States.

13 ACS, fondo PNF Servizi Vari, Serie II, Affari generali, busta 192, fasc. Offerte varie al Partito, and subfasc. Sussidi gruppi rionali; busta 194, fasc. Contributi per l'assistenza ai combattenti. The Ente Comunale di Assistenza (ECA) was a parastatal poor relief and welfare agency, instituted in 1937. Basically, the organization was to provide for 'the assisting of individuals and families who find themselves in conditions of particular need.' ASC Florence, 10443 ECA, f. 4.

14 ACS, fondo PNF Servizi Vari, Serie II, Affari generali, busta 194, fasc. Contributi per l'assistenza ai combattenti.

15 ACS, fondo PNF Servizi Vari, Serie II, Affari generali, busta 194, fasc. Istituzione nuove imposte per assistenza di guerra and fasc. Contributi per l'assistenza ai combattenti.

16 ACS, fondo PNF Servizi Vari, Serie II, Affari generali, busta 195, fasc. Richieste generi di assistenza; busta 194, fasc. Assistenza alle truppe combattenti.

17 Paul Ginsborg, *A History of Contemporary Italy*, 10–11.

18 Italy's rationing system (if not rationing itself) had in fact predated Italy's entry into the war. Instituted by the Fascist government in 1939, La Sezione Provinciale dell'Alimentazione (SEPRAL) lasted for almost ten years, finally ending in 1948. Prefects headed provincial SEPRAL sections, and each commune also had its own communal commission of *alimentazione*. In February 1943, the communal commission of *alimentazione* and its staff numbered fifteen for a commune as small as Civitella. ASC Civitella, busta 1943, cat. 8-9-10, fasc. cat. 8a, cl. 2a.

19 The *podestà* was essentially the equivalent of the mayor of a commune. In 1926, Mussolini had dissolved elected communal councils and dismissed elected mayors, or sindaci (sindaco in the singular). Communes then were administered by the *podestà*, appointed by the prefect. In Italian, the plural of *podestà* is *podestà*. I have added an 's' to make the plural clear in English.

20 Renzo De Felice, *Mussolini l'alleato 1940–1945, I. L'Italia in Guerra 1940–1943, 2. Crisi e agonia del regime* (Turin: Einaudi, 1997), 716. Megan Koreman, *The Expectation of Justice: France 1944–1946*, discusses women's food protests in postwar France.

21 ASA Pref. Gab., busta 10, fasc. 4-1 Ord. Pubbl.: Laterina.

22 ASA Pref. Gab., busta 10, fasc. 4-1 Ord. Pubbl.: Castel S. Niccolo.

23 ASA Pref. Gab., busta 10, fasc. 4-1 Ord. Pubbl. Busta 10 contains a folder for each Aretine commune, all devoted to rationing, citizens' complaints, and public order.

24 ASA Pref. Gab. busta 7, fasc. Relazione sullo stato della provincia.

25 Antonio T. Lombardo, 'Un caso di trasgressione sociale. La borsa nera in provincia di Arezzo 1939–1947,' in *Guerra di sterminio e Resistenza. La provincia di Arezzo (1943–1944)*, ed. Ivan Tognarini, 263–302 (Naples: Edizioni Scientifiche Italiane, 1990).

26 ASA Pref. Gab., busta 10, fasc. 4-1 Ord. Pubbl.: Castel S. Niccolo.

27 ASA Pref. Gab., busta 7, fasc. Relazione sullo stato della provincia. This was up from a total of fifty-one for the period from June 1, 1942, to March 31, 1943.

28 Soon after Italy entered the war on June 10, 1940, the first wave of refugees arrived in Italy – Italian nationals from Greece, 'Italian Africa,' France, Yugoslavia, and elsewhere and 'Slovene elements' escaping 'communist persecution.' Those without family in Italy generally stayed in larger cities (including Florence), though some came (or were sent) to Arezzo. ASC Florence, ECA 10446; ACS fondo PNF Servizi Vari, Serie II, busta 191, fasc. Assistenza rimpatriati dall'A.O.I.; busta 192, fasc. Pratica generale, Assistenza Sloveni.

29 ASC Florence, ECA 10443, inserto 12 (1941).

30 ASC Civitella, busta 1943, cat. 8-9-10, fasc. cat. 8a, classe 5a, document dated January 13, 1943. Iris Origo began her war diary with the arrival of refugee children from Genoa on January 30, 1943. Iris Origo, *War in Val d'Orcia: An Italian War Diary, 1943–1944* (Boston: David R. Godine, 1984) (1947).

31 ASC Civitella, busta 1943, cat. 8-9-10, fasc. cat. 8a, cl. 5a, document dated March 12, 1943.

32 ASA Pref. Gab., busta 7, fasc. Relazione sullo stato della provincia.

33 Philip Morgan, *The Fall of Mussolini.*

34 ASC Civitella, busta 1943, cat. 8-9-10, fasc. cat. 8a, cl. 5a. The prefect asked *podestàs* for exact numbers of buildings and places usable for housing refugees and evacuees – and reminded *podestàs* to employ the 'most scrupulous exactitude and realistic standards.'

35 ASA Pref. Gab., busta 24.

36 ASC Civitella, busta 1943, cat. 8-9-10, fasc. cat. 8a, cl. 5a. Owners whose property was requisitioned were promised compensation for its use. Owners who gave over their property voluntarily were permitted to set a reasonable rent, which they complained was rarely paid.

37 ASC Civitella, busta 1943, cat. 8-9-10, fasc. cat. 8a, cl. 5a (emphasis – underscoring – in the original).

38 Internment generally referred to being held in an enclosed, guarded camp and unable to leave. Confinement (*confino*, sometimes called 'free internment') was a less physically restrictive form of detention, whereby individuals and/or families lived in private houses or pensions, usually in small villages, under light surveillance (which often meant having to report to the local police station twice a day). The *confino* system predated the war and had been used against anti-Fascists since 1926. Fabio Galluccio, *I lager in Italia: La memoria sepolta nei duecento luoghi di deportazione fascisti* (Civezzano: Nonluoghi Libere Edizioni, 2003), 218–20, puts the number of wartime, civilian camps within Italy at 120, though says there may have been more. Carlo Spartaco Capogreco, who has written extensively on Italian concentration camps, counts 130. Carlo Spartaco Capogreco, *I campi del Duce: l'internamento civile nell'Italia fascista, 1940–1943* (Turin: Einaudi, 2004).

39 ASA Pref. Gab., busta 7, fasc. Relazione sullo stato della provincia. Although they were discriminated against pursuant to the racial laws of 1938, Italian Jews were not sent to concentration camps within Italy or deported to Germany until after the German occupation and the advent of the Fascist Social Republic. Those interned before the September 8, 1943, armistice would have been foreign (non-Italian) Jews, as at Oliveto.

The Aretine did not have a sizable Jewish population of its own citizens. According to the 1939 census, 34 Jews lived in the province of Arezzo, as compared to 219 in Siena; 2326 in Florence; 10,219 in Milan; and 12,799 in Rome. On June 6, 1943, after the prefect of Arezzo reminded *podestàs* to send data on the number of Jews in their communes by the third of every month, Civitella's *podestà* responded that previously, on September 12, 1942, he already had communicated that no Jews – nor anyone 'born Jewish' – lived in the commune of Civitella. Under the section titled 'Activity of the Jews' in his June 25, 1943, report, Arezzo's *Questore* provided only 'no one' (*nessuno*). ASA Pref. Gab., busta 7, fasc. Relazione sullo stato della provincia; ASC Civitella, busta 1943, cat. 8-9-10, fasc. cat. 8a, cl. 2a, subfasc. Revisione Censim. Ebrei.

As both Susan Zuccotti and Alexander Stille have asserted, the Italian state's less overtly brutal treatment towards its own Jewish citizens before 1943 ultimately served to mislead them into thinking they were safe in remaining in their homes and in Italy. See Susan Zuccotti, *The Italians and the Holocaust: Persecution, Rescue, Survival* (New York: Basic Books, 1987); and Alexander Stille, *Benevolence and Betrayal: Five Jewish Families under Fascism* (New York: Summit Books, 1991). See also Renzo De Felice, *Storia degli ebrei italiani sotto il fascismo* (Turin: Einaudi, 1993). Regarding Libyan Jews, see Renzo De Felice, *Ebrei in un paese arabo: gli ebrei nella Libia contemporanea tra colonialismo, nazionalismo arabo e sionismo (1835–1970)* (Bologna: Il Mulino, 1978). See also Settimio Sorani, *L'assistenza ai profughi ebrei in Italia (1933–1941). Contributo alla storia della Delasem* (Rome: Carucci, 1983), 195.

40 A September 15, 1943, telegram from Arezzo's prefect to the Interior Ministry seems to say (though the handwritten number is not entirely legible) that the camp at Renicci housed about 4000 internees. I have not been able to find other sources confirming this large number. See Carlo Spartaco Capogreco, *Renicci: un campo di concentramento in riva al Tevere* (Milan: Mursia, 2003). After September 8, 1943, Renicci also held Italian anarchists and anti-Fascists. Giorgio Sacchetti, 'Renicci: un campo di concentramento per slavi ed anarchici,' in *Guerra di sterminio e Resistenza*, ed. Ivan Tognarini, 225–61.

41 Fabio Galluccio, *I lager in Italia*, 118.

42 ASA Pref. Gab., busta 7, fasc. Relazione sullo stato della provincia.

43 Ibid.

44 My interviews with June Adams, Florence, June 1999. See also ASC Florence, ECA 10443, filza 4 (1938–1945) Stranieri internati che appartengano a nazioni con le quali siamo in guerra (19 Feb. 1943). For the unpublished

diary of an elderly American woman who was not interned and who spent the worst of the war years in Florence, see Frances L. Otis, 'Diary of an American Woman in Florence 1943–1944,' Hoover Institution Archives, Stanford, CA (collection title: Otis, Frances L., Diary of an American Woman in Florence 1943–1944).

45 ASA Pref. Gab., busta 7, fasc. Relazione sullo stato della provincia.

46 ASA Pref. Gab., busta 6.

47 ASA Pref. Gab., busta 7, fasc. Relazione sullo stato della provincia; and busta 6; ASC Florence, 10443 ECA, filza 4.

48 ASC Florence 10443 ECA, 1938–1945, filza 4.

49 ASC Civitella, busta 1943, cat. XII-XIII-XIV-XV, fasc. cat. 15a, cl. [blank], subfasc. Sussidi agli internati.

50 June Adams does not recall ever receiving financial assistance from the Italian government during the war and does recall that her family was in debt afterwards. Nevertheless, the regime and the state at least articulated an obligation to support the nation's resident enemies.

51 ASC Civitella, busta 1943, cat. XII-XIII-XIV-XV, fasc. cat. 15a, cl. 1a. This incident in no way attempts to describe the overall treatment of Italian and foreign Jews in Italy, or even in Arezzo, but is intended only to place Jews and other internees within the context of the war in the Aretine before October 1943. In the summer of 1943, 40,157 Jews lived in Italy; of these about 6500 were foreigners. Roberto G. Salvadori and Giorgio Sacchetti, *Presenze ebraiche nell'aretino dal XIV al XX secolo* (Florence: Olschki, 1990). For a more complete picture, in addition to Zuccotti and Stille, see Nicola Caracciolo, *Uncertain Refuge: Italy and the Jews during the Holocaust,* trans. Florette Rechnitz Koffler and Richard Koffler (Urbana: University of Illinois Press, 1995); Meir Michaelis, *Mussolini and the Jews: German-Italian Relations and the Jewish Question in Italy 1922–1945* (Oxford: Clarendon Press, 1978); Michele Sarfatti, *Mussolini contro gli ebrei. Cronaca dell'elaborazione delle legge del 1938* (Turin: Silvio Zamorani, 1994); Enzo Collotti, ed., *Razza e fascismo: La persecuzione contro gli ebrei in Toscana (1938–1943)* (Rome: Carocci, 1999).

52 ASC Civitella, busta 1943, cat. XII-XIII-XIV-XV, fasc. cat. 15a, cl. [blank], subfasc. Internati.

53 Fabio Galluccio estimates that about 150 persons died at the Renicci camp. *I lager in Italia,* 118.

54 Jonathan Dunnage, 'Conclusion: Facing the Past and Building for the Future in Postwar Italy,' in *After the War: Violence, Justice, Continuity and Renewal in Italian Society,* ed. Jonathan Dunnage, 90.

55 See James Walston, 'History and Memory of the Italian Concentration Camps,' *The Historical Journal* 40, no. 1 (1997): 169–83; and Davide Rodogno,

'*Italiani brava gente?* Fascist Italy's Policy toward the Jews in the Balkans,' April 1941–July 1943,' *European History Quarterly* 35, no. 2 (2005): 213–40.

56 See the *Journal of Modern Italian Studies* 9, no. 3 (2004) devoted to 'The Hidden Pages of Contemporary Italian History: War Crimes, War Guilt, Collective Memory.' Effie G.H. Pedaliu, 'Britain and the "Hand-over" of Italian War Criminals to Yugoslavia, 1945–48,' *Journal of Contemporary History* 39, no. 4 (2004): 503–29; and Richard Bosworth, 'War, Totalitarianism and "Deep Belief" in Fascist Italy, 1935–43,' *European History Quarterly* 34, no. 4 (2004): 475–505.

57 Percival's and other POW accounts of life at Laterina camp are at NA/PRO WO 311/679 and comprise part of the postwar Allied investigation into conditions there and into possible war crimes. Affidavit of James Percival, dated June 18, 1945. See also NARA RG 331, AFHQ, R 82. On Tobruk and El Alamein, see John Bierman and Colin Smith, *The Battle of Alamein: Turning Point, World War II* (New York: Viking, 2002).

58 NA/PRO WO 311/679, Affidavit of James Percival.

59 Iris Origo, *War in Val d'Orcia*, 31.

60 ASA Pref. Gab. busta 7, fasc. Relazione sullo stato della provincia.

61 Unpublished parish diary of Father Ferrante Bargiardi, Castelnuovo dei Sabbioni, July 25, 1943. Thank you to Emilio Polverini for giving me a copy.

62 Ivano Tognarini, ed., *La guerra di liberazione in provincia di Arezzo 1943/1944*, memorandum from prefect to interior minister, dated July 28, 1943, document no. 16, 21.

63 Diary of Father Ferrante Bagiardi, entries for July 26 and July 27, 1943.

64 ASA Pref. Gab., busta 6.

65 Ivano Tognarini, *La guerra di liberazione in provincia di Arezzo*, document nos. 18–20, 22–23.

66 Gianni Oliva, *La Repubblica di Salò* (Florence: Giunti Gruppo Editoriale – Casterman, 1997). See also ASC Florence, ECA 10443, filza 4: Atti e documenti 6 ag. '43. The king did not dissolve the Fascist Militia until December 8, 1943, by which time the Republican Fascist Militia had formed.

67 On GIL and its predecessors, see Tracy H. Koon, *Believe, Obey, Fight: Political Socialization of Youth in Fascist Italy, 1922–1943* (Chapel Hill: University of North Carolina Press, 1985).

68 Iris Origo, *War in Val d'Orcia*, 50–51.

69 ASC Civitella, busta 1943, cat. 5-6-7, fasc. cat. 6a, cl. Dopolavoro. The *dopolavoro* ('after work') clubs were social and recreational centres instituted during the Fascist regime. For the OND as a force for creating consensus, see Victoria de Grazia, *The Culture of Consent: Mass Organization of Leisure in Fascist Italy* (Cambridge: Cambridge University Press, 1981).

70 ASC Civitella, busta 1943, cat. 5-6-7, fasc. cat. 6a, cl. 1a.
71 ASC Civitella, busta 1943, cat. 5-6-7, fasc. cat. 6a, cl. Dopolavoro.
72 ASC Civitella, busta 1943 cat. 5-6-7, fasc. cat. 6a, cl. 1a.
73 The Allied decision to land in the south, rather than at Rome or farther north has been criticized ever since as an error that needlessly extended the war in Italy. The important works on the Allies' war in Italy are: Eric Linklater, *The Campaign in Italy* (London: HMSO, 1951); G.A. Shepperd, *The Italian Campaign 1943–45: A Political and Military Re-assessment* (London: Arthur Barker, 1968); Douglas Orgill, *The Gothic Line: The Autumn Campaign in Italy, 1944* (London: Heinemann, 1967); Dominick Graham and Shelford Bidwell, *Tug of War: The Battle for Italy, 1943–1945* (New York: St. Martin's Press, 1986); and Rick Atkinson, *The Day of Battle: The War in Sicily and Italy, 1943–1944* (New York: Henry Holt, 2007).
74 My interviews with Elio Scala, Montevarchi, December 1996 and February 1997. Iris Origo recorded the common sentiment on September 12, 1943: 'But how can one expect an army to fight, when its leaders have fled? The King and Badoglio are safe in Sicily: and to Italians of a different stamp, nothing is left but bitter humiliation and shame.' *War in Val d'Orcia*, 70. For Italians of that age, whether ex-soldier or civilian, September 8, 1943, is the date for which they can still remember where they were and what they were doing. Philip Cooke has said that, '8 September 1943 remains a date of almost totemic significance to Italians.' Philip Cooke, ed., *The Italian Resistance: An Anthology* (Manchester: Manchester University Press, 1997), 3. Silvio Bertoldi called September 8 the date of 'triple betrayal' by the king and Badoglio: betrayal of the Germans, the Allies, and the Italian people. Silvio Bertoldi, *Apocalisse Italiana, otto settembre 1943: fine di una nazione* (Milan: Rizzoli, 1998). See also Elena Agarossi, *A Nation Collapses: The Italian Surrender of September 1943* (Cambridge: Cambridge University Press, 1999).
75 ASA Pref. Gab., busta 7, fasc. Relazione sullo stato della provincia.
76 ASC Civitella, busta 1943, cat. 8-9-10, cat. 8a, cl. 4a. Farmers also immediately began hiding animals and produce, rather than give them to the Germans. Ivano Tognarini, ed., *La guerra di liberazione in provincia di Arezzo*, document no. 26, 28.
77 Diary of Father Ferrante Bagiardi, entry for September 10, 1943. On September 10, German troops occupied the town of Chiusi, took control of the railway, and requisitioned private automobiles on the roads. Iris Origo, *War in Val d'Orcia*, 67.
78 Diary of Father Ferrante Bagiardi, entries for September 11 and September 12, 1943.

79 Orders arrived from the camp for the guards of the British prisoners at work at the Origo estate to 'protect' the prisoners from any German attempt to seize them. Iris Origo, *War in Val d'Orcia*, 66.

80 NA/PRO WO 311/679, Affidavit of James Percival, dated June 18, 1945. See also NA/PRO WO 311/679, Affidavit of Charles Wilfred Jones, dated September 25, 1945. ASA Pref. Gab., busta 7, fasc. Relazione sullo stato della provincia.

81 Roger Neil Lewis Absalom, *A Strange Alliance: Aspects of Escape and Survival in Italy 1943–45* (Florence: L.S. Olschki, 1991) treats the relationship – or alliance – between the POWs and the local people (usually peasants) who sheltered and fed them for many months. He stresses the long-term impact of the alliance on the farmers and their families.

82 Iris Origo, *War in Val d'Orcia*, 69.

83 Ivano Tognarini, ed., *La guerra di liberazione in provincia di Arezzo*, document nos. 23 and 24, 26.

84 Diary of Father Ferrante Bagiardi, entries for September 13, 15, 19, and 23, 1943.

85 See Claudio Pavone, 'Tre governi e due occupazioni.' The central (national) CLN formed officially in Rome on September 9, 1943, by Liberal, Democratic Labour, Christian Democrat, Action, Socialist, and Communist Party representatives. On October 16, the central CLN voted to refuse orders from Marshal Badoglio.

86 ASC Civitella, busta 1943, cat. 1a, (classe unspecified). Bruno Rao Torres had been a *fascio* member since 1921. Giuseppe Bronzi, *Il fascismo aretino da Renzino a Besozzo*, 54, fn. 9. On the Fascist Republic, see Giorgio Bocca, *La Repubblica di Mussolini* (Milan: Mondadori, 1994).

87 ASC Civitella, busta 1943, cat. 3a (classe unspecified). The date again had to include the year of the Fascist era in Roman numerals (as the Fascist era had been only briefly interrupted). ASC Civitella, busta 1943 cat. 5-6-7, fasc. cat. 6a, cl. 1a.

88 ASC Civitella, busta 1943, cat. 5-6-7, fasc. cat. 6a, cl. 1a, document dated October 23, 1943, and signed by Bruno Rao Torres.

89 ACS, fondo PNF Servizi Vari, Serie II, Affari generali, busta 846, fasc. S. Giovanni Valdarno – Casa del fascio.

90 ASC Civitella, busta 1943, cat. 5-6-7, fasc. cat. 6a, cl. 1a.

91 ASC Florence, 10443 ECA, filza 4.

92 See the many categories of those assisted by ECA in Florence during 1944. ASC Florence, 10450, ECA, filza 2.

93 In central Italy, the Allies bombed the city of Grosseto in Southern Tuscany on Easter Monday in 1943, killing many civilians, including children. Iris

Origo, *War in Val d'Orcia*, 28–9. In the Aretine, the town (and rail viaduct) of Bucine and the city of Arezzo were the first places to be bombed. ASA Pref. Gab., busta 6, 7; ASC Civitella, busta 1944, fasc. cat. I-II.

94 ASC Civitella, busta 1943, cat. 8-9-10, fasc. cat. 8a, cl. 5a.

95 For the Aretine experience of the bombings, see Enzo Droandi, *Arezzo distrutta 1943–44* (Cortona: Calosci, 1995); and Almo Fanciullini, *Diario di un ragazzo aretino 1943–1944* (Florence: Edizioni Polistampa, 1996). Fanciullini recorded that the fourth bombardment took place January 7, 1944, lasting one minute at 1:05 p.m.; two died, four were wounded. On Saturday, January 15, Arezzo was bombed for the fifth time, from 12:15 to 12:25 p.m., by 34 *quadrimotori* passing in four formations. They reportedly killed nearly one hundred people. The sixth bombardment occurred on January 17 between 12:10 and 12:12 p.m., killing ten and wounding fifteen. The seventh bombardment of the city of Arezzo occurred Saturday, January 22, 1944, lasting from 12:40 to 12:42 p.m., though the alarms had sounded from 12:38 to 15:38. Twenty-four planes had participated. Thirty people were reported killed and about fifty wounded during that two minute raid.

96 ASA Pref. Gab., busta 6.

97 Aroldo Lucarini, the long-time secretary for the commune of Bucine, built his house in 1923 near the Bucine train station, in part so that his son could take the train every day to secondary school in Arezzo. His valuable, unpublished memoir of war and postwar life in the commune of Bucine, 'Ricordi di guerra, 1943–49' (written before his death in the winter of 1953) was donated to the Archivio Diaristico Nazionale in the town of Pieve Santo Stefano (Arezzo) (archive reference number MG/91). Thank you to his granddaughter (the baby referred to in the diary) who allowed me to photocopy and cite the entire memoir.

98 In that raid, eleven B-26s dropped 19.5 tons of bombs. There were no 'hits' according to the bombing unit history – meaning they missed their intended target. Air Force Historical Research Agency, Maxwell Air Force Base, (microfilm) Med. Allied Tac. AF R 8424 (old roll no. A6110), frame 1988.

99 Aroldo Lucarini, 'Ricordi di guerra, 1943–49,' 10.

100 On January 3, 1944, twenty-four B-26s dropped 47 tons of bombs over the Bucine viaduct, again with no hits. Air Force Historical Research Agency, Med. Allied Tac. AF, R 8424 (old roll no. A6110), frames 1988–1905.

101 As for the Allies' ability to carry out precision or 'pinpoint' bombing – or how all those bombers managed to miss that enormous railway bridge – see Stephen L. McFarland, *America's Pursuit of Precision Bombing, 1910–1945* (Washington, DC: Smithsonian Institution Press, 1995), especially chs. 4, 5, 7–9.

102 Don Narcisco Polvani, 'Diario anno 1944,' entry for Monday, January 3, 1944. Thank you to Emilio Polverini for giving me a photocopy of this unpublished diary.

103 Ibid., entry for Sunday, January 23, 1944.

104 Ibid., entries for Monday, January 17 and Tuesday, January 25, 1944.

105 Ibid., entry for Wednesday, January 19, 1944.

106 Ibid., entry for April 12, 1944.

107 Ibid., entries for Sunday January 16, and February 8, 1944.

108 Operation Strangle's mission was to: 'Smash the railroad yards in Central Italy, cut the bridges, strafe the motor transport, hammer the ports, knock out the shipping – in short, to "strangle" German communications through Middle Italy.' Air Force Historical Research Agency, Med. AAF, R 8386 (old roll no. A6074), frames 255–303: 'Operation Strangle – It Worked!' 'Operation STRANGLE is usually dated from 19 March 1944 when the directive for its inception was issued. It ended, strictly speaking, two months later, on 11 May, the day the Allies launched a massive ground offensive against the German lines.' F.M. Sallagar, *Operation 'STRANGLE' (Italy, Spring 1944): A Case Study of Tactical Air Interdiction* (R-851-PR; A Report prepared for United States Air Force Project Rand) (Santa Monica: Rand Corp., 1972), 7. Bombing of the Aretine actually began in November 1943 and continued into June 1944.

109 The Mediterranean Allied Air Force directive of March 19, 1944, set forth the objectives of the campaign: 'To reduce the enemy's flow of supplies to a level which will make it impractical for him to maintain and operate his forces in Central Italy.' F.M. Sallagar, *Operation 'STRANGLE,'* 18, citing AAF History, Vol. III, 373.

110 Air Force Historical Research Agency, Med. Allied Tac. AF, R 8424 (old roll no. A6110).

111 Air Force Historical Research Agency, Med. AAF, R 8386 (old roll no. A6074), frames 255–303: 'Operation Strangle – It Worked!'

112 F.M. Sallagar, *Operation 'STRANGLE,'* 11. A footnote elaborates: 'These are averages for the entire period, including many days when bad flying weather forced all or a portion of the force to stand down. The actual effort reached as high as 3000 sorties on days when conditions were favorable.'

113 'All of the planes over the target reported the majority of bombs fell in the marshaling yards with several hits on the railroad station and other buildings in the yards, causing several fires with smoke billowing up to a thousand feet. Several sticks of bombs were short of the target and some went over the target area and into the city. Two of the planes were unable to drop their bombs on the target due to mechanical difficulties, and instead

attacked targets of opportunity.' Air Force Historical Research Agency, 449
BG, R 0000001748 (old roll no. B0567), frame 928.

114 Air Force Historical Research Agency, Med. Allied Tac. AF, R 8424 (old roll
no. A6110): 'Report on Operation Strangle, 19 Mar. – 11 May 1944 – HQ
Med. Allied Tactical AF APO 650 US Army.' Dominick Graham and Shelford Bidwell said of Operation Strangle: 'Exaggerated claims were made
for [Strangle's] success at the time, and they were repeated in the US Air
Force history … One motive for the exaggerated claims made for Strangle
was to show that the Air Force was a decisive arm … Gordon Saville, a
USAAF officer, told a friend in Washington on April 20: Our waste of effort
in trying to hit railroad tracks and bridges from high altitude is *simply fan-
tastic.' Tug of War*, 231–2 (emphasis in the original).

115 Air Force Historical Research Agency, 17 BG, R 0000001169 (old roll no.
B0082), frame 1094. See also frames 1058, 1066, 1069, and 1078. Morale
suffered as a result of the lack of 'hits.' Among the transfers, parties,
dances, and movies that passed the time and aided morale, the history of
the HQ 17th Bombardment Group for the period over Arezzo is primarily
a record of 'no results' – contrary to the very positive report to the public
in 'Operation Strangle – It Worked!'

116 ASA Pref. Gab., busta 7, fasc. Relazione sullo stato della provincia.

117 Giuseppe Bronzi, *Il fascismo Aretino da Renzino a Besozzo*, 58–59, and n. 25.
The prewar population of the city of Arezzo was about 60,000. NARA RG
331 ACC Italy, 10801/115/23. When Allied troops first entered the city of
Arezzo on July 16, 1944, they found it 'much damaged by our own bomb-
ing and almost empty of civilians.' 'War diary of the HQ 1st Guard
Brigades.'

118 ASA Pref. Gab., busta 10, fasc. 4-1 Ord. Pubbl.: Anghiari. See also Diary of
Father Ferrante Bagiardi, entries for September 17 and September 20, 1943.

119 ASC Civitella, busta 1943, cat. 8-9-10, fasc. cat. 8a, cl. 5a; ASA Pref. Gab.,
busta 6; Ivano Tognarini, ed., *La guerra di liberazione in provincia di Arezzo*,
document no. 28, p. 29, and document no. 66, p. 50.

120 See Don Narciso Polvani, 'Diario anno 1944,' entry for May 5, 1944, regarding the numbers in the Valdarno who went to work for the German organization Todt. According to Father Polvani, many positions were available,
the Germans paid well, and 'what was more important,' they treated the
workers with 'every kindness.' See also Ivano Tognarini, ed., *La guerra di liberazione in provincial di Arezzo*, document no. 40, p. 37. See Bruno Mantelli,
'Italians in Germany, 1938–45: An Aspect of the Rome-Berlin Axis,' in *Italian
Fascism: History, Memory and Representation*, ed. R.J.B. Bosworth and Patrizia
Dogliani, 45–63 (Houndmills: Macmillan, 1999).

121 ASA Pref. Gab., busta 7, fasc. Relazione sullo stato della provincia.

122 Don Narcisco Polvani, 'Diario anno 1944,' entry for Thursday, March 16, 1944. Father Polvani first called them 'partisans' in his June 13, 1944, entry, when he noted that the tax collector refused to take his tax payment, saying he had been so ordered by 'the *Partisans*.' The underscoring in the original may reflect that this was the first time Father Polvani had heard the term, or that he did not agree with it, preferring to characterize them as rebels or bandits.

123 Ibid., entry for March 22, 1944.

124 Years later, Father Polvani's chaplain, Father Cuccoli, told that these 're-bels' were about ten partisans from the 3rd Company Chiatti, all locals, and well known to Father Polvani. Ibid., entry for Thursday, March 30, 1944 and added footnote 47; and entry for Friday, March 31, 1944.

125 Ibid., entry for Friday, March 31, 1944.

126 Ibid., entry for April 28, 1944 (emphasis in the original).

127 Ibid., see entry for January 6, 1944 and added footnote 9.

128 Italian historians used the term 'armed Resistance' (*Resistenza armata*) to refer to the final twenty months of what was a two decades long 'anti-Fascist resistance' (*resistenza antifascista* – without a capital 'r'). The most complete study in English on the entire anti-Fascist resistance is Charles Delzell, *Mussolini's Enemies: the Italian Anti-Fascist Resistance* (Princeton: Princeton University Press, 1961). A brief treatment of the partisan movement appears in the first two chapters of Paul Ginsborg, *A History of Contemporary Italy*. A more critical view of the partisans is presented in the less satisfactory Richard Lamb, *War in Italy: A Brutal Story* (New York: Da Capo Press, 1996), chs. 10 and 11. The presence and roles of women in the partisan movement are studied in Jane Slaughter's *Women and the Italian Resistance, 1943–1945* (Denver: Arden Press, 1997). See also Jomarie Alano, 'Armed with a Yellow Mimosa: Women's Defence and Assistance Groups in Italy, 1943–45,' *Journal of Contemporary History* 38, no. 4 (2003): 615–31. In Italian, the important older works include Guido Quazza, *Resistenza e storia d'Italia* (Milan: Feltrinelli, 1976); Roberto Battaglia, *Storia della Resistenza italiana* (Turin: Einaudi, 1970) (1953); and the writings of Piero Calamandrei, some of which have been collected in Piero Calamandrei, *Uomini e città della Resistenza* (Milan: Linea d'Ombra, 1994).

Most important of the more recent works that raised a number of previously under-considered and subsequently debated issues, is Claudio Pavone, *Una guerra civile. Saggio storico sulla moralità nella Resistenza* (Turin: Bollati Boringhieri, 1991, 1994). Both Pavone and Quazza discuss the range of choices made when joining or participating in the Resistance. See also the selection of texts relating to the Resistance, edited and annotated by Philip Cooke, ed., *The Italian Resistance: An Anthology*.

129 Many of those who volunteered early were killed by early German *rastrella-
    menti* (literally 'combings' or 'rakings,' signifying the thoroughness of Ger-
    man searches for and attacks against the partisans). In the north, by the
    end of January 1944, partisan numbers had been reduced to 9000–10,000.
    Membership rose again to about 100,000 by mid-summer, then declined
    again during the winter of 1944–5. Numbers increased dramatically after
    February 1945, 'swelled by eleventh-hour converts' and increased Allied
    material assistance. See Charles Delzell, *Mussolini's Enemies*, 296. Italian his-
    torian of the resistance, Guido Quazza, also puts the number at 9000 in
    December 1943; 20–30,000 by March 1944; 70–80,000 in May and June of
    that year; reaching 250,000 at liberation on April 25, 1945. Guido Quazza,
    'The Politics of the Italian Resistance,' in *The Rebirth of Italy*, ed. S.J. Woolf,
    1–29, especially 17; and Guido Quazza, *Resistenza e storia d'Italia*. These
    numbers are consistent with the contemporary estimates made by Allied
    Headquarters. NA/PRO WO 204/11465 (AFHQ – British Section – Report
    on German Reprisals for Partisan Activity).
130 Giuseppe Bronzi, *Il fascismo aretino da Renzino a Besozzo*, 57. With a day-by-
    day account of partisan activities and subsequent reprisals, a thorough
    (though certainly not unbiased) work on the partisan resistance in the
    Aretine is Antonio Curina, *Fuochi sui monti dell'Appennino toscano* (Arezzo:
    Tipografia D. Badiali, 1957). Many of the original reports and minutes of
    the Aretine bands' activities are housed at the Istituto Storico della
    Resistenza per Toscana (ISRT) in Florence, fondo ANPI. From early June,
    most of the Aretine partisans divided into three brigades: the XXII Gari-
    baldi Brigade; the XXIII Pio Borri Brigade (named after a young student
    killed at Vallucciole in November 1943); and the XXIV Bande Esterne
    Brigade. See Luciano Casella, *The European War of Liberation: Tuscany and
    the Gothic Line*, trans. Jean M. Ellis D'Alessandro (Florence: La Nuova Eur-
    opa, 1983), ch. 2. The Allies counted six bands and brigades in Arezzo.
    NARA RG 331 ACC Italy, 10801/115/38.
      On the Resistance in Arezzo and Tuscany, see also Nicola Labanca 'Una
    provincia tra RSI e Resistenza' in *Quando le nostre città erano macerie: Im-
    magini e documenti sulle distruzioni belliche in provincia di Arezzo (1943–1944)*,
    ed. Nicola Labanca, 42–58 (Comune Foiano della Chiana, ANPI-Sezione
    'Licio Nencetti'; Montepulciano: del Grifo, 1988); Luigi Arbizzani, ed., *Al
    di qua e al di là della linea Gotica, 1944–1945: aspetti sociali, politici e militari in
    Toscana e in Emilia-Romagna* (Bologna-Florence: Regioni Emilia-Romagna e
    Toscana, 1993); and Ivano Tognarini, ed., *Guerra di sterminio e resistenza.*

131 NA/PRO WO 204/11477, p. 1. See also ASC Cavriglia, busta AR 1946, cat. dalla 6a alla 8a, N. 129, fasc. 1946, cat. 8a, cl. IIIa, fasc. Pensioni e orfani guerra (report of activity of the 3rd Company of Chiatti).

132 There are two villages of San Pancrazio in the province of Arezzo: one in the commune of Bucine and just a few kilometres from Civitella, and the other (where Father Polvani was priest) in the commune of Cavriglia, fairly near Castelnuovo dei Sabbioni.

133 Edoardo Succhielli, 'Primi contatti con la Resistenza' in *La Resistenza nei versanti tra l'Arno e la Chiana*, ed. Edoardo Succhielli, 44–51 (Arezzo: Tipografia Sociale, 1979); Ida Balò Valli, *Giugno 1944: Civitella racconta*, 8 n. 5. The history of the Banda Renzino and CLN criticism of the band is mentioned in Giovanni Contini, *La memoria divisa*, 32–53. Antonio Curina, head of the Resistance in the Aretine, and postwar sindaco of the commune of Arezzo, mentioned the Banda Renzino only once. See Antonio Curina, *Fuochi sui monti dell'Appennino toscano*, 161.

134 NA/PRO WO 204/11479. Field Marshal Kesselring considered highway 69 a road of primary importance. NA/PRO WO 204/11467. The 'Arezzo line' crossed San Pancrazio and Civitella.

135 Albert Kesselring, *The Memoirs of Field-Marshal Kesselring*, trans. William Kimber (London: Greenhill Books 1997) (1953), 225.

136 NA/PRO WO 204/11467. The quoted and paraphrased statements that precede and follow on these pages are taken from contemporary Allied Army translations of captured or intercepted German documents.

137 NA/PRO WO 204/11496, 204/11465, 204/11467.

138 Romano Moretti, *Le donne di San Pancrazio* (Bucine: Comune di Bucine, 1994).

139 ASA Pref. Gab., busta 7: 'i numerosi bombardamenti subiti da questo capoluogo e che hanno disgregato la vita civile cittadina.'

2. Variations on a Massacre

Epigraph: Unpublished memoir of Enrico Centeni-Romani, 'L'Eccidio del popolo di Civitella della Chiana (Arezzo) per opera dei barbari tedeschi il 29 giugno del 1944,' Archivio Diaristico Nazionale, D/97 MFN 2275, 30.

1 NA/PRO WO 311/679, United Nations War Crimes Commission report, case no. UK-G/B 350. Affidavits were gathered as part of an investigation carried out by the judge advocate general, GHQ Central Mediterranean Forces, from the summer of 1945 through 1946.

2 Ibid., affidavit of John More Skelton. The sketchy history of events of the Laterina 'death march' are related in the affidavits of the POWs who took part in the marches.

3 Ibid., affidavit of Anthony Joseph Olender. The number of prisoners at Laterina in June of 1944 was variously estimated (by former inmates) between 800 and 3000.

4 Ibid., affidavit of J. Mellon.

5 Ibid., affidavit of Anthony Joseph Olender. See also the affidavits of Philip Measure, Eric Quick, Charles Gamble, and Daniel John Watson.

6 Ibid., affidavit of J. Mellon. See also the affidavits of M. Levenberg and Philip Measure.

7 Ibid., affidavit of Anthony Joseph Olender, 3.

8 Ibid., affidavits of M. Levenberg, J. Mellon, and Anthony Joseph Olender.

9 Many of the statements quoted in this chapter were taken during the Allied investigation that began November 1, 1944, and consisted primarily of interviews of the survivors and other witnesses. See NA/PRO WO 204/11479, Subject: Atrocities committed by German troops at Civitella, Cornia, and San Pancrazio. Civitella's was one of twenty large-scale massacres investigated in the area. NA/PRO WO 204/11470. A twenty-page report summarizing the Civitella massacre and events leading up to it is followed by 398 pages of witness statements. These were 'witness statements' in the sense that Allied investigators wanted particular, limited information that could be used to determine motive for the killings and to identify and prosecute the perpetrators in the event of a war crimes trial: Were the victims partisans or associated with the partisans? Had the victims received any sort of a trial? Could the witnesses identify the Germans who carried out the killings? Some of these reports are spare and seemingly dispassionate; others are lengthier narratives of the events. The statements were given in Italian and then translated into English, by either a military or a civilian interpreter, and I cite and quote the English translations. Those few witnesses who spoke English gave theirs in English. Original Italian statements are not contained in the NA/PRO materials.

As with any eyewitness evidence, particularly that relating to stressful or traumatic events, perception and recall can be faulty. The precise details of the massacre are not so important, however, as the larger picture; that is, for purposes of recounting the massacre at Civitella in this chapter, I acknowledge their weaknesses and do not hold out the statements as proof of the matter asserted (or that what the witnesses told really happened the way they told it). Nevertheless, the NA/PRO statements do offer the benefit of having been made relatively soon after the events, before they were filtered through postwar suffering and memory.

During the summer of 1945, a few months after Allied investigators took their witness statements and after the war ended, Romano Bilenchi and Marta Chiesi initiated the collection of lengthier testimonies from some of the Civitella witnesses, which Bilenchi published in 1946 in *Società*, the quarterly journal he founded the previous year. 'Strage di Civitella,' *Società* 2, nos. 7–8 (1946). See Victoria de Grazia and Leonardo Paggi, 'Story of an Ordinary Massacre: Civitella della Chiana, 29 June, 1944,' *Cardozo Studies in Law and Literature* 3, no. 2 (1991): 153–69, for Bilenchi's likely reasons for collecting and publishing the testimonies. Though fewer in number than those taken by the Allies, the witnesses were given the opportunity to say more (than Allied investigators had asked for), and so their later testimonies are more detailed. Some witnesses also characterized or interpreted the significance of the massacres. Citing Pietro Clemente, Alesandro Portelli distinguishes between 'the historian's "facts" and the anthropologist's "representations."' Alessandro Portelli, 'The Massacre at Civitella Val di Chiana (Tuscany, June 29, 1944), 140–60. Certainly, statements to Allied investigators and the testimonies collected by Bilenchi and Chiesi are more in the nature of representation than of fact, but representations of the massacre are also important to this study.

A source as important as the contemporary statements collected by the British and by Bilenchi and Chiesi, is Ida Balò Valli, ed., *Giugno 1944: Civitella racconta*. Signora Balò, whose father was killed in the massacre, spent years gathering original relevant documents, and recording the testimonies of those who were children and adolescents at the time of the massacre. Like many of those whose memories form the largest part of the book, she blames Succhielli and the partisans for the German reprisal. She is often considered the 'spokesperson' for the community regarding the massacres. Alessandro Portelli described Balò as the acknowledged 'voice of the community and its memory.' 'The Massacre at Civitella Val di Chiana,' 152. Francesca Cappelletto and Paola Calamandrei collected a number of local oral histories in 1993, and Francesca Cappelletto has published extensively on the transmission of memory of the events. See note 113 below.

The Bilenchi and Chiesi testimonies were later republished in Romano Bilenchi, *Cronaca degli anni neri* (Rome: Riuniti, 1984), 253–89 (see also Bilenchi's preface), and published in English translation in 'The Witnesses of Civitella,' trans. Cheryl Weisberg and Victoria de Grazia, *Cardozo Studies in Law and Literature* 3, no. 2 (1991): 171–95. The testimonies collected by Bilenchi and Chiesi quoted herein are from the published Weisberg and de Grazia English translation, and will be cited as 'The Witnesses of Civitella.'

In the statements collected by the Allied investigators, the women declarants are identified with their husbands' names as their surnames. When citing the NA/PRO statements, I identify the declarant as in the NA/PRO documents. In the testimonies collected by Bilenchi and Chiesi, the women identified themselves by their familial (father's) surname, prefixing the term 'widow' to the names of their dead husbands. When citing those testimonies, I identify the women as they themselves did when giving the testimonies.

10 Exactly who they were and why they were passing through the area is not known. Allied investigators after the war reasonably concluded that they were soldiers in retreat who had become separated from their unit.

11 Laura Guasti (widow Sabatini) also mentioned the four Germans shooting coloured flares in the piazza. Laura Guasti (widow Sabatini), 'The Witnesses of Civitella,' 180. These were not the first German soldiers the villagers had seen. The Germans had installed a munitions storehouse and a fuel warehouse a few kilometres away in early winter 1943.

12 NA/PRO WO 204/11479, March 28, 1945, statement of Edoardo Succhielli, hand-numbered, 20–2. Statements of other witnesses suggest that Succhielli, knowing only four Germans were in the club, decided to disarm them to obtain more weapons for his poorly armed partisan band. Ibid., statement of Dr. Luciano Gambassini, hand-numbered, 23–4. After the shooting at the club, Dr. Gambassini (as he said in his statement) 'sent several messages to partisan bands operating in the vicinity acquainting them of what had occurred and suggesting that Civitella should be occupied by partisans to prevent reprisals on the civil population; as far as I know nothing was done.' Regarding possible reasons for the differences between Gambassini's and Suchielli's versions and characterizations of the *dopolavoro* shootings and what followed, see Victoria de Grazia and Leonardo Paggi, 'Story of an Ordinary Massacre: Civitella della Chiana, 29 June, 1944.' The disputed actions of the partisans – exactly why they came to the *dopolavoro* and who shot first – have contributed to the development of the 'divided memory' (discussed later in this chapter) of the Civitella massacre and its precedents. Giovanni Contini, *La memoria divisa*, especially, 38–41, 228–37; and Ida Balò Valli, ed., *Giugno 1944: Civitella racconta*, 16–45.

13 NA/PRO WO 204/11479, statement of Giuseppina Giorgina Caldelli, hand-numbered, 60–2.

14 The impetus for the encounter (between partisans and the Germans) and for the shootings at the *dopolavoro* was later told by one of the young partisans involved, Vasco Caroti, 'Lo scontro nel *dopolavoro* di Civitella,' in

La Resistenza nei versanti tra l'Arno e la Chiana, ed. Edoardo Succhielli, 148–53. In the Bilenchi and Chiesi testimonies, several female witnesses began their statements by telling of the partisans shooting the Germans in the *dopolavoro,* even though they had not seen either the partisans or the Germans: 'During the afternoon of June 18th, five [sic] Germans came to spend the evening in Civitella and went drinking in the *dopolavoro,* where partisans came and killed them.' Maddelena Scaletti (widow Sestini), 'The Witnesses of Civitella,' 175.

15 NA/PRO WO 204/11479, statement of Giuseppina Giorgina Caldelli, hand-numbered, 60; and statement of Luigi Lammioni, hand-numbered, 39–40. Laura Guasti (widow Sabatini) recounted that the day after the shooting, a woman from Gebbia (Signora Cau) told the villagers not to abandon the town (or their 'houses would be looted and destroyed and the woods combed to find the inhabitants.' Because Signora Cau was an interpreter at the German Army Headquarters, 'she promised to take care of the matter and explain to the Germans that the culprits were not local people.' 'The Witnesses of Civitella,' 181.

16 In April, German troops had massacred civilians in the towns of Partina and Vallucciole, both located in the Casentino. Most of the women witnesses at Civitella described the fear of reprisal, the near community-wide flight from the village the day after the shooting, followed by the return some days later. 'The Witnesses of Civitella,' 171, 173–4, 176, 178, 181, 184–5, 189, 192. See also the unpublished memoir of Enrico Centeni-Romani (cited in the chapter epigraph), who lived in Caggiolo, about two kilometres from Civitella. His sister, who worked at the hospital in Civitella came home about seven-thirty in the morning on June 19 and told her family that partisans killed two Germans and wounded a third the previous evening. Centeni-Romani went to Civitella, where he saw the bodies of the dead German soldiers still in the *dopolavoro.* He too hid in the countryside, waiting for the expected reprisal.

17 San Pancrazio, in the commune of Bucine, borders the wooded zone of Montaltuzzo.

18 NA/PRO WO 204/11479, statement of Daniele Tiezzi, hand-numbered, 26; statement of Domenica Dondolini, hand-numbered, 43–4.

19 Ibid., statement of Uliana di Mario Caldelli (sic), hand-numbered, 96; statement of Luigi Lammioni, hand-numbered, 40; statement of Aldo Tavarnesi, hand-numbered, 67–9. Oral history of Lara Lammioni, 2. Laura Guasti (widow Sabatini), 'The Witnesses of Civitella,' 181–2.

20 NA/PRO WO 204/11479, statement of Daniele Tiezzi, hand-numbered, 26. The survivors and British investigators interpreted this action as a potential

reprisal, abandoned when the Germans realized not enough men were left in the village.

21 Ibid., hand-numbered, 380, 382, 389, 391, 395, 403. A couple of witnesses said German soldiers arrived as early as June 15 or June 18. Ibid., hand-numbered, 385, 400.

22 Ibid., Report 4–5, 12–13; also the statement of Edoardo Succhielli, hand-numbered, 20–2. On the 'Battle of Montaltuzzo' see Edoardo Succhielli, 'La Battaglia di Montaltuzzo,' *La Resistenza nei versanti tra l'Arno e la Chiana*, ed. Edoardo Succhielli, 175–86.

23 'Rebels' meant partisans. Oral history of Lara Lammioni, 2. Neither the German communiqué nor reassurance by the priest or *podestà* appears in any of the statements given to British investigators. This official reassurance exists in the memory of the survivors, however. Several of the women later noted having heard or been told that it was safe to return to Civitella. 'Later people told us that two nearby command posts had said that we could return without fear and we did so.' Anna Cetoloni (widow Caldelli), 'The Witnesses of Civitella,' 171. See also Elda Morfini (widow Paggi), 'The Witnesses of Civitella,' 185. Alduina Menchetti, who with her husband operated the *dopolavoro* where the Germans had been shot, told Allied investigators that the Germans did not 'publish any handbills about reprisals or Partisans. Everyone thought that some reprisal would be taken but no one knew definite[ly], to the best of my knowledge.' NA/PRO WO 204/11479, hand-numbered, 35–6.

24 In retrospect, the surviving villagers interpreted the search for radios to have been a pretext so that German soldiers could discover if the men had returned to the village. Anna Cetaloni (widow Caldelli), 'The Witnesses of Civitella,' 171.

25 NA/PRO WO 204/11479. See Carlo Gentile, 'La divisione Hermann Göring in Toscana,' in *La politica del massacro*, ed. Gianluca Fulvetti and Francesca Pelini, 213–40 (Naples: L'ancora del Mediterraneo, 2006). Three Italians – Republican Fascists – were identified as having taken part in the massacres at San Pancrazio and Cornia, and possibly at Civitella as well. NA/PRO WO 204/11479, 18–19; statement of Gino Bartolucci, hand-numbered, 32; statement of Domenica Dondolini, hand-numbered, 44; statement of Maria Assunta Lammioni, hand-numbered, 57–8. See also Maria Assunta Menchetti (widow Lammioni), 'The Witnesses of Civitella,' 193.

26 NA/PRO WO 204/11479, statement of Giuseppa Tiezzi, hand-numbered, 100–2. Giuseppa Marsili (widow Tiezzi), 'The Witnesses of Civitella,' 180. My interview with Dino Tiezzi, December 20, 1997.

27 Elda Morfini (widow Paggi), 'The Witnesses of Civitella,' 186–7. NA/PRO WO 204/11479, statement of Pia Mucciarini, hand-numbered, 182.

28 Ibid., statements of Daniele Tiezzi, hand-numbered, 27; Alduina Menchetti, hand-numbered, 35–38; Laura Guasti Sabatini, hand-numbered, 50–53. The priest's instruction to 'give them whatever they ask of you' and to let the Germans 'take what they wanted' was noted by several of the women witnesses. Maddalena Scaletti (widow Sestini), 'The Witnesses of Civitella,' 176; Laura Guasti (widow Sabatini), 'The Witnesses of Civitella,' 182. See also Ida Balò Valli, *Giugno 1944: Civitella racconta*, 91.

29 NA/PRO WO 204/11479, statement of Rino Cesarini, hand-numbered, 77–8; statement of Giovanni Bianchi, hand-numbered, 80–2.

30 Ibid., statement of Alduina Menchetti, hand-numbered, 36. See also Elda Morfini, 'The Witnesses of Civitella,' 187; NA/PRO WO 204/11479, statement of Laura Guasti Sabatini, hand-numbered, 52.

31 NA/PRO WO 204/11479, 36, 52, 58, 96. Their flight to the woods and to the orphanage is another near constant in the women's repeated testimonies. 'The Witnesses of Civitella,' 172, 175, 183, 188, 195. The orphanage had moved to Poggiali, about three kilometres west of Civitella, to avoid Allied bombings. See Ida Balò Valli, ed., *Giugno 1944: Civitella racconta*, 111.

32 NA/PRO WO 204/11479, statement of Alduina Menchetti, hand-numbered, 37.

33 Ibid., statement of Lina Rossi, hand-numbered, 65–6.

34 Ibid., statements of Daniele Tiezzi, hand-numbered, 27–8; Gino Bartolucci, hand-numbered, 31–4.

35 Alessandro Portelli discusses the memory/fact that Father Lazzeri asked the Germans to shoot him and spare the villagers, an act remembered and recounted later, but not told in the earliest statements. 'The Massacre at Civitella Val di Chiana (Tuscany, June 29, 1944),' 152 and n. 28. See Ida Balò Valli, ed., *Giugno 1944: Civitella racconta*, 95–6.

36 NA/PRO WO 204/11479, statement of Daniele Tiezzi, hand-numbered, 25–9.

37 Giuseppa Marsili (widow Tiezzi) told of searching in the woods for her wounded son, her caring for him as best she could, while he hid in a ravine for ten days until the front passed. 'The Witnesses of Civitella,' 180. Daniele Tiezzi went on to become a well-loved priest in Arezzo. He died in January 1997, and is buried in the cemetery at Civitella.

38 NA/PRO WO 204/11479, statement of Gino Bartolucci, hand-numbered, 34. See also ibid., statement of Irma Bartolucci (his daughter), hand-numbered, 104–5.

39 The British investigative report provides that the 'story of what happened in the village is a little confused as all the men except four were killed.' Ibid., 6.

40 Ibid., statement of Aldo Tavarnesi, hand-numbered, 68–9.

41 Ibid., statement of Luigi Lammioni, hand-numbered, 39–42.

42 Ibid., 78, 81. The story of the massacre at Civitella was also told in Enrico Biagini, *Civitella. Un paese, un castello, un martirio.* For the story of the massacre as told by the Banda Renzino, see Vasco Caroti, '29 Giugno 1944' and Edoardo Succhielli, 'Durante gli eccidi' and 'Gli eccidi,' in *La Resistenza nei versanti tra l'Arno e la Chiana,* ed. Edoardo Succhielli, 195–8, 198–200, 208–12, respectively.

43 NA/PRO WO 204/11479, statements of Dario Polletti, hand-numbered, 246–7; Maria Chiatti, hand-numbered, 248–9; Orazio Casini, hand-numbered, 251; Dante Pasquini, hand-numbered, 256–7; Dino Amazzoni, hand-numbered, 258–9.

44 Ibid., statement of Angiolino Biagiotti, hand-numbered, 166–7.

45 Ibid., statement of Maria Chiatti, hand-numbered, 248–9.

46 Ibid., statement of Don Natale Romanelli, hand-numbered, 209–11.

47 Ibid., statement of Dino Amazzoni, hand-numbered, 258–9.

48 Ibid., statement of Giulia Valenti, hand-numbered, 270.

49 Ibid., statements of Golsa Nannini, hand-numbered, 311–12; Bianca Panzieri, hand-numbered, 265–6; Ugo Casciotti, hand-numbered, 267–9; Giulia Valenti, hand-numbered, 270; Consiglia Del Debole, hand-numbered, 274; Elia Nannini, hand-numbered, 276; Settimia Tanfoni, hand-numbered, 279; Alfredo Serboli, hand-numbered, 283–4; Eugenia Panzieri, hand-numbered, 289–90.

50 Ibid., statement of Ugo Casciotti, hand-numbered, 268.

51 Ibid., 267.

52 Ibid., 268; statement of Arnaldo Savini, hand-numbered, 281.

53 Ibid., statement of Ugo Casciotti, hand-numbered, 268.

54 Ibid.

55 Ibid., statements of Arnaldo Savini, hand-numbered, 280–2; Alfredo Serboli, hand-numbered, 283–4.

56 Thank you to Romano Moretti for sharing with me the extensive research he has carried out on the massacre at San Pancrazio and for allowing me to quote and cite the interviews and oral testimonies he collected.

57 Aroldo Lucarini, 'Ricordi di guerra, 1943–49,' 16e.

58 NA/PRO WO 204/11479, statements of Franca Cardinali, hand-numbered, 263; Consiglia Del Debole, hand-numbered, 273; Teresa Panzieri, hand-numbered, 291; Livia Bindi, hand-numbered, 292; Emilia Arrigucci, hand-numbered, 303; Narcisca Ciofi, hand-numbered, 313; Eride Tiezzi, hand-numbered, 320; Ottavio Felicioni, hand-numbered, 340; Vittoria Pratesi, hand-numbered, 342; Leda Fiorvanti, hand-numbered, 343; Argentina Del Bellino, hand-numbered, 344–5; Father Raimondo Caprara, hand-numbered, 388.

59 Ibid., statements of Antonio Carletti, Carolina Carletti, Licia Carletti, Giorgio Gori, Lina Gori, Aurora Gori, hand-numbered, 354–71.

60 Ibid., statement of Antonio Carletti, hand-numbered, 354.

61 Ibid., 355.

62 Ibid., 355–6.

63 Ibid., statement of Maria Stangini, hand-numbered, 372.

64 Ibid., statements of Venicio Pagi, hand-numbered, 373; Dr. Antonio Celata, hand-numbered, 374.

65 Ibid., statement of Gina Polverini, hand-numbered, 349–51.

66 Ibid., statements of Argentina Del Bellino, 344–5; Dante Salvadori, hand-numbered, 346; Fernando Salvadori, hand-numbered, 348; Gina Polverini, hand-numbered, 349–50.

67 The numbers and names and exact whereabouts of who was killed vary according to the sources. The British inquest reports provides 212 victims, but included some names killed after June 29. Giovanni Contini, citing Romano Moretti, says ninety-five were killed at Civitella, sixty at San Pancrazio, and forty-eight at Cornia. Two had been killed on June 23 during the 'battle of Montaltuzzo.' Another fifty-seven died in the area after June 29 from war-related causes. See Giovanni Contini, *La memoria divisa*, 19, fn. 1.

68 NA/PRO WO 204/11479, statement of Edoardo Succhielli, hand-numbered, 20–2. See also Edoardo Succhielli, 'Durante gli eccidi' and 'I giorni della fame,' *La Resistenza nei versanti tra l'Arno e la Chiana*, ed. Edoardo Succhielli, 200, 211.

69 NA/PRO WO 204/11479, statement of Alduina Menchetti, hand-numbered, 37.

70 Ibid., statement of Giuseppina Giorgina Caldelli, hand-numbered, 61–2.

71 Ibid., statement of Alduina Menchetti, hand-numbered, 37–8.

72 Ada Sistini (widow Caldelli), 'The Witnesses of Civitella,' 173.

73 Uliana Merini (widow Caldelli), 'The Witnesses of Civitella,' 175.

74 NA/PRO WO 204/11479, statement of Alduina Menchetti, hand-numbered, 37–8.

75 Ibid., statements of Bruno Cocchini, hand-numbered, 72–3; Giuseppa Tiezzi, hand-numbered, 101; Giuseppa Bozzi, hand-numbered, 119.

76 Ibid., statement of Dino Amazzoni, hand-numbered, 258–9.

77 Ibid., statement of Dante Pasquini, hand-numbered, 256–7.

78 Ibid., statement of Don Natale Romanelli, hand-numbered, 209–11.

79 The massacres in the commune of Cavriglia were also the subject of an investigation. CSM W. Crawley (Det. 78 Section, SIB), 'on 11 September 44, in the company of Sgt. Vickers and various interpreters of this Branch, [I] commenced enquiries at Castelnuovo dei Sabbioni, Arezzo, scene of No. 1 atrocity. During this period I interviewed over 300 civilians and obtained

over 200 statements.' Crawley's forty-two page report is followed by some 400 pages of witness statements. NA/PRO WO 204/11477. Viligiardi's statements are at hand-numbered, 56–7, and 4 July 45 additional report of W. Crawley, 1–9. Like most informants, his three statements, given to British investigators several months apart, differ materially; he changed his story as necessary.

80 The interpreter Pericle Sorbi was a nineteen year old student, fluent in German, whose family had evacuated from San Giovanni to Terranuova, about three kilometres away. NA/PRO WO 204/11477, statement of Pericle Sorbi, hand-numbered, 58–60.

81 Ibid., 59.

82 NA/PRO WO 204/11477, 2. The series of events leading up to the massacres has been carefully reconstructed recently by Filippo Boni, *Colpire la comunità: 4–11 luglio 1944. Le stragi naziste a Cavriglia in terra d'Avane* (n.p. 2007).

83 NA/PRO WO 204/11477, 2–3.

84 Ibid., 4.

85 Ibid., 5.

86 Ibid., 5–6. These are remarks of the Allied investigating officer.

87 Ibid., statement of Gugliema Cristofani, hand-numbered, 258.

88 The massacre at Castelnuovo dei Sabbioni is summarized in NA/PRO WO 204/11477, 11–13. The massacres (and memories of the massacres) at Castelnuovo, and the other villages of Cavriglia are also described in *Perché la memoria non si cancelli: Gli eccidi del Luglio 1944 nel territorio di Cavriglia*, ed. Emilio Polverini and Dante Priore (Cavriglia: Comune di Cavriglia, 1994), 27–65. See also Claudio Manfroni, 'Cavriglia, luglio 1944. La memoria degli eccidi,' in *La politica del massacro*, ed. Gianluca Fulvetti and Francesca Pelini, 281–314

89 Emilio Polverini's father was not found by the Germans as they carried out their house to house search. He joined the men in the piazza, however, under the tragically mistaken belief that the Germans would burn the houses of those men who did not 'report' to the piazza. My interviews with Emilio Polverini, Castelnuovo dei Sabbioni, between May 13, 1997 and July 2007.

90 Thank you to Emilio Polverini for giving me a copy of Sister Delfino's handwritten recollections prepared soon after the events.

91 NA/PRO WO 204/11477, 11–12. See Romano Macucci, *Pane Spezzato. Breve storia di tre preti eroici: Ferrante Bagiardi, Giovanni Fondelli, Ermete Morini* (Fiesole: Servizio Editoriale Fiesolano, 1994), regarding the three priests killed during the massacres in the commune of Cavriglia. It was Father Bagiardi who had recorded in his parish diary the events of Mussolini's fall and foundation of the Salò Republic. It was also Father Bagiardi, about whose 'political sympathies' Father Polvani had written disapprovingly. See chapter 1.

92 NA/PRO WO 210/11477, 12–13, and thank you to Emilio Polverini for showing me where the events of the massacre took place in and around the village.

93 NA/PRO WO 204/11477, 11–12.

94 Ibid., 12–13.

95 Ibid., statement of Grigione (sic) Polverini, hand-numbered, 291. Two who had been killed near the cemetery and four others who lay at different spots outside the piazza escaped the burning.

96 Ibid., statement of Cesarina Camici, hand-numbered, 123.

97 Of the two men spared, one was an invalid and the other was an evacuee from San Giovanni Valdarno who carried documents signed by the German command at Montevarchi, certifying that he was engaged in essential work for the Germans and was not to be drafted into other work. Ibid., 7. The massacre at Meleto is summarized in ibid., 6–11.

98 Ibid., statements of Cesarina Camici, hand-numbered, 123–4; Maria Camici, hand-numbered, 125; Odilia Camici, hand-numbered, 126–7.

99 Father Morini was known as a supporter and helper of the partisans. The events at Massa are summarized in NA/PRO WO 204/11477, 16–19.

100 Ibid., 11.

101 The Allied investigator concluded later: 'Significantly enough Le Màtole was the home of relatives of Vannini Nello the Partisan Commander of that Area. It is also admitted locally that the inhabitants of Le Màtole were notoriously Pro-Partisan.' Ibid., 20.

102 Ibid., statement of Libera Benucci, hand-numbered, 356. See also page 8 of the later report, in which Viligiardi admitted being in Le Màtole on July 11, but denied observing the massacre.

103 NA/PRO WO 204/11477, 20–1; statement of Libera Benucci, hand-numbered, 356–7.

104 Emilio Polverini and Dante Priore, eds., *Perché la memoria non si cancelli*, 63, 137–42; my interviews with Emilio Polverini.

105 On the barbarization of war – as war's effect and as Wehrmacht policy – on the eastern front, see especially Omer Bartov, *The Eastern Front, 1941–1945: German Troops and the Barbarisation of Warfare* (New York: Palgrave, 2d ed. 2001); 'The Conduct of War: Soldiers and the Barbarization of Warfare,' *Journal of Modern History* 64, Supplement (December 1992): 32–45; Theo J. Schulte, *The German Army and Nazi Politics in Occupied Russia* (Oxford: Berg, 1989).

106 ASC Bucine, busta Danni di Guerra, fasc. Edifici Pubblici, Strade e ponti, scuole 1945. See NA/PRO WO 204/11477, 13 and 18–22, for comments made by German soldiers in the area to Italians regarding the massacres as being in retaliation for partisan actions.

107 Alessandro Portelli, *The Order has been Carried Out: History, Memory, and Meaning of a Nazi Massacre in Rome* (New York: Palgrave Macmillan, 2003); and *L'ordine è già eseguito: Roma, le Fosse Ardeatine, la memoria* (Rome: Donzelli, 1999, 2001) uses oral histories to tell about the massacre, the disputes regarding it, and Romans' 'divided memory' of it. See John Foot, 'Review Article: Via Rasella, 1944: Memory, Truth, and History,' *The Historical Journal* 43, no. 4 (2000): 1173–81. See also Robert Katz, *Death in Rome* (New York: Macmillan, 1967).

108 Ivan Tognarini described some of the massacres carried out in Tuscany during the summer of 1944, categorizing those at Castelnuovo and Meleto as cases of massacre '*in itinere.*' He also provides an appendix of documents on German atrocities and Kesselring's postwar trial. *Kesselring e le stragi nazifasciste. 1944: estate di sangue in Toscana* (Rome: Carocci, 2002).

109 NA/PRO WO 204/11479, 13; statements of Gina Polverini, hand-numbered, 349–51; Domenica Dondolini, hand-numbered, 43; and my interview with Romano Moretti, Florence, June 10, 1997.

110 The literature on the massacres, the memory of them, and the reasons for them (the connection to German occupation policies and the conduct of the war in Italy as a war against civilians) is quite vast. In addition to titles already cited, see Paolo Pezzino, 'The German Military Occupation of Italy and the War against Civilians,' *Modern Italy* 12, no. 2 (2007): 173–88; Michele Battini and Paolo Pezzino, *Guerra ai civili. Occupazione tedesca e politica del massacro. Toscana 1944* (Venice: Marsilio, 1997); Lutz Klinkhammer, *L'occupazione tedesca in Italia* (Turin: Bollati Boringhieri, 1993), arguing that German units' relative autonomy allowed them to respond to partisan attacks and to the retreat in general in various more or less violent ways (and explains why they did so); Lutz Klinkhammer, *Stragi naziste in Italia. La guerra contro i civili (1943–44)* (Rome: Donzelli, 1997); Gerhard Schreiber, *La vendetta tedesca. 1943–1945. Le rappresaglie naziste in Italia* (Milan: Mondadori, 2000); Friedrich Andrae, *La Wehrmacht in Italia. La guerra delle forze armate tedesche contro la popolazione civile 1943–1945* (Rome: Riuniti, 1997); Gianluca Fulvetti, 'Le guerre ai civili in Toscana'; Paolo Pezzino, 'Crimini di guerra nel settore occidentale della linea gotica'; and Luca Baldissara, 'Guerra totale, guerra partigiana, guerra ai civili,' all in *La politica del massacro,* ed. Gianluca Fulvetti and Francesca Pelini; Paolo Pezzino, 'Guerra ai civili. Le stragi tra storia e memoria'; and Lutz Klinkhammer, 'La politica di occupazione nazista in europa. Un tentativo di analisi strutturale,' both in *Crimini e memorie di guerra,* ed. Luca Baldissara and Paolo Pezzino, 5–88 (Naples: L'Ancora del mediterraneo, 2004). See also Luca Baldissara, 'Giudizio e castigo. La brutalizzazione della guerra e le

contradizioni della "giustizia politica,"' in *Giudicare e punire*, ed. Luca Bald-issara and Paolo Pezzino, 5–73 (Naples: L'ancora del mediterraneo, 2006); Michael Geyer, 'Civitella in Val di Chiana, 29 giugno 1944. Ricostruzione di un "intervento" tedesco,' in *La memoria del nazismo nell'Europa di oggi*, ed. Leonardo Paggi, 3–48 (Florence: La Nuova Italia, 1997).

111 In addition to *La memoria divisa*, see also Giovanni Contini, 'Toscana 1944: una storia della memoria delle stragi naziste,' in *La politica del massacro*, ed. Gianluca Fulvetti and Francesca Pelini; Paolo Pezzino, *Anatomia di un massacro: Controversia sopra una strage tedesca* (Bologna: Il Mulino, 1997); Leonardo Paggi, 'Storia di una memoria antipartigiana,' in *Storia e memoria di un massacro ordinario*, ed. Leonardo Paggi (Rome: Manifestolibri, 1996).

112 Claudio Pavone, *Una Guerra civile. Saggio storico sulla moralità nella Resistenza*, especially ch. 7 'La violenza' and subpart 4 'Le rappresaglie e le controrap-presaglie' (475–92). See also Claudio Pavone, 'La seconda guerra mondi-ale: una guerra civile europa?,' in *Guerre fratricide. Le guerra civili in età contemporanea*, ed. Gabriele Ranzato, 86–128 (Turin: Bollati Boringhieri, 1994).

113 In addition to titles already cited, see Francesca Cappelletto (using ethno-graphic methods and oral histories to consider the transmission of memo-ry and the differing memories of the massacres), 'Social Relations and War Remembrance: Second World War Atrocities in Rural Tuscan Villages,' *History and Anthropology* 17, no. 3 (2006): 245–66; Francesca Cappelletto, 'Pub-lic Memories and Personal Stories: Recalling the Nazi-fascist Massacres,' in *Memory and the Second World War: An Ethnographic Approach*, ed. Francesca Cappelletto (London: Berg, 2005); Francesca Cappelletto, 'Memories of Nazi-Fascist Massacres in Two Central Italian Villages,' *Sociologia Ruralis* 38, no. 1 (1998): 69–85.

114 Filippo Focardi, *La guerra della memoria: La Resistenza nel dibatto politico italiano dal 1945 a oggi* (Bari and Rome: Laterza, 2005). See David Ellwood, 'Intro-duction,' and Paolo Pezzino, 'The Italian Resistance between History and Memory,' *Journal of Modern Italian Studies* 10, no. 4 (2005): 385–412, and works cited therein; Andrea Mammone, 'A Daily Revision of the Past: Fas-cism, Anti-Fascism, and Memory in Contemporary Italy,' *Modern Italy* 11, no. 2 (2006): 211–26; Robert Ventresca, 'Debating the Meaning of Fascism in Contemporary Italy,' *Modern Italy* 11, no. 2 (2006): 189–209. On *Italiani brava gente*, see Filippo Focardi, *L'immagine del cattivo tedesco e il mito del bravo ital-iano: la costruzione della memoria del fascismo e della seconda guerra mondiale in Ita-lia* (Padua: Rinoceronte, 2005); David Bidussa, *Il mito del bravo italiano* (Milan: Il Saggiatore, 1994); Claudio Pavone, 'Introduction,' *Journal of Mod-ern Italian Studies* 9, no. 3 (2004): 271–9, and works cited therein; Claudio

Fogu, 'Italiani brava gente. The Legacy of Fascist Historical Culture on Italian Politics of Memory,' in *The Politics of Memory in Postwar Europe*, 147–76 (Durham: Duke University Press, 2006). See Donald Sassoon, 'Italy after Fascism: The Predicament of Dominant Narratives,' in *Life after Death: Approaches to a Cultural and Social History of Europe during the 1940s and 1950s*, ed. Richard Bessel and Dirk Schumann, 259–90, regarding the 'national collective' and postwar and 1950s' narrative of Italiani 'brava gente.' On the notion that even the Italian army was always more humane than the German, see Filippo Focardi and Lutz Klinkhammer, 'The Question of Fascist Italy's War Crimes: The Construction of a Self-acquitting Myth (1943–1948),' *Journal of Modern Italian Studies* 9, no. 3 (2004): 330–48. Adopting the narrative or myth of Resistance was not possible during the cold war decade after the war's end, Pezzino and others argue, because of the communist association with the Resistance. More general anti-Fascism, however, was acceptable earlier as a unifying theme for the new democratic republic.

115 On Saturday, June 17, 1944, an 'overcast' day, when it showered after lunch, Father Polvani wrote, 'these times are ever more saddening. Half a civil war. The English are advancing and the Germans retreating, and we feel all the *disagio* of the present moment. Here, we are safe enough, but nearby San Giovanni has fallen prey to panic and not a single person remains in the village.' He goes on to say whose houses bombs have hit. 'Not one family can claim a bit of quiet; everywhere there is uncertainty, dread, fear.' See Stuart Woolf, 'Historians: Private, Collective and Public Memories of Violence and War Atrocities,' in *Memory and World War II*, ed. Francesca Cappelletto, on the significance of the inclusive term Nazi-Fascist, and questions of memory and morality.

116 NA/PRO WO 204/11465, Report on German Reprisals for Partisan Activity in Italy.

117 The 'cabinet of shame' and its implications for postwar and contemporary Italy, and the absence of an 'Italian Nuremberg' for Italy's war crimes have now been considered in depth. See Michele Battini, *The Missing Italian Nuremberg: Cultural Amnesia and Postwar Politics*, and 'Sins of Memory: Reflections on the lack of an Italian Nuremberg and the Administration of International Justice after 1945,' *Journal of Modern Italian Studies* 9, no. 3 (2004): 349–62; Filippo Focardi and Lutz Klinkhammer, 'La questione dei "criminali di guerra" italiani e una commissione di inchiesta dimenticata,' *Contemporanea* 4, no. 3 (2001): 497–528; Mimmo Franzinelli, *Le stragi nascoste. L'armadio della vergogna: Impunità e rimozione dei crimini di guerra nazifa-*

scisti 1943–2001 (Milan: Mondadori, 2002); Franco Giustolisi, *L'Armadio della vergogna* (Rome: Nutrimenti, 2004); Filippo Focardi, 'I mancati processi ai criminali di guerra italiani, in *Giudicare e punire,* ed. Luca Baldissara and Paolo Pezzino, 185–214. See also *La Repubblica* for March 30, 2003, 'Ma in Italia Norimberga non c'è stata' ('Dialoghi' between Adriano Sofri and Michele Battini, regarding Battini's, *Peccati di memoria* (Bari and Rome: Laterza, 2003).

3. Completing the Disintegration

Epigraphs: Don Narciso Polvani, 'Diario anno 1944,' entry for August 20, 1944. From the sindaco of Cavriglia's list of verified military offensives (Allied and German) that took place in the commune, prepared January 10, 1945. ASC Cavriglia, busta Arch. Regno 1945, cat. 1a e 2a, N. 124, fasc. Decreto Indennità di Bombardamento.

1 What that communication was or how it reached the bishop in Fiesole is not now known. That something 'horrible' had happened on July 4, 1944, in Meleto, Massa, and Castelnuovo was apparent, because smoke rising from the villages could be seen from 'far away.'

2 On Sunday, November 19, 1944, Father Ciabattini returned again to Castelnuovo as the priest for the church of San Donato. He remained – fighting communism – until March 1958. In 1974, to commemorate the thirtieth anniversary of the Resistance in the diocese of Fiesole, Father Ciabattini was asked to make a report on his trip with the bishop to the sites of the massacres. He did so in the form of a reconstructed daily diary. Father Ciabattini died the year after he wrote his recollections. A portion of Father Ciabattini's 'Diario: 8–11 Luglio 1944' was later published in three instalments from July 15 to 29, 1984, in *Toscana oggi – La Parola di Fiesole,* which I quote and cite here. Thank you to Emilio Polverini for providing me with a copy.

3 According to Father Ciabattini, one villager said the Germans had prohibited the burial; however, others said that the partisans ordered them to remain unburied, so that approaching Allied troops would see the slaughter. A Radio London broadcast of October 19, 1944, telling of the massacres in the Valdarno, provided that the dead of Castelnuovo were left in the piazza with the absolute prohibition against burying them. 'London Calling Italy (*La voce di Londra*)' broadcast October 19, 1944, 16:30 BST via Bari radio. The source of the prohibition was not specified in the broadcast. In other areas (though not the Aretine), the Germans sometimes had ordered

bodies of murdered partisans (or suspected partisans) to remain unburied for twenty-four hours.

4 This is the San Pancrazio in the commune of Cavriglia, a few kilometres northwest of Castelnuovo, not the San Pancrazio in the commune of Bucine which suffered the June 29, 1944, massacre.

5 Don Narcisco Polvani, 'Diario anno 1944,' entry for Sunday, July 9, 1944. Contrary to his usual practice of recording the day's events on that day, part of the diary entry for July 4, 1944, seems to have been written some days later. Rather than noting the weather, he referred to July 4 as a 'day of blood.' He did record that on that Sunday (July 9) he said mass for the souls of three bombing victims, and that 'columns' of Germans were seen heading to Castelnuovo; the young men had fled to the woods; sounds of explosions came from the mines; and flames were seen coming from Meleto.

6 On July 11, 1944, Father Polvani wrote to the bishop, 'only Your Excellency – as both religious authority and civil authority – was able to face that difficult path, under such great hardship, to console the people.' Writing ten years after the events, Father Cuccoli noted 'the visit of the Bishop was greatly appreciated and was a great comfort to a people lacking every other civil authority.' Don Aldo Cuccoli, '4 Luglio 1944 – Come morirono,' 'Commemorazione Decennale 4 Luglio 1944,' published in six instalments in *Toscana oggi – La parola di Fiesole*, August 5, 1984–September 30, 1984. Again, thank you to Emilio Polverini for providing me with copies of all of this material.

7 Don Narcisco Polvani, 'Diario anno 1944,' entry for Monday, July 10, 1944. Regarding the bishop's visit, Father Polvani added that his 'visit is a true example of authority and of Ministership which so moved our people.' See also NA/PRO WO 204/11477.

8 Most probably, it was Nikolay Bujanov, a foreign partisan, who had been killed July 8, 1944. Thank you to Emilio Polverini for pointing out this connection.

9 'Everywhere we were received with signs of joy. It is very true that a people in pain need a priest – whom they scorn when everything is going well.' Don Narcisco Polvani, 'Diario anno 1944,' entry for July 10, 1944.

10 These events have been described in several sources: Don Narcisco Polvani, 'Diario anno 1944,' his entry for July 11, 1944; letter to the bishop of Fiesole informing him of the burial; the November 1944 British investigative report of the massacres in the commune of Cavriglia; and Don Cuccoli's recollections written ten years later. The German authorization slip for the burial is included as an exhibit in the British investigative report of the massacre. NA/PRO WO 204/11477.

11 These are Father Cuccoli's words.

12 NA/PRO WO 204/11477, statement of Don Aldo Cuccoli, hand-numbered, 259–60.

13 See ibid., statement of Gugliema Cristofani, hand-numbered, 258.

14 Don Narcisco Polvani, 'Diario anno 1944,' entry for July 11, 1944.

15 Ibid., entry for July 12, 1944.

16 NA/PRO WO 204/11477, 21; also statement of Don Aldo Cuccoli, hand-numbered, 258–60; statement of Libera Benucci, hand-numbered, 356–7.

17 Father Cuccoli went on to have a long, extremely active, and colourful life and career in the 'red' commune of Cavriglia.

18 NA/PRO WO 204/11479, statement of Alba Bonichi, hand-numbered, 107–8; statement of Modesta Magini, hand-numbered, 87.

19 Ibid., statement of Giuseppa Tiezzi, hand-numbered, 100–2; statement of Laura Guasti Sabatini, hand-numbered, 52–3.

20 My interview with Dino Tiezzi, January 3, 1998, Civitella della Chiana. In her testimony given to Bilenchi and Chiesi, Giuseppa Marsili (widow Tiezzi) spoke of finding her wounded son, Daniele, and caring for him in the woods, but not of separation from her youngest son Dino. 'We ran through the streets of the town. We saw nothing but the dead bodies of the men, but I couldn't manage to identify them because my eyes were clouded by grief and fear. I thought it was the end of the world.' 'The Witnesses of Civitella,' 179.

21 NA/PRO WO 204/11479, statement of Daniele Tiezzi, hand-numbered, 29. Giuseppa Marsili (widow Tiezzi), 'The Witnesses of Civitella,' 180.

22 NA/PRO WO 204/11479, statement of Gino Bartolucci, hand-numbered, 34.

23 The following is taken from Lara Lammioni Lucarelli's oral history, as interviewed by Valeria Di Piazza and recorded August 11, 1993, at Civitella della Chiana. The transcript of this and other oral histories of survivors of the June 29, 1944, massacre are located at the communal library, located in Badia al Pino.

24 Lara then 'gave vent' to her feelings of anger and frustration that the Allies had 'waited for days unnecessarily' before approaching Civitella and Malfiano, put off by Germans' false impression of greater artillery or by reluctance to advance into an area still held by German troops. The interpreter let her talk, 'then with great calmness, replied: "The life of one of our soldiers costs 20 years of commitment and expense, it's not possible to put it at risk and we owe it to them to always move with maximum security." ("Put themselves at risk then, to come and save you when yesterday you were our enemy?" That was clearly their unspoken thoughts.)' Lara Lammioni's oral history, 10. Hilary Footitt cites a French witness to the Allied bombing of Caen who 'recalled how she confronted a British officer after the event and

asked him to explain the reasons for the sustained later bombing of the city. His reply, she remembered with pain, was: "Mademoiselle, the life of one single English soldier is worth more than the lives of thousands of French civilians."' Hilary Footitt, *War and Liberation in France: Living with the Liberators* (New York: Palgrave Macmillan, 2004), 46–7.

25 Or so it seemed that way to Lara. Foiano actually had been in the front lines, but was liberated relatively early, on July 2, 1944. See Eric Linklater, *The Campaign in Italy*, 310.

26 All of the following section is taken from Aroldo Lucarini's, 'Ricordi di Guerra, 1943–49.'

27 Ibid.,' 19.

28 Ibid.,' 24.

29 Ibid.,' 26.

30 Ibid.,' 28.

31 'in fila indiana e silenziosi.' Ibid., 29.

32 See Douglas Orgill, *The Gothic Line: The Autumn Campaign in Italy, 1944*, 12–23.

33 Dominick Graham and Shelford Bidwell, *Tug of War: The Battle for Italy 1943–1945*; Eric Linklater, *The Campaign in Italy*, 293: 'The Germans made stands between Rome and the Gothic Line at Lake Trasimeno and Arezzo.'

34 'The Battle for Arezzo' (July 4–17) merited a few sentences in G.A. Shepperd, *The Italian Campaign 1943–45: A Political and Military Re-assessment*, 279–95. And 'The Entry into Arezzo' (via Sherman tank) did make the cover of the British magazine *The Sphere* on July 29, 1944: 'A Sherman tank passing a 47-ton German Panther knocked out during the advance of the Eighth Army. Forward Allied troops entered this town on the morning of July 16: by midday, tanks and armoured forces were moving through the town in a steady stream.' Reproduced in Enzo Droandi, *Arezzo distrutta 1943–44*, 247. Thank you to the late Enzo Droandi and to Amadeo Sereni (both former partisans in the province of Arezzo) for telling me about partisan activities and the battle and the liberation of the city of Arezzo.

The fighting in the province of Arezzo is a bit more thoroughly described in Eric Linklater, *The Campaign in Italy*, 304, 310–11, 317–20, 329–33. 'On the Eighth Army's front the lush, rolling, heavily cultivated land west of Trasimene – the naked mountains overlooking the Chiana valley south of Arezzo – and the steep confusion of the Chianti hills beyond it, all combined to underline the platitudes of Italian fighting: that ground favoured the defence, and both sides would fight for time as much as for position' (304).

35 Eric Linklater, *The Campaign in Italy*, 311.

36 Ibid., 333. Maurice Nash, a young member of the British Thirteen Corps Troops Workshop, Royal Corps of Mechanical and Electrical Engineers, serving as an electrical technician, was one of a 250 member mobile workshop that set up shop at Santa Barbara on about July 23 to deal with the damage and assist in the further advance. On the next day, he walked over to Castelnuovo and learned of the massacres there and at Meleto, Massa, and Le Màtole. I thank him for all the information he has provided me by letter and personal interview (London 1999) regarding Eighth Army troop movements in the area of Civitella, San Pancrazio, and Castelnuovo. See also Maurice G. Nash, *The Price of Innocence* (n.p., 2005).

37 These are contained on microfilm at NARA, RG 331 AFHQ, R 185 C.

38 Ibid., the frames in RG 331 AFHQ, R 185 C are not numbered. On June 21 and 23, the Allies had bombed the city of Arezzo and the area just north of it. 'Destroyed 11 motor transport and 1 trailer, and damaged 13 motor transport, 1 trailer and 4 railroad trucks. 1 Spitfire missing. 96 Kittyhawks bomed [sic] road junction northeast of Arezzo obtaining direct hits.'

39 Aroldo Lucarini, 'Ricordi di Guerra, 1943–49,' 16e.

40 Don Narciso Polvani, 'Diario anno 1944,' entry for July 13, 1944.

41 Ibid., entry for July 14, 1944.

42 Ibid., entry for July 15, 1944.

43 Ibid., entry for July 16, 1944.

44 Ibid., entry for July 17, 1944.

45 Ibid., leaving one to question the extent of their 'discipline.'

46 Ibid., entry for July 18, 1944.

47 Ibid., entry for July 20, 1944.

48 Ibid., entry for July 21, 1944.

49 Ibid., entry for July 31, 1944.

50 Ibid., entries for July 24 and 25, 1944.

51 Ibid., entry for July 31, 1944.

52 NA/PRO WO 204/11479, statements of: Giulia Valenti, hand-numbered, 270; Eugenia Panzieri, hand-numbered, 290; Laura Ciofi, hand-numbered, 335–6; Pasquale Nannini, hand-numbered, 334; Giulia Bernardi, hand-numbered, 331; Vilma Panzieri, hand-numbered, 325; Genni Panzieri, hand-numbered, 323–4; Eride Tiezzi, hand-numbered, 320; Pia Mori, hand-numbered, 318; Fernanda Nannini, hand-numbered, 295; Gina Parigi, hand-numbered, 301–2; Angiolina Rustici, hand-numbered, 317; Isola Pietrelli, hand-numbered, 315; Narcisca Ciofi, hand-numbered, 313; Gelsa Nannini, hand-numbered, 311–12; Bruna Castagni, hand-numbered, 309; Clementina Gorelli, hand-numbered, 307; Maria Buzzini, hand-numbered, 305.

53 The following is taken – with much gratitude – from Romano Moretti's *29 giugno – 16 luglio 1944: Il fronte a San Pancrazio*, published by the Commune of Bucine and the communal library in 1994 to commemorate the fiftieth anniversary of the massacre. The booklet represents only a small part of the years of research and dozens of interviews (later published) that Mr. Moretti carried out among the survivors of the June 29, 1944, massacres in San Pancrazio. I have also included information learned through my conversations and interviews with Romano Moretti and with residents of San Pancrazio during 1997 and 1998.

54 On that day, having fallen back from the Trasimene line, German forces had taken position along another defensive line that passed through San Pancrazio and Civitella, and just north of Cornia.

55 The population knew, of course, that the Germans would and did rape women; they silently acknowledged it and attempted to protect their young women. It was not something generally discussed or recorded, however. In fact, it would have been purposely not mentioned, as a number of witnesses emphasized to me. A few women who were raped did later tell the Allied investigators, and generally those portions of the women's statements are blanked out. (But see the statement of Gina Polverini in ch. 2.) According to Romano Moretti, 'it was a different time.' Village women having children out of wedlock was not uncommon, but for a woman to have been forcibly raped by the enemy occupier was something quite different and would have carried more shame and stigma – even though the victimization would have been recognized. From his many interviews, Romano Moretti has concluded that it was the young women and older girls who were marked most emotionally and most lastingly by the experience of the passage of the front, in part perhaps because of the ever-present fear of rape.

56 This is according to the recollection of Franco Panzieri. Thank you to Romano Moretti. A contemporary Allied photograph (a copy of which can be found at Bucine's communal library) documents the tank's entrance into the village.

57 Romano Moretti, *29 giugno – 16 luglio, 1944*, 12.

58 NA/PRO WO 204/11479, statement of Consiglia Del Debola, hand-numbered, 373–4.

59 Ibid., statement of Ugo Casciotti, hand-numbered, 268.

60 From one of Romano Moretti's interviews with the survivors.

61 'About 25 July, 1944, I was present when the debris was started to be removed from the cellar of the farm of Pierangeli. On the third day I was horrified to witness the remains of my husband together with those of his two brothers recovered from beneath the debris. They were all badly burned but I was able to

recognize parts of their clothing as identical to that worn by them when I saw them alive, on 29 June 1944. I was also able to recognize some of their personal effects. The body of my husband was recovered in a standing position, due I think, to the numerous other remains behind him.' NA/PRO WO 204/11479, statement of Consiglia Del Debola, hand-numbered, 373–4.

62 Ibid., statement of Angiolina Rustici, hand-numbered, 317.

63 Ibid., statement of Giulia Valenti, hand-numbered, 270.

64 Ibid., statement of Emilia Arrigucci, hand-numbered, 303–4; also, statement of Narcisca Ciofi, hand-numbered, 313.

65 Ibid., statement of Eride Tiezzi, hand-numbered, 320.

66 Ibid., statement of Eugenia Panzieri, hand-numbered, 290.

67 Ibid., statement of Maria Spini, hand-numbered, 321.

68 Ibid., statement of Santa Corsi, hand-numbered, 329.

69 My interviews with Romano Moretti, Florence, June 1997.

70 Philip Morgan makes the compelling point that to accuse Italians of 'sitting on the fence' or taking a 'wait and see' stance when they should have been more assertively anti-Fascist (or pro-partisan) is unfair, as most – like in Arezzo – faced difficult and life-threatening everyday dilemmas. Philip Morgan, *The Fall of Mussolini*, 154–5.

71 'War Diary of the HQ 1st Guard Brigades.' The AMG Provincial Supply Officer reported for July, that '[o]n arriving in Arezzo I found there were only about 400 persons, this number increased as the days went on and at the present there are an estimated number of about 8000.' NARA RG 331 ACC Italy, 10801/154/26.

72 NARA RG 331 ACC Italy, 10801/115/24.

73 Ibid., 10810/115/22 (August 14, 1944 – Weekly Report to PC).

74 The additional residents were evacuees and refugees from other communes, the city of Arezzo, and other provinces.

75 NARA RG 331 ACC Italy, 10801/105/17. The CAO also noted that an 'internment camp was located here but it was closed several months ago.' This would have been the camp at Oliveto.

76 'Civitella della Chiana has suffered from bombing, shell fire, mines and massacres of the bread winners.' NARA RG 331 ACC Italy, 10801/115/24.

77 The Red Cross supervisor suspected that the sindaco may not have been giving the village 'a fair share of the supplies sent to their area.' Ibid., 10801/105/17. 'Civitella depends on the Sindaco of Badia al Pino. The Sindaco has visited it once or twice. His representative in Civitella smells of fascism and mistrust (my impression only). The people seem to mistrust them, and expect little from them.' Ibid.

78 Ibid., emphasis (underscoring) in the original.

79 Giacomo Becattini, ed., *Lo sviluppo economico della Toscana con particolare riguardo all'industrializzazione leggera*, Istituto Regionale per la Programmazione Economica Toscana (Florence: Eurografica, 1975), 53.

80 Nicola Labanca, 'Il peso della guerra,' in *Quando le nostre città erano macerie*, ed. Nicola Labanca, 29.

81 Istituto Centrale di Statistica, *Morti e dispersi per cause belliche negli anni 1940–45* (Rome: 1957).

82 ASA Pref. Gab., busta 137; ASC Civitella, busta no. 1945, cat. X, XI, XII, fasc. cat. 10a, cl. 10a; ASC Civitella, busta 1945, cat. VI-VII-VIII-IX, fasc. cat 8, Op. Naz. Orfani di Guerra, sussidi straordinari.

83 ASC Civitella, busta 1945, cat. X, XI, XII, fasc. cat 10a, classe 1a. Reports within the same folder but prepared at different times provide slightly different figures.

84 ASA Pref. Gab., busta 137.

85 Relazione dell'attività svolta dal Sindaco di Cavriglia Dott. Arch. Leonardo Lusanna al Consiglio Comunale nella sua prima adunanza del 2 Aprile 1946, 6.

86 'The villages of Meleto, Castelnuovo, Massa and San Martino, were the scenes of fierce fighting between the Germans and the Allies ... These areas were continually under bombardment from both sides. Before the Germans left they thoroughly mined and booby trapped most of the buildings. Consequently the majority of the dwellings in these villages suffered severe damage from shell fire and exploding mines. In view of these facts it cannot be definitely stated that certain dwellings were set on fire and destroyed by the German soldiers who committed the atrocities in the areas concerned, on 4 Jul 44.' NA/PRO WO 204/11477, 38. NARA RG 331 ACC Italy, 10800/115/310.

87 ASC Cavriglia, busta no. 124: Arch. Regno 1945, cat. 1a e 2a, fasc. delle ordinanze emesse dal Sig. Sindaco.

88 ASC Cavriglia, busta no. 125: Arch. Regno 1945, cat. dalla 3a alla 11a, fasc. 1948, cat. 8a, classe IIIa, subfasc: Pensioni guerra, orfani guerra. 'Nearly all lose one leg and the other usually has to be amputated.' NARA RG 331 ACC Italy, 10801/105/125.

89 By April 1945, 161 evacuees from other provinces and 123 'occasional residents' were still in the commune. ASC Cavriglia, busta no. 127: Arch. Regno 1945, cat. 12a e 15a, fasc. 1945, cat. 12a.

90 Don Narciso Polvani, 'Diario anno 1944,' entry for July 31, 1944.

91 ASA Pref. Gab., busta 137.

92 Ibid. See also NARA RG 331 ACC Italy, 10800/115/310.

93 The commune and the village that is its communal seat played a fairly important role in postwar Italy, not only as a symbol of complete destruction, but also because the village was the birthplace and hometown of Amintore Fanfani. See Amintore Fanfani, *Una Pieve in Italia* (Milan: Mondadori, 1964).

94 Eric Linklater, *The Campaign in Italy*, 285

95 ASA Pref. Gab., busta 137, condizioni di Pieve S. Stefano, 22 Maggio 1945. The events of the war, deportation, and destruction in Pieve Santo Stefano are described briefly in Antonio Curina, *Fuochi sui monti dell'Appennino Toscano*, 479–80. A fuller version is given in Onelio Dalla Ragione, ed., *La Guerra 1940–1945 a Pieve Santo Stefano: Deportazioni, Razzie, Devastazioni, Massacri* (Pieve S. Stefano: Amministrazione Comunale di Pieve S. Stefano, 1996).

96 'As stated, all the buildings are a heap of rubble, and it can be safely described as a "dead town."' NARA RG 331 ACC Italy, 10801/105/125.

97 ASA Pref. Gab., busta 137, condizioni di Pieve S. Stefano, 22 Maggio 1945.

98 Another early Allied report provided: 'This of course means that with the exception of 18 buildings the whole town is destroyed and the 1200 present inhabitants are living in cellars and caves and lean tos in the rubble.' NARA RG 331 ACC Italy, 10801/105/97.

99 This was out of a total communal area of 15,581 hectares.

100 ASA Pref. Gab., busta 137, condizioni di Pieve S. Stefano, 22 Maggio 1945

101 Ibid., busta 137.

102 Every bridge over the Arno had been destroyed, except for the Ponte Vecchio in Florence and a single bridge in the commune of Cavriglia saved by New Zealand troops.

103 ASA Pref. Gab., busta 137. Some deportees were driven from their homes and communes, but remained in central Italy; others were sent to camps or for labour service in Germany.

104 Fifty years later, estimates were lowered, providing that approximately 1867 civilians were victims of German or Fascist atrocities, died in confinement, or were killed by bombs, artillery, and landmines in the province of Arezzo. Giuseppe Brugnoli, ed., *I civili nella Resistenza: L'apporto popolare nella Guerra di Liberazione dal Primo Risorgimento al 25 Aprile 1945* (Rome: Associazione Nazionale Vittime Civili di Guerra, 1995), 133. Both then and now, however, it is difficult to determine precisely the number of civilian victims of the war, whether killed during various massacres (*'eccidi, stragi, rappresaglie, massacri'*) carried out by German soldiers or Republican Fascists, or by the

usual 'other causes of war.' The problem of anagraphic and civil state record keeping was obviously complicated at the time.

The *Enciclopedia dell'Antifascismo e della Resistenza* (Milan: La Pietra, 1968) puts the number of Italian civilians killed in reprisals at 9180 – nearly 500 of whom were killed in the communes of Civitella, Bucine, and Cavriglia alone. See also Gerhard Schreiber, *La vendetta tedesca, 1943–1945: le rappresaglie naziste in Italia.* L'Istituto Centrale di Statistica (ISTAT) calculated that 149,496 civilians died in the war. 10 Jan. 1997 letter of Biagio Alberti, Provincial President (Florence), Associazione Nazionale Vittime Civili di Guerra, and my interviews with him, February 1997.

105 ASA Pref. Gab., busta 102: Uff. Prov. Assistenza 1944–5.
106 Ibid., busta 6.
107 Ibid., busta 6, document dated 16 Nov. 1944, titled 'Situazione della Prefettura dal dicembre 1943 ad oggi.' See also NA/PRO WO 10800/143/77.
108 ASA Pref. Gab., busta 6.

4. Life with the Allies

Epigraph: Question to S.M. Keeny, head of the UNRRA mission to Italy, at a September 1945 press conference regarding a proposed increase in UNRRA funding for Italy for the year 1946.

1 NARA RG 331 ACC Italy, 10801/115/91, 2–3.
2 Ibid., 10801/115/91.
3 Ibid.
4 The detailed investigations (which form the basis of ch. 2) were carried out some months later by a special investigative branch of the army.
5 Major Stump continued as provincial legal officer in Arezzo until the province passed to Italian government control on May 10, 1945.
6 NARA RG 331 ACC Italy, 10801/115/24 (monthly report, dated October 2, 1944). Thurburn's thoughts on the Aretine people had not been so cynical upon his arrival. At the end of August 1944 (his first full month as provincial commissioner), he had reported: 'Generally the people in this Province have suffered much in life and property from bombs, shells and mines. About 500 have been massacred. Much livestock has been carried off or destroyed ... There is not much to eat beyond the 200 grammes of bread, some vegetables and fruit, and everywhere I am begged for an increase in the bread ration ... The people have been very grateful for what supplies have been imported – but there is no doubt that this Province has been badly treated.' Ibid.
7 See for example, NARA RG 331 ACC Italy, 10801/115/21: Circular Instructions to CAOs. No. 1.
8 Ibid., 10801/115/23.

9 See for example, 'Come già ho detto, il motto del Risorgimento deve essere: LAVORARE, SUDARE, SANGUINARE (se è necessario) MA NON
CHIACCHIERARE.' ASC Civitella, busta 1947, cat. I-VII, fasc. Ricorsi contro
l'accertamento imposta di famiglia anni 1945-46-47, subfasc. Governo Militare Alleato. See also NARA RG 331 ACC Italy, 10801/105/60.

10 The dilemma was well expressed by popular American war cartoonist (and
soldier) Bill Mauldin: 'The dogfaces over here have pretty mixed feelings as
far as Italy is concerned. A lot of them – but not as many as there used to be
– remember that some of their best friends were killed by Italians, and many
of our allies can't forget that Italy caused them some grief ... But the average
dogface feels dreadfully sorry for these poor trampled wretches, and wants to
beat his brains out doing something for them ... Also, they get awfully tired of
hearing everybody – Fascists, ex-Fascists or non-Fascists – wail about how
Mussolini made them do it. Their pity is often strained by the way the Italians
seem to wait for somebody else to do something for them, but in spite of the
fact that the Italians consider the Americans a gravy train which came to bring
them pretty things to eat, the doggies still pity them.' Bill Mauldin, *Up Front*
(New York and London: W.W. Norton, 1995, 1945), 64–6.
   General Alexander issued the following statement on June 11, 1944:
'When Allied troops invaded Italy in September 1943, I issued a directive
regarding their behaviour towards the Italians. In brief, I said that their
attitude should be correct but not familiar, as befitted the soldiers of a
victorious Army entering a conquered country. The time has come when I
consider it desirable to modify this directive ... In brief, while the Italian
Government, troops and people co-operate with us in the defeat of Germany, I consider it to be proper and expedient that we should show them
good-will without familiarity and consideration without weakness.' Quoted
in Harry L. Coles and Albert K. Weinberg, *Civil Affairs: Soldiers Become
Governors* (Washington, DC: Office of the Chief of Military History, Department of the Army, 1964), 496–7 (ACC files 10000/136/192).

11 'The importance of judicious selection [of staff] was strongly borne out by the
experience of the Control Commission which, as contrasted with AMGOT,
was hastily improvised on an enormous scale, in circumstances which offered
the different army services tempting opportunities to get rid of their weaker
members, quite irrespective of any qualifications for their new tasks.' C.R.S.
Harris, *Allied Administration of Italy 1943–1945* (London: HMSO, 1957), 387.

12 The three indispensable sources on the AMG/ACC and its presence in Italy
are David W. Ellwood, *Italy 1943–1945: The Politics of Liberation* (Leicester:
Leicester University Press, 1985); C.R.S. Harris, *Allied Administration of Italy
1943–1945*; and Harry L. Coles and Albert K. Weinberg, *Civil Affairs: Soldiers
Become Governors*. All discuss the often strained British–American relations

and their differing visions for the occupation and for postwar Italy. Coles and Weinberg, especially, fully recognize the irony (and often absurd results) of a foreign military directing civil affairs in a country during wartime.

13 The ACC came into being on November 10, 1943. Intended to be less than full military occupation and government (which was AMG's job), the formation of ACC was meant to serve as an incentive to the Italians and encouragement to their assistance in the war effort against Germany. It was also a response to the stall in military advance of the Allied armies north of Naples, and to the formation of the Republic of Salò.

14 Although more accurate to refer to the Allied Military Government and/or Allied Control Commission as the ACC from that date (and from the end of October 1944 as the AC), the quotations in this chapter show how Allied officers continued to refer to ACC or AC as AMG or as AMG/ACC. Letter-heads and directives retained the AMG title.

15 Coles and Weinberg, *Civil Affairs*, 269–70.

16 C.R.S. Harris, *Allied Administration of Italy*, 114 and 379.

17 David W. Ellwood, *Italy 1943–1945*, 55. See NARA RG 331 ACC Italy, 10801/151/57.

18 'A case could certainly be made out for the conclusion that without detailed Allied control in certain departments the Italian administration would have broken down in its essential tasks, particularly in the matter of food distribution. But this does not really invalidate the principal criticism which must be brought against the Commission's constitution and working, namely that a very large proportion of its operations were concerned with matters which had only the slightest relevance, if any at all, to assisting the military task of the Commander-in-Chief.' C.R.S. Harris, *Allied Administration of Italy*, 385

19 NARA RG 331 ACC Italy, 10800/115/257 (dated July 31, 1944). Naples during the winter of 1943–4 'represents military government, let it be hoped, at its worst. During that period of time Naples was probably the worst-gov-erned city in the Western world, and it was not much better a year later.' David W. Ellwood, *Italy 1943–1945*, 49. Also see Norman Lewis, *Naples '44: An Intelligence Officer in the Italian Labyrinth* (New York: Henry Holt, 1978).

20 The advance report or survey of the province is at NARA RG 331 ACC Italy, 10801/154/25

21 Because of the war's stall south of Bologna during the fall and winter of 1944, Allied advance troops spent longer 'waiting' in Arezzo. ACC presence in all of Italy ended on December 31, 1945, except in the disputed territor-ies of Venzia Giulia and the province of Udine.

22 According to the revised listing of March 20, 1945. NARA RG 331 ACC Italy, 10801/105/106. CAOs were responsible for monitoring partisans, refugees, public utilities (water supply and electricity), the police and public safety, law and order (crime), public health, rationing, agriculture (harvesting and amassing), unemployment, physical reconstruction of public works (buildings, bridges, roads), political activities, finance, the communal administration, and 'miscellaneous.'

23 The CAO who first visited the commune of Civitella included in his '48 hour report' that he had '[p]osted proclamations 1, 2, 3, & 4; General Orders 1 & 24; Notices 1 & 2; and other miscellaneous notices.' NARA RG 331 ACC Italy, 10801/105/17. See also ibid., 10801/115/41.

24 Proclamation No. 2 'War Crimes,' Art. II, no. 39.

25 NARA RG 331 ACC Italy, 10801/105/119.

26 ASC Cavriglia, busta Arch. Regno 1945, cat. dalla 3a alla 11a, N. 125, fasc. Avvizi - Ordini e Proclami, emanati dal Governo Militare Alleato.

27 ASA Pref. Gab., busta 37 Servizi di guerra locali e altro 1940–5.

28 NARA RG 331 ACC Italy, 10801/115/108.

29 See ASC Cavriglia, Arch. Regno 1945, cat. 1a e 2a, N. 124, fasc: fasc delle ordinanze emesse dal Sig. Sindaco.

30 NARA RG 331 ACC Italy, 10801/115/23. Curfew and travel boundary lines shifted when Arezzo passed to regional command in mid-October 1944: on October 26, a curfew between seven in the evening and five in the morning was instituted, and later modified to begin at nine in the evening. See also NARA RG 331 ACC Italy, 10801/115/68. Allied officers tried cases involving violations of Allied proclamations, though as the months passed and Italian judges returned to Arezzo, more and more minor 'Allied interest' cases were tried in Italian courts.

31 NARA RG 331 ACC Italy, 10801/105/119.

32 Ibid., 10801/115/23 and 24.

33 Ibid., 10801/115/77.

34 Ibid., 10801/115/21. The actual censor was a local Aretine official 'without strong political leanings,' named by the prefect, but approved and directed by Quin Smith. Ibid., 10801/115/69. See the *Informatore Aretino* with its blank, censored sections.

35 NARA RG 331 ACC Italy, 10801/115/23 (January 4, 1945).

36 Ibid., 10801/115/95.

37 Ibid., 10801/105/118.

38 Ibid., 10801/115/23.

39 Ibid., 10801/105/60.

40 Ibid. 10801/105/47.
41 Ibid., 10801/115/74.
42 Ibid., 10801/115/23. See also 10801/105/47.
43 Ibid., 10801/115/21.
44 'Expressions of gratitude and favourable opinions toward the Allies continue, as well as references to their restrained bearing and generous character. Some complaints re: rigidity of regulations, difficulties in obtaining permits, and bureaucracy.' Ibid., 10801/115/23: Bimonthly report on Provincial Conditions, Civilian Morale & Public opinion as reflected in civil mails, February 1–15, 1945. See also the censored letter referring to the Allied governors as 'our oppressors.'
45 NARA RG 331 ACC Italy, 10801/115/21.
46 See David W. Ellwood, *Italy 1943–1945*, 56.
47 Quoted in Coles and Weinberg, *Civil Affairs*, 171–2.
48 David W. Ellwood, *Italy 1943–1945*, 56–8.
49 ASA Pref. Gab., busta 6.
50 Quin Smith did direct a memo to all his officers that they should treat Italian officials courteously, when possible, and not keep them waiting too long. 'It is realized that verbosity, indecision, vacillation and lack of the genius for organization are not only galling to busy northerners, but Italians have suffered 22 years of "wind and bombast," which is not good efficiency-training. Officers are therefore asked to be patient and constructive in their directions, for the southerner responds to courteous treatment with few exceptions ... Above all, officials should never be shouted at or abused publicly. We have no time to change their character or efficiency quotient.' NARA RG 331 ACC Italy, 10801/105/118 (November 28, 1944).
51 Ibid., 10801/115/21 (March 13, 1945).
52 Ibid., 10801/115/58.
53 Ibid. (August 4, 1944).
54 The protest provided: 'The Provincial Committee of National Liberation for Arezzo ... while reconfirming its full desire to collaborate with the Allied Government, points out the disappointment and regret of the Committee and the population that the *first Fascist Podestà of Arezzo* has been named the *first Prefect for the period of Democratic Liberty*.' NARA RG 331 ACC Italy, 10801/115/39 (emphasis in the original). See ASA Pref. Gab., busta 37 Attività dei Partigiani 1945 on the composition of Arezzo's provincial CLN.
55 Guidotti Mori's 'Scheda Personale' for epuration purposes is at NARA RG 331 ACC Italy, 10801/115/58.
56 Ibid.
57 Guidotti Mori spent the next several months attempting to collect some remuneration for his service as prefect. The Allies had no idea of how much

he should receive, and the Italian Ministry of the Interior insisted it could not determine an appropriate amount because the province had not yet been restored to Italian administration. Ibid., 10801/151/49.

58 Ibid., 10801/115/56 and 10801/115/58.

59 On July 30, 1944 (two weeks after the liberation), Arezzo's PPSO reported, '[p]atriots are handing in their firearms without any trouble, and are settling down to their normal occupations. During the first few days of our occupation they were proud to walk around the streets carrying their firearms, but now they are gradually fading away.' Ibid., 10801/115/108. See ibid., 10801/151/59 for a list of arms and ammunition recovered from partisans at Terranuova Bracciolini in early August 1944.

60 In Arezzo, a provincial committee of anti-Fascist concentration already had formed on September 2, 1943. On April 12, 1944, it changed its name to the Provincial Committee of National Liberation. The records of Arezzo's CPLN sessions are housed at the Istituto Storico della Resistenza in Toscana (ISRT, Florence), 'CLN di Arezzo' (3 volumes).

61 NARA RG 331 ACC Italy, 10800/115/257. By 'patriots' Thurburn meant partisans.

62 Ibid., 10801/115/38. As the Allies proceeded north throughout the summer of 1944, they encountered ever better organized CLNs – and CLNs even less willing to give up their authority within the communes. See ibid., 10800/115/321 for the Tuscan CLN's July 30, 1944, memorandum 'To the Allied High Command.' See also ibid., 10801/115/39.

63 Thurburn reported to headquarters: 'I have given instructions to the District CAO's that all CLN must limit their activity to giving assistance etc. to anyone who remains a patriot of any kind ... I know quite well that strong Committees exist in Grosseto and in Florence but I also know that their influence is going to be seriously restricted.' Ibid., 10800/115/233.

64 ASA Pref. Gab., busta 37 Attività dei Partigiani 1945.

65 Ibid., busta 110. The CLN explained that it spoke on behalf of the sindaco and the population of the commune.

66 NARA RG 331 ACC Italy, 10801/115/39.

67 Ibid., 10801/115/21.

68 Ibid., 10800/115/233. In his November 1, 1944, monthly report (for the month of October) to AMG Eighth Army, Quin Smith stated regarding CLNs: 'Many of these still appear to think they form part of the post-liberation scheme. They have been informed that they must carry on their normal work and dissolve as an active association.' Ibid., 10801/115/24.

69 Ibid., 10801/115/24 (December 4, 1944). At the same time Quin Smith was fighting with the Arezzo CLNs, the Supreme Allied Command for the Mediterranean Theatre (SACMED) and the Italian government under Ivanoe Bonomi

were reaching an accord with the CLN for northern Italy (CLNAI) to represent the portion of Italy as yet unliberated and unoccupied by the Allies, recognizing it as coordinator of the anti-Fascist resistance and as representative of the Italian government for the German occupied area. Ibid., 10800/115/233.

70 ASA Pref. Gab., busta 37 Attività dei Partigiani 1945; NARA RG 331 ACC Italy, 10800/115/233.

71 NARA RG 331 ACC Italy, 10801/115/23 (March 31, 1945) (emphasis in the original). See also ASA Pref. Gab., busta 7.

72 See ASA Pref. Gab., busta 37 Attività dei Partigiani 1945, for the prefect's speech. At the meeting, the congress voted that the work of the CLN would continue until the date of the convocation of the Constituent Assembly.

73 NARA RG 331 ACC Italy, 10801/151/57. See also 10801/151/36.

74 Ibid., 10801/115/24 (Quin Smith's monthly report to AMG Eighth Army for October 1944).

75 ACC officers in Arezzo had carried on 'a certain correspondence' regarding the expected arrival, 'owing to the fact that the district was in effect a "Distressed Area."' Ibid., 10800/143/37.

76 Ibid., 10800/143/37. Father Polvani recorded that many of those evicted from Santa Barbara went to Castelnuovo and to San Pancrazio searching for somewhere to stay. 'The situation is worse every day,' he wrote. Don Narcisco Polvani, 'Diario anno 1944,' entry for November 3, 1944. The CAO's report on the evacuation read: 'Naturally I had some difficulty in the first instance in persuading the people that it was necessary to clear out of their homes but on the whole I consider that they behaved admirably. I think this evacuation shows firstly that our authority is really respected and secondly that there is no serious unrest in this locality.'

77 NARA RG 331 ACC Italy, 10801/115/24.

78 Ibid., 10801/115/81.

79 Ibid., 10801/115/40.

80 There were at least four in Arezzo by December 1944, two under Eighth Army control, and two under ACC (refugee branch) control.

81 NARA RG 331 ACC Italy, 10800/154/24; 10801/115/83.

82 Ibid., 10801/115/23 (Quin Smith's monthly report for January 1945).

83 Quin Smith gave 'strict instructions' that it was time 'to get a move on with the much-delayed education programme.' Ibid., 10801/115/77.

84 The Italian inspector, the communal administration, and Quin Smith all requested unsuccessfully that Polish troops vacate. Ibid. Neither ACC nor the Eighth Army could get Polish troops to vacate other schools in some of the more northern parts of the province. Ibid., 10801/115/23.

85 In January 1945, Allied troops also occupied the seminary at Castelfranco. Ibid., 10801/115/77.
86 Ibid., 10801/154/51.
87 Don Narcisco Polvani, 'Diario anno 1944,' entry for December 7, 1944.
88 NARA RG 331 ACC Italy, 10801/154/51.
89 Ibid., 10801/105/53.
90 Ibid., 10800/154/24.
91 Ibid., 10800/161/169–171.
92 Ibid., 10801/154/24.
93 Ibid., 10801/115/83.
94 Ibid., 10801/115/81.
95 Ibid., 10800/154/24.
96 The architects and inspectors of the Italian Superintendency of Monuments and Galleries were already using part of the Casa Vasari for offices. Ibid., 10801/115/36 (February 20, 1945). Vasari was born in Arezzo, not Florence.
97 Ibid., 10801/115/36.
98 Lieutenant Frederick Hartt, the region VIII MFAA officer wrote to the director of the MFAA subcommission: 'The spectacle of the ruined forest was one of the saddest thus far seen in Tuscany, more so than that of many a ruined church. The part along the road leading from Camaldoli to the Hermitage … is almost completely destroyed … More than two thirds of the way up to the Hermitage, the picture is one of appalling devastation, which in all likelihood it will take a century to repair.' Ibid., 10801/115/36.
99 Ibid., 10801/115/36.
100 Ibid., 10801/105/73.
101 Because some 2000 tons of wood already cut was waiting to be hauled down the mountain, 'both Lieut. Kingsford and Maj. Hodge assured the undersigned that for the next two months the forest around the Eremo was in no danger, and that they would do all they could to keep from cutting it, but could promise no more than that.'
    In the nearby province of Livorno, the PC there stopped the Allied Ninety-eighth Engineers from excavating (with a gas shovel) *inside* the damaged cathedral of the city of Livorno, and using the material to feed a rock crusher (presumably for road or concrete work). 'The large stone columns of the church have actually been broken up by laborers to sizes to fit the crusher … This would appear to be a violation of common ethics and decency as well as of paras 318, 319, of "Rules of Land Warfare" FM 27-10,' the provincial commissioner commented. Ibid., 10800/115/228 (2 of 2).
102 'No petrol has been granted for industry in spite of special application.' Ibid., 10800/154/24.

103 Ibid., 10801/115/23.
104 Ibid., 10801/105/125. Three Allied military trucks (whose vehicle numbers could not be traced) carried away ninety-three tree trunks from a firm in Battifolle. Ibid., 10801/115/83.
105 Quin Smith observed a 'recent case is the requisition by a South African Engineer unit of 80,000 bricks from Terranuova Bracciolini, where the owner is in financial difficulties.' Ibid., 10801/115/83 (January 21, 1945). 'Italians able to provide fuel which is badly needed have, in many cases, stopped cutting it because their wood and charcoal is taken by military units without payment. Fuel is badly needed both by the troops and the civilian population. Every effort should be made to encourage the Italians to produce it.' Ibid., 10801/105/54.
106 Ibid., 10800/161/169–71.
107 Ibid., 10801/115/83.
108 The Allied Force headquarters financial advisor managed to shift some of the financial blame away from Army pilferers and onto the Italian government: 'However, we are calling the above to your attention as one more example in which the failure of the Italian Government to take adequate action to finance concerns which are allegedly in need of funds in order to supply the Allied Force has thrown on the Allied Force the task of deciding whether and how much financial aid is needed. You may wish to bring the matter to the attention of the Italian Government.' Ibid., 10801/151/60 Memo to HQ, Allied Commission, Finance Sub-Commission.
109 Ibid., 10801/154/24.
110 Ibid., 10801/115/47 (1 of 2).
111 Ibid., 10801/115/71; 10801/154/17.
112 Quin Smith noted that the 'illegal purchase of food is known to be a primary cause of the high cost of living here in Arezzo province. It is continually going on and varies from the purchase of foodstuffs in villages by soldiers to organized tours by units outside the province where military lorries are usually accompanied by an "interpreter" in semi-military uniform with good local knowledge and plenty of cash.' Ibid., 10801/105/54 (March 29, 1945).
113 Ibid., 10801/115/47 (1 of 2).
114 Ibid., 10801/105/119. He did not receive a jail sentence. The *carabiniere* officer who gave character evidence on the farmer's behalf, stated the 'accused was a good strong simple worker.' His attorney argued effectively, '[h]aving been accustomed to handing things over free of charge to the Germans the accused thought it was only right to give to the English military.'

115 Ibid., 10801/115/24; 10801/115/93. As when Italian women were raped by German soldiers, few reported it, both because the victims felt authorities would do nothing and because of the shame associated with having been raped.

116 The *carabinieri* report on the incident pointed out the 'incompatibility' of allowing Italian soldiers as co-belligerents in the war, but not allowing them to drink in bars with Allied soldiers. Quin Smith bluntly responded to the PPSO: 'please inform the official of the Carabinieri who forwarded it that what we require is an unvarnished statement of facts from which we can make our own deductions. He should take care that reports contain *short* notes concerning *all* aspects of the case, but should avoid expressions of personal opinion.' Ibid., 10801/115/108 (emphasis in the original).

117 Ibid., 10801/115/70.

118 Ibid., 10801/105/117.

119 Ibid., 10801/115/83.

120 See ibid., 10801/115/24.

121 Don Narcisco Polvani, 'Diario anno 1944,' entry for August 14, 1944.

122 NARA RG 331 ACC Italy, 10801/115/238 (2 of 2).

123 Even PC Quin Smith was not immune from dance fever. On March 2, 1945, he sent a memo to all CAOs: 'We are having a small dance at the Villa in Patrignone on the 10th. All CAO officers are invited (when they will be expected to share expenses). Officers in Arezzo are asked to invite one lady each, either from the staff or elsewhere. If you wish to bring a lady please let PMC (Major Drummond) know by return.' Ibid., 10801/115/1. See also ch. 7.

124 *La Nazione del Popolo*, no. 274, October 13, 1945.

125 NARA RG 331 ACC Italy, 10801/115/23; 10801/115/70.

126 ASA Pref. Gab., busta 7.

127 *L'Informatore Aretino* 1, no. 1 (September 5, 1944).

128 Don Narcisco Polvani, 'Diario anno 1944,' entry for August 31, 1944.

129 Ibid., entry for September 15, 1944.

130 Bill Mauldin, *Up Front*, 71.

131 NARA RG 331 ACC Italy, 10801/115/23 (April 30, 1945). Quin Smith apparently was given very short notice of the province's return to Italian government control. 'There are persistent rumors that this province is to be handed over to Italian control, and certainly the lack of any assigned officers points to such a conclusion. The interesting thing is that so far no single reference has been made to this office as to the advisability or possibility of such a change.'

132 On backwardness and 'amoral familism,' see, Edward Banfield, *The Moral Basis of a Backward Society* (Glencoe, IL: Free Press, 1958); and on 'familism,'

see Paul Ginsborg, *Italy and its Discontents 1980–2001* (London: Penguin, 2001), especially 97–100.

133 *La Repubblica*, April 25, 2003.

134 Ibid, April 24, 2003.

135 See the *Journal of Modern Italian Studies* 10, no. 4 (2005) on the subject and meaning of Italy's liberation. See especially David Ellwood's 'Introduction: The Never-Ending Liberation,' 385–95. See also Roberto Chiarini, *25 aprile. La competizione politica sulla memoria* (Venice: Marsilio, 2005) on a more acceptable 'grey' memory of the Resistance rather than competing 'red' and 'black' memories.

136 See the daily press coverage in *La Repubblica* and *La Nazione* in the days before April 25, 2005.

137 See the press coverage of April 26, 2005, especially *La Repubblica*.

138 He used the phrase 'la rinascita morale e materiale della nostra Patria.'

5. True Victims and the Truly Needy

Epigraphs: The heading of a letter from the sindaco of Pieve Santo Stefano to Alcide De Gasperi, President of the Council of Ministers, February 17, 1947. From the sindaco of Bucine's September 29, 1944 letter to the prefect on the situation in the village of San Pancrazio. 'Therefore, Your Excellency's urgent intervention is necessary, to come to the aid of these poor people, to mitigate in part so much ruin, so much pain.' ASA Pref. Gab., busta 110.

1 ASC Cavriglia, busta AR 1946, cat. dalla 1a alla 5a, N. 128, fasc. 1946 Giunta Comunale.

2 NARA RG 331 ACC Italy, 10801/151/57.

3 ASA Pref. Gab., busta 102, fasc. Integrazione del Governo Alleato ai bilanci ECA 1945.

4 See Peter Gibson, 'Relief Work in Italy,' *FAU Chronicle*, no. 68, February 3, 1945, 2. The American Council of Voluntary Agencies for Foreign Service (Italy Branch) included, among others, the American Jewish Joint Distribution Committee, American Relief for Italy, the Brethren Service Committee, the Congregational Christian Service Committee, the Save the Children Federation, the Unitarian Service Committee, and the War Relief Services of the National Catholic Welfare Conference. The Nobel Peace Prize of 1947 was awarded to the American Friends Service Committee and the British Friends. Thank you to Professor Massimo Rubboli for bringing the work of the FAU, the AFSC, and other voluntary organizations in postwar Italy to my attention.

5 My interview with conscientious objector and British FAU volunteer Sam
Marriage (London, July 7, 2000). The June 1943 'Starnes Amendment' prevented conscientious objectors who were U.S. citizens from engaging in humanitarian service abroad. Again, thank you to Professor Massimo Rubboli
for bringing this to my attention.

6 UN/UNRRA, PAG-4/3.0.14.3.0.:12.

7 ASC Bucine, busta cat. II, fasc. 1945. ASC Florence, 10449, filza 1, 1935–
1952; UN/UNRRA, PAG-4/3.0.14.3.0.:12.

8 ASC Bucine, busta cat. II, fasc. 1945.

9 Hoover Institution Archives, UNRRA Issuances 1943–8 (Ed. Arnold Collection), Box. 1 (accession no. 59015-9.12). '"*UNRRA'S Principle Is Helping People
to Help Themselves*."' Herbert H. Lehman, quoted in 'UNRRA in Outline and
Up-to-Date' (July 1, 1945).

10 Hoover Institution Archives, UNRRA (Ed. Arnold Collection), box 3, folder
UNRRA 1945. 'Report to the Director General to the Council for the Period
15 September 1944 to 31 December 1944,' and box 1, folder: UNRRA 1944
(outcard no. 59015-9.12).

11 The proposed programs were to begin on January 1, 1945, and were based
on a series of assumptions – most of which (including the starting date) did
not come to pass. The assumptions included that 'military operations in
Italy will end before December 31, 1944.' UN/UNRRA, PAG-4/3.0.14.3.4.:1.

12 Hoover Institution Archives, UNRRA (Ed. Arnold Collection), Box no. 1,
folder UNRRA 1943 (outcard No. 59015-9.12). For the official history, see
'A History of UNRRA in Emilia and Toscana Region,' United Nations Relief
and Rehabilitation Administration, Italian Mission, Emilia and Toscana Region – Florence (Florence, Italy, March 15, 1947). UN/UNRRA, PAG-4/4.2,
Italy #27, box 42.

13 The public information section's job was, in part, 'to ensure the most favorable presentation of UNRRA activities to the public of Tuscany and Emilia,
through the medium of the press, radio and other information outlets.' 'A
History of UNRRA in Emilia and Toscana Region,' 10–11. Italians – including the needy villagers of the Aretine – were very familiar with UNRRA
activities. A large number of the postwar diaries and memoirs in Italy's
Archivio Diaristico Nazionale in Pieve Santo Stefano mention receiving
UNRRA assistance, as did those individuals I interviewed in Civitella and
San Pancrazio.

14 UN/UNRRA, PAG-4/3.0.14.0.2.:16. (Capitals in the original.)

15 'The total UNRRA program for Italy (including $50 millions expended for
a limited relief program, partly in 1945) amounts to $425 millions.' Most of

that went for food and industrial rehabilitation. 'Economic Recovery in the Countries Assisted by UNRRA: Report Presented by the Director General of UNRRA to the Secretary General of the United Nations' (September 1946). Hoover Institution Archives, UNRRA (Ed. Arnold Collection), box 2, folder: UNRRA 1946 (outcard no. 59015-9.12).

16 UN/UNRRA, PAG-4/3.0.14.3.4.:1; PAG-4/4.2; ASA Pref. Gab., busta 102.

17 Reporting on what he learned, the newly arrived ACC regional welfare officer for Tuscany summed up ECA: 'The traditional work of ECA was to give small amounts of relief in cash or in kind to the local poor, to serve as legal guardians to abandoned children, and to administer certain legacies left for charitable purposes. In recent years it had become the agency for helping needy refugees, families whose homes and means of livelihood had been destroyed by the war, and persons whose remittances from relatives in foreign countries had been cut off.' NARA RG 331 ACC Italy, 10800/115/252.

18 Welfare branch, PHS/C, AC, Rpt., for Dec. 44, ACC files 10700/163/26, quoted in Coles and Weinberg, *Civil Affairs*, 339.

19 ACC established a new provincial office of social welfare (Ufficio Provinciale di Assistenza Sociale) in Arezzo and other liberated provinces because many 'national and provincial social welfare organizations were closely affiliated with the Fascist Party Organization which has been dissolved. Likewise, the management and functions of many local organizations had been modified in recent years to serve Fascist Party purposes rather than the needs of the local population entitled to their services.' Provincial offices thus were to provide an additional, provincial level of oversight for existing agencies. ASC Bucine, busta cat. II 1945, fasc. domande sinistrati di guerra.

20 RDL. 14 aprile 1944, n. 125.

21 ASC Bucine, busta cat. II 1945, fasc. domande sinistrati di guerra (emphasis in the original).

22 'O.N.M.I. is responsible for maternity and child welfare. The following services may be provided: a) Consultation for pregnant women. b) Meals for pregnant women and nursing mothers. c) Temporary care in Maternity Institutions. d) Care of children, e.g. Pediatric, nursing, educational and nutritional.' Appointees received no salary, but ACC stated they 'should: (a) Have knowledge of ante- and post-natal maternal welfare and child care. (b) Experience in infant feeding, and the requirements of nursing and pregnant women. (c) Administrative ability.' NARA RG 331 ACC Italy, 10800/115/221 (3 of 3). See also ibid., 10800/163/43.

23 ASA Pref. Gab., busta 128.

24 ASC Cavriglia, AR 1946, cat. dalla 1a alla 5a, N. 128, fasc. 1946 Giunta Comunale.

25 ASC Bucine, busta Passaggio Amministrazione, 1945.

26 Reporting on the commune of Bucine, the Allied psychological warfare branch (PWB) concluded that '[o]n the whole, the people are disappointed as they had hoped for more effective aid from the Allies.' NA/PRO WO 204/12629.

27 '*Sinistrati*' (singular: *sinistrato/a*) was the term most often used in contemporary official and unofficial documents to refer to individuals and entities, translatable as an adjective ('damaged,' 'harmed') or noun ('victims'). For example, the minister of public works and the office of civil engineering declared the villages of Civitella, Cornia, and Tuori in the commune of Civitella '*centri sinistrati.*' ASC Civitella, busta 1947, cat. VIII-IX-X-XI, fasc. cat. 10a, cl. 10a.

28 Relazione dell'attività svolta dal Sindaco di Cavriglia Dott. Arch. Leonardo Lusanna al Consiglio Comunale nella sua prima adunanza del 2 Aprile 1946, 6–7.

29 ASC Florence, 10446 ECA filza 7, cat. IV (1944–59).

30 ASC Bucine, busta Opere pie e beneficenze 1945; ibid., busta Corrispondenza 1945 GM. In general, Bucine notified APB that the commune calculated the number of persons needing immediate assistance of various sorts to total 284 men, 297 women, 311 children. These numbers did not include the 582 residents (including '*reduci,*' '*sfollati,*' '*bisognosi,*' '*senza tetto*') already being assisted by other organizations. ASA Pref. Gab., busta 102, fasc. Comitato Prov. UNRRA 1945.

31 Relazione dell'attività svolta dal Sindaco di Cavriglia Dott. Arch. Leonardo Lusanna al Consiglio Comunale nella sua prima adunanza del 2 Aprile 1946.

32 See, for example, detailed ECA records for the commune of Florence for the period during and after the summer of 1944, which set forth the many categories of war victims up to that point in the war. ASC Florence, 10450 ECA, filza 2.

33 On Fascist welfare generally, see Maria Sophia Quine, *Italy's Social Revolution: Charity and Welfare from Liberalism to Fascism* (Houndmills: Palgrave, 2002); and David G. Horn, *Social Bodies: Science, Reproduction, and Italian Modernity* (Princeton: Princeton University Press, 1994).

34 The Ministry of the Interior also spoke in terms of 'categories of persons' to be assisted. See ASC Civitella, busta 1947, cat. I-VII, fasc. cat. 2a, cl. 1.

35 DL June 21, 1945, no. 380. ASC Florence, 10446 ECA. APB regional and provincial offices were instituted on September 19, 1945. APB did not take exclusive jurisdiction over assisting war victims. The Ministry of Interior

continued to carry out assisting families of prisoners of war, of soldiers still under arms, and of civilians deported by the Germans. Assisting Italian refugees from 'Italian Africa' remained the province of the Ministry of Italian Africa.

36 In September 1945, when APB arranged for a distribution of clothing, potentially eligible recipients were enumerated as follows: 1) partisans; 2) veterans; 3) prisoners of war; 4) military internees and their families; 5) refugees and other civilian victims of war; 6) those repatriated from abroad. ASC Bucine, busta: Opere pie e beneficenze 1945.

37 ASC Florence, 10446 ECA Assistenza, filza 7, cat. IV Ministero dell'APB, Istruzione per gli uffici regionali e provinciali, 1945.

38 Families of soldiers killed and families of fallen partisans were considered to have a 'military' connection to the war, whereas those whose family members had been massacred by the Germans were considered to have a 'political' connection. See also ASC Florence, 10449 ECA filza 1; and ASA Pref. Gab., busta 102, fasc. Comitato Prov. UNRRA.

39 Referring to a distribution of clothing donated by ENDSI, the head of ECA for the commune of Arezzo stated: 'Unfortunately the requests far outnumbered what was available, and so the [Distribution] Committee was not able to satisfy some of the petitioners. The number of requests was considerable (1300 of them); while the number of garments was extremely limited.' ASA Pref. Gab., busta 102, fasc. Comitato Prov. UNRRA 1945.

40 'Pieve S. Stefano is without doubt the most wretched village of our Province … That commune is of course the most needy of all the others in our Province.' ASA Pref. Gab., busta 99. See also ibid., buste 102, 128, 133, 145, 188.

41 ASC Bucine, busta Opere pie e beneficenze 1945.

42 ASC Bucine, busta cat. II 1945 (Prefect's January 23, 1945 circular number 421, titled 'Sinistrati di Guerra'): 'un effettivo e reale stato di bisogno.'

43 ASA Pref. Gab., busta 137, fasc. Danni di guerra, 17-1-Massime: 'i veri e propri indigenti.' See also ASC Bucine, busta 1947, cat. 6a Azioni al Valore Civile, and busta cat. 2a, classe 4a, fasc. 1.

44 ASC Civitella, busta 1947, cat. I-VII, fasc. cat. 2a, cl. 1.

45 Civitella, for example, submitted a list of that commune's 'war wounded' and their families to the Opera Nazionale Fra Mutilati e Invalidi di Guerra divided into those suffering 'miserable economic conditions' or 'poor economic conditions.' ASC Civitella, busta 1948, cat. V-VI-VII-VIII, fasc. cat. 8a, cl. 5a. See also ASC Florence, 10449 ECA, inserto 3 Rapporti e Relazioni col Governo Militare Alleato (28 September 1944), wherein the director of ECA for Florence determined that ECA run soup kitchens would be restricted to 'the most needy' ('i più bisognosi').

46 ASC Florence, 10443 ECA, filza 4 Circolare N. 1444/6 prot. Gab.

47 ASC Bucine, busta Opere pie e beneficenze 1945.

48 ASA Pref. Gab., busta 137: 'in stato di particolare bisogno.'

49 Ibid.: 'maggiormente colpite e bisognose.' '*Colpito/a*' was another term commonly used to describe those affected by the war. The adjective means 'hit' or 'struck' as in 'hit by a blow,' certainly a valid way to describe the war's effects.

50 ASA Pref. Gab., busta 137.

51 Ibid., busta 102 Uff. Prov. Assistenza 1944–1945: 'maggiormente colpite.' The blankets would not be free, but cost 450 lire each. Even the chance to purchase a necessity like a blanket had to be rationed. Of 1980 blankets obtained by the provincial office of social assistance from ACC, 1000 were reserved for the needy of the city of Arezzo. The rest were divided between Pieve Santo Stefano (250), Civitella (200), Bucine (200), Terranuova Bracciolini (150), and Montevarchi (180).

52 ASC Bucine, busta Opere pie e beneficenze 1945.

53 ASC Cavriglia, busta Cavriglia Arch. Regno 1945, cat. 1a e 2a, N. 124, fasc. Istituzione Comitato Assistenza Pubblica - Organizzazione Funzionamento (November 1944).

54 See ASC Cavriglia, busta AR 1947, cat. dalla 7a alla 11a, N. 135, fasc. cat. 8a, cl. 3a, fasc. Pensioni guerra orfani: 'graduati per ordine di bisogno.'

55 ASC Bucine, busta Corrispondenza 1945.

56 Regarding this traditional practice, see Philip Gavitt, *Charity and Children in Renaissance Florence: The Ospedale degli Innocenti, 1410–1536* (Ann Arbor: University of Michigan Press, 1990).

57 ASC Civitella, busta 1946, cat. III-IV-V, fasc. cat. 8a, leva e truppa (January 10, 1946, letter from Opera Nazionale per gli Orfani di Guerra to the sindaco of Civitella).

58 ASC Civitella, busta 1945, cat. VI-VII-VIII-IX, fasc. cat. 8, Op. Naz. Orfani di Guerra, Sussidi Straordinari.

59 ASC Bucine, busta Opere pie e beneficenze, 1945.

60 'A History of UNRRA in Emilia and Toscana Region,' 34, UN/UNRRA PAG-4/4.2 (Bx 42).

61 ASA Pref. Gab., busta 137.

62 See for example, ASC Florence, 10443 ECA; ibid., 10449 ECA Affari in genere, fasc. 1; ASC Bucine, busta Opere pie e beneficenze, 1945.

63 UN/UNRRA PAG-4/3.0.14.2.2.3.0:3, 5–6. '[T]he number [of needy persons in Italy] is very large and unquestionably runs into the millions.'

64 ASA Pref. Gab., busta 110.

65 Ibid., busta 137.

66 Ibid., busta 168 Assistenza Post-Bellica UNRRA (emphasis in the original): 'essendo veramente tutti casi *bisognosissimi.*'

67 ASC Bucine, busta 1946, cat. IIa, cat. 2a, cl. 4a, fasc. 1: 'hanno assolutamente bisogno di assistenza.'

68 The communal CLN in Cavriglia also served briefly to compile lists of the neediest residents to receive clothing from the American Red Cross. ASC Cavriglia, busta Arch. Regno 1945, cat. 1a e 2a, N. 124, fasc. Istituzione Comitato Assistenza Pubblica - Organizazione Funzionamento.

69 ASC Bucine, busta ECA 1944–6.

70 Ibid., busta 1946, cat. IIA, cat. 2a. cl. 4a, fasc. 1.

71 ASC Florence, 10449 ECA, filza 7, cat. IV.

72 ASA Pref. Gab., busta 102 Comitato Prov. UNRRA 1945; ASC Bucine, Deliberazioni 1945–6 Giunta e Consiglio; ASC Bucine, busta cat. II 1945, fasc. Natale 1945.

73 ASC Civitella, busta 1947, cat. VIII-IX-X-XI, fasc. 8 (actually, cat. 8; not in a fasc. per se).

74 ASC Cavriglia, busta Arch. Regno 1945, cat. 1a e 2a, N. 124, fasc. Distribuzione Vestario Croce Rossa Americana.

75 Arezzo's prefect informed ECA presidents that a recent government circular set forth 'concrete' rules for the granting of subsidies to *sfollati* (evacuees or those 'dispersed'). They were neither rules nor specific standards, however, but were nothing more than another general directive to ascertain the conditions of 'absolute need' of individuals, and the possibility (or impossibility) of their returning to their home or of procuring some form of employment. ASC Bucine, busta cat. II 1945.

76 ASC Cavriglia, busta AR 1947, cat. dalla 1a alla 4a, N. 133, fasc. Comitato Naz. Pro Vittime Politiche, Roma (*carabinieri* report May 1, 1945). ASA Pref. Gab., busta 102, fasc. Comitato Prov. UNRRA 1945: 'concedendo magari indumenti a qualche famiglia poco meritevole.'; ASC Bucine, busta 1946 cat. IIa, cat. 2a, cl. 4a, fasc. 1. One woman of San Pancrazio, whose husband was not killed in the July 29 massacre at San Pancrazio, told me that those whose husbands had been killed received 'so many subsidies' and 'so much assistance' from various sources that widows were better off than families like hers (she, her husband, and young son) which also had lost everything, but received 'nothing' in the way of assistance. Interview June 16, 1997, San Pancrazio.

77 ASA Pref. Gab., busta 102: 'meno sinistrati.'

78 ASC Civitella, busta 1945, cat. XIII-XIV-XV, fasc. cat. 14a; ASC Cavriglia, busta Arch. Regno 1945, cat. 1a e 2a, N. 124, fasc. Distribuzione Vestario Croce Rossa Americana.

79 ASC Civitella, busta 1948, cat. IX-X-XI, fasc. cat. 9a, (cl. not specified).

80 ASA Pref. Gab., busta 133, Ministero Assistenza Post Bellica UNRRA: 'nel particolare momento politico che il nostro Paese sta attraversando.' Some foreign assistance was more openly 'partial,' as when blankets, sheets, and sugar came from the government of Ireland 'for fellow Catholics in need.' ASC Civitella, busta 1945, cat. XIII-XIV-XV, fasc. cat. 14a.

81 UN/UNRRA PAG-4/4.2, 33–4; ASA Pref. Gab., busta 133, fasc. Ministero Assistenza Post Bellica/UNRRA.

82 See for example, ASC Bucine, busta 1946 cat. IIa, cat. 2a, cl. 4a, fasc. 1. On the practice of *raccomandazione* during Fascism, see R.J.B. Bosworth, *Mussolini's Italy.* In his unpublished diary (which spanned the period from the war to the early 1970s), Ruggero Franci, a schoolteacher in the province of Arezzo, wrote of helping peasants (often illiterate or semi-literate) prepare their letters of request to sindaci, ECA, and various assistance organizations, though not arguing on their behalf. Ruggero Franci, 'Note di vita di scuola,' Archivio Diaristico Nazionale, DP/91.

83 See for example, ASC Bucine, fasc. ECA 1944–6; ASA Pref. Gab., buste 160, 182; ASC Florence, 10449 ECA, filza 1; ASC Bucine, busta Beneficenze 1945, classe 2a. See also letters from the UDI provincial secretary to Arezzo's prefect, the CLN, and ENDSI committee on behalf of Pieve Santo Stefano.

84 ASA Pref. Gab., busta 137.

85 ASC Florence, 10450 ECA, filza 2.

86 See ASA Pref. Gab., busta 102, fasc. Comitato Prov. UNRRA 1945; ASC Cavriglia, busta Arch. Regno 1945, cat. 1a e 2a, N. 124, fasc. Istituzione Comitato Assistenza Pubblica - Organizzazione Funzionamento; ASC Bucine, fasc. Deliberazioni 1945–6 Giunta e Consiglio; ASC Bucine, busta cat. II 1945, fasc. Natale 1945; ASC Civitella, busta Deliberazioni di Giunta 1948; ASC Montevarchi, busta ECA and busta Cartelli varie.

87 Ruggero Franci, 'Note di vita di scuola.'

88 NARA RG 331 ACC Italy, 10801/115/47.

89 ASC Bucine, busta 1946, cat. XI, cat. 11a, cl. 3a, fasc. 4.

90 Ibid., busta 1946, cat. IIa, cat. 2a, cl. 4a, fasc. 1; ibid., busta 1947, cat. 2a. cl. 5a, fasc. 3; ASC Civitella, busta 1946, cat. IX-X, fasc. cat. 9a, cl. 1; ASC Cavriglia, busta Deliberazioni 1944–5. UDI welfare and assistance work will be discussed further in ch. 12. See Angelo Ventrone, *La cittadinanza repubblicana: forma-partito e identità nazionale alle origini della democrazia italiana (1943–1948)* (Bologna: Il Mulino, 1996), especially ch. 3 on the assistance activities of women PCI members.

91 Angelo Ventrone, *La cittadinanza repubblicana.*
92 See NARA RG 331 ACC Italy, 10801/115/70.
93 ASA Pref. Gab., busta 7, fasc. Relazione sullo stato della provincia. This compared to a prewar population of 319,754 for the province.
94 NARA RG 331 ACC Italy, 10800/163/36.
95 ASC Florence, 10449 ECA, filza 1; 10450 ECA, filza 2. See also UN/UNRRA PAG-4/3.0.14.0.0.2.:3 (Regional Director's Narrative Report for the Month of October 1946), 5.
96 NARA RG 331 ACC Italy, 10801/115/34. This was in a province where 'from 20% to 30% of the houses' were estimated to have been completely destroyed. 'Living conditions are consequently bad,' said Quin Smith. Ibid. See also ASA Pref. Gab., busta 102, fasc. Uff. Prov. Assistenza 1944–5.
97 NARA RG 331 ACC Italy, 101801/115/34.
98 ASA Pref. Gab., busta 102.
99 The terms refugee and evacuee were not always used with great precision. '*Profughi*' were refugees, either Italian nationals or foreigners, who came to Italy from outside the country. Thus, *profughi* could be Italians repatriated from Greece or North Africa, as well as Poles, Germans, British, or the postwar stateless who found themselves in Italy. UNRRA soon came to refer foreigners within Italy (like the millions of foreign refugees throughout Europe after the war) as 'displaced persons' or DPs. '*Sfollati*' were evacuees: Italian citizens who had evacuated or were displaced from other provinces or other communes within Italy because of the war. Both Allied and Italian officials often used '*profughi*' to refer to refugees, displaced persons, and evacuees.
100 NARA RG 331 ACC Italy, 10801/115/34. Region VIII included Arezzo (see figure 9).
101 Ibid. In September 1944, the Regional Commissioner (for Region VIII) also tried to discourage Army HQ from sending more refugees to Arezzo, stressing the degree of damage to housing stock. Provinces were expected to accommodate refugees in the number of 10 per cent over their normal population, but Arezzo had lost more than 10 per cent of its housing. Ibid.
102 Ibid.
103 ASA Pref. Gab., busta 102.
104 Ibid.
105 NARA RG 331 ACC Italy, 10801/151/59 and 10801/115/34.
106 'I prey you too that these poor people are as soon as possible, removed from the miserable conditions in which they lay. I am sure of your interest for them so much as civil people as American and English cannot let to abandon human beings in such a condition of abrutiment.' Ibid.,

10801/115/34 (the sindaco to the American Red Cross representative – English as in the original).

107 ASA Pref. Gab., busta 102.

108 Ibid., busta 105.

109 NARA RG 331 ACC Italy, 10801/115/31.

110 Undated memo from the American Red Cross representative to the PC (most likely from November or December 1944).

111 The Army did not allow Livornese refugees to return to their city after the front had passed. A strategically important port city, Livorno had been badly damaged both by the Allies and the Germans. Any refugees who did manage to return were basically forced to work for the Allies rebuilding port facilities. 'Labour in Livorno City is being given first priority.' NARA RG 331 ACC Italy, 10801/115/34.

112 Ibid., 10800/163/36.

113 Ibid., 10801/115/34.

114 Ibid., 10801/115/34, letter dated November 30, 1944.

115 Ibid., 10801/115/34.

116 Even ACC initially considered only the six southernmost communes in Arezzo feasible for a large-scale compulsory billeting program. 'The rest of the province is impractical due to army occupation or excessive bomb damage.' Ibid.

117 The camp at Castiglion Fiorentino received between 500 and 600 new refugees each day for several days at the end of 1944. 'I expect you know that Prefect has now authorized Refugee Committees to billet people. I asked him especially to see that they do it on an ORGANIZED plan such as allowing 1 1/2 persons per room of *total* rooms habitable per house. This makes it quite clear how many refugees a house can take, once present permanent occupants is known.' Ibid. (emphasis in original). 'In addition to these [living in schools] we have over 2000 other refugees from the Provinces of Livorno and Pisa who are living in private homes throughout the Province and it is impossible to take care of any more.'

118 NARA RG 331 ACC Italy, 10800/163/36

119 Ibid., 10801/115/34.

120 Ibid., 10800/163/36 (December 30, 1944).

121 Ibid. Quin Smith later found moral fault with the villagers' decision not to use the church as a school.

122 'The refugee problem began on May 3 [1945] when a large group of Italian soldiers, ex-prisoners of war and partisans, accompanied by civilians arrived from Florence … The civilians have been arriving at the rate of about 150 per day. They are coming chiefly from Florence by "mezzi di fortuna."

Their destination is southern Italy and Sicily. They arrive without permits and with little or no baggage.' Ibid., 10801/115/34.

123 Ibid., 10800/163/36.

124 Tuscany had six large refugee camps for foreigners. UN/UNRRA PAG-4/3.0.14.0.0.2:3 (Progress Report – June 1946, Welfare Division), 5. The refugee camp in the city of Arezzo sheltered a total of 7979 persons for the year 1945, and 4530 in 1946.

125 The major groups were: stateless: 684; Polish: 534; Yugoslavs: 223; Greeks: 112; Romanians: ninety-five. UN/UNRRA PAG-4/4.2, 'A History of UNRRA in Emilia and Toscana Region,' 47.

126 UN/UNRRA PAG-4/3.0.14.0.0.2:3 (Regional Director's Narrative Report for the Month of June 1946), 6. An UNRRA aim was to eliminate out of camp financial assistance for all or most DPs, and refer them to camps where they could be more easily managed, repatriated, or resettled. UN/UNRRA PAG-4/4.2, 'A history of UNRRA in Emilia and Toscana Region,' 42–3. Out of camp assistance for DPs was finally phased out May 31, 1947.

127 Both Italians and the Allies also feared the growth of Jewish 'terroristic organisations' centred in Italy (especially Turin). NA/PRO WO 204/11001. Ferruccio Parri, then president of the council of ministers, told the Union of Italian Israelite Communities in Rome, in November 1945, that the Italian government had no objection to the entry or presence of Jewish DPs, so long as it was strictly limited in duration and so long as UNRRA assumed responsibility for their care and support. 'The Italian Government considers it just and right to give help to the Jews forced to leave other countries on account of racial persecution. Regretting that current conditions in Italy do not allow us to provide for their assistance, we trust that the immigrants will find in our country at least that spirit of liberty and of human solidarity that inspires the Italian people in their rebirth.'

128 That number was fewer than the previous month. UN/UNRRA PAG-4/3.0.14.0. 0.2:3 (Regional Director's Narrative Report for the Month of March 1946), 5.

129 Table VIII of 'War-Displaced and Homeless Persons Receiving Sussidio from Ministry of Post War Assistance … is an analysis, by regions, of current residence of this hard core of needy persons, of most of whom it can be said that they are in a state of desperate need.' UN/UNRRA PAG-4/3.0.14.2.2.3.0.:3, 6.

130 Ibid.:3, 5 (Analysis of the Ministry of Post War Assistance camp populations by Province of Origin – excluding refugees from the colonies and abroad).

131 Ibid.

132 ASA Pref. Gab., busta 133, fasc. Ministero Assistenza Post-Bellica, Affari vari: 'grave disagio.' Throughout this July 22, 1946, government circular, the terms *profughi* and *campi profughi* included Italians evacuated from

within Italy, Italians from Venezia Giulia and Dalmatia, and Italians repatriated from Tunisia, Italy's colonies and the Aegean, and from abroad.
Ibid.

133 The minister set forth: 'This Ministry trusts in the full collaboration of all
personnel responsible for promptly carrying out a plan in this delicate economic and political moment, for the return of normality and for getting
the masses of citizens currently inactive and unproductive, back to work
and to a more elevated level of life within the general framework of national reconstruction.' Ibid.

134 ASA Pref. Gab., busta 99.

135 NARA RG 331 ACC Italy, 10801/115/70.

136 References to the 'martyrdom' of Italy appear frequently in postwar writings, speeches, and documents. See, for example, 'la nostra Italia mar-
toriata' in the public report by the first post-Fascist sindaco of Cavriglia
regarding his term of office. Relazione dell'attività svolta dal Sindaco di
Cavriglia Dott. Arch. Leonardo Lusanna al Consiglio Comunale nella sua
prima adunanza del 2 Aprile 1946, 15.

6. Restitution, Reparations, and Rewards

Epigraph: ASC Bucine, busta Opere pie e beneficenze 1945.

1 ASC Cavriglia, busta Arch. Regno 1945, cat. 1a e 2a, N. 124, fasc. cat. 1a, cl.
VIa, fasc. Segretario Com.le e impiegati.

2 See the prefect's report for December 30, 1945. ASA Pref. Gab., busta 7.

3 The reference to the 'vast field of postwar assistance' was made by the
president of ECA for the commune of Florence to the general director of
APB in Rome (June 21, 1947), in noting the wide scope of ECA's postwar
activities. ASC Florence 10446 ECA 1944–59, filza 7.

4 Ibid., cat. IV, Ministero dell'APB, Istruzioni per gli uffici regionali e provinciali, 1945.

5 ASC Florence 10443 ECA, filza 4, Circolare N. 1444/6 Prot. Gab.; 10446
ECA 1944–59, filza 7: 'rientro nella vita civile.' The returnee was granted 20
lire per day, with 14 lire for each child under age fifteen who lived with the
returnee, and 17 lire for the wife and each child between fifteen and eighteen (if the child lived with the returnee and was unemployed).

6 After ninety days, it was hoped that a returnee would be back on his or her
feet and in the midst of active civil life again.

7 Prefects were to concede one subsidy or the other when a claimant held
multiple qualifications. ASC Civitella, busta 1945, cat. VI-VII-VIII-IX, fasc.
cat. 8a, Op. Naz. Orfani di Guerra, Sussidi Straordinari; ASC Bucine, busta
Opere pie e beneficenze anno 1945.

8 ASA Pref. Gab., busta 7, fasc. Relazione sullo stato della provincia, and busta 6; ASC Florence 10443 ECA 1938–1945, filza 4.

9 Ex-confinees or internees would not have been able to return home if the war was still going on in their province of origin or if ACC prohibited travel there. Subsidy amounts were calculated on a daily basis: 30 lire for the head of the family, 20 lire for the wife and every other family member living with the head. Ex-internees or confinees then residing in refugee camps were granted a smaller sum: 25 lire to the head, and 15 lire for each additional family member. NARA RG 331 ACC Italy, 10801/151/53; Ministero dell'Interno, letter no. 451/1731, August 14, 1944; ASC Civitella, busta 1943, cat. XII-XIII-XIV-XV, fasc. cat. 15a, cl. 1a; ASC Florence 10444 ECA 1944–52, filza 5; ASC Florence 10449 ECA 1935–52, filza 1.

10 NARA RG 331 ACC Italy, 10801/151/53; Prot. No. 3882, Oct. 23, 1944.

11 ASC Civitella, busta 1945 cat. XIII-XIV-XV, fasc. cat. 15a.

12 Ibid.; NARA RG 331 ACC Italy, 10801/151/53.

13 ASC Florence 10444 ECA 1944–52, filza 5.

14 NARA RG 331 ACC Italy, 10801/151/53. Prefects were to ascertain periodically whether an ex-confinee or ex-internee still could not return home, and whether his economic condition had improved enough so that further payments could be halted. ASC Bucine, no busta, unmarked fasc., Bolletino Atti Ufficiali della R. Prefettura di Arezzo, June 8, 1945.

15 ASC Civitella, busta 1945, cat. VI-VII-VIII-IX, fasc. cat. 6a, cl. 1a; ASC Cavriglia, busta Archivio Repubblica, 1946, cat. dalla 1a alla 5a, N. 128, fasc. Premio Repubblica al personale dipendente.

16 ASC Cavriglia, Deliberazioni della Giunta Comunale dall' 11 settembre 1944 a tutto l'anno 1946.

17 ASA Pref. Gab., busta 37, fasc. Attività dei Partigiani 1945. A number of women in the province of Arezzo were awarded the 'premi partigiani feriti.'

18 Italians who had assisted escaped Allied POWs between September 8, 1943, and the liberation could seek the *premio* offered by the Allied Screening Commission, as many in the Bucine area did. See ASC Bucine, busta Opere pie e beneficenze, 1945; busta 1946, cat. IIa, cat. 2a, cl. 4a, fasc. 1; busta 1947, cat. 6a, fasc. Azioni al Valore Civile; ASC Cavriglia, AR 1946, cat. dalla 13a alla 15a, N. 132, fasc. 1946, cat. 14a, cl. 1a, Affari diversi. Roger Absalom describes Allied 'certificates of gratitude' given to Italian farmers who had sheltered POWs as being 'on economy paper bearing the printed facsimile signature of Field-Marshal Alexander.' He also explains the Allied objections to recognizing, awarding, and honouring Italian helpers ('an exchange of individual honours with Italy would undoubtedly give offense to families in this country bereaved at Italian hands'). Roger Absalom, 'Allied escapers and the *contadini*

in occupied Italy (1943–5),' *Journal of Modern Italian Studies* 10, no. 4 (2005): 413–25 (see page 414 and n. 11).

19 ASA Pref. Gab. , busta 133, fasc. Min. Assistenza Postbellica, Assistenza Reduci e partigiani.

20 Ibid.: 'caduto per la lotta di liberazione.'

21 UN/UNRRA, PAG-4/3.0.14.0.2:10; ASC Civitella, busta 1945, cat. X, XI, XII, fasc. cat. 10a, cl. 1a.

22 The association had six subcommittees and eighty-seven communal offices throughout Italy. Prince Filippo Andrea Doria Pamphily (then sindaco of Rome) served as its president, and the minister of the treasury supplied the committee with a large part of its funds (100 million lire for the fiscal year 1945–6). It also sought and received funds, food, medicine, and other supplies from ACC, the American Red Cross, ENDSI, American Relief for Italy, UNRRA, and from various smaller private institutional donors and charities in the United States. It also solicited private contributions both within Italy and from the United States. ASC Cavriglia, busta Arch. Regno 1945, cat. 1a e 2a, N. 124, fasc. Assistenza famiglie vittime politiche; busta AR 1947, cat. dalla 1a alla 4a, N. 133, fasc. Comitato Naz. Pro Vittime Politiche Roma. See also ASC Bucine, busta Opere pie e beneficenze, 1945.

23 ASC Bucine, busta 1946, cat. IIa, cat. 2a, cl. 4a, fasc. 1.

24 For example, someone 'was in effect a political victim, being that he was murdered by Nazi-Fascist troops in reprisal on June 29, 1944,' and 'the below-named individuals, residents of this commune, killed in reprisal and shot by Nazi-Fascist troops, are political victims.' ASC Bucine, busta 1946, cat. IIa, cat. 2a, cl. 4a, fasc. 1. See also ASC Cavriglia, busta AR 1946, cat. dalla 1a alla 5a, N. 128, fasc. cat. IIa, cl. 1a, fasc. Assistenza e beneficenza.

25 ASC Bucine, busta 1946, cat. IIa, cat. 2a, cl. 4a, fasc. 1.

26 ASA Pref. Gab., busta 133, fasc. Min. Assistenza Postbellica, Assistenza Reduci e Partigiani.

27 Ibid., busta 110.

28 For those communes, the deadline to seek an indemnity was extended to December 31, 1944, then to February 28, 1945. ASC Cavriglia, busta Arch. Regno. 1945, cat. 1a e 2a, N. 124, fasc. Decreto Indennità di Bombardamento; ASC Bucine, busta cat. II 1945, fasc. Natale 1945.

29 This was the assessment of the inspector general for the Treasury Ministry, Direzione Generale Danni di Guerra, January 31, 1947. ASA Pref. Gab., busta 137.

30 The enormous number of unprocessed claims may be part of the reason why the national Danni di Guerra undersecretaryship continued until 1959. The 'somewhat slow rhythm of payment' may have been due not only to the

state's difficult financial situation, but also to the fact that Arezzo's provincial administrative department for Danni di Guerra had only seven temporary employees, one department head, and no bookkeeper. Only a small percentage of the thousands of claims filed had even been entered in the provincial register by the end of January 1947.

31 ASA Pref. Gab., busta 137. See ch. 5.

32 See Francesca Lagorio, 'Appunti per una storia sulle vedove di guerra italiane nei conflitti mondiali,' *Rivista di storia contemporanea* 23–4, nos. 1–2 (1994): 170–93 regarding pensions for war widows, the extension of such pensions after WWII, and women's active political roles in claiming those pensions.

33 ASC Bucine, busta 1946, cat. XIV-XV, cat. 15a, cl. 2a, fasc. 4. See also ibid., busta Opere pie e beneficenze 1945; ASC Cavriglia, busta AR 1948, cat. dalla 8a alla 15a, N. 138, fasc. cat. 8a, fasc. Pensioni orfani di guerra. In 1948, the civilian–military veteran distinction disappeared entirely. Law 135 of March 2, 1948, extended to war injured and invalided civilians and to families of fallen civilians the same past and future benefits applicable to analogous categories of killed or injured veterans.

34 See ASA Pref. Gab., busta 37, servizi di guerra, locali e altro 1940–5 for pensions for landmine victims.

35 Pension amounts varied according to the number of children (boys and unmarried girls) under the age of twenty-one, and fluctuated during the first couple of years. ASC Cavriglia, busta AR 1946, cat. dalla 6a alla 8a, N. 129, fasc. 1946, cat. 8a, cl. IIIa, fasc. Pensioni e Orfani Guerra.

36 ASC Civitella, busta 1948, cat. V-VI-VII-VIII, fasc. cat. 8, cl. 7; also busta 1947, cat. VIII-IX-X-XI, fasc. 8; ASC Bucine, busta 1946, cat. IIa, cat. 2a, cl. 4a, fasc. 1.

37 Both war injured military veterans and their civilian counterparts were divided into categories according to the severity of their injury or condition (such as loss of a hand or foot.), and given a pension in an amount based accordingly. The system was reordered in 1950 as it became clear that treating injured civilians the same as ex-soldiers (in regards to pension amounts) was not easy or straightforward. The original law requiring equal financial treatment of soldiers and civilians had not taken into account the large numbers of women and children who suffered injuries and illnesses different from male ex-soldiers. See *Nuova Solidarietà, Firenze* 2, no. 2 (Dicember 1996) (publication of the Associazione Nazionale Vittime Civili di Guerra, Florence section), and my interviews with Biaggio Alberti, Florentine provincial president of the association. See also Supplemento Ordinario all Gazzetta Ufficiale n. 16 del 18 gennaio 1982, 10–16, for a later reordering of postwar categories and classifications.

38 ASC Cavriglia, busta AR 1948, cat. dalla 8a alla 15a, N. 138, fasc. cat. 8a, fasc. Pensioni orfani di guerra.

39 These facts are as recited in judgment no. 42110, of the Corte dei Conti, Sezione Terza Giurisdizionale per le Pensioni di Guerra, dated May 26, 1961.

40 Signora Polverini's own war pension was awarded years after ministerial decree n. 1.234.791 of April 9, 1952, recognized certain pulmonary illnesses as possibly war-related, as defined in art. 10 of law no. 648 of August 10, 1950.

41 The court also commented on how Signora Polverini's wartime suffering exceeded that of most Italians. 'It is evident that because of such events, the claimant came to find herself in a special personal situation clearly different from the general condition of distress suffered by the major part of the Italian people in that sad period of war.'

42 Assistance included a state '*premio maggiore età*' for those orphans who reached the age of majority during the year 1944, admission into special colonies or camps, and partial or full scholarships for the equivalent of high school, as well as some specialized training courses. It does not appear to have been true that children who before the war would not have gone on to a higher level of schooling, now were able to do so because they received scholarships as war orphans. In the village of San Pancrazio, whose citizens were mostly small farmers and sharecroppers, very few children received state-funded scholarships, though they did receive some extraordinary subsidies and were admitted to orphanages and *collegi* where they received an education. *Borse di studio* were more numerous in Civitella, which had a more economically diverse population, and many of whose children would have gone on to secondary school or beyond had the war not occurred.

43 ASC Cavriglia, busta AR 1947, cat. dalla 7a alla 11a, N. 135, fasc. cat. 8a, cl. 3a, fasc. Pensioni guerra orfani; busta AR 1948, cat. dalla 8a alla 15a, N. 138, fasc. cat. 8a, fasc. Pensioni orfani di guerra; ASC Civitella, busta 1947, cat. VIII-IX-X-XI, fasc. cat. 8.

44 ASC Cavriglia, busta Arch. Regno 1945, cat. dalla 3a alla 11a, N. 125, cat. 8a, cl. IIIa, fasc. Pensioni guerra, Orfani guerra; ASC Bucine, busta Beneficenza 1945, cl. 2a; busta 1946, cat. IIa, cat. 2a, cl. 3a, fasc. 3; busta 1946, cat. IIa, cat. 2a, cl. 4a, fasc. 1.

45 ASC Bucine, busta Beneficenze 1945, cl. 2a; busta 1946, cat. IIa, cat. 2a, cl. 3a, fasc. 4; busta 1946, cat. IIa, cat. 2a, cl. 3a, fasc. 4.

46 A communal sindaco, police officer, or priest could provide the declaration.

47 ASC Bucine, busta Beneficenza 1945, cl. 2a, and my interviews with Romano Moretti in Florence, April 29, 1997; and June 10, 1997, in Florence; June 16, 1997, in San Pancrazio.

48 ASC Bucine, busta Beneficenza 1945, cl. 2a.

49 Ibid., busta 1946, cat. IIa, cat. 2a, cl. 3a, f. 3.

50 ASA Pref. Gab., busta 37, fasc. Attività dei Partigiani 1945.

51 Ibid., busta 133, fasc. Min. APB, Assistenza Reduci e Partigiani; DLL 21 agosto 1945, n. 518.

52 By March 1946, seeing that the work of checking credentials was necessarily going to take some time, the state authorized provincial sections of the National Partisans Association of Italy (ANPI) to grant provisional partisan or patriot certificates for use in limited purposes such as obtaining employment. ASA Pref. Gab., busta 133, fasc. Min. APB, Assistenza Reduci e Partigiani.

53 DLL del Capo Provvisorio dello Stato of September 6, 1946, n. 93. ASA Pref. Gab., busta 133, fasc. Min. APB, Assistenza Reduci e Partigiani.

54 The Ministry of War's directive on the subject lists fifteen different monetary benefits. ASA Pref. Gab., busta 133. Leaders of partisan formations could receive even more.

55 See ibid., busta 16.

56 See ibid., busta 99.

57 The Tuscan regional commission (for recognizing partisan qualifications) definitively recognized a person as 'caduto per la lotta di liberazione' within the terms of DLL 21 agosto 1945, n. 518. From Emilio Polverini's private papers.

58 NA/PRO WO 204/11479, statement of Alduina Menchetti, hand-numbered, 34–8.

59 Ibid., statement of Gina Magini, hand-numbered, 55.

60 Elio Vittorini, *Men and not men,* trans. Sarah Henry (Marlboro, VT: The Marlboro Press, 1985 (1945).

61 Ibid., 37–8.

62 Ibid., 38.

63 Ibid., 88–9.

64 Ibid., 98, 110–12.

65 Ibid., 111.

66 See Roberto Chiarini, *25 aprile. La competizione politica sulla memoria.*

7. Restoring the Community

Epigraphs: ASA Pref. Gab., busta 37, fasc. Prigionieri di Guerra e Internati 1942-1945. Local sections of the anti-Fascist parties – Communists, Socialists, Christian Democrats, Republicans – made this appeal, promising that those 'elements indisputably compromised with the past regime' would be arrested and tried through official channels, and asking that the population not exploit the 'political excitement of the moment' to 'vent personal grudges.'
Don Gino Ciabattini, parish diary, entry for August 12, 1945, c. 90 (typewritten p. 65).

1 ASA Pref. Gab., busta 7.

2 NARA RG 331 ACC Italy, 10801/115/154 (1 of 2).

3 ASA Pref. Gab., busta 133, fasc. Min. APB, Assistenza Reduci e Partigiani.

4 On the 'returnee' from deportation as western Europe's 'common victim' of WWII, see Pieter Lagrou, 'The Nationalization of Victimhood: Selective Violence and National Grief in Western Europe, 1940–1960,' in *Life after Death: Approaches to a Cultural and Social History of Europe during the 1940s and 1950s*, ed. Richard Bessel and Dirk Schumann, 243–57.

5 My interviews with June Adams, June 1999, Florence. See also NARA RG 331 ACC Italy, 10801/105/52; 10801/115/31; 10801/115/47; 10801/151/44 for communications from British subjects seeking either temporary assistance or permission to return to their residences in Italy.

6 Ibid·, 10801/115/55. PC Thurburn allowed them passage home in a railroad cattle car.

7 Relazione dell'attività svolta dal Sindaco di Cavriglia Dott. Arch. Leonardo Lusanna al Consiglio Comunale nella sua prima adunanza del 2 Aprile 1946.

8 Thank you to Romano Moretti for permission to quote the many interviews he has carried out among the citizens of San Pancrazio.

9 ASC Bucine, busta cat. II 1945, fasc. domande sinistrati di guerra.

10 Ibid., busta Beneficenza 1945, cl. 2a. See busta 1946, cat. IIa, cat. 2a, cl. 3a, fasc. 4 for Monterotondo's 'admission requirements.'

11 Ibid., busta 1945, cl. 2a. Thank you to Romano Moretti for telling me about the orphans of San Pancrazio, including himself, and for introducing me to a number of them.

12 My interview with Dino Tiezzi, January 3, 1998, Civitella.

13 ASA Pref. Gab., busta 128. Most of the citizens of Pieve Santo Stefano had not been deported to Germany for forced labour, but had been pushed north of the Gothic Line and 'distributed predominantly in the villages of the Romagna.'

14 NARA RG 331 ACC Italy, 10800/142/3419.

15 ASA Pref. Gab., busta 137; ASC Civitella, busta 1947, cat. VIII-IX-X-XI, fasc. 8.

16 ASA Pref. Gab., busta 137. The massacres in the commune of Stia during the spring of 1944, which included that in the village of Vallucciole, were the earliest carried out in the province.

17 See Brunello Mantelli, 'Italians in Germany, 1938–1945: An Aspect of the Rome-Berlin Axis,' in *Italian Fascism: History, Memory and Representation*, ed. R.J.B. Bosworth and Patrizia Dogliani, 45–63.

18 UN/UNRRA, PAG-4/3.0.14.0.0.3:2.

19 ASA Pref. Gab., busta 37, fasc. Prigionieri di guerra e internati 1942-1945; NARA RG 331 ACC Italy, 10801/115/40.

20 See Benedict S. Alper, *Love and Politics in Wartime: Letters to My Wife, 1943–45* (selected and edited by Joan Wallach Scott) (Urbana and Chicago: University of Illinois Press, 1992). The reality of the program soon became apparent: 'When I was first assigned to this job I discovered that persons selected to return home were chosen more on the basis of who requested their return than for their potential value for rebuilding the economy of Italy' (124).

21 NARA RG 331 ACC Italy, 10801/151/36.

22 Ibid., 10801/115/40.

23 Ibid., 10801/105/45.

24 ASC Cavriglia, busta AR 1946, cat. 8a, Elenchi dei prigionieri morti dispersi; Guerra per la liberazione partigiana, no. 130, 1944–7 (Contiene anche elenco volontari nell'esercito di liberazione). The text of the message was printed in *Notiziario Prigionieri* for December 31, 1945: 'Coraggio fratelli, la vostra attesa non può essere più delusa.'

25 After the end of the war, in June 1945, about a half a million Italian soldiers and 350 thousand civilians reportedly remained in German territory then occupied by the Allies. *Notiziario Prigionieri*, no. 26, June 10, 1945. On November 9, 1945, *La Nazione* reported that 502,000 soldiers, out of an original 1,245,000, still remained in Allied and German prisons at the end of October 1945; 743,000 had been repatriated. *La Nazione, Cronaca di Arezzo*, no. 301, November 9, 1945.

26 Arezzo's *Questore* reported to the prefect at the end of April 1946, that the labour market had worsened on account of the return of the *reduci*. ASA Pref. Gab., busta 118, Relazioni mensili sulla situazione della provincia. Another reason to delay the return of POWs has to do with the suggestion by Claudio Pavone and others that returned soldiers 'evoked both the shame of national military defeat and the more particular pain at the end of fascist fantasies of conquest.' Ruth Ben-Ghiat, 'Unmaking the Fascist Man: Masculinity, Film and the Transition from Dictatorship,' *Journal of Modern Italian Studies* 10, no. 3 (2005): 336–65 (quote, 339).

27 NARA RG 331 ACC Italy, 10801/115/77.

28 Ibid., 10801/115/70.

29 ASC Cavriglia, busta Archivio Regno 1946-1947, cat. Deliberazioni del Consiglio Comunale. As in this instance, in this chapter I have changed the names of those purge subjects and those charged with collaboration to whom reference appears only in communal archive records and not more publicly available documents.

30 Typically in early days of Fascism, *squadristi* either were not arrested after their violent activities, or were soon released. Often, the police either sympathized with the blackshirts, or were intimidated by them. See generally, R.J.B. Bosworth, *Mussolini's Italy*, chs. 5 and 6.

31 The commune sent a copy of its decision to his wife in Florence.

32 ASC Cavriglia, busta Archivio Regno 1946-1947, cat. Deliberazioni del Consiglio Comunale.

33 Ibid., busta (not numbered), 1946, cat. 1, cl. 6a, fasc. Epurazione dipendenti comunali.

34 The timing is interesting. Calvi was tried and convicted after the courts instituted specifically to try Fascist crimes were terminated, after the purge of public employees ended, after justice minister and Palmiro Togliatti issued the amnesty, and after the most heated manifestations of popular justice had ceased.

35 This superseded the earlier defascistization procedures instituted by the Allies after the liberation of Rome. See Roy Palmer Domenico, *Italian Fascists on Trial: 1943–1948* (Chapel Hill: University of North Carolina Press, 1991), 76–9, for an overview of decree 159's provisions. Additional decrees followed in September and October 1944, extending the reach of DLL 159 in purging Fascists from public life and public employment. An April 1945 decree established Special Assizes courts in place of earlier People's Courts. See also Hans Woller, *I conti con il fascismo: l'epurazione in Italia 1943–1948* (Bologna: Il Mulino, 1997).

36 See the March 9, 1946, memoranda to all sindaci from the president of Arezzo's provincial delegation for the High Commission for Sanctions against Fascism, regarding the commission's imminent end and requesting to know how many persons still were subject to epuration. ASC Civitella, busta 1946, cat. I-II, fasc. cat. 1a, cl. 5a.

37 All verdicts of under five years were cancelled. Death sentences were commuted to life; life sentences were reduced to thirty years; other sentences were reduced by one-third. Most financial penalties were cancelled. Roy Palmer Domenico, *Italian Fascists on Trial*, 206–11. See also Minister of the Interior *Circolare*, no. 22112/15700.1.1, May 25, 1946.

38 'The Italian program of Epuration was somewhat delayed in this Province on account of the death of Avv. [attorney] Severi who was first appointed as the Provincial Delegate of the High Commissioner for Epuration.' NARA RG 331 ACC Italy, 10801/115/23 (Major Stump's Report for the month of February 1945). Three delegates of the high commission were appointed in the province in February 1945.

39 For the twelve areas to be discerned, see ASC Bucine, busta Beneficenza 1945, cl. 2a; and busta cat. II 1945.
40 See for example, ASC Civitella, busta 1944, cat. I-II, fasc. Impiegati dichiarizione.
41 ASC Cavriglia, busta (not numbered), 1946, cat. 1, cl. 6a, fasc. Epurazione dipendenti comunali.
42 Ibid.
43 ASC Civitella, busta 1946, cat. I-II, fasc. cat. 1a.
44 The name has been changed. ASC Civitella, busta 1946, cats. I-II, fasc. cat. 1a, subd. personale.
45 The effect of the censure was that he would have had a percentage of his salary deducted temporarily.
46 The judgment stood for about four months, until the commission met again and reconsidered, and withdrew the sanction earlier imposed. ASC Civitella, busta 1946, cats. I-II, fasc. cat. 1a, subd. personale.
47 NA/PRO WO 204/11479, statement of Gina Magini, hand-numbered, 55.
48 See, for example, NARA RG 331 ACC Italy, 10801/115/47.
49 NA/PRO WO 204/11479, statement of Alba Bonichi, hand-numbered, 108.
50 'He had to belong to this party or starve but that is the only time in his life that he had belonged to any political party.' NA/PRO WO 204/11479, statement of Alduina Menchetti, hand-numbered, 38. While a victim's membership in the Fascist Party is a subject repeated in the witness statements given to Allied investigators after the massacres, neither Fascist Party membership nor Fascism itself was mentioned in the testimonies collected in 1946 by Romano Bilenchi and Marta Chiesi. Allied investigators clearly had asked about the victims' connections to the partisans, and may have asked about allegiances to Fascism as well, whereas the 1946 testimonies centre on the massacre and certainly not on local Fascism.
51 ASA Pref. Gab., busta 110.
52 She also worried about more than her husband's personal safety. As the Germans departed the area, he had hidden the family's valuables and cash in their garage. After arresting the man, the Allies requisitioned the car – which had been in the garage. Now, his wife complained, 10,000 lire they had hidden in the garage was missing, along with the car.
53 NARA RG 331 ACC Italy, 10801/105/97. Memo dated April 22, 1945. The daughter later tried another tactic; she reported to Allied authorities that one of the workers who took over her family's shop had assaulted her.
54 NARA RG 331 ACC Italy, 10800/142/3426.
55 *La Nazione, Cronaca di Arezzo*, no. 268, October 7, 1945.
56 NARA RG 331 ACC Italy, 10801/115/80.

57 Relazione sulle cause e fine dello sciopero a cura del Prefetto, ACS, Ministero dell'Interno, P.S., 1944–6 - busta 84, Affari per provincie.

58 Father Polvani recorded that Civita and the corporation's administrative director both were arrested by the British on August 19, 1944. The latter died
while in custody. Don Narcisco Polvani, 'Diario anno 1944.' NARA RG 331
ACC Italy, 10801/115/76.

59 The prefect's and *carabinieri* telegrams to the Ministry of the Interior and
others read in part: 'About 2000 miners of Castelnuovo Sabbioni began a
strike this morning to protest the reemployment of elements judged politically compromised.' ACS, Ministero dell'Interno, P.S., 1944–6 - busta 84, Affari per provincie. True to form in such telegrams, both the prefect and the
carabinieri assured Rome that public order was not threatened or disturbed
and, as usual, the prefect took full credit, asserting that the entire matter
had been peacefully resolved 'through my own personal, active
intervention.'

60 Florence was chosen because the mine's corporate offices and president
were located there.

61 ASC Bucine, busta 1946, cat. XIV-XV, fasc. XV.

62 See also ASC Cavriglia, busta (not numbered) 1946, cat. 1, cl. 6a, fasc.
Epurazione dipendenti comunali, for the case of a district doctor and
former Fascist whose conduct had been openly anti-Fascist and anti-Nazi after July 25, 1943. He had dispensed medicine and given medical assistance
to at least three injured partisans, even taking the risk of bringing one to a
hospital for treatment.

63 See NARA RG 331 ACC Italy, 10800/142/3419.

64 This and what follows is taken from Aroldo Lucarini, 'Ricordi di Guerra
1943–49.'

65 Aroldo Lucarini, 'Ricordi di Guerra 1943–49,' 34. See ASC Cavriglia, Deliberazioni 1944-1945, Estratto dal Protocollo delle Deliberazioni della Giunta
Comunale no. 19, for November 18, 1944, in which Cavriglia's communal
giunta 'recognized the need immediately to reorganize the personnel ros-
ters so that the communal administration could begin to function again.' A
'good part of the old personnel had abandoned their posts, because of their
political precedents or because they were enrolled in the Fascist Republican
Party.' The *giunta* agreed to choose replacements 'especially from amongst
the Patriots, anti-Nazis, anti-fascists, etc.'

66 Aroldo Lucarini, 'Ricordi di Guerra 1943–49,' 35.

67 Ibid.

68 See NARA RG 331 ACC Italy, 10801/105/44, 10801/105/45, for many intercepted letters describing such assaults, and see *La Nazione, Cronaca di Arezzo*

for the period. In Ciggiano (in the commune of Civitella), the many bombs and shots had 'fortunately not yet had any serious consequence.' *La Nazione, Cronaca di Arezzo*, no. 192, July 28, 1945. On July 20, 1945, for example, people had gathered outside Vincenzo Mencuccini's house in Ciggiano, calling for him to come out. When he opened his window, machinegun and pistol shots were fired. Ciggiano, along with Soci, Poppi, and the entire Casentino area were particularly active places for reprisals against former Fascists.

Massimo Storchi, 'Post-war Violence in Italy: A Struggle for Memory,' *Modern Italy* 12, no. 2 (2007): 237–50, discusses postwar violence against Fascists in Reggio Emilia, and the changing memory of the Resistance. See also Sarah Morgan, 'The Schio killings: A Case Study of Partisan Violence in Post-war Italy,' *Modern Italy* 5, no. 2 (2000): 147–60, and citations, therein on partisan postwar anti-Fascist violence. See Giampaolo Pansa, *Il sangue dei vinti: Quello che accadde in Italia dopo il 25 aprile* (Milan: Sperling and Kupfer, 2005) and Giorgio Pisanò and Paolo Pisanò, *Il triangolo della morte: La politica della strage in Emilia durante e dopo la guerra civile* (Milan: Mursia, 1992) for more provocative treatments of postwar retributive violence.

69 Aroldo Lucarini's daughter, Antelma, had worked in the communal rationing office. She may have been unpopular amongst some of their neighbours for her own activities, as well as because of the familial relationship with Signor Lucarini. ACC received a number of anonymous letters and denouncements regarding the activities of certain women during the Fascist era. See NARA RG 331 ACC Italy, 10801/115/77.

70 The Allied PWB report on political activity for February 1945 noted that Italian youths were cutting the hair of girls and young women who had associated with Allied troops. NARA RG 331 AFHQ, R 486C (microfilm frames not numbered). See the discussion of hair cutting in postwar France in Megan Koreman, *The Expectation of Justice: France 1944–1946*, 108 *et seq.* In *Shorn Women: Gender and Punishment in Liberation France* (Oxford: Berg Press 2002), Fabrice Virgili argues that, in France, the majority of those popularly punished for collaboration were women, and that many if not most of those punished were innocent of sexual involvement with the Germans.

71 *La Nazione, Cronaca di Arezzo*, no. 172, July 14, 1945. See also figure 10, showing two women in a doorway in the background, both wearing scarves. The reference to typhus comes from the practice of shaving one's head or cutting off one's hair to help reduce a fever, such as would occur if one really did have typhus.

72 See *La Nazione, Cronaca di Arezzo* for the months of June, July, and August 1945 especially. See also *L'Informatore Aretino*, Arezzo's locally published biweekly.

73 *La Nazione, Cronaca di Arezzo*, no. 131, June 2–3, 1945 (emphasis in the original). Laterina had also been the site of a POW camp for Allied soldiers.

74 *La Nazione, Cronaca di Arezzo*, no. 143, June 16–17; no. 160, July 5, 1945.

75 He had participated in killing three patriots. Ibid., no. 222, August 22, 1945.

76 ASA Pref. Gab., busta 7; *La Nazione, Cronaca di Arezzo*, no. 223, August 23, 1945.

77 ASA Pref. Gab., busta 7.

78 NARA RG 331 ACC Italy, 10801/105/44.

79 Ibid., 10801/105/44, 10801/115/93. His murder, on March 6, 1945, was the second within four days in that district.

80 ASA Pref. Gab., busta 7.

81 Ibid.

82 Don Gino Ciabattini, parish diary, entries for May 30 and July 3, 1945.

83 ASA Pref. Gab., busta 118, Relazioni mensili sulla situazione della provincia.

84 *La Nazione, Cronaca di Arezzo*, no. 146, June 22, 1946.

85 Ibid., no. 147, June 23, 1946.

86 ASC Cavriglia, busta (not numbered), 1946, cat. 1, cl. 6a, fasc. Epurazione dipendenti comunali. The back pay and benefit issue depended in part on whether a former Fascist communal or public employee had been given a period of suspension or received an 'act of discrimination.'

87 ASC Cavriglia, busta Archivio Regno, 1946-1947, cat. Deliberazioni del Consiglio Comunale.

88 Ibid., busta Arch. Repubblica, 1948, cat. Deliberazioni della Giunta Comunale.

89 See DL 7/2/1948, n. 48, and *Circolare* no. 6561/10124.140/2/1.7, February 25, 1948. Those who had been hired in their stead then had to be let go. See ASC Cavriglia, busta Arch. Repubblica, 1948, Deliberazioni della Giunta Comunale.

90 ASC Bucine, busta 1948, delib. CC & GC.

91 ASC Cavriglia, Relazione dell'attività svolta dal Sindaco Onor. Priamo Bigiandi e dal Consiglio Comunale nei 5 anni di carica dal marzo 1946 ad oggi, 16–17.

92 ASA Pref. Gab., busta 145.

93 The purge of schoolteachers had been the focus of a separate subcommission. See for example, *La Nazione, Cronaca di Arezzo*, no. 301, November 9, 1945.

94 R.J.B. Bosworth, *Mussolini's Italy*.

95 Ruggero Franci, 'Note di vita di scuola,' 46.

96 Ibid., 47.

97 Franci noted that the most often retold themes (as opposed to individual stories) were the interruption of the mass that morning, the murder of the archpriest, the escape of the wounded young seminary student (Daniele Tiezzi), and the burning of the village (47–9).

98 ASC Bucine, busta 1946, cats. XIV-XV, fasc. cat. 15a, cl. 2a, fasc. 4.

99 ASC Civitella, busta 1944, cat. XII-XIII-XIV-XV, fasc. cat. 15, sicurezza pubblica, cl. 1. See *La Nazione, Cronaca di Arezzo*, no. 43, February 20, 1946.

100 *La Nazione del Popolo*, no. 236, September 5, 1945. The writer of that article also raised the 'thorny question' why organizations that gave dances to raise money for reconstruction and political parties which called for equal rights for women and men did not charge women an entrance fee – 'not even a contribution of 5 or 10 lire' – to help with reconstruction.

101 *La Nazione, Cronaca di Arezzo*, no. 47, February 24, 1946.

102 ASC Bucine, busta 1946, cats. XIV-XV, fasc. cat. 15a, cl. 3a, fasc. 3. ENAL is the Ente Nazionale Assistenza Lavoratori, or National Labourers' Assistance Association. It was connected to the Communist Party.

103 ASC Civitella, busta 1945, cat. XIII-XIV-XV, fasc. cat. 15a.

104 See ASA Pref. Gab., busta 145, fasc. 32-4, for many such letters to various sindaci.

105 Ibid.

106 ASC Civitella, busta 1947, cat. I-VII, fasc. cat. 2a, cl. [blank].

107 Don Gino Ciabattini, parish diary, entry for August 12, 1945, c. 90 (typewritten, 65).

108 Oral history of Lara Lammioni, 11.

109 NARA RG 331 ACC Italy, 10801/115/70.

110 ASA Pref. Gab., busta 149, fasc. M-APB, UNRRA,

111 *La Nazione del Popolo*, no. 162, July 7, 1945.

112 Don Narcisco Polvani, 'Diario anno 1944,' entry for September 10, 1944. On Sunday, October 15, he noted that the church was nearly empty that day for the Festival of the Rosary, while the rooms of the social circle (where they were holding a dance) were filled.

8. Rebuilding the Commune

Epigraph: Father Polvani noted that he sent the sindaco a letter to that same effect.

1 See for example, NARA RG 331 ACC Italy, 10801/115/70.

2 ASA Pref. Gab., busta 7.

3 The literature on – or which touches on – the truism of Italian 'localism' (or the attitude of *campanilismo*) is vast. See, as only two examples, Joseph LaPalombara, *Democracy Italian Style*, 85–7; Sydel Silverman, *Three Bells of Civilization*, and the additional works they cite.

4 Norman Kogan, *The Government of Italy* (New York: Thomas Y. Crowell, 1962), 149–64.

5 See Martin Clark, *Modern Italy, 1871–1995*, 2nd ed. (London: Longman, 1996), 235.

6 Article 1 of RDL 14 aprile 1944, n. 111, provided for the reconstitution of communal administrations, with a sindaco and a municipal *giunta* whose members would vary in number according to the population of the commune, but no communal council. Any decree during this period was very much a product of the Allied Control Commission.

7 Don Narcisco Polvani, 'Diario anno 1944.' See, for examples, entries for September 12; September 21; September 25, 1944.

8 Aroldo Lucarini, 'Ricordi di Guerra 1943–49,' 53–4.

9 ASA Pref. Gab., busta 118, Relazioni mensili sulla situazione della provincia.

10 ASC Bucine, Registro delle deliberazioni Podestarili dal mese di agosto 1939 al 19 dic. 1944, no. 1.

11 ASA Pref. Gab., busta 97, fasc. Lavoro e P.S. The committees were to have four partisan members (among others) and their task was to find work for 'all the unemployed' – 'with an absolute preference for patriots and partisans.'

12 Ibid., busta 129, fasc. 39-6, Disoccupazione operaia, Prestito comunale, Finanziamento lavori.

13 The former was the Commissione Comunale Accertamento Lavoratori Agricoli. See ASC Bucine, Deliberazioni della Giunta Municipale dell'Anno 1945, no. 37; busta 1948, cat. [too faded to read], fasc. Commissione Accertamento Lavoratori Agricoli. See also ASC Civitella, Deliberazioni di Giunta dal 1945 al 1948 (deliberation for March 29, 1945), naming Civitella commune's four person committee.

14 ASC Cavriglia, busta Arch. Regno 1945, cat. 1a e 2a, N. 124, fasc. delle ordinanze emessa dal Sig. Sindaco.

15 ASC Cavriglia, busta Deliberazioni 1944–1945 (deliberation 76 for July 18, 1945, naming Commissioni Vigilanza Prezzi for Cavriglia, Castelnuovo, Meleto, and Montegonzi. The Cavriglia and Castelnuovo committees had member representatives from UDI, CLN, artisans, labourers' organizations, merchants, and cooperatives).

16 ASC Bucine, Deliberazioni della Giunta Municipale dell'Anno 1945, no. 17; Registro G.M. 26.1.1946 al 3.7.47.

17 ASA Pref. Gab., busta 133.

18 Elio Scala would also serve on committees that had to do with education. I interviewed Elio Scala several times between 1997 and 1999. He died in 2001.

19 Thank you to Elio Scala, Enzo Droandi, Goffredo Cinelli, and Ugo Jona for discussing this aspect of postwar life with me. Interviews throughout 1996, 1997, and 1998, especially.

20 Relazione dell'attività svolta dal Sindaco di Cavriglia Dott. Arch. Leonardo Lusanna al Consiglio Comunale nella sua prima adunanza del 2 Aprile 1946.

21 See NARA RG 331 ACC Italy, 10801/105/104. 'We don't have even enough oil to make soup; and the bread is like something you would give to a dog.' 'Can you do me a favour? Next time you are in Perugia [Arezzo's neighbouring province], if you find olive oil, can you get me 5 or 6 kilos? I'll pay up to 300 lire [per kilo].' See also ibid., 10801/105/45 for letters relating various rationing and price violations.

22 Ibid., 10801/115/70.

23 ASA Pref. Gab., busta 7.

24 Ibid., busta 118, Relazioni mensili sulla situazione della provincia.

25 Ibid., busta 135, Relazioni mensili sullo stato della provincia.

26 Ibid., busta 7; busta 118, Relazioni mensili sulla situazione della provincia.

27 See, as only a single example, the October 10, 1945, report of the provincial alimentation section of the High Commission for Alimentation, which spelled out in detail the Aretine's worsening situation for grain amassing; the price of beef, veal, and pork; supplies of chicken, rabbits, eggs; the 'absolute lack' of butter, cheese, and rice; the 'serious situation' of fats and oil; the 'preoccupation' with dried beans and potatoes; and the high price of wine. ASA Pref. Gab., busta 7.

28 See NARA RG 331 ACC Italy, 10801/105/45.

29 Ruggero Franci, 'Note di vita di scuola.'

30 'The population demonstrates disregard for the measures adopted by the government in the field of rationing and provisioning.' ASA Pref. Gab., busta 118, Relazioni mensili sulla situazione della provincia.

31 SEPRAL's director told ACC and the prefect, in October 1944, that the 100 grams of oil per person as allotted in the city and commune of Arezzo was not sufficient to satisfy the needs of the population, and would lead to evasions and illegal purchases. NARA RG 331 ACC Italy, 10801/154/17.

32 Quin Smith suspended him as sindaco. NARA RG 331 ACC Italy, 10800/142/3421. It is doubtful that Father Polvani was ever prosecuted,

something he does not mention in his diary. See Don Narcisco Polvani, 'Diario anno 1944,' entries for September 23, 1944; October 21, 1944; November 14, 1944.

33 NARA RG 331 ACC Italy, 10801/115/23. 'This can be traced directly to lack of public confidence in the administration both in Rome and in the Provinces.' Ibid., 10800/142/342.

34 Ibid., 10801/105/60.

35 ASC Cavriglia, Deliberazioni 1944-1945.

36 NARA RG 331 ACC Italy, 10801/154/20.

37 Sindaci were to urge municipal guards to 'intensify their activity' in making sure price limits were observed and that merchants publicly posted their prices. ASC Bucine, busta 1946, cat. XI, cat. 11a, cl. 3a, fasc. 4.

38 Ensuring compliance required additional communal expense. One communal guard, for example, earned 400 lire in overtime for two months of 'night service' 'watching over' the olive presses during the 1944–5 pressing in the commune of Cavriglia, to reduce the likelihood of producers keeping more of their own oil than allowed. ASC Cavriglia, Deliberazioni 1944-1945.

39 Aroldo Lucarini, 'Ricordi di Guerra, 1943–49,' 47–8.

40 ASA Pref. Gab., busta 7.

41 Ibid., busta 118, Relazioni mensili sulla situazione della provincia.

42 Ruggero Franci, 'Note di vita di scuola.'

43 ASC Bucine, busta cat. XI, cat. 11a, cl. 2a, fasc. 1.

44 See ASA Pref. Gab., busta 135; ASC Civitella, busta 1946, cat. XI-XII, fasc. cat. 12a, cl. 1; busta 1947, cat. XII, XIII, XIV, XV, fasc. cat. 12a, cl. 2.

45 See for example, ASC Bucine, busta Delib. G. & C. 1947, fasc. Delib. del Consiglio. See also ASC Civitella, busta 1945, cat. III, IV, V, fasc. cat. 5a, cl. 1a.

46 ASC Cavriglia, Deliberazioni della Giunta Comunale dall'11 settembre 1944 a tutto l'anno 1946, deliberation no. 27, March 17, 1945.

47 ASC Bucine, Deliberazioni della Giunta Municipale dell'Anno 1945, no. 60. See also ASC Bucine, Deliberazioni Giunta e Consiglio, Anno 1947, regarding San Pancrazio.

48 UNRRA and ACC expressed this sentiment as well. At his 1945 press conference, UNRRA Italian mission head, S.M. Keeny, spoke of UNRRA's goal to rebuild and refurbish schools: 'The moral effect of getting children back to school means a good deal for the families ... especially with so many men away from home, and the discussions about delinquency tend to fade out fairly rapidly when the organization of very day [everyday] life begins to be restored again.'

49 NARA RG 331 ACC Italy, 10800/144/84; 10801/115/77; 10800/144/67. While the Allied Army displaced students from their school buildings, ACC

concerned itself with 'defascistizing' school textbooks and the curriculum on a national and local level. Ibid., 10800/115/77; 10800/144/84; 10800/144/3.

50 ASC Civitella, busta 1945, cat. VI, VII, VIII, IX, fasc. cat. 9a, cl. 1a.

51 ASC Civitella, busta 1946, cat. IX-X, Istruzione pubblica, fasc. anno 1946, cat. 9.

52 Ibid.

53 ASC Civitella, busta 1947, cat. VIII-IX-X-XI, fasc. cat. 9a.

54 Interviews with Romano Moretti, Emilio Polverini, and Elio Scala during 1996–8.

55 ASC Bucine, busta delib. G & C 1947, fasc. 1947 Delib. della Giunta approvate o restituite senza provvedimento.

56 Ibid., busta Deliberazioni Consiglio e Giunta Comunale, Anno 1948. Deliberation for November 18, 1948.

57 Ibid., busta Deliberazioni G & C 1947, fasc. Delib. del Consiglio 1947.

58 Ibid., Copia di Deliberazioni della Giunta Comunale, January 8, 1945.

59 See Ibid., busta 1947 cat. II, fasc. cat. 2a, classe 3a, fasc. 1.

60 Ibid., busta Deliberazioni Giunta Consiglio 1947.

61 Ibid., busta Deliberazioni della Giunta Municipale dell'Anno 1945.

62 Rabid dogs, dogs biting children, and communes hiring unemployed men to catch stray dogs were common postwar happenings in a number of villages. See ASC Cavriglia, busta AR Rep. 1946-1947, Delib. della Giunta.

63 ASC Bucine, Deliberazioni G.M. 11.01.46 - 20.7.49.

64 Ibid., busta 1948, delib. CC e GC. If a resident was not inscribed on the commune's poverty rolls, technically the commune was not financially responsible for his hospital stay or other medical care. Nevertheless, often communes would vote to pay a resident's outstanding hospital or medical bill. See for example, ASC Bucine, Registro Deliberazioni Giunta Municipale 21.6.1946 al 31.7.1947 for deliberations on payments to hospitals in Civitella, Montevarchi, and elsewhere for various poor residents of the commune. And see ASC Civitella, busta Deliberazioni di Giunta dal 1945 al 1948.

65 ASC Bucine, busta 1947 cat. II, fasc. classe 1a.

66 Ibid., busta 1946 cat. II, fasc. cat. 2a, classe 2a. See also busta Deliberazioni Giunta Consiglio, Anno 1947.

67 ASC Bucine, fasc. Passaggio Amministrazione 1945. See (no busta) fasc. Mutuo di L. 3.000.000 anno 1946 for pages and pages of the commune's debts for, among other things, transporting the sick to hospitals outside the commune, purchasing a bicycle, school supplies and benches for schoolrooms, election materials, funeral caskets, wood for rebuilding bridges, paper for communal offices, medicines, disinfectant.

68 ASC Bucine, loose fasc, Beneficenza 1945; ASA Pref. Gab., busta 118, Relazioni mensili sulla situazione della provincia.

69 Every commune noted the theft of its typewriters, but what retreating German troops needed with typewriters is a mystery. Canadian liberation forces took the typewriters in one commune. ASC Bucine, Registro Deliberazioni Giunta Municipale 21.6.1946 al 31.7.1947. In the few months between the time the commune of Bucine first deliberated about setting aside money to buy a new typewriter and the time they voted to buy one, the price almost doubled. See also ASC Cavriglia, busta AR 1946, cat. dalla 1a alla 5a, N. 128, fasc. 1946, cat. Va, cl. 1a, fasc. proprietà com.li; busta Arch. Repubblica 1948, Deliberazioni della Giunta Comunale. On the shortage of bicycle tires, see ASC Cavriglia, busta Arch. Regno 1945, cat. 1a e 2a, N. 124, fasc. cat. 1a, cl. VIa, fasc. Segretario Com.le e Impiegati; busta AR 1946, cat. dalla 1a alla 5a, N. 128, fasc. 1946, Segretario e Dipendenti Com.li.

70 ASC Cavriglia, Deliberazioni 1944-1945.

71 This tax primarily affected cafes. ASC Civitella, busta Deliberazioni di Giunta dal 1945 al 1948.

72 Cavriglia, in 1947, reduced its impost on domestic help by half for families who had a single domestic who worked only a few hours a day. ASC Cavriglia, busta AR Rep. 1946-1947, Delib. della Giunta.

73 ASC Bucine, Deliberazioni 1945-1946, Giunta e Consiglio. In 1945, Cavriglia abolished its communal impost on pianos, and altered its impost on billiard tables to 500 lire per private table, and 1000 lire for tables in public places and recreational circles. ASC Cavriglia, Deliberazioni 1944-1945.

74 ASC Civitella, busta Deliberazioni di Giunta dal 1945 al 1948; ASC Cavriglia, busta Arch. Regno 1945, cat. dalla 3a alla 11a, N. 125, fasc. cat. 5a.

75 ASC Bucine, busta Delib. G. & C., fasc. 1947, Delib. della Giunta approvate o restituite senza provvedimento.

76 Cavriglia, busta Arch. Regno 1945, cat. dalla 3a alla 11a, N. 125, fasc. cat. 5a.

77 Emphasis in the original.

78 ASA Pref. Gab., busta 94, fasc. Commissione prov. e comitati comunali per la ricostruzione 1945, and busta 128; ASC Civitella, busta 1946, cat. Xa, cl. 1.

79 ASC Civitella, busta 1946, cat. Xa, cl. 1.

80 NA/PRO WO 204/12629.

81 See generally ASC Bucine, Registri Deliberazioni Giunta dal 26 gennaio 1946 al 31 luglio 1947 dal n.1 al n. 99.

82 These photographs, originally taken by studio Foto Vestri of Montevarchi in March 1946, made up part of an anniversary exhibit on the reconstruction

of the bridge, mounted at the Bucine communal library during 1996. Contemporary archival records make no mention of residents from other provinces employed on the rebuilding, and given the tenor of the time, local protests at hiring outsiders over locals most definitely would have taken place. Nevertheless, one resident recalled that the carpenters who built the frames for the viaduct arches were 'all from Friuli.'

83   *La Nazione, Cronaca di Arezzo*, no. 77, March 31, 1946.

84   Because it marked the end of the reconstruction project, the lunch was 'a worry' as much as a celebration: it meant that the labourers again would be unemployed. Within a week of the viaduct's completion, unemployed workers demonstrated.

85   Giorgio Sacchetti, *Il minatore deputato*, 12.

86   Factual information in the following section, except as supported by archival citations, is taken from Sezione Fotografica ARCA, Santa Barbara (Cavriglia), ed., *Il bacino lignitifero del Valdarno Superiore: Storia di una terra toscana* (San Giovanni Valdarno: ARCA CCD Toscana, 1999); and Giorgio Sacchetti, *Il minatore deputato: Priamo Bigiandi 1900–1961.*

87   *Il bacino lignitifero*, 39.

88   Don Gino Ciabattini, parish diary, entry for December 4, 1945, c. 91 (typewritten, 66).

89   Coal is also a higher quality fuel than lignite, in that it is denser, burns longer, and provides greater heat.

90   Don Gino Ciabattini, parish diary, entry for December 4, 1946, c. 102 (typewritten, 75).

91   ACS, GMI (Ministero dell'Interno, Gabinetto) 1947, busta 101, fasc. 5806, Agitazioni lavoratori.

92   Giuseppe Romita, a socialist, was minister of labour and social security for the hundred days of De Gasperi's third government.

93   The minister of the interior, on the other hand, wanted the names of those responsible for the occupation of the mine. Arezzo's prefect attempted to calm the situation, informing Rome that the miners' actions were justified by the need to provide lignite for Valdarno industrial firms and (as heating fuel) for local institutes of assistance and charity. Thus, the workers, in keeping with assurances 'to maintain the most perfect order and discipline,' took up their posts during their occupation of the mine 'without any violence towards the equipment or property.' ACS, GMI 1947, busta 101, fasc. 5806, Agitazioni lavoratori.

94   Don Gino Ciabattini, parish diary, entry for December 4, 1947, c. 106 (typewritten, 77).

95 ACS, GMI 1949, busta 105, fasc. 6002, Arezzo, Società Mineraria Valdarno.

96 Don Gino Ciabattini, parish diary, entry for May 1, 1948, c. 110 (typewritten, 80).

97 See CGIL Montevarchi, busta V (Firenze Convegno – sulla lignite), fasc. Valdarno Mineraria.

98 See *La Nazione, Cronaca di Arezzo* for May 8, 1948, regarding 'the mass dismissals' that marred the May 1 festival of labour. By the end of 1948, the corporation owed about 247,000,000 lire to creditors (most of whom were employees). CGIL Montevarchi, busta V (Firenze Convegno – sulla lignite), fasc. Miniere.

99 CGIL Montevarchi, busta V (Firenze Convegno – sulla lignite), fasc. Miniere. See Alfio Savini, Guido Occhini, and Carlo Salvicchi, *Ricordi, immagini, documenti: 1944–1989, pezzi di storia sindacale nell'aretino* (Cortona: Grafica L'Etruria, 1989), 39–58, regarding the ongoing crisis of the Valdarno mines during the 1950s.

100 Don Gino Ciabattini, parish diary, entry for December 4, 1948, c. 113 (typewritten, 87).

101 ASA Pref. Gab., busta 152, Relazioni mensili sulla provincia.

102 Don Gino Ciabattini, parish diary, entry for February 28, 1949, c. 115 (typewritten, 87). See also entry for December 4, 1949, c. 122 (typewritten, 93), regarding the continued occupation of the mines.

103 See Alfio Savini, Guido Occhini, and Carlo Salvicchi, *Ricordi, immagini, documenti*, 39–58.

104 Relazione dell'attività svolta dal Sindaco di Cavriglia Dott. Arch. Leonardo Lusanna al Consiglio Comunale nella sua prima adunanza del 2 Aprile 1946.

105 Ibid.

106 ASC Cavriglia, busta Archivio Regno 1946-1947, cat. Deliberazioni del Consiglio Comunale.

9. Private Property, Public Good, and the Housing Crisis

Epigraphs: Don Narcisco Polvani, 'Diario anno 1944,' entries for Sunday, October 8 and Tuesday October 10, 1944, regarding the gathering – or theft – of chestnuts from farmers' privately owned woods.
UN/UNRRA PAG-4/3.0.14.2.2.3.0.:3, UNRRA Italian Mission Memorandum on the Expanded UNRRA Lire Fund Housing Reconstruction Program, Proposed Program and Budget, February 1947.

1 An English translation of the 1948 Italian constitution is included in Norman Kogan, *The Government of Italy* (New York: Thomas Y. Crowell, 1962), 188 et seq. (from United States Department of State, *Documents and State Papers*, Vol. I, No. 1, April 1948, 46–63).

2 Hoover Institution Archives, Collection title: UNRRA (Ed. Arnold Collection), box no. 3, folder UNRRA 1945, Press Conference of Mr. S.M. Keeny, October 9, 1945, 5.

3 ASC Bucine, busta 1945, cats. IV-VII, cl. IV-VII.

4 Ibid., busta 1946, cat. XIV-XV, fasc. XIV.

5 NARA RG 331 ACC Italy, 10801/105/117. The request was written in English, and dated November 7, 1944.

6 'Capt. Goulding, at that time [Allied] Governor of Sansepolcro, was informed of this controversy and duly intervened by blocking the lorry and ordering the application of a board with the word "*reserved.*" In the occasion he was so kind as to declare to me that, if somebody was entitled to the possession of the contested lorry, the man *was I*, considering the ... troubles I had suffered.' NARA RG 331 ACC Italy, 10801/105/117 (emphasis in the original).

7 See the second entry from the first sitting of the reconstructed Bucine communal council after the passage of the front, August 12, 1944. ASC Bucine, Registro delle deliberazioni Podestarili dal mese di agosto 1939 al 19 dic. 1944. The commune also named a caretaker/administrator for the *fattoria* Pierangeli, whose estate manager had been massacred by the Germans on June 29.

8 NARA RG 331 ACC Italy, 10801/115/73.

9 ASC Cavriglia, Deliberazioni 1944–5.

10 ASA Pref. Gab., busta 110.

11 ASC Bucine, busta 1946, cats. XIV-XV, fasc. cat. XV.

12 ASA Pref. Gab., busta 129, fasc. 39-2, Ministero Lavoro e Previdenza Sociale, Ufficio Provinciale del Lavoro.

13 Ibid., busta 94, fasc. Ricostruzione: lavori 1944–5.

14 Ibid., busta 37, fasc. Attività dei Partigiani.

15 ASC Cavriglia, busta AR 1947, cat. dalla 5a e 6a, N. 134, fasc. Beni mobili provenienti dalle ex case del fascio.

16 ASC Civitella, busta 1945, cat. VI-VII-VIII-IX, fasc. cat. 6a, cl. 1a.

17 A desk and file cabinet belonging to the ex-*fascio* in Viciomaggio eventually were located in June 1948. ASC Civitella, busta 1948, cat. V-VI-VII-VIII.

18 To turn the building into a school also had been the commune's plan in 1943 when the Fascist Party had been dissolved. See chapter 1.

19 ASC Bucine, busta 8a, fasc. Danni di guerra privati.

20 ASC Cavriglia, busta Arch. Regno 1945, cat. 1a e 2a, N. 124, fasc. fasc. delle ordinanze emesse dal Sig. Sindaco.
21 See Don Narciso Polvani, 'Diario anno 1944,' entries for September 12, 16, 17, 22, regarding mandated sharing and arguments over priority for use of a thresher.
22 Ibid., entry for Friday, September 15, 1944.
23 ASC Cavriglia, busta Arch. Regno 1945, cat. 1a e 2a, N. 124, fasc. fasc. delle ordinanze emesse dal Sig. Sindaco.
24 ASC Bucine, busta 1946, cats. XIV-XV, fasc. cat. XV.
25 Ibid., Registro Deliberazioni Giunta Municipale 26.1.1946 al 31.7.1947.
26 The property was worth more than 20,000 lire, but the family agreed to accept that amount now, with more to be paid over time. ASC Cavriglia, busta AR 1946–7, Delib. della Giunta.
27 ASC Civitella, Giunta 1946.
28 Ibid.
29 ASC Bucine, busta 1946, cats. XIV-XV, fasc. cat. XV.
30 ASC Bucine, Deliberazioni della Giunta Municipale.
31 ASC Civitella, busta 1946, cat. IX-X, fasc. cat. 9a, cl. 1a.
32 ASA Pref. Gab., busta 145, fasc. 32, Ministero Pubblica Instruzione, 32-4 - Accademie - Istituti Scientifici - Biblioteche.
33 Ibid., busta 182.
34 ASC Civitella, busta 1946, cat. IX-X, fasc. cat. 10a.
35 The phrase 'crisi degli alloggi' appears with great frequency in official and unofficial documents of the period. The total number of rooms destroyed and damaged in Italy as a whole, and not yet rebuilt or repaired as of February 1947, was estimated to be 4,138,000. See UN/UNRRA PAG-4/ 3.0.14.2.2.3.0.:3. 'The effect of this is that to-day, over a year and a half after the end of the war in Italy, hundreds of thousands of such Italians, who were displaced or left homeless by the war, are still displaced from their home environments or without habitable homes, and are living under severely demoralizing conditions in Italian refugee camps, in overcrowded public buildings and shacks, or in often unsafe and unsanitary parts of their damaged houses. The damaging effect of this, physically and morally, upon these persons, and upon the national recovery, need not be enlarged upon.'
36 ASC Bucine, busta cat. XIV, fasc. Commissario Alloggi 1945-7.
37 Ibid. ASA Pref. Gab., busta 138, fasc. Alloggi e Negozi Massime; ASC Cavriglia, Arch. Regno 1945, cat. 1a e 2a, N. 124, fasc. fasc. delle ordinanze emesse dal Sig. Sindaco.
38 ASA Pref. Gab., busta 37, fasc. Servizi di guerra, locali e altro 1940–5.

39 Ibid., busta 160.
40 Ibid., busta 182, fasc. 19-4.
41 See ibid., busta 182, fasc. 19-4 for additional letters, petitions, and documents regarding families sharing housing.
42 DLL 28 dicembre 1944, n. 415. ASA Pref. Gab., busta 160, fasc. Alloggi e Negozi, Massime. The extent of the commissioner's powers was not entirely clear. Some communes pointed out that the text of the law did not appear to confer the power to requisition entire houses or apartments that were unoccupied, but only obligated those residing in houses with more rooms than they absolutely needed to accommodate another family and share the kitchen.
43 ASA Pref. Gab., busta 160, fasc. Alloggi e Negozi, Massime.
44 Ibid., busta 138, fasc. Alloggi e Negozi, Massime.
45 ASC Bucine, Registro Deliberazioni Giunta Municipale 26.1.1946 al 31.7.1947; busta cat. XIV, fasc. Commissario Alloggi 1945–7; ASC Cavriglia, AR 1946–7, Delib. della Giunta. See RDL 25 maggio 1946, n. 425, which created the new Commissione per le Opposizioni ai Provvedimenti del Commissario per gli Alloggi.
46 DL 30 giugno 1947, n. 548.
47 ASA Pref. Gab., busta 160, fasc. Alloggi e Negozi, Massime.
48 Ibid.
49 Ibid.
50 Ibid. (emphasis, capitals, in the original).
51 Refugees from other communes were counted separately. ASA Pref. Gab., busta 37, fasc. Servizi di guerra, Locali e Altro 1940–5.
52 They might be living 'in storerooms, caves, huts, or in schools, offices, theatres, etc.' ASA Pref. Gab., busta 37. The 'senza tetto' designation did not include those whose own homes had been destroyed but who had been assigned to share housing, who were living in residences that had been requisitioned, who were renting a residence, or who had found shelter with relatives or friends.
53 This and the excerpts that follow all date from 1945, and are contained in ASC Bucine, busta cat. II 1945, fasc. ECA - Domande sinistrati di Guerra.
54 ASA Pref. Gab., busta 160.
55 Ibid.
56 ASA Pref. Gab., busta 94, fasc. Ricostruzione: Lavori 1944–5; busta 110.
57 See Ibid., busta 128; busta 225, fasc. Lavoro e Prev. Sociale, INA-Casa, 39-1-1C; ASC Civitella, busta 1945, cat. X, XI, XII, fasc. cat. 10a, cl. 1a.
58 See DLL 17 novembre 1944, n. 366; DLL 18 gennaio 1945, n. 4; and DLL 1 marzo 1945, n []; DLL 9 giugno 1945, n. 305 (especially art. 10 of the 9 June 1945 decree). UN/UNRRA PAG-4/3.0.14.2.2.3.0.:3.

59 See NARA RG 331 ACC Italy, 10801/105/49; ASA Pref. Gab., busta 37, fasc. Servizi di guerra locali e altro, 1940–5.

60 ASA Pref. Gab., busta 128, fasc. 38-2, Comitato Provinciale per la Ricostruzione.

61 ASC Bucine, busta Deliberazioni 1945-6, Giunta e Consiglio. See also ASC Civitella, busta 1946, cat. IX-X, fasc. 10a; ASC Bucine, busta Deliberazioni Giunta e Consiglio 1947.

62 UN/UNRRA, PAG-4/3.0.14.2.2.3.0.:3, UNRRA Italian Mission report on the CASAS program, October 15, 1946.

63 In the commune of Bucine, one man spent 72,234 lire on repairing damage caused by shelling, completing the work by October 31, 1946. His 50 per cent state repayment finally was authorized on July 12, 1948. ASC Bucine, busta 1948, fasc. 1948 Evidenza dell'Uff. Lavoro. See ASC Bucine, busta Danni Guerra - Privati 1945 for other early claims. For Civitella, see ASC Civitella, busta 1948, cat. Perizie danni bellici pagate dal Comune di Civitella Chiana.

64 Pursuant to TU 9 guigno 1945, n. 305. ASA Pref. Gab. busta 128, fasc. Ministero per la Ricostruzione, Lavori per la Riscostruzione.

65 This was how some who had not owned homes before the war were able to buy them. My June 16, 1997, interview with Signora M of San Pancrazio.

66 See ASA Pref. Gab., busta 170. Decree 9.6.1945, n. 305. When raised to 500,000 lire, the system by which the state's contribution was calculated became even more complicated, varying according to the amount of an owner's patrimony. UN/UNRRA, PAG-4/3.0.14.2.2.3.0.:3, Memorandum on the Expanded UNRRA Lire Fund Housing Reconstruction Program, Proposed Program and Budget, February 1947.

67 See ASC Civitella, busta 1947, cat. 12.13.14-15, fasc. 14a, Oggetti diversi.

68 Ibid., busta 1947, cat. 12.13.14.15, fasc. 14a, Oggetti diversi; busta 1947, cat. VIII-IX-X-XI, fasc. Risarcimento danni di guerra. See busta 1948, cat. IX-X-XI, fasc. cat. 10a, cl. 6a, subfasc. Case popolari per i senza tetto a Civitella.

69 DLL 9 giugno 1945, n. 305. ASC Cavriglia, busta Danni di Guerra, Modelli e Stampati, Pagamenti, Contributi; AR 1946, cat. dalla 9a alla 12a, N. 131, fasc. cat. 10a, cl. IXa, fasc. Ufficio Tecnico (emphasis in the original). See also ASC Bucine, busta 1948, fasc. Commissione Accer. Lavoratori Agricoli.

70 ASC Cavriglia, AR 1946, cat. dalla 9a alla 12a, N. 131, fasc. cat. 10a, cl. IXa, fasc. Ufficio Tecnico.

71 ASA Pref. Gab., busta 170.

72 ASC Cavriglia, AR 1946, cat. dalla 9a alla 12a, N. 131, fasc. cat. 10a, cl. IXa, fasc. Uffico Tecnico.

73 Ibid.

74 Funds first became available from the Solidarity Fund in April 1946. Over a period of May, August, and September 1946, a total of 1,371,000,000 lire was allocated to the provinces that had suffered reprisals. ASC Civitella, busta 1946, cat. IX-X, fasc. cat. 10.

75 ASA Pref. Gab., busta 128, fasc. Ministero per la Ricostruzione, Lavori per la Ricostruzione; and fasc. Pieve S. Stefano, Ricostruzione paese, Lavori.

76 In October 1946, the minister of public works outlined the ministry's future plans, which envisioned spending 280 billion lire over the following two or three years on large scale, nationwide repair and construction programs. Of the 280 billion, 129 billion was to be allocated for housing, 20 billion for public buildings, and the rest for roads, bridges, ports, etc. Obtaining the 280 billion in the first place depended on Prime Minister De Gasperi's success in seeking a loan from the United States during his 1946 visit to Washington, DC.

77 By February 1947, 42,000 rooms had been completed, and 57,000 were under construction throughout Italy. UN/UNRRA, PAG-4/3.0.14.2.2.3.0.:3.

78 See ASA Pref. Gab., busta 24, fasc. Case Popolari.

79 See UN/UNRRA, PAG-4/3.0.14.2.2.3.0.:3, especially 'Memorandum on The Expanded UNRRA Lire Fund Housing Reconstruction Program (Proposed Program and Budget)' (February 1947) (UN/UNRRA, Italian Mission, Bureau of Requirements and Distribution, Sub-Bureau of Industrial Rehabilitation). That program came to direct much of its attention to the south.

80 ASC Civitella, busta 1948, cat. IX-X-XI, fasc. cat. 10a, cl. 6a, subfasc. Case popolari per i senza tetto a Civitella.

81 ASC Cavriglia, Archivio R. 1946–7, cat. Deliberazioni del Consiglio Comunale.

82 ASC Civitella, Consiglio Comunale 20 novembre '49, sessione straord., prima convocaz. See also ASC Civitella, busta 1948, cat. IX-X-XI, fasc. cat. 10a, cl. 6a, subfasc. Case popolari per i senza tetto a Civitella; ASC Civitella, Consiglio com.le sessione straordinar., 1a convocaz. - urgente, 17.7.949.

83 ASA Pref. Gab., busta 37.

84 ASC Civitella, busta 1948, cat. IX-X-XI, fasc. cat. 10a, cl. 6a, subfasc. Case popolari per i senza tetto a Civitella.

85 A member of the UNRRA-CASAS Italian mission phrased the selection process somewhat more optimistically: 'Great care is taken to see that the persons chosen are from among the most needy, that they are of a type that is capable of taking the best possible advantage of the premises and opportunities offered, and that the family unit concerned is suitable to the type of

dwellings provided.' UN/UNRRA, PAG-4/3.0.14. 2.2.3.0.:3. UNRRA viewed the new houses as a means of 'family rehabilitation,' whereby families that had been living in camps or in otherwise 'deplorable conditions' for the previous few years on account of the war, would be able to return 'to normal lives of responsibility and self-support.' UNRRA-CASAS had 'the aim of re-establishing healthy and happy relationships within the family unit, and of integrating the family life within that of the community.'

86 ASA Pref. Gab., busta 182, fasc. 19-4.

87 See for example, ibid., busta 160, busta 182.

88 ASC Civitella, busta 1947, cat. VIII-IX-X-XI, fasc. cat. 10a, cl. 12.

89 Another family had lived there (without injury) during a period when the family was absent. On their return, the *professoressa* had succeeded in having that family evicted.

10. *Mezzadria* Struggle and Social Change: The 'Haves' and 'Have-Nots'

Epigraphs: From ACC Provincial Commissioner Quin Smith's March 31, 1945, report to region VIII headquarters. NARA RG 331 ACC Italy, 10801/115/23. CGIL Toscana, fondo Confederterra Toscana (1944–78), busta 68, fasc. 1: Convegno Nazionale Sindacale della Mezzadria Classica (Firenze, 12-13 aprile 1947).

1 NARA RG 331 ACC Italy, 10801/115/37.

2 CGIL Toscana, fondo Confederterra Toscana (1944–78), busta 68, fasc. 1, Documenti relativi al Progetto di Nuovo Capitolato Colonico, hand-numbered, 98–112.

3 The *mezzadria* contract was an annual one between farmer and farm owner, the latter of whom could give the sharecropper unilateral notice of termination before the month of July and then evict the *mezzadro* and family in January, though the same family sometimes worked a particular plot for a generation or more. Farm accounts were supposed to be settled at the end of every year, but often were not. The failure (on the part of landowners) to reckon accounts regularly often resulted in annually increasing debts on the part of the *mezzadro* family, which was one of the long-term complaints about the system on the part of the *mezzadro*. For an overview of the *mezzadria* system, see Jeff Pratt, *The Rationality of Rural Life: Economic and Cultural Change in Tuscany* (Chur, Switzerland: Harwood Academic Publishers, 1994), chs. 2 and 3; David Kertzer, *Family Life in Central Italy, 1880–1910: Sharecropping, Wage Labor, and Coresidence* (New Brunswick: Rutgers University Press, 1984),

17–85. See also Sydel Silverman, *Three Bells of Civilization*, 46; Giorgio Giorgetti, *Contadini e proprietari nell'Italia moderna: rapporti di produzione e contratti agrari dal secolo 16 a oggi* (Turin: Einaudi, 1974), 413 et seq.; and 'Contratti agrari e rapporti sociali nelle campagne,' in *Storia d'Italia* (Turin: Einaudi, 1973), 745 et seq.

4 Perry Willson describes the 'rigid hierarchical structure according to age and gender' within the *mezzadria* relationship in *Peasant Women and Politics in Fascist Italy: The Massaie Rurali* (London: Routledge, 2002), ch. 1.

5 See Iris Origo's very personal view, *Images and Shadows: Part of a Life* (London: John Murray, 1970).

6 Catia Sonetti, 'The Family in Tuscany between Fascism and the Cold War,' in *After the War: Violence, Justice, Continuity and Renewal in Italian Society*, ed. Jonathan Dunnage, 75–88 (quote, 77).

7 See Jomarie Alano, 'Armed with a Yellow Mimosa: Women's Defence and Assistance Groups in Italy, 1943–45,' *Journal of Contemporary History* 38, no. 4 (2003): 615–31. Alano argues that women's participation in the Resistance resulted in both increased political activism and relatively unchanged social roles after the war.

8 The sharecropping system of farming and the hard, seemingly unchanging rural way of life it encompassed both before and after the Second World War have been the subject of both historical and anthropological study. In addition to the titles in note 3 above, see also Ivo Biagianti, 'Condizioni della mezzadria Toscana nel secondo dopoguerra,' in *Annali dell'Istituto Alcide Cervi*, n. 3, 1981; Ferruccio Fabilli, *I mezzadri*. In addition to gender and social hierarchical considerations, the *mezzadria* system was often given a Marxist analysis because of the obvious landlord-capital and sharecropper-labour division, or treated as a 'transition to capitalism' variant. *Mezzadri* were not simply the equivalent of industrial labourers in an agricultural setting, however, because the *mezzadria* system implicated the land itself, together with customs, law, social relations, social ordering, and a way of life not transferable to the factory floor. Moreover, the *mezzadria* system is very much about the history of property – and the history of the lack of ownership.

9 See Paul Corner, 'Fascist Agrarian Policy and the Italian Economy in the Interwar Years,' in *Gramsci and Italy's Passive Revolution*, ed. J.A. Davis (London: Croom Helm, 1979), regarding Fascist agricultural policies.

10 See Frank M. Snowden, *The Fascist Revolution in Tuscany, 1919–1922*.

11 The new contract also 'prevented a total subordination of the *mezzadro* to every arbitrary act' of the landowner. Ferruccio Fabilli, *I mezzadri*, 37. See also J.S. MacDonald, 'Agricultural Organization, Migration and Labour Militancy in Rural Italy,' *The Economic History Review* 16 New Series, no. 1 (1963): 61–75.

12 In addition to Frank M. Snowden, *The Fascist Revolution in Tuscany*, see Adrian Lyttelton, *The Seizure of Power: Fascism in Italy 1919–1929*; Paul Corner, *Fascism in Ferrara, 1915–1925* (London and New York: Oxford University Press, 1975); Claudio Segrè, *Italo Balbo: A Fascist Life*, 22–90; Anthony L. Cardoza, *Agrarian Elites and Italian Fascism: The Province of Bologna, 1901–1926* (Princeton: Princeton University Press, 1982).

13 Vera Zamagni, *The Economic History of Italy 1860–1990*, 264. The number of sharecroppers and, especially, tenant farmers increased significantly between 1921 and 1936. The percentage of day labourers in agriculture declined from 55.1 per cent in 1911, to 43.8 per cent in 1921, to 27.2 per cent by 1936. Although paying *braccianti* by the day or season, only as needed, made more economic sense for landowners (than did 'permanent' *mezzadri* families) in the years before and after WWI, *braccianti* were more likely to strike or engage in other concerted labour unrest. Sharecroppers were much less likely to strike and place their crop and contract at risk. See David Kertzer, *Family Life in Central Italy*, 56.

14 CGIL Toscana, fondo Confederterra Toscana (1944–78), busta 68, fasc. 1, Documenti relativi al Progetto di Nuovo Capitolato Colonico, hand-numbered, 98–112.

15 Ibid., hand-numbered, 108.

16 Ferruccio Fabilli, *I mezzadri*, 44. On the restoration of the old contract terms during the early Fascist years, see Giorgio Giorgetti, *Contadini e proprietari nell'Italia moderna*, 453–505.

17 See Giorgio Sacchetti, *Camicie nere in Valdarno* and *Il minatore deputato*, ch. 1.

18 'Leghe dei contadini baluardi di difesa delle condizioni di vita e di lavoro di tutti i lavoratori della terra.'

19 NARA RG 331, AFHQ R 486C (microfilm frames not numbered). The report also provided: 'The district … has a high percentage of communists. This is NOT due to their political views only, but to unrest caused through very bad living conditions, low rates of pay, unemployment and real fears of further unemployment. Consequently being a mining district, they look to the Communist party to give them by force what they cannot obtain in a normal manner.' The same report estimated the Communist Party locally possessed 150 automatic weapons, 600 'rifles, etc.,' 300 pistols, and 1000

hand grenades, though the writer assured that the party secretaries 'are as a whole very reasonable men and well thought of. They are NOT the type to take the law into their own hands.'

20 NARA RG 331 ACC Italy, 10801/115/37.

21 Ibid.

22 PC Quin Smith's monthly report to Region VIII Headquarters for February 1945 provided: 'In view of the levity of offence and the danger of "martyrising" one Sassi, a prominent political, prosecution against him and committee suspended.' Ibid., 10801/115/23.

23 See NA/PRO WO 204/12629.

24 NARA RG 331 ACC Italy, 10801/115/23.

25 Ibid., 10801/115/37.

26 CGIL Archive for the Province of Arezzo (CGIL Arezzo), busta Ricostruzione CGIL 1944-1949. The documents in CGIL's Arezzo archive for this period are not organized into files.

27 'No farm house should be left without toilets, lights, water, etc. Where it is impossible to outfit a farmhouse immediately with electric lights, the owner ought to agree to provide for it as soon as electricity is available.'

28 '[L]ast week, an association of agriculturalists have endeavored to hold private meetings with a view to organizing committees for future activities which will presumable [sic] attempt to counter mezzadria reform propaganda. In Poppi, the local communists broke up the meeting and have managed to intimidate local sympathisers so that there seems little likelihood of their getting anything organised. Next day, a similar action occurred at Bibbiena ... No actual violence occurred, but it was plain that the communists were determined to use force to prevent their suspected political opponents from organising.' NARA RG 331 ACC Italy, 10801/115/95.

29 CGIL Toscana, fondo Confederterra Toscana (1944–78), busta 2, fasc. 4. See Paul Ginsborg, *A History of Contemporary Italy*, 60–3, 106–8, on the Gullo decrees and the south.

30 By May, Arezzo's Camera del Lavoro noted that, '[I]n the Valdarno, for some time, we have been agitating for a new *patto colonico*,' but exactly what form that agitation or unrest took it did not describe. CGIL Toscana, fondo Confederterra Toscana (1944–78), busta 1, fasc. 2, Arezzo.

31 Alfio Savini, Guido Occhini, and Carlo Salvicchi, *Ricordi, immagini, documenti*, 19–20.

32 CGIL Toscana, fondo Confederterra Toscana (1944–78), busta 68, fasc. 1.

33 An adequate discussion of the historical and political meaning of the Camera del Lavoro is too complex (and long) to attempt here. When CGIL fractured in 1948, the Camera del Lavoro remained with the communist-socialist CGIL.

The new post-secession labour confederations (CISL and UIL) formed their own versions of the Camera del Lavoro. For definitions in English and for treatment of CGIL, see Gino Bedani, *Politics and Ideology in the Italian Workers' Movement: Union Development and the Changing Role of the Catholic and Communist Subcultures in Postwar Italy* (Oxford: Berg, 1995). For essays on the postwar Camera del Lavoro of Florence, which also have relevance for the Camere del Lavoro in the rest of Tuscany, see Zeffiro Ciuffoletti, Mario G. Rossi, Angelo Varni, eds., *La Camera del Lavoro di Firenze dalla Liberazione agli anni settanta* (Naples: Edizioni Scientifiche Italiane, 1991).

34 In his February 1945 report to region VIII headquarters, Quin Smith wrote: 'Legality of [the Camera del Lavoro] has been referred to Region. Not known if ever formed officially by Italian Govt. It *is* known they are cells of communism, and are NOT apolitical bodies they pretend. Local head office has had to be disciplined more than once while Montevarchi branch has issued unauthorised publication re mezzadria reform.' NARA RG 331 ACC Italy, 10801/115/23.

35 See CGIL Toscana, fondo Confederterra Toscana (1944–78), busta 1, fasc. 2, Arezzo; and busta 3, IV, fasc.1.

36 CGIL too had a precedent in the pre-Fascist General Confederation of Labor, the Confederazione generale del lavoro, or Cgl. Founded in 1906, by the Socialist Unions and the Camera del Lavoro, Cgl was to serve as a confederation of all workers organizations, unions, and federations, and to address social reform. On the postwar founding of CGIL, see Gino Bedani, *Politics and Ideology in the Italian Workers' Movement*, chs. 1 and 2. See also B. Salvati, 'The Rebirth of Italian Trade Unionism, 1943–54,' in *The Rebirth of Italy, 1943–50*, ed. S.J. Woolf, on the formation of CGIL; and Maurice F. Neufeld, *Italy: School for Awakening Countries; The Italian Labor Movement in its Political, Social, and Economic Setting from 1800 to 1960* (Ithaca: New York State School of Industrial and Labor Relations, Cornell University, 1961).

37 See CGIL Toscana, fondo Confederterra Toscana (1944–78), busta 3, VI, fasc. 2 for the text of the 'Patto di Roma per l'Unità Sindacale, Giugno 1944.'

38 *Sindacale* and *Sindacato* (*sindacati* in the plural) are also difficult to translate and explain. *Sindacato* is most often translated as union – as I sometimes refer to *sindacati* or have translated the term in this text. Italian–English dictionaries provide 'trade union' or 'labour union' for *sindacato*. *Sindacato* may be used to refer to an individual union – the *Sindacato mezzadri*, or *mezzadri* union, for example, or to a part of the labour or workers' movement in general – such as the communist syndicate, or communist 'bloc' within the labour movement, or *rappresentati sindacali*, to mean the union representatives of various unions within a larger organization. It can also mean the labour

movement or workers' movement as a whole. See Alfio Savini, Guido Occhini, and Carlo Salvicchi, *Ricordi, immagini, documenti.*

39 CGIL Arezzo, fondo Ricostruzione CGIL 1944–9.

40 CGIL Toscana, fondo Confederterra Toscana (1944–78), busta 1, fasc. 1, varie.

41 Ibid., busta 1, fasc. 50, Siena.

42 CGIL Toscana, fondo Confederterra Toscana, busta 3, IV, fasc. 1. The DC began organizing direct cultivators (ostensibly including *mezzadri* and tenant farmers, but focusing primarily on smallholders) as early as the end of October 1944. See Perry Willson, *Peasant Women and Politics in Fascist Italy: The Massaie Rurali,* epilogue, regarding Coldiretti. See also Orazio Lanza, 'L'agricoltura, la Coldiretti e la DC,' in *Costruire la democrazia. Gruppi partiti in Italia,* ed. Leonardo Morlino, (Bologna: Il Mulino, 1991).

43 CGIL Toscana, fondo Confederterra Toscana (1944–78), busta 3, VI, fasc. 1.

44 For the connection between CGIL and land reform, see Paul Ginsborg, *A History of Contemporary Italy,* 61–2. Ginsborg succinctly explains in parts of his chs. 2, 3, and 4 some of what I elaborate here based on CGIL archival sources.

45 They elected a commission made up of ten Communists and four Christian Democrats. No Socialist or female candidates 'presented themselves,' according to the first provincial secretary. Later during 1945, however, a Socialist member was added to the Aretine commission, as was a women's panel or board. Alfio Savini, Guido Occhini, and Carlo Salvicchi, *Ricordi, immagini, documenti,* 18.

46 CGIL Toscana, fondo Confederterra Toscana (1944–78), busta 51, fasc. 12. For the agenda of that first regional meeting, see CGIL, Toscana, fondo Confederterra Toscana (1944–78), busta 51, fasc. 15, Riunioni Regionali Verbali. See also Paul Ginsborg, *A History of Contemporary Italy,* 108.

47 CGIL Toscana, fondo Confederterra Toscana (1944–78), busta 51, fasc. 1, Arezzo.

48 Ibid.

49 CGIL Toscana, fondo Confederterra Toscana (1944–78), busta 52, fasc. Confederterra (II,I), Naz.le (II).

50 ASC Civitella, busta 1946, cat. XIa, cl. 1.

51 'In any case, let it be very clear that no act of intimidation, of abuse, or of violence, by whomever carried out, will be tolerated or will remain unpunished.' Ibid.

52 For a contemporary Federterra analysis of points in question and dispute within the existing *mazzadri* contract and that contract as proposed, see CGIL Toscana, fondo Confederterra Toscana (1944–78), busta 68, fasc. 1, Documenti relative al Progetto di Nuovo Capitolato Colonico.

53 On August 18, 1945, during the third meeting of its directing committee, Arezzo's Federterra agreed, among other things, to the 'intensification of

the labor struggle' until such time as the sharecroppers reached an accord that satisfied the 'aspirations' of the peasants for a more 'equal and just' division of the crops. CGIL Toscana, fondo Confederterra Toscana (1944–78), busta 1, fasc. 2, Arezzo.

54 Ibid., busta 3, VI, fasc. 1.

55 See the letters from sharecroppers to Federterra and between Federterra and political party representatives regarding sharecroppers' inability to get needed immediate assistance, subsidies, or indemnification from local or national Italian or American authorities. Ibid., busta 4, IX, fasc. 1 and fasc. 2.

56 Ibid., busta 51, fasc. 1, Arezzo.

57 Ibid., busta 51, fasc. 1, Arezzo.

58 Ibid., busta 51, fasc. 17.

59 In 1946, Federterra had 20,000 members in the province. Alfio Savini, Guido Occhini, and Carlo Salvicchi, *Ricordi, immagini, documenti,* 18. In the province of Siena, the union had 33,556 members by 1947. Paul Ginsborg, *A History of Contemporary Italy,* 478, n. 86.

60 ASA Pref. Gab., busta 7, December 30, 1945, Relazione sulla situazione della provincia.

61 See CGIL Toscana, Opuscolo M 331 89 Giu., 'Il "Giudizio dell'On. De Gasperi" sulla vertenza mezzadrile,' art. 2.

62 Works of improvement or reconstruction were to be carried out by non-agricultural labourers (rather than by *braccianti* or *mezzadri* themselves), when possible in order to generate employment for unemployed labourers. See CGIL Toscana, Opuscolo M 331 89 Giu., 'Il "Giudizio dell'On. De Gasperi" sulla vertenza mezzadrile,' art. 3.

63 Ibid., art. 4.

64 Article 2 specified that the current contract and the 50 per cent division of the farm product were to remain as they were. Article 1 directed that negotiations towards a new contract were to begin October 1, 1947. See also article 7.

65 For an explanation of the term '*lodo*' and its semi-legal use in this context, see the *Grande Dizionario della Lingua Italiana* (Turin: UTET 1961-2002); C. Battisti and G. Alessio, eds., *Nuovo Etinologico* (Florence: Barbèra, 1975). Articles 6 and 8 called for arbitration of controversies by an arbitration commission composed of a landowner's representative, a *mezzadro* representative, and a third member nominated by the president of the local tribunal.

66 ASA Pref. Gab., busta 118, Relazioni mensili sulla situazione della provincia.

67 See CGIL Toscana, Opuscolo M 331 89 Giu., 'Il "Giudizio dell'On. De Gasperi" sulla vertenza mezzadrile,' art. 8.

68 See ibid., art. 7.
69 ASA Pref. Gab., busta 130, Prefect's report for August 1946.
70 CGIL Toscana, fondo Confederterra Toscana (1944–78), busta 53, fasc. Provincial Arezzo.
71 ASA Pref. Gab., busta 118, Relazioni mensili sulla situazione della provincia. See also Ferruccio Fabilli, *I mezzadri*, 120. This ultimatum also was published in the Florence CTLN newspaper *La Nazione del Popolo*.
72 ASC Bucine, busta 1946, cat. 15, cl. 5.
73 ASC Civitella, busta 1946, cat. XIa, cl. 1; ASC Cavriglia, busta AR 1947, cat. dalla 7a alla 11a, N. 135, fasc. Lodo mezzadarile De Gasperi. Federterra and the association of farm owners for each province in Tuscany eventually reached its own accord or agreement regarding the application of the 'Giudizio De Gasperi' in individual provinces. See CGIL Toscana, M 331 89 Giu.
74 ASA Pref. Gab., busta 118, Relazioni mensili sulla situazione della provincia.
75 Now that the disputes had been resolved, the prefect believed that the 'struggle' was over and the *mezzadri* should return to their traditional labours and turn attention and efforts to other aspects of reconstruction. ASC Civitella, busta 1946, cat. XIa, cl. 1; ASC Cavriglia, busta AR 1947, cat. dalla 7a alla 11a, N. 135, fasc. Lodo mezzadrile De Gasperi.
76 CGIL Toscana, fondo Confederterra Toscana (1944–78), busta 52, fasc. Confederterra (II,1), Naz.le (II). In February 1947, in anticipation of the '*lodo* De Gasperi' becoming law, as well as an extension of the law stabilizing the terms of tenant farm contracts, Amintore Fanfani, as president of Coldiretti, from the organization's seat in Arezzo, thanked De Gasperi and the minister of agriculture on behalf of all members of Arezzo's provincial federation of 'Coltivatori Diretti e Piccoli Proprietari.' DL 27 maggio 1947, n. 495, article 1, instituted province-wide arbitration commissions charged with the task of applying the *lodo*'s provisions and deciding controversies relating to *mezzadria* contracts.
77 CGIL Toscana, fondo Confederterra Toscana (1944–78), busta 52, fasc. Confederterra Naz.le (II) and fasc. Confederterre provinciali (II). See also Alfio Savini, Guido Occhini, and Carlo Salvicchi, *Ricordi, immagini, documenti*, 10.
78 ASA Pref. Gab., busta 135, Relazioni mensili sullo stato della provincia.
79 ASC Civitella, busta 1947, cat. VIII-IX-X-XI, fasc. 1947, cat. XI.
80 On the ongoing attempts to reach a new contract, see CGIL Toscana, fondo Confederterra Toscana (1944–78), busta 55, fasc. 4/C, Arezzo, and fasc. 1, 4/C, Verbali Riunioni.

81 See the many lists of members of *fattoria* councils in CGIL Toscana, fondo Confederterra Toscana (1944–78), busta 2, III, fasc. 1. See also Alfio Savini, Guido Occhini and Carlo Salvicchi, *Ricordi, immagini, documenti*, 18, and Ferruccio Fabilli, *I mezzadri*, 104–8.

82 See ASC Bucine, busta (none), fasc. Consiglio Tributario 1946-48, 11.1.1.

83 Although Arezzo's membership numbers (both for *mezzadri* alone, and all members) were well below those of Florence and Siena provinces, they about equalled those of Grosseto and Pisa, and surpassed Livorno, Carrara, Lucca, and Pistoia. CGIL Toscana, fondo Confederterra Toscana (1944–78), busta 69, fasc. Tabelle Generali Dati Organizzativi 1948-49.

84 Ibid.

85 'It was a painful, distressing period, in which all the evils – economic and social – that had been latent in the whole system of the *mezzadria* for so many centuries, came to the surface.' Iris Origo, *Images and Shadows: Part of a Life*, 246–7. See also Sydel F. Silverman, '"Exploitation" in Rural Central Italy: Structure and Ideology in Stratification Study,' *Comparative Studies in Society and History* 12, no. 3 (1970): 327–39. Silverman wrote of the central Italian *mezzadri*'s perception (in 1969) of the *mezzadria* system as one of 'exploitation' by the landowners, thereby leading to 'crisis,' despite 'real changes' in the *mezzadria* system since WWII.

Real legal change in the property relationships underlying the *mezzadria* system was made possible with the enactment of three bills in 1950. See Amintore Fanfani, *Land Reform in Italy* (Rome: Ministry of Agriculture and Forestry, 1953) (Fanfani was minister of agriculture and forestry in 1953); Ministry of Agriculture and Forestry, *Land Reform in the Maremma: Fundamental Facts* (Rome and Grossetto: Ministry of Agriculture and Forestry, Ente Maremma, 1952); G. Barbero, *Land Reform in Italy: Achievements and Perspectives* (Rome: Food and Agricultural Organization of the United Nations, 1961); Davis McEntire, *Land Reforms in Italy* (Washington DC: Agency for International Development, 1970).

86 Iris Origo wrote that by 1970, only six out of their fifty-seven farms were still inhabited by their old tenants and run on the *mezzadria* system. *Images and Shadows: Part of a Life*, 248.

87 In 1952, 15,767 *mezzadri* families lived in the province of Arezzo. The number decreased every year after that – as did the number of members within each family that remained on the land – both because of the flight from family-centred agricultural work and farm life to non-agricultural wage work in more urban areas and, to a lesser extent, because of land reform which enabled former sharecroppers to purchase land. By 1969, 5822

families remained *mezzadri* in the province of Arezzo. Alfio Savini, Guido Occhini, and Carlo Salvicchi, *Ricordi, immagini, documenti*, 36–7.

88 Paul Ginsborg, *A History of Contemporary Italy*, 108–10.

89 The 'have-nots' and 'have-littles' as PC Quin Smith put it. NARA RG 331 ACC Italy, 10801/115/95.

11. Unemployment

Epigraphs: Registro delle Deliberazioni della Giunta for the commune of Civitella, August 23, 1945.
Circular N. 49941/43620/1/1/26 of 23 October 1945, as quoted by Arezzo's prefect in Bolletino Atti Ufficiali della R. Prefettura di Arezzo, 14 dicembre 1945, Div. Gab. N. 4763.

1 Relazione dell'attività svolta dal Sindaco di Cavriglia, Dott. Arch. Leonardo Lusanna al Consiglio Comunale nella sua prima adunanza del 2 Aprile 1946.

2 ASC Bucine, Registro delle deliberazioni Podestarili dal mese di agosto 1939 al 19 dic. 1944, No. 5, Provvedimente per il personale.

3 See for example, ASC Bucine, Deliberazioni della Giunta Municipale dell'Anno 1945, no. 18.

4 'maschili competenti, bisognosi e politicamente a posto.' ASA Pref. Gab., busta 99, fasc. Alto Commissariato Aggiunto per l'epurazione.

5 ASA Pref. Gab., busta 99 (emphasis in the original).

6 ASC Cavriglia, busta Arch. Regno 1944, N. 122, cat. dalla 1a alla 10a, fasc. cat. 1a, cl. 6a, Segretario – Dipendenti Personale Straordinario, Cassa Previdenza.

7 ASA Pref. Gab., busta 99.

8 Ibid.

9 Ibid., fasc. Alto Commissariato Aggiunto per l'epurazione.

10 ASA Pref. Gab., busta 99 (decree prot. no. 631); ASC Civitella, busta 1944, cat. I-II; ASC Bucine, busta cat. II 1945.

11 See ASA Pref. Gab., busta 99, fasc. 1-6, Licenziamento personale Femminile e sostituzione con disoccupati, 1944–5.

12 ASA Pref. Gab., busta 99 (emphasis in the original).

13 Ibid.

14 Ibid.

15 Ibid. (emphasis in the original).

16 The Buitoni pasta factory, located in Sansepolcro, was a major employer of women for the area. See ASA Pref. Gab., busta 7. In that commune, female

unemployment often remained higher than male through 1950. ASA Pref. Gab., busta 234.

17 ASA Pref. Gab., busta 99, fasc. 1-6, Licenziamento personale Femminile e sostituzione con disoccupati, 1944–5.

18 ASA Pref. Gab., busta 99.

19 Ibid.

20 He also noted the national postwar High Commission for Veterans Affairs was then in the process of formulating provisions for the mandatory 'absorption' of veterans and partisans into the national economic life, pointing out that he was merely anticipating what the national government soon would mandate. ASA Pref. Gab., busta 99, fasc. 1-6, Personale Femminile; busta 133, fasc. 40-4, Assistenza Reduci e Partigiani.

21 ASA Pref. Gab., busta 99.

22 Ibid. (emphasis in the original). *L'Unità* had published the general secretary's statement on September 22, 1945.

23 ASC Cavriglia, busta AR 1946, cat. dalla 1a alla 5a, N. 128, fasc. 1946, Segretario e Dipendenti Com.li.; busta A. Rep. Anno 1946–7, Delib. della Giunta.

24 On the postwar dismissal of women workers elsewhere, see generally, Alice Kessler-Harris, *Out to Work: A History of Wage-Earning Women in the United States* (New York and Oxford: Oxford University Press, 1982), 217–99; Penny Summerfield, *Women Workers in the Second World War: Production and Patriarchy in Conflict* (London: Croom Helm, 1984).

25 On October 11, 1945, the newspaper *La Nazione, Cronaca di Arezzo* reported that the number of female personnel in the administrative offices of the commune of Arezzo last year 'amounted to' thirty-eight. Since January 1945, twenty-two women had been 'relieved from service in consequence of the application of the provisions concerning the employment of male labour.'

26 'The struggle against unemployment' was a phrase in common use. In 1946, the prefect instituted a 'special Commission' whose object was '*la lotta contro la disoccupazione.*' Communes also had communal Committees against Unemployment. See ASA Pref. Gab., busta 129, fasc. 39-6, Disoccupazione Operaia nei comuni.

27 ASA Pref. Gab., busta 129, fasc. Disoccupazione operaia, Prestito Comunale, Finanziamento lavori; and fasc. 39-6, Disoccupazione Operaia nei comuni; and busta 130, fasc. Relazioni Mensili 1946.

28 NARA RG 331 ACC Italy, 10801/115/24. See also 10801/115/34 for PC Thurburn's citation of 5000–6000 unemployed as reason why the area could not absorb any more refugees.

29 NARA RG 331 ACC Italy, 10801/151/59.

30 Ibid., 10801/115/23 (from the Allied Censor Control Office, Feb. 1–15, 1945)

31 The *Questore*'s report to the prefect regarding the 'general situation in the province' for the month of July 1945, provided that 1873 persons were un-employed in the city of Arezzo. 'Such an unemployment figure reflects the dismissal of labourers by Allied units.' ASA Pref. Gab., busta 7.

32 ASA Pref. Gab., busta 99, fasc. Statistica, Disoccupazione Operaia.

33 Ibid., busta 97, Relazioni mensili, 1944–5.

34 As seen, numbers frequently changed between the ten day reporting periods. Ibid., busta 99.

35 Ibid., busta 130.

36 Ibid., busta 129, fasc. Disoccupazione operaia, Prestito Comunale, Finanziamento lavori; busta 99, fasc. Statistica, Disoccupazione Operaia; ASC Bucine, busta cat. 2a, cl. 4a, fasc. 1. Such small numbers also were reported for the other almost totally agricultural communes.

37 ASC Bucine, busta 1946, cats. XIV-XV, fasc. cat. XV.

38 ASC Bucine, busta 1946, cat. XI, cl. 11a, fasc. 1.

39 See ASA Pref. Gab., busta 146, fasc. Ministero Lavoro e Previdenza Sociale, Disoccupazione operaia, lavori in genere; busta 163, fasc. Lavori Pubblici, Opere pubbliche e lavori in genere.

40 ASA Pref. Gab., busta 234, fasc. Statistici Disoccupati.

41 NARA RG 331 ACC Italy, 10801/115/24 (provincial commissioner's monthly report for Oct. 1944: Nov. 1, 1944).

42 ASA Pref. Gab., busta 7.

43 Ibid., busta 99, fasc. Pieve S. Stefano - Disoccupazione operaia.

44 Ibid., busta 12, fasc. Partiti politici.

45 See generally, *La Nazione, Cronoca di Arezzo* for coverage of party rallies and public meetings during this period.

46 ASA Pref. Gab., busta 129, fasc. Disoccupazione operaia, Prestito Comunale, Finanziamento lavori.

47 Ibid., busta 118, Relazioni mensili sulla situazione della provincia.

48 Ibid., busta 129, fasc. 39-6, Disoccupazione Operaia nei comuni.

49 See ibid., busta 118, Relazioni mensili sulla situazione della provincia; and busta 135, Relazioni mensili sullo stato della provincia.

50 ASC Bucine, busta 1946, cat. XI, cl. 11a, fasc. 1.

51 ASA Pref. Gab., busta 129, fasc. Disoccupazione operaia, Prestito Comunale, Finanziamento lavori.

52 Ibid., busta 129, fasc. 39-6, Disoccupazione Operaia nei comuni.

53 Ibid., busta 129, fasc. Disoccupazione operaia, Prestito Comunale, Finanziamento lavori.

54 ASC Civitella, busta 1946, cat. IX-X, fasc. cat 10; busta Delib. Consiglio 1946.

55 ASA Pref. Gab. busta 129, fasc. 39-6, Disoccupazione Operaia nei comuni.

56 Ibid., busta 146, fasc. Ministero Lavoro e Previdenza Sociale, Disoccupazione operaia, Lavori in genere.

57 ASC Bucine, busta 8a, fasc. Mese di Maggio 1947.

58 Unemployed labourers were not the only ones to go on strike during these years. So did many clerks and white-collar workers employed by state agencies, who demanded higher wages to keep up with the cost of living. See, for example, ASC Civitella, busta 1948, cat. I, II, III, IV, fasc. cat. 1, cl. 6.

59 The head of Arezzo's provincial labour office noted, in August 1946, that the lack of employment – connected to the slow undertaking of public works reconstruction – and together with the increasing cost of living 'has created a very serious impatience on the part of the unemployed, who almost permanently besiege the commune and the Prefecture.' ASA Pref. Gab., busta 130.

60 ASA Pref. Gab., busta 129, fasc. 39-6, Disoccuapzione Operai nei comuni.

61 Ibid., busta 130.

62 Ibid., busta 130 (emphasis in the original).

63 Ibid., busta 99.

64 Ibid., busta 94, fasc. Commissione prov. e comitati comunali per la ricostruzione, 1945.

65 Ibid., busta 99.

66 Ibid., busta 146, fasc. Ministero Lavoro e Previdenza Sociale, Disoccupazione operaia, Lavori in genere.

67 ASC Bucine, busta 1946, cat. XI, cl. 11a, fasc. 1.

68 ASC Cavriglia, busta AR Anno 1947, cat. dalla 7a alla 11a, N. 135, fasc. cat. 10a, cl. IXa, fasc. Ufficio Tecnico.

69 Fanfani wrote to Arezzo's prefect regarding the money as 'a further refutation of the reproaches made.' ASA Pref. Gab., busta 129, fasc. Disoccupazione operaia, Prestito Comunale, Finanziamento lavori.

70 ASA Pref. Gab., busta 163, fasc. Lavori Pubblici, Opere pubbliche e Lavori in genere.

71 ASC Civitella, busta 1946–7, 1948–9, Deliberazioni del Consiglio.

72 ASC Bucine, busta 1948, cat. I, fasc. cat. 1a, cl. 4a, fasc. 1.

73 ASC Bucine, busta 1948, cat. XI, cat. 11a, cl. 5a, fasc. 6.

74 ASA Pref. Gab., busta 163, fasc. Lavori Pubblici, Opere pubbliche e Lavori in genere.

75 This program was called the 'assunzione mano d'opera nell'agricultura' or 'asorbimento mano d'opera.' ASA Pref. Gab., busta 129, fasc. 39-6, Assunzione mano d'opera nell'Agricultura.

76 See Aroldo Lucarini, 'Ricordi di Guerra, 1943–49,' 49–50.
77 On a day 'a bit windy,' but 'otherwise nice,' the priest met with Cavriglia's sindaco (who did not seem to Father Polvani to be a 'communist,' as others had said, but rather 'a man who sacrificed himself for the good of the people') to discuss the 'orders' given by the communal authorities. The two men had an amicable discussion and reached a 'perfect accord,' even though it required the priest's 'great sacrifice' as he did not have a 'large income.' Don Narcisco Polvani, 'Diario anno 1944,' entry for September 25, 1944.
78 ASA Pref. Gab., busta 99 (emphasis in the original).
79 ASA Pref. Gab., busta 129, fasc. Assunzione mano d'opera nell'Agricoltura; ASC Civitella, busta 1947, cat. I-VII, fasc. cat. 6.
80 The amount would be determined according to the 'taxable land income as shown on the past year's (1945) tax payment form.' The commission could assign labourers to farms outside their own commune.
81 ASC Civitella, busta 1948, cat. IX-X-XI, fasc. cat. 11, cl. 7a; ASC Bucine, busta 1946, cat. XI, cl. 11a, fasc. 1. See also ASA Pref. Gab., busta 146, fasc. Ministero Lavoro e Previdenza Sociale, Disoccupazione operaia, Lavori Agricoli.
82 See for example, ASA Pref. Gab., busta 129, fasc. Assunzione mano d'opera nell'Agricoltura (emphases in the originals).
83 The sindaco of Terranuova Bracciolini determined that one labourer should be hired for every two plots, or *poderi*. Thus, the owner of a fairly large farm divided into twenty-four *poderi* would have to take on twelve labourers, despite the fact that twenty-four *mezzadri* families already lived and worked on those plots. In the commune of Bibbiena, one farm made up of twelve equal *poderi*, which had been quite prosperous before the war, but was now badly damaged (eighty cows and ninety-six pigs had been carried off by the Germans, and two farm houses had been completely destroyed), was ordered to take on thirteen labourers.
84 ASA Pref. Gab., busta 146, fasc. Ministero Lavoro e Previdenza Sociale, Disoccupazione operaia, Lavori Agricoli; ASC Civitella, busta 1947, cat. VIII-IX-X-XI, fasc. 11; ASC Civitella, busta 1948, cat. IX-X-XI, fasc. cat. 11, cl. 7a. The assumption of unemployed labourers was indeed obligatory: landowner violators could and would (according to the prefect) be punished under article 650 of the Penal Code. Whether any farmers actually were prosecuted for circumventing or ignoring the prefect's absorption decree is not apparent from the archives.
85 Aroldo Lucarini, 'Ricordi di Guerra, 1943–49,' 50.
86 Ibid., 51.
87 Ibid., 52.

88 NARA RG 331 ACC Italy, 10801/115/24.

89 Ibid., 10801/115/37; 10801/151/65.

90 ASA Pref. Gab., busta 99; ASC Civitella, busta 1945, cat. X-XI-XII.

91 ASA Pref. Gab., busta 99.

92 ASC Civitella, busta 1945, cat. X-XI-XII (emphasis in the original).

93 ASA Pref. Gab., busta 133, fasc. 40-4, Assistenza Reduci e Partigiani.

94 ASA Pref. Gab., busta 97, fasc. Ufficio Provinciale Lavoro, Relazione Annuale 1945.

95 ASA Pref. Gab., busta 99, fasc. Pieve S. Stefano - Disoccupazione operaia.

96 Possession of a worker's registration card, or employment card or booklet (*libretto di lavoro*) remained a requirement in Italy to obtain and hold a job legally. *Libretti* were issued by one's commune of residence, and were a register of all jobs carried out, a record of starting and stopping dates of each job, and types of duties carried out.

97 ASC Civitella, busta 1945, cat. X, XI, XII, fasc. cat. 11, cl. 1a.

98 Ibid. Dozens of such applications to leave the agricultural worker category can be found at ASC Civitella, busta 1946, cat. XI-XII, fasc. cat. XIa, cl. 1; busta 1947, cat. VIII-IX-X-XI, fasc. 1947, cat. XI; ASC Bucine, busta 1946, cat. XI, fasc. cat. 11a, cl. 11a, fasc. 2 – and probably in the communal archives of most farming areas.

99 ASC Civitella, busta 1946, cat. XIa, cl. 1.

100 These were not large farms. One hectare is 10,000 square metres, or the equivalent of about 2.47 acres.

101 ACLI Archive, Montevarchi, 'ACLI 1948–1952.'

102 ASC Civitella, busta 1947, cat. VIII-IX-X-XI, fasc. (not a fasc. per se, but a sheet of paper) 11.

103 Ibid., busta 1948, cat. IX-X-XI, fasc. cat. 11, cl. 8. See also busta 1946, cat. XIa, cl. 1.

104 ASA Pref. Gab., busta 133, fasc. 40-4, Assistenza Reduci e Partigiani.

105 On Fascist era laws restricting labour mobility, see Vera Zamagni, *The Economic History of Italy, 1860–1990*, 312, n. 27. See also A. Treves, *Le migrazioni interne nell'Italia fascista* (Turin: Einaudi, 1976).

106 On October 17, 1946, Rome's prefect decreed all industries, firms, cooperatives, and similar operations were bound to hire new personnel only through Rome's communal employment office, which functioned in conjunction with the provincial labour office. In particular, the Roman prefect pointed out, provisions in the law against urbanization prohibited employers from taking on workers previously resident in others communes. The prefect of Arezzo notified the local press to publish notice and warnings for those who might be contemplating looking for work in the capital. ASA

Pref. Gab., busta 129, fasc. Disoccupazione operaia, Prestito Comunale, Finanziamento lavori.

107 ASC Bucine, busta 1946, cat. XV.

108 ASC Cavriglia, busta Arch. Regno 1945, cat. 1a e 2a, N. 124, fasc. delle ordinanze emesse dal Sig. Sindaco.

109 ASC Civitella, busta 1946, cat. IX-X, fasc. cat. 10.

110 'Licenziamento di personale non di ruolo ed assunzione di reduci' (DLL 26 marzo 1946, n. 138). ASC Cavriglia, busta AR 1948, cat. dalla 8a alla 15a, N. 138, fasc. cat. 8a, fasc. pensioni orfani di Guerra. The decree also required communes to list existing employees' 'characteristics' to determine if they could keep their jobs: for example, if they were war invalids, had been wounded in the war, were veterans (from either WWI, the Ethiopian War, the war of 1940–3, or the war of Liberation), if they had any family members killed in reprisals, if they were war orphans, if they owned real property, if they had been members of the Fascist Republican Party, collaborated with the Nazi-Fascists, and if their work for the commune was satisfactory. See ASC Civitella, busta 1946, cat. I-II, fasc. cat 1a, Amministrazione. See also ASC Bucine, Deliberazioni Giunta Consiglio, 1947.

111 Circolare prefettizia n. 4763, 10 dicembre 1945; DLLs 4 agosto 1945, n. 453 and 22 marzo 1946, n. 148 on 'l'assunzione obbligatoria dei reduci nelle pubbliche Amministrazioni.' See ASC Cavriglia, busta AR Rep. Anno 1946–7, Delib. della Giunta; ASC Bucine, Deliberazioni 1945–6, Giunta e Consiglio; ASA Pref. Gab., busta 99, fasc. Statistica, Disoccupazione Operaia.

112 ASC Bucine, Deliberazioni 1945–6, Giunta e Consiglio.

113 ASC Cavriglia, busta AR 1948, cat. dalla 8a alla 15a, N. 138, fasc. cat. 9a, cl. IIa, Istruzione pubblica. See also busta AR 1946, cat. dalla 9a alla 12a, N. 131, fasc. cat. 9a, cl. I e IIa, Scuole. All of the 131 temporary and substitute teachers for the 1946–7 school year for the province of Arezzo were *combattente, reduce, partigiano* or *partigiana, vedova guerra, invalido guerra, orfano guerra* or *orfana guerra*, or *deportato*.

114 ASC Civitella, Giunta 1946.

115 The council specified that she was a widow of the 1940–3 war – rather than the war of Liberation (1943–5). ASC Civitella, busta Anno 1946–7, 1948–9, Deliberazioni del Consiglio, fasc. Deliberazioni Consiglio del 1947.

116 Ibid.

117 See, for example, ASC Civitella, busta 1944, cat. III-IV-V; and busta 1945, fasc. cat. 1a.

118 Ibid., busta 1944, cat. I-II, fasc. cat. 1a, cl. 6a, subfasc. Impiegati avventizia Uff. Annonario.

119 ASA Pref. Gab., busta 167.

120 CGIL Arezzo, Ricostruzione CGIL 1944–9.

121 See ASA Pref. Gab., busta 167, fasc. Domande di occupazione, for letters from De Gasperi to Arezzo's prefect and to the provincial labour office, and from the prefect to sindaci and to private employers about specific individuals.

122 See CGIL Arezzo, Ricostruzione CGIL 1944–9.

123 CGIL Montevarchi, scatola 10 (loose papers).

12. Pure Politics

Epigraphs: 'He should make a very capable Sindaco.' NARA RG 331 ACC Italy, 10801/151/59.
Don Gino Ciabattini's parish diary, regarding the June 2, 1946 election for the institutional referendum and for the Constituent Assembly.

1 ASA Pref. Gab., busta 7, from the prefect's December 30, 1945, monthly 'Report on the Provincial Situation' to the minister of the interior.

2 ASA Pref. Gab., busta 7.

3 PC Lieutenant Colonel Thurburn reported as early as October 1944 that 'all parties are becoming better organized. This is especially true of the Communists, who have been working hard, mainly on the unemployed by promising legislation to pay subsidies to those who have not worked since the industrial plants were closed.' NARA RG 331 ACC Italy, 10801/115/24.

4 ASA Pref. Gab., busta 7.

5 See Joseph LaPalombara, *Democracy Italian Style*, especially ch. 3 – 'Life as Politics' – for the best formulation of that proposition. More recently, some (including authors of several recent books about Berlusconi) have argued that life in Italy has ceased being political, or at least is not political in the way it once was.

6 ASC Cavriglia, busta Deliberazioni 1944–5.

7 ASA Pref. Gab., busta 135, fasc. Culti.

8 Ibid., busta 174, fasc. Relazioni Mensili 1949.

9 Giovanni Guareschi wrote dozens of Don Camillo stories. See especially *Mondo Piccolo, Don Camillo* (Milan: Rizzoli, 1948), trans. Una Vincenzo Troubridge as *The Little World of Don Camillo* (Garden City, NY: Image Books, 1986 ed.).

10 Joseph LaPalombara, 'Italy: Fragmentation, Isolation, and Alienation,' in *Political Culture and Political Development*, ed. Lucian W. Pye and Sidney Verba, 282–329 (quote, 291) (Princeton: Princeton University Press, 1965).

11 There are far too many to list even a representational sample here. A very few of the most useful studies include: David I. Kertzer, *Comrades and Christians: Religion and Political Struggle in Communist Italy* (Cambridge and New York: Cambridge University Press, 1980) (see his excellent bibliography); Angelo Ventrone, *La cittadinanza repubblicana: Forma-partito e identità nazionale alle origini della democrazia italiana (1943–1948)* (Bologna: Il Mulino, 1996); Giorgio Galli, *I partiti politici in Italia, 1943–1994* (Turin: UTET Libreria, 1994); Simona Colarizi, *Storia dei partiti nell'Italia repubblicana* (Bari and Rome: Laterza, 1996).

12 See Don Gino Ciabattini, parish diary, especially for July 4, 1946.

13 Garibaldi's head superimposed on a green star was the symbol of the Fronte Democratico Popolare (Democratic Popular Front) joining the PCI and the PSI in a single list (but not a single party) for the April 18, 1948, parliamentary election. The Christian Democrat victory in that election is sometimes referred to as 'when Garibaldi betrayed Togliatti.'

14 ASA Pref. Gab., busta 145, fasc. 32-4.

15 Ibid., busta 129, fasc. 39-2, Ministero Lavoro e Previdenza Sociale, Ufficio Provinciale del Lavoro. The Fronte dell'Uomo Qualunque did surprisingly well in the province of Arezzo 'among the vast category of those discontented and disillusioned with the democratic movement established in Italy.' Ibid., busta 118, Relazioni mensili sulla situazione della provincia. See also busta 135, Relazioni mensili sullo stato della provincia, for the party's gains during 1947.

16 ACLI, the Associazioni Cristiane Lavoratori Italiani was founded in August 1944, almost a year before the war's end. According to its founding charter, ACLI established Christian expression in the field of labour association, and offered a social institution to carry out its own appropriate activity in the formative field of labour, as well as in the realms of social assistance and re-creation. ACLI thus mixed religion, labour, some economic assistance, leisure, and politics together in one social casserole – like ARCI, but with religion. Within a year, ACLI had a women's section, holding a national convention for women workers, soon followed by a youth section and a conference of 'young-aclisti.' In Arezzo, ACLI-terra sections for sharecroppers, farm workers, and smallholders existed in all of the province's zones. Theatre and music groups within local ACLI circles socialized and competed with one another in and outside the province. Arezzo, like elsewhere, had an ACLI consumer cooperative. ACLI circle members distributed food packages to needy families for the holidays, and together with the Catholic women's organization Centro Italiano Femminile (CIF), they ran seaside

summer camps for workers' children. See folder '1948–1952' maintained by the ACLI centre, Arezzo.

17 David I. Kertzer, *Comrades and Christians*, 41. Angelo Ventrone says that UDI 'was born in the second half of 1944, thanks to the commitment of some communist and socialist leaders, such as Rita Montagnana and Giuliana Nenni, or those near the left, such as Marisa Cinciari Rodano.' Angelo Ventrone, *La cittadinanza repubblicana*, 126. On the history of UDI, see Silvana Casmirri, *L'Unione donne italiane (1944–1948)* (Rome: Quaderni della Fiap, 1978); Maria Michetti, Margherita Repetto, and Luciana Viviani, *Udi: laboratorio di politica delle donne: idee e materiali per una storia* (Rome: Cooperativa Libera Stampa, 1984).

18 David I. Kertzer, *Comrades and Christians*, 41. DLL 1 febbraio 1945, no. 23 'extended' the right to vote to women.

19 Angelo Ventrone discusses how the Communist and Christian Democrat parties built their 'social presence' through a variety of recreational, assistance, and other activities. *La cittadinanza repubblicana*, ch. 3, 109–67. He has borrowed the 'social presence' reference (as have I) from Agopik Manoukian, ed., *La presenza sociale del Pci e della Dc* (Istituto di studi e ricerche Carlo Cattaneo. Vol. 4, Ricerche sulla participazione politica in Italia) (Bologna: Il Mulino, 1969).

20 *La Nazione, Cronaca di Arezzo*, no. 124, May 25, 1945. UDI commenced its first national congress in the city of Florence on October 23, 1945. Ibid., no. 284, October 23, 1945.

21 NARA RG 331 ACC Italy, 10801/115/47 (1 of 2). See also the *Questore*'s report to the prefect for July 1945, that UDI had, 'as is known,' democratic leanings and aimed above all for the spiritual elevation of women. ASA Pref. Gab., busta 7.

22 Kertzer describes UDI during the early 1970s as '[h]eavily influenced by the PCI at the national level, with a Socialist minority, UDI's areas of highest membership correspond with those of the PCI, reaching an apex in the Red Belt.' *Comrades and Christians*, 42, citing Agopik Manoukian, ed., *La presenza sociale del Pci e della Dc*. Margherita Repetto Alaia has emphasized that even at UDI's beginning, the organization was considered one for communist women, rather than communist and socialist women or for all women of the left. Margherita Repetto Alaia, 'Women and Mass Politics in the Republic,' in *Italian Socialism, Between Politics and History*, ed. Spencer M. Di Scala, 126–41 (Amherst: University of Massachusetts Press, 1996).

23 ASA Pref. Gab., busta 7.

24 ASC Cavriglia, busta Deliberazioni 1944–5.

25 *La Nazione, Cronaca di Arezzo*, no. 162, July 7, 1945; ibid., no. 171, July 13, 1945. Summer health camps had been the work of ECA (and its predecessor EOA) during Fascism.

26 ASA Pref. Gab., busta 99.

27 *La Nazione, Cronaca di Arezzo*, no. 16, January 19, 1946. Distribution of Befana gifts had also been the work of EOA and ECA female volunteers during Fascism.

28 Angelo Ventrone, *La cittadinanza repubblicana*, 127–9.

29 ASC Civitella, busta 1947, cat. 1-6, fasc. cat. 6a, cl. 3; ASC Bucine, busta 1947, cat. 2a, cl. 5a, fasc. 3.

30 ASA Pref. Gab., busta 7.

31 Angelo Ventrone, *La cittadinanza repubblicana*, 124, citing A. Rossi-Doria, *Le donne sulla scena politica*, in *Storia dell'Italia repubblicana* vol. I (Turin: Einaudi, 1994), 799. See also Agopik Manoukian, ed., *La presenza sociale del Pci e della Dc*, 437; and Nina Rothenberg, 'The Catholic and the Communist Women's Press in Post-War Italy – An Analysis of *Cronache* and *Noi Donne*,' *Modern Italy* 11, no. 3 (2006): 285–304.

32 Arezzo's Commissione Femminile della Federazione Comunista had organized the visit, with communist UDI women (and mothers) of the Valdarno. *La Nazione, Cronaca di Arezzo*, no. 76, March 30, 1946.

33 The other parties, especially the Action Party, had made early assistance attempts, but did not have the resources or volunteers to continue to compete with the PCI and the DC. ASA Pref. Gab., busta 12, fasc. Partiti Politici.

34 Ibid., busta 133, fasc. Ministero Assistenza Post Bellica, UNRRA.

35 Ibid., busta 149, fasc. Ministero Assistenza Post-Bellica, Massime (emphasis in the original).

36 Don Gino Ciabattini, parish diary, entry for August 14, 1949. The newspaper clipping is attached to the diary entry. '*Udine*' spells out UDI.

37 More than fifty years later, some women in the massacred village of San Pancrazio did tell me they had no interest in the local or national politics and elections of the time, and did not even remember if they voted.

38 ASA Pref. Gab., busta 118, Relazioni mensili sulla situazione della provincia.

39 Stone's memo to the file for September 13, 1944, noted that Bonomi agreed with the French provisional government that it was a good idea to postpone local administrative elections until the end of hostilities, the return of prisoners, and the return of refugees to their homes. NA/PRO WO 204/9747. See also the memorandum prepared for the United States' ambassador to Italy in January 1946 making the U.S. government's position clear. NA/PRO WO 204/9743.

40 Suffice it to say, however, that copies of the famous 'communism is like a rat' letter from the American anti-communism mass letter writing campaign can be found even in Arezzo's communal archives.

41 'Secret Memorandum as to the Desirability and Possibility of Holding Local Government Elections in Italy at Present,' NA/PRO WO 204/9717.

42 NA/PRO WO 204/9743.

43 Arezzo's state archive (fondo Gabinetto Prefettura) houses many dozens of notices to the prefect, sindaci, the *Questore*, and the *carabinieri* regarding formation of local sections of political parties, and planned political rallies and proposed speakers from the various political parties. See especially ASA Pref. Gab., busta 12, fasc. Partiti Politici. The prefect reported to Rome at the end of 1945 that there were no able local (meaning Aretine) party orators who could persuade or convince their listeners. Therefore, the parties had to rely on 'outside speakers.' Ibid., busta 7.

44 Ibid., busta 12, fasc. Partiti Politici.

45 Ibid.

46 *La Nazione del Popolo*, no. 39, February 16, 1946; no. 40, February 17, 1946.

47 He also spoke that afternoon in Cortona, while lesser names spoke at the other major centres of the province. Ibid., no. 109, May 10, 1946.

48 ASA Pref. Gab., busta 7.

49 Ibid. This is in a general population of about 319,000. Two years later, in 1947, the 'mass parties' in the province of Arezzo counted (and rounded off) their enrolled members: the Communist Party 14,000; the Christian Democrats 12,000; the Socialists 7000; the Socialisti dei Lavoratori Italiani (Socialist Workers) 2000; and the Fronte dell'Uomo Qualunque 1400. ASA Pref. Gab., busta 213. The numbers were not that far off from the *Questore*'s estimates in 1945, except that he had reckoned 2000 more Communist Party members.

50 ASA Pref. Gab., busta 7.

51 Ibid.

52 ASC Civitella, busta Deliberazioni di Giunta dal 1945–8.

53 ASA Pref. Gab., busta 118, fasc. Servizio ispettivo.

54 Frequent telegrams passed from the communes to the prefect on the status of the electoral lists, the number of voters inscribed, and distribution of electoral certificates. See ASC Bucine, busta Governo 1946, 6.6.1.

55 ASC Bucine, busta Elezioni 1948, fasc. norme per la Elezione dei deputati.

56 ASA Pref. Gab., busta 117.

57 ASC Bucine, busta Elezioni 1948.

58 In Cavriglia, nineteen persons were suspended from voting because they were compromised by connections with the past regime. ASA Pref. Gab., busta 118, fasc. Servizio ispettivo, Servizi elettorali dei comuni 1945–46.

59 'Bollettino Atti Ufficiali della R. Prefettura di Arezzo,' Div. 2 - N. 2624, January 31, 1946.

60 ASA Pref. Gab., busta 118, fasc. Servizio ispettivo, Servizi elettorali dei comuni 1945–6.

61 Ibid.

62 ASA Pref. Gab., busta 117.

63 Ibid.

64 ASC Cavriglia, busta Risultati delle varie Elezioni dal 1946 al 1972 e verbali della CEM anni vari.

65 ASA Pref. Gab., busta 117, fasc. Ordine pubblico.

66 ASC Civitella, busta 1946, cat. VI-VII-VIII, fasc. cat. 6a, Governo; ASC Bucine, busta Elezioni 1946, fasc. Elezioni telegrammi.

67 *La Nazione del Popolo*, no. 32, February 7, 1946. The number of councillors depended on a commune's population.

68 ASA Pref. Gab., busta 118, fasc. Servizi elettorali dei comuni.

69 See *La Nazione, Cronaca di Arezzo*, nos. 66–75, March 19–March 29, 1946, for election results and commentary for Arezzo, Tuscany, and all of Italy.

70 ASC Bucine, busta Elezioni 1948, norme per la Elezione dei deputati.

71 On later symbols in a more complex sense, see David I. Kertzer, *Politics and Symbols: The Italian Communist Party and the Fall of Communism* (New Haven: Yale University Press, 1996).

72 ASC Bucine, busta Elezioni 1948, fasc. Telegrammi. The minister of the interior also ordered sindaci to telegraph the election results the day after the election, according to: a) the number of those on the electoral list, divided according to gender; b) the number of those who cast votes, also counted by gender; and c) the candidates elected. ASC Bucine, busta Governo 1946, 6.6.1.

73 Communal records show the results as follows: 4141 individual votes for the Communists, 1082 for the Socialists, and 776 for the Independents; voting by list, the Communists received 3721 votes, the Socialists 673, and the Independents 751. ASC Cavriglia, busta Risultati delle varie Elezioni dal 1946 al 1972 e verbali della CEM anni vari.

74 *La Nazione del Popolo*, no. 63, March 15, 1946. The Republicans had won eight communes, the Liberals seventeen, Democratic Labor eleven, the Action Party ten, L'Uomo Qualunque three, 'Concentration of the Right' nine, and Independents sixty-seven.

75 ASC Cavriglia, busta Risultati delle varie Elezioni dal 1946 al 1972 e verbali della CEM anni vari.

76 ASC Civitella, busta 1946 Amministrative Elezioni.

77 ASC Cavriglia, busta Resultati delle varie Elezioni dal 1946 al 1972 e verbali della CEM anni vari. The two Castelnuovo polling sections included more than just the villages of Castelnuovo.

78 ASC Civitella, busta 1946 Amministrative Elezioni. Fewer women than men voted as a whole, but that was true not only in the widowed villages. During the 1946 election on the referendum and for the Constituent Assembly, some of the women of San Pancrazio seem to have stayed away from the polls, though the number of male registered voters was higher than the number of female registered voters – more so than in the other sections in that commune. Of 935 registered voters, 502 were men and 433 were women; 476 men and 378 women voted in the June 2, 1946, elections – meaning fifty-five women did not vote. (Only nineteen votes were cast for the Christian Democrats in that section during that election.)

79 ASC Cavriglia, busta Risultati delle varie Elezioni dal 1946 al 1972 e verbali della CEM anni vari.

80 ASA Pref. Gab., busta 160.

81 Ibid., busta 117. The candidate with the highest number of popular votes did not automatically become sindaco. Sindaci were elected from among council members, by council members. That system meant that the party whose candidates had received the most votes might not see one of their own as sindaco. In Arezzo, where the Communist Party candidates received the most votes overall, it made for the odd result of twenty-four Socialist sindaci, eleven Communist, three Independent, and one Christian Democrat.

82 ASA Pref. Gab., busta 160.

83 See ibid. for the make-up of the first elected councils for all of the communes. In the city and commune of Arezzo, as expected, many of the Communist and Socialist council members were more educated and included white-collar clerks, a lawyer, doctors, surveyors, engineers, and business owners. The commune of Arezzo, where forty were elected, also showed a wider range of party members elected. Most were Communists and Socialists, but eight were Christian Democrats; three were Liberals; one was PSLI; one had been an Actionist, but also was now PSLI; one was Democratic Labour; and one was a member of L'Uomo Qualunque.

84 NARA RG 331 ACC Italy, 10801/151/67.

85 Don Gino Ciabattini, parish diary, entry for February 11, 1945, c. 86 (typewritten, 62).

86 Emilio Polverini, who first showed me these photographs, pointed out the fine fabric and excellent cut of the Prince's coat, compared to the uniforms

of the other soldiers, and to the village women who are not wearing coats on that February day.

87 *La Nazione, Cronaca di Arezzo*, no. 107, May 8, 1946.

88 NA/PRO WO 204/9743.

89 The provinces were divided into thirty-two electoral colleges. See ASC Bucine, busta Elezioni 1948, fasc. Norme per la Elezione dei deputati. See also PRO WO 204/9717.

90 See Elvio Paolini and Alberto Douglas Scotti, *Da Badoglio a Berlusconi* (Carnago, Varese: Sugarco, 1995).

91 ASA Pref. Gab., busta 118, Relazioni mensili sulla situazione della provincia.

92 Don Gino Ciabattini, parish diary, c. 95 (typewritten, 68).

93 Don Gino Ciabattini, parish diary, entry for April 9–13, 1946, c. 94 (typewritten, 67).

94 Ruggero Franci, 'Note di vita di scuola,' 37–8. On the monarchy's attempt to bring the church onto its side and to ensure that Italians equated the monarchy with democracy and republic with communism, see Norman Kogan, *A Political History of Postwar Italy*, 37–8.

95 ASC Bucine, busta Elezioni 1948, fasc. Telegrammi.

96 The Fronte dell'Uomo Qualunque received 130 votes, the Liberal Party ninety-six, the Action Party sixty-seven, and the Republican Party thirty-seven. The electoral section in which San Pancrazio was situated cast 341 votes for the Communist Party, 221 for the Socialists, and nineteen for the Christian Democrats. ASC Bucine, busta Elezioni 1948, fasc. Costituente dati già segnalati.

97 The electoral section in which the village of Civitella is located cast only fifty-six votes for the Communist Party, but 155 for the Christian Democrats and 183 for the Socialist Party. ASC Civitella, busta 1948, cat. V-VI-VII-VIII, fasc. cat. 6a, cl. 2a.

98 In that commune, the Communist Party received 3947 votes, the Christian Democrats 864, and the Socialists 823. In the two electoral sections for the village of Castelnuovo, the Communists received 1217 votes, Socialists 244 votes, and Christian Democrats 241. ASC Cavriglia, busta Resultati delle varie Elezioni dal 1946 al 1972 e verbali della CEM anni vari, subfasc. Resultati delle varie Consultazioni Elettorali del 24 Marzo 1946 a oggi 1972.

99 The Communist Party received 55,613 votes; the Socialist Party 49,586 votes; and the Christian Democrat Party 49,360. Such a result for L'Uomo Qualunque was 'completely unforeseen,' the prefect stated. The authorities had not believed that the movement enjoyed much prestige locally. The Democratic Union, which had placed its hopes on a single list, gathered 3879 votes, while the Action Party had received only 2749 votes. ASA Pref. Gab.,

busta 118, Relazioni mensili sulla situazione della provincia. Complete election results for Arezzo and the other provinces of Tuscany are provided in *Dalla Costituente alla Regione, Il comportamento elettorale in Toscana dal 1946 al 1970* (Florence: Regione Toscana, Giunta regionale, Dipartimento statistica informazione documentazione, 1972).

100 Paul Ginsborg, *A History of Contemporary Italy*, 99. See also Norman Kogan, *A Political History of Postwar Italy*, 38: 'The election of members to the Constituent Assembly verified the previous electoral indications.'

101 In Arezzo, the Communist party received 34.45 per cent of the votes, the Socialists and the Christian Democrats about 30 per cent each. Of the more than 600 members of the Constituent Assembly, only twenty-one were women.

102 Don Gino Ciabattini, parish diary, c. 95 (typewritten, 68).

103 Paul Ginsborg wrote, the 'defeat of the monarchy at the referendum was without doubt the single greatest achievement of the progressive forces in Italian society in these years. Looking back at the debacle of the years 1945–8, the left-wing protagonists of that time could always find consolation in the establishment of the republic.' *A History of Contemporary Italy*, 99.

104 See Norman Kogan, *A Political History of Postwar Italy*, 35–8, for the more 'sinister' reason for deciding the monarchy question by referendum.

105 Ruggero Franci, 'Note di vita di scuola,' 38.

106 *Dalla Costituente alla Regione, Il comportamento elettorale in Toscana dal 1946 al 1970* refers to the Aretine as 'certainly more timid' in its referendum voting than were the other provinces of Tuscany. Province-wide, 67.4 per cent of the electorate voted for the republic, and 32.6 voted for the monarchy. In the commune of Cavriglia, with 5775 valid votes, 5031 (or 87.11 per cent) voted for the republic, while only 744 (or 12.89 per cent) voted for the monarchy. In Bucine, the monarchy received 1785 votes, more than half as many as the 3166 cast for the republic. ASC Bucine, busta Elezioni 1948, fasc. Referendum, dati gia segnalati. Only a single Aretine commune – Castiglion Fiorentino – voted to retain the monarchy (by 52.3 per cent), though two others came close, with Castiglion Fibocchi with 381 votes for the republic and 320 (or 45.6 per cent) for the monarchy, and Pratovecchio voting 44.6 per cent for the monarchy. ASA Pref. Gab., busta 118, fasc. Relazioni mensili sulla situazione della provincia.

107 ASA Pref. Gab., busta 118. Umberto left Italy for exile on June 13, 1946. He did not make a graceful exit, first claiming that the election results were not accurate and that many of the votes for the republic were invalid.

108 ASC Bucine, busta 1946, cat. XV. June 2 was declared a national holiday in May 1947, on which day public buildings were to display the national flag.

ASC Civitella, busta cat. 1-6, fasc. cat. 6a, cl. 3; ASC Cavriglia, busta AR Rep. 1946–7, Deliberazioni della Giunta. Italian towns of any size have a street named '2 giugno.'

109 *La Nazione, Cronaca di Arezzo,* no. 138, June 13, 1946.

110 ASA Pref. Gab., busta 118, Relazioni mensili sulla situazione della provincia.

111 Communal councils for the various communes of Arezzo (including the communes of Cavriglia and San Giovanni Valdarno) made lengthy praise of the constitution and its guarantees of human rights the substance of their first session for January 1, 1948 – the date on which the constitution went into effect. See ASA Pref. Gab., busta 171.

112 The Christian Democrats and the Communists were the groups 'most inflexible in their programmatic positions,' the prefect concluded. ASA Pref. Gab., busta 118, Relazioni mensili sulla situazione della provincia.

113 In the province of Arezzo, the Democratic Popular Front received 101,507 votes, and the Christian Democrat party 72,705 votes in the election for the chamber of deputies. ASA Pref. Gab., busta 152, fasc. Elezioni. Nationally, the Christian Democrats received 12,741,299 votes (or 48.5 per cent), the Democratic Popular Front 8,137,047 votes (or 31 per cent), and the Socialist Union 1,858,346 votes (or 7.1 per cent) for the chamber candidates. For senate candidates, the Christian Democrats won 48.1 per cent, and the Democratic Popular Front 30.8 per cent. See Elvio Paolini and Alberto Douglas Scotti, *Da Badoglio a Berlusconi,* 22–3.

114 A couple of contemporary incidents supplied the Social–Communists with ammunition against priests in general: 'Two incidents are contributing to swell the anticlerical propaganda: the Cippico case and the Don Cancelli case. The first committed grave irregularities in the administration of Church property at the Vatican, while the second is accused of immoral acts with some little girls. In the village of Castelnuovo especially the working people are talking about it and commenting ironically about these things.' Don Gino Ciabattini, parish diary, entry for March, c. 107 (typewritten, 78).

115 Don Gino Ciabattini, parish diary, entry for March 7, 1948, c. 107–8 (typewritten, 78–9).

116 Don Gino Ciabattini, parish diary, c. 108, (typewritten, 79).

117 Don Gino Ciabattini, parish diary, entry for April, c. 108 (typewritten, 79).

118 Ibid.

119 Don Gino Ciabattini, parish diary, entry for April 11, 1948, c. 108 (typewritten, 79).

120 Ibid., entry for April 18, 1948, c. 109 (typewritten, 79).

121 ASA Pref. Gab., busta 183.

122 Don Gino Ciabattini, parish diary, entry for April 18, 1948, c. 109 (typewritten, 79).
123 ASC Bucine, busta Elezioni 1948, fasc. Telegrammi.
124 Don Gino Ciabattini, parish diary, entry for April 19, 1948, c. 109 (typewritten, 80).
125 ASC Cavriglia, busta Resultati delle varie Elezioni dal 1946 al 1972.
126 Giorgio Sacchetti, *Il minatore deputato*, ch. 3. Sacchetti relates the pre-election campaigning somewhat differently from Father Ciabattini.
127 Don Gino Ciabattini, parish diary, entry '14 Luglio,' c. 113 (typewritten, 81).
128 Marco Innocenti, *L'Italia del 1948 ...quando De Gasperi batté Togliatti* (Milan: Mursia, 1997), 73.

13. Honouring the Dead

Epigraph: The list of names of those massacred at San Pancrazio follows. ASC Bucine, busta Deliberazioni della Giunta Municipale dell'Anno 1945; deliberation no. 42 of the communal *giunta*, April 9, 1945.

  1 See chapter 2.
  2 NA/PRO WO 204/11479, statement of Antonio Carletti, hand-numbered, 354–6. See also the statements of Carolina Carletti, Licia Carletti, Giogio Gori, Lina Gori, and Aurora Gori, hand-numbered, 357–71.
  3 NARA RG 331, ACC Italy, 10801/115/70.
  4 ASC Cavriglia, busta AR 1946, cat. 8a, fasc. Elenchi dei prigionieri morti dispersi; Guerra per la liberazione partigiana, N. 130 1944–7 (Contiene anche elenco volontari nell'esercito di Liberazione); and fasc. Guerra 1940–5, Civili morti per cause di guerra o per rappresaglie da parte delle Truppe Tedesche - Elenchi ecct.
  5 ASC Civitella, busta 1947, cat. VIII-IX-X-XI, fasc. 8 [not in a fasc. per se].
  6 See also Alessandro Portelli, *The Order has been Carried Out: History, Memory, and Meaning of a Nazi Massacre in Rome.*
  7 See Giovanni Contini, *La memoria divisa*, 251, regarding that controversy.
  8 N.R. Kleinfield, 'As 9/11 Nears, a Debate Rises: How Much Tribute Is Enough?,' *The New York Times*, September 2, 2007: 1 and 21.
  9 ASC Civitella, busta 1947, cat. VIII-IX-X-XI, fasc. 8 [not in a fasc. per se]. See also ASC Bucine, busta 1946, cat. XV (14.9.1) regarding providing 'the number of dead, disabled, and wounded.'
 10 Thomas Laqueur has discussed the importance of 'naming' and individualizing the dead in the context of war and memory in 'Memory and Naming

in the Great War,' in *Commemorations: The Politics of National Identity*, ed.
John R. Gillis, 150–67 (Princeton: Princeton University Press, 1994). See
also Thomas Laqueur, 'Names, Bodies, and the Anxiety of Erasure,' in *The
Social and Political Body*, ed. Theodore R. Schatzki and Wolfgang Natter
(New York and London: The Guilford Press, 1996).

11 ASC Cavriglia, busta AR 1946, cat. 8a, N. 130, fasc. Guerra 1940–5, Militari e
Civili Morti durante la Guerra del 1940–5 e dispersi.

12 ASC Cavriglia, AR 1947, cat. dalla 7a alla 11a, N. 135, cat. 8a, cl. 2a, Servizi
militari in genere.

13 'Bollettino Atti Ufficiali della R. Prefettura di Arezzo,' no. 2447, June 6,
1946.

14 ASC Cavriglia, busta AR 1946, cat. 8a.

15 Ibid., busta AR 1947, cat. dalla 1a alla 4a, N. 133, fasc. Comitato Naz. Pro
Vittime Politiche Roma.

16 ASC Bucine, busta 1945, deliberation number 44 of the communal *giunta*,
May 11, 1945. The *giunta*'s deliberation read: 'It being held right and proper to remember with a marble tablet the barbarous slaughter of some
SEVENTY-TWO persons carried out by the Germans June 29, 1944 at the
Pierangeli *fattoria* in San Pancrazio, to render to the glorious martyrs the
tribute of veneration and gratitude by all the population of the commune,
the communal *giunta* by unanimous vote decides to place at communal expense a marble tablet at the Pierangeli *fattoria* with the following epigraph
[quoted at the beginning of this chapter].'

17 ASC Bucine, busta 1945, cats. IV-VII.

18 Ibid., busta Beneficenza 1945, cl. 2a.

19 July 16, 1944, was the day Bucine was liberated.

20 ASC Bucine, busta Deliberazioni. 1945–6, Giunta e Consiglio; busta Registro
Deliberazioni Giunta Municipale 26.1.1946 al 31.7.1947; busta 1946, cat. II,
fasc. cat. 2a, cl. 4a, fasc. 1.

21 Aroldo Lucarini, 'Ricordi di Guerra 1943–49,' 47. Signor Lucarini described
the amount spent as a 'sizable figure from the communal budget.'

22 NARA RG 331 ACC Italy, 10801/115/82. The letter was written in English to
'The Provincial Commissioner A.M.G. Arezzo.'

23 ASC Cavriglia, busta AR 1946, cat. 8a, N. 130, fasc. Guerra 1940–5, Civili
morti per cause di guerra, per rappresaglie da parte delle Truppe Tedesche
- Elenchi ecct.

24 ASC Civitella, busta 1948, cat. I, II, III, IV, fasc. cat. 2a, cl. 3a.

25 Ibid., busta 1947, cat. I-II-III-IV-V-VI-VII, fasc. cat. 4a. See more such requests
also in busta 1946, cat. III-IV-V, fasc. cat. 4a, sanità ed igiene.

26 ASC Bucine, busta 1946, cat. 15, cl. 5, fasc. cat. 1.

27 Ibid., busta 1948, Deliberazioni CC e GC; busta Danni di Guerra, Edifici pubblici, strade e ponti, scuole 1945.

28 ASC Bucine, busta 1945.

29 ASA Pref. Gab., busta 37, fasc. Attività dei Partigiani, 1945.

30 ASC Civitella, busta 1947, cat. VIII-IX-X-XI, fasc. cat. 8.

31 Ibid.

32 There are too many relevant titles to list; many have been set forth in earlier notes. See also the bibliography.

33 On 'gaps' in memory, see Ruth Ben-Ghiat, 'A Lesser Evil? Italian Fascism in/and the Totalitarian Equation,' in *The Lesser Evil: Moral Approaches to Genocide Practices in a Comparative Perspective*, ed. H. Dubiel and G. Motzkin (London: Frank Cass, 2003–4).

34 R.J.B. Bosworth and Patrizia Dogliani, eds., *Italian Fascism: History, Memory, and Representation*, 6.

35 Robert Ventresca, 'Debating the Meaning of Fascism in Contemporary Italy,' *Modern Italy* 11, no. 2 (2006): 189–209. See also Andrea Mammone, 'A Daily Revision of the Past: Fascism, Anti-Fascism, and Memory in Contemporary Italy,' *Modern Italy* 11, no. 2 (2006): 211–26, on creation and manipulation of memory from above.

36 Alessandro Portelli, 'The Massacre at Civitella Val di Chiana (Tuscany, June 29, 1944) (quote, 142). The 'divided memory' reference is to Giovanni Contini, *La memoria divisa*. Francesca Cappelletto, 'Social Relations and War Remembrance: Second World War Atrocities in Rural Tuscan Villages,' *History and Anthropology* 17, no. 3 (2006): 245–66; 'Public Memories and Personal Stories: Recalling the Nazi-fascist Massacres,' in *Memory and World War II: An Ethnographic Approach*, ed. Francesca Cappelletto, 101–30; and 'Memories of Nazi-Fascist Massacres in Two Central Italian Villages,' *Sociologia Ruralis* 38, no. 1 (1998): 69–85.

37 In this vein, memory creation from below does not differ from memory creation from above: both tend to (or affirmatively choose to) remember and forget selectively.

38 Parish diary, entry for August 4, 1944, entitled 'Il trentesimo in suffragio dei Martirizzati,' c. 82 (typewritten, 59).

39 Don Narcisco Polvani, 'Diario anno 1944,' entry for October 23, 1944.

40 Father Polvani noted that the women of Le Màtole (see chapter 3) went to mass and took the sacrament at Massa on November 14, 1944, bringing Father Cuccoli 'a beautiful altar cloth' as a gift. Father Polvani was pleased by the gesture made to his former curate by 'those poor women deprived of husbands, fathers, and brothers by the German hordes.' Ibid., entry for November 14, 1944.

41 And, most took communion. Don Gino Ciabattini, parish diary, entry for
   July 4, 1945, c. 89 (typewritten, 64). *La Nazione, Cronaca di Arezzo*, no. 145,
   for July 4, 1945, set forth the planned program, which began at eight that
   morning with religious services in the parish church, then a commemoration at the massacre site at nine, at which 'various orators' would speak. At
   nine-thirty, a religious ceremony began at the parish church in Meleto, followed at ten-thirty by a commemoration in the village's main piazza.
42 Although the speaker was unknown to Father Ciabattini, Emilio Polverini
   points out that he was most likely Virgilio Diomiri, who was well known to
   the villagers. He had once been a member of a religious order who then became a socialist. He had worked for the mining company and had actively
   participated in the labour struggles there since 1919.
43 Don Gino Ciabattini, parish diary, February 1946, c. 92 (typewritten, 66).
44 Ibid., entry for July 4, 1946, c. 97–8 (typewritten, 69).
45 Ibid., c. 101 (typewritten, 69).
46 Ibid., c. 97, attachments, figs. 3; c. 98, attachments, figs. 4a and 4b. See also
   ibid., c. 99–100, attachments, figs. 5–7.
47 See chapter 12 regarding Father Benedetti of Subbiano who during the war
   had blessed the partisans' weapons (and been persecuted by the Germans
   on account of it) but who postwar was vehemently anti-communist.
48 Don Gino Ciabattini, parish diary, c. 99, attachment, fig. 6.
49 Ibid., c. 104 (typewritten, 76).
50 See ASA Pref. Gab., busta 171, regarding the ceremony in the village of Fon-
   taccia in the commune of Castiglion Fibocchi, called off by the sindaco, because she (this was the only commune with a woman sindaco) stated that
   the event had become too politicized.
51 See ibid., busta 37, fasc. Attività dei Partigiani 1945; busta 135; busta 171;
   ASC Civitella, busta 1947, cat. VIII-IX-X-XI, fasc. cat. 8; ASC Bucine, busta
   Beneficenza 1945, cl. 2a.
52 See ASC Civitella, busta Deliberazioni Consiglio 1946; busta Deliberazioni di
   Giunta 1947; busta Deliberazioni di Giunta 1948.
53 ASC Civitella, busta 1944, cat. XII-XIII-XIV-XV, fasc. 15a, sicurezza pubblica,
   cl. 1a.
54 ASC Bucine, busta Riconoscimenti e qualificati Partigiani 1946. Bucine's
   communal council voted a few days later to give 500 lire for a 'solemn mass'
   at San Leolino for the souls of those killed by the Germans in that village.
   Ibid., busta Deliberazioni 1945–6, Giunta e Consiglio.
55 San Pancrazio would receive the gold medal for civilian valour in February
   1975. Two years later, the Ministry of the Interior awarded the gold medal
   for civilian valour to the memory of Father Giuseppe Torelli, San Pancrazio's

priest killed in the June 29, 1944, massacre. Father Ferrante Bagiardi, massacred with his parishioners and fellow citizens on July 4, 1944, in Castelnuovo, and Father Giovanni Fondelli, massacred with his parishioners and fellow citizens in Meleto that same day, were both awarded silver medals for military valour under the auspices of the Ministry of Defence in July 1991. Father Ermete Morini and Dante Pagliazzi, who had been murdered and burned together in Massa dei Sabbioni were given silver medals in their memory the following year. The commune of Cavriglia was decorated for military valour. Documents from Emilio Polverini's collection. See also Romano Macucci, *Pane Spezzato: Breve storia di tre preti eroici.*

56 At that time, people were visiting Assisi where a statue of the Madonna was said to have been seen weeping. Father Ciabattini had organized one such trip for his parishioners.

57 Don Gino Ciabattini, parish diary, entry for July 4, 1948, c. 111 (typewritten, 81).

58 Ibid., c. 112, attachment, figs. 11a–d.

59 Don Gino Ciabattini, parish diary, c. 123, fig. 17 (*Il Mattino* for September 30, 1949) (typewritten, 94).

Conclusion: After War and Massacre

1 Don Narcisco Polvani, 'Diario anno 1944,' entry for September 27, 1944.

2 Italo Calvino, *The Path to the Nest of Spiders*, trans. Archibald Colquhoun; preface trans. William Weaver (New York: Ecco Press, 1976) (1947).

3 Don Narcisco Polvani, 'Diario anno 1944,' entry for August 6, 1944.

Bibliography

Absalom, Roger. 'Allied Escapers and the *Contadini* in Occupied Italy (1943–5).' *Journal of Modern Italian Studies* 10, no. 4 (2005): 413–25.

– *Gli Alleati e la ricostruzione in Toscana (1944–1945): Documenti Anglo-Americani.* 2 vols. Florence: Olschki, 1988–2001.

– 'Il mondo contadino toscano e la guerra: 1943–1945. Alcune modeste proposte per una storia da fare.' *Passato e presente* 4, no. 8 (1985): 157–74.

– 'A Resistance to the Resistance? The Italian Peasant in History 1943–1948.' In *Moving in Measure: Essays in Honour of Brian Moloney*, edited by J. Bryce and D. Thompson, 169–79. Hull: Hull University Press, 1989.

– *A Strange Alliance: Aspects of Escape and Survival in Italy 1943–45.* Florence: Olschki, 1991.

Acquarone, Alberto. *L'organizzazione dello stato totalitario.* Turin: Einaudi, 1995.

Acquarone, Alberto, and Maurizio Vernassa, eds. *Il regime fascista.* Bologna: Il Mulino, 1974.

Agar Hamilton, J., and L.C.F. Turner. *Crisis in the Desert, May to July 1942.* Oxford: Oxford University Press, 1952.

Agarossi, Elena. *A Nation Collapses: The Italian Surrender of September 1943.* Translated by Harvey Fergusson II. Cambridge: Cambridge University Press, 1999.

Alaia, Margherita Repetto. 'Women and Mass Politics in the Republic.' In *Italian Socialism, Between Politics and History*, edited by Spencer M. Di Scala, 126–41. Amherst: University of Massachusetts Press, 1996.

Alano, Jomarie. 'Armed with a Yellow Mimosa: Women's Defence and Assistance Groups in Italy, 1943–45.' *Journal of Contemporary History* 38, no. 4 (2003): 615–31.

Allied Control Commission and Istituto Centrale di Statistica. *Censuses and Surveys for the National Reconstruction carried out in September 1944.* Rome: 1945.

Alper, Benedict S. *Love and Politics in Wartime: Letters to My Wife, 1943–45.*
Selected and edited by Joan Wallach Scott. Urbana and Chicago: University
of Illinois Press, 1992.

Andrae, Friedrich. *La Wehrmacht in Italia. La guerra delle forze armate tedesche contro la popolazione civile, 1943–1945.* Rome: Riuniti, 1997.

Antze, Paul, and Michael Lambeck, eds. *Tense Past: Cultural Essays in Trauma and
Memory.* New York: Routledge, 1996.

Arbizzani, Luigi, ed. *Al di qua e al di là della linea Gotica, 1944–1945: Aspetti sociali, politici e militari in Toscana e in Emilia-Romagna.* Bologna and Florence:
Regioni Emilia-Romagna e Toscana, 1993.

Ascarelli, Attilio. *Le fosse Ardeatine.* Rome: Edizioni ANFIM, 1992.

Ascoli, Ugo. *Analysis of the Italian Welfare System: Some Implications for Current
Australian Issues.* SWRC Reports and proceedings, no. 49, August 1984.

Atkinson, Rick. *The Day of Battle: The War in Sicily and Italy, 1943–1944.* New
York: Henry Holt, 2007.

Bagnasco, Arnaldo. *Tre Italie. La problematica territoriale dello sviluppo italiano.*
Bologna: Il Mulino, 1991. First published 1977.

Baldissara, Luca, and Paolo Pezzino, eds. *Crimini e memorie di guerra. Violenza contro
le popolazioni e politiche del ricordo.* Naples: L'ancora del mediterraneo, 2004.

– eds. *Giudicare e punire. I processi per crimini di guerra tra diritto e politica.* Naples:
L'ancora del mediterraneo, 2005.

Ballini, Pier Luigi, ed. *La Nazione del Popolo: Organo del Comitato Toscano di
Liberazione Nazionale (11 agosto 1944–3 luglio 1946).* Florence: Regione Toscana,
Consiglio Regionale, 1998.

Ballini, Pier Luigi, and Giacomo Becattini. *La Toscana nel secondo dopoguerra.*
Milan: Franco Angeli, 1991.

Balò Valli, Ida, ed. *Giugno 1944: Civitella racconta.* Cortona: Grafica L'Etruria, 1994.

Banfield, Edward. *The Moral Basis of a Backward Society.* Glencoe, IL: Free Press,
1958.

Barbero, Giuseppe. *Land Reform in Italy: Achievements and Perspectives.* Rome:
Food and Agricultural Organization of the United Nations, 1961.

Barnes, Samuel H. *Party Democracy: Politics in an Italian Socialist Federation.* New
Haven and London: Yale University Press, 1967.

Bartov, Omer. 'The Conduct of War: Soldiers and the Barbarization of Warfare.'
Journal of Modern History 64, Supplement (December 1992): S32–S45.

– *The Eastern Front, 1941–1945: German Troops and the Barbarisation of Warfare.*
2nd ed., Basingstoke and New York: Palgrave, 2001.

– *Hitler's Army: Soldiers, Nazis, and War in the Third Reich.* New York and Oxford:
Oxford University Press, 1991.

– *Mirrors of Destruction: War, Genocide, and Modern Identity.* New York and Oxford: Oxford University Press, 2000.

– 'Trauma and Absence.' In *European Memories of the Second World War*, edited by Helmut Peitsch, Charles Burdett, and Claire Gorrara, 258–71. New York and Oxford: Berghahn Books, 1999.

Battaglia, Roberto. *Storia della Resistenza italiana.* Turin: Einaudi, 1970. First published 1953.

Battini, Michele. *The Missing Italian Nuremberg: Cultural Amnesia and Postwar Politics.* Translated by Noor Giovanni Mazhar and edited by Stanislao G. Pugliese. New York: Palgrave Macmillan, 2007.

– 'Sins of Memory: Reflections on the Lack of an Italian Nuremberg and the Administration of International Justice after 1945.' *Journal of Modern Italian History* 9, no. 3 (2004): 349–62.

Battini, Michele, and Paolo Pezzino. *Guerra ai civili: Occupazione tedesca e politica del massacro. Toscana 1944.* Venice: Marsilio, 1997.

Battisti, C., and G. Alessio, eds. *Nuovo Etinologico.* Florence: Barbèra, 1975.

Becattini, Giacomo. *Il bruco e la farfalla. Prato: Una storia esemplare dell'Italia dei distretti.* Florence: Le Monnier, 2000.

– *Prato storia di una città. 4. Il distretto industriale (1943–1993).* Florence, Comune of Prato: Le Monnier, 1997.

– 'Riflessioni sullo sviluppo socio-economico della Toscana in questo dopoguerra.' In *Storia d'Italia, Le regioni dall'Unità ad oggi: La Toscana*, edited by G. Mori. Turin: Einaudi, 1986.

– ed. *Lo sviluppo economico della Toscana con particolare riguardo all'industrializzazione leggera.* Florence: Eurografica, 1975.

Bedani, Gino. *Politics and Ideology in the Italian Workers' Movement: Union Development and the Changing Role of the Catholic and Communist Subcultures in Postwar Italy.* Oxford: Berg, 1995.

Bell, Rudolph M. *Fate and Honor, Family and Village: Demographic and Cultural Change in Rural Italy since 1800.* Chicago: University of Chicago Press, 1979.

Bendotti, Angelo, Giuliana Bertacchi, Mario Pelliccioli, and Eugenia Valtulina. '"Ho fatto la Grecia, l'Albania, la Jugoslavia …". Il disagio della memoria.' In *L'Italia in guerra 1940–43*, edited by B. Micheletti and P.P. Poggio, 964–79. Vol. 5, Annali della Fondazione 'Luigi Micheletti,' 1992.

Ben-Ghiat, Ruth. 'A Lesser Evil? Italian Fascism in/and the Totalitarian Equation.' In *The Lesser Evil: Moral Approaches to Genocide Practices in a Comparative Perspective*, edited by H. Dubiel and G. Motzkin, 137–53. London: Routledge, 2004.

– 'Unmaking of the Fascist Man: Masculinity, Film, and the Transition from Dictatorship.' *Journal of Modern Italian Studies* 10, no. 3 (2005): 336–65.

Berezin, Mabel. *Making the Fascist Self: The Political Culture of Interwar Italy.* Ithaca and London: Cornell University Press, 1997.

Bertoldi, Silvio. *Apocalisse Italiana, otto settembre 1943: Fine di una nazione.* Milan: Rizzoli, 1998.

Bessel, Richard, ed. *Fascist Italy and Nazi Germany: Comparisons and Contrasts.* Cambridge: Cambridge University Press, 1996.

Bessel, Richard, and Dirk Schumann, eds. *Life after Death: Approaches to a Cultural and Social History of Europe during the 1940s and 1950s.* Publications of the German Historical Institute, Washington, DC. Cambridge: Cambridge University Press, 2003.

Biagianti, Ivo. 'Condizioni della mezzadria Toscana nel secondo dopoguerra.' 'Le campagne italiane e la politica agraria dei governi di unità antifascita (1943–1947),' *Annali dell' Istituto Alcide Cervi*, no. 3 (1981): 111–38.

Biagini, Enrico *Civitella. Un paese, un castello, un martirio.* Arezzo: Centrostampa, 1981.

Bidussa, David. *Il mito del bravo italiano.* Milan: Il Saggiatore, 1994.

Bierman, John, and Colin Smith. *The Battle of El Alamein: The Turning Point, World War II.* New York: Viking, 2002.

Bilenchi, Romano, ed. *Cronache degli anni neri.* Rome: Riuniti, 1994. First published 1984.

Biocca, Dario. 'Has the Nation Died? The Debate over Italy's Identity (and Future).' *Daedalus* 126, no. 3 (1997): 223–39.

Blackmer, Donald, and Sidney Tarrow. *Communism in Italy and France.* Princeton: Princeton University Press: 1975.

Blaxland, Gregory. *Alexander's Generals. The Italian Campaign 1944–1945.* London: William Kimber, 1979.

Bocca, Giorgio. *La Repubblica di Mussolini.* Milan: Mondadori, 1994.

Bock, Gisela, and Pat Thane, eds. *Maternity and Gender Policies: Women and the Rise of the European Welfare States, 1880s–1950s.* London and New York: Routledge, 1991.

Bondanella, Peter. *Italian Cinema from Neorealism to the Present.* New York: Continuum, 1995 edition.

Boni, Filippo. *Colpire la comunità: 4–11 luglio 1944. Le stragi naziste a Cavriglia in terra d'Avane.* N.p. 2007.

Bosworth, R.J.B. 'Everyday Mussolinism: Friends, Family, Locality and Violence in Fascist Italy.' *Contemporary European History* 14, no. 1 (2005): 23–43.

– 'Explaining "Auschwitz" after the End of History: The Case of Italy.' *History and Theory* 38, no. 2 (1999): 84–99.

– *The Italian Dictatorship. Problems and Perspectives in the Interpretation of Mussolini and Fascism.* London and New York: Arnold, 1998.

– *Mussolini*. London: Arnold, and New York: Oxford University Press, 2002.

– *Mussolini's Italy: Life Under the Fascist Dictatorship, 1915–1945*. New York: Penguin, 2006.

– 'War, Totalitarianism and "Deep Belief" in Fascist Italy, 1935–43.' *European History Quarterly* 34, no. 4 (2004): 475–505.

Bosworth, R.J.B., and Patrizia Dogliani. Introduction to *Italian Fascism: History, Memory, and Representation*, edited by R.J.B. Bosworth and Patrizia Dogliani. London: Macmillan, 1999.

Botjer, George F. *Sideshow War: The Italian Campaign, 1943–1945*. College Station: Texas A&M University Press, 1996.

Bourke, Joanna. *Dismembering the Male: Men's Bodies, Britain and the Great War*. Chicago: University of Chicago Press, 1996.

Bracken, Patrick J., and Celia Petty, eds. *Rethinking the Trauma of War*. London: Free Association Press, 1998.

Bravo, Anna. 'Armed and Unarmed: Struggles without Weapons in Europe and in Italy.' *Journal of Modern Italian Studies* 10, no. 4 (2005): 468–84.

Bravo, A., and A.M. Bruzzone. *In guerra senza armi. Storie di donne. 1940–1945*. Bari and Rome: Laterza, 1995.

Brenner, Michael. *After the Holocaust: Rebuilding Jewish Lives in Postwar Germany*. Translated by Barbara Harshav. Princeton: Princeton University Press, 1997.

Bronzi, Giuseppe. *Il fascismo aretino da Renzino a Besozzo (1921–1945): Proposta di ricerca su studi e fonti d'archivio*. Cortona: Grafica l'Etruria, 1988.

Brugnoli, Giuseppe, ed. *I civili nella Resistenza: L'apporto popolare nella Guerra di Liberazione dal Primo Risorgimento al 25 Aprile 1945*. Rome: Associazione Nazionale Vittime Civili di Guerra, 1995.

Budani, Donna M. *Italian Women's Narratives of Their Experiences During World War II*. Vol. 9, Mellen Studies in Anthropology. Lewiston, NY: Edwin Mellen Press, 2003.

Caesar, Michael, and Peter Hainsworth. 'The Transformation of Post-war Italy.' In *Writers and Society in Contemporary Italy: A Collection of Essays*, edited by Michael Caesar and Peter Hainsworth, 1–34. Leamington Spa: Berg, 1984.

Calamandrei, Piero. *Uomini e città della Resistenza*. Milan: Linea d'Ombra, 1994.

Calvino, Italo. *The Path to the Nest of Spiders*. Translated by Archibald Colquhoun. Preface translated by William Weaver. New York: Ecco Press, 1976. First published 1947.

Cantagalli, Roberto. *Storia del fascismo fiorentino 1919–1925*. Florence: Vallecchi, 1972.

Capogreco, Carlo Spartaco. *I campi del Duce: L'internamento civile nell'Italia fascista, 1940–1943*. Turin: Einaudi, 2004.

– *Renicci: Un campo di concentramento in riva al Tevere*. Milan: Mursia, 2003.

Cappelletto, Francesca. 'Long-term Memory of Extreme Events: From Autobiography to History.' *Journal of the Royal Anthropological Institute* 9, no. 2 (2003): 241–60.

– 'Memories of Nazi-Fascist Massacres in Two Central Italian Villages.' *Sociologia Ruralis* 38, no. 1 (1998): 69–85.

– 'Public Memories and Personal Stories: Recalling the Nazi-Fascist Massacres.' In *Memory and World War II: An Ethnographic Approach*, edited by Francesca Cappelletto, 101–30. Oxford: Berg, 2005.

– 'Social Relations and War Remembrance: Second World War Atrocities in Rural Tuscan Villages.' *History and Anthropology* 17, no. 3 (2006): 245–66.

Caracciolo, Nicola. *Uncertain Refuge: Italy and the Jews during the Holocaust.* Translated and edited by Florette Rechnitz Koffler and Richard Koffler. Urbana: University of Illinois Press, 1995.

Cardoza, Anthony L. *Agrarian Elites and Italian Fascism: The Province of Bologna, 1901–1926.* Princeton: Princeton University Press, 1982.

Carocci, Giampiero. *The Officers Camp.* Translated by George Hochfield. Evanston, IL: Marlboro Press, 1995.

Casella, Luciano. *The European War of Liberation: Tuscany and the Gothic Line.* Translated by Jean M. Ellis D'Alessandro. Florence: La Nuova Europa, 1983.

Casmirri, Silvana. 'Le Acli-terra (1947–1950).' 'Le campagne italiane e la politica agraria dei governi di unità antifascita (1943–1947),' *Annali dell' Istituto Alcide Cervi*, no. 3 (1981): 391–8.

– *Cattolici e questione agraria negli anni della ricostruzione, 1943–1950.* Rome: Bulzoni, 1989.

– *Un'economia per la ricostruzione: Riflessione teorica e azione politica dei cattolici italiani, 1943–1956.* Rome: Studium, 2000.

– *L'Unione donne italiane (1944–1948).* Rome: Quaderni della Fiap, 1978.

Cavallo, Sandra and Lyndan Warner, eds. *Widowhood in Medieval and Early Modern Europe.* London: Longman, 1999.

Cheles, Luciano, and Lucio Sponza. *The Art of Persuasion. Political Communication in Italy from 1945 to the 1990s.* Manchester: Manchester University Press, 2001.

Chiarini, Roberto. *25 aprile. La competizione politica sulla memoria.* Venice: Marsilio, 2005.

Chiurico, Giorgio Alberto. *Storia della rivoluzione fascista (1919–1922).* 5 vols. Florence: Vallecchi, 1929.

Ciuffoletti, Zeffiro, Mario G. Rossi, and Angelo Varni, eds. *La Camera del Lavoro di Firenze dalla Liberazione agli anni settanta.* Naples: Edizioni Scientifiche Italiane 1991.

Clark, Martin. *Modern Italy: 1871–1995.* 2nd ed. London and New York: Longman, 1996.

Clough, Shephard. *An Economic History of Modern Italy.* New York: Columbia University Press, 1964.

Cohn, Samuel K., Jr. *The Cult of Remembrance and the Black Death: Six Renaissance Cities in Central Italy.* Baltimore and London: Johns Hopkins University Press, 1992.

Colarizi, Simona. *Biografia della prima Repubblica.* Bari and Rome: Laterza, 1998.

– *Dopoguerra e fascismo in Puglia, 1919–1926.* Bari and Rome: Laterza, 1977.

– *L'opinione degli italiani sotto il regime, 1929–1943.* Bari and Rome: Laterza, 2000.

– *La seconda Guerra mondiale e la Repubblica. Storia d'Italia dall' Unità alla fine della prima Repubblica.* Vol. 4. Milan: Editori Associati (TEA), 1996; 1984.

– *Storia dei partiti nell'Italia repubblicana.* Bari and Rome: Laterza, 1996.

Coles, Harry L., and Albert K. Weinberg. *Civil Affairs: Soldiers Become Governors.* Washington DC: Office of the Chief of Military History, Department of the Army, 1964.

Collo, Luigi. *La resistenza disarmata. La storia dei soldati italiani prigionieri nei lager tedeschi.* Venice: Marsilio, 1995.

Collotti, Enzo, ed. *Razza e fascismo: La persecuzione contro gli ebrei in Toscana (1938–1943).* Rome: Carocci, 1999.

Collotti, Enzo, and Lutz Klinkhammer. *Il fascismo e l'Italia in Guerra. Una conversazione fra storia e storiografica.* Rome: Ediesse, 1996.

Contini, Giovanni. *La memoria divisa.* Milan: Rizzoli, 1997.

Contini, Giovanni, Gabriella Gribaudi, and Paolo Pezzino. 'Forum: Revisionismo e ortodossia. Resistenza e guerra in Italia 1943–'45.' *Quaderni Storici* 111, no. 3 (2002): 785–816.

Cooke, Philip. 'Recent Work on Nazi Massacres in Italy during the Second World War.' *Modern Italy* 5, no. 2 (2000): 211–18.

– ed. *The Italian Resistance: An Anthology.* Manchester and New York: Manchester University Press, 1997.

Coppa, Frank J., and Margherita Repetto-Alaia, eds. *The Formation of the Ialian Republic (Proceedings of the International Symposium on Postwar Italy).* New York: Peter Lang, 1993.

Corner, Paul. *Fascism in Ferrara, 1915–1925.* London and New York: Oxford University Press, 1975.

– 'Fascist Agrarian Policy and the Italian Economy in the Interwar Years.' In *Gramsci and Italy's Passive Revolution,* edited by J.A. Davis. London: Croom Helm, 1979.

– *Riformismo e fascismo. L'Italia fra il 1900 e il 1940.* Rome: Bulzoni, 2002.

Croce, Benedetto. *Quando l'Italia era tagliata in due. Estratto di un diario (luglio 1943–giugno 1944).* Bari and Rome: Laterza, 1948.

Curina, Antonio. *Fuochi sui monti dell'Appennino toscano.* Arezzo: Tipografia D. Badiali, 1957.

Dalla Ragione, Onelio, ed. *La Guerra 1940–1945 a Pieve Santo Stefano: Deportazioni, Razzie, Devastazioni, Massacri.* Pieve S. Stefano: Comune di Pieve S. Stefano, 1996.

Dallas, Gregor. *1945: The War that Never Ended.* New Haven and London: Yale University Press, 2005.

Davis, John A. *Conflict and Control: Law and Order in Nineteenth-Century Italy.* Atlantic Highlands: Humanities Press International, 1988.

– ed. *Gramsci and Italy's Passive Revolution.* London: Croom Helm, 1979.

Deák, István, Jan T. Gross, and Tony Judt, eds. *The Politics of Retribution in Europe: World War II and its Aftermath.* Princeton: Princeton University Press, 2000.

Deakin, F.W. *The Brutal Friendship: Mussolini, Hitler, and the Fall of Italian Fascism.* Part 1, revised. Garden City, NY: Anchor Books, 1966; 1962.

De Felice, Renzo. *Ebrei in un paese arabo. Gli ebrei nella Libia contemporanea tra colonialismo, nazionalismo arabo e sionismo (1835–1970).* Bologna: Il Mulino, 1978.

– *Mussolini l'alleato 1940–1945.* Vol 2. *La guerra civile 1943–1945.* Turin: Einaudi, 1997.

– *Mussolini l'alleato 1940–1945.* Vol. 1, part 2. *L'Italia in Guerra 1940–1943. Crisi e agonia del regime.* Turin: Einaudi, 1997.

– *Mussolini il Duce.* Vol. 2. *Lo Stato totalitario: 1936–1940.* Turin: Einaudi, 1996.

– *Storia degli ebrei italiani sotto il fascismo.* Turin: Einaudi, 1993 edition.

De Grand, Alexander J. *Fascist Italy and Nazi Germany: The 'Fascist' Style of Rule.* London and New York: Routledge, 1995.

De Grazia, Victoria. *The Culture of Consent, Mass Organization of Leisure in Fascist Italy.* Cambridge: Cambridge University Press, 1981.

– *How Fascism Ruled Women: Italy, 1922–1945.* Berkeley: University of California Press, 1992.

De Grazia, Victoria, and Leonardo Paggi. 'Story of an Ordinary Massacre: Civitella della Chiana, 29 June, 1944.' *Cardozo Studies in Law and Literature* 3, no. 2 (1991): 153–69.

Delzell, Charles. 'The Italian Anti-fascist Resistance in Retrospect: Three Decades of Historiography.' *Journal of Modern History* 47, no. 1 (1975): 66–96.

– *Mussolini's Enemies: The Italian Anti-Fascist Resistance.* Princeton: Princeton University Press, 1961.

Derossi, Laura, ed. *1945: Il voto alle donne.* Milan: Franco Angeli, 1998.

Di Nicola, Patrizio. *Quarant'anni di tesseramento Cgil, 1944–1988.* Rome: Ediesse, 1989.

Di Scala, Spencer M., ed. *Italian Socialism: Between Politics and History.* Amherst: University of Massachusetts Press, 1996.

Domenico, Roy Palmer. *Italian Fascists on Trial, 1943–1948.* Chapel Hill and London: University of North Carolina Press, 1991.

Dondi, Mirco. 'The Fascist Mentality after Fascism.' In *Italian Fascism: History, Memory and Representation*, edited by R.J.B. Bosworth and Patrizia Dogliani. London: Macmillan, 1999.

Dossetti, Giuseppe. 'Fine del tripartite.' In *Cronache sociali (1947–1951)*, edited by Marcella Glisenti and Leopoldo Elia. San Giovanni Valdarno and Rome: Landi, 1961.

Droandi, Enzo. *Arezzo distrutta 1943–44*. Cortona: Calosci, 1995.

Duchen, Claire, and Irene Bandhauer-Schöffmann, eds. *When the War was Over: Women, War and Peace in Europe, 1940–1956*. London and New York: Leicester University Press, 2000.

Duggan, Christopher. 'Italy in the Cold War Years and the Legacy of Fascism.' In *Italy in the Cold War. Politics, Culture and Society 1948–1958*, edited by Christopher Duggan and Christopher Wagstaff. Oxford: Berg, 1995.

Duggan, Christopher, and Christopher Wagstaff, eds. *Italy in the Cold War. Politics, Culture and Society 1948–1958*. Oxford: Berg, 1995.

Dunnage, Jonathan. *The Italian Police and the Rise of Fascism: A Case Study of the Province of Bologna*. Westport, CT: Praeger, 1997.

– *Twentieth-century Italy: A Social History*. New York and London: Longman, 2002

– ed. *After the War: Violence, Justice, Continuity and Renewal in Italian Society*. Market Harborough: Troubador and University of Hull, 1999.

Edkins, Jenny. *Trauma and the Memory of Politics*. Cambridge: Cambridge University Press, 2003.

Ellwood, David W. *L'Alleato nemico*. Milan: Feltrinelli, 1977.

– 'Introduction: The Never-Ending Liberation.' *Journal of Modern Italian Studies* 10, no. 4 (2005): 385–95.

– *Italy 1943–1945: The Politics of Liberation*. Leicester: Leicester University Press, 1985.

– *Rebuilding Europe: Western Europe, America, and Postwar Reconstruction*. London and New York: Longman, 1992.

Fabilli, Ferruccio. *I mezzadri: lavoro, conflitti sociali, trasformazioni economiche, politiche e culturali a Cortona dal 1900 ad oggi*. Cortona: CGIL Valdichiana, 1992.

Fanciullini, Almo. *Diario di un ragazzo aretino 1943–1944*. Florence: Edizioni Polistampa, 1996.

Fanfani, Amintore. *Land Reform in Italy*. Rome: Ministry of Agriculture and Forestry, 1953.

– *Una pieve in Italia*. Milan: Mondadori, 1964.

– *The Twelve Year Plan for the Development of Agriculture*. Rome: Ministry of Agriculture and Forestry, 1953.

Fargion, Valeria. *Geografia della cittadinanza sociale in Italia: Regioni e politche assistenziali dagli anni Settanta agli anni Novanta*. Bologna: Il Mulino, 1997.

Farmer, Sarah. *Martyred Village: Commemorating the 1944 Massacre at Oradour-sur-Glane.* Berkeley: University of California Press, 1999.

Favuzza, Salvatore, ed. *Gli archivi della Confederterra Toscana (1944–1978): Inventario.* Florence: Giunta Regionale Toscana; Milan: Bibliografica, 1990.

Fenoglio, Beppe. *Johnny the Partisan.* Translated by Stuart Hood. London: Quartet Books, 1994.

Fimiani, Enzo. *Guerra e fame. Il secondo conflitto mondiale e le memorie popolari.* Itinerari, 1997.

Fishman, Sarah. *We Will Wait: Wives of French Prisoners of War, 1940–1945.* New Haven and London: Yale University Press, 1991.

Focardi, Filippo. *La guerra della memoria. La Resistenza nel dibattito politico italiano dal 1945 a oggi.* Bari and Rome: Laterza, 2005.

– *L'immagine del cattivo tedesco e il mito del bravo italiano: La costruzione della memoria del fascismo e della seconda guerra mondiale in Italia.* Padua: Rinoceronte, 2005.

Focardi, Filippo, and Lutz Klinkhammer. 'La questione dei "criminali di Guerra" italiani e una Commissione di inchiesta dimenticata.' *Contemporanea* 4, no. 3 (2001): 497–528.

– 'The Question of Fascist Italy's War Crimes: The Construction of a Self-acquitting Myth (1943–1948).' *Journal of Modern Italian Studies* 9, no. 3 (2004): 330–48.

Fogu, Claudio. *The Historic Imaginary: Politics of History in Fascist Italy.* Toronto: University of Toronto Press, 2003.

– '*Italiani brava gente*. The Legacy of Fascist Historical Culture on Italian Politics of Memory.' In *The Politics of Memory in Postwar Europe,* edited by Richard Ned Lebow, Wulf Kansteiner, and Claudio Fogu, 147–76. Durham and London: Duke University Press, 2006.

Foot, John. 'Review Article: Via Rasella, 1944: Memory, Truth, and History.' *The Historical Journal* 43, no. 4 (2000): 1173–81.

– 'Words, Songs and Books. Oral History in Italy. A Review and Discussion.' *Journal of Modern Italian Studies* 3, no. 2 (1998): 164–74.

Footitt, Hilary. *War and Liberation in France: Living with the Liberators.* Basingstoke and New York: Palgrave Macmillan, 2004.

Forgacs, David. 'Fascism and Anti-fascism Reviewed: Generations, History and Film in Italy after 1968.' In *European Memories of the Second World War,* edited by Helmut Peitsch, Charles Burdett, and Claire Gorrara, 185–99. New York and Oxford: Berghahn Books, 1999.

Förster, Alice, and Birgit Beck. 'Post-Traumatic Stress Disorder and World War II: Can a Psychiatric Concept Help Us Understand Postwar Society?' In *Life after Death: Approaches to a Cultural and Social History of Europe During the 1940s and 1950s*, edited by Richard Bessel and Dirk Schumann. Publications of the German Historical Institute, Washington, DC. Cambridge: Cambridge University Press (2003).

Forti, Carla. *Dopoguerra in provincia. Microstorie pisane e lucchesi (1944–1948).* Milan: Franco-Angeli, 2007.

Fraddosio, Maria. 'The Fallen Hero: The Myth of Mussolini and Fascist Women in the Italian Social Republic (1943–5).' *Journal of Contemporary History* 31, no. 1 (1996): 99–124.

Franzinelli, Mimmo. *L'amnistia Togliatti: 22 giugno 1946, colpo di spugna sui crimini fascisti.* Milan: Mondadori, 2006.

– *Le stragi nascoste. L'armadio della vergogna: Impunità e rimozione dei crimini di Guerra nazifascisti 1943–2001.* Milan: Mondadori, 2002.

Fulvetti, Gianluca, and Francesca Pelini, eds. *La politica del massacro. Per un atlante delle stragi naziste in Toscana.* Naples: L'ancora del mediterraneo, 2006.

Gallerano, Nicola. 'A Neglected Chapter in Italy's Transition from Fascism to the Republic: The Kingdom of the South (1943–1944).' *Journal of Modern Italian Studies* 1, no. 3 (1996): 390–9.

Galli, Giorgio. *I partiti politici in Italia, 1943–1994.* Turin: UTET, 1994.

Galli della Loggia, Ernesto. *La morte della Patria. La crisi dell'idea di nazione tra Resistenza, antifascismo e Repubblica.* Bari and Rome: Laterza, 1996.

Galluccio, Fabio. *I lager in Italia: La memoria sepolta nei duecento luoghi di deportazione fascisti.* Civezzano: Nonluoghi Libere Edizioni, 2003.

Gambino, Antonio. *Storia del dopoguerra dalla liberazione al potere DC.* Bari and Rome: Laterza, 1975.

Gavitt, Philip. *Charity and Children in Renaissance Florence: The Ospedale degli Innocenti, 1410–1536.* Ann Arbor: University of Michigan Press, 1990.

Gayre, G.R. *Italy in Transition. Extracts from the Private Journal of G.R. Gayre.* London: Faber & Faber, 1946.

Gentile, Carlo. 'La divisione Hermann Göring in Toscana.' In *La politica del massacro. Per un atlante delle stragi naziste in Toscana* edited by Gianluca Fulvetti and Francesca Pelini, 212–40. Naples: L'ancora del Mediterraneo, 2006.

– ed. *La Wehrmacht in Toscana: Immagini di un esercito di occupazione (1943–44).* Rome: Carrocci; Florence: Regione Toscana, 2006.

Gentile, Emilio. *Il culto di littorio. La sacralizzazione della politica nell'Italia fascista.* Bari and Rome: Laterza, 1993.

– 'Fascism in Italian Historiography: In Search of an Individual Historical Identity.' *Journal of Contemporary History* 21, no. 2 (1986): 179–208.

– *Fascismo: Storia e interpretazione.* Bari and Rome: Laterza, 2002.

– *La via italiana al totalitarismo: Il partito e lo Stato nel regime fascista.* 2nd ed. Rome: Carocci, 2001; 1995.

Geyer, Michael. 'Civitella in Val di Chiana, 29 giugno 1944. Ricostruzione di un "intervento" Tedesco.' In *La memoria del nazismo nell'Europa di oggi,* edited by Leonardo Paggi, 3–49. Florence: La Nuova Italia, 1997.

Gibson, Peter. 'Relief Work in Italy.' *FAU Chronicle* 68, no. 3 (1945).

Gildea, Robert, Olivier Wieviorka, and Anette Warring, eds. *Surviving Hitler and Mussolini: Daily Life in Occupied Europe.* Oxford and New York: Berg. 2006.

Gillis, John R., ed. *Commemorations: The Politics of National Identity.* Princeton: Princeton University Press, 1994.

Ginsborg, Paul. *A History of Contemporary Italy: Society and Politics 1943–1988.* London: Penguin, 1990.

– *Italy and Its Discontent: Family, Civil Society, State, 1980–2001.* London: Penguin, 2001.

Giorgetti, Giorgio. *Contadini e proprietari nell'Italia moderna: Rapporti di produzione e contratti agrari dal secolo 16 a oggi.* Turin: Einaudi, 1974.

– 'Contratti agrari e rapporti sociali nelle campagne.' In *Storia d'Italia,* 745. Turin: Einaudi, 1976.

Giustolisi, Franco. *L'Armadio della vergogna.* Rome: Nutrimenti, 2004.

Goldstein, J. *War and Gender.* Cambridge: Cambridge University Press, 2001.

Gordon, Robert S. C. 'The Holocaust in Italian Collective Memory: *Il giorno della memoria,* 27 January 2001.' *Modern Italy* 11, no. 2 (2006): 167–88.

Graham, Dominick, and Shelford Bidwell. *Tug of War: The Battle for Italy, 1943–1945.* New York: St. Martin's Press, 1986.

Grande Dizionario della Lingua Italiana. Turin: UTET. 1961–2002.

Grazianti, Augusto, ed. *L'economia italiana dal 1945 a oggi.* New edition. Bologna: Il Mulino, 1979.

Gribaudi, Gabriella. *Guerra totale. Tra bombe alleate e violenze naziste. Napoli, il fronte meridionale, 1940–1944.* Turin: Bollati Boringhieri, 2005.

– 'Guerra, violenza, reponsabilità. Alcuni volumi sui massacri nazisti in Italia.' *Quaderni Storici* 100, no. 1 (1999): 135–49.

– ed. *Terra bruciata. Le stragi naziste sul fronte meridionale.* Naples: L'ancora del mediterraneo, 2003.

Griffin, Roger. 'The Primacy of Culture: The Current Growth (or Manufacture) of Consensus within Fascist Studies.' *Journal of Contemporary History* 37, no. 1 (2002): 21–43.

Gross, Feliks. *Il Paese: Values and Social Change in an Italian Village.* New York: New York University Press, 1973.

Guareschi, Giovanni. *Mondo Piccolo, Don Camillo.* Milan: Rizzoli, 1948.

Guderzo, Giulio. *L'altra guerra. Neofascisti, tedeschi, partigiani, popolo in una provincia padana. Pavia, 1943–1945*. Bologna: Il Mulino, 2002.

Hamilton, J. Agar, and L.C.F. Turner. *Crisis in the Desert, May to July 1942*. Oxford: Oxford University Press, 1952.

Hammerman, Gabriele. *Gli internati militari italiani in Germania, 1943–1945*. Bologna: Il Mulino, 2004.

Harper, J.L. *America and the Reconstruction of Italy 1945–1948*. Cambridge: Cambridge University Press, 1986.

Harris, C.R.S. *Allied Administration of Italy 1943–1945*. London: HMSO, 1957.

Heineman, Elizabeth D. *What Difference Does a Husband Make?: Women and Marital Status in Nazi and Postwar Germany*. Berkeley: University of California Press, 1999.

Herman, J.L. *Trauma and Recovery*. New York: Basic Books, 1992.

Hine, David. *Governing Italy. The Politics of Bargained Pluralism*. Oxford: Clarendon Press, 1993.

Hitchcock, William L. *The Bitter Road to Freedom: A New History of the Liberation of Europe*. New York: Free Press, 2008.

Hood, Stuart. *Pebbles from my Skull*. London: Hutchinson, 1963.

Horn, David G. *Social Bodies: Science, Reproduction, and Italian Modernity*. Princeton: Princeton University Press, 1994.

Hughes, H. Stuart. *Prisoners of Hope: The Silver Age of the Italian Jews 1924–1974*. Cambridge and London: Harvard University Press, 1983.

Hyde, J.K. *Society and Politics in Medieval Italy: The Evolution of Civil Life, 1000–1350*. New York: St. Martin's Press, 1973.

Imbriani, Angelo Michele. *Gli italiani e il Duce: Il mito e l'immagine di Mussolini negli ultimi anni del fascismo, 1938–1943*. Naples: Liguori, 1992.

Innocenti, Marco. *L'Italia del 1948 ... quando De Gasperi batté Togliatti*. Milan: Mursia, 1997.

Italy (postwar government). *Atti del Convegno per Studi di Assistenza Sociale*. Sotto gli auspici del Ministero Assistenza Post-Bellica della delegazione del governo italiano per i rapporti con l'UNRRA e della missione italiana UNRRA. Milan: Carlo Marzorati, 1946.

Ipsen, Carl. *Dictating Demography: The Problem of Population in Fascist Italy*. Cambridge: Cambridge University Press, 1996.

Istituto Centrale di Statistica. *Morti e dispersi per cause belliche negli anni 1940–45*. Rome: ISTAT, 1957.

Istituto nazionale per la storia del movimento di liberazione in Italia. *Atti del Convegno internazionale organizzato a Firenze il 26–28 marzo 1976 con il concorso della Regione Toscana, L'Italia dalla liberazione alla repubblica*. Milan: Feltrinelli, 1976.

Journal of Contemporary History 39, no. 4. Special Issue: Collective Memory. (2004).

Journal of Modern Italian Studies 9, no. 3. 'The Hidden Pages of Contemporary Italian History: War Crimes, War Guilt, Collective Memory.' (2004).

– 10, no. 4. 'The Never-ending Liberation.' (2005).

Judt, Tony. *Postwar: A History of Europe Since 1945*. New York: Penguin, 2005.

Katz, Robert. *Death in Rome*. New York: Macmillan, 1967.

Kelikan, Alice. *Town and Country under Fascism: The Transformation of Brescia, 1915–1926*. Oxford and New York: Oxford University Press, 1986.

Kertzer, David I. *Comrades and Christians: Religion and Political Struggle in Communist Italy*. Cambridge and New York: Cambridge University Press, 1980.

– *Family Life in Central Italy, 1880–1910: Sharecropping, Wage Labor, and Coresidence*. New Brunswick, NJ: Rutgers University Press, 1984.

– *Politics and Symbols: The Italian Communist Party and the Fall of Communism*. New Haven: Yale University Press, 1996.

Kertzer, David I., and Richard P. Saller, eds. *The Family in Italy from Antiquity to the Present*. New Haven and London: Yale University Press, 1991.

Kesselring, Albert. *The Memoirs of Field-Marshal Kesselring*. Translated by William Kimber. London: Greenhill Books, 1988. First published 1953.

Kessler-Harris, Alice. *Out to Work: A History of Wage-Earning Women in the United States*. New York and Oxford: Oxford University Press, 1982.

Klinkhammer, Lutz. *L'occupazione tedesca in Italia*. Turin: Bollati Boringhieri, 1993.

– *Stragi naziste in Italia. La guerra contro i civili (1943–44)*. Rome: Donzelli, 1997.

Knox, MacGregor. 'Expansionist Zeal, Fighting Power, and Staying Power in the Italian and German Dictatorships.' In *Fascist Italy and Nazi Germany: Comparisons and Contrasts*, edited by Richard Bessel, 113–33. Cambridge: Cambridge University Press, 1996.

– *Mussolini Unleashed, 1939–1941: Politics and Strategy in Fascist Italy's Last War*. Cambridge: Cambridge University Press, 1982.

Kogan, Norman. *The Government of Italy*. New York: Thomas Y. Crowell Co., 1962.

– *Italy and the Allies*. Cambridge, MA: Harvard University Press, 1961.

– *A Political History of Postwar Italy*. New York and Washington: Frederick A. Preager, 1966.

Koon, Tracy H. *Believe, Obey, Fight: Political Socialization of Youth in Fascist Italy*. Chapel Hill and London: University of North Carolina Press, 1985.

Koreman, Megan. *The Expectation of Justice: France 1944–1946*. Durham and London: Duke University Press, 1999.

Labanca, Nicola. 'Una provincia tra RSA e Resistenza.' In *Quando le nostre città erano macerie: Immagini e documenti sulle distruzioni belliche in provincia di Arezzo*

(1943–1944), edited by Nicola Labanca, 42–58. Comune di Foiano della Chiana; A.N.P.I.-Sezione 'Licio Nencetti'; Montepulciano: del Grifo, 1988.

– ed. *Fra sterminio e sfruttamento. Militari internati e prigionieri di guerra nella Germania nazista (1939–45)*. Florence: Le lettere, 1992.

– ed. *La memoria del ritorno. Il rimpatrio degli internati militari italiani, (1945–1946)*. Florence: Giuntina, 2000.

Lagorio, Francesca. 'Appunti per una storia sulle vedove di guerra italiane nei conflitti mondiali.' *Rivista di storia contemporanea* 23–4, nos. 1–2 (1994): 170–93.

Lagrou, Pieter. *The Legacy of Nazi Occupation: Patriotic Memory and National Recovery in Western Europe, 1945–1965*. Cambridge: Cambridge University Press, 2000.

– 'The Nationalization of Victimhood: Selective Violence and National Grief in Western Europe, 1940–1960.' In *Life after Death: Approaches to a Cultural and Social History of Europe during the 1940s and 1950s*, edited by Richard Bessel and Dirk Schumann, 243–57. Publications of the German Historical Institute, Washington, DC. Cambridge: Cambridge University Press, 2003.

Lamb, Richard. *War in Italy 1943–1945: A Brutal Story*. New York: Da Capo Press, 1996.

Lanza, Carlo, ed. *Ricostituzione delle amministrazioni comunali su base elettiva: D.L.L. 7 gennaio 1946, n. 1*. Milan: D. Salvatores, 1946.

Lanza, Orazio. 'L'agricoltura, la Coldiretti e la D.C.' In *Costruire la democrazia, Gruppi e partiti in Italia*, edited by L. Morlino. Bologna: Il Mulino, 1991.

LaPalombara, Joseph. *Democracy Italian Style*. New Haven and London: Yale University Press, 1987.

– 'Italy: Fragmentation, Isolation, and Alienation. In *Political Culture and Political Development*, edited by Lucian W. Pye and Sidney Verba. Princeton: Princeton University Press, 1965.

Laqueur, Thomas W. 'Memory and Naming in the Great War.' In *Commemorations: The Politics of National Identity*, edited by John R. Gillis, 150–67. Princeton: Princeton University Press, 1994.

– 'Names, Bodies, and the Anxiety of Erasure.' In *The Social and Political Body*, edited by Theodore R. Schatzki and Wolfgang Natter, 123–44. New York and London: Guilford Press, 1996.

– '"The Sound of Voices Intoning Names": A Review of Serge Klarsfeld, *French Jewish Children of the Holocause: A Memorial.*' *London Review of Books* 19, no. 11 (June 5, 1997): 3–8.

Laurie, Clayton D. *Rome-Arno: 22 January–9 September 1944*. The U.S. Army Campaigns of World War II. Washington, DC: US Government Printing Office, 1994.

Lebow, Richard Ned, Wulf Kansteiner, and Claudio Fogu, eds. *The Politics of Memory in Postwar Europe*. Durham and London: Duke University Press, 2006.

Leone, Massimo. *Le organizzazioni di soccorso ebraiche in età fascista (1918–1945)*. Rome: Carocci, 1983.

Lepre, Aurelio. *Le illusioni, la paura, la rabbia. Il fronte interno italiano (1940–1943)*. Rome: Edizioni Scientifiche Italiane, 1989.

Levi, Arrigo. *La DC nell'Italia che cambia*. Bari and Rome: Laterza, 1984.

Levi, Carlo. *Christ Stopped at Eboli: The Story of a Year*. Translated by Frances Frenaye. New York: Farrar, Straus & Young, 1963.

– *The Watch: A Novel*. South Royalton, VT: Steerforth Press, 1999; New York: Farrar, Straus & Young, 1951.

Levy, Carl. 'From Fascism to "Post-Fascists": Italian Roads to Modernity.' In *Fascist Italy and Nazi Germany: Comparisons and Contrasts*, edited by Richard Bessel, 165–96. Cambridge and New York: Cambridge University Press, 1996.

– ed. *Italian Regionalism: History, Identity and Politics*. Oxford and New York: Berg, 1996.

Lewis, Norman. *Naples '44: An Intelligence Officer in the Italian Labyrinth*. New York: Henry Holt and Company, 1978.

Linklater, Eric. *The Campaign in Italy*. London: HMSO, 1951.

Liotti, Caterina, Rosangela Pesenti, Angela Remaggi, and Delfina Tromboni, eds. '*Volevamo cambiare il mondo': Memorie e storie delle donne dell'UDI in Emilia Romagna*. Rome: Carocci, 2002.

Lomartire, Carlo Maria. *Insurrezione. 14 luglio 1948: L'attentato a Togliatti e la tentazione rivoluzionaria*. Milan: Mondadori, 2006.

Lombardo, Antonio T. *Un caso di trasgressione sociale. La borsa nera in provincia di Arezzo 1939–1947*. In *Guerra di sterminio e Resistenza. La provincia di Arezzo (1943–1944)*, edited by Ivan Tognarini, 263–302. Naples: Edizioni Scientifiche Italiane, 1990.

Lottman, Herbert R. *The People's Anger: Justice and Revenge in Post-Liberation France*. London: Hutchinson, 1986.

Lyttelton, Adrian. *Liberal and Fascist Italy 1900–1945*. The Short Oxford History of Italy. Oxford and New York: Oxford University Press, 2002.

– *The Seizure of Power: Fascism in Italy 1919–1929*. London: Weidenfeld and Nicolson, 1973.

– ed. *Italian Fascisms from Pareto to Gentile*. London: Cape, 1973.

MacDonald, J.S. 'Agricultural Organization, Migration and Labour Militancy in Rural Italy.' *The Economic History Review*, New Series, 16, no. 1 (1963): 61–75.

Macucci, Romano. *Pane Spezzato. Breve storia di tre preti eroici: Ferrante Bagiardi, Giovanni Fondelli, Ermete Morini*. Fiesole: Servizio Editoriale Fiesolano, 1994.

Mafai, Miriam. *Pane nero: Donne e vita quotidiana nella seconda guerra mondiale.* Milan: Mondadori, 1987.

Mammarella, Giuseppe. *Italy after Fascism 1943–1965.* South Bend, IN: University of Notre Dame Press, 1966.

Mammone, Andrea. 'A Daily Revision of the Past: Fascism, Anti-Fascism, and Memory in Contemporary Italy.' *Modern Italy* 11, no. 2 (2006): 211–26.

Manfroni, Claudio. 'Cavriglia, luglio 1944. La memoria degli eccidi.' In *La politica del massacro. Per un atlante delle stragi naziste in Toscana,* edited by Gianluca Fulvetti and Francesca Pelini, 281–314. Naples: L'ancora del mediterraneo, 2006.

Manoukian, Agopik, ed. *La presenza sociale del PCI e della DC.* Istituto di studi e ricerche Carlo Cattaneo. Vol. 4, Ricerche sulla participazione politica in Italia. Bologna: Il Mulino, 1969.

Mantelli, Bruno. 'Italians in Germany, 1938–45: An Aspect of the Rome-Berlin Axis.' In *Italian Fascism: History, Memory and Representation,* edited by R.J.B. Bosworth and Patrizia Dogliani, 45–63. Houndmills: Macmillan, 1999.

Maraspini, A.L. *The Study of an Italian Village.* Paris and The Hague: Mouton, 1968.

Martin, Simon. *Football and Fascism: The National Game under Mussolini.* Oxford and New York: Berg, 2004.

Marwick, Arthur. *War and Social Change in the Twentieth Century: A Comparative Study of Britain, France, Germany, Russia and the United States.* London: Collier-Macmillan, 1974.

– ed. *Total War and Social Change.* New York: St. Martin's Press, 1988.

Mauldin, Bill. *Up Front.* 1945. Reprint, New York and London: W.W. Norton & Co. 1995.

Mazower, Mark. Introduction. In *After the War: Violence, Justice, Continuity and Renewal in Italian Society,* edited by Jonathan Dunnage. Market Harborough: Troubador, 1999.

McCarthy, Patrick, ed. *Italy since 1945.* The Short Oxford History of Italy. Oxford and NY: Oxford University Press, 2000.

McFarland, Stephen L. *America's Pursuit of Precision Bombing, 1910–1945.* Washington and London: Smithsonian Institution Press, 1995.

Meintjes, Sheila, Anu Pillay, and Meredith Turshen, eds. *The Aftermath: Women in Post-Conflict Transformation.* London: Zed Books, 2001.

Michaelis, Meir. *Mussolini and the Jews: German-Italian Relations and the Jewish Question in Italy 1922–1945.* Oxford: Clarendon Press, 1978.

Michetti, Maria, Margherita Repetto, and Luciana Viviani. *Udi, laboratorio di politica delle donne: Idée e materiali per una storia.* Rome: Cooperativa Libera Stampa, 1984.

Miller, J.E. *The United States and Italy 1940–1950. The Politics and Diplomacy of Stabilization.* Chapel Hill and London: University of North Carolina Press, 1986.

Minow, Martha. *Between Vengeance and Forgiveness: Facing History after Genocide and Mass Violence.* Boston: Beacon Press, 1998.

Modern Italy 12, no. 2. 'Italy at War, 1935–2005.' (2007).

Moretti, Romano. *Le donne di San Pancrazio.* Bucine: Comune di Bucine, 1994.

– *Il giorno di San Pietro: Volume primo, l'eccidio di San Pancrazio (le memorie e la storia): L'eccidio nazifascista del 29 giugno del 1944 a Civitella in Val di Chiana, Cornia, San Pancrazio (provincial di Arezzo).* Montepulciano: Le Balze, 2005.

– *29 giugno–6 luglio 1944: Il fronte a San Pancrazio.* Bucine: Comune di Bucine, 1994.

Morgan, Philip. *The Fall of Mussolini: Italy, the Italians, and the Second World War.* Oxford: Oxford University Press, 2007.

– '"I Was There Too": Memories of Victimhood in Wartime Italy.' *Modern Italy* 14, no. 2 (2009): 217–31.

– 'The Prefects and Party-state Relations in Fascist Italy.' *Journal of Modern Italian Studies* 3, no. 3 (1998): 241–72.

Morgan, Sarah. 'The Schio Killings: A Case Study of Partisan Violence in Postwar Italy.' *Modern Italy* 5, no. 2 (2000): 147–60.

Mortara, Alberto, ed. *Le associazioni italiane.* Milan: Franco Angeli, 1985.

Mosse, George L. *Fallen Soldiers: Reshaping the Memory of the World Wars.* New York and London: Oxford University Press, 1990.

Mulligan, Timothy Patrick. *The Politics of Illusion and Empire: German Occupation Policy in the Soviet Union, 1942–1943.* New York and London: Praeger, 1988.

Naimark, Norman M. *The Russians in Germany: A History of the Soviet Zone of Occupation, 1945–1949.* Cambridge and London: Belknap Press of Harvard University Press, 1995.

Nash, Maurice G. *The Price of Innocence.* N.p., 2005.

Neri Serneri, Simone. 'A Past to be Thrown Away? Politics and History in the Italian Resistance.' *Contemporary European History* 4, no. 3 (1995): 367–81.

Neufeld, Maurice F. *Italy: A School for Awakening Countries. The Italian Labor Movement in its Political, Social, and Economic Setting from 1800 to 1960.* Ithaca: New York State School of Industrial and Labor Relations, Cornell University, 1961.

Newby, Eric. *Love and War in the Apennines.* London: Picador, 1983. First published 1971.

Nichols, Peter. *Italia Italia.* Boston: Little Brown, 1974.

Nizza, Enzo. *Autobiografia del Fascismo.* Milan: La Pietra, 1962.

Oliva, Gianna. *La Repubblica di Salò.* Florence: Giunti Gruppo Editoriale – Casterman, 1997.

Orgill, Douglas. *The Gothic Line: The Autumn Campaign in Italy, 1944.* London: Heinemann, 1967.

Origo, Iris. *Images and Shadows: Part of a Life.* London: John Murray, 1970.

– *War in Val D'Orcia: An Italian War Diary, 1943–1944.* Boston: David R. Godine, 1984. First published 1947.

Paggi, Leonardo. 'Storia di una memoria antipartigiana.' In *La memoria del nazismo nell'Europa di oggi,* edited by Leonardo Paggi, 49–80. Florence: La Nuova Italia, 1997.

– ed. *Storia e memoria di un massacro ordinario.* Rome: Manifestolibri, 1996.

Pansa, Giampaolo. *Il sangue dei vinti. Quello che accadde in Italia dopo il 25 aprile.* Milan: Sperling & Kupfer, 2005 edition.

Paolini, Elvio, and Alberto Douglas Scotti. *Da Badoglio a Berlusconi: Tutto sulla Prima Repubblica.* Carnago, Varese: Sugarco, 1995.

Paris, Roland. *At War's End: Building Peace after Civil Conflict.* Cambridge: Cambridge University Press, 2004.

Passerini, Luisa. *Fascism in Popular Memory: The Cultural Experience of the Turin Working Class.* Cambridge and New York: Cambridge University Press, 1987.

– 'Memories of Resistance, Resistance of Memory.' In *European Memories of the Second World War,* edited by Helmut Peitsch, Charles Burdett, and Claire Gorrara, 288–96. New York and Oxford: Berghahn Books, 1999.

Pavese, Cesare. *The House on the Hill.* Translated by R.W. Flint. New York: Farrar, Straus and Giroux, 1968. First published 1949.

– *The Moon and the Bonfires.* Translated by Marianne Ceconi. New York: Farrar, Straus and Young, 1953.

Pavone, Claudio. 'The General Problem of the Continuity of the State and the Legacy of Fascism.' In *After the War: Violence, Justice, Continuity and Renewal in Italian Society,* edited by Jonathan Dunnage, 5–20. Market Harborough: Troubador, 1999.

– *Una guerra civile. Saggio storico sulla moralità nella Resistenza.* Turin: Bollati Boringhieri, 1991.

– Introduction. *Journal of Modern Italian Studies* 9, no.3 (2004): 271–9.

– *Alle origini della Repubblica: Scritti su fascismo, antifascismo e continuità dello Stato.* Turin: Bollati Boringhieri, 1995.

– 'La seconda guerra mondiale: Una guerra civile europea?' In *Guerre fratricide. Le guerre civili in età contemporanea,* edited by Gabriele Ranzato, 86–128. Turin: Bollati Boringhieri, 1994.

– 'Tre governi e due occupazioni.' In *L'Italia nella seconda guerra mondiale e nella Resistenza,* edited by Francesca Ferratini Tosi, Gaetano Grassi, and Massimo Legnani, 423–52. Milan: Franco Angeli, 1988.

– 'La violenza e le fratture della memoria.' In *Storia e memoria di un massacro ordinario*, edited by Leonardo Paggi, 15–23. Rome: Manifesto Libri, 1996.

Payne, Stanley G. *A History of Fascism 1914–1945*. Madison: University of Wisconsin Press, 1995.

Pedaliu, Effie G.H. 'Britain and the "Hand-over" of Italian War Criminals to Yugoslavia, 1945–48.' *Journal of Contemporary History* 39, no. 4 (2004): 503–29.

Peitsch, Helmut, Charles Burdett, and Claire Gorrara, eds. *European Memories of the Second World War*. New York and Oxford: Berghahn Books, 1999.

Pestellini, Tito. *La Mezzeria e le sue consuetudini nelle province di Siena, Firenze e Pisa*. 1905. Reprint *Rivista di storia dell'agricoltura*, Numero Speciale. Florence: Accademia Economico, Agraria dei Georgofili, 1980.

Pezzino, Paolo. *Anatomia di un massacro: Controversia sopra una strage tedesca*. Bologna: Il Mulino, 1997.

– 'The German Military Occupation of Italy and the War against Civilians.' *Modern Italy* 12, no. 2 (2007): 173–88.

– 'Guerra ai civili. Le stragi tra storia e memoria.' In *Crimini e memorie di guerra. Violenza contro le popolazioni e politiche del ricordo*, edited by Luca Baldissara and Paolo Pezzino, 5–58. Naples: L'ancora del mediterrraneo, 2004.

– 'The Italian Resistance between History and Memory.' *Journal of Modern Italian Studies* 10, no. 4 (2005): 396–412.

Pisanò, Giorgio, and Paolo Pisanò. *Il triangolo della morte: La politica della strage in Emilia durante e dopo la guerra civile*. Milan: Mursia, 1992.

Poggi, Gianfranco. *Catholic Action in Italy: The Sociology of a Sponsored Organization*. Stanford: Stanford University Press, 1967.

Polverini, Emilio, and Dante Priore, eds. *Perché la memoria non si cancelli. Gli eccidi del luglio 1944 nel territorio di Cavriglia*. Cavriglia: Comune di Cavriglia, 1994.

Portelli, Alessandro. 'The Massacre at Civitella Val di Chiana (Tuscany, June 29, 1944): Myth and Politics, Mourning and Common Sense.' Chap. 10 in *Oral History and the Art of Dialogue*. Madison: University of Wisconsin Press, 1997.

– *The Order Has Been Carried Out: History, Memory, and Meaning of a Nazi Massacre in Rome*. Houndmills and New York: Palgrave Macmillan, 2003.

– *L'ordine è già eseguito: Roma, le Fosse Ardeatine, la memoria*. Rome: Donzelli, 2001; 1999.

Porter, Bruce D. *War and the Rise of the State*. New York: Free Press, 1995.

Pratt, Jeff. *The Rationality of Rural Life: Economic and Cultural Change in Tuscany*. Chur, Switzerland: Harwood Academic Publishers, 1994.

Putnam, Robert D., with Robert Leonardi and Raffaella Y. Nanetti. *Making Democracy Work: Civic Traditions in Modern Italy*. Princeton: Princeton University Press, 1993.

Quazza, Guido. 'La guerra partigiana: Proposte di ricerca.' In *L'Italia nella seconda guerra mondiale e nella Resistenza*, edited by Francesca Ferratini Tosi, Gaetano Grassi, and Massimo Legnani, 453–508. Milan: Franco Angeli, 1988.

– 'The Politics of the Italian Resistance.' In *The Rebirth of Italy 1943–50*, edited by S.J. Woolf, 1–29. London: Longman, 1972.

– *Resistenza e storia d'Italia. Problemi e ipotesi di ricerca.* Milan: Feltrinelli, 1976.

Quine, Maria Sophia. *Italy's Social Revolution: Charity and Welfare from Liberalism to Fascism.* Houndmills and New York: Palgrave Macmillan, 2002.

Ragionieri, Ernesto. 'La storia politica e sociale.' In Vol. 4, part 3, *Storia d'Italia, Dall'Unità ad oggi*, 1667–2832. Turin: Einaudi, 1976.

Revelli, Nuto. *Le due guerre. Guerra fascista e guerra partigiana.* Turin: Einaudi, 2003.

– *Il mondo dei vinti. Testimonianze di vita contadina: La pianura. La collina. La montagna. Le Langhe.* Turin: Einaudi, 1997. First published 1977.

Roberts, David D., and Alexander De Grand, Mark Antliff, and Thomas Linehan. 'Comments on Roger Griffin, "The Primacy of Culture: The Current Growth (or Manufacture) of Consensus within Fascist Studies."' *Journal of Contemporary History* 37, no. 2 (2002): 259–74.

Rodogno, Davide. '*Italiani brava gente?* Fascist Italy's Policy Toward the Jews in the Balkans, April 1941–July 1943.' *European History Quarterly* 35, no. 2 (2005): 213–40.

– *Il nuovo ordine mediterraneo. Le politiche di occupazione dell'Italia fascista in Europa (1940–1943).* Turin: Bollati Boringhieri, 2003.

Rossi, A. (pseudo.). *The Rise of Italian Fascism.* Translated by Peter and Dorothy Wait. London: Methuen, 1938.

Rotelli, Ettore, ed. *La ricostruzione in Toscana dal CLN ai Partiti.* Bologna: Il Mulino, 1980.

Rothenberg, Nina. 'The Catholic and the Communist Women's Press in Postwar Italy – An Analysis of *Cronache* and *Noi Donne*.' *Modern Italy* 11, no. 3 (2006): 285–304.

Rousso, Henry. *The Vichy Syndrome: History and Memory in France since 1944.* Translated by Arthur Goldhammer. Cambridge: Harvard University Press, 1991.

Rusconi, Gian Enrico. *Resistenza e postfascismo.* Bologna: Il Mulino, 1995.

Sacchetti, Giorgio. *Camicie nere in Valdarno. Cronache inedite del 23 marzo 1921 (guerra sociale e guerra civile).* Pisa: Biblioteca Franco Serantini, 1996.

– *Ligniti per la Patria. Collaborazione, conflittualità, compromesso. Le relazioni sindacali nelle miniere del Valdarno Superiore (1915–1958).* Rome: Ediesse, 2002.

– *Il minatore deputato: Priamo Bigiandi 1900–1961.* Florence: Manent, 1998.

Sallagar, F.M. *Operation "STRANGLE" (Italy, Spring 1944): A Case Study of Tactical Air Interdiction.* Santa Monica: Rand, 1972.

Salvadori, Roberto G., and Giorgio Sacchetti. *Presenze ebraiche nell'aretino dal XIV al XX secolo.* Florence: Olschki, 1990.

Salvati, B. 'The Rebirth of Italian Trade Unionism, 1943–54,' In *The Rebirth of Italy 1943–54,* edited by S.J. Woolf, 181–211. London: Longman, 1972.

Salvati, Mariuccia. *Stato e industria nella ricostruzione.* Milan: Feltrinelli, 1982.

Salvatici, Silvia. *Contadine dell'Italia fascista: presenza, ruoli, immagini.* Turin: Rosenberg & Seller, 1999.

Sarfatti, Michele. *Mussolini contro gli ebrei. Cronaca dell'elaborazione delle legge del 1938.* Turin: Silvio Zamorani, 1994.

Sarti, Roland. *Long Live the Strong: A History of Rural Society in the Apennine Mountains.* Amherst: University of Massachusetts Press, 1985.

Sassoon, Donald. *Contemporary Italy. Politics, Economy and Society since 1945.* London and New York: Longman, 1986.

– 'Italy after Fascism: The Predicament of Dominant Narratives.' In *Life after Death: Approaches to a Cultural and Social History of Europe during the 1940s and 1950s,* edited by Richard Bessel and Dirk Schumann, 259–90. Publications of the German Historical Institute, Washington, DC. Cambridge: Cambridge University Press, 2003.

Savini, Alfio, Guido Occhini, and Carlo Salvicchi. *Ricordi, immagini, documenti: 1944–1989, pezzi di storia sindacale nell'aretino.* Cortona: Il Progresso, 1989.

Schatzki, Theodore R., and Wolfgang Natter, eds. *The Social and Political Body.* New York and London: Guilford Press, 1996.

Schreiber, Gerhard. *La vendetta tedesca. 1943–1945. Le rappresaglie naziste in Italia.* Milan: Mondadori, 2000.

Schulte, Theo J. *The German Army and Nazi Politics in Occupied Russia.* Oxford and New York: Berg, 1989.

Scoppola, Pietro. *25 aprile. Liberazione.* Turin: Einaudi, 1995.

Segrè, Claudio. *Italo Balbo: A Fascist Life.* Berkeley: University of California Press, 1987.

Sereni, Emilio. *Il capitalismo nelle campagne (1860–1900).* Turin: Einaudi, 1968. First published 1947.

– *History of the Italian Agricultural Landscape.* Translated by R. Burr Litchfield. Princeton: Princeton University Press, 1997.

Sezione Fotografica ARCA, Santa Barbara (Cavriglia), ed. *Il bacino lignitifero del Valdarno Superiore. Storia di una terra toscana.* San Giovanni Valdarno: ARCA CCD Toscana, 1999.

Shepperd, G.A. *The Italian Campaign 1943–45: A Political and Military Re-assessment.* London: Arthur Baker, 1968.

Silverman, Sydel. '"Exploitation" in Rural Central Italy: Structure and Ideology in Stratification Study.' *Comparative Studies in Society and History* 12, no. 3 (1970): 327–39.

– *Three Bells of Civilization: The Life of an Italian Hill Town.* New York: Columbia University Press, 1975.

Slaughter, Jane. *Women and the Italian Resistance, 1943–1945.* Denver: Arden Press, 1997.

Snowden, Frank M. *The Fascist Revolution in Tuscany, 1919–1922.* Cambridge and New York: Cambridge University Press, 1989.

– *Violence and Great Estates in the South of Italy: Apulia, 1900–1922.* New York and Cambridge: Cambridge University Press, 1986.

Sonetti, Catia. 'The Family in Tuscany between Fascism and the Cold War.' In *After the War: Violence, Justice, Continuity and Renewal in Italian Society,* edited by Jonathan Dunnage, 75–88. Market Harborough: Troubador, 1999.

Sorani, Settimio. *L'assistenza ai profughi ebrei in Italia (1933–1941): Contributo alla storia della Delasem.* Rome: Carucci, 1983.

Spriano, Paolo. *Storia del Partito Comunista Italiano.* 5 vols. Turin: Einaudi, 1965–1975.

Stille, Alexander. *Benevolence and Betrayal: Five Jewish Families under Fascism.* New York: Summit Books, 1991.

Storchi, Massimo. 'Post-war Violence in Italy: A Struggle for Memory.' *Modern Italy* 12, no. 2 (2007): 237–50.

Strachan, Hew. 'Total War in the Twentieth Century.' *The International History Review* 22, no. 2 (2000): 341–70.

Strawson, John. *The Italian Campaign.* London: Secker & Warburg, 1987.

Succhielli, Edoardo, ed. *La Resistenza nei versanti tra l'Arno e la Chiana.* Arezzo: Tipografia Sociale, 1979.

Suleiman, Susan Rubin. *Crises of Memory and the Second World War.* Cambridge and London: Harvard University Press, 2006.

Summerfield, Penny. 'Women, War and Social Change: Women in Britain in World War II.' In *Total War and Social Change,* edited by Arthur Marwick, 98–118. New York: St. Martin's Press, 1988.

– *Women Workers in the Second World War: Production and Patriarchy in Conflict.* London: Croom Helm, 1984.

Teitel, Ruti G., *Transitional Justice.* Oxford: Oxford University Press, 2000.

Tognarini, Ivano. *Kesselring e le stragi nazifasciste, 1944. Estate di sangue in Toscana.* Rome: Carocci, 2002.

– ed. *La guerra di liberazione in provincia di Arezzo 1943/1944: Immagini e documenti.* Arezzo: Provincia di Arezzo, 1987.

– ed. *Guerra di sterminio e Resistenza: La provincia di Arezzo 1943–1944.* Naples: Edizioni Scientifiche Italiane, 1990.

Tonkin, Elizabeth. *Narrating Our Pasts: The Social Construction of Oral History.* Cambridge: Cambridge University Press, 1992.

Torriglia, Anna Maria. *Broken Time, Fragmented Space: A Cultural Map for Postwar Italy.* Toronto: University of Toronto Press, 2002.

Toscana, Giunta Regionale, Dipartimento statistica informazione documentazione. *Dalla Costituente alla Regione. Il comportamento elettorale in Toscana dal 1946 al 1970.* Florence: Regione Toscana, 1972.

Treves, Anna. *Le migrazioni interne nell'Italia fascista: Politica e realtà demografica.* Turin: Einaudi, 1976.

Unione donne italiane: Congresso Nazionale, Firenze, 20–21–22 ottobre. Florence: UDI, 1945.

van Creveld, Martin. *The Rise and the Decline of the State.* Cambridge and New York: Cambridge University Press, 1999.

Ventresca, Robert. 'Debating the Meaning of Fascism in Contemporary Italy.' *Modern Italy* 11, no. 2 (June 2006): 189–209.

– *From Fascism to Democracy: Culture and Politics in the Italian Election of 1948.* Toronto: University of Toronto Press, 2004.

Ventrone, Angelo. *La cittadinanza repubblicana: Forma-partito e identità nazionale alle origini della democrazia italiana (1943–1948).* Bologna: Il Mulino, 1996.

Vigorelli, Ezio. *Sei anni di amministrazione dell'ECA di Milano (25 aprile 1945 –25 aprile 1951).* Milan: Vitagliano, 1951.

Vittorini, Elio. *Men and Not Men.* Translated by Sarah Henry. Marlboro, VT: Marlboro Press, 1985. First published 1945.

Vogt, Timothy R. *Denazification in Soviet-Occupied Germany: Brandenburg, 1945–1948.* Cambridge: Harvard University Press, 2001.

Waller, Maureen. *London 1945: Life in the Debris of War.* New York: St. Martin's Press, 2004.

Walston, James. 'History and Memory of the Italian Concentration Camps.' *The Historical Journal* 40, no. 1 (1997): 169–83.

White, Caroline. *Patrons and Partisans: A Study of Politics in Two Southern Italian Comuni.* Cambridge: Cambridge University Press, 1980.

White, Steven. *Progressive Renaissance: America and the Reconstruction of Italian Education, 1943–1962.* New York: Garland Press, 1991.

Whitman, John. 'Review Article. Fascism and Anti-fascism in Italy: History, Memory and Culture.' *Journal of Contemporary History* 36, no. 1 (2001): 163–71.

Willson, Perry. *Peasant Women and Politics in Fascist Italy: The Massaie Rurali.* London and New York: Routledge, 2002.

Woller, Hans. *I conti con il fascismo: L'epurazione in Italia 1943–1948.* Bologna: Il Mulino, 2004. First published 1997.

Wood, Nancy. *Vectors of Memory: Legacies of Trauma in Postwar Europe.* Oxford and New York: Berg, 1999.

Woolf, Stuart. 'Historians: Private, Collective and Public Memories of Violence and War Atrocities.' In *Memory and World War II, An Ethnographic Approach,* edited by Francesca Cappelletto, 177–93. Oxford and New York: Berg, 2005.

Woolf, S.J., ed. *The Rebirth of Italy 1943–50.* London: Longman, 1972.

Zamagni, Vera. *The Economic History of Italy 1860–1990: Recovery after Decline.* Translated by Patrick Barr. Oxford: Clarendon Press, 1993.

Zuccotti, Susan. *The Italians and the Holocaust: Persecution, Rescue, Survival.* New York: Basic Books, 1987.

Index